The Great Ideas

Man
Mathematics
Matter
Mechanics
Medicine
Memory and Imagination
Metaphysics
Mind
Monarchy
Nature
Necessity and Contingency
Oligarchy
One and Many
Opinion
Opposition
Philosophy
Physics
Pleasure and Pain
Poetry
Principle
Progress
Prophecy
Prudence
Punishment
Quality
Quantity
Reasoning
Relation
Religion
Revolution
Rhetoric
Same and Other
Science
Sense
Sign and Symbol
Sin
Slavery
Soul
Space
State
Temperance
Theology
Time
Truth
Tyranny
Universal and Particular
Virtue and Vice
War and Peace
Wealth
Will
Wisdom
World

"Target with Plaster Casts" (1955), by Jasper Johns. Encaustic and collage on canvas with objects (plaster casts), 51″ x 44″ x 3½″.

The Great Ideas Today

1986

Encyclopædia Britannica, Inc.

CHICAGO
AUCKLAND • GENEVA • LONDON • MANILA • PARIS • ROME • SEOUL • SYDNEY • TOKYO • TORONTO

Library of Congress Catalog Card Number: 61-65561
International Standard Book Number: 0-85229-440-9
International Standard Serial Number: 0072-7288
Printed in the U.S.A.

A NOTE ON REFERENCE STYLE

In the following pages, passages in *Great Books of the Western World* are referred to by the initials '*GBWW,*' followed by volume, page number, and page section. Thus, '*GBWW,* Vol. 39, p. 210b' refers to page 210 in Adam Smith's *The Wealth of Nations*, which is Volume 39 in *Great Books of the Western World*. The small letter 'b' indicates the page section. In books printed in single column, 'a' and 'b' refer to the upper and lower halves of the page. In books printed in double column, 'a' and 'b' refer to the upper and lower halves of the left column, 'c' and 'd' to the upper and lower halves of the right column. For example, 'Vol. 53, p. 210b' refers to the lower half of page 210, since Volume 53, James's *Principles of Psychology*, is printed in single column. On the other hand, 'Vol. 7, p. 210b' refers to the lower left quarter of the page, since Volume 7, Plato's *Dialogues*, is printed in double column.

Gateway to the Great Books is referred to by the initials '*GGB,*' followed by volume and page number. Thus, '*GGB,* Vol. 10, pp. 39–57' refers to pages 39 through 57 of Volume 10 of *Gateway to the Great Books*, which is James's essay, "The Will to Believe."

The Great Ideas Today is referred to by the initials '*GIT,*' followed by the year and page number. Thus '*GIT* 1968, p. 210' refers to page 210 of the 1968 edition of *The Great Ideas Today.*

Contents

Preface

Readers who glance at the table of contents of this year's issue of *The Great Ideas Today* will see, among the articles on "Current Developments in the Arts and Sciences," that we include a discussion of recent graphic art, chiefly painting. Such an article is long overdue, and we can only plead that the one which now appears, by the distinguished critic Donald Kuspit, is at any rate both sound and comprehensive in its treatment of the subject. This is so despite the fact that the focus of the piece, as its title indicates, is on American art. For it is widely accepted, and Mr. Kuspit himself argues, that the story of painting since mid-century has in fact *been* an American one for the most part, although the most interesting work in the field recently has been coming again from Europe, as up to the beginning of the period covered by the article had always been the case.

A second, somewhat shorter essay in this section of the book is on an aspect of the physical sciences known as chaos, or complexity. Chaos theory is a relatively new branch of physics, though one that may be said to emanate from, or at least be related to, thermodynamics, regarded as the science of stable states. Chaos in this meaning of the word refers rather to unstable states, or rather, to the process by which stable ones become unstable—by which order in nature becomes disordered, as when a stream of water flowing from a faucet loses its tubular form with increasing force and shatters into a random spray. Such a phenomenon, which is readily observed, is interesting because according to recent research there is an order in the approach to disorder which can now be mathematically described. The mathematics are, however, rather difficult to explain to nonmathematicians, so that we are fortunate in having been able to persuade Leo Kadanoff, of the University of Chicago, to undertake the task, as well as to suggest the implications of what has been discovered, in this year's volume.

In the section devoted to "Reconsiderations of Great Books and Ideas" will be found an essay we long ago arranged to have from Anthony Quinton on the subject of animals, specifically the relationship between animals and men. The essay was suggested by Lord Quinton himself, who pointed out that the discussion of animals and animal nature in the *Great Books* is no longer satisfactory in the light of modern research and opinion and was therefore in need of being updated. This he has managed to do, notwithstanding the press of other obligations, with his customary elegance of thought and style, which readers of previous issues of *The Great Ideas Today,* where his writings have also appeared, will particularly appreciate.

In this section are, as well, two pieces by Dr. Adler. One is a discussion of dialectic, the method of inquiry that, as here defined, underlies the *Syntopicon,* where the anatomy of the method is indicated by the topical outlines and references and its application is shown in the chapter introductions. Other illustrations of it with which readers may be familiar are embodied in the *Encyclopædia Britannica* and in *The Great Ideas Today* itself, where the attempt is made to discuss ideas and issues without insisting upon a particular view of them, as to which a different kind of discussion, involving argument and seeking to convince, must be pursued.

Dr. Adler writes following this of the difference between two ways of reading the Great Books—that of the scholar and that of the philosopher—which will be seen as related to his remarks on dialectic. They will be seen also as two kinds of reading that each of us must practice at times, the important thing being not to confuse them, supposing that the methods proper to the one will achieve the aims of the other, and failing to remember that they differ with the two kinds of reading themselves.

Also in this section is an essay on the reading of Euclid by Otto Bird, our contributing editor. Euclid's work on geometry was until this century regarded as the greatest teaching tool among all the writings in *Great Books of the Western World,* and both its structure and the methods of study it requires are still the basis of systematic understanding in nearly every field, not just mathematics. This being so, taking the work as a great teaching model Dr. Bird shows how it can be read—no doubt in some parts more easily than in others—by anyone willing to give it close attention, and suggests the excitement that certain of its propositions generate when we grasp them.

We have, in addition, three "Special Features" in this year's volume. The first and longest of these is a discussion by Thomas K. Simpson of James Clerk Maxwell's *Treatise on Electricity and Magnetism,* a work inaccessible to most readers because of its intricate mathematics, but one that Mr. Simpson treats without resorting to a single equation. At the same time he indicates convincingly the immense contribution it has made to scientific thought, and notes certain ideas in it that scientific thought might have done well to accept but did not.

A second feature is by Maurice Cranston, who writes again this year on Rousseau, taking as his topic the conflict between Rousseau and Jean-Philippe Rameau as to the merits of eighteenth-century French opera, a controversy that acquired philosophic dimensions when it expanded to take on the whole nature of music.

And we have once again Professor George Anastaplo writing on still another great Eastern book, this time the *Gilgamesh* epic, so-called, a Mesopotamian heroic poem from the second millennium B.C., fragments of which were recovered in the last century and have been added to since, though the complete work has not yet been found and probably never will be. This poem, which has been compared to the work of Homer, to which it bears certain similarities, but which in its fragmentary shape it hardly equals, is nevertheless of great interest as the expression of its otherwise vanished civilization and the elements of permanent human truth it contains. Readers will note that, as usual with these essays by Professor Anastaplo, we reprint the work he discusses, in this case the epic itself, or as much of it as survives, in the back of the book.

Of the remaining works in this year's "Additions to the Great Books Library," the chief one is also by Clerk Maxwell, his *Matter and Motion,* first published in 1876 as an elementary (which is not to say simple) text in physics for beginning students. This book, which is something of a classic in its own right, is now inevitably dated in some respects, but as Mr. Simpson's introductory remarks suggest, it offers a conception of physical science that must still intrigue all who contemplate the subject, even if they believe, as science now mostly does, that mathematical equations are the only true language with which to understand nature.

Following *Matter and Motion* are three short papers by Maxwell which help to clarify his thought both on science and on its philosophical underpinnings—Maxwell, who knew science, knowing a great deal else besides, being indeed as competent in Greek as he was in quadratic equations. These papers are devoted to the subject of analogy, to action at a distance, and to the question of the ether.

And for readers of the volume who by this time have had quite as much scientific and mathematical discussion as they can bear, we provide at last another story—an early one—by Henry James, "The Madonna of the Future," which in its preoccupations brings us round full circle to Professor Kuspit's essay on art, though James has, as usual, his own views on that subject, and his peculiar eloquence in rendering them.

PART ONE

Current Developments in the Arts and Sciences

American Art Since Mid-Century

Donald B. Kuspit

Donald Kuspit is professor of art history and philosophy at the State University of New York at Stony Brook. He has a doctorate in philosophy from the University of Frankfurt and one in art history from the University of Michigan. He edits three series of books for the University of Michigan's Research Press: *Contemporary American Art Critics, Art Criticism,* and *Art Theory*.

Professor Kuspit has amassed a large body of work as an art critic, having written some 400 articles, exhibition reviews, and book reviews; he has also curated 35 exhibitions. In 1983 he received the Frank Jewett Mather Award for Distinction in Art Criticism, given by the College Art Association of America. He is editor of *Art Criticism,* contributing editor of *Art in America,* a staff member at *Artforum,* and a regular contributor to *Artscribe, Arts,* and *Wolkenkratzer*.

Among his books are *Clement Greenberg, Art Critic* (1978), *The Critic Is Artist: The Intentionality of Art* (1984), and *Leon Golub, Existentialist/ Activist Painter* (1985).

Introduction: The Americanness of American Art

Since colonial days, American art has been troubled by a sense of inferiority to European art. It was rarely as innovative as European art, and rarely as interesting in its outlook. It had no clear sense of its own identity—of what it meant to be uniquely American. Only in the period after World War II did American art come into its own against European art, transcending, if also utilizing, European models of art-making. For the first time, it achieved international importance, inseparable from the general prominence of American society and culture in the postwar period. Its development became rich, complicated, and unprecedented.

In the process of becoming a specifically "American" art, postwar American art became the leading avant-garde art as well. It picked up where prewar European avant-garde art left off, taking it in a new American direction, without denying indebtedness to it. While for postwar European artists the development of prewar avant-garde art was a finished history, American artists were able to find fresh creative stimulus in it. In general, the new American art filled the cultural vacuum left by devastated postwar Europe and lifted the curse that Hitler put on avant-garde art by his abusive labeling of it as "degenerate" and crypto-Communist. America became the new home for advanced art.

If this sounds chauvinistic, one has only to recall the well-known art critic Clement Greenberg's dismissal of most postwar School of Paris painting as "self-evident confectionary" in contrast to vital American painting.[1] Similarly, Harold Rosenberg's famous "Parable of American Painting" distinguishes between the professional European artist, wearing a ready-made uniform of style ("Redcoatism"), and the "sharp-shooting" American artist, working without stylistic preconceptions, even without style—retaining the inventive individualism of the pioneer ("Coonskinism").[2] His art is based on existential experience of the "raw *scene*" of the new American world.

Rosenberg's distinction resembles that which Greenberg makes between the postwar Parisian attempt to make Abstract Expressionist painting "more acceptable to standard taste" by giving it a finish and unity that destroys its force—which, as Greenberg says, tames rather than disciplines it—and "the fresher, more open, more immediate surface" of American Abstract Expressionist painting. "Standard [European] taste is offended by what looks like undue looseness, and as usual, mistakes a new [American] spontaneity and directness for disorder or at best, solipsistic decoration." In fact, for Greenberg it is American artists who carry forward what has been the "productive impulse in [modern] painting"—the bellwether art—since its discovery by the European artist Édouard Manet: the attempt to give "aesthetic purpose" to the seemingly "too intractable, too raw and accidental."[3] Again, for Rosenberg, it is postwar American art that retains "the surprise of the new" that Charles Baudelaire regarded as of the essence of modernity, not postwar European art. After World War II, it was the energetic Americans rather than the exhausted Europeans who had the power to, in Ezra Pound's words, "make it new."

"Raw" is the key concept for both Greenberg and Rosenberg; the pursuit of rawness gave American art authority, and independence from European art. American rawness was the antidote to European polish. Already in 1837, Ralph Waldo Emerson, in his address "The American Scholar," stated the problem of American art and culture: "We have listened too long to the courtly muses of Europe. The spirit of the American freeman is already suspected to be timid, imitative, tame." A few lines later he stated the solution to the problem of becoming uniquely, and a truly "free," American: "the single man [must] plant himself indomitably on his instincts"—on the rawest part of his nature.[4] This is the same solution offered a century later by American Abstract Expressionist painters, as when Jackson Pollock, the greatest of them, asked where the nature was in his abstract paintings, replied "I am nature." It is as though, because one is an American—the inhabitant of a raw, young, land—one is necessarily more natural—instinctive and individual—than the cultivated, conformist European.

Similarly, in 1871, in *Democratic Vistas,* Walt Whitman wrote: "America has yet morally and artistically originated nothing. She seems singularly unaware that the models of persons, books, manners, etc., appropriate for former conditions and for European lands, are but exiles and exotics here."[5] As in Emerson, the secret of American originality is "the all-varied, all-permitting, all-free theorem of individuality," inseparable from a sense of infinite, "common" nature—"ever the most precious in the common."[6] Following in Whitman's as well as Emerson's footsteps, Pollock carried the "theorem of individuality" to an extreme, creating a seemingly "all-varied, all-permitting, all-free" art, which encompassed the antipodes of American nature. "Living is keener, more demanding, more intense and expansive in New York than in the West. . . . At the same time, I have a definite feeling for the West: the vast horizontality of the land, for instance."[7] Pollock's holistic, so-called all-over paintings fuse verticals and horizontals in a

"Number 1, 1948" (1948), by Jackson Pollock. *"Losing all sense of clear direction in a Pollock painting, one is left with a sense of vast, raw space—a very American kind of space."*

momentum that seems to abolish the difference between them. Losing all sense of clear direction in a Pollock painting, one is left with a sense of vast, raw space—a very American kind of space.

At the same time, Pollock attempted to reconcile this naturally raw American space with naturally raw human nature, by using the one to evoke the other. Again, it is because one is a raw American, rather than a cultivated European, that one is in a better position to grasp and articulate raw human nature. "I am particularly impressed with their concept of the source of art being the unconscious," Pollock said of the Europeans. "This idea interests me more than these specific [European modern] painters do."[8] The unconscious is the internally raw, much as American nature is exceptionally raw external nature. Pollock's painting seems authentically American because it combines the rawest internal and external nature in a completely "instinctive"—totally natural—painterliness. Its forceful fluidity metaphorically represents the primordially—"originally"—human as well as mythically primordial American nature.

But Pollock was acutely aware of the difficulty, even the impossibility and the undesirability, of making a strictly "all-American" painting. Such a provincial, isolationist painting would be unrealistic and irrelevant in the modern world. Rebelling against the idea of a hermetic, self-generating American art—the idea of the necessary, even superior, provincialism of American art—Pollock acknowledged, and advocated, a "universal"—international—art.

This rebellion, and the insistence upon a broadly based, generally modern art, less specifically if finally inescapably American, is a direct response to the isolationism and chauvinism of the American Social Realist painters of the thirties, especially Pollock's own teacher, Thomas Hart Benton, whose work he described as "important as something against which to react very strongly." The new cosmopolitanism of American art is the other side of its peculiarly American rawness, and as usual, in his greatness, Pollock reconciles these apparent opposites, showing their dialectical relationship. In 1944, at the beginning of his meteoric career, Pollock remarked: "The idea of an isolated American painting, so popular in this country during the 'thirties, seems absurd to me, just as the idea of creating a purely American mathematics or physics would seem absurd. . . . And in another sense, the problem doesn't exist at all; or, if it did, would solve itself: An American is an American and his painting would naturally be qualified by that fact, whether he wills it or not. But the basic problems of contemporary painting are independent of any one country."[9]

As William Rubin has pointed out in his series of articles on "Jackson Pollock and the Modern Tradition," Pollock's extraordinary achievement—the achievement that has made him either an inspiration or obstacle to every subsequent advanced artist, American or European—consisted in his ability to concentrate and integrate in his own development that of what Rubin regarded as the major movements in modern art, from Impressionism through Cubism to Surrealism.[10] Pollock's ontogeny recapitulated the entire basic phylogeny of modern art. It is worth noting that his kind of "ecumenical," assimilative approach is as inseparable from being American as is the celebration of, and the sense of having privileged access to, raw nature. Thus Whitman, in the same breath in which he celebrates and correlates American individuality and naturalness, insists that in attempting to "promulgate her own new standard," America has the responsibility of "accepting the old, the perennial elements, and combining them into groups, unities, appropriate to the modern, the democratic, the west."[11] Postwar American art is freshly raw, but simultaneously sophisticated in its awareness of past traditions of art, especially of the movements that constitute what Rosenberg called the "tradition of the new."

It is for this reason—because of the extraordinary diversity of sources and interests that inform postwar American art, both aesthetic and ideological—that it cannot be said to have a uniform, continuous development, with one movement privileged as a mainstream from which all others derive as tributaries. There are what can be regarded as climactic moments, and it is the case that Abstract Expressionism is the seminal movement. But most of the movements are at cross-purposes, however secretly connected by a dialectical umbilical cord. I will attempt to show their connection without compromising the theoretically "raw" individuality of any movement. In any case, the methodological difficulty of putting all the pieces together is testimony to the vital diversity of postwar American art. This diversity has its logic—it is not a hollow, chaotic pluralism, in which everything is possible and valuable—but the logic is not easily articulated. At the same time, conventional categorizations of it remain useful as guidelines, like ropes on the deck of a ship in a storm.

A general division must be made between first-generation (1947–55) and second-generation (1956–60) Abstract Expressionism. A sharper division must be made between Abstract Expressionism as a whole, and the sixties rebellion against it of Pop art and Minimalism, fraternal twins in attitude despite their difference in appearance. The sixties close with Conceptual or Idea art, which rebels against both as well as Abstract Expressionism, while acknowledging the subtle influence of Minimalism.

In general, the interaction of all the players in the field is evident at first glance, and even the blank spaces in the historical field—such as Op art—do not deny the fact that every player has a tendentious relation to every other and desires total dominance of the field. As the philosopher and sociologist of art Theodor Adorno has written, no serious art cares to live comfortably with any other, but desires to refute and devalue the others in the name of its own superordinate value. Moreover, the emergence in the seventies of a new sociopolitically oriented art, more important for its attitude to world-historical events than for aesthetic innovation—so-called Protest art—complicates matters. Protest art is not a stylistic movement, although it has stylistic implications. It develops in response to such consciousness-raising events in American society as the women's rights movement, the black civil rights movement, and the Vietnam War. It is a major attempt to abolish what Baudelaire called the "puerile"—yet long-lived—idea of art for art's sake, and to make art once again human.

Partly reportorial and topical, partly an emotional call-to-arms and autobiographical sign of social activism, Protest art utilized and reconceived all kinds of traditional styles to make its point. It was the *dernier cri* of modernist, avant-garde art in the original sense of the term: a brutal revelation of a brutal society.[12] At the same time, it prepared the way for the eighties, when all styles have come to seem equally valid, in part because art has become the victim of its own consumer success, with the art world expanding far beyond what it was in the Abstract Expressionist forties and fifties.

In the current situation, art history has become a cross between a bank vault full of securities and a warehouse of theatrical props, to be exploited at will. It is hard to tell whether such conscious borrowing from tradition is a sign of failure of nerve or a creative opportunism tinged with ancestral worship. In any case, the brief American dominance of the international art scene is over, even if there are still serious, important American artists. "European art is 'back'," at least since the 1981 exhibition of "A New Spirit of Painting" at the Royal Academy of Arts in London.[13] Yet the energetic new internationalism of the eighties, in which European—especially German and Italian—art has become freshly prominent, testifies to the staying power of postwar American art, for the European artists have assimilated its various aspects the way the Abstract Expressionists once assimilated important European styles. Such dependence implicitly acknowledges the value of what is assimilated.

The American era of art has not closed. Rather, in the so-called postmodernist eighties modernist American art has become the atmosphere in which all other art is made, showing its success. As the contradictions which informed the development of modern art in general—the tense competition between nonrepresentational and representational art, between aesthetic and ideological conceptions of art, between tradition and individual talent,[14] and between museum art and media or street "art" as resources and general models for art-making[15]—have broken down, artists have attempted to invent what Van Wyck Brooks called a personally "usable past." Significant past styles have come to be regarded as culturally sound forms of authentic selfhood. To appropriate them was to begin to establish one's own selfhood. The new culture of quotation, as it has been called, has a peculiarly subjective purpose. To quote is to create a center where there is none. This new sophisticated way of becoming "rooted" is not unrelated to the earlier, heroic Abstract Expressionist pursuit of rawness, which also implies an insecure, temporary—if more tempestuous—sense of selfhood. However, there is no doubt that suffering for the sake of individuality has changed its meaning in the change from modernism to postmodernism, and the idea of "naturalness" has been completely lost to American art.

Abstract Expressionism

Clement Greenberg, one of the movement's early and major advocates, almost always used the term "Abstract Expressionism" in quotation marks.[16] His point was that the "plenitude of presence" Abstract Expressionist paintings offer was not "a newfangled thrill, but something whose equivalent I find in the successful art of the past."[17] Thus, Greenberg could write: "A good deal of what is so rashly called 'abstract expressionism' amounts essentially to a kind of Late Cubism (which takes nothing away from it in principle)."[18]

In playing up the art historical heritage of Abstract Expressionism, Greenberg played down just what Harold Rosenberg, the movement's other major advocate, emphasized: its role as a means of articulating a specifically American sense of selfhood.[19] Debate about the correct interpretation of Abstract Expressionism continues to the present day, with one side insisting upon the movement's purely stylistic significance, and the other its depth of psychological implications. Jackson Pollock has become the focus of the debate, which is really about the valid methodology for understanding art.[20]

Both sides are correct, by the testimony of the artists themselves. Abstract Expressionism is inseparable from the development of modern art in general, but it is an original response to that development, synthesizing its major innovations to give them new import. As the painter John Ferren wrote, Abstract Expressionism was a marriage between "the essential principles of Abstraction, that 'pure form and color have emotional significance,' and of Surrealism, 'that human experience of life goes inwardly in depth as well as outwardly' . . . but in their fusion they were radically altered."[21]

This fusion was a heroically creative achievement against great odds. It showed the error of the all-powerful School of Paris's assumption that abstraction and Surrealism were irreconcilable. Because they originated in different attitudes and had different stylistic ideals, the two supposedly could not be made to work together. That assumption led each to dead-end in a stereotype. Their fusion in Abstract Expressionism, as absurd and incoherent as it looked at first, lifted the curse of limitations that each had imposed on itself out of resistance to the other. Each had defined its integrity in a deliberately narrow way out of self-conscious recognition of the alien presence of the other, reducing its own sense of possibilities. Insisting upon its pristine integrity, each had become sterile.

Their American synthesis (America has always been the place where opposites hoped to work out their union fruitfully) involved not only a repudiation of the European stereotyping of abstraction and Surrealism as one-dimensional but of the one-dimensionality of American Regional painting, with its *retardataire* representational style and lack of emotional depth. Nonetheless, Abstract Expressionism integrated the most salient aspects of modern American and European art and mentality, while stripping both of their provinciality. "In the general ferment of a new point of view . . . the stubborn temper [of] the Middle West" and the major aspects of European modernism converged in a grand synthesis: "the two-dimensional surface of Cubism, the free form of Miró and Kandinsky, the primitivism of Klee, the end-all of Mondrian, the color of Matisse and Bonnard, the genius pure and simple of Picasso."[22] In a sense, modern art was reinvented in American terms, and the modern outlook reaffirmed in the context of American life.

As Robert Motherwell wrote—he was the youngest first-generation Abstract Expressionist painter, and their intellectual spokesman—"The function of the *modern* artist is by definition the felt expression of modern reality," and the major problem of modern reality is the "individual's freedom." The freedom the modern artist seeks implies "rejection

. . . of the values of the bourgeois world. In this world modern artists form a kind of *spiritual underground*" or resistance.[23] In a sense, from the perspective of Abstract Expressionism, bourgeois Europe had destroyed itself—confirming the bankruptcy of its values—in World War II. The values of bourgeois America had therefore to be challenged. Abstract Expressionist style—primitive, abstract, radically individualistic—was in effect a critique of the bourgeois American life-style.

Meyer Schapiro sharpened the contrast by formulating it in terms of a distinction between bourgeois communication and radically spiritual art: between familiar representational art, which "transmits an already prepared and complete message to a relatively indifferent and impersonal receiver," and radically spiritual abstract art, which "induce(s) an attitude of communion and contemplation" and offers "an equivalent of what is regarded as part of religious life: a sincere and humble submission to a spiritual object, an experience which is not given automatically, but requires preparation and purity of spirit."[24] This polarization is a constant of postwar American art. It states the basic terms of the argument which postwar American art is—the extremes between which it oscillates, sometimes violently, sometimes subtly.

On the one side, there are artists who advocate an easily assimilable, seemingly facile art of communication which requires little emotional or intellectual preparation—special engagement—on the part of the spectator, and which takes its point of departure from the stream of everyday appearances and media-derived images that inundate us in American society. On the other side, there are artists who insist, as Motherwell puts it, on the modern necessity of an art that is "remote" not only because it has developed a specialized abstract language but because it is spiritually demanding, a challenge to the conventional values articulated through the communication arts.[25]

The development of Abstract Expressionism is inseparable from the emergence of New York as the world center of art. Because of World War II, many important European artists and architects came to New York, if later moving elsewhere. From the Bauhaus alone came Josef Albers, Lyonel Feininger, Laszlo Moholy-Nagy, Naum Gabo, Walter Gropius, Marcel Breuer, and Ludwig Mies van der Rohe. From France came Amédée Ozenfant and Fernand Léger. Perhaps most important, Piet Mondrian came, with his uncompromisingly abstract or pure painting. Finally, such major Surrealist masters as Roberto Matta, Salvador Dalí, Max Ernst, and André Masson came, together with André Breton, who had written the first Surrealist manifesto (1924).

Peggy Guggenheim, Max Ernst's wife, opened the important gallery-museum Art of This Century (1942–46), which became a showcase for European abstract and Surrealist art. Guggenheim also first showed such young American Abstract Expressionists as Pollock, Motherwell, William Baziotes, Mark Rothko, Clyfford Still, Adolph Gottlieb, Richard

Pousette-Dart, and David Hare—artists who tried to fuse the two major kinds of modern European art. Hans Hofmann, along with Arshile Gorky instrumental as a mediator of modern European art (both acknowledged Cubism as its major tradition, while using it to pursue surreal effect), had his first one-person show at Guggenheim's gallery. The stage was set for the transmutation of modern European into modern American art.

In a sense, the problem of Abstract Expressionism can be understood as an attempt to create purely abstract, generally painterly works whose metaphoric power was enhanced by memory traces of the figure that remained embedded in the painterliness. The problem was not to lose sight of the figure, yet not to let it exist realistically—banally. Looked at from the other side, the problem was to create a painting that was nothing but a brilliantly executed painting—an autonomous object—while retaining the spiritual or psychodramatic implications associated with the figure. The figure was camouflaged, making it freshly mysterious. In fact, Gorky taught a wartime class in camouflage, learning that "if the realistic object can be camouflaged, so can the unreal, or 'surreal' object be decoded and decamouflaged."[26] Eventually the figure was

Pollock painting in his studio. *"Abstract Expressionism has been called variously action painting, process painting, and gestural painting: the figure is in the process of dissolving into gesture through the action of the painting."*

relinquished, but not before its aura was exhausted. As Mark Rothko stated, "It was with the utmost reluctance that I found the figure could not serve my purposes. . . . But a time came when none of us could use the figure without mutilating it."[27]

If one looks at "Mural" (1943), a work crucial both in Pollock's particular and Abstract Expressionism's general development, one sees a grouping of attenuated, totemlike figures in the process of dissolving into the painterly flow. The figures are ambiguously powerful, pure paint strokes and grotesque, haunting, visionary images. One can see why Abstract Expressionism has been called variously action painting, process painting, and gestural painting: the figure is in the process of dissolving into gesture through the action of the painting—in the process of becoming a pure painterly act. (These concepts elaborate the Surrealist idea of automatism: uncensored, spontaneous articulation.) Yet the pure painterly gesture seems to connote the figure—can be unconsciously read as a figure, which charges it with unconscious meanings. The old problem of the relationship of figure and ground is faced with a new sense of their dramatic interaction, even interchangeability. The surreal figure is charged with the energy of the field of paint, and the field of paint takes on a surreal dimension by reason of its incorporation of the figure. It is as though the picture is a python digesting the whole history of the figure and the long chain of conscious and unconscious associations attached to it.

The superior flatness of Abstract Expressionism's "all-over, 'decentralized,' 'polyphonic' picture that relies on a surface knit together of identical or closely similar elements which repeat themselves"[28] is the result of profound repression of the figure. The figure becomes a latent texture, a ghost haunting the quasi-decorative surface with its energy, which fuses with that of the surface's manifest texture. Imploded figure and explosive surface become one. The fusion of the abstracted figure and the animated material surface gives the work an especially intense concreteness. Pollock's ghosts in "Mural" are formalized sedimentations of unconscious energy. They recur in all his works, even the purest ones.

It was in 1948, with "Number 1," that these hyper-pure paintings of Pollock's emerged. Such immediate ancestors as "Full Fathom Five," "Cathedral," and "Eyes in the Heat II"(all 1947) have implicit figural allusions, as signaled by their titles. While the figure seems to disappear entirely until 1951, when fragments of figures openly return, as in "Number 23, 1951" ("Frogman"), one can trace its residual effect through works such as "Summertime" (1948) and "Out of the Web" (1949) to "Blue Poles" (1953). In these works the figure exists in the extra-density—the transiently ecstatic standing-out—of the dervishing vertical elements. These paintings, extravagantly spatialized durations, seem to demand a figurelike element as a way of "marking" internal time.

After Pollock, Willem de Kooning has been acknowledged as the most important Abstract Expressionist painter. De Kooning has always remained openly loyal to the figure, as his extended series of paintings of women indicates. Even in his purely landscape paintings there is a sensual implication, which is easily associated with the eternal feminine, and later in his development he explicitly merges landscape and woman, as if by sympathetic magic. De Kooning is important because his rough-hewn painterliness seems particularly exemplary of Abstract Expressionist all-over style at its most self-contradictory. His virile early female figures look as if they were hacked out of some obdurate material, like unfinished sculptures, not always distinguishable from the chips of paint that litter the ground of the painting as the spatial waste of their creation. It is a style which seems to bespeak manual labor, the lowest kind of labor, the labor of the impoverished, such as the painters were when they made their most famous works. (Recognition of this aspect of Abstract Expressionism has been repressed in its bourgeois assimilation.)

The labor-intensive character of de Kooning's style is inseparable from the struggle between figure and space in his works. In his later works this struggle sometimes seems facilely resolved, but it is renewed with new Expressionist import in his sculptures. In de Kooning, painterly release seems more troubled and convulsive—modern beauty must be convulsive, as Breton asserts at the end of his novel *Nadja*—than in Pollock, and so, less subject to what Freud called the Nirvana principle. In some ways more explicitly than Pollock, de Kooning shows the dialectical character of "the principle of congestion" operational in the most tough-minded, fanatical Abstract Expressionism. It is perhaps in his important black-and-white paintings of the late forties and early fifties that a pregnant density is most vigorously and unnervingly realized. These works approach chaos without dissolving—always a major test of modern art. The paintings seem not only a special climax of the general Expressionist use of black and white—the classic noncolors for the articulation of internal necessity, the drama of inner life—but a climax as well of the history of "the anxious object," the term Harold Rosenberg uses to characterize the modern work of art in general.[29]

Of all the Abstract Expressionists, Motherwell seems closest to the European heritage and mentality. His ongoing series of elegiac homages to the Spanish Republic (begun in the forties) recapitulates the Surrealist heritage in abstract terms, and his later Open series (begun in the mid-sixties) recapitulates the heritage of pure abstraction in a quasi-surreal way. Gorky struggled with this heritage, disciplining himself by repeated acts of pictorial devotion to it, so much so that until his death a perceptive critic such as Greenberg could think he was merely a camp follower. Only after death was Gorky's extraordinary synthesizing achievement appreciated. For the more passively nostalgic Motherwell, the modernist heritage seemed painlessly—sentimentally—available, and the synthesis appeared a pleasurable, facile accomplishment. In a sense, Gorky and Motherwell represent the poles of Abstract Expressionist attitude to the European heritage. Motherwell was ready to be Europeanized without understanding the full depth of the European accomplishment, and Gorky, despite his obvious debt to the modern European masters, deepened the sense of what American painting could be.

If one compares the black-and-white paintings of Franz Kline to both, one sees what explicitly American Abstract Expressionist painting embodies: a radical sense of directness and concreteness, even more radicalized by a determined renunciation of metaphoric implications. While Kline's works have been moralized as "Manichaean"[30] (many puritanized American minds cannot tolerate sensually straightforward paintings but must spontaneously fill what seems like their vacuum of meaning with transparent associations), they in fact show the affinity between the European pursuit of pure painting and the American pursuit of direct experience. Kline forces criticism back to laconic appreciation and description, in a sense showing that consciousness is at its most critical when it is seeing without comment. Consciousness' own intense directedness can be the only proper comment on paintings as directly and exclusively sensual as possible. Susan Sontag's call for an "erotics of art" was really a demand that consciousness understand itself.[31]

Even among artists it was not possible to tolerate the apparent meaninglessness that arose from determinedly pure painting—painting that, in its complete repudiation of the extra-artistic, was the most convincing signal of modernist art's autonomy. Much Abstract Expressionist painting can be understood as a search for poetic or unconscious meaning by way of the so-called pictograph and biomorphic form, which alludes to organic form but cannot be found in nature. Pictographic and biomorphic form often fuse in a singular image. Both make explicit the primitive linguistic character of abstract form and its power to evoke primitive emotions. Their poetry has been understood to extend the primitivizing side of Surrealism—to try, through primitive image-forms, to articulate directly the primitive unconscious. Cave paintings were understood to be constructed of pictographs, and mandalas to be biomorphs of heavenly creatures. (Were biomorphic forms attempts to give organic appearances the status of abstract mandalas?) More immediately, the pictograph and biomorph were derived from certain singular forms that seem to have been invented by Miró and extended by Picasso. Nonetheless, they are peculiarly American attempts to create a kind of primitive or irreducible picture and organic form. The pictograph reflects an American sense of reductive simplification,

"Voyager's Return" (1946), by Adolph Gottlieb. *"The pictograph reflects an American sense of reductive simplification, as biomorphic form shows an American sense of the mysterious Gothic possibilities of nature."*

as biomorphic form shows an American sense of the mysterious Gothic possibilities of nature. (This is evident in Edgar Allan Poe but is not unrelated to Odilon Redon (1840–1916), who fantasized creatures that Louis Pasteur said deserved to live. Redon, incidentally, invented protobiomorphs to illustrate Poe.)

Adolph Gottlieb is credited with the first use of pictographs, and a work such as "Voyager's Return" (1946) seems like a basic alphabet of them. Sexually allusive biomorphic form is much in evidence in Gorky's late works (1940s) and in such early works by Rothko as "Prehistoric Memories" (1946). The pictograph and biomorph demonstrate the pursuit—partly inspired by the psychoanalytic outlook—of the prehistoric and mythological ("primitive mentality") typical of much Abstract Expressionism. The one issue of the magazine *Possibilities* (Winter 1947/48), illustrated with poetic Abstract Expressionist pictures and full of scholarly and speculative articles dealing with the idea as well as the actuality of the primitive, shows just how comprehensive and determined was the effort to reconstruct—and make poetic capital out of—primitivism at the time. There was a headlong attempt to resurrect—reinvent—the archaic. At one time or another all the Abstract Expressionists willingly endured a rite of passage through the poetically

"Black, Pink, and Yellow Over Orange" (1951–52), by Mark Rothko. Rothko, as well as other Abstract Expressionist artists, *"moved beyond primitivism, adding a major new dimension to Abstract Impressionism. . . . The picture lost all its descriptive, and theoretically even its evocative, power. But it became all the more pure a painting."*

conceived primitive. Some of them, such as Baziotes and Theodore Stamos, never came out of it. Archaic image-form, rich with archaic connotation, became the absolute goal of their art, bringing a major aspect of Abstract Expressionism to ripeness.

Other artists, such as Barnett Newman, Clyfford Still, and Mark Rothko, moved beyond primitivism, adding a major new dimension to Abstract Expressionism, if it can still be called that. The term "Abstract Impressionism" has been used to describe their achievement, but, as Greenberg points out, that is as misleading as "Abstract Expressionism." He uses the more neutral " 'American-Type' Painting." If, as Greenberg says, it is "a law of modernism . . . that the conventions not essential to the viability of a medium be discarded as soon as they are recognized,"[32] then what the American-type painters did was discard the convention of vestigial illusionistic space that was the Cubist heritage. Shallow space, in which subliminal images could exist, was completely flattened out. The pictorial surface was uncompromisingly reduced to its original flatness, which was finessed by pure color in the process of being articulated by it. The picture lost all its descriptive, and theoretically even its evocative, power. But it became all the more pure a painting. As Greenberg wrote, Still's paintings were "the first *serious* abstract pictures . . . almost entirely devoid of decipherable references to Cubism."[33] Late Monet inspired this change, proving Greenberg's point that "the devolution of tradition cannot take place except in the presence of tradition."[34]

Barnett Newman was the leader in this purification of the all-over painting into the field painting. His "forthright verticality as well as . . . activated, pregnant 'emptiness' . . . constitute[d] perhaps the most direct attack yet on the easel convention."[35] Newman's provocative gestural "zip" in a flat color void remains an extreme of purity, even though Newman meant his picture as a poetic evocation of a primitive state of being. Rothko's structures of scumbled colors are less aggressive articulations of the medium's limits, and have been more readily interpreted as "mystical"—evocative—in import than Newman's works. That is, they regress more easily to a poetic, and so less pure, condition. Gottlieb and Pousette-Dart, moving beyond the pictograph, developed an imagery which tried to reconcile the field painting's purity of surface with its poetic potential. Despite the powerful and meditative results, they show that it is not easy to have it both ways. One tends to read their pictures one way or the other. It is perhaps best to remain openly caught on the horns of the dilemma, enjoying one's precarious position, as Bradley Walker Tomlin, Mark Tobey, Milton Resnick, Joan Mitchell, and Lee Krasner seem to do.

In field painting, which soon became *de rigeur* and institutionalized in what Greenberg called "post-painterly abstraction," painting reached both an apogee of self-reflexivity and a nadir of cultural meaning.

Despite the effort of such independent field painters as Ad Reinhardt to attribute mystical import to their works—easier to do in Reinhardt's case because of his use of a grid as a mandala—the works were generally understood entirely in terms of their manipulation of their empirically given physical attributes: flatness and edge (shape), and the color and line used to articulate them. A whole group of artists, often producing very different looking works, can be traced to the common aesthetic root of field painting.

In recent years various artists and critics have argued that the bankruptcy or exhaustion of abstraction began with its post-painterly triumph in the early sixties. Recent exhibitions of the once universally acclaimed work of Morris Louis, Kenneth Noland, Jules Olitski, Larry Poons, and Frank Stella, among many others, have met with skepticism. The works of Still, Newman, and Rothko have sustained their significance, perhaps because they still resonate poetically—still have a primitive aura. In post-painterly abstraction and affiliated works, purity, in becoming completely realized, unexpectedly subverted itself. In killing off the poetic and primitive, it committed slow suicide. In becoming completely sophisticated and civilized, pure painting lost the inner dialectic or contradiction that was its dynamic.

Frank Stella, deliberately antihumanistic—that is, antifigural and antipoetic, or generally anticonnotative—argued for a purely perceptual art: "what you see is what you get." But the collapse of the abstract picture's inner dialogue between "humanistic"—however diluted—and perceptual values led to the collapse of abstraction as a value and

"Ifafa II" (1964), by Frank Stella. *"Frank Stella, deliberately antihumanistic—that is, antifigural and antipoetic, or generally anticonnotative—argued for a purely perceptual art: 'what you see is what you get.' "*

goal in itself. Post-painterly abstraction took the pursuit of purity to an extreme at which it became meaningless—at which the sensuality it articulated became empty sensation. A hollow, completely denotative—self-denoting—picture was created. The journey of perceptual discovery initiated by Impressionism's, and especially Cézanne's, articulation of the mystery of "vibrating sensation" was over. There was no more mystery left in modern sensation.

There have been a number of important Abstract Expressionist sculptors, the most prominent being David Smith. Smith was always preoccupied with the problem of uniting painting and sculpture, and his early works were a kind of idiomatic fusion of generalized Expressionist and Surrealist styles. The most important of these works, the "Medals for Dishonor" (1937–40), were explicitly political in character. It is hard to tell whether their Expressionistic Surrealism was grafted on to their searing Social Realism, or vice versa.

After World War II Smith began producing a number of wonderfully lyrical sculptural landscapes, many of which incorporated found objects. "Blackburn—Song of an Irish Blacksmith" (1950) and "Hudson River Landscape" (1951) are major examples. These welded works show a linear tautness and complexity inseparable from gesturalism. Their illusionistic, pictorial quality—they are like calligraphic poems painted in three dimensions—is confirmed by their framed look. They have been called a kind of "drawing-in-space," and they seem to flatten out internally and externally. The object-images in them seem more like knots in the grain of a flat space than truly space displacing.

This self-contained—peculiarly pictorial—concentration remains throughout Smith's development, even in his three major series, "Voltri-Bolton," "Zig," and "Cubi." While the Voltri-Bolton series (begun 1962) is supposedly the last based explicitly on the human figure, the tumbling verticality of the Zig and Cubi works clearly has figural connotations, even though they are purged of organic elements. And yet traces of the organic remain in the polished touch and dramatic light effects of the Cubi series surfaces.

All of Smith's works make most sense when located in a landscape. This is true even of the explicitly geometrical Zig and Cubi works. Smith shows his Americanness in his fusion of the tinker's and frontiersman's attitudes. His works seem to be the products of a machine shop set up in the American wilderness, reflecting raw nature as they defy it. His works have a hybrid look; they seem manufactured and organically grown at once, realizing a modernist ideal.

Other Abstract Expressionist sculpture, such as that of Ibram Lassaw, David Hare, Herbert Ferber, Seymour Lipton, Theodore Roszak, and Reuben Nakian, seems more decidedly organically grown than manufactured, even though it is welded metal. John Chamberlain uses manufactured material—crushed automobile parts—and Mark Di Su-

"Factum I" (1957, above), and "Factum II" (1957, opposite), by Robert Rauschenberg. *"Pop art . . . began to develop when the possibilities of the Abstract Expressionist sensibility seemed exhausted, whether*

because of rebellious dissatisfaction with its character by young artists, or because it no longer promised as creative and independent an artistic future for them as it had done for its progenitors."

vero uses equally "heroic" material—giant wooden beams—but the effect in both is of organic structure even though Di Suvero's sculpture is assembled. The same can be said of Louise Nevelson's wooden assemblages, with their mostly black grid structures full of small wooden objects, sometimes erratically, sometimes neatly, displayed. In all these works a certain surreal figural impact remains, for all their abstractness. They seem more Surrealistic than pure. Few of the sculptors struggle as intensely with the dilemma of Abstract Expressionism as the painters do. The results are often ingratiating. Abstract Expressionist sculpture is generally valuable as a demonstration of the difficulty of making art that integrates character and consequence—abstract integrity and unconscious power—rather than as an example of work that unquestionably does so.

Pop art

Pop art—along with Minimal art, as we will see—began to develop when the possibilities of the Abstract Expressionist sensibility seemed exhausted, whether because of rebellious dissatisfaction with its character by young artists, or because it no longer promised as creative and independent an artistic future for them as it had done for its progenitors. As often occurs in the history of art, the refusal of young artists to be the epigones of an existing movement—to be decadent—led to innovative practice. Lawrence Alloway said of artists emerging in the mid-1950s that they

> turned away from gestural art or never entered it. Jasper Johns's targets from 1955, [Kenneth] Noland's circles from late 1958, and [Frank] Stella's symmetrical black paintings of 1958–59 are . . . significant shifts from the directional brushwork and projected anxiety of the Expressionists. [Robert] Rauschenberg's twin paintings, "Factum I" and "Factum II," 1957, along with duplicated photographs, included almost identical paint splashes and trickles, an ironic and loaded image. A gestural mark was turned into a repeatable object.[36]

Alloway is credited with inventing the term "Pop art" in 1954 to describe the art of the so-called Independent Group of English artists.[37] Lucy Lippard regards Johns's "depersonalizing [of] his own action-painting techniques"[38] as "simplified composition," a Duchampian sense of the ready-made object, ambiguously or ironically art and nonart (Lippard thinks he made the painting itself into one[39]), as the beginning of the new aesthetic that eventually became Pop art style. In other words, Johns is the major figure showing the way from Abstract Expressionism to Pop art, if never himself arriving or wanting to arrive there.

Johns points away from the sense of unconscious depth Abstract

"Three Flags" (1958), by Jasper Johns. *"Johns is the major figure showing the way from Abstract Expressionism to Pop art, if never himself arriving or wanting to arrive there. Johns points . . . toward Pop art's sense of social surface."*

Expressionism tried to evoke toward Pop art's sense of social surface. Johns's representation in painting of such socially familiar objects as the American flag and the map of the United States, and in sculpture of ale cans and a flashlight, leads directly to the flat affect of Roy Lichtenstein's impersonal, all-American images. Alain Robbe-Grillet regarded Lichtenstein as implying that his " 'flat images conform far more to what really goes on inside our heads, than those false depths' of lyrical abstraction or abstract expressionism."[40]

The point is that Johns, and in a different way Rauschenberg, with his obsession with "heterogeneity" of image—they have been viewed as roped together the way Pablo Picasso and Georges Braque were during the development of Cubism—introduce a new outlook as well as sensibility: a turn away from personally created gesture toward ready-made popular imagery.

A fundamental reorientation of art, even change in the basic conception of its means and function, is involved. It is a change from Abstract Expressionism's view of the work of art as so radically individual that it successfully resists being socially assimilated to the Pop art conception of it as highly socialized—inseparable from society—to begin with. Pop art implies that art is a manipulated perception of socially given visual facts, while Abstract Expressionism implies that it is an imaginative act of self-creation whose public product is the metaphoric record of the private, but existentially exemplary, process. Abstract Expressionism emphasizes the original "work" that went into the work of art, while Pop art emphasizes its reality as a social object. Most Abstract Expressionist art looks as if it has been relentlessly worked over, while much Pop art looks as if it has hardly been worked at. It is the difference between "hot" and "cool"—emphatic and detached—approaches. They are not necessarily irreconcilable, but taken together they do seem to point to a basic dichotomy in art-making as well as different expectations from art.

Abstract Expressionism, in its preoccupation with the private achievement of selfhood, seemed blind to the givenness of the public world; Pop art, in its exploration of the character of the world's givenness through popular or commercial representations of it, seemed indifferent to the self's anxious condition in it. In effect, Abstract Expressionism, which implicitly claimed universal existential validity and impact for its gesture, was superseded by an art which expected familiarity with explicitly American media styles and images. The change from Abstract Expressionism to Pop art can also be regarded as a modernization of the methods of art-making—a shift away from the handmade work of art to the machine-made one, or one that looks machine-made, like Lichtenstein's paintings. Andy Warhol said he wanted to *be* a machine. Art, instead of being an original production, becomes or emulates mechanical reproduction, as when Lichtenstein endlessly copies and fetishistically isolates the handmade gestures of Abstract Expressionist art or the original compositions of Picasso, Miró, and Leger, among others.

Lucy Lippard admits to "only five hard-core Pop artists in New York"—Roy Lichtenstein, Claes Oldenburg, James Rosenquist, Andy Warhol, and Tom Wesselman. Despite their dissimilar styles, "they all employ more or less hard-edge, commercial techniques and colours to convey their unmistakably popular, representational images."[41] Alloway offers a more differentiated conception of proto-Pop and Pop art.

> It will always include at least one of the following characteristics. . . . 1. Syntactic complexity: under this heading belong the interplay of written and pictorial forms, such as Johns' letters, numerals, or words, and [Robert] Indiana's numbers and sentences. 2. Range of media: Rauschenberg's combine-paintings (which relate to assemblage and to Happenings in their incorporation of diverse objects); extension of medium, as in the case of Rosenquist introducing billboard techniques into experimental easel painting. 3. Familiarity of subjects (Lichtenstein's comics or Warhol's newsprint sources); the literal presence of the object (Wesselman's bathrooms and [Jim] Dine's objects attached to canvases). 4. Connections with technology: Rauschenberg in particular, but machines are also an essential term of Oldenburg's metamorphic forms.[42]

Common to all Pop artists is a preoccupation with clichés and sign-systems. Pop art "by and large, [is] an art of quotations, translations, imitations, and double-takes," Alloway writes.[43] Alloway understood Pop art in terms of what he called "a fine art–Pop art continuum, in which the enduring and the expendable, the timeless and the timely, coexisted, but without damage either to the senses of the spectator or to the standards of society." Pop art was the major example of "the new role for the fine arts [as] one of the possible forms of communication in an expanding framework that also includes the mass arts."[44]

In general, Pop art tends "toward a public message or statement,"[45] often presented with "humor."[46] However, there continues to be a good deal of debate as to whether that humor has a satiric cutting edge or is a goodwilled indulgence in the American vernacular. In any case, Pop art can be regarded as a witty extension of public communication—an adventurous appropriation of popular modes of articulation.

Pop art is far from exclusively American. In fact, the English artist Richard Hamilton's collage "Just What Is It that Makes Today's Homes so Different, so Appealing?" (1956) is regarded by some historians as the first genuinely Pop art work. But even that work, like Hamilton's "first painting with sources in Pop culture,"[47] "Hommage à Chrysler Corp" (1957)—later Oldenburg was also to deal with the Chrysler, if more nostalgically—is heavily indebted to American image-artifacts. In the collage, "an inventory of popular culture,"[48] the Ford Motor Company logo on the lampshade, the cover of the *Young Romance* magazine framed and mounted on the living room wall, the can of ham on the coffee table, and visible through the window the billboard image of Al Jolson as *The Jazz Singer* are clearly American in origin. The images of the male bodybuilder and the female nude (both soft porn), as well as of the magnetic tape recorder and the vacuum cleaner that reaches farther than ordinary vacuum cleaners, are probably American products. The close-up photograph of the moon on the ceiling was probably another triumph of American technology and can be understood as an allegorical representation of the ominously all-encompassing, dominant—or so it seemed in the 1950s—American presence.

There is in this, and in many other English Pop art images—such as Peter Blake's "Self-Portrait" (1961) showing himself holding a copy of an Elvis Presley fan magazine—a fascination with the image-artifacts and mass media technology of American culture, which is seen as an overwhelmingly popular culture. This fascination sometimes seems to be tinged with envy or disgust, sometimes with reluctant acceptance verging on unconscious admiration. It also clearly involves enormous curiosity about the American world, a cognitive exploration of an alien yet fresh modernity. Whatever its mood, the fascination with things American inevitably leads to their artistic appropriation and mastery.

In all Pop art the dynamic surface of American popular life becomes the raw material of a high art in search of its special identity in a modern world which seems to have no urgent need for high art or individualistic artists, given the prevalence of popular or mass art. The hidden meaning of Pop art, underneath its veneer of extraordinary rapport with the world of popular culture (some critics could not see the art for its subject matter[49]), is that it represents the crisis of a high culture no longer certain of its destiny or purpose in a world dominated by popular culture, a world in which to be modern means to be mass.

Abstract Expressionism may have conveyed the individual's anxiety and alienation in the modern American world, which for all its media-created appearance of being the best of all worlds—a glossy, happy Disneyland—was hardly that. But it was confident of itself as high art, and of the purpose of high art in the American world. Its role was to preserve the emotional rights, and to cultivate the ego strength of the individual—to protect and voice heroic individual existence. But Pop art, for all its determination to belong to the mainstream of media America, masked a sense of serious art's insufficiency or diminution of purpose in the American world. For all its apparent brazenness and skill in appropriating popular images and popularizing high art images, Pop art can be understood as high art's failure of nerve—an ingenious, camp way of making the best of a failure of seriousness and of getting on the bandwagon of the seemingly inevitable clean sweep of popular culture. Pop art capitulates to mass culture's power to determine consciousness.

Pop art certainly was servile to the mainstream. It suggested that there was no American tragedy and had never been any. Rosenberg's demonstration of the continuity between Abstract Expressionist painters and nineteenth-century authors with a tragic sense of American life—Hawthorne and Melville—was beside the point of Pop art, which seemed to epitomize America's postwar optimism and omnipresence. But underneath this chauvinism (Pop art served the purposes of American narcissism and grandiosity, celebrated the triumph of American materialistic values in the postwar world) was a sense of uncertainty about the future of high American art. Abstract Expressionism celebrated individuals who while social losers were yet personally victorious through their singular art, while Pop art celebrated a winning society in which there was no place for misfit individuals and artists—for anyone who didn't conform. Pop art suggested that Abstract Expressionist pursuit of spiritual values—Rothko's search for the "timeless and tragic," which was explicitly intended as a dissent from American materialistic values—was not simply criticism but a betrayal of America. Baudelaire had asserted that banality was the only vice in art. Pop art, however mischievously, celebrated banality, along with the rest of America.

If one looks at a number of Lichtenstein works produced during the 1960s—"Blam" and "Golf Ball" (both 1962), "As I opened fire" (1964), the Picassoesque "Woman with Flowered Hat" (1963), and "We rose up slowly" (1964)—one notes a consistency of technique. Whether a modernist style or an American event or object is the subject mat-

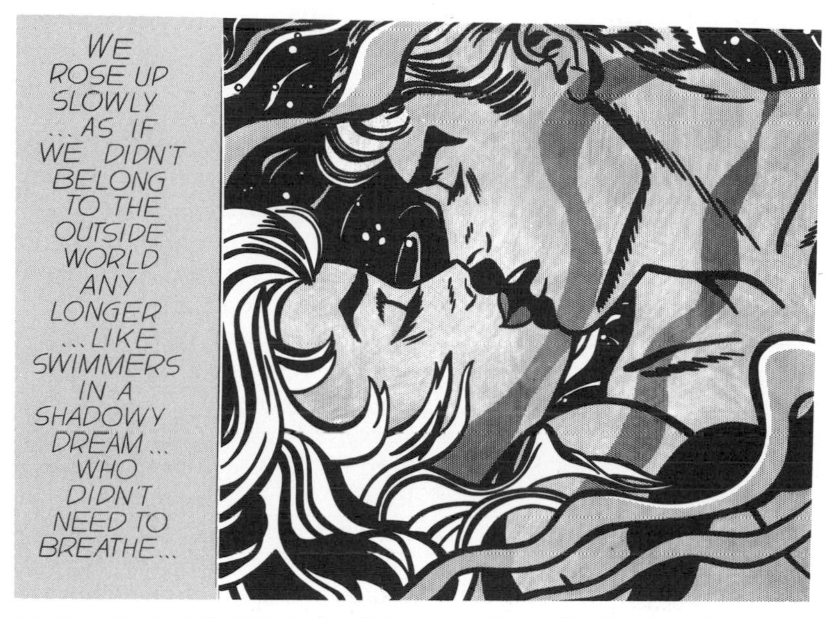

"We Rose Up Slowly" (1964), by Roy Lichtenstein. *"These [Ben Day] dots, like everything else in the mechanical looking picture, have been subject to a process of 'elaborate formalization,' which at once sublimates the content, de-Americanizing it . . . yet makes it more pointed and universal in implication."*

ter, there are the same mechanically repetitious Ben Day dots, which develop during the process of printing the comic strip but look more conspicuous in the Lichtenstein picture—more like an emotional punctuation of the narrative image than a neutral surface. These dots, like everything else in the mechanical looking picture, have been subject to a process of "elaborate formalization,"[50] which at once sublimates the content, de-Americanizing it, as it were, yet makes it more pointed and universal in implication—more emblematic and hallucinatory. Lichtenstein is concerned both to put some aesthetic distance between his work and its content, and to make that content more telling—even to use it allegorically for personal purposes, the way the Surrealists did with their "street content."[51] Lichtenstein himself has said that the comic strip "intends to depict and I intend to unify."[52] He has also said that "the closer my work is to the original, the more threatening and critical the content."[53] He clearly wants and has it both ways.

Nothing seems immune to Lichtenstein's vacuum cleaner, which sweeps up everything in its path. There is an omnivorousness to his interests which matches the obsessiveness of his handling, evident also in his tendency to work in series. Alloway has pointed out that "Pop art is neither abstract nor realistic, though it has contacts in both directions."[54] That is, it is neither as idealistic nor as concrete as might be supposed. Perhaps nowhere does this subtle sense of doubleness, of touch-and-go convergence, make itself more felt than in Lichtenstein's mirror paintings, and secondarily in his entablature series. Lichtenstein's handling is not as "deadpan" as Alloway thinks,[55] nor is the mirror "unpaintable."[56] Rather, the abstractness of the mirror's surface is "realistically" represented according to comic-strip code—articulated as an end in itself. The effect is very much like that Lemuel Gulliver experienced when a Brobdingnagian woman put him upon her chest: he nearly fell into the holes (pores). The mirror works show us just how deeply Lichtenstein draws us into the essence of a subject matter and at the same time pushes us away from it into a rigidly matter-of-fact awareness of its existence, mediated by a taken-for-granted yet formal and politic public style of presentation (which is of course always a representation).

Lichtenstein has three-dimensionalized his approach in sculpture and furniture-sculpture—the Art Deco-derived pieces are especially faithful to his approach—suggesting that what counts with him is less the medium than the coolly ironic attitude and the method used to realize it. His sculpture often seems like a nostalgic recapitulation of his painting, of his American-type subject matter and populist style. In Abstract Expressionism there seemed a greater unity of "message" and stylistic method, which hardly detracts from Pop art, for it seems to realize more readily the modernist ambition of making art out of contemporary subject matter—or of making any subject matter, including the art of the past, contemporary. This is done by embalming the subject matter in what seems like an eternally popular and so omnipresent and eternally vital style, that is, mass media. Of course Abstract Expressionism also aims for the surprise and novelty of a stylized immediacy of effect, but unlike Pop art it does not rely heavily on what seems like an immediately and effectively communicative subject matter. Pop art depends upon our immediate grasp of the popularity of its subject matter, while Abstract Expressionism depends upon the immediate sensation of the artist's touch.

The "outrageousness" of Oldenburg's sculpture comes from his "choosing banal objects to memorialize."[57] Oldenburg takes everyday things—among them, a "Bedroom Ensemble" and pay telephone (1963), shoestring potatoes spilling from a bag (1965), and even a whole store (1961)—and makes them threateningly monumental. His sculptures are sometimes hard (plaster, metal), sometimes soft (vinyl), and generally sexual in implication—erotic puns. Oldenburg has said "the erotic or the sexual is the root of 'art,' its first impulse."[58] He is determined that his objects bespeak the unconscious, function as a field in which the tense dialectic between id impulses and restraining superego can operate as playfully and freely as possible.

Oldenburg's anxious objects reveal the discontents of civilization and

"Bedroom Ensemble" (1963), by Claes Oldenburg. *"Oldenburg's anxious objects reveal the discontents of civilization and of all Pop art works show the most debt to an Abstract Expressionist outlook, for all their humor."*

of all Pop art works show the most debt to an Abstract Expressionist outlook, for all their humor. The most prominent examples of his sexual orientation are his Ray Guns (1959 on), which show their hallucinatory doubleness by being coyly legible as grossly phallic. There is also a practical aspect to Oldenburg's hyperbole of the object: he makes literally large, or earmarks as outstandingly ordinary, objects which loom "fantastically" in our unconscious and social lives. They loom large in the imagination because they are necessary to modern living in an elementary way, or they are forced upon us by a consumer society as the ultimately seductive objects of desire. Oldenburg combines Duchamp's and Magritte's attitudes to objects, fetishizing them so they seem to dominate the spectator—their possessor. Oldenburg demonstrates that there is more to possession of an object than we might suppose: there is possession by it.

Oldenburg's works are inseparable from an understanding of Happenings, a peculiarly American phenomenon transitional between the European Surrealistic theater of the 1920s and American performance art of the 1950s and 1960s. Oldenburg was greatly interested in the ideas of Allan Kaprow, a major force in the production of Happenings. In a famous statement reminiscent of Breton's ideas, Kaprow compared the random turbulence of Manhattan's Fourteenth Street with the somewhat less chaotic, dynamic experience of an art exhibition, preferring the former to the latter. The first Happenings had the more or less carefully produced atmosphere of Fourteenth Street's incoherence and clutter. They were an odd mix of expressionist spontaneity and fervor, and streetwise behavior. Indeed, the Happening has been understood as a demonstration of the way art is simultaneously object-making and public behavior.

The Happening often "objectified" strange, antisocial fragments of behavior. From 1952 to 1959 Kaprow and the sculptor George Segal—tangentially associated with Pop art (his Edward Hopperesque figural scenarios combine a melancholy street look with a high art reductionism, related to Mondrian)—ran the cooperative Hansa Gallery, where various Happenings were performed. Oldenburg seemed particularly interested in their outreach into the environment, and indeed his "performing objects" have obvious environmental implications. His store, at 107 East Second Street in New York City, was not only an environment of objects but the environment as an object. Oldenburg's early work also had a strongly antisocial aspect to it.

James Rosenquist has been called the most Surrealist of the Pop artists. He often paints close-up details of ordinary objects in "dangerous" juxtapositions, reminiscent of the Surrealist idea of generating a charge between incommensurate objects by metonymically uniting them, so that they become unconsciously congruent in a potentially metaphoric relationship. Rosenquist works large, often quasi-billboard-sized canvases. His style has become increasingly meticulous and polished. His single most famous work, which seems to epitomize his whole oeuvre, is the arbitrarily sectionalized "F-111" (1965; 10 by 86 feet; 51 parts, each meant to be sold separately), which documents the American mentality at a certain complex moment in its history. Rosenquist shows how the apparent fragmentary character and contradictoriness of this mentality—its simultaneous pursuit of the good life and military dominance—are reconciled through a pervasive slick style, a kind of idealistic streamlining which is the real sign of American might. Rosenquist's Cold War painting is a mix of the aggressive and the cute (i.e., the banal sentimentalized), all made palatable by slickness.

The documentary character of Rosenquist's work, and of Pop art in general, is not to be underestimated. In works such as "Untitled, Joan Crawford Says" (1964) the documentary use of contemporary material makes it seem intellectually necessary as a symptom of the times. The documentary look also conveys a patina of use—of instant obsoleteness—so that the image is instrumentalized as an archaeological fragment of a dead civilization. In a sense, Pop art shows us how dead our world already is—how so much of it that looks vital really is alive only in appearance. Pop art shows the zombielike character of popular images—the deadening impact of sterotypes. At its best, Pop art turns stereotypes into psychosocially profound revelations.

Andy Warhol is perhaps the most prominent of the Pop artists, as much for his persona as for his art. The aura of neutrality he creates—beyond the simply blasé or nonchalant—has been read as symbolizing capitalism's ultimate indifference to the human. Indeed, Warhol has explicitly adopted a businessman's philosophy—a kind of use and be used. He certainly seems available for social use wherever it promises to pay off most, and his work, articulating every kind of prominent person or thing, or certifying them as prominent by archly "artifying" them, shows the aesthetic documentability and socioeconomic profitability to which anything whatsoever can be put. Warhol makes clear Pop art's parasitic relationship to the typical; by not pushing it toward the archetypal he confirms its banality. Timing—a precise sense of social appropriateness—is crucial to his art. This is his art's "expressive" dimension; it is generally understood as masterful in its inexpressivity—its deadpan probity. Warhol keeps a sober, straight face in every situation, suggesting that the negativity central to modernism has reached a kind of dead end in his person and work.

It is hard to know whether to take Warhol as a new Buster Keaton or as a decadent; he has been understood both ways. He has used enlarged comic strips, photographs of famous people—especially female celebrities such as Marilyn Monroe, Elizabeth Taylor, and Jackie Kennedy—as the basis of his work, which often has an "expressionist" touch. He has an F. Scott Fitzgerald curiosity about celebrity, and his subjects represent "topical climaxes of glamor . . . Warhol is a master of the goldfish-bowl effect that modern communication has produced."[59] There has been much effort expended to show his "social relevance," as though he was a super-sly debunker of the status quo he in fact is militantly committed to. None of it has proved convincing. What remains is the sense of Warhol as a relentless exploiter of already exploitive imagery—a super-exhibitionist of social exhibitionism. He is the conformist par excellence.

His "redeeming social value" is that he makes us aware of how overexhibited we are—how we have come to be our own entertainment. It has been argued that Warhol extends Rauschenberg's obsession with the "sustained flow of images" as itself social metaphor[60] to its logical conclusion, showing how caught we are in the blind flux of manufactured appearances. I think this is true, except that the flow in the last analysis seems not to be a metaphor for social reality but the social reality itself. Warhol shows us a society narcissistically entranced with its image of itself, which seems to exhaust its possibilities; it can achieve nothing other than more self-exhibition. In the end, Warhol's celebrities perform only for themselves. He shows us a society in which actor and audience are one—which thinks it can witness itself and miss nothing, which has nothing more to say about itself—perhaps the unfortunate truth. Warhol's art really never departs, except in technical detail, from the graphic art and store-window displays with which he began his career. Even when his sources become "vigorous 'low' " rather than "commercial genteel,"[61] his art remains simplistically American in its overelaborated materialism.

Tom Wesselman is best known for his "Great American Nude" series (1961 on), which seems endless in its permutations of the streamlined or abstracted female figure. His later displays of fragments of the female nude seem an inevitable extension of them. Like Lichtenstein, Wesselman ambitiously converts low—but also traditional—subject matter into high art. In his case, this involves "fusing the arabesque and brilliant colour of Matisse with the sinuous line of Modigliani and a more rigorous framework traceable to Mondrian."[62] His pictures have a certain bright outlook to match their bright color. Many of them are successful extensions of the collage to gargantuan portions; whole rooms are integrated into the picture, making it, literally, a "slice of life." Indeed, Wesselman points to the indirect naturalism of Pop art, with its attempt to swallow life whole—to quote it without really digesting it. As with Segal and other Pop art-related artists, the art sometimes seems a veneer—sometimes thick, sometimes thin—on an importunate subject matter which the artist wants to let speak for itself. Yet the artistic staging of the subject matter does more than give us the necessary social distance for viewing it. The staging seems to place it in the limbo of the laboratory as a specimen, waiting to be dissected. Form chloroforms subject matter in Pop art, showing a certain impatience with it. But it is not clear that Pop artists are truly and sufficiently scientific in their detachment, that they offer a true analysis of it.

There are many artists who have affinities with the Pop outlook and manner, especially in California. The work of Billy Al Bengston, Edward Kienholz, Mel Ramos, Edward Ruscha, and Wayne Thiebaud is particularly noteworthy. The Pop approach became a vogue which has not yet run its course, and indeed seems to be going through a revival of sorts in postmodernism, which emphasizes the anonymity of the artist as a field on which social codes are inscribed, the dependence of all representations on sign and social systems, and the positive value of mechanical reproduction as a general basis for art-making. Indeed, Pop art has been reconceived as prototypically postmodernist—the beginning of an understanding of art-making that emphasizes art as a form of social copying rather than an original individual creation.

Yet there is an imaginative dimension to Pop art, even in the Baudelairean sense of imagination as articulating a childhood vision of the world with the analytic methods of the adult mind. For all their sophistication, such Pop artists as Lichtenstein and Warhol show a kind of infantile fixation on ordinary social appearances, as though these were inherently wondrous. Pop artists seem to be in a state of intoxication with the banal or standardized, not because it is saturated with hidden meaning, but simply because it is so obviously the case. It may be another kind of worship of success for success's sake—of popularity because it is a sign of success.

This suggests the stultification of consciousness—the popularization that falsifies it—typical of mass-media man. Psychic stultification and physical standardization may be served up appealingly on an elegant (merely cleverly designed?) artistic platter, but it shows that Pop art is on a certain level infatuated with the dim-witted. Pop art may show the intellectual artist stooping to conquer. Indeed, it may be that the Pop artists are apotheosizing a mass consciousness that reveals nothing more than the blindness of ordinary American consciousness to the existential realities Abstract Expressionism wanted to articulate.

Minimal art, Conceptual art, and Earth art

It may seem strange to put Minimal art, Conceptual art, and Earth art together on the same continuum. Yet each attempts to renew the modernist sense of art's autonomy and the uniqueness of the "art experience" by making an art that seems impossible to appropriate—to be at ease with, to treat familiarly. Each freshly articulates the radical modernist idea that the "art" in the work of art does not reside in its material character but in the spectator's relationship to, or way of, conceiving it. Each creates works of art that cannot be regarded simply as superior objects, or even as objects at all. Not only does each show the bankruptcy of the conventional wisdom that decrees art to exist in discreetly given, conclusive objects, but each ingeniously demonstrates that art cannot be said to be given in a clear and distinct way. It is at once elusive and mysteriously absolute. In the name of a revitalized vision of art's sacredness, each subverts the traditional idea that there are specifically artistic media. In each, art floats free of its usual moorings to become a kind of revolutionary consciousness.

Minimal art, by reducing the art object to a "minimal" object in a specific space (placement is crucial for the Minimalist work, which functions more to punctuate a space than to assert its own integrity), attempts to make art's objectness the basis for a metaphysical awareness of concreteness as such. By this last is meant as deep and immediate an apprehension as is possible of what it means to be inescapably given.

Conceptual art dismisses art's objectness altogether, insisting that art exists authentically as an idea rather than an entity—that a work of art's material particularity is a "metaphoric" way of articulating a general conception of art. From the point of view of Conceptual art, an artistic "advance" means the development of a new idea of art. Conceptual art—sometimes called "Idea art"—holds that a work of art can exist entirely in the form of an idea, that is, in immaterial form. (Conceptual art has been spoken of as the " 'dematerialization' of the art object."[63])

Earth art implies that art's objectness is tied to a particular natural environment and space, that it expresses an attitude to the life-world and biosphere; art can never be moved into the sterile utopia—the "nowhere"—of the man-made museum, with its limbo of faceless, general space.

Ironically, each of these kinds of art uses elaborate theoretical means to justify its sense of art's special concreteness. This is perhaps as it should be, since in the end each is an investigation of the transformative effect of art on consciousness. Each wants to give the work of art a new moral and intellectual integrity—a new critical identity. All seem to imply, in Gregory Battcock's words, "a rejection of the 'bourgeois' aspects of traditional art," especially of "the usual commercial, marketplace aspects of artmaking."[64] Battcock is speaking of Conceptual art, but the attitude he describes originated in Minimal art and reached its most determined expression in Earth art. Each can be understood as a different facet of a general reaction or rebellion—at once resentful and defensive—against an accelerating materialistic, exploitive attitude to art (Pop art seems to cater to it), which includes museum as well as market appropriation of it. All three imply art's desire to outrace its reification and assimilation as a capitalistic/cultural treasure. In ret-

"Untitled" (1965), by Robert Morris. *"Minimal art—called ABC art by Barbara Rose, in recognition of its 'fundamentalism'—is best understood through its sculpture, which takes the form of a geometrical gestalt."*

"St. John's Rotary Arc" (1980), by Richard Serra. *"Both Minimalist sculpture and painting appear at first glance to be . . . naively objectlike. . . . But this appearance is deceptive, for Minimalist art . . . demonstrates the famous dictum that 'less is more.' "*

rospect, the development of these movements in the 1960s seems to signal a desperate, last-ditch attempt by art to retain its avant-garde isolation, in Renato Poggioli's sense of the term—to re-articulate its basic alienation from and negation of the status quo.

Minimal art—called ABC art by Barbara Rose, in recognition of its "fundamentalism"[65]—is best understood through its sculpture, which takes the form of a geometrical gestalt. Robert Morris, one of Minimalism's most articulate and exemplary practitioners, has written that

> While the work must be autonomous in the sense of being a self-contained unit for the formation of the gestalt, the indivisible and undissolvable whole, the major aesthetic terms are not in but dependent upon this autonomous object and exist as unfixed variables that find their specific definition in the particular space and light and physical viewpoint of the spectator. . . . Control is necessary if the variables of object, light, space, body, are to function. The object itself has not become less important. It has merely become less *self*-important."[66]

Lawrence Alloway, who describes Minimal painting as "systemic" and "One-Image," has written: "In style analysis we look for unity within variety; in One-Image art we look for variety within conspicuous unity."[67] Alloway is responding to the charge that Minimal art is monotonous or one-dimensional. The Minimalist paintings Alloway examines are generally constituted by a single field of color and based on a modular unit such as the grid.

Both Minimalist sculpture and painting appear at first glance to be simple, direct, and easily comprehensible—naively objectlike. Many of the Minimalist sculptures are in fact constructed of ordinary materials. Morris has used felt, plywood, and pilings; Carl Andre has used metal plates, bricks, and bales of hay; Richard Serra has used lengths of rolled steel; Dan Flavin has used fluorescent fixtures—dismantled after their exhibition, reconstructed for re-exhibition. But this appearance is deceptive, for Minimalist art, like the ideas behind the architecture of Mies van der Rohe—which is not unrelated to it, theoretically—demonstrates the famous dictum that "less is more," and argues that "God exists in the details." The impression of the physical simplicity of the Minimalist structure, and of the simplemindedness of the idea behind it, fades with intimate experience of the Minimalist object. Or rather, simplicity is discovered to be very complex.

Some scholars regard Minimal art as the climactic exemplification of Duchamp's notion that the spectator "completes" the work of art with his consciousness. In a sense, the Minimal work of art forces the spectator to complete it, for its apparent simplicity is a kind of vacuum which invites us to read meaning and complex detail into it. As the saying goes, nature abhors a vacuum. The spectator fills it by serving as the star witness—absolute "judge"—of the Minimalist work's being as he conscientiously moves around it. The general point is that the intense synthesis of acute sense awareness and shrewd analytic intellectuality demanded by the Minimalist object—its determined specificity seems to physically capsulate the concentration and directedness of consciousness—reminds us that works of art cannot simply be "picked up" by a quick glance or facile enjoyment of their sensuous surfaces. Minimalist art is an austere, renunciatory, ascetic art, reminding us of the inherent difficulty of art and the intensity of the art experience.

Minimal art is narrow, but presumably steep. However, Clement Greenberg argues—suggesting the connection between Minimal art and Conceptual art—that it

> remains too much a feat of ideation, and not enough anything else. Its idea remains an idea, something deduced instead of felt and discovered. The geometrical and modular simplicity may announce and signify the artistically furthest-out, but the fact that the signals are understood for what they want to mean betrays them artistically. There is hardly any aesthetic surprise in Minimal Art, only a phenomenal one, . . . which is a one-time surprise. . . . Behind the expected, self-canceling emblems of the furthest-out, almost every work of Minimal Art . . . reveals in experience a more or less conventional sensibility. The artistic substance and reality, as distinct from the program, turns out to be in good safe

taste. I find myself back in the realm of Good Design, where Pop, Op, Assemblage, and the rest of Novelty Art live."[68]

Greenberg has put his finger on a problem that affects Conceptual art and Earth art as well as Minimal art: are they a programmatic pursuit of novelty, or, as Gregory Battcock thought, explorations in "a new area of aesthetic speculation"?[69] Suppose they are both—a calculated pursuit of novelty to have a far-out avant-garde look and at the same time a kind of aesthetic exploration of the limits of art. Does that make them art, that is, in Greenberg's words, a source of "aesthetic surprise [that] comes from inspiration and sensibility as well as from being abreast of the artistic times"?[70] Greenberg seems willing to acknowledge that Minimal art is art, that it aims to " 'project' objects and ensembles of objects that are just nudgeable into art."[71] That may make them aesthetically speculative, as Battcock says, but it hardly makes them aesthetically significant art. The problem for Greenberg is that once the novelty has worn off, the sensibility seems thin or null.

In Conceptual art the question of sensibility seems to be entirely beside the point. Art can only be significant when it is aesthetically speculative—speculative about the nature of art. As Joseph Kosuth, writing on "Art After Philosophy"—at once a Conceptual art manifesto and justification, and itself a Conceptual work of art—has said, the artist is "an analyst . . . not directly concerned with the physical properties of things. He is concerned only with (1) the way in which art is capable of conceptual growth and (2) how his propositions [works of art] are capable of logically following that growth."[72] What follows from this is the assertion of the basically linguistic character of art: "the propositions of art are not factual, but linguistic in *character*—that is, they do not describe the behavior of physical or even mental objects; they express definitions of art, or the formal consequences of definitions of art." Thus, "art operates on a logic."[73] Consistent with this, Kosuth says that "actual works of art are little more than historical curiosities."[74] They are merely illustrations of art. He can argue then, and does, that Robert Smithson's real work was "his articles in magazines," that his material works served as "illustrations for them."[75]

A central aspect of Conceptual art for Kosuth is the "questioning of the nature of art," which is "a very important concept in understanding the function of art."[76] This function has nothing to do with "the presentation of visual (or other) kinds of experience," which "may have been one of art's extraneous functions in the preceding centuries."[77] Rather, "in this period of man, after philosophy and religion, art may possibly be one endeavor that fulfills what another age might have called 'man's spiritual needs.' "[78] This is why "art's only claim is for art," why "art is the definition of art"[79]—art satisfies the spiritual need for something that "exists for its own sake."

"One and Three Chairs" (1965), by Joseph Kosuth. *"A central aspect of Conceptual art for Kosuth is the 'questioning of the nature of art,' which is 'a very important concept in understanding the function of art.' "*

Kosuth acknowledges the connection of Minimal art and Conceptual art when he remarks that Sol LeWitt—a major Minimal artist—"is notably responsible for creating an environment which made [Conceptual] art acceptable, if not conceivable."[80] Ad Reinhardt, Duchamp, Johns, and Judd are also important predecessors for Kosuth. That the same artist can be both Minimal and Conceptual is signaled by Kosuth's assertion that "added to Conceptual Art's history would be certain early works by Robert Morris, particularly the "Card File" (1962)."[81]

All of these artists point to the understanding of the work of art as an "analytic proposition," Kosuth calls it, appropriating Kant's distinction between analytic and synthetic propositions. An analytic proposition, e.g., a mathematical one, is tautological, while a synthetic proposition is empirical. (It should be recalled that Kant thought of the *Critique of Pure Reason* as an investigation into a priori synthetic propositions, that is, into what has been called the "metaphysics of experience" or the logic basic to it.) For Kosuth, "one is always tempted to 'verify' the [art] proposition empirically" when it is framed "in synthetic terms,"[82] that is, when it seems to exist materially "before" it exists conceptually. (When art is not presented a priori in linguistic terms but rather a posteriori in physical terms Kosuth describes it as a synthetic proposition. He seems to suggest, erroneously from Kant's point of view, that there can be no a priori synthetic propositions, although perhaps there can be none in art.) The point is to avoid what has been called "visual *Muzak*"[83]—the articulation and understanding of art as first and last a strictly visual experience, indeed, an experience rather than an idea. (For Kosuth, experience always exists for the sake of something else; an idea exists for its own sake.)

Kosuth lists many Conceptual artists, perhaps notably the English group associated with and named after the publication *Art and Language,* devoted to the analysis of the language of art and the demonstration of art as language. Terry Atkinson and Michael Baldwin are two of its most prominent members. Here is Kosuth's description of the works produced by their collaboration, which began in 1966. They produced

> a rectangle with linear depictions of the states of Kentucky and Iowa, titled "Map to not include: Canada, James Bay, Ontario, Quebec, St. Lawrence River, New Brunswick" . . . and so on; conceptual drawings based on various serial and conceptual schemes; a map of a thirty-six-square-mile area of the Pacific Ocean, west of Oahu, scale three inches to the mile (an empty square). Works from 1967 were the "Air Conditioning" show and the "Air show." The "Air show" as described by Terry Atkinson was, "A series of assertions concerning a theoretical usage of a column of air comprising a base of one square mile and of unspecified distance in the vertical dimension." No particular square mile of the earth's surface was specified. The concept did not entail any such particular location.[84]

Sometimes Conceptual works of art involve "performances," such as traveling to a remote place to perform a certain activity, e.g., to the Arctic to throw stones across the line—clearly conceptual—that demarks the Arctic Circle. It is not always clear what a Conceptual work of art is, even when we are told that a certain work is Conceptual in character. It seems impossible to articulate any common characteristics that all Conceptual works of art would have. Yet the point is that they deal with a concept rather than a material actuality: like the line of the Arctic Circle or a map, the column of air is a concept or, as a Conceptual artist would say, has a theoretical existence—one which does not necessarily entail a "practical" existence. It is "art" in that it exists for its own sake and raises the question of what art is.

Perhaps the most exemplary Earth artist—one who shows the overlap of Earth art, Minimal art, and Conceptual art most clearly—is Robert Smithson, a brilliant thinker as well as revolutionary artist, who died prematurely in his thirties (1973). (In the modern world, many voices have attempted to take possession of art because of the collapse of consensus about its nature and function, leading revolutionary artists to write complex theoretical tracts and outspoken manifestos to justify and make room for their work.) Smithson brings together so many of the ideas basic to modernism and pointing toward postmodernism that it is hard to categorize him. In terms of the production of objects, he began as an expressionistically oriented, fantasist painter, achieving initial prominence with his Minimalist works. But he truly came into his own with his Earth art and projects, including his writings. His single most famous work is "Spiral Jetty" (1970), a structure of salt crystals, stone, and earth projecting into the Great Salt Lake (Utah) from its shore. It is in the process of eroding back into the water. For many art historians and critics it is the classic Earth work, both in its reparative if transient relationship to the Earth and in its theoretical implications.

Smithson was in pursuit of "a new kind of monumentality," an articulation of space which would show it to be constituted by time and energy.[85] He spoke of Minimal art as "entropic," and, in his project of placing mirrors in nine locations in the Yucatán—perhaps his most famous work after "Spiral Jetty"—he pursued a sense of timelessness,[86] which he saw as a quality of "primordial consciousness."[87] His work not only became site-specific but specific to what seemed prehistoric sites, that is, places which seemed to have been untouched or bypassed by history, or even discarded by it—lake sites such as the one for "Spiral Jetty" and the one for the "Amarillo (Texas) Ramp" (1973, his last work), or the abandoned quarry near Emmen, Holland, where he built "Broken Circle—Spiral Hill" (1971). He saw in the spiral form a symbol of cosmic order—a symbol innate to and brought forth by the cosmos as its self-articulation. For Smithson, the spiral integrated space and time in a dynamic simplicity. The spiral was at once an abstract emblem and the literal embodiment of the eternal cosmos, representing in its single figure the simultaneity of its simplicity and complexity.

Smithson's ambition was both personal—a religious search for oceanic experience or a sense of unity with the cosmos beyond the small world of human beings[88]—and sociopolitical. He made "public art" in the profoundest sense; in fact, he can be understood as the artist who most successfully integrated the work of art into public space, making them almost seamlessly one. In his own words, "By reclaiming land in terms of earth art, he felt that art could be economically and politically integrated into society. In his mind this could best be accomplished by working with mining companies to reclaim devastated strip-mined land as earth art."[89]

Smithson's work can be understood, as he himself did, as continuing, within the context of, and in response to, twentieth-century industrial society, the nineteenth-century tradition of landscape art articulated by Frederick Law Olmsted. For Smithson, the twentieth century necessitates a dialectical mode of presenting landscape, so that the uneasy coexistence of the modern technological world and nature can be made manifest in a structure of coexistence.[90] Dialectical representation of social and cosmic reality does not guarantee their integration, their necessary harmony. Perhaps Smithson's idea of his works as simultaneously referring to a natural site while being non-sites in themselves most clearly shows the dialectical irony and tension that animate his work in general.

It is worth noting that efforts have been made to establish continuity between the work of Earth artists and the "art" of prehistoric times—Stonehenge is a typical example—associated with religious rituals.[91] This is certainly one way of subsuming the great number of Earth works into a clear and simple pattern of significance, but it ignores their contemporary significance—their ideological basis as an extension of the modernist aesthetic and ethos of autonomy that is inevitably in the background of art-making today. It must be emphasized that for all their diversity the Earth artists, and Minimal art, Conceptual art, and Earth art, truly integrate only when understood as new strategies for demonstrating the paradoxical separateness of art from life—its special way of standing out from life while seeming to be immovably embedded in it.

The many faces of seventies art

The seventies was a period of contradiction. It was a time of exploding paradigms, in which the art values of the previous two decades were seriously undermined but not clearly replaced by new values; it was a time also of revivals, of a sometimes desperate extension of known values—

"neo" this and "neo" that, as one critic described it.[92] The seventies have been called "the pluralist era,"[93] and many critics have thought of it as transitional—but to what has never been made clear. Pluralism is simply an acknowledgment of diversity; to regard it as indicating that all stylistic options are equally valid is to declare bankruptcy. To admit to pluralism is in effect to admit to the absence of any decisive revolutionary idea. Paul Gauguin once said that "in art, there are only two types of people: revolutionaries and plagiarists."[94] The seventies seemed to be a period of such intense plagiarism as to appear almost revolutionary. What was plagiarized was not simply a style or a subject matter but an old idea of art: that it is life concentrated and filtered through a temperament (style).

One of the major changes that occurred in the seventies was the collapse of the idea of art's autonomy, which in the sixties was given new credibility by being carried to an extreme that afterward became impossible to sustain. Clement Greenberg has argued that innovative change takes place in art through a process of "dialectical conversion."[95] A development is pursued to its limit; it arrives somewhere different from what was anticipated—some place completely unanticipated. Thus Cézanne, agonizingly in search of true-to-experience articulation of the sensation of nature, produces pictures which end up alluding less to nature than to the making of art itself—involuntarily producing abstract pictures. Reaching for the *ne plus ultra* of representational art, he unexpectedly became nonrepresentational. In the same manner, Minimal art, Conceptual art, and Earth art, reasserting art's autonomy with new subtlety, unwittingly show it to be completely inseparable from extra-artistic reality—from environmental and thought processes. They show it to be interactive at root, radically dependent on, and a disguised indication of, the world-historical, whether in the form of subject matter or ideology. In a sense, the major development of art in the seventies had to do with the world rather than with art—with the way the Vietnam, black, and women's protest movements made themselves felt in art, exploding preconceptions of it. It became impossible to make art without realizing not only that contemporary history impinged upon it but that art was implicated in that history. If art didn't witness inescapable history—if art took a detached, *noli me tangere* position—it would share history's guilt.

One can make a tripartite categorization of seventies art that perhaps seems overly broad yet is the least confusing way of comprehending it. There is (1) art related to politics; (2) art that matter-of-factly utilizes both representational and abstract means to effect a kind of truce between—rather than a profound synthesis of—the two; and (3) art that transcends the conventional conception of high art, and that seems to extend, or spill over from, life.

In the first category, there is the work of various so-called protest artists—a term first used for work, such as that by Leon Golub and Rudolf Baranik, which was critical of American engagement in Vietnam, but which seems extendable to the whole category of socially critical art. This has also been called an "art of conscience." It has been described as attempting to synthesize journalistic and high art approaches—to idealize the vigorously mundane. The second category would include phenomena as different as pattern painting and superrealism (painting and sculpture), so-called New Image and "Bad" painting, as well as such examples of supposedly absolute abstraction as the work of Brice Marden, Robert Mangold, and Joel Shapiro. Their work is not only abstract but a representation of abstraction, that is, a neo-abstract idealization or hypostatization of abstract art. The third category includes performance art, video art, and photography—art which transgresses the conventional conception of the high art medium as well as of high art's "transcendental" intention. One might say that each of these kinds of art is life intensive rather than art intensive, although there is more art to them than is customarily realized.

To take them one by one, there was no way in the seventies to escape consciousness of the black, women, and anti-Vietnam War protest movements. In the art world this manifested itself in a variety of social responses. In 1969–70 the Artworkers Coalition (officially called the Artists Coalition) held a series of weekly meetings. Determined to politicize art, this influential group worked together with various peace groups and groups concerned with black and women's rights. In 1970 "The New York Art Strike Against War, Racism, Fascism, Sexism and Repression"—for a time it had the support of almost everyone in the art world—organized a variety of activities, ranging from a protest at the Kent State deaths to an "Alternative Venice Biennale" to raise money to support the antiwar movement. In 1967 the Smokehouse Associates, a group of black artists, was formed to improve Harlem by painting its walls with abstract art. The Black Emergency Cultural Coalition was involved in various protests, including one against the Metropolitan Museum's "Harlem on My Mind" exhibition (1969), which was regarded as a display of black memorabilia rather than as an exhibition of work by black artists. During this period museums exhibited more work by black artists than they had previously, but there was still protest that it had been chosen by white curators.

The art that was related to this and other protest activities cannot be thought entirely Protest art, as the abstract art the Smokehouse Associates exhibited indicates. It is important to realize that putting abstract art on city walls gives it a new lease on life—extends it beyond the museum, innovatively gives it a kind of vernacular muscle—as much as it registers black protest. The fact that much of the work makes more sense as art than as protest activity is made clear by the black artist Melvin Edwards's "Homage to the Poet Leon Gontran Damas"

(1978–80), an innovative sculpture—in its environmental spread and strategy of integrating individual units—that, because it uses a chain symbolic of slavery and tribal bricolage method of construction, claims a black content for itself. This work gains more from being understood in formal terms than in political terms. Similarly, Romare Bearden, for all the explicit black content of his works, is perhaps more important for the photomontage technique by which he creates an effect of stratification, with its evocation of unconscious depth and disordering of space. Similarly, such works by Betye Saar as "The Liberation of Aunt Jemima" (1972) and "Bessie Smith" (1974) are as important for their innovative use of the box—Saar was inspired by Joseph Cornell's use of the box to create an emotional microcosm—as they are for their politically explosive treatment of white stereotypes of black persons.

The question of how a political work of art can also be aesthetically significant haunts all Protest art. In the history of art there are works such as Goya's "Disasters of War" (1810–14) and Picasso's "Guernica" (1937) that are powerful works of conscience as well as aesthetically advanced productions. One way of understanding the question of the quality of socially critical works of art, especially works which are so loudly about a disturbing content that they seem to have no significant form—effect no aesthetic transformation of their material—is through T. W. Adorno's dialectical conception of quality. Adorno writes: "The quality of an art work is largely determined by whether or not it meets the challenge of the irreconcilable. In the so-called formal moments content, far from being expunged, surfaces again as a result of form's relation to the irreconcilable."[96] For Adorno, the irreconcilable is associated with the historically contingent world, full of "divergences or antagonisms." Quality has to do with the way these are forced into the open, "figured." "Figuration of antagonisms is not the same as reconciliation or a definitive overcoming of antagonisms."[97] Thus, in the modern world the qualitatively significant work of art is one that dares to show the scars of its own making—dares to reveal its failure to integrate content into form despite intense effort to effect their unity. A qualitatively significant work has to show both: powerful pressure toward formal integration, and powerful resistance from content. The qualitatively significant modern work of art must demonstrate this dialectical tension.

In Protest art it is content, rather than stylistic form, that is advanced. If we can argue that every important art is a unity of symbiotic and autonomous elements—of antagonistic elements, one implying profound connection with tradition, and the other revolutionary separation from it—then Protest art tends to be stylistically traditional but revolutionary and separatist in its content. At a time when it no longer seemed possible to wrest autonomous style from tradition, autonomy was redefined in terms of content. Thus, to deal with racism and sexism, as Faith Ringgold did in her paintings of the American flag—"the only truly subversive and revolutionary abstraction one can paint"[98]—shows a greater autonomy than to paint abstractly, even if one is a black artist. (Jasper Johns's use of the American flag was also subversive, but stylistically, in that it toyed with our complex awareness of the flag as simultaneously symbolic representation and abstract form.)

Judy Chicago and Miriam Schapiro are major innovators in the feminist art movement. Chicago, who taught the first feminist art course (Fresno State College in California, 1970), began, with Schapiro, to team teach in the Feminist Art Program they set up at the California Institute of the Arts (1971). They were also responsible, along with other women artists, for establishing the communal Womanspace Gallery in the Women's Building in Los Angeles (1973). Chicago and Schapiro were also instrumental in developing the important 1972 project called "Womanhouse," in which students used the rooms in an old mansion in Los Angeles to create displays pertinent to women's experiences. The "Nurturant Kitchen" sported a fleshy pink paint skin covering the walls, floors, ceilings, and all the objects and appliances; "Sheet Closet" held a closeted female mannequin by Sandra Orgel. A "Menstruation Bathroom," done by Chicago herself, was "very sterile, all white," and offered "under a shelf full of all the paraphernalia with which this culture 'cleans up' menstruation . . . a garbage can filled with the unmistakable marks of our animality" so conspicuously absent from the rest of the house.[99] "Womanhouse" was a militant assertion of female presence, a kind of keynote address to the art world by women artists determined to change it.

Chicago's "The Dinner Party" (1973–79) is perhaps the single most important feminist work—more like a "demonstration"—of the period. It is "an equilateral triangle 48 feet on a side . . . which . . . [holds] some 390 separate pieces: the 39 plates, each with its own chalice, flatware, runner and napkin; three table cloths; three corner runners; six banners and a 2,300-tile floor which comes in 144 sections."[100] Each plate symbolizes the spirit of a mythic or historical woman. Georgia O'Keeffe was the only modern one; historical figures include Sojourner Truth and Emily Dickinson, and among mythic figures the goddess Isis. The work's most controversial aspect is each plate's vaginal appearance, which brings out into the open the implicit meaning of the emphatic central shape of Chicago's abstract paintings.

Chicago's work is not unrelated to what Schapiro called "Femmage," collage utilizing women's materials—decorative fabric, including women's handkerchiefs—to create female imagery. Many of Schapiro's femmages communicate a sense of vibrant tenderness unique in today's art, and her fan and kimono works advance the idea of collage apart from their allusion to woman. Schapiro, together with the painter Robert

Zakanitch, helped form the Pattern and Decoration Group of artists in New York, to which she moved in 1976.

In discussing women's art, it is important to distinguish between artists who are women but do not produce feminist works, and overtly antisexist women artists. There are more of the former than the latter. In addition to Chicago and Schapiro, other representative feminist

"[Judy] Chicago's 'The Dinner Party' (1973–79) is perhaps the single most important feminist work—more like a 'demonstration'—of the period. . . . [It] is not unrelated to . . . 'Femmage,' collage utilizing women's materials . . . to create female imagery."

artists include the sculptors Hannah Wilke and Harmony Hammond, the painters Judith Bernstein and May Stevens, and Nancy Spero and Dotty Attie, who work on paper. As early as the late sixties, Wilke made sculptures that were essentially vaginal signs. Hammond's work—like Wilke's, materially original—alludes to female mentality or persona. Bernstein makes expressionistic hairy screws which can be read as penises and understood as appropriative of masculine phallic power. Stevens, similarly preoccupied with male power in her "Big Daddy" series (early seventies), in her "Ordinary/Extraordinary" series (late seventies) contrasts the lives of the Marxist revolutionary Rosa Luxemburg and her own mother, who spent the last twenty-five years of her life in a mental hospital. Stevens discloses the devastating alternatives of female life in the modern world. Spero, in her long paper scrolls mixing language and image, all of it quotation, deals with woman as consistently abused victim in terms of man's conception of her, and as a victim of rape and murder in various countries, particularly in South America. (Spero uses cases documented by Amnesty International.) Her "Torture of Women" (1976) is particularly noteworthy. Attie meticulously executes drawings alluding to female reality, usually involving quotations from famous works of art. She arranges them in a subversive, ironical narrative. All of these artists are concerned with the issue of female identity, which no longer seems a settled matter. Their work is critical in that it both subverts old stereotypes of female identity and shows a new sense of militant female selfhood.

The sculptor Jackie Winsor and the painter Jennifer Bartlett are among the many important nonfeminist women artists who emerged in the seventies. The work of each is innovative within its medium, as well as Conceptually oriented. Winsor has made wrapping and binding pieces, usually serial in character, showing her Minimalist origins. "#2 Copper" (1976) arranges in rows balls of copper coil wrapped around standing wooden sticks. Bartlett also works serially. Her "Rhapsody" (1976) spreads 988 square steel plates over nearly 154 feet of gallery wall space. Taken together, the plates appear to summarize schematically every abstract and representational visual possibility. It is essentially a systemic work that alphabetizes known formal and imagistic ideas.

Various women's groups, particularly the Women's Caucus for Art and *Heresies,* have continued to further the interests of women artists and to provide forums for discussion of issues relevant to women's art and situation. The large historical exhibition "Women Artists: 1550–1950," opening at the Los Angeles County Museum in 1976 and closing at the Brooklyn Museum in 1977, was a major acknowledgment of important women artists of the past. The exhibition, with its important catalog, was a corrective to traditional art history, which has generally ignored women artists.

Much as feminist art criticized American sexism, antiwar art criticized American militarism. As with women's art, many artists were involved in protest against the Vietnam War, but not every artist made works that were antiwar in content. Among the most representative who did are Leon Golub and Rudolf Baranik, who make an interesting comparison in that the work of the former is realistic and the work of the latter is abstract.

Golub's group of paintings entitled "Assassins" (early 1970s), depicting American soldiers and their Vietnam victims, is stylistically interesting for its mural size, cutout sections, and crude surfaces—its generally raw look, as though the horror of war was embedded in the concrete material of art. Golub has continued to paint large pictures dealing with torture, the use of mercenaries in various small undeclared wars, and the South American "white squads" responsible for the murder and disappearance of many people. Baranik's "Napalm Elegies" series of paintings attempts to integrate the tradition of field painting—in their blackness Baranik's paintings sustain what Rothko began with his black paintings (his last works)—with politically realistic images. Baranik incorporates a photograph of the melted head of a still alive victim of napalm bombing into an immaculately muted surface, creating a profoundly mournful and melancholy effect. Since the "Napalm Elegies," which are comparable to Robert Motherwell's series of "Elegies to the Spanish Republic," Baranik has become more exclusively elegiac and abstract in his development, if not without an impacted world-historical allusion.

Subsequent to and in part simultaneous with the Protest art of the seventies, there has been an intense development of political art, much of it involving the transformation of images from various media sources—posters, newspapers, and TV—to make political commentary. It has sometimes been described as political sniping in a competitive "image war."[101] Much of it utilizes information available from the media and in general attempts to turn the media against itself. Post-seventies political art criticizes all facets of American society and usually attempts to make its criticism entertaining, that is, to use a populist style associated with entertainment to deliver and sugarcoat an angry, bitter sociopolitical message.

As for art incorporating abstract and representational elements—giving them parity in the same work—a good deal of it was made in the seventies. Much pattern and decorative work, such as that of Robert Kushner, includes strong figural elements, embedded in an abstract field—in effect, abstractly conceived. Much superrealist work is also abstract in impact; the realistic scene often seems like a platform for heightened formal effects. Even so-called "Bad Painting"—the name of an exhibition at the New Museum (1978)—and "New Image Painting"—the name of an exhibition at the Whitney Museum of American

Art (1978)—seem to deal as much with issues of abstraction as with representation. None of this art creates a new sense of significant, tense unity between the two but rather seems to propose a facile if not uninteresting reconciliation between them. From the perspective of the eighties, much of this art seems subtly inconclusive or unresolved, and in fact many of the artists have moved on to produce stronger work. They were in effect proposing a new kind of figuration, but it was more designed than stylistically realized.

A sense of the dominance of design over style—that is, of preordained rather than achieved form, facile formula rather than hard-earned innovation—seems to me typical of much of the art in this second seventies category. It is perhaps most obvious in the pattern and decorative painting of the period, such as the work of Joyce Kozloff, Zakanitch, Kim MacConnel, Cynthia Carlson, Mary Grigoriadis, and Valerie Jaudon. What looks inventive and ideologically trendy—pattern painting claims to overcome the hierarchical distinction between high and popular art—in fact turns out to be mechanical. After the immediate sensual impact wears out—which it quickly does—much of this art reveals its emptiness, its inability to mediate a more than surface meaning. It lacks the transcendental power and visual subtlety of earlier abstract field painting. It tended to mask this inadequacy by becoming useful. Many of the artists decorated subway walls and furniture. This is an appropriate finale for pattern painting. Very few artists—Kushner is one—rise above the prettiness and sentimentality of seventies decorative art, producing work that sustains itself as complex art.

What seems antithetical to pattern and decorative painting, yet is essentially similar to it in import, is superrealism, sometimes called sharp focus realism or photo-realism. The effect here again is of design—often very superior design, but nonetheless design. The illustrative nature of this art matters as little as the abstract nature of pattern painting. The one betrays the goals of realism—a revelation of true reality, not simply of interesting appearances (the difference between Goya and Reginald Marsh, for example)—as much as the other betrays the transcendental goals of abstraction. Both the decorative and the superrealistic create temporarily exciting surfaces, but without durable effect.

Even advocates of superrealism acknowledge that it offers little more than "a reassuring sense of craftsmanship"—well-crafted things for a "culture [that] believes in things and little else."[102] However, it can be argued that in so thoroughly echoing American culture, in both method and concept—the way the Pop artists do—superrealism is redeeming as art. It does not simply make visually memorable what we perceive in the everyday world but forces us to consciousness of our own culturally encouraged investment in things, our culturally encouraged way of treating people like things, our culturally encouraged tendency to regard technique as substance.

Indeed, the superrealists tend to be brilliant technicians and to be preoccupied with technique, seemingly as the be-all and end-all of art. This is particularly evident in the photograph-based painted portraits of Chuck Close and the mannequinlike sculpture of Duane Hanson. In his later development Close makes the technical basis of his work transparent by bringing to the fore the grid which underlies his images, revealing them to be carefully calculated constructions. In Hanson's work the verisimilitude is so startling in its precision that we can't help realizing the artist's extraordinary control. Control is the byword of the best of this art. In Hanson's case this control has been put in the service of social criticism, as in his hyperrealistic gaunt corpse called "Welfare 2598" (1967) and in the subsequent series of works dealing with violence, including Vietnam violence. There is an angry edge to Hanson's sharp observation of reality that is inseparable from his pursuit of verisimilitude.

The impact of superrealistic verisimilitude was made clear by Harold Rosenberg, who in commenting on John de Andrea's naked, alluring figures—soft porn to some—remarked that "to the extent [the works] seem to be made of flesh, they are a bit grisly in their prettiness."[103] It is precisely this grisliness which is the critical cutting edge of superrealistic art—which makes it telling. At first glance this implicit ghastliness seems missing from Richard Estes's meticulous pictures, but the absence of figures in them makes the monstrousness of the things depicted all the more subtle—makes their indifference more aggressive. Paradoxically, superrealistic pictures seem to realize nineteenth-century Symbolist painting's pursuit of hallucinatory effect in an unexpectedly exemplary way, which is made particularly clear in Audrey Flack's work. So excruciatingly precise is the execution in these works that our perception seems to be somnambulist—wide-eyed yet unconsciously terrified as it moves effortlessly among these unexpectedly strange familiar things. While superrealism's iconography ranges from the banal to the intimate—Flack is a feminist who paints a very personal subject matter—its main point seems to be that the apparently banal can be hypnotic, like the best abstract art opening the way to another kind of consciousness, if different in kind.

Both Bad Painting and New Image Painting supposedly take as their point of departure Philip Guston's new figural style, inaugurated about 1970. The rough, cartoonlike figures, derived from images of hooded Ku Klux Klansmen, led Guston to cartoon self-portraiture, equally crude. Guston produced images that were at once absorbingly outlandish and awkward, yet simplistically narrative in import. They were American in their vernacular character yet high style in the way they used the expansive abstract field that had been developed during the sixties.

A similar placement of the vernacular image in a high art setting of abstract space characterizes most Bad Painting and New Image Painting. Joe Zucker and Neil Jenney have a similar interest in American imagery, and Nicholas Africano places tiny populist figures in a comparatively vast neutral space. Susan Rothenberg calls herself as much of an "image breaker" as an "image maker." Her heavy paint—its turgidity seems to bespeak a deep turbulent current—seems to drain her image as much as fill it. In the eighties Rothenberg has come to be regarded as a neo-Expressionist, which makes clear the high art ambition of her paintings.

While Bad Painting and New Image Painting have been said to bring into question academic standards of painting and drawing, and have a certain—sometimes preposterous—primitivism to them, they in fact are acutely aware of art historical precedents, and they represent a new version of the old attempt to revitalize high art by integrating low sources into it. The motivation remains avant-garde rather than kitschy. The anarchism of Bad Painting and New Image Painting has been overstated.

Seventies abstract painting and sculpture, in general, seem to me to offer a representation of abstract art rather than abstract art informed with a transcendental purpose, such as the pioneering abstractionists had. Richard Diebenkorn's "Ocean Park" series of paintings (1967 on) and Joel Shapiro's figurelike abstract sculptures partly make this clear, in that they show a certain exhaustion of motivation for the making of abstract art. Their work implies the slackness or insufficiency of abstraction as an end in itself; abstraction compensates by superficial reconciliation with representation.

To say this is not to deny that a freshly adequate abstraction results but to acknowledge its tenuous raison d'être. In such very different abstract painters as Brice Marden, Elizabeth Murray, Milton Resnick, Frank Stella, and Deborah Remington, among others, abstraction, for all its professed self-sufficiency, shows a new pursuit of dramatic, sometimes merely stagy, effect almost as though abstract formalization was inherently theatrical—as though the abstract object was a performer. In these artists abstraction dresses itself in a worldly veil to make itself more seductive. It becomes a kind of designed and illustrated abstraction—abstraction self-conscious not because it has just been discovered but because it has become freshly sensational. Seventies abstraction can be regarded as decadent, in the best sense of the term: an attempt to squeeze a rare sensation out of the overfamiliar. Seventies abstraction is a dramatization, rather than a revelation, of abstraction—a dramatization of an old idea of abstraction rather than a revelation of new abstraction.

As for the third kind of seventies art I have mentioned, there was a major surge of attention to photography. It acquired new prestige, new commercial value, and new theories about it. Photography in

"Lucas Samaras, well known for his neo-Surrealist sculptural constructions, is also a master of psychodramatic, suggestive photography. His 'Autopolaroids' (1969–73) are a masterpiece within the genre and make explicit the narcissism implied by it."

the "Directorial Mode," as it was called by A. D. Coleman, began to develop: photographers became imaginative rather than merely reportorial, staging scenes that would state a vision. Duane Michals is generally regarded as the pioneer of "photographic serial narrative."[104] Such works as "Things Are Queer" (1972) and "Self-Portrait with My Guardian Angel" (1974) make clear Michals's pursuit of *Real Dreams* (the title of his 1976 book). He wants photography to deal not merely with external appearances but with inner life, "especially the difficult things of our lives: anxiety, childhood hurts, lust, nightmares." Like Surrealist painters, Michals wants photography to acknowledge that "the things that cannot be seen are the most significant." While "they cannot be photographed," they can be "suggested."[105] Michals in effect wants photography to become "poetic."

Lucas Samaras, well known for his neo-Surrealist sculptural constructions, is also a master of psychodramatic, suggestive photography. His "Autopolaroids" (1969–73) are a masterpiece within the genre and make explicit the narcissism implied by it. This exhibitionistic narcissism is also evident in the performances—on video and in person—of Vito Acconci, who has made his erotic/anxious response to his own body the subject matter of much of his work. Similarly, Robert Mapplethorpe focuses on the exterior eroticism and interior anxiety of his "outsider" types, ranging from black men and women bodybuilders to rock stars and gays. Like Samaras's photographs, Mapplethorpe's have a certain formal beauty to them. Eve Sonneman emphasizes narrative sequence more than narcissistic "verification" of the disturbed self—she subverts the idealized "decisive moment" Henri Cartier-Bresson waited for—but she too deals with the condition of the modern self, if in more sociopolitical terms. Her interest in "gesture, innuendo and small changes" in behavior[106] indicates a focus on the other self.

In general, all these photographers conceive of photography as an active, rather than a passive, art. The photographer no longer waits for an appropriate subject matter to move into view in front of the camera but searches for or creates it.

Nam June Paik almost single-handedly is responsible for the acceptance of video as a serious art form. Associated with the neo-Dadaist, performance-oriented Fluxus group of artists in the early sixties—a movement which emphasized, as Paik put it, change for change's, rather than beauty's, sake—Paik tended to a conceptual use of video. Seriously interested in contemporary music, he had cellist Charlotte Moorman use two small TV monitors as a bra in a 1969 performance. His "Fish Flies in the Sky" (1976) consisted of twenty TV monitors hanging face down from a gallery ceiling. The spectator was expected to lie on the floor to watch them. On one channel small fish seemed to swim from set to set; on the other channel, a jet airplane left a smoke trail. "The Moon Is the Oldest TV Set" (1976) had fifteen TV monitors each displaying a phase of the moon. Paik's work combines an Oriental sense of poetry with modern technology.

Many artists use video to document performances as well as as an instrument of performance itself. (In Hannah Wilke's work the video camera follows her around like a lover.) There has been an enormous development of video art—pursuit of the electronically created image, an image which pulsates from within, rather than exists as, the outside of a surface, like paint and photograph images. Video has covered a great diversity of subject matter and created a great diversity of formal effects. The number of video artists has steadily increased, partly because equipment costs have dropped but also because video affords extraordinary opportunities for visual manipulation. In the work of Bill Viola, it seems to have reached aesthetic maturity and to articulate inner vision without any loss of critical awareness of the varieties of visual rhetoric—without losing its special powers of deconstruction. It is this ability to generate aesthetic effect through deconstructive awareness that makes video art so fraught with possibilities for the future.

The eighties

To describe accurately the American art of the eighties one would have to describe the European art so much of it depends on. Beginning with the exhibition of "A New Spirit of Painting" at the Royal Academy of Art in London (1981), German and Italian art have seemed more innovative, adventurous, or dynamic than American art. The new expressionism and figuration, the new interest in mythology and narrative, the new fusion of avant-garde and kitsch imagery as well as of painterly and photographic methods that have come to be regarded as central to postmodernism, the new interest in both major and minor styles of the recent and distant past, the new interest in cultural content—all these have come to be understood as originating in European art.

The European artists have been the vigorous conquerors of new territory; the Americans have followed in their path, broadening and paving it, but not laying down its essential lines. Before one can attend to the American artists, one must attend to Georg Baselitz, Jörg Immendorff, Anselm Kiefer, K. H. Hödicke, Helmut Middendorf, Francesco Clemente, Enzo Cucchi, and Mimmo Paladino, among other German and Italian artists. This does not mean there is no significant, strong American art that has developed in the eighties, only that most of it is not completely comprehensible without awareness of European developments.

Describing the development of American art from the perspective of 1981, Robert Morris argued that it "could be divided roughly between four attitudes or positions, the aggressive, expansionist abstract (Pollock); the cynical, ironic concerned with systems (Duchamp); the realistic, reflecting alienation (Hopper); and the decorative, accumulative, repetitive (Cornell)." He found the last to be "the most mindless and least challenging, but the one, unfortunately, to be dominant in American art."[107] Morris regarded its popularity as a sign of the bankruptcy of modernist art and as a defensive response to the conditions of modern life.

"Muscular Paper" (1985), by David Salle. Suggesting an articulation of classic Freudian neurosis, *"the contents of the pictures . . . reveal themselves as unconscious, confirmed by Salle's obsessive repetition of certain 'commonplace' themes, such as the figure of the female and the blue-tipped pegs of an abstract grid."*

> An emotional weariness . . . has occurred. I would suggest that the shift has occurred with the growing awareness of the more global threats to the existence of life itself. Whether this takes the form of instant nuclear detonation or a more leisurely extinction from a combination of exhaustion of resources and the pervasive, industrially based trashing of the planet, that sense of doom has gathered on the horizon of our perceptions and grows larger every day. Concomitantly, credible political ideologies for the ideal future no longer exist and the general values underlying rationalist doctrines for an improved future through science and technology are crumbling fast. . . . In any case the future no longer exists and a numbness in the face of a gigantic failure of imagination has set in. The decorative is the apt mode for such a sensibility, being a response on the edge of numbness.[108]

The eighties have proved Morris wrong, despite his own pursuit of a neo-decorative art that attempts to incorporate all the other modes in its own would-be prophetic articulation of the apocalypse. In fact, Julian Schnabel has created a new aggressive, expanionist art, integrating the abstract and the representational in a dynamic new unity. Schnabel's work has the energy of revitalized primitivism. There has been a renewal of strong realistic art dealing with alienation in Eric Fischl's paintings. There has been a revitalization of cynical, ironic systems-oriented art in David Salle's work.

The difference between the modernist and postmodernist use of these stylistic modes is that in the postmodernist eighties the artists are aware that all positions are fictions that make a certain rhetorical point. That is, they are aware that they are using certain languages of art, which must be stretched to make a point—even to discover what point there is to be made. All of these artists are engaged in a double activity: to deconstruct the artistic conventions they use, and to manipulate them to achieve psychodynamic effect—to end the "emotional weariness" Morris notes, or rather to reach the emotional reality behind it.

The issue for these artists still remains inner vision, but they recognize that inner vision is a fiction using fictional methods to make its vital point. In this they show their desperate sophistication and the homelessness of their art. They inhabit past artistic attitudes the way sand crabs inhabit the discarded shells of their fellow creatures, hoping the stylistic shells of dead artists will fit, at least until they are outgrown.

While there are obviously numerous artists one can talk about in the eighties, these three—Schnabel, Fischl, and Salle—remain the most representative and crucial for American art. Others, however different they may be—the neo-Surrealists Jedd Garet and Robert Longo and the neo-Protest artists Barbara Kruger and Jenny Holzer represent the extremes—are essentially decorative, if with a new trickiness. That is, they offer an art that confirms our numbness rather than breaks through it to arouse the life beneath, which is not to deny that it tries to do so, often using theatrical methods. Schnabel, Fischl, and Salle show the possibility of a new imaginative radicality in American art: not simply a revival of imagination, but a recognition of its inherent radicality and power to articulate the invisible through the visible, to penetrate the "depths."

Schnabel's most characteristic works are his plate paintings, which create a radically violent, broken surface that summarizes what has been called Pollock's "muddiness" and Rauschenberg's combine paintings. Indeed, Schnabel's use of collage—antlers, e.g.—is strongly reminiscent of Rauschenberg's use. On his charismatically hyperactive, violent and violating, surface Schnabel presents a more or less ghostly figure, usually mythological or historical, and identifiable, but reduced to a vehement trace by the harsh surface—that is, given the status of a highly charged unconscious memory. The tension between surface and figure is crucial for Schnabel. A Schnabel picture seems to articulate the experience of a stereotypical unconscious content spontaneously rising to consciousness. This sense of a content or image or form being released from repression is crucial to the best modern art.

A similar "transferential" effect is generated, in very different ways, by the paintings of Salle and Fischl. Salle's juxtaposition of stereotyped and matter-of-factly rendered abstract and representational forms—displayed with no attempt at reconciliation—establishes a tension which threatens to disintegrate the picture totally. This represents a disintegration of consciousness, or rather, an articulation of a neurotic consciousness, in the classic Freudian sense of neurosis as indicating the inability to reconcile irreconcilable thoughts. In neurosis, conflict or contradiction is hypostatized. Salle's pictures articulate this state of discontent, of oppositions which can barely be coordinated let alone integrated. The contents of the pictures thus reveal themselves as unconscious, confirmed by Salle's obsessive repetition of certain "commonplace" themes, such as the figure of the female and the blue-tipped pegs of an abstract grid. It is almost as though Salle has caught the moment of displacement of psychic energy from one object—and style—to another, or watched it bouncing between them.

Fischl, who has stated his concern with adolescent states of loneliness and the adolescent difficulty of facing love and death, presents realistic allegories of anxiety. What counts in "Birthday Boy" (1983) is not so much the nakedness of the boy and the adult female with him, nor her ambiguously inviting/threatening (potentially engulfing) position, but his pondering, melancholy state. (The hand holding up the head is standard iconography for melancholy.) The boy confronts the puzzles of existence and the riddle of the female—he is Oedipus with the Sphinx. Like Gauguin, but in a banal American context, he is asking "Where Do We Come From? What Are We? Where Are We Going?" (1897–98).

The power of the best American art of the eighties is that it has the

"[Eric] Fischl . . . presents realistic allegories of anxiety. What counts in 'Birthday Boy' (1983) is . . . his [the boy's] pondering, melancholy state. . . . The boy confronts the puzzles of existence and the riddle of the female."

courage to ask the fundamental existential questions in the American world, and to ask them without forfeiting a profound, sophisticated awareness of the methods of modern art. The discovery of the best artists of the postmodernist eighties is not simply that the past can be appropriated for present effect—the way the Romans ransacked a Greek art as ancient to them as early European and American modernist art is for us, in search of trophies that would give them the illusion of contemporary glory—but that all of the American and modern tradition's novel possibilities can still be of use in articulating the timeless existential questions. The past has once again disclosed itself to be the royal road to the fundamental. As paradoxical as it may seem, eighties American art revives, in a devious, self-conscious way, the existential and psychodramatic concerns that Abstract Expressionism had seemed to deal with naively, or rather, directly, two generations before.

---

[1]Clement Greenberg, "The School of Paris: 1946" and "Contribution to a Symposium," *Art and Culture* (Boston: Beacon Press, 1965; paperback), pp. 123–24.

[2]Harold Rosenberg, "Parable of American Painting," *The Tradition of the New* (New York: McGraw-Hill, 1965; paperback), pp. 15–18.

[3]Greenberg, pp. 124–25.

[4]Ralph Waldo Emerson, "The American Scholar," *Selections from Ralph Waldo Emerson* (Boston: Houghton Mifflin, 1957; Riverside Edition), p. 79.

[5]Walt Whitman, "Democratic Vistas," *The Great Ideas Today* (Chicago: Encyclopædia Britannica, 1984), p. 450.

[6]Whitman, pp. 454–55.

[7]"Jackson Pollock," *Arts & Architecture* 41 (February 1944): 14–15.

[8]Ibid.

[9]Ibid.

[10]William Rubin, "Jackson Pollock and the Modern Tradition," *Artforum,* Part I, 5 (February 1967); Part II, 5 (March 1967); Part III, 5 (April 1967); Part IV, 5 (May 1967).

[11]Whitman, p. 454.

[12]Gabriel-Désiré Laverdant, virtually the first thinker to speak of "avant-garde art," stated that it must "lay bare with a brutal brush all the brutalities, all the filth, which are at the base of our society." Quoted in Renato Poggioli, *The Theory of the Avant-Garde* (New York: Harper & Row, 1971; Icon Edition), p. 9.

[13]Elizabeth C. Baker, "Editorial: The 'Return' of European Art," *Art in America* 70 (September 1982): 5. This is one of two special issues devoted to the new European art.

[14]T. S. Eliot, "Tradition and the Individual Talent," *The Sacred Wood* (London: Methuen, 1920), pp. 47–59. Eliot argues that it is impossible for a poet [artist] to realize his individuality without "the historical sense . . . not only of the pastness of the past, but of its presence" (p. 49).

[15]André Breton, "Surrealism and Painting" (1928) in Herschel B. Chipp (ed.), *Theories of Modern Art* (Berkeley: University of California Press, 1968), pp. 402–9. Breton contrasts

"the enchantments of the street" to those of "the slippery-floored halls of museums" (p. 405). His preference for the former is echoed in Rosenberg's preference for "the appetites of the street" (Rosenberg, "Parable of American Painting," p. 16).

[16]Greenberg, *Art and Culture,* pp. 90, 166, 193, 195, 210–17, 219, 224, 228, 233. In a note on p. 209 Greenberg remarks that "abstract expressionism" is "very inaccurate as a covering term." He uses it because it is "the most current term."

[17]Greenberg, *Art and Culture,* p. 125.

[18]Greenberg, *Art and Culture,* p. 195.

[19]Rosenberg argues this particularly in "Parable of American Painting" and "The American Action Painters," both included in *The Tradition of the New* (see n. 2), pp. 13–39.

[20]*See* William Rubin, "Pollock as Jungian Illustrator: The Limits of Psychological Criticism, Part I," *Art in America* 67 (November 1979): 104–23; and "Part II," *Art in America* 67 (December 1979): 72–91.

[21]John Ferren, "Epitaph for an Avant-garde," *Arts* 32 (November 1958), quoted in Barbara Rose, ed., *Readings in American Art Since 1900* (New York: Frederick A. Praeger, 1968), p. 137.

[22]Ibid.

[23]Robert Motherwell, "The Modern Painter's World," *Dyn* 6 (1944), quoted in Rose, pp. 130–31.

[24]Meyer Schapiro, "Recent Abstract Painting," *Modern Art: 19th and 20th Centuries* (New York: George Braziller, 1978), pp. 222–24.

[25]Motherwell, p. 131.

[26]Julien Levy, "Foreword" in William Seitz, *Arshile Gorky* (New York: Museum of Modern Art, 1962), p. 8.

[27]Mark Rothko, quoted by Dore Ashton in the *New York Times,* Oct. 31, 1958.

[28]Greenberg, *Art and Culture,* p. 155.

[29]Harold Rosenberg, *The Anxious Object* (New York: Collier Books, 1966, 2nd edition). On p. 17 Rosenberg writes: "The anxiety of art is a philosophical quality perceived by artists to be inherent in acts of creation in our time. It manifests itself . . . in the questioning of art itself. . . . This can only mean that the object persists without a secure identity, as . . . an 'anxious object.' "

[30]Barbara Rose, *American Art Since 1900* (New York: Frederick A. Praeger, 1967), p. 205.

[31]Susan Sontag, "Against Interpretation," *Against Interpretation* (New York: Farrar, Straus & Giroux, 1966), p. 14.

[32]Greenberg, *Art and Culture,* p. 208.

[33]Ibid., p. 221.

[34]Ibid., pp. 208–9.

[35]Ibid., p. 225.

[36]Lawrence Alloway, "Systemic Painting," *Minimal Art: A Critical Anthology,* ed. Gregory Battcock (New York: E. P. Dutton & Co., 1968), p. 39.

[37]Lawrence Alloway, "The Development of British Pop," *Pop Art,* ed. Lucy R. Lippard (New York: Frederick A. Praeger, 1966), p. 27.

[38]Lucy R. Lippard, "New York Pop," *Pop Art,* p. 69.

[39]Ibid., p. 70.

[40]Quoted in Lawrence Alloway, *American Pop Art* (New York: Collier Macmillan Publishers and the Whitney Museum of American Art, 1974; exhibition catalog), p. 78.

[41]Lippard, "New York Pop, " p. 69.

[42]Alloway, *American Pop Art,* p. 19.

[43]Ibid., p. 78.

[44]Alloway, "The Development of British Pop," pp. 36, 38.

[45]Jeanne Siegel, "Roy Lichtenstein: Thoughts on the 'Modern' Period," *Artwords: Discourse on the 60s and 70s* (Ann Arbor, Mich.: UMI Research Press, 1985), p. 195.

[46]Ibid., p. 191.

[47]Alloway, "The Development of British Pop," p. 41.

[48]Ibid., p. 40.

[49]Quoted in Lippard, *Pop Art,* p. 94.

[50]Alloway, *American Pop Art,* p. 75.

[51]Donald B. Kuspit, "Lichtenstein and the Collective Unconscious of Style," *The Critic*

Is Artist: The Intentionality of Art (Ann Arbor, Mich.: UMI Research Press, 1984), pp. 221–26.

[52]Lippard, *Pop Art,* p. 95.

[53]Ibid., p. 90.

[54]Alloway, *American Pop Art,* p. 7.

[55]Ibid., p. 84.

[56]Ibid., p. 86.

[57]Jeanne Siegel, "Claes Oldenburg: How To Keep Sculpture Alive In and Out of a Museum," *Artwords,* p. 181.

[58]Alloway, *American Pop Art,* p. 101.

[59]Ibid., p. 109.

[60]Ibid., p. 114.

[61]Ibid., p. 109.

[62]Lippard, *Pop Art,* p. 111.

[63]Lucy R. Lippard, *Six Years: The Dematerialization of The Art Object from 1966 to 1972* (New York: Praeger Publishers, 1973), p. 5.

[64]Gregory Battcock, Introduction to *Idea Art: A Critical Anthology,* ed. Gregory Battcock (New York: E. P. Dutton & Co., 1973), p. 1.

[65]Barbara Rose, "A B C Art," *Minimal Art: A Critical Anthology* (see n. 36), pp. 274–97.

[66]Robert Morris, "Notes on Sculpture," *Minimal Art: A Critical Anthology,* p. 234.

[67]Lawrence Alloway, "Systemic Painting," *Minimal Art: A Critical Anthology,* p. 56.

[68]Clement Greenberg, "Recentness of Sculpture," *Minimal Art: A Critical Anthology,* pp. 183–84.

[69]Gregory Battcock, Introduction to *Idea Art,* p. 1.

[70]Greenberg, "Recentness of Sculpture," p. 184.

[71]Ibid., p. 183.

[72]Joseph Kosuth, "Art After Philosophy I and II," *Idea Art,* p. 84.

[73]Ibid.

[74]Ibid., p. 82.

[75]Ibid., p. 100.

[76]Ibid., p. 80.

[77]Ibid., p. 88.

[78]Ibid., p. 91.

[79]Ibid., p. 92.

[80]Ibid., p. 99.

[81]Ibid.

[82]Ibid., p. 85.

[83]Lucy R. Lippard, quoted by Kosuth, p. 79.

[84]Kosuth, pp. 97–98.

[85]Robert Smithson, *The Writings of Robert Smithson* (New York: New York University Press, 1979), p. 9.

[86]Smithson, "Incidents of Mirror-Travel in the Yucatan," *The Writings of Robert Smithson,* pp. 94–103.

[87]Smithson, *The Writings,* p. 155.

[88]Donald B. Kuspit, "The Pascalian Spiral: Robert Smithson's Drunken Boat," *Arts Magazine* 56 (October 1981): 82–88.

[89]Smithson, *The Writings,* p. 6.

[90]Smithson, "Frederick Law Olmsted and the Dialectical Landscape," *The Writings,* pp. 117–28.

[91]Lucy R. Lippard, *Overlay: Contemporary Art and the Art of Prehistory* (New York: Pantheon Books, 1983).

[92]Joseph Masheck, "Neo-Neo," *Historical Present: Essays of the 1970s* (Ann Arbor, Mich.: UMI Research Press, 1984), pp. 231–48.

[93]Corinne Robins, *The Pluralist Era: American Art 1968–1981* (New York: Harper & Row, 1984).

[94]Paul Gauguin, *The Writings of a Savage,* ed. Daniel Guérin (New York: Viking Press, 1978), p. 107.

[95]Donald B. Kuspit, "Dialectical Conversion," *Clement Greenberg, Art Critic* (Madison, Wis.: University of Wisconsin Press, 1979), p. 20.

[96]T. W. Adorno, *Aesthetic Theory* (London: Routledge & Kegan Paul, 1984), p. 271.

[97]Ibid., p. 272.

[98]Quoted in Elsa Honig Fine, *The Afro-American Artist* (New York: Holt, Rinehart, Winston, 1973), p. 209.

[99]Judy Chicago, *Through The Flower* (New York: Doubleday & Co., 1975), p. 106D.

[100]Roberta Smith, " 'The Dinner Party': Nuts and Bolts," *Art in America* 68 (April 1980): 121.

[101]Lucy R. Lippard, *Get The Message? A Decade of Art for Social Change* (New York: E. P. Dutton, 1984), p. 275.

[102]Henry D. Raymond, "Beyond Freedom, Dignity and Ridicule," *Arts Magazine* 48 (February 1974): 26.

[103]Harold Rosenberg, "Reality Again," *Super Realism: A Critical Anthology,* ed. Gregory Battcock (New York: E. P. Dutton & Co., 1975), p. 139.

[104]Andy Grundberg, "Duane Michals at Light," *Art in America* 63 (May/June 1975): 78.

[105]Duane Michals, *Real Dreams* (New Hampshire: Danbury House, 1976), p. 10.

[106]David Schapiro, *Eve Sonneman's Photography: Splitting and Integrity* (Minneapolis: Minneapolis Institute of Arts, 1980; exhibition catalog), n.p.

[107]Matthew Baigell, "Robert Morris's Latest Works: Slouching Toward Armageddon," *Art Criticism* 2 (Fall 1985): 7.

[108]Robert Morris, "American Quartet," *Art in America* 69 (December 1981): 104.

Chaos: A View of Complexity in the Physical Sciences

Leo P. Kadanoff

Leo Kadanoff is a theoretical physicist who has contributed widely to research in the properties of matter and upon the fringes of elementary particle physics. Most recently he has been involved in the understanding of the onset of chaos in simple mechanical and fluid systems.

He was born and received his early education in New York City. He did his undergraduate and graduate work at Harvard University, and after some post-doctoral work at the Niels Bohr Institute in Copenhagen he joined the staff at the University of Illinois in 1962. In 1966 and 1967 he did research on the organization of matter in "phase transitions," which led to a substantial modification of physicists' ways of looking at these changes in the state of matter. For this work he received the Buckley Prize of the American Physical Society (1977) and the Wolf Foundation Prize (1980).

He went to the University of Chicago in 1978 and became John D. MacArthur Distinguished Service Professor of Physics there in 1982.

Professor Kadanoff is a member of the National Academy of Sciences, a Fellow of the American Physical Society, and a member of the American Academy of Arts and Sciences.

Introduction

Definition of chaos: complexity and order

The word *chaos* has suddenly come to be popular in the physical sciences. It is used to describe situations in which we can see a very complex behavior in space and time. Because the term is used imprecisely, it is best explained by example (*see* illustrations on the following two pages). Figure 1 shows a kind of atmospheric disturbance which, over the course of many years, has been observed on the surface of the planet Jupiter. This close-up shows a quite intricate pattern of atmospheric swirling or turbulence. Observers of the TV news will recognize that somewhat similar swirling patterns also exist in the Earth's atmosphere. On both planets, the turbulence takes on fantastic forms in which we can nonetheless see some underlying regularity and order. One kind of regularity is that the storm, according to what we believe, has continued to exist on the surface of Jupiter for millions of years. Another kind of regularity is that the storm contains large, rather uniform regions.

The predominant impression that one gets from weather maps on either planet is nevertheless one of considerable complexity. Chaotic patterns are characteristically quite varied in their details, but they may have quite regular general features. For example, clouds are sufficiently orderly so that one can give a meaningful classification of their general types, but each type exhibits endless variations in its detailed shapes.

Look at another example. Figure 2 shows a dried-up lake in which mud has hardened itself into a complex pattern. We can see that the pattern is almost the same in different places, but it repeats itself with apparently unpredictable variations and is hence "chaotic." Additional familiar examples of chaotic behavior are provided by the fantastically rich patterns of snowflakes or of the frost which can appear on the inside of a window in winter. Figure 3 shows the result of the solidification of water on a cool, flat surface. New ice forms in contact with the old. Because a piece of the ice surface which sticks out can more effectively move forward, projections upon the ice surface grow into longer and longer branches. But then, if a branch has a little bump on

Figure 1. A "storm" in the atmosphere of Jupiter.

it, that bump will also tend to grow and become a branch itself. And, by the same logic, branches will grow on branches, and so on indefinitely until a beautiful treelike shape arises.

All these examples of chaos have several striking features in common. One, which I wish to emphasize now, is the outcome's sensitivity to the conditions under which the pattern is formed. A degree's change in temperature today, and next week's weather map would change totally. If you blow upon the windowpane, you can completely change the details of a branching pattern like that of Figure 3.

Chapter I: Simple laws, complex outcomes

The physical sciences are divided into many disciplinary subfields, among them meteorology, astronomy, aerodynamics, and physics. Except for physics, all these subfields try to gain a deep and solid understanding of particular areas of nature. Thus, if an astronomer looks at a galaxy and sees it to be chaotic, his or her natural reaction is likely to be a desire to understand that particular problem. Concentration on a complex behavior is natural to fields of activity like astronomy.

Physicists, on the other hand, consider themselves to be looking for the fundamental laws of nature. They seek basic principles, ideas, and mathematical formulations on which all further understanding can be

Figures 2 and 3. "*Chaotic patterns are characteristically quite varied in their details, but they may have quite regular general features.*" The pattern of the dried up lake, in Figure 2 (top), and frost on a flat surface, in Figure 3, are examples.

built. To look at complexity is to some extent a new endeavor for physicists. It runs counter to the idea of physics as the science that seeks to understand nature in simplest terms. Newton gave us three simply stated laws to describe all the motions of the heavenly bodies—and many aspects of earthly motion as well. The laws of general relativity or of quantum mechanics are also simple to state. Moreover, such laws tend to result from a study of their "simplest," most elementary realizations. For Newton's gravity this realization is found in Kepler's rules for the motion of two gravitating bodies; for general relativity it is found in black holes; for quantum mechanics it lies in hydrogen atoms.

For the student of physics, or the practitioner, the science is interesting and beautiful precisely because it summarizes the complexity of the world in a few simple laws and then describes the consequences of these laws by almost equally simple examples. However, many students and even some practitioners suspect that something is lost in the process. When physics concentrates on three laws, or five, or seven, when those laws are mostly applied only to the very simplest examples, we have lost something of the real world. We have chosen to ignore the wonderful diversity and exquisite complication that really characterize our world. This choice has led to wonderful descriptions of nature in our theories of quantum mechanics, relativity, cosmology, and so forth. But, these theories are so focused upon the simple and "basic" that they run the danger of providing a peculiar caricature of nature. Focus upon simplicity and you leave out Jupiter's storms, the diversity of galaxies, the intricacies of organic chemistry, and indeed life itself.

In recent years there has been some change in the attitude of many physicists toward complexity. Indeed, the very existence of this article reflects the change. Physicists have begun to realize that complex systems might have their own laws, and that these laws might be as simple, as fundamental, and as beautiful as any other laws of nature. Hence, more and more the attention of physicists has turned toward nature's more complex and "chaotic" manifestations, and to the attempt to construct laws for this chaos.

In some sense, this change in attention has resulted from a natural attempt to understand interesting situations such as the ones I have shown in the figures. In another sense, the concentration upon chaos has been a part of a change in our understanding of what it means for a law to be "fundamental" or "basic." Physical scientists have sometimes been tempted to take a reductionist view of nature. In this view, there are fundamental laws and everything else follows directly and immediately from them. Following this line of thought, one would construct a hierarchy of scientific problems. The "deepest" problems would be those connected with the most fundamental things, perhaps the largest issues of cosmology, or the hardest problems of mathematical logic, or maybe the physics of the very smallest observable units in the universe. To the reductionist the important problem is to understand these deepest matters and to build from them, in a step-by-step way, explanations of all other observable phenomena.

Here I wish to argue against the reductionist prejudice. It seems to me that considerable experience has been developed to show that there are levels of aggregation that represent the natural subject areas of different groups of scientists. Thus, one group may study quarks (a variety of subnuclear particle), another, atomic nuclei, another, atoms, another, molecular biology, and another, genetics. In this list, each succeeding part is made up of objects from the preceding level. Each level might be considered to be less fundamental than the one preceding it in the list. But at each level there are new and exciting valid generalizations which could not in any very natural way have been deduced from any more "basic" sciences. Starting from the "least fundamental" and going backward on the list, we can enumerate, in succession, representative and important conclusions from each of these sciences, as Mendelian inheritance, the double helix, quantum mechanics, and nuclear fission. Which is the most fundamental, the most basic? Which was derived from which? From this example, it seems rather foolish to think about a hierarchy of scientific knowledge. Rather, it would appear that grand ideas appear at any level of generalization.

With exactly this realization in mind, one might look at the rich variety of chaotic systems and wonder whether there are broad and general principles which can be derived from them. In fact, I have already mentioned one such "law": *chaotic systems show a detailed behavior which is extremely sensitive to the conditions under which they are formed.* The consequences of this sensitivity are further examined in the next section.

Practical predictability

Many of the modern concepts of chaos were formed by Henri Poincaré, a nineteeth-century French astronomer and mathematician. He recognized very clearly that there was a qualitative difference between the motion of two gravitating bodies (Earth-Sun, for example) and that of three (Moon-Earth-Sun). In the former case, when we have two bodies each moving under the gravitational influence of the other, the orbits are simple and easily predictable. They are Kepler's ellipses, and these orbits are certainly not chaotic. The latter situation, the famous "three-body problem," is chaotic. Three bodies develop complex orbit structures in which the positions of the objects in the distant future are extremely sensitive to their positions now. And this sensitivity and complexity is not just theoretical nonsense. It has practical consequences. To predict the future, one needs information about the present, and the longer the forecast, the better the information required. In the chaotic problem, the accuracy required of the input data must be very sharply improved as the forecasting period becomes longer and longer.

For astronomical systems, the data initially needed are the position and velocities of the gravitating bodies. Imagine that we are looking ahead and trying to forecast the positions of the planets, perhaps with a view to predicting the time of eclipses. Imagine further that there is a certain error in our present knowledge of planetary positions, perhaps by only a few feet. In both the nonchaotic and the chaotic cases our forecasting uncertainty will get larger as we look further forward into the future. The difference is in the type of growth. In the nonchaotic case, for each further year of forecast, the uncertainty grows by the addition of an increment proportional to the original uncertainty. In the chaotic case, for each additional year of forecast, the uncertainty grows by an increment proportional to the uncertainty in *that year's* forecast. The latter type of growth, so-called exponential growth, is akin to compound interest and is very rapid compared with the growth in the nonchaotic case, which is akin to simple interest. In the long run, the uncertainties in the "compound interest" case are far, far larger than in the corresponding case of "simple interest."

Thus our ability to forecast, for example, eclipses, is far, far worse in the chaotic case than in the more orderly example of the motion of two gravitating bodies.

This line of thought was picked up by a meteorologist from the Massachusetts Institute of Technology, Edward Lorenz. He was interested in the implications of the idea that Earth's atmosphere might exhibit a sensitivity to initial conditions similar to the one which had been thought about in the gravitational case. His work, published in 1963,* in some sense marked the beginning of our "modern era" in the study of chaotic systems. He looked at convection, that is, flows in which a heated fluid rises because it is less dense than its surroundings. He set up a simple mathematical model for convection, solved it on a computer, and showed that even in this oversimplified case the system's behavior was wonderfully rich and complex. In addition, he showed that its long-term behavior exhibited the kind of sensitivity to initial conditions that was described above for chaotic planetary systems. He made the point that if actual weather prediction were like the model he studied, it would be terribly hard to predict very far ahead.

Naturally, this practical unpredictability has very important implications for all kinds of engineering arts involving chaotic situations—not only weather prediction, but also airplane wing design, the flow of fluids through chemical plants, and many other cases. It has also inspired

*E. N. Lorenz, "Deterministic Non-Periodic Flows," *Journal of the Atmospheric Sciences* 20 (1963): 130.

some rethinking about such familiar philosophical questions as free will and determinism. For several different reasons, then, we may wish to understand this result in somewhat more detail.

In the next chapter I shall further discuss the nature of chaos by showing how it arises. In the final chapter I shall describe how chaos reflects itself in beautiful and complicated geometrical structures and illustrate this with an example from Lorenz's work.

Chapter II: Routes to chaos

One way of understanding the nature of chaos is to ask how it arises. One can start from a very orderly situation, gradually change the situation, and then see chaos set in little by little. Consider, for example, the flow of water that might occur in a river as it flows past an obstacle. Imagine that we are standing on a bridge, looking down at the water as it flows past a buttress of the bridge sitting in the water. If the water is flowing slowly, it flows in smooth and unswirly paths like those in Figure 4a. The rate of flow is listed in the different parts of Figure 4 by giving the value of a "parameter," R, which is proportional to the rate or speed at which the river is flowing. (The word *parameter* is often used in the sciences to mean a numerical value which defines a natural situation; for example, the birthrate is an important parameter for determining the future quality of life on our planet.)

Successive rows in Figure 4 show the situation for successively higher values of the flow rate. As this parameter is increased, the flow gets successively more complex. This increase in complexity is depicted in two ways. The first column shows spatial patterns by depicting the flow path of typical particles in the water—or of debris on the surface—as the particles (or the debris) move around the buttress. In the second column we plot the speed of the water at a particular spot, the one marked with an x in Figure 4a. For small speeds, as in 4a, the flow pattern would be completely time-independent and totally lacking in swirls. If the river were running a bit faster, as in Figure 4b, there would be a few swirls or vortices fixed in place near the bridge, but because these are fixed, the pattern would remain time-independent. Increase the speed still more, as in Figure 4c, and the swirls come loose and start moving slowly downstream, away from the bridge. New swirls are produced near the buttress at a regular rate, and these too move downstream in a regular progression. In this case, our instrument, which measures the speed at point x, will show a repetitive time dependence in which the speed goes through a maximum as the swirl passes by.

Such periodic behavior simply repeats itself again and again as time goes by and is certainly not chaotic. But a further increase in the speed does produce chaos. Figure 4d indicates that at this higher value of R

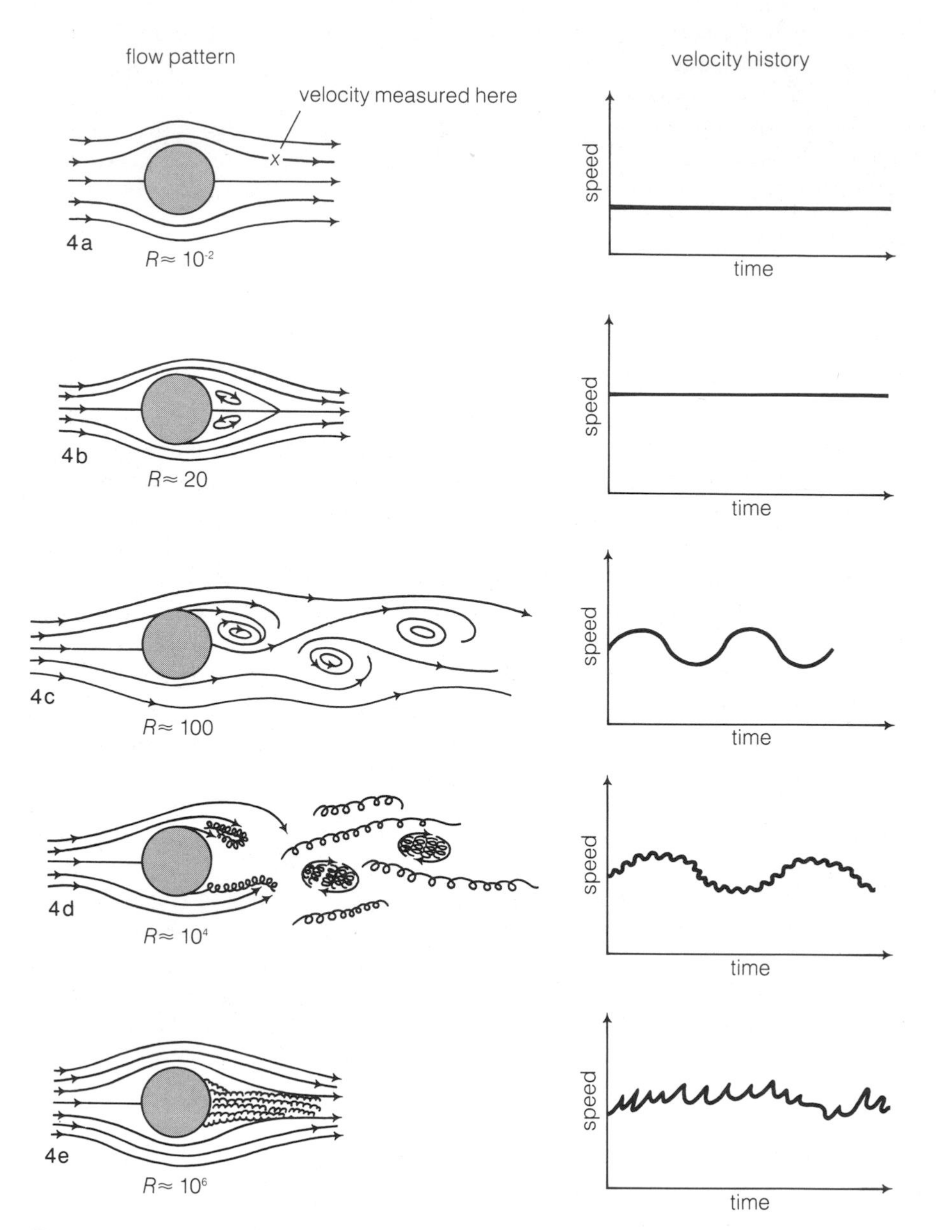

Figures 4a–e. Flows of water past a cylinder for successively larger values of the velocity, or flow rate, defined by the parameter, *R*. The first column shows flow patterns, the second, time histories of the velocity at the point marked by an *x* in Figure 4a.

the individual swirls have begun to look a bit ragged and chaotic. The time dependence shows a basically periodic pattern, similar to that of Figure 4c, but there is a small amount of chaotic jiggling superposed upon the regular motion. Finally, if the river is moving very fast indeed, as in Figure 4e, the turbulent region moves out and fills the entire wake behind the bridge. Then the time dependence seems totally unpredictable and chaotic.

A model of chaos

Next, I would like to explain in somewhat more detail and with greater precision exactly how the chaos arose in the hydrodynamic system just described. I would like to, but I cannot. Nobody has a real understanding of chaos in any fluid dynamical context. So, instead of that, I shall turn my attention to a simpler problem, one with a very simple mathematical structure which we can encompass and understand. (A simpler problem used to illuminate a more complex one is called a "model.")

This chapter and the next are largely concerned with the description of several mathematical models of chaos. These models are sets of equations which are easier to understand and study than the realistic cases which are our actual concern. However, if deftly chosen, such a model might just capture some important feature of the real system and exhibit it in a transparent form. In fact, in the best of cases the model will capture the essential nature of the physical process under study and will leave out only insignificant details. In this best situation, the model can be used to predict the results of experiments in the real system.

Our present interest is in the onset and development of chaos in fluid mechanical systems like the one depicted in Figure 4. Our model system for understanding this onset is so simple that one might, at first glance, assume that it contains nothing of interest. But I ask the reader to suspend disbelief, at least for a time. The model is interesting and does have a connection to hydrodynamic systems.

Consider, therefore, an island with a population of insects. In every year, during one month, the insects are hatched, they eat, they mate, they lay eggs, and they die. In the next year the whole process is repeated over again.

A mathematical model for this kind of process is a formula by which we can infer each year's population from the population in the previous year. We can repeat this inference again and again, and thereby generate a list of populations in the different years. We can then examine the list and see whether the result is orderly or chaotic. An orderly pattern might, for example, be one in which the population increased year by year but, after a while, started to "level out" so that, in the long run, the population approached closer and closer to some final value. A chaotic pattern could be one in which the population went up and down in an apparently disorderly way, like a stock market average. A given island might behave in either fashion, depending upon the formula used to generate one year's population from the last.

Now imagine a whole group of islands, each of which provides a different kind of environment for our insects. The different islands are distinguished by a growth-rate parameter, called r, which is a qualitative indication of how well the particular island supports the insect population. We must visualize two basic processes going on. One is the natural increase in population year by year in a manner rather similar to compound interest. The other is the effect of overcrowding. If the population gets too large, destructive competition ensues and the next year's population is considerably smaller than it would otherwise have been.

Given these two processes, there are several outcomes we may imagine. I will describe these outcomes verbally here and mathematically later on:

Case a. (The lowest values of r.) A poor environment provides a negative natural increase for the insects; year by year the population decreases until, finally, no insects remain. This pattern is totally orderly and not at all chaotic. The time-evolution of the population for this case is depicted in Figure 5a.

Case b. (Very high population increase. Large r.) In this case, a quite disorderly pattern may ensue. For example, imagine that in the first year the population is small. With a large growth factor, it could well be true that the next year's population will be very large. Then the unfavorable effects of crowding could cause a precipitous drop in the population for the third year. Over the next few years the population could grow again, and then once again collapse due to overcrowding. We could thus have a situation in which the population increased and decreased in a disorderly and apparently chaotic fashion. This kind of behavior is depicted in Figure 5b for two separate islands.

Case c. (Intermediate values for the population increase.) Imagine a natural growth rate just large enough to sustain a slow population growth in the absence of any overcrowding effect. In this kind of island, we would see a population that increases year by year until overcrowding limits its growth. In the end, the population would settle down to a steady value in which crowding and natural growth balance each other. Such a population pattern is quite orderly. The pattern is shown in Figure 5c.

We have said, in sum, that different islands might be described by the same kind of model, but that each island would have to be distinguished by different values of the population growth parameter, r. Depending on the value of this parameter, a given island might show either orderly behavior (for low rates of population increase) or chaos (for high rates).

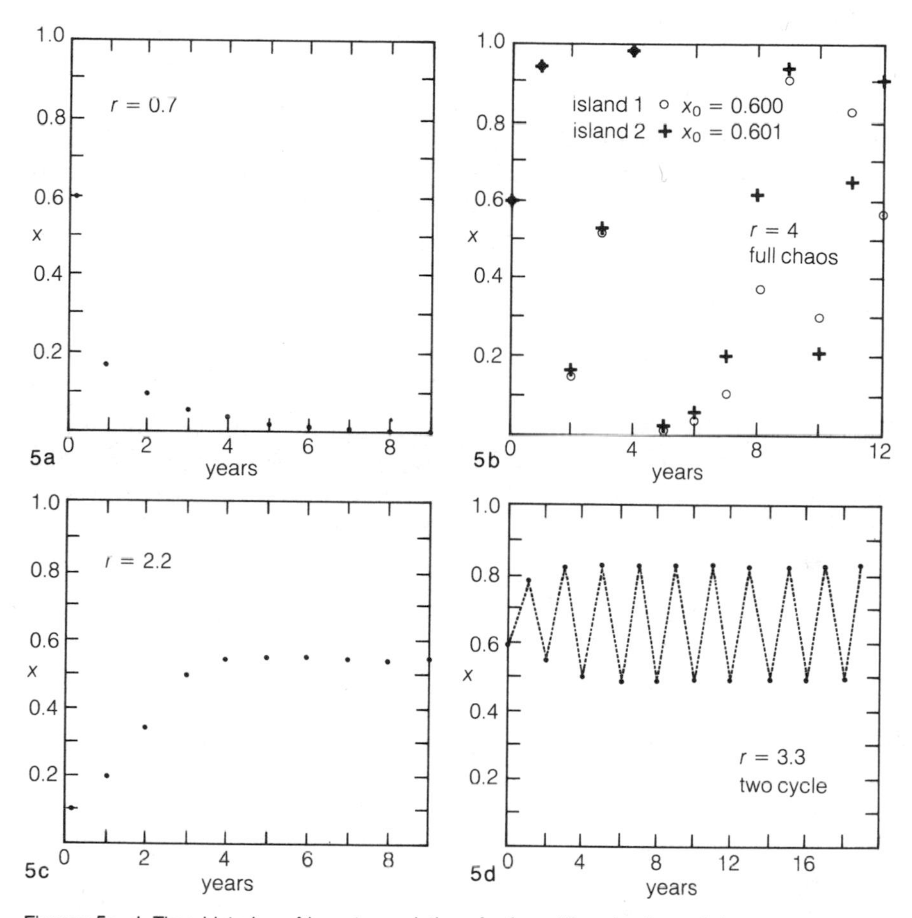

Figures 5a–d. Time histories of insect populations for four different values of the parameter, r. Figure 5b shows two histories with slightly different starting populations. In the course of time this difference becomes larger and larger. For the other r-values shown, the effect of such a small mutual difference would never become noticeable. The case shown in 5b is chaotic, the other cases depicted are not. Dotted lines in Figure 5d highlight the fact that the diagram is one oscillating insect population, not two.

Now we wish to convert the verbal argument into a mathematical one by giving a well-defined formula to determine one year's population from that of the year before.

The mathematical description of this situation will enable us to give a far more detailed account of the possible outcomes than I could give in the verbal descriptions above. There is a further advantage however. We can imagine a succession of different islands, each with a slightly larger value of the growth-rate parameter. In our minds, we can examine the history of each of these islands. Those with small values of r will be orderly; those with the largest will be chaotic. By studying the intermediate values of r we can ask ourselves, "just how does the chaos first arise?"

The model in mathematical form

One can describe an island in terms of a variable, p, which tells you the population of insects in a given year. The mathematical model is an equation that gives the population next year, p_{next}, in terms of the population this year, p. For example, the simplest such model might predict that the population will increase by 10% during each year. This process would be represented by a simple equation for next year's population, namely,

$$p_{next} = rp. \tag{1}$$

To represent the 10% per year increase in population, we will choose the growth-rate parameter, r, to be 1.1. To look for chaos, we will take the equation that predicts each year's population from the last and then use it to generate a list of populations in different years,

$$p_0, p_1, p_2, \ldots, p_j, \ldots. \tag{2}$$

Here the subscripts 0, 1, and 2 are used to describe the populations in years 0, one, and two, . . . ,while p_j represents the population in the jth year. The game then is to use an equation like equation (1) to calculate each year's population in terms of the last and thereby generate, in year-by-year fashion, a list like that in expression (2). (The problem, and its solution, is exactly the same as the one for compound interest.) We then look for patterns in the list and ask whether the pattern is orderly or chaotic, and why. We especially ask whether the different islands, which are represented by different values of r, show different types of behavior. The answer is yes. There are three different categories of behavior corresponding to three qualitatively different types of environments for the insects and consisting of three different ranges of r. These are:

First case: A poor environment. Here the growth-rate parameter, r, lies in the range between zero and one. For these islands the population is smaller each year until eventually it becomes invisible. The resulting population pattern is orderly but dull.

Second case: An equally orderly and dull result will ensue in an island described by equation (1) with $r = 1$. In this balanced environment the population would simply remain unchanged year by year.

Third case: In a favorable environment, r would be greater than one. An island with this environment would have a population that increases year by year. The population would grow without limit.

This last case is unrealistic, of course. In the long run, something must limit the insect population. Thus, the simple model of equation (1) is unsatisfactory as a natural prediction. Furthermore, it shows no chaos. We must go on to develop a slightly more complex model.

The next simplest model could show that when the insect population gets large the reproductive process is inhibited and next year's population is diminished. This reduction might occur because individuals would compete for food or for nesting space. Or maybe the insects are simply shy and do not reproduce well when they are crowded. In any case, the model we need is one that reduces the population predicted in equation (1) by an amount proportional to the number of possible interactions among the different individuals in the population. Since the number of possible interactions is proportional to the population squared, we might try a model of the form:

$$p_{next} = rp - sp^2, \tag{3}$$

where s is another parameter which measures the effectiveness of the various interactions in a diminishing population.

Note that equation (3) only makes sense if the population is smaller than r/s. If the population is larger than this value, equation (3) gives the non-sense result of a population in the next year as negative. For this reason, we limit our attention to situations in which the population is a positive number but smaller than r/s.

One final step is required to convert this model into a form suitable for further study. Instead of using a variable, p, for population, we will use instead a variable x and say that $x = (s/r)p$. By this we mean that x measures the ratio of the actual population of the island to its maximum possible one. Thus, x varies between zero and one, for the population cannot be less than zero, nor greater than the maximum population the island can sustain. According to equation (3), the population ratio next year is determined from the population ratio this year as follows:

$$\begin{aligned} p_{next} &= rp\,(1 - sp^2/rp) \\ p_{next} &= rp\,[1 - (s/r)\,p] \\ (r/s)\,x_{next} &= r\,(r/s)\,x\,(1 - x). \qquad [\text{since } p = (r/s)\,x] \end{aligned}$$

We can now cancel out the common factor, r/s, and find

$$x_{next} = rx\,(1 - x). \tag{4}$$

Once again, r has the significance of a growth factor. When the population is small, i.e., x is close to zero, then $(1 - x)$ is close to one, and the population will be multiplied only by a factor of r during each year. Here then is our model. Next we can look at its consequences.

Order and chaos

For r (the growth-rate parameter) less than one, our first model, equation (1), gave a uniformly diminishing population. Since the modification that led to equations (3) and (4) will further decrease the population through decreased reproductive ability, it is reasonable to expect that this decline will also occur in our new model. To see how it works, consider, for example, the case in which $r = 0.7$. Choose some initial value of the population ratio x, for example $x_0 = 0.6$. Then it is very easy to use equation (4) to calculate the next year's population ratio to be $x_1 = rx_0 (1 - x_0) = .7 \times .6 \times .4 = 0.168$. The next year's calculation gives $x_2 = 0.0978$, showing that the population has diminished. It continues to diminish, as shown in Figure 5a.

In contrast, consider an island in which the growth-rate parameter, r, has the value 4. Then, by equation (4), if the population starts out low, it will in the next year quadruple. Hence, it cannot stay low long. However, if the ratio of the actual population to the maximum ever gets close to its highest possible value, 1, then in the next year the population will become very small (from the combined obstacles to reproduction). The resulting population pattern can be seen with the data points shown as circles in Figure 5b. It goes up and down in an apparently unpredictable manner. To see this unpredictability in even more detail, compare the circle-points to the data points shown as plus signs. The only difference between the population patterns in the two cases is the starting value of the population. The circle-points represent an island in which the ratio of the initial population to the maximum is given by $x_0 = 0.600$. The plus points represent another island which has a very slightly different starting value, $x_0 = 0.601$. At the beginning and for the first few years, we cannot tell the difference between the two islands. The plus points lie on top of the circle ones. However, after a few years the difference between the two cases becomes noticeable. By the end of the twelve-year period shown in Figure 5b, there seems to be no correlation between the populations of the two islands. The diverging behavior of the population patterns, which were at first so similar, is a demonstration of the sensitivity to initial conditions that I described in the first chapter as a sign of chaos.

Now we have two situations which we can describe in words. For a growth factor, r, between zero and one the pattern is very orderly: the population simply dies down to zero. At $r = 4$, the behavior is highly chaotic; the population pattern keeps jumping around, and for most starting values of the population ratio, x, it never settles down to any orderly behavior. So this system exhibits both order and chaos. What lies in between, or how do we get from one to the other?

Period doubling and the onset of chaos

To repeat, for a growth-rate parameter, r, less than one, eventually the population dies away and x settles down to a specific value, namely, 0, by equation (4). Try to visualize what happens for r just greater than one. Imagine that for this case, too, a settling down occurs. Use the

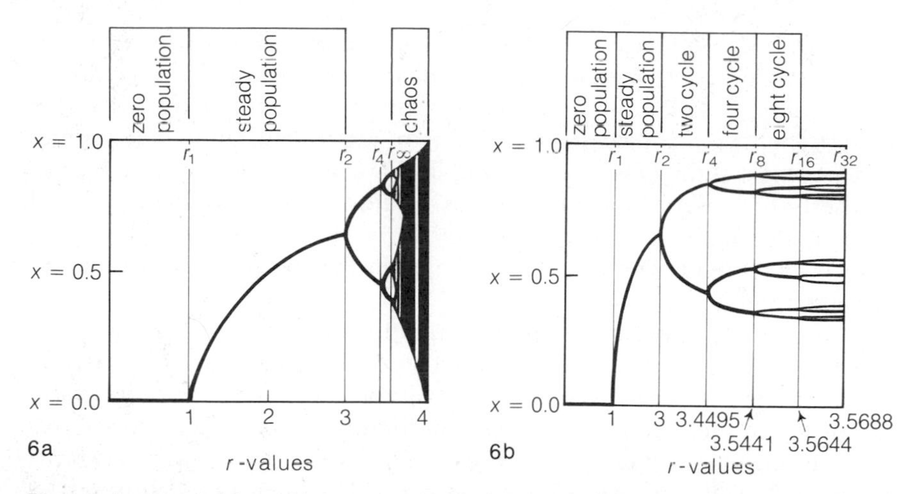

Figure 6. A summary of possible long-run behavior of insect populations for islands with different values of the growth-rate parameter, r. Two views of the same basic plot are shown. The left view has an ordinary linear scale for r in which the distance between $r = 1$ and $r = 2$ is the same as that between $r = 3$ and $r = 4$. At right, the scale of r is distorted to emphasize the region in which the higher order period doublings occur.

symbol x^* to denote the long-run value of x, i.e., the value into which the population settles after many years. Then, if the value of x this year is x^*, the value next year will also be x^*. What is the possible value of x^* itself? Look back at equation (4), substitute x^* for both x and x_{next} and we find that x^* must obey

$$x^* = rx^* (1 - x^*). \tag{5}$$

There are two possible solutions,

$$x^* = 0 \quad \text{and} \quad x^* = 1 - 1/r. \tag{6}$$

We observe that for r greater than one, the first solution is unstable in the sense given by Malthus: Even if the initial population is small, since r is greater than one, the population will grow until it is limited by overcrowding. We can see this behavior by looking at Figure 5c. This plots the population change starting from the very small value $x_0 = 0.1$ for the case in which $r = 2.2$. If we substitute this value for r in equation (6), we find x tending to 0.5454 . . . after a long period of time. From Figure 5c, we see that this value for the population ratio, x, has essentially been achieved after ten years.

In Figure 6 I will summarize the knowledge we have gained so far. This plot shows what x-values are obtained in the long run for different values of the growth-rate parameter, r. We know that at $r = 4$, all x-values between zero and one show up (fig. 5b), while for r between zero and one, only $x^* = 0$ is possible, i.e., in the long run the population will decline to nothing (fig. 5a). For r between one and three, the only possible long-term value of the insect population is the x^* given by the second part of equation (6). These three regions of behavior—$r = 4$, $0 < r < 1$, and $1 < r < 3$—correspond, respectively, to the chaotic behavior shown for the fluid in Figure 4e, and to the time-independent fluid behaviors shown in Figures 4a and 4b. In Figure 6, these three regions are marked as "chaos," "zero population," and "steady population." However, in the actual fluid, when the flow rate, R, was increased beyond the value shown in Figure 4b, then the motion became time dependent.

The analogy between the model example and the real system continues to work. As r is further increased, beyond the value 3 the steady behavior represented by equation (6) disappears. As in the fluid example of Figure 4c, a time dependence suddenly appears. One can see this time dependence by looking at Figure 5d, where the growth rate, r, is given as 3.3. Notice that after a few years the insect population settles down into a regular pattern. But the pattern is time dependent. There are *two* eventual population values: one high, one low. In good years the insect population is low and they reproduce avidly. The next year is a bad one in the sense that there is much overcrowding. Hence, reproduction is impaired, so that the following year's population is low. This alternation continues forever. Such a situation, in which the behavior repeats after two steps, is called a two cycle or a cycle of length two. The cycle is depicted in Figure 6 by showing two values of x for each r in this region.

But time dependence is not chaos. Chaos will not arise until the x-values cease to settle into a regular pattern. To see how that happens, imagine increasing r still further. As r increases above 3.4, a cycle of four years dominates the long-run behavior of the population. For almost all starting values of x in this region, the insect population will, after many years, fall into a pattern in which the population cycles through four different values before it repeats. This pattern is also shown in Figure 6 in the region marked four cycle. Increase r a bit more and you get an eight cycle, a tiny bit more and the period doubles yet again, until at $r = 3.59946 \ldots$ an infinite number of period doublings have occurred and we reach a situation which might fairly be described as chaos. In this system, chaos first appears as a result of many successive doublings of the period of the cyclic population pattern. Hence, we call what we have just described the period-doubling route to chaos.

The successive values of r at which cycles of length 1, 2, 4, 8, . . . first appear are denoted in Figure 6 by r_1, r_2, r_4, r_8, . . . , while the r-value for which the cycle of infinite length appears is denoted by r_∞. At r_∞ the insect population never repeats itself, never settles down to a fixed value or values. We say then that we have reached the onset of chaos. Likewise, for most *higher* values of the growth-rate parameter, r, those between r_∞ and 4 (i.e., the region marked chaos in fig. 6a), the typical behavior of the insect system is one in which it does not repeat itself but shows a chaotic behavior. The crucial value of r is thus r_∞, since it is at this value that chaos first appears. We call this point on the x versus r curve a Feigenbaum point, for Mitchell J. Feigenbaum, who first elucidated its properties and thus enabled us to understand the period-doubling route to chaos.

Universality and contact with experiment

It may seem that we have lost contact with the hydrodynamic systems that served as our starting point. The last section's argument about the onset of chaos seems very specific to population problems, or at most to problems that involve a single variable, x, and a dynamics in which x is determined again and again in a step-by-step fashion. However, the work on our simple model offered a hint that the results obtained might be more generally applicable. For there are some aspects of the answers which seem quite independent of the exact form of the problem under study.

Recall that we studied a problem in which the population was determined by the equation:

$$x_{next} = rx\,(1 - x).$$

But, we could have used a slightly different equation, for example,

$$x_{next} = rx\,(1 - x^2).$$

If it were true that the answers obtained were equally valid for both types of equations, and for many others like them, we might guess that these answers would have the potential for being much more general than the particular starting point we used would suggest. They might even be applicable to real systems, in the laboratory or in nature. When some result is much more general than its starting point, the situation is described by mathematicians as one of *structural stability.* Physicists describe a similar situation by saying that it exhibits *universality.*

Where can we find universality in the period-doubling route to chaos? There are two places. First, the overall structure of Figure 6, with its doublings and chaotic regions, is insensitive to the choice of the exact equation that will determine x_{next}. Changing the equation will distort the picture somewhat, as if it were drawn upon a piece of rubber and stretched, but will leave its essential features quite unchanged. Since this picture describes a variety of different mathematical problems that lead to an infinite period doubling, perhaps it also describes some real physical cases that show infinite period doubling.

In this way, we can hope to make contact between the "insect system" and real experimental systems. For example, we can set up electrical circuits that are unstable and "go chaotic" as some control parameter, roughly analogous to r, is changed. The most familiar example is an audio system, where r would describe the position of the microphone relative to the speaker. As these are brought closer together, the system may become unstable, that is, a hum may develop.

Analogous purely electrical circuits have been constructed to test the theory described above. For example, Testa, Perez, and Jeffries* performed an experiment in which an electrical circuit containing a transistor was controlled with a voltage, v_c, which played a role analogous to our parameter r. They noticed that their circuit had a natural oscillation that changed character as v_c varied. As v_c was increased, the period of the oscillation doubled, and doubled, and doubled again. By observing peak voltages, v_p, at one point in the circuit, they were able to trace out a v_p versus v_c picture that looked very much like Figure 6. Thus the electrical circuit showed a behavior very much like the one we have described. We can say, therefore, that we understand the period-doubling route to chaos in the real electrical system because we understand it in the insect model, and the two are very much the same.

Feigenbaum pointed to another way in which universality would manifest itself. As r approaches r_∞, he said, some aspects of the time pattern would remain the same even if insect behavior was different. For example, he looked at r-values for which cycles of length 1, 2, 4, 8, 16, . . . , ∞ first appeared. In Figure 6 these are denoted by r_1, r_2, r_4, r_8, r_{16}, . . . , r_∞. There is nothing universal or general about the appearance of the first few cycles. Hence there is nothing very useful to say about r_1 or r_2 or r_4. But the r-values at which very long cycles would appear turned out to be much more predictable. As the cycles get longer and longer, the spacing between successive r-values gets smaller and smaller (*see* the numbers at the bottom of fig. 6b). Indeed, for long cycles, the spacing forms a geometrical series in which the successive terms are divided by a constant factor called δ. It is surprising but true that *this constant has a value which is universal,* i.e., independent of insect behavior specifically. The spacing ratio, δ, takes the value $\delta = 4.8296$ . . . for *all* growth of the type indicated here, the type, that is, which follows a pattern of period doubling.

At first, other workers in the field were resistant to Feigenbaum's work, and particularly to the proposition that a number like δ could be universal. Feigenbaum derived an elaborate theory of this universality, based upon the "renormalization group" theory that Kenneth Wilson† had invented for quite another area of physics. The argument

*J. Testa, J. Perez, and C. Jeffries, "Evidence for Universal Chaotic Behavior of a Driven Non-Linear Oscillator," *Physical Review Letters* 48 (1982): 714.

†Kenneth G. Wilson, "Problems in Physics with Many Scales of Length," *Scientific American* 241 (August 1979): 158.

was settled by two developments: (1) a mathematical proof that in an appropriate sense the result *was* universal, and (2) experimental verifications that Feigenbaum's predictions about the quantitative aspects of successive period doubling held in other examples far removed from simple population growth models. In fact, δ-values are obtained for experiments involving instabilities in electrical circuits and also fluid systems. Within the limited accuracy of the experiments, Feigenbaum's predictions were fully verified.

The end result is a remarkable intellectual achievement. We can say with some truth that we understand how chaos arises in the simple model system described by equation (4). This is a satisfying achievement, and even though the system is simple, it is impressive. But we also have evidence, partially based upon theory and partially upon experiment, that exactly the same route to chaos is obtained in other much more complex systems. We believe that if we took one of these complex systems, measured the period doublings, and thereby found the value of δ, that number would be exactly and precisely the same number as the corresponding δ-value obtained from the simple model of equation (4). Thus the pattern of the simpler system is exactly duplicated in the more complex ones, and we can see that in understanding one case, we understand many.

In the years since Feigenbaum's work, several other scenarios for the onset of chaos have been explored both experimentally and theoretically. Each of these "routes to chaos" is universal in the sense that many different systems will exhibit the same pattern. We can therefore say that we are beginning to understand how chaos arises.

In the next chapter we will look at fully developed chaos and ask how well *that* is understood.

Chapter III: The geometry of chaos

In the last chapter the onset of chaos was considered. A full understanding of chaos, beyond its onset, still eludes us. However, we have built up a few substantial ideas about its geometrical structure. The purpose of this chapter is to discuss these geometrical ideas.

Well-developed turbulence

Chaos has been defined here as a physical situation in which the basic patterns never quite repeat themselves. One vivid example of such a nonrepetitive pattern is in a flow pattern depicted by Leonardo, shown in Figure 7. Notice how within this big swirl there are smaller ones and within them smaller ones yet. This kind of flow within flow within flow is called well-developed turbulence. The nonrepetitive nature of the pattern arises precisely because it is a Chinese box in which structures

Figure 7. Turbulent flow patterns as drawn by Leonardo da Vinci. Note how the large swirls break into smaller ones, and these again break up.

appear within structures. This point was later made into a little poem by L. F. Richardson, who wrote:

Big whorls have little whorls,
Which feed on their velocity;
And little whorls have lesser whorls,
And so on to viscosity
(in the molecular sense).*

The Soviet mathematician A. N. Kolmogorov picked up on this picture and developed a useful theory of such behavior by writing down the mathematical consequences of the idea that similar structures reappear again and again inside of one another. We do not believe that Kolmogorov's theory is entirely right, but we don't yet have a replacement for it.

The Chinese box example has to contend with two major complications. One is that any well-developed chaos is hard to understand. The other is that this particular chaos of flow within flow occurs in space.

*This poem is quoted in Benoit B. Mandelbrot, *The Fractal Geometry of Nature* (New York: W. H. Freeman and Company, 1983), p. 402.

To describe it fully, we would have to specify the velocity at every single point in the entire system. Since there are an infinite number of points, we would have to have an infinity of different numbers just to specify the chaotic situation at one time! But we have already seen a chaotic situation that could be specified by giving only one number, x, at each time. (A number like x, which can change in time, is called a "variable.") We were able to understand this example reasonably well and to see how chaos arose in it. Of course this situation was intentionally constructed to be simple. When we go out and look at the real world, we can find situations which are intermediate in complexity between the one-variable case described in the last chapter and the cases with an infinite number of variables depicted by Leonardo. These cases can often be described by specifying the time dependence of just a few variables, perhaps two, x and y, or three, x, y, and z. In the next sections, we will try to describe the kinds of behavior that could arise in these few-variable systems.

Attractors, strange and otherwise

To describe these relatively simple systems, we will direct our attention to the mathematical world in which they live. In the case of our insect island, we can fully specify its future behavior by giving one number, which describes this year's population in relation to the maximum possible one. This ratio, x, must be a number between zero and one. Indeed, for the mathematician studying our example, the relevant world is not the hypothetical island upon which the insects live, it is the mathematical world which is the set of all numbers between zero and one. That kind of world is called the "phase space" for the problem, so as to distinguish it from the physical space (the island) in which the events occur. In this example, we can depict the phase space by drawing a line segment, as in Figure 8, *case a,* and imagining that a specific value of x is depicted by putting a point upon that segment. Notice that this segment is drawn as a line that goes up and down, instead of the more conventional drawing that would go from left to right. I ignore the conventions so as to have my pictures look like the ones drawn in the previous chapter, that is, Figures 5 and 6.

Now let us return to the kind of thinking that we used in constructing these earlier figures. Consider some fixed value of the growth-rate parameter, r, say the $r = 2.2$ of Figure 5c. Then, as shown in that figure, year by year x, the ratio of the existing population to the maximum one, approaches a specific value, namely, 0.5454 . . . . For almost any value of the initial population, the long-term result is precisely the same. As the years go by, the population ratio will get closer and closer to that particular value of x. This is graphically described by drawing a point at $x = 0.5454$ within the phase space of Figure 8, as in *case c.* We then say that this point is the "attractor" for

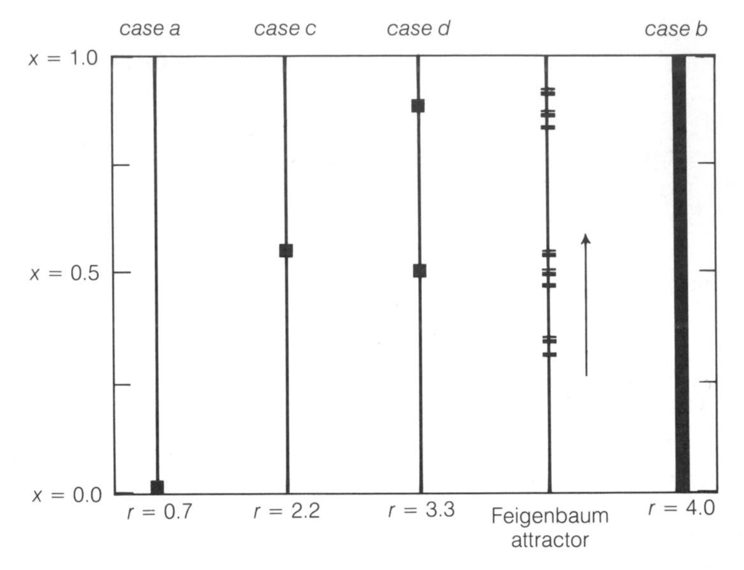

Figure 8. A description of some attractors for different r-values in our insect system. The vertical axis on the far left describes the "space" in which the attractor will fit, namely, the line between $x = 0.0$ and $x = 1.0$. The line labeled *case a* describes what happens when $r = 0.7$. It has a point at $x = 0.0$, showing that for this r-value the insect population ratio goes to zero. The filled-in regions for the other r-values similarly depict the possible population ratio values for each one of these situations.

the insect system at $r = 2.2$. By this we mean that in the year-by-year development of the insect systems, their population ratios approach or "are attracted to" this point.

For a higher growth-rate parameter, the attractor might be more complicated. For example, as we already know from Figure 5d, at $r = 3.3$ the long-term behavior of the population is a two-cycle one. Hence, the motion is attracted to a pair of points, as shown in Figure 8, *case d.* In this way, for each value of r, we can plot out the attractor, that is, the value to which the population ratio converges. In fact, Figure 6 is simply a plot that shows the attractors for all values of r.

For a still higher growth-rate parameter, the population graph exhibits chaotic behavior. The attractors in the chaotic regions of this parameter, r, are not collections of points, as in the last example, but instead *regions.* For example, in the full chaos of $r = 4.0$, as shown in Figure 8, *case b,* all values of the population ratio, x, between zero and one arise within the course of a typical pattern of time development. Hence, for this value of r, the attractor is the entire interval between zero and one. Whenever there is chaos, the attractor is an interval, or perhaps a collection of different intervals. This behavior can also be seen in the right-hand portion of Figure 6a.

In the cases described so far, the attractors are relatively simple and straightforward: a point, a few points, an interval, or a few intervals.

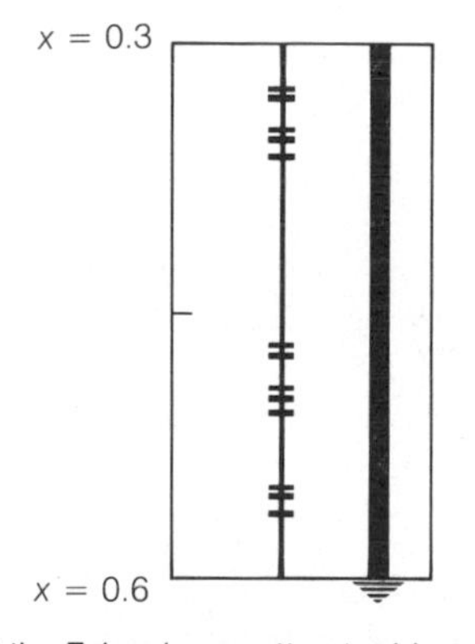

Figure 9. A portion of the Feigenbaum attractor blown up and replotted. This portion looks essentially identical to the entire attractor (*see* fig. 8).

However, when we follow Feigenbaum and look at the point for which a cycle of infinite length first appears, we see a much stranger and richer behavior. What we must do is draw the attractor for a two cycle, as in Figure 8, *case d,* then for a four cycle, next for an eight cycle, next sixteen. Then, in the limit, one gets the picture shown in the part of Figure 8 labeled "Feigenbaum attractor." This configuration contains an infinite number of points arranged in a rather interesting pattern. Such an attractor, in which there is structure inside of structure inside of structure, is called a "strange" attractor. The reader will notice that I have just defined *strange* as a technical word. In doing this, I am following the standard terminology in the field. The term *strange attractor* is due to David Ruelle of the Institut pour Haut Étude Scientifique in Paris.

Before going further, I should compare the structure within structure of Figure 7, Leonardo's drawing, with that of the Feigenbaum attractor in Figure 8. They are both "strange." However, the pictures show two different types of worlds. Leonardo draws a picture of one time in our real three-dimensional world. Figure 8, on the other hand, is drawn in phase space and is a superposition of infinitely many pictures at different times.

To see the strange character of the Feigenbaum attractor, we take the portion of it indicated by the arrow in Figure 8, blow it up, turn it over, and plot it again. The result is shown in Figure 9. Notice that, except for the values of the *x*-coordinates, the picture looks essentially identical to the one in Figure 8. This identity strongly suggests that there is a succession of almost identical structures nested within the Feigenbaum attractor, in the same way that Russian dolls are nested within one another.

Such nested behavior is very common in physical systems. Look back at the solidification patterns shown in Figure 3. Notice once again how

Figure 10. An example of a fractal object. Notice how the fine treelike object is represented again and again at different sizes.

the ice consists of a group of arms, upon which lie smaller arms and upon them smaller ones yet. This kind of behavior was first described by the nineteenth-century mathematician Georg Cantor, and later on by Felix Hausdorff and others. In more recent work, such nested behavior is often described by the terms *scale-invariant* or *fractal.* Figure 10 shows such a pattern. The term *scale-invariant* merely says that when you blow up the picture in Figure 9 (i.e., change its scale) and look at a portion of the result, you get much the same thing as before. Thus it is unchanged or invariant. The word *fractal* was introduced by Benoit Mandelbrot of IBM, who has discovered and publicized many examples of scale-invariant behavior. The term is intended to remind us of another property of these strange objects. They can be described by using a variant of the concept of a dimension. It is commonplace to say that a point has no dimension, a line is one-dimensional, an area two-dimensional, and a volume three-dimensional. For strange objects, we extend the meaning of *dimension* to include possibilities in which a dimension is not just an integer (1, 2, or 3) but instead any positive number (say 0.41). There is then a technical definition that enables us to calculate this fractional or "fractal" dimension from the picture of the object, as, for example, Figure 9. (This particular attractor has dimension 0.538 . . . which, as one might expect, is larger than the value for a point and smaller than the value for a line.)

Incidentally, I should note that the motion upon the Feigenbaum attractor is really rather orderly and cannot be described in any sense as chaotic. For example, imagine starting off with a population ratio of $x_0 = 0.5$, which is indeed a point lying on the attractor. We can look at the points that arise after 1, 2, 4, 8, 16, or 32, successive iterations of equation (4), using the value of the growth-rate parameter,

r, appropriate to the Feigenbaum attractor. The placement of these x-values is very orderly. The points x_1, x_2, x_4, x_8, x_{16}, . . . approach $x_0 = 0.5$, with alternate members of the list lying above and below x_0. Thus the Feigenbaum attractor may be "strange," but the motion on it is certainly not chaotic.

*Chaos on strange attractors**

In our insect example, chaos and strange attractors tend to occur for different values of r. However, in slightly more complicated systems, chaotic behavior almost always produces a strange attractor. So far, we have worked mostly with an example in which the present and future behavior of the system could be defined by giving the value of one number, x, representing a population ratio. In the next, more complicated, example the future state of the system is defined by two numbers, called x and y. For example, these might be the populations of two different age-groups in a given year. A model system could be defined by saying how the values of x and y in the next year depended upon the values this year.

Another example of such a dependence is given by the following equations:

$$x_{next} = rx\,(1 - x) + y, \text{ and} \qquad (7)$$
$$y_{next} = xb.$$

We might arrive at such equations by visualizing a case in which there is once again an insect population and where x is the population in a given year. (For simplicity's sake we will here talk of x as if it were the population, rather than a population ratio, as previously.) But we could introduce one difference. We could suppose that a proportion, b, of the insects would live for two summers. Call the number of "old" insects y. In that case, the same analysis as before would lead us to a result like equation (7).

The point here is that, to define the situation fully, we now need to specify two numbers: the existing population, x, and the previous year's population, y. This can be rendered geometrically by drawing a common kind of graph with x and y axes and specifying some situation by a point on the graph, as shown in Figure 11. An attractor for this situation can be constructed by starting out with some initially chosen value of x and y, constructing successively the next values via equation (7), and then imagining that after some large number of steps the values of the pair (x,y) have moved in toward the attractor.

This model, or rather one equivalent to it, has been constructed by

*For a slightly more technical presentation of similar material about Hénon's and Feigenbaum's work, *see* Douglas R. Hofstadter, "Metamagical Themas," *Scientific American* (November 1981): 22.

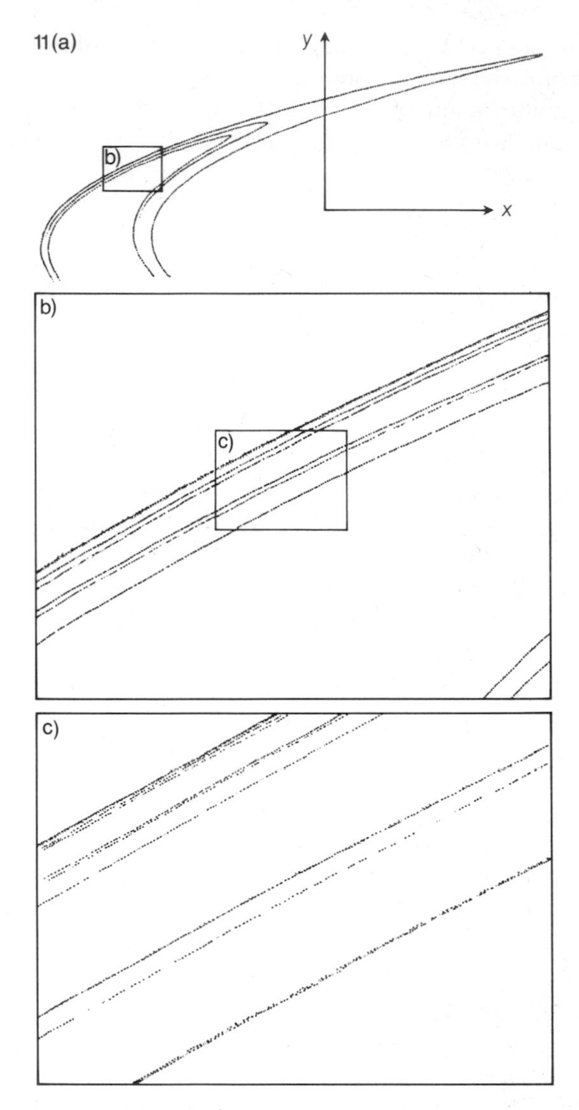

Figures 11a–c. Figure 11a shows the Hénon attractor. The other pictures are successive blowups of this attractor, with 11b being an expanded version of the boxed region in 11a, and 11c a similarly expanded version of the box in Figure 11b.

a French astrophysicist, Michel Hénon. He focuses his attention upon particular values of the parameters b and r; chooses initial values of x and y; calculates several hundred thousand successor points; throws away the first twenty thousand; and plots the rest. The result is shown in Figure 11a. This looks simply like a geometric structure containing a few parallel lines. But look more closely. Figure 11b is an expanded view of the box shown in Figure 11a. This expanded view also contains lines, but when one blows up a box within that figure, obtaining as a result 11c, one sees a familiar looking picture with a few lines within it. In this way, Hénon demonstrated that the attractor from his map could be scale-invariant and fractal. And, in contrast to the previous example, we do not have to do any careful adjustment of r to find a strange attractor. On the contrary, strange attractors will pop up for many reasonable and arbitrarily chosen values of b and r.

In contrast to the motion on the Feigenbaum attractor, the motion on the Hénon attractor is chaotic. In the first case, it is easy to predict the x-value that will be achieved after a large number of iterations. For example, if the large number is a high power of two, e.g., 2^{99}, the achieved x-value will be almost identical to the starting x-value. In the Hénon example, if we start off on the attractor, we know that the (x,y) point will continue to lie within the attractor, but there is no similarly simple rule that permits accurate prediction of just where the points will lie after many steps. Moreover, the result is extremely sensitive to initial conditions.

Hence, in Hénon's model chaos and strange attractors exist together. In fact, they are believed to have a causative relaxation: the attractors are strange exactly because they are chaotic.

Hénon is an astrophysicist. He is interested in motion in the solar system and galaxies. His work on the model described above is not just the construction of a mathematical toy, unrelated to his astronomical interests. On the contrary, all kinds of astronomical systems—for example, our own solar system—can be usefully thought of as being described by a few variables that in the course of time trace out a chaotic motion on a strange attractor. The real attractors are more complicated than the one in Figure 11, but probably in many ways not essentially different.

Tracing chaos through time

Return to Figure 7, and the complicated swirls of Leonardo's picture of chaos in a fluid. From a practical point of view, it is distressing that we do not have a decent understanding of these turbulent flows. The flow of energy through real fluids like the atmosphere of the Earth, or the water cooling a nuclear reactor, or the air flowing around a body entering the Earth's atmosphere is dominated in each case by turbulent swirls. The fact is that our understanding of these swirls has hardly progressed beyond Leonardo's. Without additional understanding, we lack the tools to make predictions and reliable engineering designs in all kinds of interesting and/or technically important situations.

The meteorologist Edward Lorenz was very acutely aware of this imperfection, since it is a meteorologist's business to understand flows in the Earth's atmosphere. To describe a flow in this or any other fluid, we write equations for the rate of change of such properties as the fluid velocity, the temperature, and the pressure at each point in the fluid. As I have already mentioned, since there are an infinite number of

The Lorenz Equations

A solution of these equations is depicted in Figure 12. In this set of equations $\mathring{x}$, $\mathring{y}$, and $\mathring{z}$ stand for the rate of change of x, y, and z with respect to time:

$$\mathring{x} = 10\,(y - x)$$
$$\mathring{y} = 28x - y - xz$$
$$\mathring{z} = 8z/3$$

"points" in every geometrical body, we must solve an infinite number of equations. Lorenz sought a ruthless simplification of the problem. Instead of describing his fluid by giving the values of an infinite number of quantities, he assumed that the fluid could be described by three, which he called, naturally enough, x, y, and z. His phase space could then be described in terms of the three coordinates. I show the exact form of his equations in the box on this page.

This detailed form is irrelevant to all the arguments that follow. The main idea, however, is not at all irrelevant. Lorenz's goal was to describe the particular kind of swirling motion called "convection." In this flow, the lower layer of a fluid heated from below rises because it is lighter (less dense) than the material above it. As the air above one portion of the Earth rises, air in another region flows downward. The net result is a complicated swirling flow. Lorenz's equations were an attempt to catch the essence of a swirling region in the very simplest fashion.

The major point about these equations is that if you give numerical values for x, y, and z at a particular time, the system will determine the values of these quantities at subsequent times. Hence, we can picture the system at a given time by drawing a point on a standard x, y, z coordinate system of the kind shown in Figure 12a. The subsequent motion of the system is shown by giving the x, y, z coordinates at later times (fig. 12b) and then connecting up these points with arrows that show the direction of increasing time along the trajectory. After an initial time to settle down, the motion approaches an orbit that covers only a small portion of the x, y, z space (*see* fig. 12c). This orbit is, of course, a strange attractor. The path traced out by the time development of the system is an object of both impressive simplicity and imposing complexity.

First, the simplicity. Two basic kinds of motions are shown in Figure 12c. There are loops tilted leftward and loops tilted rightward. These

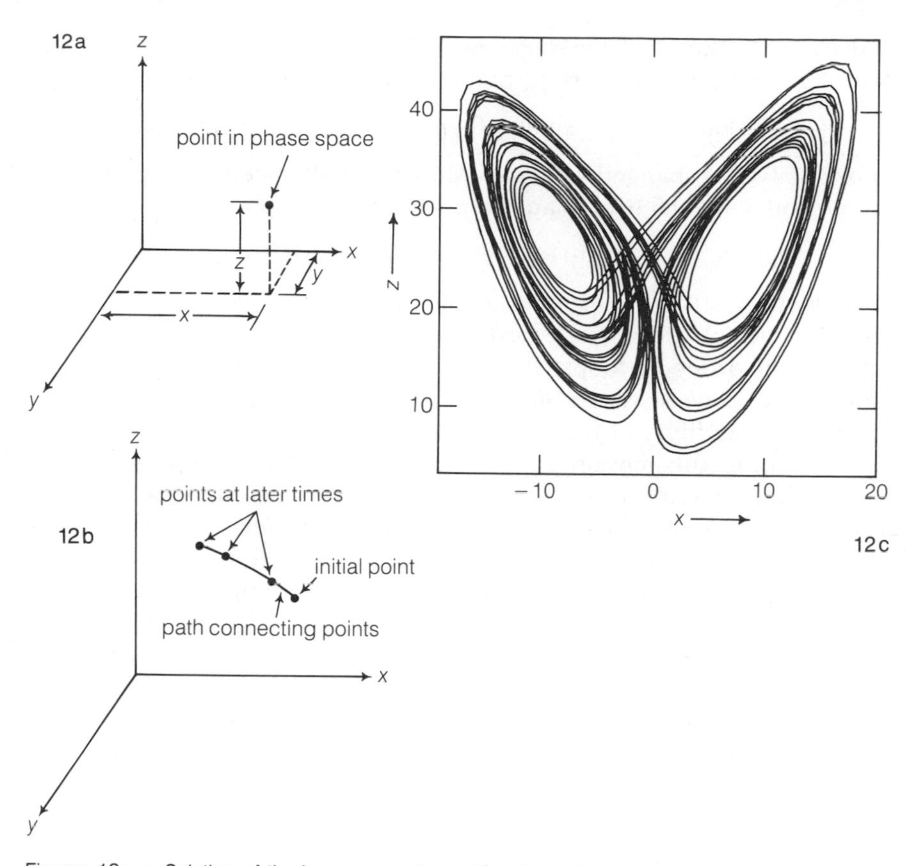

Figures 12a–c. Solution of the Lorenz equations. 12a shows the *x*, *y*, *z* space in which the equations are solved, 12b shows a fragment of the solution, while 12c is a projection upon the *x*, *z* plane of the solution over a long period of time.

come together in the region near the bottom of the diagram. As the system develops, it goes through each of these two kinds of loops in turn. To describe the sequence of events, we may list, in order, the loops that are traversed. For example, to describe the orbit in Figure 12c, which covers first a rightward loop and then two leftward ones, we may write "right-left-left." Over a very wide range of starting points, that is starting values of *x*, *y*, and *z*, the system will go through this loop-type behavior.

Now, the complexity: Depending upon the exact starting values of *x*, *y*, and *z*, the subsequent motion will be different. For one set of starting values, the motion might be

right-left-left-right-right-left-right-right-left-left-right- . . . .

Change the starting values just a little and the initial looping will change hardly at all. But the later stages may change quite considerably. Thus, with a small change in starting point we might have

right-left-left-right-right-left-right-right-left-left-**left-** . . . .

(For clarity, the changed values are shown in bold face.) A larger change in starting point will lead to an early change in the looping, for example,

right-left-left-right-right-left-**left-left-left-left-right-** . . . .

The looping structure is fully predictable in the sense that for any initial values of the x, y, z coordinates we can know and calculate the subsequent order of loops. But the structure is very sensitive to the initial conditions in that a small change in the beginning will cause a complete reshuffling of the loops at later times.

Calculating the motion in the Lorenz model is a quite nontrivial undertaking. We must carry through all the work of solving a set of differential equations. That requires a larger computer and considerable skill in its use. But the real fluids and the real world must be described with many many more variables than the three used by Lorenz. Nobody knows whether the more complicated "realistic" situations will show the same kind of complicated algebraic and geometric structure as the simplified models described here. I suspect and hope that many of the features presented here will reappear in the "real world." But now I have reached about as far as our present knowledge of the subject runs.

PART TWO

Reconsiderations of Great Books and Ideas

Animals and Men

Anthony Quinton

Anthony Quinton, who has had a distinguished academic career including writing, lecturing, and administration, has recently been made vice-chairman of the Board of Editors of Encyclopædia Britannica. He is also chairman of the British Library, vice-president of the British Academy, and president of Trinity College, Oxford. In 1982 he was granted a title and is now Lord Quinton.

He began his higher educational studies at Christ College, Oxford, studying first history and then philosophy. He was a fellow at All Souls College, Oxford, and later at New College before becoming president of Trinity in 1978. He has, at various times, been visiting professor at Swarthmore College, Stanford University, and the New School for Social Research in New York. He has also lectured extensively throughout England.

Lord Quinton's interests include social and political philosophy, intellectual history, and the theory of knowledge, all of which he has written books about. Among his writings are: *The Nature of Things* (1973), *The Politics of Imperfection* (1978), and *Thoughts and Thinkers* (1982).

He contributed an article on the philosophy of Kant to the 1977 volume of *The Great Ideas Today* and took part in the "Disputation on the Future of Democracy" that was published in the 1978 volume.

I. Introductory

In the century and a quarter since Darwin's *Origin of Species* (1859) came out, man's conception of the relation of his own species to others in the animal kingdom has greatly changed. The progress and effective popularization of zoology on the one hand, particularly of work on animal intelligence and behavior, and the decline of supernatural religion on the other, have loosened the hold of the idea that there is an absolute and fundamental difference in kind between animals and human beings.

In this essay I begin by presenting the general evolutionary case for the continuity of animals and men in a historical form. I am a complete layman in this field, and the authorities on whom I have relied may well be superannuated in some detailed respects. But the general picture is the important thing. It is needed if we are to discount the overwhelmingly large place taken by human beings in our conception of the world in which we live. In all sorts of ways we rely on and make use of animals, treating them in a manner which is morally open to serious question. But, for most of us, our direct relationships with animals are confined to those we make pets and companions of and, by and large, treat reasonably well. In stockyards and laboratories much less agreeable conditions prevail. A memorable account of this fearful belowstairs or engine room is given in Peter Singer's *Animal Liberation*.

Our lack of moral consideration for animals is underpinned by a variety of questionable beliefs about the nature of the differences between animals and men. It is to these that I go on to address myself, arguing, generally, that there are really no hard and fast distinctions between the minds or reasons or wills or moral capacities or qualifications for direct moral consideration between the two. I return at the end to the moral question and finish on a doubtful note, questioning the capacity of our habitual attitudes toward the permissible treatment of animals to withstand rational investigation.

II. On the history of the animal kingdom

1. Before the mammals

When we talk conversationally about animals, what we usually have in mind are mammals, the dramatis personae of children's stories and picture books: the dogs and cats of the home, the cows and horses of the farm, the lions and elephants of the wild. But mammals are only one class (out of five) in the subphylum of vertebrates, which is by far the most important element in the phylum of Chordata—which, in its turn, however, is one of twenty-four phyla of the animal kingdom as a whole. From our point of view as human beings, mammals are the most interesting animals. To start with, we are ourselves mammals. Secondly, the great majority of the significant interactions that we are ordinarily conscious of having with animals are with mammals. We eat and sometimes hunt birds and fish, we watch birds, we eat crustaceans and mollusks, we keep bees and dispel other insects with chemical sprays. But most of our involvement with nonhuman animals is with mammals, whether practical, when they are our meals or companions, or symbolic, in religion, art, and literature.

A gesture of nonanthropomorphic respect for the comprehensive width and variety of the animal kingdom is appropriate. A good form for it to take would be to survey the kingdom in a historical, or, at any rate, narrative, way. The vast range of animal species, living and extinct, has all evolved from a particular, elemental kind of ancestor: one-celled protozoans, who reproduce themselves by fission and with whom we have little more in common than we have with plants. But, on account of this common ancestry, the species that make up the animal kingdom are all part of one family, genealogically speaking. To approach the animal kingdom through its history, is, then, explanatory, as well as being more graphic than a mere systematic inventory.

Plants seem to have come into existence on the earth, or, more precisely, in the sea, about three billion years ago, when the first bacteria and algae made their appearance. A billion years later the first animals emerged, the protozoans mentioned above. Four or five hundred million years ago the first plants and animals to leave the sea for the land made their move; mosses and ferns in the one case, spiders in the other. After another hundred million years or thereabouts, plants with seeds first evolved. In this comparatively busy epoch amphibians (frogs and toads), retaining strong connections with the water they had emerged from, and reptiles (turtles, crocodiles, snakes, and lizards) took to the dry land. They left the crustaceans to dominate the sea. The first insects date from much the same period, as do the first fish.

From around two hundred million years ago the great age of the reptiles lasted for about seventy million years. In the course of it the first birds evolved from reptiles. The archaeopteryx was a two-legged reptile that was able to glide from tree to tree with the aid of its feathers, developed, presumably, from scales. Meanwhile, at the very beginning of the period of reptile greatness, they had given rise, through another line of development, to the first, rudimentary mammals. Their closest surviving descendants are the egg-laying platypuses, something of a taxonomist's nightmare, with their improper assemblage of defining traits. More important for the future development of life on earth were small insectivores, very much of the nature of shrews, from which the main body of mammals—the placentals—descend. Small tree-dwelling mammals led to the marsupials, which now survive only in Australia and the Americas.

It was only toward the end of the Jurassic period (190 to 135 million years ago) that flowering plants first appeared on the earth. They provided a colorful background for the dinosaurs, with whose still unexplained collapse sixty-five million years ago the age of reptile dominance finally came to an end. There are two hundred and fifty thousand species of flowering plants, and they make up about two-thirds of the world's plant life.

Some statistics of the same kind help to put the place of mammals in the general scheme in perspective. Nineteen species out of twenty in the animal kingdom are invertebrates. Three species out of four are of arthropods, creatures with segmented bodies and external skeletons, such as insects and arachnids (spiders, scorpions, and so on). Among vertebrates most species are fish. In this bewildering array mammals bulk fairly small, and primates, the kind of mammals of most concern to us, even smaller.

All living things nourish themselves and reproduce themselves. But plants supply their needs by photosynthesis of inorganic materials. Animals live off organic foods, plant life, and other animals. They are equipped to get hold of food, to take it into themselves—often by some form of processing such as chewing—to digest it, and to excrete the ingredients in it they do not need. They have sense organs and a nervous system to inform them of the whereabouts of food (and also of various kinds of danger, notably predators). They have means of locomotion—fins, wings, legs—to enable them to come within reach of the food they perceive and to get out of the reach of what might kill or injure them.

Many animal species are characteristically social in their behavior. In some cases the social order they have evolved is sophisticated and almost metropolitan in its elaborate division of labor, complexity of interaction, and general multitudinousness, most notably among the hymenoptera: ants, bees, and wasps. An ant colony can be half a million strong. Birds seek food in flocks; wolves and wild dogs hunt in packs; fish typically form schools. According to E. O. Wilson, the only societies larger than China are those that are found among locusts and pigeons.

Proximity is not by itself social organization; it simply creates a crowd. But creatures at a distance from one another are still socially related if they take account of and react to each other. In many species there are stable relationships of dominance and submission among deer, sheep, and bumblebees, for instance. In many, too, there is division of labor, most conspicuously in the societies of the hymenoptera. Animals communicate, and not just with generalized expressions of hostility, sexual interest, and fear. The bee's dance gives detailed factual information.

Animals move in groups, resist predators in groups, hunt in packs, graze in herds. Beavers and ants cooperate with their fellows in building works. Reptiles are perhaps the most unsocial of the major classes of vertebrates. But that is not to be ascribed to their evolutionary antiquity. They are not as old as the most elaborately social of all nonhuman animals, the social insects. It is true, the social life of the hymenoptera has its limitations. Ants and bees do not recognize individuals—only members of their own group.

The extinction of the dinosaurs at the end of the Jurassic period sixty-five million years ago was followed by the spread of the mammals all over the world, and their dominance. Mammals of a sort had first appeared three times as far back in time as that. A tree creature ancestral to modern rodents appeared around fifty million years ago, the first primates twenty million years after that. Thus, before examining our own order in the animal kingdom, we should first consider the class of mammals as a whole.

2. *The mammals*

Mammals and birds are the only two classes among the vertebrates that are warm-blooded. This fact, taken together with their possession of adjustable body covering—hair in one case, feathers in the other—is in a way the most important thing about them. It enables species to colonize previously unoccupied regions and thus, under new kinds of environmental pressure, to evolve in novel, imaginative ways. It enables individuals to move from one sort of region to another, since they are not dependent on a thermally stable environment. Birds most conspicuously deal with seasonal environmental change by migration, often over very great distances. The warm-blooded animals are the most adaptable.

There is probably a connection between this adaptability and the fact that birds and mammals are the only animals with which it is possible for human beings to have some sort of personal relationship. Part of the connection must lie in the highly visual nature of birds and mammals, a characteristic that fits them to take account of individuals, whether friend or foe, at a distance. A pet ant or tortoise is a bit of a joke, at best a nonreciprocating companion.

Rodents are the most numerous of mammals, both in species and in individuals. They are closest of all mammals to the earliest members of the class, from which the whole variegated array of monotremes (e.g., the platypus), marsupials, bats, whales, rabbits, carnivores, horses, cloven-hoofed artiodactyls (e.g., pigs, hippopotamuses, camels), primates, and still others evolved. An immense variety of habitats, diets, sizes, and shapes is associated with these different orders of the mammal.

"The warm-blooded animals are the most adaptable. There is probably a connection between this adaptability and the fact that birds and mammals are the only animals with which it is possible for human beings to have some sort of personal relationship."

Apart from being warm-blooded and suckling their young, mammals are, for the most part, quadrupedal and hairy. Most of them are placental, giving birth to live offspring, not laying eggs or keeping their young in pouches in the manner of marsupials. The long infancy of the placental mammal creates the family, by requiring a comparatively long period of protected dependence. That allows for a good deal of imitative learning, for the practicing of routines of behavior in play. The newly hatched fish has to fend for itself from the start, and to succeed must be equipped with a fixed repertoire of imperative instincts. Placental mammals have the largest brains, comparatively speaking. That feature is associated in part as cause and in part as consequence with the opportunities for learning provided by their manner of coming into the world. The most impressive cerebral equipment is that of the primates; the cetaceans (dolphins, whales, and porpoises) being not far behind.

Mammals maintain themselves in an enterprising fashion. They develop acute and sophisticated sense organs to help them detect food and to warn them of predators. They develop teeth and claws to make it possible to ingest a wide variety of foods and complex digestive systems to convert that food into energy. They are, of course, by no means the only social animals. Although reptiles are fairly solitary, birds and insects tend to live in large social groups. But insect society is rigid and mechanical, bird society swarmingly multitudinous and undifferentiated. Mammals are highly differentiated sexually. There is a general tendency among the higher mammals for females to be monopolized by particular dominant males, who have to defend their harems against the younger males they exclude from access to the females. A harem is advantageous from the point of view of perpetuating one's genes among species where the females are capable of conceiving only for limited periods now and then.

The mammal's specially developed teeth enlarge its range of possible foods, a biological anticipation of cooking, just as the mammal's adjustable surface of hair is a biological anticipation of clothing. Their characteristically long infancy is associated with small litters and the possibility of a more discriminating, individualized relationship between parent and child. Those mammals who took to the trees, to escape the predatory attentions of larger, stronger carnivores, had to develop a particularly high degree of hand and eye coordination. This was the evolutionary surge that led to the primates, in due course to inherit the earth because of their larger brains. In the manner of an edifying folktale, a weakness led after a time to an invincible strength.

3. The primates

Primates descend from tree-dwelling mammals who lived between sixty and forty million years ago. Between thirty and twelve million years ago the descendants of these more or less ratlike tree-dwellers divided into three main varieties. First, there were the comparatively small prosimians, whose light weight made it possible for them to move about on small branches and twigs; the ancestors of modern lemurs and lorises. Second, on the larger branches, there were the earliest monkeys, ancestors of the modern baboons and mandrills of the Old World and the marmosets and spider monkeys of the New World. Third, and, to us, most importantly, there were the dryopithecines, from whom descend both apes and men.

Primates, including man, have hair on their bodies (although in man it is more or less vestigial), hands, and stereoscopic color vision. They live in troops. They are sexually promiscuous and copulate with females who are not in heat. The ape and hominid descendants of the dryopithecines have no tails. Their bodies and brains are larger than those of other primates. Their eyes look forward. They can adopt an upright posture.

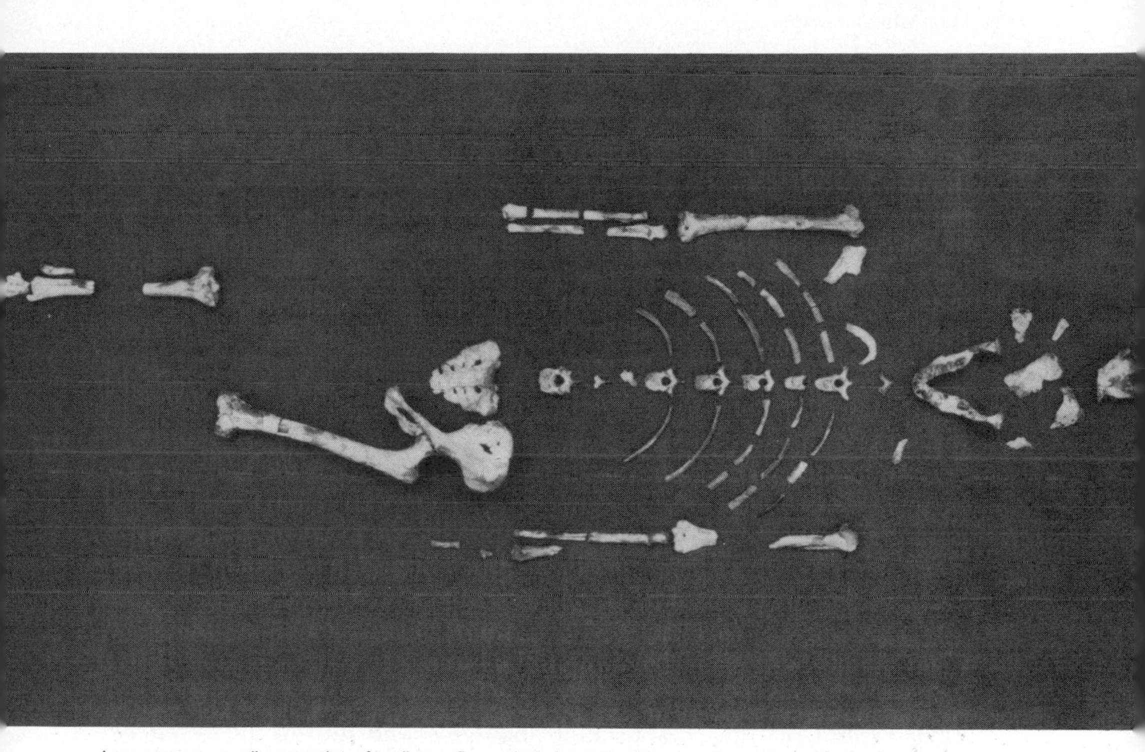

Lucy, an unusually complete fossil, confirms that *Australopithecus afarensis* walked upright on two feet. *"At one time it was believed that there must be some missing link between him and those we should be willing to call men. But it now seems that he was a dead end in primate evolution."*

The apes, like most other primates, continued to live in the trees after they and the hominids had separated from the dryopithecine stem common to them. Their method of moving among the branches was brachiation, swinging from hand to hand, from one branch to another. Hominids came down from the trees and moved out into the savannas and abandoned a purely vegetarian diet in a setting less well supplied with plant food but with plenty of small game. They came to walk upright, exploiting the ability of dryopithecines to stand up. They had shorter arms than apes, having no need to swing from branch to branch. Their thumbs were more agile and manipulable than those of any other animal, a development that proceeded in step with the use of sticks and stones as tools and weapons. Their feet evolved along with the practice of walking upright.

Between fifteen and eight million years ago the first known hominid, *Ramapithecus,* lived on earth, manlike in not being an ape, but not yet a man. There may perhaps have been a hundred thousand of them. Between five and four million years ago *Australopithecus* lived in caves in South and East Africa. He was four or five feet high, used simple tools, but did not wear any sort of clothing. He was mainly vegetarian in his diet. At one time it was believed that there must be some missing link between him and those we should be willing to call men. But it now seems that he was a dead end in primate evolution and that man descended by some other route from *Ramapithecus* and, beyond him, *Dryopithecus*.

Around two and a half million years ago a further step forward was registered with the very early manlike individual discovered near Lake Rudolph in Kenya in 1972 by Richard Leakey. He, and the *Homo habilis* found in Olduvai Gorge by Leakey's father, Louis, years before, appear both to have been approximately contemporaneous with *Australopithecus*, but to have been more advanced. The Lake Rudolph man lived in the open and did not just find tools, he made them. He was a meat eater and hunted cooperatively. That style of hunting brought a whole new range of game within his reach and greatly enhanced his diet.

It was hominids of this kind who first left Africa to spread eventually all over the earth, at least in the form of their descendant, *Homo sapiens*. More efficient food gathering by this time made a population of about half a million possible. Getting on to a million years ago, mere hominids at last gave way to man proper: *Homo erectus*, not, in fact, the first to go upright, but the first, it appears, to have fire and thus to secure energy more widely and more efficiently from food by cooking it.

In this evolution from earlier mammals through primates to creatures who are truly men it is noteworthy how biological developments have fostered, and themselves no doubt been further accelerated by, institutions: reproductive, nutritive, and protective—the first rough intimations of family, economy, and state. Mammal, and especially primate, families are small, with offspring needing much attention. Primates, able and willing to copulate whether in heat or not, do not favor the harem arrangement so widely spread among mammals in general. But there are still dominant males in primate troops who feed first and take their pick of the females.

With the earliest men something new occurs. The hunters bring their catch back to the place where the females have been left with the children, and to the fire on which it can be cooked, and then share it with those left behind. Many animals live on what is left over by their gorged leaders, but that is only sharing by accident of superfluity. The conspicuous sexual differentiation characteristic of mammals in general is greater still among primates and greatest of all in men. The large brains of primates require the pelvis of the female to be wide enough to give birth without injury or death to mother or child. As a result females do not run as fast as males. Unfitted physically for hunting by that limitation, they are also unfitted socially by the need, which

"With the earliest men something new occurs. The hunters bring their catch back to the place where the females have been left with the children, and to the fire on which it can be cooked, and then share it with those left behind."

they are most disposed to supply, for someone to look after the dependent, defenseless, and accident-prone young. What they can contribute economically is the gathering of vegetables and fruit, something that can be carried on slowly and without attention being distracted from everything but the pursuit of the quarry. In that way the great sexual division of labor was set up between male hunters and female gatherers, an arrangement that has persisted for at least ninety-eight, and perhaps ninety-nine, percent of the history of mankind so far.

The greater physical strength of human and prehuman males, together with their habit of combative collaboration in hunting, fitted them for the main protective or political task of keeping dangerous predators or competitors—of other species or their own—at bay.

With *Homo erectus,* then, there are adumbrations of family, economy, and state. *Homo erectus* is a toolmaker and a fire-user. There are stable institutions and a rude technological tradition. As man proper continues to develop in the ensuing million to eight hundred thousand years, a third strand in culture comes into existence with religion and art and, beyond them, with the Neolithic revolution which led to crop farming and the domestication of animals, to science and civilization.

III. On the history of mankind

1. *The emergence of* Homo sapiens

The appropriate time units for discussing the animal kingdom are millions of years. When we come to the history of man, a much larger time scale is needed, since the entire episode so far is contained within only about one million years. For a while, then, the unit of discussion will be the millennium, in its less apocalyptic, merely chronological sense of a thousand years.

Homo erectus may have appeared on the earth as long as one and a half million years ago. His tools were made and not simply found, in particular the hand ax. Chopping, and not just pounding and crushing, were within his power. As has been mentioned before, he had got hold of fire, an achievement full of consequences. Beyond the cooking of food, it served to make caves habitable, to protect small human groups from predators, to act as a center or focus for the communal sharing of the hunters' catch. With better weapons the hunters were able to cooperate in the pursuit of really big game: elephants and mammoths, for instance. Among the large animals now within their reach as hunters were creatures whose skins were big enough to be used as clothing: bears, lions, tigers. The exigencies of hunting may have prompted the first development of communication in the direction of language proper, as something more than emotional expression, serving contingently to warn, threaten, or excite.

Homo erectus has been found in many places: in Africa, south and north, in eastern Europe, in China. His remains first came to light in 1891/92 in Java. Then, in the 1930s, in some caves a few miles from Peking, at Chou-k'ou-tien, the relics of more than forty members of the species were discovered. Some seemed clearly to have died violent deaths. There were evidences, not conclusive, of cannibalism. The species endured until three hundred or two hundred and fifty millennia ago, a period that included within it the first two ice ages. These large climatic variations had a great influence on the movements of *Homo erectus* on the face of the earth as the conditions of temperature and of the availability of food became more or less propitious.

The earliest known specimens of *Homo sapiens,* found at Swanscombe in England and Steinheim in Germany, show that by two hundred and fifty millennia ago, toward the end of the period between the second and third ice ages, a new and more advanced type of man had emerged to dominate the world, the immediate ancestor both of Neanderthal man and of modern man. With Neanderthal man the lower, i.e., earlier, Paleolithic gives way to the middle Paleolithic period, marked by increased refinement of toolmaking. That progress is revealed by finds of flint scrapers (to detach the meat and pelt from his hunting bag), of spearheads and traps to make that bag larger, of artifacts of bone that constitute a pregnant move forward from more or less roughly fashioned stone.

Neanderthal man was soon widely spread from his first appearance about a hundred thousand years ago. He was well adapted for the cold conditions that prevailed in Europe during the fourth ice age, which ran from eighty to fifteen thousand years ago. By contrast with modern man, he was hairy and stocky. What is of most cultural interest about him is that he is the first man to have achieved a measure of spiritual, rather than simply technical or institutional, culture. There is clear evidence in his case of ceremonial burial practices, which imply not only personal affection or concern, but also some conception of life after death.

His end came, comparatively rapidly, about thirty-five thousand years ago, when our own species, *Homo sapiens sapiens,* seems completely to have displaced him. The manner of his elimination is not clear. Anthropologists have a tradition of emphasizing the less morally attractive aspects of human nature and have usually assumed that our species killed off its Neanderthal predecessor. That idea is given powerful imaginative development in William Golding's novel *The Inheritors,* where the gentle and kindly Neanderthalers are liquidated by ferocious and relentless supplanters. But it may be that they succumbed to disease or that they were absorbed by interbreeding into a more numerous community of *Homo sapiens* proper. The two groups would seem, at any rate, to have overlapped for some considerable time. Our species was in existence for some fifteen thousand years before it became the only species of man on earth thirty-five thousand years ago.

2. *The ages of man*

Modern man seems to have begun in and around the eastern Mediterranean, in a region running from southeastern Europe to the near East. When he became dominant, at a time that defines the beginning of the upper, i.e., most recent, Paleolithic epoch, he may have numbered from five to ten million. With him, substantial genetic change in man comes to an end. Despite all the varieties of habitat and manner of life he has since experienced he remains physically—in brain size, in hairiness, in habitual posture, in the structure of his face and teeth—what he was then.

He has proved to be the most adaptable, versatile, and resourceful of all types of man. It is his capacity to adjust his environment to his physically determined needs—by his technology, his social organization, his skill in getting hold of food, and his bodily ability to nourish himself on a very varied diet—that has enabled him to survive successfully under various sorts of environmental pressure and thus to avoid major genetic modification. The different races of mankind show some minor physical differences: in skin color, in size, in texture and curliness of hair. But there has been no differentiation into distinct species.

It is generally agreed that the very first manlike creatures appeared in Africa. From there successive species of man spread out to populate much of Europe and Asia, their region of occupation responding to the alternations of ice ages and the warmer periods between them. It was left to modern man to populate Australia, some thirty thousand years ago, where the aboriginal inhabitants displayed a culture not importantly different from that of the first arrivals to the Europeans who settled there two centuries ago, a kind of ethnological Whipsnade (the London Zoo) with Paleolithic men in their natural surroundings. Modern men may have got to North America, crossing over to Alaska from eastern Siberia, at about the same time (Australia must have been reached by boat). The oldest traces prove them to have arrived twelve thousand years ago, and not long after that, by nine thousand years ago, they were installed at the southernmost tip of the southern American continent. The islands of the Pacific, including New Zealand, were not occupied by man until between three thousand and one thousand years ago.

Where hominids found tools and weapons, and *Homo erectus* made tools, *Homo sapiens sapiens* developed tools with which to make tools, notably the stone chisel. A comparably distinguished achievement is his invention of art. First, about thirty thousand years ago decoratively carved antlers appeared. Then, there were the exaggeratedly feminine and pregnant figures, like the Venus of Willendorf, which are commonly taken to be fertility symbols, lying on the border of art and religion. Finally, less than twenty thousand years ago, western Europe gave an unrivaled display of cultural preeminence, almost on the scale of its origination of natural science in the early modern period, if only a live, continuing tradition of art had been initiated.

This was the amazing creative outburst of naturalistic cave painting, chiefly of animal subjects, at Lascaux in France, for example, and Altamira in Spain. Those of Lascaux, at least, were particularly striking for their power as representation, the Altamira paintings being more fluent and sketchlike. In both cases they differ from the efforts at visual representation of children and those who are "primitive" in having had no artistic training, which show things, not as they strike the eye, but, in a sense, as they actually are.

It is usually supposed that these remarkable works—hidden away from convenient viewing—had some ritual purpose in connection with the hunting of the animals depicted in them, for these hunts had an importance that would make a reverent and ceremonial attitude toward them appropriate. Other observers have been led by their exuberance and vitality to see them as instances of pure artistic expression, the

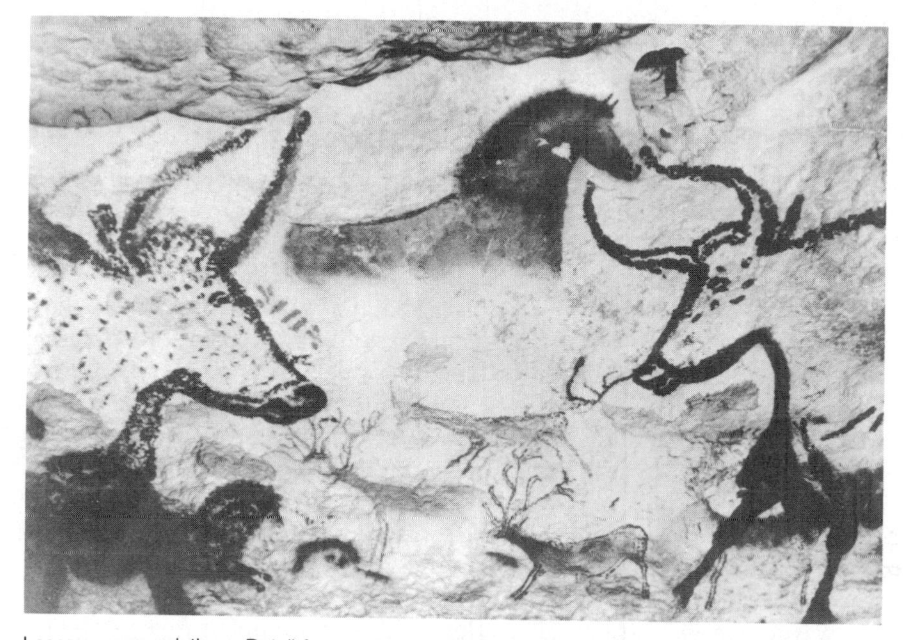

Lascaux cave paintings. Detail from main rotunda discovered in 1940, Dordogne, France. The paintings are believed to be as old as 15,000 B.C.

outflow of emotions of delight and admiration excited by the animals among whom and, in a way, through whom men lived. As was said earlier, these paintings did not lead on to a persisting artistic tradition. They were the fruit of an isolated episode, a long one, as long as that which links the elegant Egyptian reliefs of 3000 B.C. to the Abstract Expressionism of the present age and the riot of trivial fads to which it has given way, but one in which there was little development of style or subject, and which was replaced in its turn by an altogether less powerful, more conventionally primitive kind of art.

Some fifteen thousand years ago the last ice age came to an end in Europe. Already the first considerable buildings had been erected. The first stirrings of the most important change in the technical culture of mankind in a million years took place with the domestication of dogs, presumably wolves and wild dogs of particular amiability and docility, who had hung round the fires of hunting groups in the hope of scraps. Twelve thousand years ago a new mode of domestication brought sheep and goats into the service of man as herded suppliers of meat, milk, and wool. At much the same time cereal cultivation seems to have begun. The agricultural revolution had brought in the Neolithic age.

The amount of land required to support a given population by agriculture was about a thousandth of what was needed if that population was to be kept alive on the products of hunting and gathering. A style of economy that had prevailed, through many important variations of technique, for a million years was replaced by a mixture of nomadic pastoralism and comparatively settled crop raising, one that was often tense, as is shown by the story of Cain, the cultivator, and Abel, the herdsman, or, coming nearer the present, by a host of Western movies. Where conditions were suitable for agriculture, population rapidly increased, even if the ruling class persisted, as they do recreationally even today, in the old fashions of activity.

Some ten thousand years ago cattle were domesticated in the Middle East and the horse in western Asia. The first fortified towns were established: Jericho and, somewhat later, Çatalhüyük in southern Turkey. While the first crops were being planted and harvested in Europe, men finally reached the southern extremity of the Americas. Metallurgy began, as did trade—in such useful and rare materials as obsidian. The first boats were made. Older techniques of chipping stone to make tools were refined into grinding and polishing. In the flooded river valleys of Mesopotamia irrigation helped to enhance agricultural output.

Five thousand years ago mankind was about to advance into civilization, first in Mesopotamia, then in Egypt. Basketmaking and pottery were added to the technical repertoire. More important, perhaps, writing was invented, presumably to deal with the administrative problems of comparatively large urban communities. The main ingredients of modern life were all present, apart from mechanical and electrical power.

3. Animals and men

The main object of this selective survey of the history of animal and human life from the protozoa to the beginnings of civilization six or seven thousand years ago is to present the leading features of the scientific case for the essential continuity between men and the nonhuman animals. Throughout most of the history of philosophy it is the difference between them that has been stressed, indeed to a very great extent simply taken for granted. For most philosophers, as for most unreflective people, the great division of the concrete constituents of the world is that between persons and things.

What I have described as the first element of spiritual (as distinct from technical and institutional) culture, namely religion, has, at any rate in its higher forms, been the great social enforcer of this particular dualism. Judaism, Christianity, and Mohammedanism, the great monotheistic religions, have endorsed it without qualification. In religions in which reincarnation is recognized, above all in Hinduism, change from animal to human and from human to animal at turning points in the sequence of lives is accepted, as it is also by comparatively minor mystery sects such as Pythagoreans, Orphics, and Gnostics. In Egyptian religion and Hinduism there are animal gods, or, some would say, gods in animal form.

As human history has progressed, the importance and pervasiveness of human relationships with animals have steadily diminished. The lives of hunters are completely bound up with those of animals; so, in a different—in some respects more intimate—way are the lives of pastoralists and plowmen. On the other hand, animals have only a precarious foothold in the urban settlements in which civilized men have more and more come to congregate. But the conviction of an impermeable barrier between human and animal prevailed long before serious urbanization.

A somewhat ambiguous evidence of the hold of the distinction on the human mind is to be found in what is often now seen as the most important ingredient in the humanity of human beings: grammar. First of all, there is the distinction between personal pronouns and the impersonal "it." Then, associated with it, is the practice of bestowing proper names on human beings and only very fitfully and infrequently on animals. However, in uneducated speech anything whatever—a car, a spade, a cat, a snake—may be referred to as "he" or "she." Only the weather remains obstinately "it," an implicit but perfectly correct recognition of the fact that in "it is raining," the word *it* is not used referentially, as is shown by the obvious impropriety of the response "*what* is?" Furthermore, while some animals are given proper names, people are often referred to, even addressed, in general terms: "Boy," "Waiter," "Nurse."

Anthropism, as I shall call the idea that the most fundamental distinction between the concrete contents of time and space is that between human beings and everything else, is comparable to an idea most people tend to have from time to time about themselves: that they are utterly distinct from all other human beings, who are themselves, by and large, pretty much like each other. We know that that kind of instinctive metaphysical egoism is an illusion whenever we look back over our own pasts in memory, in a home movie or photograph album, or in attending to the conceptions of us formed by others. Nevertheless, when so to speak *inside* our own lives, we find it hard to resist the notion that we are, individually, unique. Something comparable, some peculiarity of perspective seems to be at work in anthropism.

The findings of zoology and anthropology, articulated in an evolutionary manner, can be drawn on to loosen its hold upon us. The main point is that, although there are breaks in the evolutionary narrative as one species is followed by another, the overall sequence is continuous. Men are linked to other primates as the latter are to the prosimians from which they evolved. What is more, there is no clear boundary between the men we are today and our predecessors, on the other side of which all are nonhuman. I think it is fair to say that anthropologists neither agree very precisely as to where the line between mere anthropoids or hominids and men should be drawn nor do they think it of any great importance to decide the issue. Most would say that *Homo erectus* is a man, some that only with *Homo sapiens* do we get true man. It is generally agreed that our species, the supplanter of Neanderthal man, *Homo sapiens sapiens,* appeared on the earth fifty thousand years ago.

The continuity of men and animals is no doubt most pronounced and incontestable in their anatomies. In a dim light and at a distance an ape and a hairy man are easily confused. An ape is very much more like a man than it is like a lynx or a turtle or a tuna, to confine the comparison to animals of the same order of magnitude. Continuity is still present when we turn from anatomy to behavior. Animals use tools; creatures as marginally human as *Homo habilis* seem to have made tools; *Homo erectus* certainly did. Our species is marked off by a further step forward: we began the use of tools to make tools. Most mammals are social, as are animals of many other classes. Cooperative hunting, the protective and educative mammalian family, division of labor, a hierarchy of dominance and submission, are all to be found in animal species that everyone would agree are nonhuman. What is peculiar to man is what I have called spiritual culture: religion (first seen in the burial practices of the Neanderthalers), art (the invention of our own species twenty or thirty thousand years ago), writing (in the wake of the first development of urban living), and science.

The older varieties of reflective anthropism took man's spiritual culture to be the outward expression of his fundamental distinguishing mark: the soul. At the opposite extreme of the spectrum of beliefs, the Marxist takes technical culture, which, along with natural resources, constitutes the "conditions of production," to be an essential factor in the socioeconomic basis of human existence, indeed to be the dynamically crucial one. What I have called institutional culture is one aspect of the superstructure whose nature is determined by the socioeconomic basis. The other is the realm of "ideas and beliefs," of ideology or, in my terminology, spiritual culture. The Marxist, taking spiritual culture to be dependent and epiphenomenal, a mere by-product of the serious productive business of society, does not make it the defining characteristic of mankind. He finds that characteristic in technical culture, in the consciously designed production of the necessities of life with tools that man has himself made.

A number of distinct tendencies in contemporary thought converge on the idea that the ultimate distinguishing mark of man is his mastery of language. There are two difficulties about its application. One is that there is no agreed way of deciding what makes a method of communication into a language proper. The other is that we have no clear idea when what would generally be held to be truly linguistic communication began. Certainly no nonhuman animal now living communicates linguistically so far as we know. We have no idea how many of our extinct forebears did.

But before confronting the question directly of how definite and how important the distinction between humans and nonhuman animals is (in the light of the evident physical, psychological, and social continuities between them), it will be as well to supplement the historical account of their evolution with a survey of the very varied and often very close relations between them.

IV. The relations between men and animals

1. Man's use of animals

Animals pay very little attention to fellow animals of other species except when they hope to make a meal of them or fear that they will be a meal for them. Men watch birds, but birds largely ignore men unless they get worryingly near. Special concerns interest them in worms and cats; with birds of other species they indifferently coexist.

But man, the most curious and most omnivorous of creatures, beside the theoretical concern of zoology with absolutely all animals, has a variety of practical concerns with a great many of them. He eats far more kinds of them than the members of any animal species do: mammals, of course, as well as birds, fish, and crustaceans. He comes into possession of them by hunting and by rearing. He uses some animals—most conspicuously dogs and falcons—to help him in hunting; dogs, again, assist him in the control of his flocks of domesticated animals. Dogs and cats help him to get rid of the rats and other nuisances who make off with the crops he has plowed for and harvested with oxen, horses, or camels.

Man does not kill animals merely to eat them (or to avoid being eaten by them) as other animals do. He uses their hides for all sorts of purposes, from clothing and containers to the making of tents, and, less lethally, drinks their milk, or turns it into butter and cheese, and clips their wool to make clothes and blankets. A particularly important aspect of the Neolithic revolution that brought in farming was the use of strong animals as energy sources: to pull loads, to draw plows and, in due course, to carry men themselves about when hunting, fighting, on trading voyages, nomadically traveling to new pasture, herding stock, emigrating, or simply making social visits.

Until the domestication of dogs inaugurated the great Neolithic step forward into agriculture, man's relations with animals were distant and, although often respectful, generally hostile. Men hunted animals in order to eat them and to make themselves safe from them. Their dependence on animal flesh gave them an interest in the biological success of its suppliers, in an abundance of game. The great cave paintings of France and Spain twenty thousand years ago are widely supposed to have played a part in magical ceremonies designed to ensure the

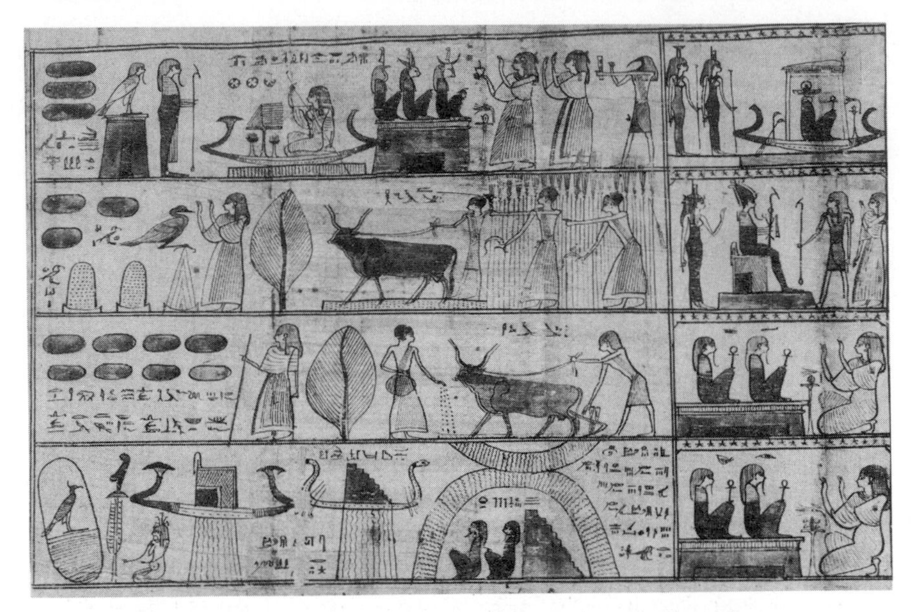

"By the time men had the skill and occasion to build permanent dwellings, there were animals trained to be welcome members of the family circle and, in the routine of milking, herding, feeding, and plowing, men were occupied with them throughout the working day."

fertility of the objects of the chase, and, perhaps, to express admiration for their powers, even to propitiate them for the injuries done to them.

In the long hunting period of human history—something like ninety-nine percent of its duration so far—men had to know a good deal about animals, about how they behave and what could be done with them. But only in the few thousand years of agriculture, which lasted until the nineteenth century in Europe and is still the dominant form of life in many places, have men and animals been intimately involved. By the time men had the skill and occasion to build permanent dwellings, there were animals trained to be welcome members of the family circle and, in the routine of milking, herding, feeding, and plowing, men were occupied with them throughout the working day.

At this stage of human development the purely practical use of animals by men merges into a companionable one. A hunter and his dog, a falconer and his hawk will evolve a measure of mutual trust and affection from their collaboration in a common purpose. Similarly the regularity of the relationship between a plowman and his team, a mahout and his elephant, or a rider and his mount will take on the individualized quality of intimate human relationships. The grief at such an animal collaborator's death will be something more than the distress appropriate to a major economic misfortune; it will also be sadness at the loss of a friend. Even the less individualized members of a herd of cattle, always driven or milked as a group, and probably destined for slaughter in the end, will evoke warm feelings by their mildness and amenability.

It cannot have been long after men had settled homes and the habit of keeping animals in them that the purely companionable keeping of animals, as pets, began. It is right that the first animal to be domesticated should still be man's supreme animal companion. The dog's unrivaled combination of friendliness and intelligence, his freedom from suspicion and resentment, his sublime suggestibility, the intensely individual quality of his affection together equip him outstandingly for his familiar role in human life. The cat is too private and independent, the horse too nervous and, because of his size, too cumbrous and inconvenient, to offer serious competition. The power of men to make something out of practically nothing is shown in some of the less responsive animals they show affection to, or at least take interest in: white mice, goldfish, turtles, canaries, rabbits, gerbils, and stick insects.

The industrialization of the world has not stopped short of agriculture. In the factory farm where cows are mechanically milked or battery chickens pass their lives in small cages under artificial light, the individual, more or less personal relation that prevailed between men and animals in the agriculture of the past is extinguished. Apart from the keeping of pets and the purely spectatorial business of visiting zoos, there are few activities left in which men and animals come together: hunting for sport, riding for exercise. Man's ingenuity has created an environment for him in which he need have nothing to do with animals at all. Nutritionists warn him against animal flesh for its high content of cholesterol and calories. His clothing is increasingly the product of industrial chemistry. Bureaucratic frenzies about hygiene exclude animals from more and more places. Vegetarians and conservationists, concerned for the well-being of animals, seek to keep them out of men's meals and region of influence. For our good and theirs, it seems, we must have as little to do with one another as possible.

2. Animals and the human imagination

Men's ideas about animals, beyond the practical lore of the farmer or trainer and the scientific findings of the zoologist and the veterinarian, both of which are none too well known professional specialisms, take an imaginative form in certain religions (and in aspects of most religions), in art and literature, and in a widely spread deposit of common assumption and belief, a compound of proverbial or symbolic wisdom and illusion.

We must derive our conceptions of the earliest religions of mankind, first, from the religions of people still living on the earth who share the upper Paleolithic culture of the first men we have reason to suppose to have been religious and, second, from such evidences as we can exhume that are reasonably susceptible of religious interpretation. The

"Apart from the keeping of pets and the purely spectatorial business of visiting zoos, there are few activities left in which men and animals come together."

most important social relic in still existing primitive societies of a large place for animals in religion is totemism. A totem is usually an animal, and it serves as a symbol for a group or individual. In its group form, totemism, by clubbing people together, helps to unify society. But there is more to it than its socially functional cash value. In the light of the cave paintings of men who, twenty thousand years ago, had reached a stage of development comparable to that of the totemic aborigines of Australia, we may infer that it derives from some kind of religion in which animals were worshiped.

Once we arrive at the religions of civilized mankind, we are met at the beginning with the gods of Egypt. These are notable for being exceedingly numerous and for being, for the most part, in more or less animal form, animal-headed, at least. Experts in the field are reluctant to suppose that this theriomorphism about the gods amounted to theriolatry, the worship of animals. Certainly to conceive the objects of worship in animal form is not in itself the worship of animals. But to separate the two definitely it is necessary to claim that the Egyptians thought of the gods as beings, essentially human or personal in nature, who chose to dress up or present themselves in the form of animals. It may well be doubted whether, in terms of the conceptions available to them, the ancient Egyptians were able to distinguish between seeing the gods as persons in the form of animals or as animals with the mental attributes of persons.

Osiris, the suffering god, is the most human member of the Egyptian pantheon. Horus is usually a falcon, Set a pig, Anubis a jackal, Hathor a cow, Bastet a cat. The only comparably animalistic major religion is Hinduism. Not only does it recognize a host of animal gods, its doctrine of reincarnation allows the soul, on the death of a human body it has been inhabiting, to enter into the body of an animal. However, since the passage of the soul from a human to an animal body is conceived as a punishment, there is a tension between this idea and the notion that some gods—inevitably conceived as being higher than man—are really animals.

The series of Mesopotamian religions whose high god is Marduk or Bel seem to have conceived him and his fellow deities as essentially human—from some points of view, a little all too human, perhaps. And, as was mentioned before, the religion of the Hebrews, the first of the great monotheistic religions, has always been resolutely anthropomorphic. We read in the first chapter of Genesis: "God said, Let us make man in our image, after our likeness." Soon after, the man thus created is adjured to set himself up as a despot over all species: "have dominion over the fish of the sea, and over the fowl of the air, and over every living thing that moveth upon the earth." The devil appears to Adam in the guise of a serpent.

On the whole the Old Testament displays an unrelenting hostility to animals. The dove who brought the olive branch to the ark is not unsympathetic, and the ravens who fed Elijah served an approved purpose. But the more usual tone is that of Goliath's remark to David: "am I a dog that thou comest to me with staves?" or "is thy servant a dog that he should do such a thing?" As for Nebuchadnezzar, on going mad, "his dwelling shall be with the beasts of the field." At least Balaam's ass is allowed to complain about the way in which he is treated, but he does not get an apology.

The New Testament is not much better. Its most memorable animal story is that of the Gadarene swine. It is extraordinary that in this vast compilation of the literature of a pastoral people there should be no sympathetic account of a relationship between a human being and an animal. Only in metaphor are animals presented in an agreeable light.

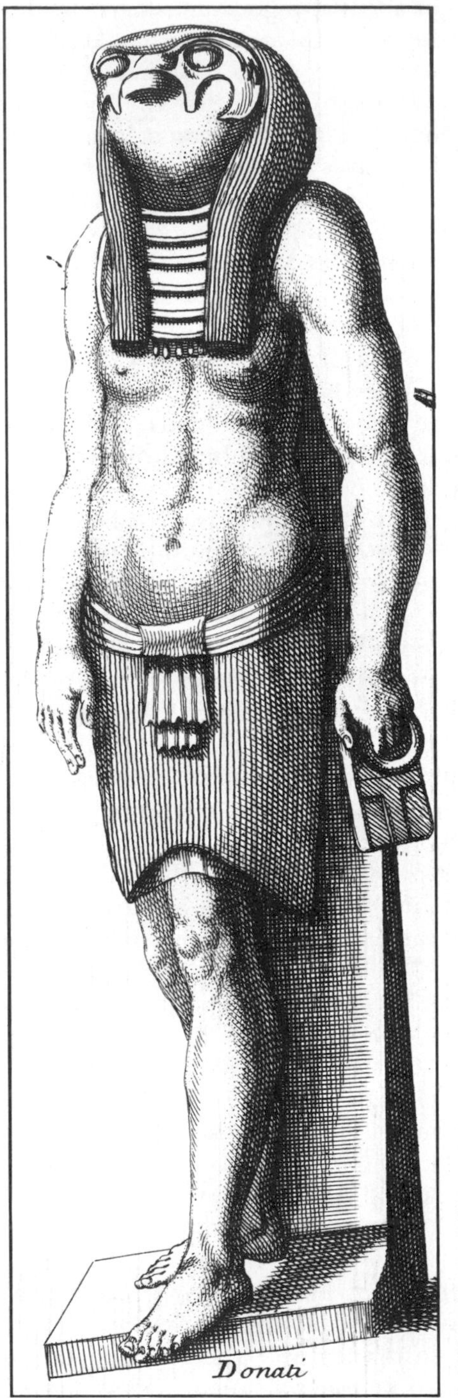

"[The Egyptian gods] are notable for being . . . in more or less animal form." The god Horus, shown here, is usually depicted with the head of a falcon.

There a literary convention serves to keep them at a distance from us, safely immured in a kind of zoo by a figure of speech. Repelled withdrawal prevails wherever animals are described as interacting with human beings.

Christianity, we may conclude, imposed anthropism on Western man. It has been assisted in the task by a leading tradition in philosophy: the exorbitant dualism of mind and body affirmed by Plato, which was reanimated in the early modern period by Descartes and is still extremely lively today in the thought of a variety of philosophers who agree that man, and man alone, is not a proper subject for science. Between Plato and Descartes there was, for five hundred years, a strong countervailing force in the scholastic articulation of Christianity in terms of the philosophy of Aristotle, who maintained the continuity between men and animals. Between Descartes and the most recent revival of dualism lies Darwin's doctrine of evolution, which sees all living things as part of one family.

Anthropism is not only an error about "our" place in nature, as will be argued later. It is also, perhaps, in conflict with our nature. An older and better founded conception of the continuity between men and animals shows itself in all sorts of ways in which animals have been represented as persons, as beings with experiences and temperaments in many respects like our own.

The most prominent of these is literature, in many of what may be felt to be its less central manifestations. Folktales and fairy tales abound with intelligent and talking animals. These are nowadays largely read by children, apart from those whose business it is to study them professionally. Most modern books in which personified animals figure are of this comparatively undifferentiated kind: *The Wind in the Willows, The Just So Stories,* the stories of Beatrix Potter. In them, animals are represented in their normal surroundings, engaged to a considerable extent in activities natural to the kinds of animals involved. Mr. Toad lives on a riverbank, Squirrel Nutkin in a wood. The animals, although personified, are not detached from their natural setting.

Two distinct forms of development from that kind of story move in very different directions. The first is that of the fable, begun by Aesop, at its best in La Fontaine and Krylov, where the animals are no more than symbols for certain types of human being, in which an alleged characteristic of a kind of animal is used to pass moral comments on the same characteristic as present, or over-present, in human life. The second is the novel of attempted naturalistic empathy with animals, such as Henry Williamson's *Tarka the Otter* or Richard Adams's *Watership Down,* or, to take older examples, Kipling's *Jungle Books,* Fitzpatrick's *Jock of the Bushveld,* and the stories of Ernest Thompson Seton.

Unless they are sophisticated fables, serving a satirical purpose, and having no serious implication whatever about the kinds of animals that

"The devil appears to Adam in the guise of a serpent."

ostensibly figure in them, animal stories draw on a large submerged mass of conventional assumptions about the nature and leading traits of character of the animals they mention. In the empathetic books there is an attempt to represent animals as they in fact are. But in most nonfabulous, nonsatirical fiction about animals, the assumptions about the characteristics of animals are very often profoundly mistaken.

The wolf, in common belief and animal stories alike, is viewed as a direct danger to human life. Farley Mowat, in his *Never Cry Wolf,* tried to correct this gross misapprehension which has led to efforts at extermination entirely out of proportion to the dangers involved. Wolves can, indeed, be a nuisance by preying on animals men wish to eat themselves, but evidence of their attacking human beings is exceedingly hard to find. Man's intimate relationship with domestic animals has given him reasonably accurate notions of what they are like. About wild animals he is, for the most part, grossly misinformed.

The extent of his misinformation is entertainingly set out by Boyce Rensberger in his *The Cult of the Wild* (1977). Lions are not particularly noble. They do not kill only for food. Like lesser cats they often kill slowly. (Wild dogs kill much more quickly.) They are spongers, eager to live off the kills of others. They are lazy; females do most of the work of hunting. Cubs are often left to starve. Fights between lions do not end in the rational capitulation Konrad Lorenz observed in dogs; they often fight to the death.

Wolves are highly sociable animals who are so averse to fighting that they will go to great lengths to avoid it. With them the Lorenzian machinery of submission works and preserves peaceable social cohesion. The few authenticated stories of wolves attacking humans almost certainly involve wolves with rabies. Most of the animals they attack withstand or escape them.

The common attitude to the gorilla as the most extreme incarnation of aggression and violence is equally wide of the mark. Gorillas are shy, timid, easily put to flight. As for their alleged sexual excessiveness, male gorillas have very small genitals and are the least sexually active of primates. They spend most of their time pottering around in pursuit of vegetable matter to eat.

Elephants are, indeed, highly intelligent animals. They live in complex matriarchal societies. When there is trouble males are the first to run away. They live in families for the same reason that we do, because of a long period of infant dependency in which knowledge and skill are passed on. Elephants are profoundly affected by the death of their relations.

Hyenas are much less given to scavenging than lions and kill most of what they eat, a fact long obscured by the hyena's practice of hunting at night. They are, indeed, particularly gifted hunters and are helped in

"Folktales and fairy tales abound with intelligent and talking animals."

this by a social order that is at once sophisticated and companionable. Unlike lions they kill quickly and dine politely.

Bears, especially brown bears, are the carnivores most directly dangerous to man in the parts of the world they inhabit. Grizzlies are very dangerous but do much less damage than black bears, which are far more numerous. Dolphins, although they can learn tricks and, like parrots, are excellent mimics, are not really all that intelligent. The altruism they display in coming to the rescue of injured members of their species is by no means peculiar to them. The mechanism of kin selection has established it as well among elephants, baboons, and wild dogs.

Conservationist enthusiasm, encouraged by the teachings of Lorenz, has fostered the idea that man is uniquely aggressive, that, as is sometimes said, he is the only creature that kills for other reasons than self-defense and food. In fact, as E. O. Wilson observes, "Murder is far more common and hence 'normal' in many vertebrate species than in man." The fact that the tide of informed opinion has completely reversed itself in the twenty years since Lorenz's ideas were first generally available shows how limited the development of the scientific study of animal behavior is.

It was pointed out earlier that during the vastly greater part of the duration of the human species so far, the period of hunting and gathering, men's relations to animals were important but distant. Only in the agricultural epoch did the relations between them become close. But, even then, close relations were confined to domesticated animals. Wild animals were, if anything, remoter than ever. Men's ideas about horses and cows, dogs and cats became reasonable enough once these animals had been domesticated. But the earlier fear of wild animals persisted in its error-fostering role, even if it was no longer intensified by anxiety about there being enough wild animals around for men to hunt and feed on.

Misconceptions of animal nature have been at least partly redeemed by aesthetic benefits in the visual arts. Kenneth Clark's casual but typically elegant essay that introduces the fine reproductions in *Animals and Men* (1977) runs through the main motives underlying the human interest in animals as it reveals itself in art. Clark lists fear, admiration (as in cave paintings), greed, cruelty (as in the bullfight and its celebrators in paint, Goya and Picasso), and love. Animals are prominent in ancient and classical art. But what I have called Christian anthropism excluded all but a few species picked out as religious emblems—lion, fox, eagle—from most medieval art. Leonardo's concern was formal rather than emotional. Only with Titian and Veronese are animals regular features of the human scene; they are not to be found in the work of Michelangelo and Raphael. It is the strength and energy of animals that usually attract the painter's eye. But some are concerned with animals as living things, not as visible structures: Dürer, Stubbs, and Bewick. With Landseer, and others in the nineteenth century, that measure of sympathy topples over into sentimental anthropomorphism.

V. Are men really animals?

1. Two short answers

As things stand colloquially the correct answer to the question whether men are really animals is very simple. It is no. In ordinary conversation we use the word *animal* to distinguish from men those living things that can move themselves about and are not men. What is that moving around in the next room, crashing about in the undergrowth, disappearing over the skyline—a man or an animal? we ask. The two possibilities are taken to be mutually exclusive. Animal food is not appropriate for human consumption. Animal acts on the stage or at the circus must involve nonhuman beings. Remarks like *he prefers animals to men* or *they were behaving like animals,* phrases like *animal trainer* or *research animal* would make no sense unless the fields of application of *man* and *animal* were distinct.

Those who say that men are really animals are not unaware of this fairly trivial, lexicographical fact. The first sentence of Mary Midgley's admirable *Beast and Man* is "We are not just rather like animals; we *are* animals." But, of course, not only does she understand the everyday and exclusive use of the two words perfectly well, she also adheres to it herself with the laudable purpose of being readily intelligible and of avoiding the cumbrous expression *other animals* to which her bold initial proclamation would appear to commit her.

A moderately unhelpful move at this point is to circumvent the collision between the two points of view by saying that it is simply the result of the word's having two different senses, an everyday one and a technical, zoological one. A familiar comparable case is that of the word *fish.* Most people are inclined to describe as fish any living creature whose usual habitat is the water. But many of them realize that those who have given most attention to the denizens of the water deny that whales are fish, although whales live in the sea. It is natural to acknowledge this fact by saying that although whales are often called fish, they are not *really* fish. A special authority is given to the technical sense of the word. It may be convenient for conversational purposes to call all water dwellers *fish,* but it is admitted that this is a formally defective way of speaking.

In the fish case, no one who is aware of the technical concept is much disposed to question its superiority to its everyday competitor. Apart from the single feature of their common habitat, whales have much less in common with sharks or cod than they do with elephants and cows. Whales, like the latter, give birth to live young, not eggs; they breathe air; they are warm-blooded. The superiority of the technical concept is admitted without protest because there is nothing much at stake. It incorporates a large number of important if not immediately obvious similarities between whales and other mammals, while the everyday concept takes note of a single, obvious likeness. The first is richer; it tells you more about something it is correctly applied to than the everyday concept does.

That peaceful state of affairs does not prevail in the case of *animal* and *man*. There is an impulse to say that men really are animals and a contrary one to say that they are not. It is not a case where the superior authority of a technical over an everyday sense is contentedly admitted. Nor, again, is it a case where two different senses can be allowed to coexist without a claim being made for the primacy of either, as is suggested by the move I described as unhelpful a little while ago. That kind of placid pluralism is to be found among those who do and do not take wildflowers to be flowers, admirals to be sailors, or library steps to be ladders. The animal and man case is more like disagreement as to whether or not Anglican clergymen are priests. Obviously they are not Catholic priests, but those combative Catholics who doubt the validity of Anglican orders would deny that they are really priests at all.

Modern studies of animal behavior have indirectly illuminated one factor that may have contributed to the refusal to let the two senses peacefully coexist or to admit the superiority of the technical sense, in other words to an insistence that men are really not animals. Colloquially to describe someone as an animal or as behaving like one is to dispraise him for grossness. Much the same is true of the older synonyms for *animal: brute* and *beast.* To be brutal is to be cruel; to be beastly, to be disgusting. The adjective *wild,* with which we pick out animals who have not been rendered more or less acceptable by domestication, is also generally unfavorable, implying tumultuous violence.

Attentive and persistent observation of nonhuman animals in their natural state has shown that the conventional picture of them as violent, cruel, and disorderly is a gross misrepresentation. It was probably fostered by the fact that most casual observation of undomesticated animals was made by people who were attempting to kill them, a point of view to which no one is likely to give either an agreeable or a representative impression. Animals are not, in general, wild, beastly, or brutal, in the ordinary senses of these terms. Like men they can be violent in the pursuit of food, in self-defense, and in seeking and enjoying erotic satisfaction. But these, with them as with us, are exceptional episodes, standing out from a background of orderly routine, domestic affection, and simple torpor.

But, even if the emotional obstacle set up by this system of misconceptions is removed, reluctance to admit that animals are men will persist. The admission that there are numerous similarities between men and animals may be made less grudging if the libel that they are monstrous images of our worst passions is refuted. Still, it is maintained, these likenesses are outweighed by the much more important differences between animals and men.

2. The problem of classification

There is an assumption, embodied in talking about similarities outweighing differences in importance as the justification for preferring one way of drawing conceptual boundaries to another, that should be brought into the open. This is that it is a matter of human convention, up to us, to draw conceptual boundaries as we choose. That is by no means the traditional view of the matter, which is that there are fixed natural kinds, and that these must be discerned by the intelligent observer. The observer's only element of choice in the matter is the selection of sounds and marks to give spoken or written expression to the general, classificatory conceptions he registers.

The world, on this, more or less Platonic, view, is like a warehouse of motorcar parts in which there is a finite variety of kinds of item, each item falling squarely and unequivocally into one of the kinds in the inventory. The fixity of kinds in such a warehouse is the result of the fact that everything brought into it has been deliberately manufactured in accordance with previously formulated specifications. In the real world, of course, no warehouse is so perfect. Other oddments creep in with the people who work there; there are the ingredients of the warehouse itself. But if the world is conceived as the product of an intelligent creator, the notion of a fixity of kinds in it is a congruous one. Items that do not fit into the inventory are spoiled or anomalous and so detract, by implication, from the creator's perfection.

There are features of the world that lend some color to the theory of fixed kinds. Many of the things we deal with are human artifacts, although they will pose classificatory problems from time to time, since their creators, or, more properly, fashioners, are imperfect. Another large group of things are members of living species of whom, in general, it is true that they can come into existence only through the sexual collaboration of two other, previously existing members of the same species. If that were absolutely true, together with the species-defining principle that every member of a given species has a set of properties that is uniquely definitive of that species, all living things without remainder would fall into fixed kinds. But since species evolve, it cannot be absolutely true. Finally, chemistry has established that all matter, living and nonliving, is made up from a limited repertoire of chemical elements, each of which itself consists, to oversimplify slightly, of a nucleus and an element-defining number of electrons.

There is, then, a lot of fixity about, simply as a matter of very general, natural fact. But it prevails at the level of element and species in a way that it does not at the level of the more general kinds under which the primary kinds are classified (metals or hawks, for example) or, again, at the level of classifications that are independent of the primary ones (into inflammable substances or carnivores, for example). Man is a species, but animal is not.

The doctrine of fixity of kinds has an extreme contrary opposite from whose evident unacceptability it may derive some undeserved support. This is the arbitrary variety of conventionalism which holds that the way we classify the things we come across is entirely of our own making, a purely subjective contrivance whose subjectivity is concealed by the fact that we all agree to adopt much the same conventions. It may well be doubted whether this is even a coherent thesis. Are our individual conventions really the same or do we merely surreptitiously agree to call them the same? And do we really call them the same . . . ? It is surely plain that many likenesses and differences are just matters of given, experienced fact: the likeness in color of these two ripe tomatoes and the difference in color between them and the lemon nearby.

But beyond this basic level we have room for maneuver. A traditional idea about classification associated with that of the fixity of kinds is that of their simplicity, the idea that each kind is defined by a unique set of characteristics. A strong form of this doctrine is that all but the most general kinds are defined by reference to the more general kind of which they are a species and the differentiating property that distinguishes them from the other species within that more general kind.

That idea cannot be sustained. Most actual kinds are defined by clusters of characteristics which do not all have to be possessed by an item if it is to count as a member of the kind, only a reasonable number or quorum, and then only to some extent or within a certain range. Lemons, for example, do not all have the same color or the same shape or the same size. The concepts of kinds it is useful to have are those that are widely applicable. So they must embody clusters of characteristics that are frequently found in association. But in the actual world characteristics do not associate as neatly as the doctrine of simplicity assumes. As we get to know more about the way characteristics occur together, we can revise our notions of kinds in various different ways. Thus, old words get new senses, like *fish,* and new words come into use, like *neurosis* or *semantics,* which are not words for new or newly discovered things, such as *television* and *quasar*.

In experience, then, we find in the world a number of objective likenesses and differences which serve as the foundation of all our subsequent classificatory ordering of what there is. In moving on to more general and specific classifications we can choose what general sums and specific products of characteristics we shall pick out to give names to. They are not irresistibly thrust on us by the nature of the world, but there are objective reasons for preferring some choices to others.

3. The tradition of dualism

When one considers how closely alike men and apes are, both in physical appearance and in behavior—how much, indeed, men have in common with many of the mammals they have had good opportunities for observing—it is extraordinary how little headway the idea that men are animals has made. It is not just that the idea that man is a part of nature has been rejected as absurd when it *has* been advanced, as by Hobbes and, in a much more convincingly based way, by Darwin, two hundred years later. It is that it has seldom been given serious consideration.

The main practical reason for this curious state of affairs has been, of course, the power of institutional Christianity. For Christianity, men are distinguished absolutely from animals and from everything else in the natural world by the fact that they have, or even essentially *are,* souls. The human body, animals, plants, and lifeless matter are all, according to Christian doctrine, provided by God for men to live with or among for a while, to make discriminating use of, to be tempted by, and, ultimately, to transcend, to leave altogether behind them at the end of the soul's earthly career.

The church could exercise control over the expression of thought and thus, to some extent, over thought itself, which is helped to flourish by explicit formulation and debate. But it was also able to call on intellectual support of a distinguished kind in its unrelenting resistance to naturalism of any kind. There have been two main streams of doctrine to uphold the division of the world into men and everything else. The first is the dualism philosophically articulated by Plato in his *Phaedo,* developed and incorporated into Christianity by St. Augustine, and revived with brilliant dialectical force and economy by Descartes so as to become the almost universal persuasion of philosophers, even non-Christian and anti-Christian ones, until comparatively recent times. The second is the philosophy of Aristotle, which in its original form did not accord an overwhelming importance to the distinction it recognized between men and animals but came to do so in the Christianized form it was given by Aquinas, which has been for many centuries the official philosophy of the Catholic church.

The philosophical dualism of soul and body does not inevitably imply that there is a fundamental difference between men and animals. In view of the excellent grounds we have for ascribing consciousness, sensibility, and intelligence to animals, it would be more natural to associate it with the view that both men and animals are on one side of the major division it affirms within the domain of what exists, while plants and lifeless matter are on the other. Descartes, clearheaded enough to see that this was a formally possible way of following out the consequences of the soul–body dualism to which he was committed, took the bold step of asserting that animals are automata and the mentality they seem to exhibit is only illusory appearance. More usually the problem of categorization posed by the fact of animal life has simply been ignored. Nothing is acknowledged to exist in the world surveyed by most philosophers but men and the material things they perceive and handle.

The continuity of men and animals is repudiated by the two most widely influential philosophers of the middle part of this century: Wittgenstein and Sartre, the most thoroughgoing of anti-Cartesians and the most uncompromising of atheists, respectively. Wittgenstein pertinaciously fought against Descartes's idea that mind and body are utterly different kinds of things because differently known. According to him, when we talk about the mind and its contents what we say must be connected to the observable behavior of human bodies. Yet he ascribed only the most meager mental life to animals, denying that they could form intentions or harbor any but the most rudimentary beliefs, on the ground that they are not users of language. Second, he maintained that human actions are radically distinct in character from what he called "natural happenings," including all the activities of animals, on the ground that human actions, being done for reasons, are not susceptible of causal explanation. Sartre divides the field of existing things into those that exist for themselves and those that exist in themselves. The former, which are conscious of themselves and determine their own character, are exclusively human beings. The latter have fixed given natures. It has been suggested that the blindness of these philosophers to the close likenesses between men and animals is due to their respective sophisticated metropolitan backgrounds in Vienna and Paris. It seems unlikely that either of them ever owned a dog.

Aristotle influentially distinguished men, animals, and plants from lifeless matter in terms of the rational, animal, and vegetative souls they each possessed. These souls are what underlies reason; also self-movement, perception, desire, and emotion; also nutrition and reproduction. Aristotle took reason to be peculiar to mankind (and to any "higher" intelligent creatures there may be), but no unfathomable abyss separated men from animals in his view. Men alone have rational souls, but they have animal souls as well. They are, in the words of the celebrated definition, rational animals. Reflection on his terminology prompts the thought that it is really very strange of Cartesian dualists to deny that animals have souls, given that the word *animal* is derived from *anima,* the Latin synonym of the Greek *psyche* or soul.

In order to incorporate Aristotle into Christianity, and, in particular, to find a place for human immortality within a system of thought that made no real provision for it, some casual remarks about the active intellect, suggesting that on the death of its possessor it would rejoin the universal reason, had to be elaborately developed and insisted on. A Christianizing revision, then, obliterated the naturalistic tendency of

Aristotle's philosophy, with its emphasis on the graded continuity of all existing things.

The dualistic doctrine of the soul affirms not only that the soul is distinct from the body in a fundamentally important way and that human beings alone have souls. It also holds that human beings are essentially or intrinsically souls, capable of being attached to bodies but equally capable of existence independently of them. This prepares the way for the idea that the soul actually does continue to exist after the death and disintegration of a body to which it has been attached. The most general argument for that conclusion was put forward by Plato. The soul is simple and indivisible (perhaps because it is not in space); only what is composite and divisible can go out of existence (at any rate in the natural order of things and without divine intervention): therefore, the soul cannot go out of existence.

Descartes's argument for the thesis that I, or any human being, am essentially a soul, and only contingently a body, is that it is impossible for me to suppose that I do not exist, but I can suppose, without contradiction, that my body does not exist, so that it is possible for me to exist although my body does not. For the purposes of this discussion it is not necessary to ask if the argument is valid or not. If, as seems obvious, animals are conscious beings and have beliefs, it would simply follow that, if the argument were valid, then animals are essentially souls and only contingently embodied too.

The naturalist alternative to these dualistic ways of thinking may be of a strong, materialistic variety, holding that mental events and processes just are material events and processes of a particular, presumably cerebral, sort. It may, more moderately, admit a distinctness of character between the mental and the physical but contend that the mental never occurs without, and is causally dependent on, the existence of a physical organism in which it is embodied. But it will deny that any mental activity could go on without a physical basis, whether it were the mental activity of men or of animals.

VI. The soul: its parts and purposes

1. The alleged uniqueness of man

The traditional dualism of soul and body was not advanced by philosophers with any particular interest in distinguishing men from animals. Its main underlying purpose was to distinguish man, or an essential ingredient in man, from nature. Animals, unreflectively assumed to be parts of nature, were, by an easy transition of thought, supposed, for the most part with the same lack of reflection, to be without souls. Only when Descartes took the step of explicitly asserting that animals are automata did it become necessary to draw some distinctions, to work out in just what respect animals fall short of man.

What is it to have a soul? At its most inclusive a soul is simply a consciousness, a sensibility, in particular the capacity to enjoy pleasure and suffer pain. The disconcerting view of Descartes was that animals, despite appearances, lack even this. They cannot, of course, tell us in so many words that they are enjoying themselves or that they are suffering. Nor can a baby, or a retarded person, or someone suffering from aphasia, or even a foreigner whose language we do not understand. A monkey may well look much more like an adult human being then a baby does. Its behavior when in pain may be much more like an adult human's than a baby's. It can identify the painful spot and rub it for alleviation. We have, then, much better reason for saying that the monkey is in pain than that the baby is. Indeed, it seems to me that we can reasonably suppose that we have a better idea of what it is like to be a monkey in pain than to be a baby in pain, despite the fact that in our unrecallable pasts we have all been babies in pain.

As philosophical investigators of the problem of our knowledge of other minds often remind us, we do not know the pains of others as we know our own. We feel our own pains, we directly experience them. But, for all the sympathetic wincing the pains of others may excite in us, we have to tell that they are in pain from our observations, which are painless in themselves, of their pain-giving circumstances and their pain-expressing behavior, the cut finger and the sharp cry. The baby's cry may come from stomachache or frustration. The monkey's expressions of physical pain and of anger are much more clearly differentiated. Our adult compatriots can, of course, tell us that they are in pain. But they do not always tell us the truth. Circumstances and behavior are the ultimate, if seldom appealed to, tests of their veracity. Furthermore, they can and do deceive us by pretending to be in pain, or, more commonly, because of the exigencies of social life, to be enjoying themselves. Animal pretense is on a much more modest scale. Our evidence for animal pain is, then, much more unequivocal than that we have for the pains of our fellow human beings. To turn this point in the direction of Descartes: we have no less reason to think that other human beings are automata than we have to think that animals are, and no more either. And since the first belief is absurd, so is the second.

The Cartesian account of the nature of animals is clearly a philosophical grotesque, a paradox to be used simply as an incitement to further thought about the way in which we ascribe feelings to other sensitive beings. Any account of the difference between men and animals plausible enough to be taken as a serious contender for our acceptance must be Aristotelian. Aristotle ascribed to animals sensation and appetite (comprising desire, passion, and wish) but denied that they had reason

Chimpanzee expressing anger. *"They cannot, of course, tell us in so many words that . . . they are suffering."*

or the power of thought. His position is not as clear as it looks. The familiar contrast of thought and feeling is not a sharp one; there is a debatable middle ground of mental activities that partake of both, essentially the region of perception and belief. Aristotle acknowledges that animals can perceive but denies that they have beliefs, denies also that they have the power of "calculation and thought."

Belief and thought are closely connected, as is suggested by the colloquial use of *think* for *believe*. "I think he is married" means the same as "I believe he is married." Perception, again, is commonly distinguished from mere sensation, a wholly passive sensory receptiveness, as a matter of the formation of beliefs at the prompting of sensation. We do not need to explore these refinements, since it is quite evident that animals are capable of perception and belief. H. H. Price sensibly observes:

> The point of being conscious, of having experiences, is that it enables one to *recognize* one's food or one's enemies when they are within the range of one's sense-organs, or to recognize other things which are biologically helpful or harmful (for example, a suitable place for concealment, a safe place for building a nest). . . . It is possible that in some creatures the capacity of recognizing their food or their enemies is unlearned, "instinctive" as we say. . . . But in most animals, perhaps

> in all, sensation has another function as well. It enables one to learn from experience, and thereby to respond more effectively to one's environment. (*Thinking and Experience,* pp. 41–42.)

We all know perfectly well that a dog can believe, quite rightly, that its ball has rolled under the sofa; a cat, that one is about to feed it; a squirrel, that it can jump safely from one branch to another.

Belief and the kind of perceptual thought from which all our fundamental beliefs about matters of fact derive are plainly within the capacity of animals. So Locke is wrong when he says that "brutes abstract not," that animals do not make sense of their experience with general ideas. Of course they do not use general *words.* But their behavior gives overwhelming evidence of their ability to recognize things as being of particular kinds and of having predictive beliefs—expectations, set up by their recognitions, together with learned beliefs about the further characteristics of what they recognize.

Where Aristotle and many others since have firmly dug their feet in is in their insistence that human beings alone have reason. But animals identify problems—the need to find a way out of a disagreeably confined environment, for example—which they go about solving much as human investigators do, namely, by the experimental procedure of trial and error. Nor are their inquiries always directed toward the solution of some immediately pressing problem. A predator may spend a long time carefully observing the regular movements of its prey in order to choose a good moment to strike. Animals reason, draw inferences, and display intelligence.

What they do not do is think for the sake of thinking. They are not speculative theorists but practical investigators. We may agree that science, or, more broadly and accurately, *theory,* is a special and distinguished achievement of our species without concluding that it amounts to some vast and estranging abyss between men and animals. After all, it is an activity of rather few human beings even now, and it is reasonable to think it has emerged only rather late in the evolutionary history of the human species.

The most favored differentiator relied upon by those who still wish to maintain that the difference between men and animals is the most fundamental partitioning of the actual contents of the world is language. Its invokers have to admit that animals communicate. On the one hand there is the very precise signaling system of bees, with its admittedly limited repertoire; on the other, the chimpanzees who have been taught to say a large number of things in gesture. The bees can be discounted since their communications about the distance and direction from the hive of supplies of nectar has something of the mechanical rigidity of the thermometer or barometer. These minds are too one-track to count as minds at all. But the talkative chimpanzees are another matter. They

Chatting with herself, Koko, a gorilla, signs "eye" while looking at a picture of a big-eyed frog. She was taught sign language as part of a scientific project.

can make up new sentences out of the elements of gesture-language they have been taught. In doing so, they have moved beyond mere signaling to an articulated, syntactical manner of using language which has hitherto been, so far as we know, a human monopoly.

It must be admitted that these linguistic achievements, although real, are very rudimentary although the chimpanzees' new sentences show that there is no incapacity in principle in nonhuman animals to use a means of communication that is a true language in being conventional and creative. I mentioned earlier that in the social life of animals there are to be found, in comparatively primitive form, the stable family, the organized economy, and the law-enforcing state. These are needed for the continuation of the species, its sustenance, and its protection from external enemies and internal conflict. But the other three great human institutions have no correlates in the animal world. We are unique in possessing theory, religion, and art. Theory comprises much more than science as Bacon conceived it, a body of methodically acquired and systematically organized natural knowledge for the more effective satisfaction of our desires. A main part of religion is theory, about the world as a whole and man's place in it, in large measure a response to the knowledge of the inevitability of death. Animals fear death when the danger of it is near at hand; they do not contemplate it from afar. They also have in some form the other main parts of religion: ritual and the instilling of codes of conduct. They have aesthetic preferences but do not seem deliberately to make things for the purpose of gratifying them.

Although it will be admitted that animal societies instill and enforce codes of conduct, many would rest their case for the uniqueness of man on the fact that he is a moral agent, that his conduct is, at least partially, governed by conscientious choice rather than instinct or the powerful sanctions of the tribe. But if we consider the content of morality, the forms of action and the types of virtue it generally enjoins, underneath all its anthropologically celebrated variations the contrast between us and animals is far from irresistibly evident. Animals are courageous, patient, affectionate, good parents, loyal companions, forgiving—very much in the way we are, that is to say, not all, not all the time, and in some cases never.

When the whole range of allegedly differentiating human powers and achievements is surveyed, the old ideas that animals are quite other than men because devoid of soul or reason shrink to manageable proportions. Of course there are differences. The modest peculiarities of human anatomy and physiology—the large brain, the comparative hairlessness, the habitually upright posture, and so forth—are associated with more substantial differences of mentality and culture. But these are not of a completely different order from the differences that separate species of nonhuman animals. What is strongly suggested by the straightforward physical likenesses of men and other animals is confirmed by the continuities of behavior and of social life. It is plain that man is a special kind of animal. But it is blindness to believe that he is not an animal at all, or that some animals, at least, are not in most respects like him.

2. The real points at issue

What are the underlying reasons for the deeply entrenched habit of considering men and animals to be in all that matters utterly distinct, a habit that, when challenged, turns into an anxious determination? The most fundamental has already been briefly mentioned in connection with philosophical dualism about soul and body: immortality. The survival of the death of his body by what is essential to his personal identity is the most metaphysically grandiose element in what is supposed to be the special dignity of man. Of almost equal antiquity and importance is the idea that men alone have free will. Animals, as much as running water and falling stones, are taken to be rigidly governed in their behavior by causal laws. Given their natures and their circumstances they cannot but do what they do do. But men, it is believed, are different. They have free choice and are, generally, responsible for their actions. A libertarian or indeterministic conception of man seems inconsistent with the programs of the human and social sciences, at least if these are conceived as undertakings of the same kind as the natural sciences.

Despite the relevance of human freedom of will to morality it is not, in itself, a moral issue. But there is a large array of connected moral problems about man's relation to and treatment of animals. He hunts, breeds, kills, and eats them. He compels them to work for him in various ways, as providers of food and muscular energy, for the most part. For the sake of entertainment, and a dash of instruction, he trains them to perform in circuses and locks them up in zoos. For purposes of scientific research he subjects them to all sorts of painful, mutilating, and lethal experimentation. These are all modes of treatment that are more or less unthinkable as applied to human beings. Some of them would be acceptable provided that the subject's consent had been obtained, perhaps in exchange for some consideration, monetary or other. Most of them would not be regarded as things for which consent could permissibly be sought or given. The issues must be looked at in a little more detail.

Immortality. The main philosophical point of mind–body dualism has always been the immortality of the soul, even if dualism has often been accepted by philosophers such as Hume and A. J. Ayer, who do not believe in the soul's survival of death. There has been a great deal of very involved discussion about the nature of the soul, which is held to survive the death and disintegration of the body, that is, its completely going out of existence as a body. Is the soul or mental aspect of a person the total set of his experiences, of the passing mental states of

Sir Henry Hesketh Bell, governor of Northern Nigeria from 1909 to 1911, poses with his trophies in Uganda, 1908. *"Most casual observation of undomesticated animals was made by people who were attempting to kill them."*

which he is conscious? Is it, as Aristotle hinted—in a way that made it possible to reconcile his philosophy with Christian doctrine—a part of his mental equipment, in Aristotle's case, the "active reason," the bit of the mind that goes in for theoretical reasoning? Is it, as some have said, a mysterious something or other, a pure ego, as it is sometimes called, which has or underlies all the conscious states that make up a mind's history? A further difficulty is presented by the universally admitted, if not always explicitly acknowledged, existence of unconscious mentality—mental states and processes, that is to say, whose subjects are not consciously aware of them.

Even if sense can be made of the notion of a pure ego, which I do not think it can, its persistence after the death of the body would not be enough to count as a real continuation of an individual person's life. Locke and Leibniz, two major philosophers who disagreed about almost everything except that there was such a thing as spiritual substance or the pure ego, agreed also that survival required that souls should be connected to their previously embodied selves by memory of their former states. That is, the soul after the body's death would have to have conscious experiences, in particular memory experiences of former conscious experiences.

An obvious objection to the idea that a person's mental life can go on after the death of his body is that all the mental life we know of, or even have good evidence for, is associated with living bodies (and not, of course, only human bodies). Furthermore, some parts of it seem to be more closely and directly dependent on the body than others. Perception and sensation seem to require physical organs of sense. Emotion and desire, the domain of what used to be called the passions, have evident bodily manifestations and accompaniments. Aristotle's theoretical reason, on the other hand, is comparatively self-contained. It can be exercised without bodily expression and upon purely mental stores of information, without reliance on any immediate bodily stimulus. This lends some color to the idea that the human reason, at any rate, can intelligibly be supposed to exist without a bodily support. But it does not do much more than that. It is plain that our reasoning powers are subject to bodily influence. For one thing they can be damaged or completely destroyed by injury to the brain, a fact that throws a somber light on their prospects when the brain has completely disintegrated. They are also susceptible to the influence of drugs and other chemical substances that are introduced into the body.

What is more, the reason on its own suffers from the same defect as the pure ego or soul substance. Its survival would not preserve the individuality of its previous possessor. Separated by bodily death from the rest of his mental apparatus, it would be, as Aristotle himself saw, entirely impersonal, a consideration that led him to view it as being absorbed back, after embodiment in a particular human individual, into some kind of universal mind.

The fact that much of our mental life is unconscious is a further support for the thesis that an individual's mental life is causally dependent on his body. If I step carefully over an obstacle in my path when too interested in something else to be consciously aware of the fact, there is the same relation between the physical exposure of the sense organs to the obstacle and the ensuing avoidance of it that is present in the conscious case where I am actually aware of perceiving it. What can the unconscious perception of the obstacle be that we believe to have occurred but a registration of the obstacle in the brain which leads to a nerve impulse that alters my mode of walking?

Immortality, then, is an obscure notion and a somewhat protean one. All the same, it is something that many, perhaps most, people have passionately desired, and nearly as many have passionately believed in. It is also something that has been generally ascribed by those who believed in it to *all* human beings and *only* to human beings. Whatever view is taken of the nature of mind, the reasonableness of this restrictive belief will have to be examined.

Free will. Human beings, it is generally held, are the only moral agents, the only creatures that are morally responsible for their actions. That is really too sweeping. No human being is morally responsible for everything he does. All of us are sometimes subject to duress, irresistible physical force, breakdowns of consciousness of one sort or another. Some human beings are excused from responsibility, not just for particular acts by reason of special exculpating conditions, but for part or all of their lives: the badly retarded permanently, the insane from the time of going mad. Nevertheless, it does seem reasonable to say that most human beings are morally responsible for a good deal of what they do, and that nothing that is not a human being is morally responsible for anything it does.

It is a common conviction that a moral agent is absolved from responsibility for something he has done if he could not have done otherwise. But if there is a causal explanation, in terms of my nature and the circumstances, for my acting as I did, it follows that it is impossible that, given that nature and those circumstances, I should have done anything different from what I did do. If the scope of causal law, in other words, extends to cover the whole range of human conduct, nothing humans do is ever done freely, and for nothing that they do are they ever really morally responsible. *Ought* implies *can,* as the phrase is; it is incorrect to say that I ought to have done something other than what I actually did unless I could have done otherwise. But if I am a part of nature conceived as a deterministic system, then I can never do anything other than what I actually do do.

I believe, with many other philosophers, that this conclusion is incorrect, the result of a muddle. But many philosophers think otherwise, and they are by no means less well qualified to have an opinion on the subject. I do not intend to enter into debate with them directly since either view—that determinism is, or that it is not, compatible with moral responsibility—is itself compatible, I shall argue, with the view that men are enough like other animals to be counted as animals themselves.

Nevertheless, the attribution to men, by the libertarian opponents of determinism, of free will, of a faculty of making choices or decisions that are not causally determined by the nature and circumstances of the agent, has been thought to mark a crucial aspect of the distinction between men and animals. Animals behave, but men act. Animals are driven by instincts, brought into operation by immediately perceived stimuli. An animal that appears to be steadily working toward the realization of a plan, deliberately prepared in advance, like a spider spinning a web, a beaver building a dam, or a bird building a nest, is not a genuine agent but is simply going through a behavioral routine for which it has been programmed by evolution.

The possession by men of a genuine, that is to say, free, will is closely tied up by those who believe in it with man's allegedly unique possession of reason. Where the animal is instinctually driven to go through its built-in program, we consciously formulate and adopt more or less long-term ends and select means to them in the light of our stores of general knowledge about how things are connected and from our calculations of the costs of these alternatives and their side effects. To do this we must be able to reason and to acquire and retain a good deal of more or less theoretical knowledge. Will and reason, in short, go together; will, properly so called, is simply reason in its practical employment, as Kant put it. Both are higher, distinctively (even if not quite universally) human faculties of the mind. The uniqueness of man as an agent preserves him in his deterministic natural environment as the sole bearer of moral responsibility.

The sciences of man. A disquieting implication of the thesis that men, as morally responsible agents, frequently act in independence of causally determining factors is that to the extent that man acts freely his conduct is not susceptible of scientific explanation. It follows that psychology and the social sciences, understood as they usually are, are doomed to failure as attempts to discover the causal laws of human conduct. Man can be a subject for science only in respect of those of his activities that occur independently of his will. These are for the most part bodily: breathing, the circulation of the blood, digestion, growth. There may be room for a science of abnormal behavior, that of the naturally deficient in whom the will does not operate—the retarded and the mad—and also, perhaps, for child psychology, of the mental life and behavior of those in whom the will has not yet emerged. Human freedom of will is part of what underlies the doctrine that history is not a science and is perverted by those who try to pursue it as if it were.

Two recent tendencies in philosophy, the Wittgensteinian and the existentialist, strongly opposed to one another in many respects, agree that human beings are not a proper or possible topic for causal inquiry in the way that, apart from man but including animals, nature is. The Wittgensteinian view is that human conduct has to be understood as issuing from motives or reasons and that these explanatory factors are not causes connected by law to the actions they explain. The existentialist asserts that man has no fixed nature for the supposed causes of his conduct to be found in. Men create themselves by free acts of will. Wittgensteinians share with structuralists the idea that the possession of language is the essential distinguishing mark of mankind, and they are led by this to the conclusion that to understand men and their institutions is more like interpreting a text than a matter of registering a natural regularity.

One recent attempt to bring men within the scope of a universally acknowledged natural science which has excited violent controversy is the sociobiology of E. O. Wilson. Wilson is an expert on the social insects and has brought the most sophisticated forms of evolutionary biology and population genetics to the business of explaining how a particular form of natural selection operates in favoring the development of various peculiarities of structure and behavior. This is "kin selection," the way in which evolutionary advantage goes to organisms that act so as to maximize the chances of survival of the genes that are distinctive of them, and which they share in varying degrees with their blood relations.

Wilson's offense in the eyes of his most vehement critics has been to extend the application of his theories to the human species. In the interests of various ideological fads, such as antisexism and antiracism, they have subjected him to a torrent of invective well outside the usually recognized limits of academic brawling.

It is not that they hold that human nature and conduct cannot be causally explained. Many of them are Marxists, constrained by their interpretation of that system of doctrine to hold that the historically varying properties of men are due to society and culture, more specifically to the interaction between the way in which economic production is carried on and the social organization that corresponds to it. Generally, they hold that man's genetic inheritance, a matter that falls within the scope of biological science, determines largely what is common to the species, while the variations that have taken place since the establishment of the species are largely due to culture. What culture has brought about, a changed culture can change in the direction of its heart's desires. To attribute aspects of the social life of mankind—an important instance is the comparatively specialized roles of males and females—to inherited factors excludes, or at any rate limits, the possibilities of what they see as desirable reform. No adherent of supernatural religion has assailed with greater ferocity than critics of sociobiology the idea that men and animals can be investigated in the same way.

The treatment of animals. The interests which have been considered so far as underlying the distinction between men and animals have all been concerned with safeguarding the dignity of man. He alone, among all that is to be found in the universe, can survive the death of his body, act freely as a morally responsible agent, and elude the net of scientific interpretation; thus, he alone can escape the dangers of having his actions predicted and, worse than that, brought under the control of technical manipulation. Another, more practical interest is human convenience. To see animals as wholly distinct from human beings is, among other things, to exclude them from the moral constituency, from the range of those whose well-being we ought morally to take into account.

Man's convenience dictates that animals should be used as part of the general bounty of nature in whatever way suits us, provided that we respect the property rights in them of other human beings. We use them, first of all, for food, as an unrivaled source of protein. With this in mind, we hunt and fish them in their natural habitats, breed, rear, and slaughter them in various environments—farms, batteries, and abattoirs. Second, we use them to provide us with dairy products and eggs, with wool and silk for clothing. Third, we use them for purposes

"We hunt and fish them in their natural habitats, breed, rear, and slaughter them in various environments—farms, batteries, and abattoirs."

of research, a work for which they are the more suited the more like us they are. We test drugs on them, use them to examine the course and effects of diseases that we induce in them, try out industrial products on them to see if they have unpleasant side effects. Fourth, we make use of them in a large number of ways for pleasure and recreation. We hunt, shoot, and fish them when we do not need or even intend to eat what we kill. We breed and train them to race against each other. In a more furtive way we still set them up to fight against each other, in spite of fairly widespread legal prohibition. We train them to appear as circus acts. We capture them in order to display them in zoos, frequently in conditions of unpleasant confinement. More genially we keep them as pets, but as well as the companionable side of this relationship there is also much cruelty, neglect, and abandonment. Finally, we use them to work for us, as draft animals, as aids in hunting, to guard factories and sniff out drugs, to herd sheep, to guide the blind, to control rodents, even, although to a decreasing extent, to take us about, but more for exercise than for purposive travel.

Traditionally, those who have reflected philosophically on the morality of man's treatment of animals have either, in the spirit of Descartes's theory of animals as mindless natural objects, taken the view that there is no moral issue here at all—that we are morally permitted to treat animals in any way that we like—or they have held that we ought not to ill-treat animals because to do so is to fall into habits of cruelty that could be harmful to other men. The first position is adopted unreservedly by Spinoza. "The law against the slaughtering of animals is founded rather on vain superstition and womanish pity than on sound reason. . . . I do not deny that beasts feel; what I deny is, that we may not consult our own advantage and use them as we please, treating them in the way that best suits us." The same belief is found in St. Augustine, who defends it by reference to the incident of Christ's miraculous transfer of devils into the Gadarene swine.

The second position is that of Kant, who argued that we could have no duties to animals since they are not rational beings, but that we should not treat them cruelly because it fosters a habit of inhumanity to do so. That is not a very defensible point of view. Either animals are enough like us to deserve moral consideration because of what they actually are, or it is simply a sentimental illusion to worry about them, like pitying an old car as it grinds up a steep hill.

Many Eastern religions have condemned the killing and eating of animals, sometimes because they believed that the souls of human beings could be reincarnated in the bodies of animals. In the West, a concern for the well-being of animals for their own sake has been fitful. St. Francis is a lonely medieval exception. In the Enlightenment, Voltaire and others revived the generous ideas of Montaigne, but, as Mary Midgley points out in *Animals and Why They Matter* (1983), this initiative was to some extent smothered by the preoccupation of the thinkers of the Enlightenment with reason. Most philosophers, she remarks, are town dwellers, have little to do with animals, and easily forget about them, despite their steaks and salmon and woolen sweaters.

VII. Human dignity and convenience examined

Now that the supposed marks of distinction between men and animals have been themselves distinguished and made more explicit, it is time to see whether they have the favorable implications that have given men an interest in drawing them. The idea that men have souls, a mental aspect that could be the form in which they survive the deaths of their bodies, has been interpreted as referring principally to three things: the whole of a subject's conscious experience, the pure ego or soul substance, and the reason, which is multiform, being indentified as the ability to think, or the ability to theorize, or the possession of language. Then there is the idea that men are, or that most of them, at any rate, sometimes or even often are, truly free agents, moved by will and not merely by instinct, on the one hand morally responsible for what they choose to do and, on the other hand, because of their freedom, not to be made predictable and manipulable by having their conduct explained by their nature and circumstances together with laws of human and social science. Finally, there is the idea that men alone are the appropriate objects of direct moral consideration, the only bearers of rights, the only moral ends in themselves.

With regard to each of these ideas, I shall ask whether the actual differences between men and animals give an adequate foothold to the exclusive status accorded to human beings. I shall argue that in no case is the total exclusion of animals from the respect and consideration men are accustomed to giving themselves justified, although the differences that really exist between men and animals can be reasonably argued to have some qualifying consequences for the morality of our treatment of the latter. If that is right, there are, in the case of each of the interesting ideas involved, two possibilities. Either we can conclude that animals too have immortal souls, free wills, and moral rights. Or we can conclude that since they do not, we also do not.

1. The immortal soul in men and animals

The soul in men, which has been supposed to be the essential element capable of surviving the death of their bodies, can be understood in several different ways. The most comprehensive identifies the soul with the totality of an individual's conscious experience, the entire stream of beliefs, imaginings, desires, emotions, deliberations, and choices of which an individual can be introspectively aware as making up his inner, mental life. A soul in this sense can be denied to animals, and in particular to the primates and more evolved mammals who are physically and genetically closest to us, only by the heroically absurd expedient of maintaining that animals have no conscious experiences at all. The plain fact is that we have precisely the same sort of grounds for ascribing consciousness to many human beings—to babies, to the very old, to the mentally abnormal, to those, also, who are very alien to us in language and behavior—as we have for ascribing it to many animals. And we have very much the same evidence, but some more besides, for ascribing it to people with whom we can communicate linguistically and whose customs and preferences we share. If consciousness is a reason for supposing immortality to be possible or actual for people other than ourselves, then we must admit that animals are immortal too.

The same conclusion follows from the assumption that the immortal element in a human being is a pure ego or spiritual substance. We can attribute such a thing to ourselves or anyone else only indirectly, inferring it from the fact that they are conscious together with some general principle to the effect that conscious states are inconceivable without a substantial something or other of which they are the states. If men have pure egos, then so do animals.

The idea that reason is the immortal ingredient in the constitution of men can itself be taken in at least three ways. The simplest is that a being has reason if it can draw inferences from the beliefs it acquires by perception. That is suggested by the adoption of appropriate means to bring about desired ends but is not clearly established by it. The well-adjusted routine of behavior might be purely instinctive yet it is plain that much complex satisfaction-producing behavior in animals is not simply instinctive but has been learned, and not by a process of conditioning imposed by some external trainer, but rather as a result of the animal's own observations and trials.

There is, however, another, narrower conception of reason in which it does seem to be largely peculiar to human beings. This is theoretical reason, the power of developing logically articulated bodies of general beliefs about the world, carried on, for the most part, reflectively and by thinkers not in direct perceptual contact with a problematic situation. The purest product of theoretical reason is mathematics, of which animals plainly have no inkling. The special intellectual glory of our species is the theoretical natural science elaborated in the last three centuries in which mathematics is applied to the world by bringing calculation to bear on the results of measurement.

It was something like this that Aristotle had in mind with his conception of "active reason," in his view the only possibly immortal element in the soul. Its impersonality was his ground for thinking it to be not really the property of the individuals who have the use of it, and so really universal and capable of surviving the death of the rest of the individual. At any rate, if it is distinctive of the human species, it is not distinctive of particular individuals. What those who find the thought of immortality attractive want for themselves and those they are attached to after death is not this thin and abstractly intellectual residue of personality. Immortality confined to this would not be worth having. Many human beings would not achieve it anyway; as a criterion it restricts immortality to a cognitive elite.

The most favored conception of the distinctive reason of men at the present time is the type of rationality that is embodied in the possession of language. Animals, it is admitted, have signaling systems, but these are not languages proper. What is undeniable is that animal "languages" are much poorer and more rudimentary than human language. It is much less clear that, as is often claimed, animal languages have no real grammar but are just a desultory repertoire of unrelated message-units and, again, that animal communication is not the expression of an intention to communicate. And we must remember that many human beings, from great youth or age or some other reason, have no capacity to use language, so they could be denied humanity on this ground. Thus, the possession of language has all the weaknesses as a criterion that theoretical reason has, and more, since it is far from clear that animals are wholly without it.

Defenders of immortality are not usually very precise about what it is that they expect to survive death. One who did try to think the matter through was C. S. Lewis. In his book *The Problem of Pain* he felt constrained to admit that animals had something of what he hoped would survive death in human beings. He consistently drew the conclusion that animals, or at least animals that had been to some extent humanized by human companionship, would survive death too.

Although animals are conscious, often intelligent, and modestly rational as well as, it seems, the intentional users of systems of communication, there is one important limitation to their mental lives which must be considered. This is that their awareness is generally restricted to what is going on in their immediate spatial and temporal environment. They are not given to what is variously called "free thinking" or "thinking in absence." To the extent that they do think about what is absent, it has to be tied by a strong associative link to what is present to their senses. It is the currently visible lead that makes the dog think of a walk and a swim, the heard sound of the refrigerator door that puts the cat in mind of a drink of milk. It might be said that a dog who snuffles and whimpers and shakes his legs in a dream is thinking about rabbits pursued long ago and, at any rate, not sensibly present to him. But this familiar speculative possibility does not undermine the point. The dreaming dog thinks of the rabbits, if he dreams about them, as actually present to him, just as we should.

A consequence of this parochialism of conscious scope in animals is that their memories are limited in a way that ours are not. They remember how to do things that they have learned, in particular to recognize individual people and places. Past experiences can affect their current reactions. But, like the burned child, they do not have to recall the particular fire that burned them and caused them to dread this fire now. In other words, they do not appear to have much in the way of a personal memory, the power to recollect particular events in their own pasts. Philosophers have often seen the power to recall past experience as an essential element in the identity of a person, sometimes as *the* essential element. It was animal deficiency in this respect that led Leibniz's follower Wolff to deny that animals are persons. They do not have, he said, "a consciouness of having been the same thing previously in this or that state."

Locke defined a person as "a thinking intelligent being, that has reason and reflection, and can consider itself as itself, the same thinking thing, in different times and places." I should hold that some continuity of character is also part of the idea of a person, but some continuity of personal memory is at least a necessary condition. It is this and the memories they do have, particularly of us and of what we are like, that makes companionable relationships possible with animals that at least marginally approximate to those we have with human beings we are attached to. The limitations of animal memory cast doubt on the conceivability of animals' survival of bodily death. A convenient way to think about the problem is to compare the ways in which we might be led to suppose that a man or an animal, known to have died, has been reincarnated. If the new animal enthusiastically recognized us and displayed the same character as the dead one, we might well identify the two. But we should lack the corroborating evidence of specific recollections of our shared past which would be available in the parallel human case. This little thought-experiment is not as farfetched as it might seem. It has a realistic analogue in the problem of identifying a physically unrecognizable man or animal, who, in the way appropriate to him, claims to be a man or animal we have known in the past but have long lost touch with.

I conclude that the limits of animal memory do not absolutely exclude, as Wolff believed, the conception of animals as continuing personalities of a rudimentary kind, nor do they make the survival of death inconceivable for them in a way that it is not inconceivable for men. But, like the animal's lack of theorizing power, a form of intellectual detachment from the immediate environment comparable to personal memory, it is a real difference between the two.

2. *Freedom and moral agency*

Before we can ask whether animals are free agents we must ask whether they are agents at all. The contrary view is that their behavior is entirely driven by instinct, by fixed and innate dispositions manifested under the influence of perceived external stimuli—the mouse in the cat's field of vision—and internal ones, such as a felt emptiness of the stomach. There are two points to be made here. The first is that it is certainly not true that all animals are wholly run by instinct. Many of them plainly learn from experience—from early life, in which they imitate or are trained by their elders, onward. Second, it is certainly not true that instinct plays no part in human life. There is no hard and fast dividing line between instinctive animals and deliberative men. We start with an instinctive set of dispositions, these are conditioned in various ways by our culture, that is to say by parents, by companions, by schools, by the state. Over and above this passively undergone modification of our springs of action, we also actively modify our own modes of conduct through experimentally pursued experience of life. Animals, too, try out new things and new ways of doing things.

But, just as they lack explicit theory, so they lack explicit codes of conduct—technical, prudential, and moral. Since their codes are not explicit and, so to speak, externalized, they are not available readily for critical examination, and animal means of communication are not rich enough for them to be discussed. That, however, is not to say that they do not have such codes, in the form of rules, or, if the word is preferred, habits of action, which are susceptible of change through intelligent adaptation to the experienced results of acting in accordance with them. It is not anthropomorphic fantasy on our part to speak of the cunning of the dog who comes to know how to shame us into taking

"They show self-sacrificing concern for their offspring, suppress aggressive impulses, tolerate the tiresomenesses and minister to the needs of one another."

him for a walk, or the cleverness of the cat who slips out of the house when we want him to stay in.

Animals, like us, envisage alternative possibilities of choice and, after reflection and perhaps some tentative tests, make their selection. Sometimes they just do things, but at others it seems more reasonable to say that they decide to do them. We can tell what they are thinking about and that they spend some time at it before they do it. Often, like us again, they are impulsive or act in an automatic, unreflective fashion. They passively acquire and also actively develop more efficient ways of doing things. They also come to be more prudent with the passage of time, take care to avoid pain and achieve pleasure, to maximize their long-run advantage, even if they have no conception of such a thing.

Do they have wills? The will, as such, is something of a philosopher's speciality. In ordinary life we talk about good and bad will, strong and weak will, but not of the will on its own. Animals can unquestionably be compared in respect of the relative goodness or strength of their wills. They are more or less amiable, more or less resolute and determined. They have characters. Kant confined will to human beings on the ground that to act on will is to act in accordance with the *idea* of a rule, and not merely in accordance with a regularity. But that is a perverse limitation; the relevant point is whether the rule is part of the agent's given constitution or is an intelligent acquisition, susceptible of intelligent amendment.

Are animals moral? They exhibit forms of behavior that would undoubtedly be accounted moral in human beings and have what are very like virtues and vices. They show self-sacrificing concern for their offspring, suppress aggressive impulses, tolerate the tiresomenesses and minister to the needs of one another. In all this naive, primitively moral activity they are, after all, like a great many unsophisticated human beings who do not reflect about moral issues in the abstract but know what they ought to do and try to do it with more or less success. It is no more true of animals than it is of human beings that, in general, they behave in formal accordance with the generally recognized principles of morality only in order to avoid trouble and secure material rewards. They, like us, are capable from time to time of a disinterested concern for the well-being of others.

I do not want to suggest, however, that animals are fully fledged moral agents. For that, I think, a capacity to stand outside oneself and consider one's conduct and character in a critical manner is required. For that, in turn, a kind of self-consciousness is needed which animals do not possess because of their lack of personal memory and also, perhaps, because, if they have language at all, it is confined to the particular features of the here and now. What I do maintain is that there are the preliminaries of moral agency in animals, just as there are in young children, a fact that makes both of them susceptible to moral training in good habits and proper objects of praise and blame, to which both animals and young children are responsive.

None of this implies that the wills of animals are free, in the sense that any of their actions are intrinsically unpredictable, unconnected by law with their character and circumstances. Much of what they do is, of course, unpredictable in practice, but that can be attributed to the limitations of our knowledge, not to an objective deficiency in what there is to know. It is true that their repertoire of conduct is narrower than that of human beings, particularly of civilized human beings in the modern world. The gap is narrower between them and primitive human beings. It can be reasonably held that human beings are uniquely creative, as long as it is acknowledged that only a few human beings actually are.

But, if animals are not free agents in the sense of being able to act in an uncaused way, neither, I should argue, along with many other philosophers, are human beings. It is not necessary, fortunately, to discuss the problem here. In general, the reasons adduced for attributing this kind of freedom to human beings, like true creativeness or the habit of explicit moral self-criticism, apply to few, or at best a minority. Or, as with the power of deliberation and choice, the possession of wills of varying degrees of strength and goodness, the habit of acting efficiently, prudently, and virtuously as much may be said of many animals as of human beings.

A science does not require that the field to which it is applied be perfectly deterministic. All that is presupposed as a condition of possibly fruitful scientific investigation is some measure of order. As with the other kind of law, the one which human societies impose on their members, the whole undertaking is not undermined by the fact of a number of exceptions, so long as they are exceptions and not the usual case. Social and human science in general, and sociobiology in particular, are compatible with a measure of contra-causal freedom. Although such freedom has, in my view, nothing to do with moral responsibility (I agree with Hume that responsibility presupposes determinism—or a good deal of it—and is inconceivable without it), human creativeness and some novelties in nature do count in favor of there being such a thing in fact.

But the usual objection to sociobiology is not that it is deterministic. It is, rather, that it rules out all sorts of beneficial changes in the human world as impossible, or immensely costly, by connecting things it would be good to change—the relations of the sexes, classes, and races—with aspects of genetic inheritance which cannot in practice be altered. The most vociferous critics of sociobiology hold that human nature is not a constant, unalterably fixed in our genetic constitution, but, at the present stage of human evolution at any rate, is a product of culture, which is various and within our power to change. E. O. Wilson's extrapolations from the genetically programmed features of the social life of the hymenoptera are undoubtedly rather extravagantly speculative. More reasonably applicable lessons would be available from study of our closer relatives, the mammals and, particularly, our fellow primates. These higher animals, as we have seen, have a culture too, of an elementary and, as it might be put, nonspiritual kind. There is no absolute gulf between men and animals that rules the project of sociobiology out in principle. Its speculative excesses should be curbed by rational criticism, not quasi-religious hysteria.

3. The treatment of animals

Very much the greater part of our conduct that affects animals contravenes principles that would universally be agreed to apply to our treatment of human beings. We kill them, eat them, cause them great pain for no compensating advantage of their own, and enslave them. There is in many advanced countries, where the keeping of pets is much more widespread than participation in the hunting and rearing of animals for food and sport, a general persuasion that animals should not be treated cruelly. Laws against cruelty to animals are enforced and offenses against them are energetically sought out and prosecuted by voluntary societies. Many people are induced by moral considerations, and not for the sake of their own health, to abstain from the eating of animal flesh. In our moral environment, alive and well, there is to be found a whole range of attitudes from that of the dedicated vivisectionists and happy steak enthusiasts at one extreme to that of the committed vegetarians at the other.

The animal-users have the weight of our moral tradition behind them. If called on to justify their exclusion of animals from the domain of moral consideration, they would appeal to the familiar distinguishing features. If the Cartesian view were correct, their position would be impregnable. Since it is not, they must rely on the allegedly nonrational nature of animals in one of its forms.

But the relevant fact is that animals suffer and feel, can experience pain. If that is denied, it follows that it is morally permissible to eat, hunt, torment, and work to death nonrational human beings. The fact that animals are not moral agents is sometimes invoked to support our manner of treating them. I have admitted that the moral agency of animals is at most rudimentary and, for the purposes of this argument, I am quite content to allow that it does not exist at all. Animals have no rights, it is said, because rights imply duties and animals, not being moral agents, can have no duties. Therefore animals have no rights; there can be no moral aspect to any action of ours that affects an animal except to the extent that the rights of another human being are involved—its owner, perhaps.

This is just a sophism. Rights imply duties, not in the sense that I can have rights only if I can also have duties, but in the sense that if A

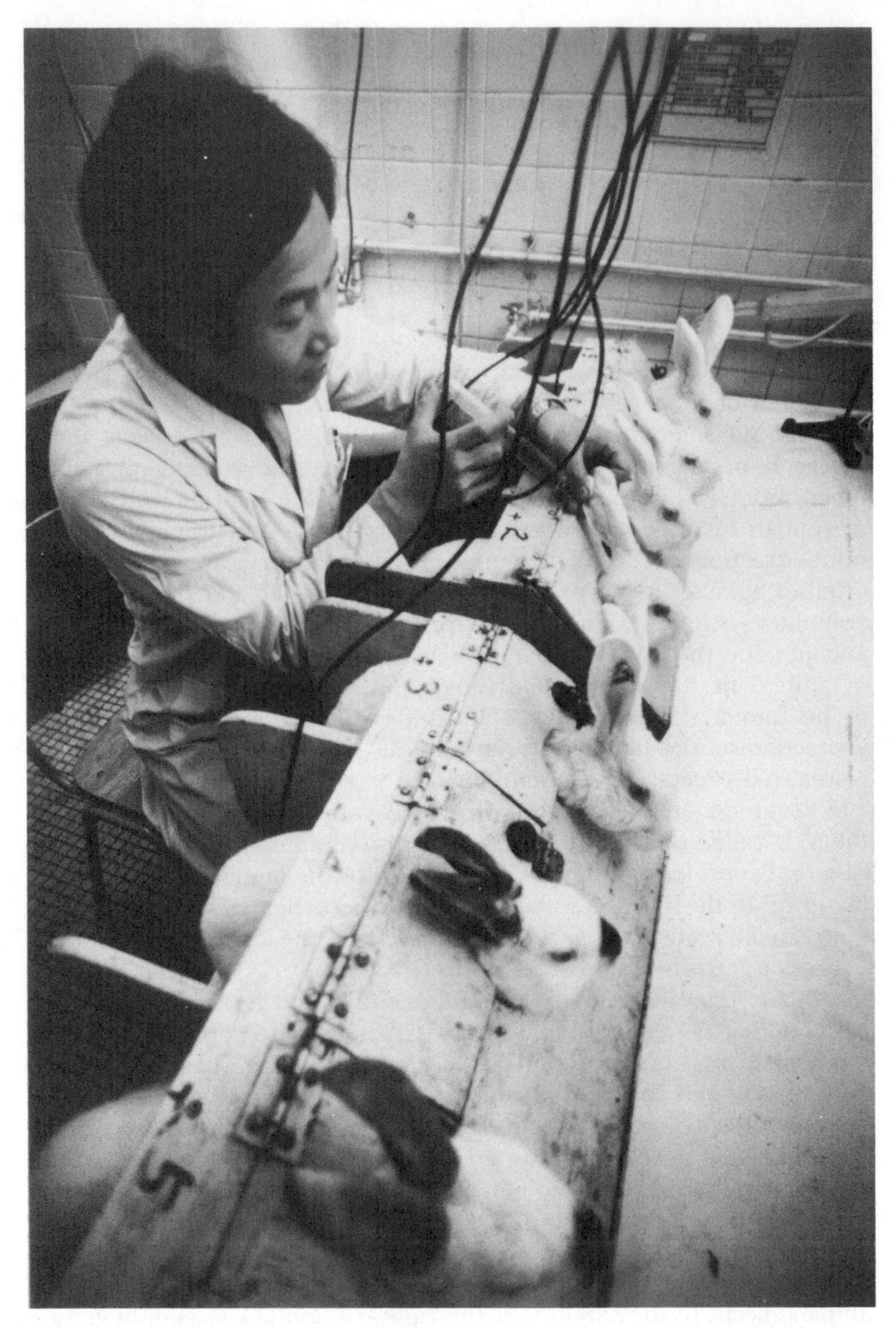

Millions of animals are used in laboratories annually. *"We kill them, . . . cause them great pain for no compensating advantage of their own, and enslave them."*

has a right against B, then B has a duty toward A. Children too young to have duties obviously have rights; there are things we have a duty to do for them and things we have a duty not to do to them.

A more defensible point of view relies on the fact that animals in general, having no personal memory, have no real self-conscious awareness of their own identity as continuing things. (They lack the existentialist's most dramatic human feature; they have no conception of the ultimate inevitability of their own death.) This may also have implications about the nature of an animal's experience of pain. Preoccupied with our own continuing futures, we fear and dislike pain, at least in part because of our fear of its consequences in terms of disablement, mutilation, and death. An outward-reaching anxiety is added in our case to the painful sensation. The lives of human beings are seen by them as continuing projects, where those of animals are a sequence of immediacies.

The moral prohibition of killing people is so fundamental that it seems almost absurd to try to make the reasons for it explicit. Its primordial nature is shown by the fact that in order to show that some forms of killing are morally permissible, we normally appeal, with more or less plausibility, to their being the means to the prevention of other deaths. That justification is most powerful as applied to killing in self-defense. It is weaker as a basis for capital punishment. Even if confined to those who have killed others or tried to do so, it has to assume that that makes it likely that they will kill, or try to kill, again. Once a war has started, the self-defense argument applies, in a collective fashion, although, for one side at least, it is not available as war breaks out.

The fact of being killed abolishes the system of expectations within which the individual's conduct of his life was carried on. That will be of no (earthly) disadvantage to him, but it will to all those who were rewardingly involved in that system, most acutely those who loved or liked him. The fear of an unnaturally precipitate death, not quietened by the effects of mortal illness or old age, must shadow and undermine his life. The right to life is traditionally given first place in lists of the supposed natural rights of man. Its being respected is, after all, an indispensable condition of the exercise or enjoyment of any other rights. Perhaps an underlying assumption is that the future will contain a positive balance of satisfaction over suffering. Even where we are convinced that this is incorrect in some particular case, we do not give serious consideration to the thought that, since the person would be better off dead, we should take steps to kill him, unless mental collapse has unfitted him for running his own life. *Arsenic and Old Lace* was a farcical comedy, not a dramatized policy recommendation.

Insofar as we kill animals for food or sport we can reconcile this with our convictions about the taking of human life only by relying on the difference between a man's conception of his future and an animal's, and as far as the indirect effects of killing are concerned, on the belief that the individual attachments of animals to one another are of an altogether different order of magnitude in intensity from those that connect human beings. It is not a very substantial moral basis for the meat industry, but it is at least an open and rational one. Vegetarians are right to reject the suggestion that kindly treated meat animals would not have the pleasant, even if foreshortened, lives they do—fed, warmed, protected from harm—unless men wished to eat them. We should hardly endorse the practice of replacing abortion by the rearing of unwanted children for the table.

The not unreasonable idea that animal pain is very different from ours, for the same reason that animal fear of death is, must also be invoked in any rational attempt to defend vivisection. The genuine, if often circuitous, contribution it makes to the saving of human lives is not enough, any more than it would be for a practice of using involuntary human subjects—prisoners, for example.

Moral progress, in its most important dimension, has always been a matter of enlarging the moral constituency: from family to tribe, from men to women, from adults to children, from compatriots to mankind at large. It is probable that, as we shake ourselves free from our habitual illusions about the differences between men and animals, we shall increasingly regard both as members of a single moral community.

Bibliography

Mortimer J. Adler. *The Difference of Man and the Difference It Makes.* New York, 1967. A forceful and extremely lucid statement of the case for the existence of a real distinction of kind between human beings and any other things with mindlike characteristics, whether animal or mechanical.

David Barash. *Sociobiology: The Whisperings Within.* London, 1980. A very detailed popular introduction to the sociobiology of animals.

Keith Campbell. *Body and Mind.* London, 1971. A superbly lucid and concise treatment of the philosophical problems of the relation between mind and body.

Arthur Caplan (ed.). *The Sociobiology Debate.* New York, 1978. A large and wide-ranging collection of articles.

Stephen R. L. Clark. *The Moral Status of Animals.* Oxford, 1977.
The Nature of the Beast. Oxford, 1984.
These are passionate expositions of the claims of animals to moral consideration by an expert philosopher who is also a Christian.

Donald Griffin. *The Question of Animal Awareness.* New York, 1976. A thorough, methodical, and persuasive account of animal mental life, with particular reference to animal powers of communication.

Mary Midgley. *Beast and Man.* Ithaca, N.Y., 1978.
Animals and Why They Matter. Harmondsworth, 1983.
Entertaining, very wide-ranging inquiries into human–animal differences and their implications for morality and our understanding of it.
Leonora C. Rosenfield. *From Beast-Machine to Man-Machine.* New York, 1941.
Learned, detailed study of seventeenth-century conceptions of the nature of men and animals.
Michael Ruse. *Sociobiology: Sense or Nonsense.* 2nd ed. Dordrecht, 1985.
Very well-balanced and well-informed philosophical assessment of the claims of the sociobiologists and their critics. Admirably lucid and intelligible.
Peter Singer. *Animal Liberation.* New York, 1975.
Arrestingly written survey of the facts and the morality of our treatment of animals.
The Expanding Circle. Oxford, 1981.
Luminous account of sociobiology and its philosophical implications.
Stephen Walker. *Animal Thought.* London, 1983.
Expert introductory account, including much physiology.
Edward O. Wilson. *Sociobiology; the New Synthesis.* Cambridge, Mass., 1975.
The original, canonical text of the new discipline.
On Human Nature. Cambridge, Mass., 1978.
Interesting, fairly rash, speculative extrapolations.

The Idea of Dialectic

Mortimer J. Adler

In addition to being editor of *The Great Ideas Today,* Mortimer Adler has been chairman of the Board of Editors of Encyclopædia Britannica since 1974. His lifelong interest in education through seminars on great books has led to many projects, including the editing, along with Robert M. Hutchins, of *Great Books of the Western World* for Britannica.

Born in New York City, Dr. Adler earned his Ph.D. from Columbia University, where he taught before going on to the University of Chicago. He has been visiting lecturer at several universities. Since 1953 he has annually conducted seminars during the summer months at the Aspen Institute for Humanistic Studies, of which he is a trustee.

In 1952 Dr. Adler founded the Institute for Philosophical Research in Chicago and became its director. The Institute's most recent project has been an educational reform called the Paideia Proposal, designed in part to involve grade school and high school children in learning through discussion. Several pilot schools have sprung up since the appearance of *The Paideia Proposal,* written in 1982 by Dr. Adler and members of the Paideia Group.

Dr. Adler is the author of more than 30 books, among them *How to Read a Book* (1940), *The Conditions of Philosophy* (1965), *The Difference of Man and the Difference It Makes* (1967), and *Aristotle for Everybody* (1978). His most recent book is *A Guidebook to Learning* (1986).

I. The great conversation

It is a commonplace that men differ on fundamental subjects. They differ in their beliefs about God, in their conceptions of man and his place in nature, and in their views of the cosmos. They differ in their opinions about the goals men should seek and the way they should behave, in their standards for judging political institutions or economic policies, and in their evaluation of forms of government. They differ about the meaning of justice, the nature and uses of freedom, the limits of knowledge, the attainability of truth, the purport of history, and the destiny of the human race.

Most of us have been involved in such differences of opinion with our friends and acquaintances. But few of us feel satisfied with our experience of the discussions that resulted. We too frequently have been left in doubt about who agrees or disagrees with whom; and even when a disagreement has seemed plain enough at the beginning, we have been left in the dark as the argument proceeded. We have found ourselves and other men talking together, but not thinking together, because we have been talking without listening and arguing without responding to arguments. Yet we realize that the reason why we are engaged in discussion—the fact that we do not all think alike—is the very reason why we should try to think together.

Schopenhauer, in his *Art of Controversy*, offers the following advice: When you are involved in a discussion, he says, do not allow yourself to be distracted by listening to your opponent's argument, but utilize the time to collect your thoughts and to plan what you are going to say when he has finished speaking. What Schopenhauer intended as irony is, unfortunately, the general practice of men. Our discussions of serious and difficult themes tend to take the form of alternating monologues. Whatever pleasure we may derive from soliloquizing in public, we can hardly learn much from listening only to ourselves. We cannot profit intellectually, as we might from good conversation. We cannot hope to get nearer to the truth unless discussion has something of the character of rational debate.

When we are serious about our fundamental beliefs or convictions, we are concerned with their truth. That is why we are also seriously concerned about agreement and disagreement. Anyone who claims truth for the opinions he holds must wish to persuade others; and if he regards his opinions as reasonable, he should be willing to offer reasons why others ought to agree with him. Anyone who does not regard himself as infallible should also be open to persuasion by those who disagree with him; he should be willing and anxious to hear the reasons that might be offered by those who claim truth for contrary opinions.

Discussion takes the form of rational debate when reasonable men talk to one another in the hope of persuading those who disagree, yet with a willingness to be persuaded by them. The first step toward such efforts at thinking together about what is true may take the form of conversation that merely explores the differences of opinion, in order to determine the points of agreement and disagreement. But once disagreements are discovered, the course of further conversation should be controlled by the issues on which men hold clearly opposed views.

Aware that a good discussion of basic issues frequently ends without agreement, we are prepared to admit that disagreement about fundamental matters will probably continue to prevail. Yet we expect a good discussion to clarify our differences, even when it fails to resolve them, and to bring about mutual understanding and a finer interplay of minds.

When our deepest convictions are at stake, we can hardly be satisfied with conversation that is just an exchange of opinions. Such talk tends to be desultory, even when it is about trivial matters. Who is not familiar with the experience described by the painter Degas? "We exchanged some ideas," he said, "and now I feel quite dull."

Our discussions of questions about freedom, justice, and the principles of conduct usually leave us with an uneasy sense of failure. The arguments get us nowhere, we say; nor has there even been a meeting of minds. We know, however, that these and many other fundamental questions have been discussed by the greatest thinkers in Western history. They, we assume, at least understood one another and conducted their disputes with clarity and precision.

This assumption is shared by scholars and laymen alike. Histories of thought in any field—philosophy, religion, science, politics, economics—take it for granted that the great writers throughout the centuries joined issue and carried on an intelligible dispute of their differences. Though in most cases they never met or talked with one another, and were separated in time and place and by the barriers of nationality, language and culture, they are nevertheless not regarded as isolated figures, indulging in lonely and magnificent self-expression. On the contrary, historians in any field of thought picture the great thinkers as if they were in communication, even about matters on which they did not explicitly refer to one another. They are placed side by side in agreement, or on opposite sides in disagreement, with respect to the fundamental issues which every century and every generation must face. Thus portrayed, the history of thought appears to be a history of controversy which, whatever its faults, presents us with the best example of men discussing their differences.

It was Scott Buchanan who, in 1927, first proposed that the diverse philosophies of the West be conceived "as if they were voices in the great conversation that has been going on for the last three thousand years."[1] He expressed an idea that others had had before, but the phrase "the great conversation" conveys in a striking manner what all of us have in mind when we imagine the history of thought as a magnificent debate. It epitomizes Professor Arthur O. Lovejoy's insight that "dialogue, discussion, the pursuit of truth through the interaction of two or more minds—this is the very essence of [the] method"[2] by which men must think about basic ideas. This continuing process Professor E. A. Burtt has described as "the sociable enterprise of philosophic debate."[3]

The idea of the great conversation provides us with a bold but inspiring view of the cultural heritage which liberal education tries to transmit from generation to generation. In terms of it, we can see that the cultural pluralism of the West—its tolerance of a variety of beliefs about fundamental subjects—need not destroy our sense of its unity. As the prime contributors to Western thought, those who participated in the great conversation discoursed on the common themes or problems that have been persistent topics of that conversation across the centuries. By regarding these topics as the meeting places of minds that differ, we can find one continuous and coherent tradition in the history of Western thought, in spite of all the disagreements it contains. The threads of the great conversation supply the unifying warp through which intellectual differences have woven an intelligible and coherent pattern.

If a great debate has been going on in the great books of Western thought, each generation can find there the instruction it needs concerning the basic issues that confront men in every age, as well as the starting points for its own original thinking about those issues. What better way is there for us to take account of both the unity and the diversity of our culture, and to reap the intellectual heritage it affords us? Hence the proposal that the reading and discussion of the great books should be an essential part of liberal education for everyone, in school and after. The idea behind that proposal was the conception of the great conversation—as something to be listened to first, and then participated in.

When, in 1952, the Encyclopædia Britannica published *Great Books of the Western World* as an instrument of liberal education, it was highly appropriate that the first of the fifty-four volumes should be an introductory essay on the great conversation.[4] It was no less appropriate that the second and third volumes should be an effort to make the great conversation more accessible to readers by providing them with something like a map of the ideas, the problems, and the issues that the Great Books discussed. These two volumes, which I edited, were called *The Great Ideas* or *Syntopicon.*

The *Syntopicon,* as the name suggests, consists in an orderly collection of topics, each a subject of discussion by the great writers of the West. We found writers in all centuries discussing the same fundamental themes, even writers as dissimilar as Dostoevsky and Thomas Aquinas, or Freud and Plato. The variety of those themes can be briefly indicated by listing some of the ideas under which they fall: art, beauty, chance, constitution, democracy, duty, God, good and evil, government, happiness, honor, immortality, justice, knowledge, labor, law, liberty, love, man, matter, mind, nature, opinion, pleasure and pain, progress, religion, sin, slavery, state, time, truth, virtue and vice, war and peace, wealth, wisdom, world. To the questions raised by such ideas, the Great Books and other books of signal importance in the Western tradition offer a wide variety of answers, which are indexed in the *Syntopicon.* The relevance of these answers to one another seems to be as plain as their diversity.

When, after eight years of work, in which a large research staff cooperated, we completed the *Syntopicon,* I felt that we had demonstrated the existence of the great conversation. "If the notion of the great conversation had been a myth," I wrote, "the *Syntopicon* could not have been constructed at all. To say that these two volumes of *The Great Ideas* make possible a syntopical reading of the great books, is to say also that they bear witness to the actuality of the great conversation."[5]

In the great conversation, there are many controversies, many disputed issues. These controversies can be constructed out of the raw materials to be found in the *Syntopicon.* The method to be employed in contrasting them and appraising the truth to be found in them is dialectic. In order to understand this method, we must first consider the nature of dialectical truth, then what is involved in dialectical neutrality, and finally the idea of dialectic itself. But before we do that, it is proper to state, in summary fashion, the aim we pursue by such a method, and the result that can be achieved by a successful employment of it.

Through dialectical inquiry, regarded in the most comprehensive terms, we can appraise ourselves of the extent and character of the agreements that are possible among men who disagree about what is true. That is our aim, briefly stated, and the result we seek to produce.

II. Dialectical truth

Let us first, in showing how this can be done, consider the nature of dialectical truth—in particular, and by way of illustration, the discussion of law. When the dialectician succeeds in constructing the controversies about law, both special and general, which he finds implicit in the literature of that subject, he knows from his formulations the points at issue, or the matters about which conflicting claims of truth are made. For example, the legal naturalists who claim truth for their views about law are opposed by the legal positivists who make a similar claim for their contrary views. The dialectician knows that certain authors are in nonagreement simply because they do not discuss the same subject; and that other authors, who can be construed as taking the same side of this or that issue, are in categorical agreement. Together they claim truth for the same views about law.

If we overlook for a moment such categorical agreements, it would appear that the chief effect of the dialectician's construction of a controversy is to indicate how men are divided, either in their disagreement about what is true in fact or in their nonagreement about the subject to be considered. But that is far from being the whole story. Before a controversy was made to emerge by a dialectical clarification of the discussion of law, that discussion showed how men are divided by the diversity of their conceptions or views. The constructed controversy not only shows more plainly how they are divided, but in addition it also shows how they are united. It reveals the things they can agree about in spite of all the things they do not agree about.

They can agree on the description of the subjects about which they disagree in various ways. They can agree about the questions at issue on which they take opposite sides. They can agree about the content of the issues—the statement of the positions that are opposed. They can even agree about the connection of one issue with another, though in debating these issues they may argue against one another, as each reasons from the position he takes on the one to the position he takes on the other.

Their agreement on all these matters still permits them to disagree categorically about what is true in fact; more than that, they could not disagree at all unless they were in agreement in at least the first three of these four ways. But when men disagree, we regard them as differing about what is true. So, too, we must regard them as sharing some truth when they agree. What, then, is the nature of the truth they share when they agree in every way short of agreeing categorically on what is true in fact about the subject under discussion?

The answer is that such agreements are about what is dialectically true of the subject under discussion, in contradistinction to what is doctrinally true about that subject.

The naturalists' *doctrine* of law contradicts the positivists' *doctrine* of law at many points. On those points, one doctrine must be true in fact and the other false. Whichever is true as a doctrine is true in the sense that it accords with the facts or realities of the subject—in this case law.

But, divided as they are by their conflicting claims of truth for opposed doctrines, legal naturalists and positivists can together affirm such *dialectical truths* as the following: (i) that human law as the subject under consideration can be described as a body of violable man-made rules of conduct enforceable by the state through sanctions for disobedience; (ii) that the question "Should positive law be based on natural law?" is a question to be answered; (iii) that taking opposite sides on the issue raised by this question has a bearing on the position to be taken on other issues about human law, such as the issues about its sanctions, its justice, its authority, etc. The truth of these statements about law, to which the disputants can agree, is unaffected by whether or not the naturalists' or the positivists' doctrine of law is true.

The foregoing exemplifies the general relation that obtains between (a) the dialectical truths to which disputants in a controversy can agree, and (b) the soundness or accuracy of the dialectician's construction of that controversy. If the dialectician's hypothesis about the discussion of law is tenable or, better, is the hypothesis most probable in the light of the observable facts of that discussion, then the soundness or accuracy of each of his constructive statements indicates a dialectical truth about law that can be shared by those who disagree doctrinally about it. Though he adds not one iota to the doctrinal truth about law, the dialectician can be credited with uncovering a large number of dialectical truths about it when he has succeeded in constructing a generally acceptable hypothesis about the discussion of that subject.[6]

The reason for this relation is not far to seek. The dialectician's constructive statements indicate the dialectical truths on which the disputants in a controversy can agree, precisely because his formulations are neutral with respect to the truth and falsity of opposed *doctrines* or theories. Only to the extent that the dialectician's constructions accommodate, without prejudice or embarrassment, the variety of doctrines that appear in a discussion, do they have the neutrality requisite for uncovering dialectical truth.

III. Dialectical neutrality

Neutrality is not a virtue exclusively possessed or displayed by the dialectician. It is exercised by others who do not normally look upon themselves in that way. It is, for example, a virtue which the encyclopedist regards as a necessity of his profession; it is also displayed by the historian of ideas who wishes to preserve the purity of his historical approach to controversial subjects by maintaining his detachment from the truth or falsity of the theories, of which he aims to give only a historical account. Though the encyclopedist and the historian are not professed dialecticians, the neutrality they try to achieve is, nevertheless, like that of the professional.[7]

Nor is impartiality an ideal only for those who are engaged in reporting other men's thought. It is also the ideal of the thinker, insofar as he is concerned with the thought of other men in relation to his own. This holds for every field—history and science as well as theology and philosophy. Anyone who proposes a theory for which he claims truth is obligated to consider the rival claims of other theories. Wherever such rivalry makes anyone a partisan for the view he holds against the partisan views held by others, such partisanship needs to be supplemented by impartiality in order to get at what is dialectically true about the disputed matters.

Some philosophers have shown themselves able to achieve a modicum of impartiality in their understanding of theories they reject. Such impartiality, whenever and to whatever extent it is achieved, is akin to the neutrality that is essential to the dialectician. In a sense, the philosopher who manages to be impartial in his treatment of theories he rejects as false does so by functioning like a dialectician. It may be thought that in this respect he does not differ from the historian of ideas or the encyclopedist who also manages to be impartial toward the views he is considering. But to say no more than this would be to overlook a crucially significant difference between them.

The historian of ideas and the encyclopedist are not *as such* engaged in propounding philosophical theories of their own. But the philosopher, precisely in virtue of being a philosopher, takes that to be his principal task. To combine being a philosopher with being something of a dialectician requires the individual, who would try to do both, to overcome a tension between two different kinds of work that does not exist in the case of the historian and the encyclopedist. That is why it is more difficult for one man to be both a philosopher and a dialectician or, what is even harder, to be equally good at both tasks. Hence it can be said that the pursuit of truth requires a division of labor, not only to get the dialectical task itself done well, but also to enable philosophers, assisted by the independent work of dialecticians, to achieve more fully the impartiality that philosophers themselves acknowledge as ideal.[8]

But we are here concerned with quite another problem, the reverse of the problem of combining partisanship with impartiality. The question is whether impartiality can be separated from all partisanship. There are really two questions here. (1) Does the dialectician's effort to be neutral require him to be totally without any doctrinal commitments, totally devoid of any point of view of his own? And (2) can anyone who is concerned with truth be so completely detached or open-minded?

Let us acknowledge at once that a completely open mind is the mind of an infant, not a man. To be completely without commitments is an unearthly and inhuman state of intellectual innocence. Since the dialectician is ordinary flesh and blood, the answer to the first question cannot be that dialectical neutrality requires the dialectician as a person to achieve absolute point-of-viewlessness or complete detachment from every vestige of philosophical doctrine. There is no reason why a man who engages in dialectical work should not have philosophical views of his own. In fact, if philosophizing is the general vocation of every man regardless of his more specialized profession, the man who engages in dialectical work is no more exempt from this common calling than is the physician or the engineer, the scientist or the historian.

Nor can there be any question whether it is possible for the dialectician to achieve the neutrality requisite for his work in spite of his own personal philosophical views, whatever they may be. We have already affirmed that, though difficult, it is certainly possible for the philosopher to combine an impartial understanding of his adversaries with partisanship for his own point of view.

In one sense, it should be easier for the dialectician, because he is more nearly in the position of the engineer or the physician. Philosophizing may be his vocation as a man, but it is not part of his work. He can perform his tasks as a dialectician, just as the engineer and the physician can perform their professional duties, without having to be active partisans for a particular philosophical point of view. The professional philosopher, on the other hand, cannot do his work without being an active partisan for the philosophical theories or doctrines he holds to be true.

In another sense, the dialectician faces a greater difficulty. Impartiality may be an ultimate ideal for the philosopher to aim at, but he can do his work without achieving it or even if he only approximates it to some degree. As history amply shows, a man may be a great philosopher in the originality and power of his work and, at the same time, have failed signally to combine impartiality with his partisanship. Impartiality, in other words, is an ideal for the philosopher, not a basic necessity. But it is a basic necessity for the dialectician, not an ideal. Unless he can maintain neutrality throughout every phase of his work, he cannot produce the result his method aims at.

These things being so, the problem is not whether the dialectician can maintain the neutrality that is indispensable to his work in spite of having some philosophy of his own. The real problem is whether the assumptions implicit in the dialectician's method and aim bring him inevitably into conflict with certain points of view. If that were the case, then the very use of the method itself would elicit from certain quarters the charge that the dialectician cannot accommodate all points of view without prejudice or embarrassment to some of them, at least.

To estimate the seriousness of this problem, let us consider a few of the most obvious cases in which the exponent of a certain point of view might object to the dialectician's attempt to treat his doctrine, on the grounds that the dialectical method itself inevitably violates its integrity.

The extreme skeptic, for example, might say that the dialectical method assumes that incompatible positions cannot both be true and that, when these are contradictory, one must be true and the other false. This assumption the extreme skeptic rejects. According to his position on truth, either no opinion is true or false or all opinions are equally true or equally false. If the dialectician were to construct the controversy implicit in the discussion of truth itself, the skeptical position would be one he would have to represent on certain basic issues. But this, the skeptic claims, is precisely what he cannot do, at least not fairly, because his method requires him to treat the skeptic's position as if it were either true or false. To treat it that way is to misrepresent the skeptic's intention.

The trouble is not that the dialectician as a person holds a point of view contrary to that of the skeptic. The fact that he personally holds a theory of democracy, law, or freedom that is contrary to certain points of view represented in the controversies on those subjects need not prevent him from preserving neutrality in his treatment of them. However difficult that may be, humanly speaking, it is by no means impossible. But if his method itself requires him to override or distort what is essential to a doctrine, like that of the skeptic, then it is absolutely impossible for him to apply that method to the doctrine and at the same time to claim that the doctrine has been treated with the requisite neutrality.[9]

The mystic, to take another example, might raise an objection more general than the skeptic's. He might say that the dialectical method assumes that discursive thought is the only approach to knowing the truth. It is, therefore, able to deal only with thought that proceeds in terms of definitions and propositions, premises and conclusions, and the whole apparatus of analysis and reasoning or argumentation. But the mystic's approach to reality is by intuition or vision—an immediate grasp of the whole without analysis or dissection of any sort, a knowledge of truth that can be expressed without resort to any of the logical articulations involved in discursive thought. Hence if the dialectician were to construct a controversy about any subject on which the mystic claims to have insight, he could not represent what the mystic claims to know without distorting it. The dialectical method itself would make it impossible for him to be fair in his treatment of the mystic.

In the foregoing example, the conflict seems to be one between the general methodological assumptions of the dialectician and a methodology (if one can speak of the "method" of a mystic) that denies those assumptions. The mystic is not the only one who might raise an objection of this sort. A similar objection might be raised by any philosopher whose method involves a logic which either transforms or transcends the principles of ordinary logic, such as the familiar "laws of thought"—the laws of identity, excluded middle, and contradiction.

The objecting philosopher can with justice point out that the logic of controversy, which underlies the dialectician's method of constructing one, presupposes (a) that a subject of discussion can be identified and thereafter retain its identity unchanged throughout a prolonged and varied consideration of it; (b) that the answers to a given question are either compatible or incompatible; and (c) that if they are incompatible, either they are contradictory and so exclude a middle ground, or they are not and so permit other alternatives. But according to the method of the objecting philosopher, contradictory positions are seldom if ever exhaustive and exclusive. Their antithetical points can be reconciled in a synthesis that embraces both and includes the partial truths they represent.

Therefore, by its acknowledged logical assumptions, the dialectical method inevitably violates a philosophy whose method does not honor those assumptions. In constructing any controversy in which that philosophy should be treated as an important point of view, the dialectician cannot accord it the treatment its own method demands.

Closely related to the objection just considered is the objection of the philosopher who insists that the only way his doctrine can be understood is as a whole. To treat any part of it in isolation as a position which can be understood in separation from the systematic context of the whole is to distort the meaning of that part. Yet the dialectician's method of constructing a controversy requires him always to represent the position an author takes on a particular issue, in isolation from that author's whole philosophy. He can never bring an author's whole philosophy to bear on a particular issue. In constructing each issue, he can only formulate positions that are opposed answers to the particular question at issue. He must, therefore, do injustice to any philosophy whose proponent insists that his views on particular subjects cannot be fairly treated when they are wrenched from the whole of which they are integral parts.[10]

Finally, since the dialectician's method involves him in dealing with the language of thinkers, not for its own sake but for the sake of comparing their thought, he may meet objections from still another quarter. Concerning language in relation to thought or meaning, the presuppositions of his method are (a) that men can have the same conceptions or meanings in mind even when they use quite different words; (b) that they can have different conceptions or meanings in mind even when they use the same words; and (c) that it is possible to discover which is the case from the way in which they employ whatever words they use. In addition, that phase of his method by which he identifies general subjects of discussion, like democracy, freedom, or law, assumes that the words that name such subjects refer to objects of thought that have reality.

These assumptions underlying his method might be challenged by those who hold that language can be made to serve as a medium of emotional or practical communication, but that it sets up an almost insuperable barrier to intellectual communication; and who, in addition, maintain that when words do not refer to particular things, they can only refer to other words or to fictions in the mind itself. From their point of view, the dialectical method rests on a questionable metaphysics if it assumes that two men who are discussing democracy, for example, are referring to anything other than the word itself or the ideas each has in his own mind.

It might be said in reply that the method of the semanticist also rests on a questionable metaphysics if it assumes that when two men are talking and thinking about democracy in general, there is no reality whatsoever to which their words and conceptions refer (except, perhaps, such particular things as the democracy of Athens or of the United States, which they were *not* discussing). But far from removing the objection, this reply makes it clear. The semanticist's objection is precisely that the dialectical method cannot impartially treat his view of language and thought, since the dialectician's use of language rests on a contrary view. In constructing controversies on subjects to which the semanticist's view might be relevant, the dialectician cannot use his method and still remain neutral to all relevant points of view.

The foregoing examples of conflict between certain points of view and points of view implicit in the dialectical method itself may not exhaust all the typical cases in which the dialectician's neutrality seems to be destroyed or impaired by his own method. But even if an exhaustive enumeration of such cases had been made, it would still represent a small set of exceptional instances. In other words, the dialectician is not embarrassed by his method in handling most of the points of view with which he must deal on most of the subjects he wishes to treat. That still leaves these exceptions to be considered as a limitation or a blemish on the method, for which the dialectician might otherwise be inclined to claim universal scope or the possibility of unqualified success.

Confronted with these exceptions, the dialectician seems to have only two alternatives. (1) In order to preserve his neutrality unimpaired, he can concede the limited applicability of his method. It cannot be applied to all points of view on every subject, but only to those that are unaffected by the application of the method itself. (2) In order to achieve universal scope or comprehensiveness of application, he can explicitly acknowledge that his method is prejudicial to certain points of view. When he treats these points of view, he can compensate to some extent for his inevitable loss of neutrality by acknowledging it. On either alternative, the fact remains that the dialectician must, like any other investigator, pay a certain price for the use of his method.[11]

As between these alternatives, the dialectician does not need to make a fixed and unalterable choice. It might conceivably be prudent for him to adopt the first procedure in dealing with a subject like truth or language and omit any reference to the skeptic or the semanticist whose views he cannot treat with the requisite neutrality. But in treating a subject like democracy, law, or freedom, the other choice might be wiser; that is, to treat all relevant points of view even if the method of treating some of them distorts them somewhat, but calling attention, of course, to what is prejudicial in the treatment.

One subject that has not so far been mentioned might be thought to raise special difficulties for the dialectician, and that is the nature of dialectic itself. The discussion of dialectic across the centuries contains various, apparently conflicting, theories of what dialectic is and what it does.

IV. Theories of dialectic

A theory of dialectic is, like a theory of science or of art, a philosophical theory. If the dialectician has a conception of dialectic itself, in addition to having and using a certain method, he does so in virtue of being a philosopher, not a dialectician. On the other hand, his conception of dialectic must square with the principles and objectives of his method. We have already seen that his method commits him to certain philosophical positions—about truth, human reason, the laws of thought, language and meaning. It also commits him to a certain theory of dialectic.

If theories of dialectic are philosophical theories, and if the dialectical method we have been describing is applicable to the diversity of philosophical theories about any subject, then it should be applicable to the apparently conflicting theories of dialectic which are to be found in the discussion of that subject. But the fact that the method commits its user to one of these theories would seem to impair, if not destroy, the neutrality he is obligated to preserve. Here is a case, therefore, where prudence might recommend not venturing on the unfeasible—a dialectically neutral treatment of dialectic.

Let us, however, risk the imprudence and see what can be said about the diverse theories of dialectic. The most likely hypothesis is that these theories only *appear* to be in conflict but are actually in nonagreement rather than disagreement. In the name of dialectic, they are really treating three different things and therefore cannot disagree. This does not exclude the possibility that those who are talking about the same theory of dialectic may disagree among themselves.

To apply the foregoing hypothesis in detail to the whole discussion of dialectic would require us to do extensive research. But, perhaps, that is not necessary for our present purposes. It may suffice to sketch the general outlines of the hypothesis from such acquaintance as we already have with the historic discussion of dialectic.[12]

Our hypothesis is that the word *dialectic* is used in the literature by three distinct groups of theories. Each group of theories may include diverse and even conflicting conceptions of dialectic, but we are immediately concerned with the subject that each group of theories is considering. How shall these three subjects, each called "dialectic," be identified?

We can identify one by saying that certain authors who use the word *dialectic* have in mind the process of philosophical inquiry itself together with the kind of knowledge in which such inquiry results. Let us refer to the subject thus identified as "noetic dialectic," because all conceptions of this subject regard it as a unique way of knowing reality. Plato's conception of dialectic, in those passages in *The Republic* in which he identifies dialectic with philosophy as knowledge of the ultimate realities, is the archetypical representative of this group of theories.[13]

We can identify a second by saying that certain authors who use the word *dialectic* have in mind the fundamental laws that govern all processes of development in nature and history, such laws as the unity of opposites, the transformation of quantity into quality, and the negation of the negation. Let us refer to the subject thus identified as "regulative dialectic," because all conceptions of this dialectic regard it, not only as a way of knowing reality, but also as the way reality itself behaves according to the dialectical principles that regulate its processes.[14] Hegel's conception of dialectic is, in one sense, the leading representative of this group of theories, though it must be added at once that the Marxist conception, while following that of Hegel, is also its leading opponent.[15]

We can identify a third subject by saying that certain authors who use the word *dialectic* have in mind a method auxiliary to philosophy by which men think about things, not as they are in themselves, but as they are reflected in human thought. Let us refer to the subject thus identified as "reflexive dialectic," because all conceptions of this dialectic regard it, not as a way of knowing reality directly nor as the regulation of reality itself, but as an independent discipline, separate from philosophy, which deals reflexively with all the things that philosophy deals with directly. It deals with them only as they appear in the context of diverse philosophical theories or doctrines. Aristotle's statement that "dialectic is merely critical where philosophy claims to know" is typical of this group of theories.[16]

The conception of dialectic set forth in this article clearly belongs to the third group of theories. Dialectic, as we have been treating it, is not identical with philosophy as knowledge of reality, nor is it even one of the methods of conducting philosophical inquiry. It could hardly be mistaken for the inner logic of reality itself, whose laws regulate all developments in nature, history, and thought. It might, however, be thought to resemble logic insofar as the science or art of logic also deals with thought; but unlike formal logic, it is not a science of the forms of thought; and unlike the art of logic, it is not a method of correct thinking. It is none of these. It is simply a method of dealing with what men have actually thought on the wide variety of fundamental subjects about which they manifestly differ in their views.

Before we consider how this conception of dialectic relates to Aristotle's conception of the same subject, let us first examine the three subjects that we have just identified. They are clearly distinct. In this respect, they are like man-made law, natural law, and divine law. Just as those who discuss only man-made law are simply in nonagreement with those who discuss only divine law, so those who consider only noetic dialectic or only regulative dialectic are in nonagreement with those who consider only reflexive dialectic. But in the case of law, there is disagreement as to whether there is only one kind of law or more. Some, for example, hold that man-made law is the only law, and deny that "natural law" is law or a kind of law, while others affirm that natural law and man-made law are both law, though of different kinds. Is there a similar disagreement about dialectic and its kinds?

There does not seem to be. Unlike theories of law, no theory of dialectic holds, for example, that regulative and reflexive dialectic are two kinds of dialectic. No author can be construed as asserting that some two or all three of these subjects, all bearing the name "dialectic," must belong to one general class as kinds. Hence no issue about kinds of dialectic can be constructed.

In the absence of controversy about dialectic in general and in the absence of disagreement about its kinds, exponents of the three major types of theory are simply in nonagreement. Each is concerned with a different subject. Yet all bear the same name. A question arises, therefore, about the name itself. Does it connote any elements that are common to the three distinct subjects?

Any generic characterization of dialectic would probably mention at least two things as common to noetic, regulative, and reflexive dialectic: (1) some principle whereby a diversity is unified or opposites are reconciled;[17] and (2) the assumption that dialectic effects or facilitates the achievement of truth. But no one claims that this, or any other, generic characterization of dialectic identifies a general class, of which noetic, regulative, and reflexive dialectic are kinds. On the other hand, no proponent of a particular theory of dialectic would accept the two points stated above as sufficiently precise to identify the dialectic he is trying to define. What significance, then, does such a generic characterization have?

The answer would seem to be that it throws light on what is at least the nominal agreement that exists among those who discuss dialectic. It explains how they all happen to use one word to designate the different subjects they are writing about. Thus used, that word is not as plainly equivocal as is the word *bull* when it is used to refer to an animal and a proclamation. Some threads of common meaning connect the three uses of the word. But the word may have some systematic ambiguity even though there is no controversy about dialectic in general nor about its kinds, at least not between exponents of one major type of theory and exponents of another.[18]

This fact has critical significance for the theory of dialectic set forth in these pages. It means that there is no need to defend the dialectic with which we have been concerned against theories of noetic or regulative dialectic, for they on their part do not deny the possibility or validity of a reflexive dialectic. It also means that we can apply our own dialectical method to different theories of dialectic in the same way that we can to other problems, for the fact that the method commits its user to one of these theories does not impair its neutrality. The theory of reflexive dialectic does not challenge the validity of the other theories of dialectic since these deal with different subjects. The hypothesis that exponents of the three major types of theory are simply in nonagreement is not prejudicial to the sense or truth of any of them.[19]

One problem remains, which we mentioned earlier but postponed. It is the problem of the relation between the conception of dialectic set forth in this article and Aristotle's conception of the same subject. The identification of that subject as a reflexive dialectic—a method of considering the content of thought itself—is acceptable to both theories. But do they, considering this same subject, (i) conceive it differently? If they do, (ii) must we regard them as offering incompatible definitions of dialectic? And if we have to construct a definitional issue, (iii) can we do so in a neutral manner?

The embarrassment of the third question can be avoided if the two conceptions of reflexive dialectic are not incompatible. It is certainly possible for them to be different without being incompatible, for one may simply be more complete and precise than the other. The more adequate conception can then be regarded as including rather than rejecting the less adequate conception. Unless the exponents of the less adequate conception insisted upon its adequacy as stated, no issue would arise between them and the exponents of the more adequate conception, for they would see that both held the same one, the latter in an improved form.

Let us, then, compare the two conceptions—the Aristotelian conception and the conception presented in this article. Because both regard dialectic as reflexive, both are concerned with the diversity of views that men hold on any subject. Since both conceive dialectic as a method of dealing, not with reality itself, but with the subjects of human thought, it is inevitable that both should be concerned with conflicts of opinion, apparent or real; for the realm of thought is the place where all contraries coexist. Finally, both agree that dialectic, while not itself a method of philosophical inquiry or a way of knowing reality, is auxiliary to philosophy and serves the philosopher in his pursuit of truth about the reality or nature of things.[20]

How, then, do they differ? The difference between the two conceptions must be said to lie in how they further specify the purpose of the dialectical method and its use. Is the method to be used (1) by a participant in discussion, and for the sake of getting at the doctrinal truth of the matter under consideration, or (2) by an observer of discussion, and for the sake of getting at the dialectical truth about the controversy that such discussion involves?

The dialectical method proposed in this article clearly takes the second alternative. Its primary aim, in constructing the controversy that is implicit in a diversity of views, is to get at the dialectical, not the doctrinal, truth about the subject under discussion.[21] Because this is its aim, detachment from all competing doctrines and neutrality with respect to them are essential to its proper use. Such detachment and neutrality are usually better maintained by an observer of discussion than by a participant in it.

To be different, the Aristotelian conception of dialectic would have to take the first alternative, and this in fact it appears to do. If that alternative makes the dialectical method essentially polemical and partisan, then the two conceptions are not only different but are also clearly opposed; for, on this hypothesis, they would attribute contrary properties to a reflexive dialectic. One and the same method cannot be both essentially neutral and polemical; it cannot be simultaneously used for nonpartisan and partisan purposes.

The hypothesis stated above must be rejected. It violates what is common to the two conceptions, however else they differ; namely, that dialectic is auxiliary to the philosopher in his pursuit of truth. Thus, no theory of reflexive dialectic can consistently conceive such dialectic as purely polemical and wholly partisan. Insofar as a method is purely polemical in its aim and partisan in its use, it may assist its user stubbornly to maintain the truth he claims for his own doctrine; it may help him to win forensic victories over his opponents; but far from assisting him in getting at the doctrinal truth about things, it will probably prevent him from doing so if any part of the truth resides in some doctrine other than his own. A philosopher's loyalty is to the truth no matter where it resides, not to the claims of truth he has made for his own doctrine. If the ultimate objective of a particular individual is to maintain the truth of his own doctrine at all costs, then he is no philosopher.

Hence it follows that a method which is polemical and partisan, in the extreme sense indicated above, does not meet the first requirement of any theory of reflexive dialectic. Polemic defeats rather than promotes the ultimate objectives of philosophical inquiry. Indulgence in polemics on all sides degrades discussion and prevents fruitful debate from ever emerging when men appear to differ.

These things being so, we return to the question of how Aristotle's conception of the dialectical method differs from the one set forth in this article. We have already pointed out that Aristotle conceives the method with which he is concerned as an instrument to be used by a participant in discussion, and with the primary aim of getting at the doctrinal truth about matters on which there is an apparent or real difference of opinion. If the participant is a philosopher, not a sophist or a merely disputatious person seeking a forensic triumph, his being a participant will not make his use of the method purely polemical and partisan.[22]

He will try as a philosopher to temper his partisanship with some effort at fairness and impartiality in his treatment of conflicting views. Nevertheless, he remains a partisan of the particular doctrine to which he is attached. Detachment from all conflicting doctrines is not, therefore, essential to his use of dialectic; nor, in Aristotle's conception, need the philosopher as dialectician attempt to achieve such a thoroughgoing neutrality. His primary aim is not to get at the dialectical truth about a controversy but rather at the doctrinal truth about the matters in dispute, and though he may try to defend the truth of his own doctrine, he remains hospitable to whatever elements of truth can be found elsewhere.[23]

As used by the philosopher for doctrinal, but not polemical, purposes, dialectic, according to Aristotle, is critical or exploratory. The philosopher uses it to explore, from the point of view of his own doctrine, the diversity of views on whatever subject he is treating. He uses it critically to examine and weigh divergent opinions, in order to take from them whatever truth he can find and thus perfect the truth of his own doctrine. Aristotle himself exemplifies such use of dialectic when he undertakes "to call into council the views of those of our predecessors who have declared any opinion on this subject, in order that we may profit by whatever is sound in their suggestions and avoid their errors."[24]

The difference between the two conceptions being clear, one question remains. Are the two theories of reflexive dialectic opposed? Do they advance incompatible definitions of one and the same subject? Only if the two theories exclude one another are we faced with the embarrassing question of whether we can use our own method to construct in a thoroughly neutral manner the resultant issue about the definition of dialectic.

In the light of what has been said, two hypotheses suggest themselves, on neither of which are we faced with that embarrassing question. The first hypothesis is that each of the theories defines a distinct kind of reflexive dialectic. The second hypothesis is that there is only one kind of reflexive dialectic, of which one of the two theories offers a more explicit and adequate conception than the other. Let us consider these two hypotheses in turn.

On the first hypothesis, the two kinds of reflexive dialectic would be distinguished by their primary aim and use. To name the kind of dialectic with which Aristotle is concerned, we can use the key word in Aristotle's description of it—"critical." In contrast, "constructive" is the key word in the description we have given of the other kind of reflexive dialectic. A critical dialectic deals with the diversity of views from the point of view of a doctrine that itself contributes to the diversity; a constructive dialectic deals with diversity without attachment to any particular point of view. Whereas the primary aim of one is to get at doctrinal truth, though it may incidentally uncover some dialectical truth, the primary aim of the other is to discover dialectical truth, while at the same time indirectly serving the philosopher's main quest of doctrinal truth. Complete neutrality is, therefore, not essential to the one as it is to the other.[25]

On this hypothesis, the two conceptions, each of a different kind of dialectic, are not opposed. They are no more incompatible than are the conceptions of human and divine law, for instance, when it is granted that these are two kinds of law. But would the proponents of these two conceptions be willing to grant that each defines a distinct kind belonging to the same general class, characterized as reflexive dialectic? There seems to be no reason why proponents of the Aristotelian theory would not admit that it defines only one of two possible kinds. We, on our part, can also accept the hypothesis that, while having certain generic features in common, a critical and a constructive dialectic are distinct kinds, differentiated by their primary objectives and by the way in which they are used. Yet we have one reason for favoring a different hypothesis.

This other hypothesis lays greater emphasis on what is common to the two theories. Both regard the dialectical method as *auxiliary* to the philosophical pursuit of truth about the nature of things. Its ultimate purpose is to assist the philosopher in ascertaining the doctrinal truth about any matter under consideration. Now if dialectic is not itself a method of philosophical inquiry, which both theories admit, then perhaps it can be said that its primary objective should be to get at dialectical truth through the construction of the controversy that is implicit in a diversity of views about a particular subject. For this primary purpose, complete neutrality is essential, whether the method is used by a dialectical observer or by a philosophical participant in the discussion. To be a dialectician, in other words, the philosophical participant must become, for a time at least, as detached and impartial as he could be if he were merely an observer.

According to this hypothesis, the theory of the dialectical method as essentially constructive and neutral offers the more explicit and adequate conception of what a reflexive dialectic should be. Insofar as the procedure is seen as critical rather than constructive, and insofar as impartiality is recommended rather than made obligatory, the conception of the method fails to make explicit and definite what is essential to dialectic as auxiliary to philosophy. A critical method, used directly for doctrinal purposes, is not a distinct kind of reflexive dialectic. It represents only a stage in the development of a constructive method, used directly for dialectical purposes and only indirectly for the attainment of doctrinal truth.

This hypothesis about the relation of the two theories seems to us preferable for the basic reason that dialectical rather than doctrinal truth should be the immediate and primary objective of a method which is admittedly dialectical rather than philosophical, because it is not itself a method of philosophical inquiry but only auxiliary to such inquiry. That reason, we think, justifies us in regarding the traditional statement of the Aristotelian theory as an inadequate conception of the method. It is inadequate to the extent that it fails to describe the procedure as constructive, fails to insist upon neutrality as essential, and fails to define the aim as the discovery of dialectical truth, first for its own sake, and ultimately for the sake of promoting the pursuit of doctrinal truth.

If proponents of the Aristotelian theory were to grant its inadequacy in these respects, then we would have no reason to reject the Aristotelian conception as false.[26] We would simply take the position that our more adequate conception includes their less adequate conception and improves upon it by making explicit and precise what should be said in a true definition of reflexive dialectic.

The most important consequence of having achieved the more adequate statement is the present formulation of the method itself as a method of constructing controversies with complete neutrality. Yet the truth of the conception that underlies the method by no means guarantees its workability or its production of the results at which it aims. These must be independently judged.

---

[1]Scott Buchanan, *Possibility* (New York: Harcourt, Brace & Co., 1927), pp. 180–81.

[2]"On Some Conditions of Progress in Philosophical Inquiry," Presidential Address before the American Philosophical Association in 1916, published in *The Philosophical Review* 26 (March 1917): pp. 123–63.

[3]"The Generic Definition of Philosophic Terms." In *The Philosophical Review* 62 (January 1953): pp. 42–44. "The fact that this debate goes steadily on, and that philosophers of all schools and convictions engage in it, is easily forgotten," Professor Burtt declares, "because of its ubiquitous presence."

[4]*The Great Conversation* was written by Robert M. Hutchins, who was also editor in chief of *Great Books of the Western World*. "The goal toward which Western society

moves," Hutchins declared, "is the Civilization of the Dialogue. The spirit of Western civilization is the spirit of inquiry. Its dominant element is the *Logos.* Nothing is to remain undiscussed. Everybody is to speak his mind. No proposition is to be left unexamined. The exchange of ideas is held to be the path to the realization of the potentialities of the race" (*op. cit.,* p. 1). Alfred North Whitehead once said that the history of Western thought can be viewed as a series of footnotes to Plato. To regard the West as the Civilization of the Dialogue, Hutchins suggested, is to conceive it as the ever-expanding conversation that was initiated in the West by the dialogues of Plato.

[5]*GBWW,* Vol. 3, p. 1234.

[6]Thus seen as able to discover dialectical truth about a subject, the method of the dialectician does more than transform the diversity it finds in an extended and elaborate discussion. It not only turns that diversity into clear-cut disagreements and nonagreements, but it also reveals the unity that underlies the diversity. The extent and character of that unity is made explicit by the indicated agreements on dialectical truth, just as the extent and character of the initial diversity is made explicit by the formulated disagreements and nonagreements about what is doctrinally true. Because it is based on the sharing of dialectical truth, we can speak of such unity as "dialectical unity." It is a dialectical unity that makes the whole intellectual tradition of the West the tradition of *one* culture, in spite of all its doctrinal diversity. It may even be that enough dialectical truth can be discovered to unify the diverse cultures of mankind.

[7]In his Prefatory Notice to the Ninth Edition of the *Encyclopædia Britannica,* the editor, Thomas S. Baynes, wrote that, in the conflict of opinion, "a work like the Encyclopedia is not called upon to take any direct part. . . . It cannot be the organ of any sect or party in Science, Religion, or Philosophy. Its main duty is to give an accurate account of the facts and an impartial summary of results in every department of inquiry and research" (p. viii). Referring to this statement by Baynes, Hugh Chisholm added, in the Editorial Introduction to the Eleventh Edition, that "every effort has been made to obtain, impartially, such statements of doctrine and belief in matters of religion and similar questions as are satisfactory to those who hold them, and to deal with these questions, so far as criticism is concerned, in such a way that the controversial points may be understood and appreciated, without prejudice to the argument" (p. xxi).

[8]The main reason for a division of labor is that the philosophical and the dialectical tasks are each arduous and exacting and so make demands on time and energy that it would be very difficult for a single individual to fulfill adequately. It is the tension between the pulls of two different kinds of creative work, not the impossibility of combining partisanship with impartiality, that calls for a division of labor.

[9]What is said above about the dialectician's attempt to construct the controversy about truth would hold as well for attempts to deal dialectically with the discussion of certain other subjects on which the skeptic takes an extreme position, such as knowledge or the power of human reason. It would also hold for a dialectical treatment of the discussion of the nature of philosophy, on which subject the contemporary logical positivist or semanticist holds the moderate skeptical view that science is involved with objective truth but that philosophy is not and cannot be. Since the problem about the nature of philosophy is itself a philosophical problem, the dialectician's attempt to construct a controversy about this subject would itself be prejudicial to the view held by the positivist or semanticist, for his method of doing so presumes that objective truth is at stake in philosophical issues—about philosophy or anything else.

[10]In his essay "On Some Conditions of Progress in Philosophical Inquiry," Professor Lovejoy mentions this objection to the dialectical dissection of whole philosophies, when they are treated problem by problem and issue by issue. He quotes, without naming, a colleague who said that philosophical knowledge is characterized by "its incapacity to answer any one of its problems, without anticipating in broad outline the kind of answer that has to be given to all the others. In other words, it deals with problems for which no method of successful isolation has yet been formulated. . . . The various philosophical problems cannot be treated as so many separate issues." Commenting on this, Professor Lovejoy points out, first, that only a few philosophers hold a view of philosophy that regards every philosophical issue as "inextricably intertwined with all of the others." And, second, he suggests that by a process of hypothetical reasoning, it is possible to deal piecemeal with doctrines whose exponents insist upon their irrefragable wholeness. See *The Philosophical Review* 26, 2 (March 1917): pp. 155–58.

[11]Modern physics provides us with a striking instance of the general rule that every method imposes certain limitations or has certain defects. Over a large area of the phenomena that the physicist investigates, his methods do not embarrass him in any way. But at the fringes, where he deals with astronomical speeds and distances or with subatomic quantities, the contemporary physicist explicitly recognizes that his techniques of observation affect and limit the results he can obtain. The same thing is, of course, true of the biologist who experiments with living organisms, or of the psychologist who tries to observe mental phenomena under laboratory conditions.

[12]We can, in other words, do something like what we have done in the case of law. Though we have referred to the discussion of law as an "imaginary discussion," its main lines were obviously drawn from the actual discussion of that subject. We called it "imaginary" to indicate that the dialectical hypothesis we presented was merely a sketch based on our general acquaintance with the historic discussion of law, and not a detailed working out of the hypothesis in the light of data supplied by protracted research.

[13]See *The Republic,* Book VI (511), Book VII (532–34). [*GBWW,* Vol. 7, pp. 387c, 397a–98c.] Other dialogues emphasize the method or process of knowing rather than the knowing itself; *see* the *Sophist, Statesman,* and *Philebus* [*GBWW,* Vol. 7]. Plato's identification of the philosopher with the dialectician gives rise to one conception of philosophy and its method of inquiry. According to an interesting analysis by Richard McKeon, the dialectical philosopher, in Plato's sense of "dialectical," is in method and character only one of four types, the others being characterized by other methods, which he calls "logistic," "problematic," and "operational." For McKeon's description of the dialectical philosopher, *see* his essay "Dialectic and Political Thought and Action," in *Ethics* 65, 1 (October 1954): pp. 1–33; for his classification of the four types of philosophy and philosophical method, *see* his *Thought, Action, and Passion* (Chicago: University of Chicago Press, 1954), pp. 85–88, and his *Freedom and History* (New York: Noonday Press, 1952).

[14]For Hegel, the real is the rational and the rational the real. Consequently, for Hegel, dialectic is at once the inner logic of both mind and reality; the laws of dialectic regulate the development of thought and the development of things. See *Encyclopedia of the Philosophical Sciences, Logic,* chap. 6, sec. 81. "Wherever there is movement," Hegel writes, "wherever there is life, wherever anything is carried into effect in the actual world, there Dialectic is at work. It is also the soul of all knowledge which is truly scientific." Cf. *Philosophy of Right,* Introduction, ¶31 [*GBWW,* Vol. 46, p. 19d], where Hegel says that his dialectic "is not an activity of subjective thinking applied to some matter externally, but is rather the matter's very soul putting forth its branches and fruit organically." For the full exposition of the principles of Hegel's regulative dialectic, see *The Science of Logic* and *Phenomenology of Mind.* And for Hegel's account of the history of dialectic, in which he attributes certain anticipations of his own theory to Plato and others, *see* the section cited above in the *Encyclopedia of the Philosophical Sciences,* and also his *Philosophy of History* [*GBWW,* Vol. 46].

[15]For Marx and Engels, the dialectic of nature or of history is to be found in the laws governing the transformations of matter only. Borrowing from Hegel the conception of a regulative dialectic and its laws, but differing from Hegel about whether the laws of dialectic are laws of matter or of mind, the Marxists developed what they called a "dialectical materialism." *See* F. Engels, *Dialectics of Nature* (New York, 1940); *Ludwig Feuerbach and the Outcome of Classical German Philosophy* (New York, 1934); and compare *A Textbook of Marxist Philosophy,* prepared by the Leningrad Institute of Philosophy and translated by A. C. Moseley (London, 1937).

[16]See *Metaphysics,* Book IV, chap. 2, 1004^{b}25 [*GBWW,* Vol. 8, p. 523d]. For Aristotle's conception of dialectic as "a process of criticism," *see* his *Topics;* especially Book I, chap. 2 [ibid., pp. 143d–44a], where he explains the usefulness of the method as auxiliary to philosophy. Kant's theory of dialectic is related to Aristotle's. In the passage from the *Metaphysics* quoted above, Aristotle distinguishes sophistry from philosophy as well as dialectic. "Sophistry," he writes, "is what appears to be philosophy, but is not." Kant identifies ancient dialectic with sophistry. "This art," he writes, "presented false principles in the semblance of truth, and sought, in accordance with these, to maintain things in semblance. Amongst the Greeks the dialecticians were advocates and rhetoricians who could lead the populace wherever they chose, because the populace lets itself be deluded with semblance. . . . In Logic, also, it was for a long time treated of under the name of the *Art of Disputation,* and for so long all logic and philosophy was the cultivation by

certain chatter-heads of the art of semblance" (*Introduction to Logic* [London: Longmans, Green & Co., 1885], sec. ii). Kant then goes on to say that in his own Logic he proposes to introduce "a critical examination of this semblance" or sophistry under the head of dialectic. In his *Critique of Pure Reason* [*GBWW*, Vol. 42], he called this division of his Transcendental Logic a "*Transcendental Dialectic.*"

[17]As, for example, the opposition of the One and Many in Plato's dialectic, the opposition of thesis and antithesis in Hegel's dialectic, and the opposition of conflicting theories or arguments in Aristotle's dialectic or Kant's.

[18]The word *induction* provides us with another example of the same situation. It is not completely equivocal as it is used in inductive logic and in algebra, yet those who are concerned with mathematical induction and those who are concerned with induction in the experimental sciences are simply in nonagreement. They do not think of mathematical and experimental induction as belonging to the same general class; they do not argue the question whether these two subjects are both kinds of induction.

[19]A particular individual who uses the dialectical method as auxiliary to philosophy may also be a philosopher who rejects Plato's or Hegel's theory of dialectic as a false philosophical theory of knowledge or reality. But he would do so on philosophical grounds, not because he used the dialectical method. As using the method, he is not called upon to judge the philosophical truth of these other theories of dialectic. He can, therefore, remain dialectically neutral in treating them, just as he can remain dialectically neutral in treating theories of freedom with which, *as an individual philosophizing about freedom, not as a dialectician,* he may disagree.

[20]The *Topics,* that part of his *Organon* in which Aristotle expounds the rules of dialectic as a method to be used, also contains a great deal that does not properly belong to the art or method of dialectic at all. The analysis of definitions which Aristotle gives there, and his famous classification of the types of predicates or "predicables," belongs rather to the science of logic itself, in that division of the science which Aristotle's medieval followers called "material," as opposed to "formal," logic. The justification for treating such matters in a book ostensibly devoted to an art of disputation, and to a critical method of dealing with the conflict of opinions, may be that the arguments for opposed positions often appeal to definitions and often turn on how the disputants employ their fundamental terms or predicates.

[21]The fact that its primary aim is to get at dialectical rather than doctrinal truth does not exclude all interest in the latter. On the contrary, if the discovery of dialectical truth did not ultimately serve the pursuit of doctrinal truth, the method would not be auxiliary to philosophy as a pursuit of such truth about the nature of things. But it aims at such truth indirectly, not primarily or directly.

[22]In the second chapter of Book I of the *Topics* [*GBWW*, Vol. 8, pp. 143d–44a], Aristotle distinguishes between two main uses that can be made of the art or method of dialectic. The first is the use that can be made by men generally in "casual encounters," wherein they are engaged in disputation with one another and in efforts to argue effectively or persuasively for their own views. This use of dialectic associates it with rhetoric. In fact, Aristotle declares, "rhetoric is a branch of dialectic. . . . Both are methods of providing arguments." (*Rhetoric,* Book I, chap. 2, 1356^{a}30–34 [*GBWW*, Vol. 9, pp. 595d–96a].) And in another place, he says that "all men make use of both (i.e., rhetoric and dialectic); for to a certain extent all men attempt to discuss statements and to maintain them, to defend themselves and to attack others." (Ibid., Book I, chap. 1, 1354^{a}3–6 [*GBWW*, Vol. 9, p. 593a].) This first use of dialectic—by men generally in casual encounters—verges on the disputatious or polemical. But it is also clearly distinct in Aristotle's mind from the use of dialectic by philosophers. Aristotle describes that second use as enabling the philosopher "to raise searching difficulties on both sides of a subject . . . to detect more easily the truth and error about the several points that arise." (*Topics,* Book I, chap. 2, 101^{a}34–37 [*GBWW*, Vol. 8, p. 144a].) Aristotle's dialectic is sometimes spoken of as the art of reasoning from merely probable premises in the form of widely accepted opinions or the opinions of experts, but that applies only to the use of dialectic in casual encounters and for forensic purposes. It does not apply to dialectic as a method used by philosophers to get at the doctrinal truth about a subject. If philosophers were to engage in reasoning from accepted or expert opinion, they would be arguing from authority rather than from facts and principles.

[23]This primary aim does not exclude the possibility that indirectly or incidentally the philosopher's doctrinal use of dialectic may uncover or lead to the discovery of some dialectical truths about the controversy in which he is engaged. Cf. note 21.

[24]*On the Soul,* Book I, chap. 2, 403^{b}22–24 [*GBWW,* Vol. 8, p. 633a].

[25]As we have already seen, the philosopher's doctrinal use of dialectic can and should be tempered by some effort to be impartial, or at least to avoid the unfairness and subjectivity of merely polemical criticism or refutation. In one place, Aristotle speaks of dialectic as "an art of drawing opposite conclusions *impartially.*" (*Rhetoric,* Book I, chap. 1, 1355^{a}36 [*GBWW,* Vol. 9, p. 594d].) Furthermore, his statement that the purpose of dialectic is "to raise searching difficulties on both sides of a subject" and "to detect . . . truth and error about the several points that arise" (*loc. cit.*) suggests some measure of impartiality. It is only when dialectic is used, not by the philosopher but in "casual encounters," that it is, as an art of disputation, polemical in its partisanship. Cf. note 21.

[26]We can offer one reason why proponents of the Aristotelian theory should grant, in terms of that theory itself, the inadequacy of their conception of reflexive dialectic. In their view, as well as in ours, the line between a polemical misuse of the dialectical method and a proper philosophical use of it lies in the fairness and impartiality with which the philosopher, who is making a doctrinal use of dialectic, treats the doctrines of others. If he is truly a philosopher rather than a polemicist, open to the truth wherever it is found and not just a stubborn defender of the claims he makes for the truth of his own doctrine, then he is also truly a dialectician to the extent that he achieves impartiality in his treatment of whatever philosophical diversity he finds. To recommend neutrality, but not to make it obligatory, is therefore an imperfect conception of the method. It follows also that the philosopher should not use dialectic in a merely critical manner to deal with other doctrines from the point of view of his own. He should try constructively to see the controversy in which his own doctrine is included merely as one among others.

Two Approaches to the Authors of the Great Books

Mortimer J. Adler

In certain of his dialogues, especially in the *Gorgias* and the *Sophist,* Plato is at pains to distinguish between the philosopher and the sophist or between the philosopher and the kind of rhetorician who is at heart sophistical. In his view, the criterion that separates them is the relation in which they stand to truth.

The sophist, according to Plato, attempts to win an argument regardless of whether the conclusion reached is true or not. So, too, the sophistical orator attempts to persuade an audience regardless of whether the action or attitude recommended is right or not. There may be many similarities between the method of the philosopher and the method of the sophist so far as the logical devices they employ are concerned. But they do not employ these devices for the same purpose. The philosopher employs them only and always to get at the truth. The sophist, in sharp contrast, puts them to use in order to succeed in getting others to adopt this or that view even if the view advocated is incorrect or false.

I mention this differentiation between the sophist and the philosopher as background for the distinction I wish to make between two approaches to the authors of the Great Books. One is the philosophical approach to reading and interpreting them; the other is the scholarly approach. The difference between these two readings, I would like to suggest, is that one of them has truth for its object, whereas the other does not—that in this sense the scholar is like the sophist, not because he tries to make what is false appear to be true, but because he is not for the most part concerned with whether the views or positions taken by the author under consideration are true or false.

I appreciate that in suggesting this I may seem to be putting scholarship down, though that is not my intention. For as between the philosopher and the sophist, or even one who is said to be like the sophist, the latter must sound to our ears the less noble figure. He is so because we regard him as one who seeks to gain victory—that is, to convince us of something—at any cost, and particularly at the cost of that for which the contest ought to be waged, which is truth.

We are likely to think of the sophist in this way even if, in other discussions, we subscribe to the proposition that there is no such thing as "the truth," or if we insist that, after all, there is no substitute for victory, or hold that Socrates himself was a kind of dialectical trickster who in the end was the greatest sophist of all, as his enemies said.

None of these contentions really makes us comfortable or happy with the sophist, but only defensive of him as the best that ignorance allows, or that a ruthless world affords, or as an instance of one rather low-ceilinged truth we admit, which is the truth of the great figure who has been debunked.

Of course we admire, or we should, the kind of presentation that seeks to prevail when the question of truth is beyond human capacity to decide absolutely, as in the trial of an issue of fact that cannot be reenacted, and as to which subsequent accounts differ; or the kind that a teacher adopts when he invites contention from his students on a matter of which the truth can be known, and is, but which for the moment he hides to the end that they may ferret it out themselves, for the good of the exercise (a somewhat debased version, be it said, of the "learned ignorance" that Socrates himself adopts in the Platonic dialogues); and so we admire, too, the exposition that a scholar makes when his object is to set forth the views of some writer as consistently as they will allow, to the end that they may make the best case for themselves and be best understood.

Why then our felt reservation with respect to such practices? Surely it is that they are acceptable only in special cases of one sort or another, the cases having as their common feature that in them truth is unavailable, or for didactic reasons has been temporarily suspended, or is regarded as something subject to a prior condition. Where the situation is not of this sort, we have much greater difficulty allowing sophistry, or anything like sophistry, to prevail, if we allow it at all.

Thus the lawyer who knows, or thinks he knows, that his client is guilty of the crime with which he has been charged is faced at the very least with an ethical dilemma when it comes to defending him. Similarly, whatever the devices of the teacher may be with respect to dissembling as to the truth of what he teaches, no one would say he had not some ultimate responsibility to see that it is recognized by his students, especially if they do not perceive it—if they are in fact quite misled by the pretense of ignorance or error which he has adopted.

And so with the scholar, whose summary of the opinions and arguments of the writer he has undertaken to expound we think wholly proper, indeed altogether necessary to the further task of deciding whether what the writer says is true or not—yet we say, or we should say, that our sense of that writer is incomplete when the further inquiry into the truth of what he asserts is not undertaken; and we should add that when, as sometimes happens, we are diverted by the authority of the scholarship from making any such inquiry at all, we have been badly served by it.

Where we are well served by scholarship is in the reading of difficult works, particularly those of ancient writers, which none of us could read—which could not even be translated—were it not for the patient labors of generations of scholars who have established their texts, so far as possible.

Even more recent writers who have written in our own language are such as we come to with the benefit of comments by those who have gone before, and whose interpretations form part of our own reading, though we may think it necessary on occasion to correct them, and though, having satisfied ourselves that they fairly represent what the author has said, we still must go on to decide whether or not in our judgment it has any validity. Indeed, the greater the author, the more likely he is to need rereading from time to time—by readers who perceive something in them which they did not perceive before, or which they had long since forgotten.

Nevertheless, this kind of reading is always to be distinguished from the kind that seeks to determine the truth of what an author says, or its value. For the aim of this kind of scholarly writing is never anything more (or less) than *comprehension,* and the difference between that and the philosophical reading to which I have referred is just the difference between comprehension and *judgment*—between a grasp of the statement and a conclusion as to the truth of the statement. It is because the scholarly kind of reading has as its aim the comprehension of what the author says, and not its truth, that I presume to liken it to the sophistry of which Plato wrote.

I do not mean that the scholar *is* a sophist. I mean that he is *like* one in that he is interested in something besides truth—something we may call accuracy, or consistency, or even coherence, but not truth. Because that is so, the scholar as such is never, at least in my view, a philosopher, nor is the kind of reading he gives to a scholarly task a philosophical one.

Hence I presume also to say that, the scholarly reading of a work having been completed, the philosophical one must begin, and precisely at the point where the scholarly reading leaves off—at the point where the fact of the statement (or its consistency, or coherence) has been established, but where its truth has not yet been considered.

How important philosophical reading is will be evident when we remember that the authors of the Great Books are fallible human beings, and that no matter how great they are, their works are likely to contain, in some proportion, both truth and error. We should never expect to find a great book that is completely and perfectly true, true in every principle it appeals to or in every conclusion that it reaches. Nor should we ever expect to find one that is false throughout—false in every point it makes or proposition that it advances. If that were the case, it would hardly have the status of a great book. But it could easily be a great book if it contained some admixture of truth and error, particularly if the truths it enunciates are fundamental and the errors it also contains are extremely important ones to avoid making.

With this in mind, the philosophical approach to the reading of a great author concentrates on sifting the truths to be found in his works from the errors that are also present there. Aristotle, in two passages, succinctly summarizes the essence of the philosophical approach. The first passage occurs in chapter 1 of Book II of his *Metaphysics.* There he tells us that

> The investigation of the truth is in one way hard, in another easy. An indication of this is found in the fact that no one is able to attain the truth adequately, while, on the other hand, we do not collectively fail, but everyone says something true about the nature of things, and while individually we contribute little or nothing to the truth, by the union of all a considerable amount is amassed. [*GBWW,* Vol. 8, p. 511.]

The second passage comes from chapter 2 of Book I of his treatise *On the Soul.* There he writes as follows:

> It is necessary . . . to call into council the views of . . . our predecessors . . . in order that we may profit by whatever is sound in their suggestions and avoid their errors. [*GBWW,* Vol. 8, p. 633.]

Among the authors of the Great Books, Aristotle is the one in whom I find a great many truths of fundamental importance, but I also find errors in his writings, among them two of the greatest importance—his error about the division of mankind into those who are by nature intended for freedom and those who are by nature intended for slavery, and his error about the inferiority of women to men. There are, of course, other errors in Aristotle, but many of these are errors about matters of fact that represent the inadequacy of the scientific investigation of nature in his day.

In contrast to Aristotle, I find more errors than truths in the major philosophical works of David Hume—errors of the greatest importance because they are errors in fundamental principles, which, carried out to their logical conclusions, lead to very serious consequences that ought to be avoided like the plague. I also find some truths in Hume—particularly the insight that even complete knowledge of the way things are in reality cannot yield a single conclusion about what goals human beings ought to seek in life or how they ought to be sought.

What I have just said about my reading of Aristotle and Hume is offered as an example of what I regard as a philosophical approach to the authors of the Great Books. If I had chosen other authors to comment on—Plato and Rousseau, for example—the proportion of truth to error would have been more nearly balanced than it is in the case of Aristotle and Hume; but I would still be proceeding philosophically in the same way—sifting truth from error and profiting by the discovery of both, for finding errors to be corrected is as profitable as finding truths to be espoused.

The scholarly approach to the authors named, and other authors as well, is quite different. I am acquainted with scholarly interpretations of Aristotle that, instead of rejecting his views about natural slaves and about women as flagrant errors, attempt to put them somehow in a good light. This kind of approach to Aristotle apparently proceeds on the assumption that every fundamental position in Aristotle must be regarded as having the aspect of truth, as if it were an oracular instead of a human utterance.

I am also acquainted with scholarly interpretations of Hume, of Plato, and of Rousseau, which proceed in the same way, even when the scholarly commentators do acknowledge the presence of what looks like contradictions in the authors they are writing about. They give us the impression that these contradictions must be more apparent than real, and that a deeper understanding of the author can somehow remove them.

In thus describing the scholarly approach, I am not accusing scholars of overlooking or concealing errors and contradictions that they plainly recognize. I am only asserting that the scholarly approach is controlled by the aim of putting the best face on, or seeing in the most favorable light, everything that the author being considered has to say. The aim, in short, is *apologetic* rather than *critical*. It is certainly not directed to the sifting of truths from errors, adopting the former and rejecting the latter.

Are both approaches to the reading of the great authors recommended? Do both make significant contributions to the education we seek in reading the Great Books?

My answer to these questions is affirmative. They are both to be recommended because they both do make contributions to the learning we seek in reading the Great Books. But their contributions are quite different.

The scholarly approach contributes to our understanding of a great author, usually an understanding that encompasses all or most of his writings, not just one book or another. The philosophical approach contributes to our knowledge of the truth and to the wisdom we come to possess as our knowledge of ourselves and of the world we live in is enlightened by more truth and by truths that are more fundamental than those we first understood.

On Reading Euclid

Otto Bird

Born and raised in Ann Arbor, Michigan, Otto Bird attended the university there, graduating in 1935 with honors in English. He added a master's degree in comparative literature the following year. He took his doctorate in philosophy and literature at the University of Toronto in 1939.

From 1947 to 1950 he served as associate editor of the *Syntopicon* for *Great Books of the Western World,* working with Mortimer Adler. In the latter year he joined the faculty at the University of Notre Dame, where he was director of the general program of liberal studies until 1963. He was executive editor of *The Great Ideas Today* from 1964 to 1970, when he was appointed university professor of arts and letters at Notre Dame, from which he retired in 1977. In 1986 he was distinguished visiting professor of the humanities at the University of Dallas.

He has written four books, *The Canzoné d'Amore of Guido Cavalcanti with the Commentary of Dino del Garbo* (1942), *Syllogistic Logic and Its Extensions* (1964), *The Idea of Justice* (1967), and *Cultures in Conflict* (1976), besides articles on the history and theory of the liberal arts. In addition, he was a major contributor to the *Propædia,* or Outline of Knowledge, of the current (fifteenth) edition of the *Encyclopædia Britannica.*

Mr. Bird now spends much of the year in Shoals, Indiana, where he has built a house and grows grapes for making wine. He continues to be active in editorial projects of Encyclopædia Britannica, Inc., and remains consulting editor of *The Great Ideas Today.* He has contributed to many of our volumes. His essay on Montaigne appeared last year.

The great books of mathematics and science are not read as much or as frequently as are those in other subject matters. One reason is that they are no longer living resources for the professionals working in those fields. Poets, dramatists, novelists, philosophers, theologians, all return to the works of the ancients, not only for inspiration and enlightenment, but also for principles and matter. But scientists attend to the works of their ancient predecessors only if they also happen to have an interest in the history of their discipline.

The general common reader turns to them almost as seldom, but for a still different reason: the belief that the great books of science are so specialized in subject and language that they can be read only by the specialist or one who possesses a particularly "mathematical mind." Yet this belief is in many cases a cheat, one that causes the common reader to miss rich opportunities for extending and deepening his understanding as well as for pleasure and excitement. Many of these books were composed at the very beginnings of science, when the experience from which it started was close to the experience shared by every man. Of this, the work of Euclid provides especially eloquent testimony.

Euclid's *Elements* is certainly one of the most successful books ever written. From the time of its writing, somewhere around 300 B.C., down until this twentieth century, it provided the basic text from which everyone learned mathematics if he knew any mathematics at all—and not only the pagans of ancient Greece and Rome, but Jews, Christians, and Mohammedans as well. Its value, however, is not limited to providing an entry into the world of mathematics. It also offers one of the clearest examples of the art of logical thinking. It may almost be said that from it, mankind learned what constitutes a proof.

It is also a book that is available to the common reader, even to one who has little training in mathematics. I can testify to that from my own personal experience. Having had only a high school education in mathematics, I took up the reading of Euclid some seventeen years afterward and continued it for almost a year with immense delight. Then, after another seventeen years had passed, I returned to it again, and again came to know the traces of that old flame (*Agnosco veteris vestigia flammae—Aeneid:* IV.23; *GBWW,* Vol. 13, p. 167b).

Its contents

At the start of any work, it is helpful to know what the work as a whole is about. In the case of Euclid's *Elements* such knowledge is easily acquired, for almost all of its thirteen books begin by giving definitions which lay down the subject matter to be treated, and merely by paging through the books we can obtain a good idea of their principal concerns.

Thus Book I, after preliminary definitions regarding point, line, plane surface, and angle, proceeds to define circle, triangle, and square, ending up with a definition of parallel straight lines. On paging through this first book we find that its first twenty-six propositions are mainly concerned with triangles. Proposition 27 takes up the consideration of parallel lines, and Propositions 33 through 46 deal with parallelograms, the 46th being devoted to the square. Book I ends with the Pythagorean theorem and its converse—that in right-angled triangles the square on the hypotenuse is equal to the sum of the squares on the other two sides.

Proceeding in like fashion through the remaining books, we learn what are the main concerns of the entire work, the contents of which can be summarized as follows:

I.	Of triangles mainly, also parallel lines and parallelograms	(48 Props.)
II.	Of rectangular parallelograms	(14 ")
III.	Of circles	(37 ")
IV.	Of inscribing and circumscribing one plane figure in or about another	(16 ")
V.	Of ratios and proportions	(25 ")
VI.	Of proportions in plane figures	(33 ")
VII.	Of numbers, odd, even, prime, square, cube and their proportions	(39 ")
VIII.	Of numbers in continued proportion, i.e., in geometrical progression	(27 ")
IX.	More of numbers in proportion and of primes	(36 ")
X.	Of commensurable and incommensurable magnitudes, i.e., of the rational and irrational	(115 ")
XI.	Of solid figures	(39 ")
XII.	Of the relation between solid figures	(18 ")
XIII.	Of the five regular solids	(18 ")
		(Total 465 Props.)

This table makes clear that the *Elements* as a whole divide into three distinct parts according to the matter of which they treat. Books I–VI are devoted to plane geometry, Books VII–IX to the arithmetic of whole numbers, Books X–XIII to solid geometry. Books V and X are *sui generis* in that they develop the theory of proportion that is needed for examining, first, the relation between plane figures and whole numbers, and then, that between various solid figures. It also shows and thereby corrects the sometimes mistaken notion that Euclid treats only of geometry, for the method, while geometrical throughout in that it proceeds always with reference to magnitudes represented by lines and figures, allows treatment of the theory of whole numbers or integers in Books VII–IX.

Having obtained a view of the whole, we can turn now to the actual reading of the text and begin appropriately with the beginning, that is, Book I. I shall devote more attention to this book than to any of the others and consider in some detail how it constitutes a whole by itself. In the other books I shall direct attention only to a few selected propositions that are important and interesting both in themselves and for the light they cast upon Euclid's method of doing mathematics.

The axiomatic method

This method provides perhaps the clearest example of "reason reasoning," i.e., of the process of reason itself. It has been widely accepted as constituting the best and most rigorous form for the exposition of a science. Newton adopted it for physics in his *Mathematical Principles of Natural Philosophy,* Russell and Whitehead took it for their *Principia Mathematica* of logic as well as of mathematics, and Spinoza, convinced that it provided the best form even for the exposition of philosophy, adopted it for his *Ethics.* Yet of all the examples of its use, Euclid's Book I offers the easiest and clearest introduction to an understanding of it.

Euclid was not the inventor of the method. Plato gave an outline of it in his analysis of the kinds of knowledge in the sixth book of the *Republic,* and Aristotle not only made an extensive analysis of it but also was the first actually to use it. He presented his theory of the syllogism in axiomatic form by showing how all the valid moods of the syllogism can be derived from a few taken as primary. His analysis of the method in the *Posterior Analytics* is a good introduction to a discussion of Euclid's use of it. Both Aristotle and Euclid were members of Plato's Academy, but Euclid was younger by perhaps a generation; hence there is a possibility that Euclid knew Aristotle's theory of the method.

According to the account given in the *Posterior Analytics* (I.10; *GBWW,* Vol. 8, p. 105b), every demonstrative science (*epistéme*) is concerned with three things: (1) the subject matter or that with which the science is concerned, (2) the things proved about it, its attributes, and (3) that from which the demonstration begins. These last are indemonstrable principles, or starting points, indemonstrable since not everything can be proven, nor need be. They are of two kinds: Some are common to many sciences; an example is the axiom that if equals are taken from equals, equals remain. Others are special or peculiar to a given science, and of these Aristotle distinguishes three again: (a) the subject matter of which both the meaning and existence is assumed, such as points and lines in geometry; (b) the attributes of the subject, of which only the meaning is assumed, whereas their existence is demonstrated by means of the axioms and previously established conclusions taken as premises; and (c) postulates the existence of which is assumed and from which something can be assumed regarding the subject.

When we turn to Euclid's Book I, we find much of what Aristotle had taught us to expect, but it is much more fully developed, since we are now embarked upon the course of a demonstrative science. The book begins by distinguishing three different kinds of principles, or starting points: definitions, postulates, and common notions, the last of which correspond to what Aristotle called "axioms," as is seen from the fact that Euclid's Common Notion 3 is the same as the example cited above by Aristotle.

The three different principles also differ in their relation to meaning and existence. That the definitions are intended only to establish meaning is evident once Definition 4 is compared with Postulate 1, since the latter postulates that a straight line can be drawn from any point to any point, whereas the definition says only that a straight line is a line that lies evenly with the points on itself. This definition may not seem very illuminating, and it may be appealing to our visual experience of sighting along an even row of objects; if so, the postulate would also imply that only one straight line can join two points. At any rate, the appeal to sense experience can at most serve only as a crutch to help us grasp the meaning of the definition, since a line that is defined as a breadthless length is not a thing that can be observed by sight.

A still different relation between meaning and existence appears when the definition (20) of an equilateral triangle is compared with the proof of its construction in Proposition I.1. For in this case it is shown that, given the postulated possibility of drawing a straight line and describing a circle about it, we can prove that an equilateral triangle is possible by actually constructing one, although again the diagram drawn is but a crutch for the intellect.

That the definitions establish the subject matter of Book I is evident merely from the two just considered. Yet we might reflect a little further on just what kind of an object is given to us. It is obviously not a visual object, or one that can be sensed, as is clear from the definitions of point, line, surface. Perhaps these objects can be imagined, even though they cannot be seen. When we reach the definition (23) of parallel straight lines, however, we have also gone beyond the imaginable, for these are lines that are produced indefinitely, i.e., without end, and never meet. The subject matter is neither sensible nor imaginary, but conceptual. Yet it is by means of—with the help of—words and diagrams, which *are* sensible things, that we can think about and discover the properties of these purely conceptual objects. It is also clear that Euclid is beginning from what is logically or conceptually prior and moving from there to the later and more complex, since a point or line as he defines it is certainly not the sort of thing we first encounter. Indeed, among objects of sense experience closest to his geometrical ones, the ones he treats last are those of which we have the most immediate experience, namely solids of three dimensions.

Euclid's postulates are, if anything, even more important than his definitions for establishing the objects of geometry. The postulates so constitute their existence that properties or attributes about them can be inferred or deduced. In effect, the postulates establish a unique kind of space. The first three, concerning the straight line and circle, lay down the only kind of lines to be dealt with, and, in postulating that they can be of any magnitude, imply that the space is continuous and not discrete; for if it is possible to describe a circle of any size, it can be indefinitely small, in which case there is no room for any gaps in the space it occupies.

However, of the five postulates it is the fourth and fifth that make Euclid's geometry uniquely Euclidean. Postulate 4 asserts that the right angle is a determinate magnitude and so can serve as a standard or criterion by which to measure other angles either as less (acute), or greater (obtuse); and since all right angles are equal, it in effect says that the space in which they exist is homogeneous or all of the same kind. That makes it possible to test figures by coincidence, or application of one on another, and thus gives us the fourth axiom to the effect that things which coincide with one another are equal. Postulate 4 is also necessary for the statement of the great fifth postulate.

Of this, the so-called parallel postulate, it has been written that it "must ever be regarded as among the most epoch-making achievements in the domain of geometry." To appreciate this claim we must see how the postulate is used and why it is necessary, but for that we must first understand what it says. Parallel lines have been defined in Definition 23 as straight lines which never meet, however far they are extended. The fifth postulate now provides a criterion by which to determine when two straight lines are *not* parallel but will intersect if extended sufficiently far enough. The test consists in letting a single straight line fall across the two lines and determining whether the interior angles that it makes between the two lines are less than two right angles; for if so the lines are postulated to meet if produced far enough on the side on which the two angles are less than two right angles (*see* fig. 1).

Readers of Euclid from a very early date took exception to this postulate about parallels from the belief that it should be proved rather than assumed. They had at least two reasons for this belief. One is that Euclid himself proves the converse of it in Proposition I.28, namely, that if a transverse line crosses two lines so as to make the interior angles equal to two right angles, the lines are parallel. The other reason is that it is by no means necessary that if lines converge they must ultimately meet, for there are lines that continually get ever closer *without* ever meeting, namely asymptotes. Hence, from antiquity until the nineteenth century, attempts were made to prove and not assume the proposition asserted in Postulate 5. What ultimately was proved, however, was rather that the postulate could not be demonstrated using Euclid's methods, and his genius came to be better appreciated for having recognized what had to be assumed for his geometry. Why that assumption must be made and something of what it involves, can be gathered from seeing how Euclid uses the postulate.

Euclid seems to have wanted to postpone as long as possible the treatment of parallels, for he does not begin it until the 27th proposition, more than halfway through the first book. Up to this point he has been investigating properties of the triangle. He then devotes five propositions to the consideration of parallels, the first two of which make no appeal to Postulate 5, which is invoked for the first time in I.29. The need for the postulate becomes apparent when he returns to the triangle in I.32, the very important proposition that the three interior angles of a triangle are equal to two right angles. There is thus an intimate, indeed essential, connection and interdependence between the Euclidean triangle, the theory of parallels, and the meeting of lines asserted in Postulate 5, which is why it has come to be known as the "parallel postulate."

In effect, the proposition about triangles, I.32, is the equivalent of

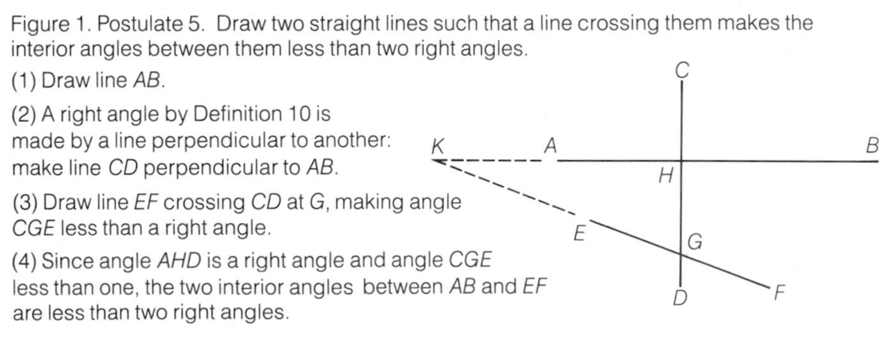

Figure 1. Postulate 5. Draw two straight lines such that a line crossing them makes the interior angles between them less than two right angles.

(1) Draw line *AB*.

(2) A right angle by Definition 10 is made by a line perpendicular to another: make line *CD* perpendicular to *AB*.

(3) Draw line *EF* crossing *CD* at *G*, making angle *CGE* less than a right angle.

(4) Since angle *AHD* is a right angle and angle *CGE* less than one, the two interior angles between *AB* and *EF* are less than two right angles.

Postulate 5 then asserts that if *AB* and *EF* are produced on the side where the interior angles are less than two right angles, they will meet, as at *K*.

Lines are parallel then, only if the transverse line makes the interior angles equal to two right angles, as is proven in I.28.

Postulate 5. If one goes, the other goes too, and it was by letting both go that the non-Euclidean geometries came to be developed. If the sum of the interior angles is greater than two right angles, as it is in the case of a triangle on the surface of a sphere, we obtain the non-Euclidean geometry of Riemann; if it is less than two right angles, we have the geometry of Lobachevsky, with his so-called space of negative curvature. Hence, by means of his fifth postulate Euclid in effect specifies that his is a geometry of a space that is flat or of zero curvature. But enough of the wonders of the parallel postulate.

Of Euclid's third kind of principle, that of the common notions or axioms, no such lengthy consideration is needed. In calling them "common," he implies, as already expressly noted by Aristotle, that they are used in more than one science. This is obviously the case with all except possibly the fourth. For Common Notion 1, that two things equal to the same thing are equal to each other, is as true of number as it is of size, and that the whole is greater than the part (Common Notion 5), when said of finite things, is a typical example of a self-evident truth, since it is evident once the meaning of "whole" and "part" are understood.

Common Notion 4, however, concerning coincidence, seems to be peculiar to geometry. It certifies the superposition of one figure on another as a test for the equality of the figures. It would not seem to be common to arithmetic, for example, for one does not prove the equal numerosity of two groups of things by placing the items of one group upon those of the other unless coincidence is taken to be matching, as when we know that the number of chairs in a room equals the number of people in it if every chair is occupied by one person and no one is without a chair. Aristotle claimed that axioms are indemonstrable and require no proof or postulation since they are self-evident. There seems no doubt that Euclid's common notions have more evidence in themselves than the postulates do.

It is sometimes objected that Euclid fails to state explicitly in this preliminary matter all the principles that he uses when he comes to prove his propositions, and we will soon see examples of this. Consequently, geometers have frequently added to the number of postulates and axioms (which accounts incidentally for the different numbering found in differing editions of the *Elements*). Euclid, of course, may not himself have been aware of such a lack and assumed principles without knowing that he did so. Yet one should not rule out the possibility that he *was* aware and himself decided not to make explicit some of such principles. Aristotle noted, in the text already referred to, that there is no need to make everything explicit that is obvious and well known.

Since it is the postulates that are special and peculiar to geometry—the axioms being common to many sciences—why, it might be asked, should Euclid be said to be using an axiomatic rather than a postulational method? Wouldn't it be more accurate to use the latter name? Euclid might well agree. But for many modern mathematicians, logicians, and philosophers his axioms are no less postulational than his postulates. In denying that there *are* any self-evident axioms, they are denying that there exist any axioms at all in the old sense of principles distinct from postulates, with the result that the two words *axiom* and *postulate* have come to be used interchangeably. In any case, an axiomatic system is one that begins with indemonstrable principles from which certain propositions can be deduced as conclusions. That describes what Euclid does, for although further definitions are required in the *Elements,* the postulates and axioms given here apply to all thirteen books.

Construction and demonstration

To read Euclid demands making and doing. The book calls for a straight-edge and compass, and hand as well as eye must be put to work. It is true, the knowledge we obtain is not strictly speaking about the physical diagrams that we draw, but by making the diagrams that are called for, we can more readily come to understand the properties and relations that are being established. Much can also be learned about the investigation merely from observing and tracing the interrelations between the various propositions: why one comes after another, and, where the order is not one of logical dependence (proof of one proposition being needed before another can be proven), what other reason there can be for its position in the sequence of propositions.

The first thing Euclid does is to show that from the principles laid down it is possible to produce or construct a triangle. This is the simplest plane figure (Definition 10) bounded by straight lines. A circle is simpler, in that it consists of only one line, but that is a curved, not a straight, line. Two lines also enclose a space if one is curved and the other straight, as in a semicircle (Definition 18). And two straights cannot make a bounded figure, as is implied by the first postulate and the definition of a straight line. Hence the most elementary plane figure composed of straight lines is an equilateral triangle consisting of three equal straights, and such is the first proposition that opens the demonstration in the *Elements.*

The two immediately following propositions are also constructions in that they enable us to cut off or make equal lines. It might be asked why a simpler procedure than Euclid's would not be the use of a graduated ruler or a fixed compass length. Evidently, Euclid wanted his mechanical instruments to be as simple as possible and so supposes an ungraduated straight-edge and compasses that close when lifted.

These propositions calling for constructions are in effect problems:

they set a task to be done, something to be made, which is why they close with the expression "Being what it was required to do" (often abbreviated to Q.E.F. from the Latin for it). In this they are distinguished from propositions that are theorems (the first of which is 1.4), which establish a property of a thing so as to show what it is, and for this reason the proposition is concluded with the words "Being what it was required to prove" (shortened after the Latin to Q.E.D.). The difference between the two kinds of propositions corresponds to that between asking *whether* a thing is—that is, can exist—and asking *what* it is: between its existence (mathematically) and its properties or attributes.

Fourteen of the forty-eight propositions in Book I are problems. After the first ones on constructing equal lines, there come those dealing with bisecting an angle and constructing a right angle and erecting a perpendicular to a line (I.9–12). Then there is one on constructing a triangle from three given lines (I.22), one on making equal angles (I.23) and parallel lines (I.31), followed by a series on applying to a given angle or line one figure equal to another (I.42, 44–45), the final one being the construction of a square (I.46).

The great virtue of the axiomatic method lies in the way it makes perspicuous the deduction or drawing of a conclusion from what has been laid down in the premises. It is now time to see how Euclid accomplishes this. To achieve even greater clarity, even at the risk of emphasizing the obvious, I will fill in details Euclid did not bother about and number each separate step.

As an example of the treatment of a problem, let us consider the very first proposition, I.1. It begins with a statement of what is given and what is sought, thus:

(1) Given is a straight line, which is known to be possible from Postulate 1, and which is represented by drawing line *AB* (fig. 2). Note that no length is specified, although the line drawn of course has a definite length, which is

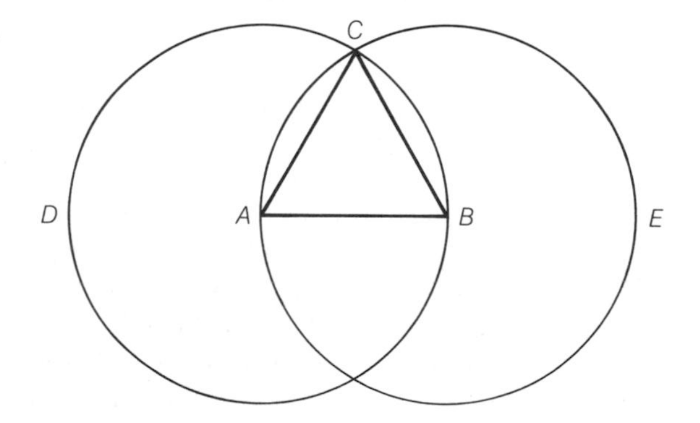

Figure 2. Book I, Proposition 1.

only to emphasize again that the proposition is not about or restricted to the line in the diagram.

(2) What is sought is to construct an equilateral triangle (Definition 20) on line *AB*.

Construction:

(3) With center *A* and distance *AB* the circle *BCD* is described, which is possible by Postulate 3.

(4) With center *B* and distance *BA* describe circle *ACE* (Postulate 3). Note that in each case the lettering proceeds from the center on which the compass is placed to the point at which it begins to describe; in this case from point *B* to point *A* around *C* to *E*.

(5) From point *C*, where the circles cut one another, to points *A* and *B* join the straight lines *CA* and *CB*, again by Postulate 1.

The triangle *ABC* is the one sought.

Proof:

(6) $AC = AB$ since both are lines from the center to the circumference of circle *CBD* and by Definition 15 are equal.

(7) $BC = BA$ for the same reason in circle *CAE*.

(8) $CA = CB$ since both are equal to *AB* and things equal to the same are equal to each other by Common Notion 1.

(9) $CA = AB = BC$ forming triangle *ABC*.

Therefore triangle *ABC* is equilateral and has been constructed upon the given line *AB*. Q.E.F.

Note that, with one exception, in both the construction and the proof reasons are given for each step, the reasons for the former being Postulates 3 and 1, which allow us to do something, and in the latter Definition 15, which identifies the equality among the radii of a circle and Common Notion 1 as the equality among the three sides.

The exception is that no reason is given for knowing that the two circles will intersect at point *C*. This is a geometrical, not a logical, property, and its omission is therefore surprising. Perhaps Euclid thought it obvious, but if so, he must have had in mind what happens when we draw the diagram, and that can be said to be a fault, since it involves dependence upon something besides the principles laid down, the laws and rules of logical deduction (which are taken for granted), and the language used to describe the whole operation.

The first theorem to be *demonstrated* is I.4, concerning the equality of two triangles having two corresponding sides and the contained angle equal. Again, although simple, the proposition is worth considering closely so as to understand what is involved in a proof. But there is no need to go into the same detail as in reading I.1, for the proof is accomplished essentially by two steps. By appeal to Common Notion 4, equality by coincidence, which involves imagining one triangle superimposed upon the other, the two corresponding sides and the angle they contain are shown to be equal, and all that remains is to show that the third side, or base, and the base angles are also equal. The proof consists in supposing that they do not coincide, which is impossible, for two straight lines having the same extremities will then enclose a space, and that contradicts Postulate 1 and Definition 4. Hence the opposite must be true, namely that the bases do coincide and that the two triangles are equal in all respects.

With this, the consideration of congruence, which is a major theme of the first book, has begun. But there is no need to linger over this proposition, for Euclid avoids proof by coincidence as much as possible, and the method of proof employed here can be better understood from the analysis of another theorem.

Consider Proposition I.6, to the effect that if a triangle has two equal angles, the sides subtending them will also be equal:

(1) Given triangle *ABC* in which angle *ABC* equals angle *ACB* (fig. 3).
(2) Sought: to show that side *AB* equals side *AC*.

Proof:
(3) If $AB \neq AC$, one of them is greater. Suppose it is *AB*, i.e., $AB > AC$.
(4) From *AB* cut off $DB = AC$, by I.3.
(5) Join *DC* by Postulate 1.

We now have two triangles, *DBC* and *ACB*.
What do we know about them?

Figure 3. Book I, Proposition 6.

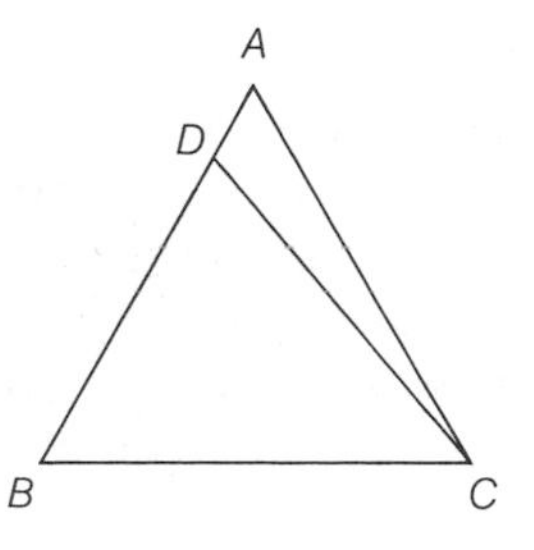

(6) $DB = AC$ by (4) above.
(7) $BC = CB$ since it is the same line.
(8) Angle DBC = angle ACB since angle DBC is the same angle ABC which equals angle ACB by (1).
(9) $DC = AB$ by I.4 since triangles ACB and DCB have two equal sides and the contained angle equal by (6, 7, 8).
(10) Triangle DBC = triangle ACB by the same I.4.
(11) But triangle DBC < triangle ACB since $AB > AC$ by (3).
(12) Therefore the less equals the greater (10–11), which is absurd.
(13) AB then is not unequal to AC.

Therefore $AB = AC$, which is what was sought. Q.E.D.

In this proposition the proof is not direct from premises as it was in I.1, where we proceeded by a series of reasoned steps to reach the conclusion sought for. Here the conclusion is reached indirectly by the proof known as *per impossibile* or *reductio ad absurdum.* It is indirect in that it begins by assuming the opposite of what is wanted, namely that side AB is greater than side AC. Then by a series of reasoned steps it reaches a conclusion that is absurd in being a contradiction which both affirms and denies the same thing. Hence the opposite must be true, which is what we wanted to show. No reason is given for this step. It is the law of contradiction that a thing cannot both be and not be at the same time and in the same respect. Since contradictories cannot both be true, a proposition that leads to a contradiction must be false and its opposite must be true. The strength of the logic lies in the fact that if contradictories *could* be true (at the same time and in the same respect), we could prove anything at all, which would destroy the very idea of proof and so also of reasoning itself. Proof by this indirect method is a favorite with Euclid, as it is with many mathematicians. The logic of it is not expressly stated but is taken for granted.

Before leaving Proposition I.6, we should note its relation to the previous proposition, I.5. They are so-called geometrical converses of one another in that the given and sought in the one are reversed in the other. Thus in I.6 the given is a triangle with two equal angles and what is sought is the equality of the sides, whereas in I.5 the equality of the sides is given and what is sought is the equality of the angles (plus, in this particular case, a further property regarding the angles beneath the base). Euclid frequently places close together the proof of converse propositions because of their intimate relation to one another rather than because of any immediate mathematical need. This is indicated by the fact that he does not appeal to I.6 until the second book at II.4. With this we come to the question of the organization of the work, or of what might be called—

The plot of Book I

It may seem exaggerated and overly poetic to refer to a book of geometry as having a plot. Yet if the organization of the *Elements* is carefully examined, it can be seen that Euclid obviously plotted to place certain propositions where they would achieve a certain effect, or at least for reasons other than logical dependence. That this is so is clear from the fact that he chose to arrange the propositions in such a way as to end with the Pythagorean theorem and its converse (I.47, 48). For if we look at the propositions actually used in their proof, we can see that he could have placed these two propositions much earlier in the book, as is evident once the logical dependencies are tabulated:

I.48	depends	on	47 and 8.
47	"	"	46, 41, and 4.
46	"	"	34 and 31.
41	"	"	37 and 34.
37	"	"	35 and 34.
35	"	"	34 and 29.
34	"	"	29, 26, and 4.
31	"	"	27 and 23.
29	"	"	13 and Postulate 5.
27	"	"	16.
26	"	"	16, 4, and 3.

Before I.16, the propositions are more closely linked logically. Yet, as the table makes evident, Euclid could have started the steps leading up to the Pythagorean theorem immediately after I.16, had he wanted to, by proving 26 in the 17th place, 27 in the 18th place, 29 in the 19th, and so on. I.47 and 48 could then have occupied the 26th and 27th places in Book I, only a little past the middle instead of occurring at the very end. Euclid evidently wanted the Pythagorean theorem to appear as the climactic conclusion of his first book.

There are several possible reasons for this. If the best and most important should be reserved for the last, that provides one of them. For Book I is mainly concerned with the properties of the triangle, and of all the propositions dealing with triangles I.47 is undoubtedly the most important. Another reason for the deferral, perhaps even more significant, is that the theorem exposes a mystery, even a scandal, in mathematics, that of the irrational and the incommensurable. This is a separate topic, to which we now turn.

The incommensurable and irrational

These terms are not defined until Book X, since it is not until then that Euclid begins to investigate their relation and classify various kinds of irrational straight lines. However, the existence of the irrational is implicit from the first book on, and the Pythagorean theorem may have led to its discovery. That theorem still remains the simplest way of showing its existence. But first we need some definitions.

Magnitudes are said to be *commensurable* if they can be measured by one and the same measure, *incommensurable* if they have no common measure (Book X, Definition 1). Quantities that are commensurable are *rational,* while those that are incommensurable are *irrational.*

Propositions X.5–8 clarify the meaning of these definitions. Magnitudes are commensurable when they have to one another the ratio which a number has to a number, where by *number* Euclid understands an integer or whole number. The incommensurable then are those quantities that do not stand to one another in the ratio of one whole number to another, and since they cannot be expressed by such a ratio they are irrational.

Euclid's meaning of *rational* is wider than that in modern usage, inasmuch as he admits as rational those quantities which are commensurable only in square and incommensurable otherwise, whereas now such quantities would also be considered irrational, since their base cannot be expressed as the ratio of two whole numbers. It is of this sense of irrational that I.47 provides a proof.

This theorem, expressed algebraically, asserts that $c^2 = a^2 + b^2$, where c represents the side opposite the right angle in a right-angled triangle (the hypotenuse) and a and b the other two sides. There are then two different cases to consider, since sides a and b can be either equal or unequal to one another. Let them be unequal, say $a = 3$ and $b = 4$, then $c^2 = 3^2 + 4^2$, or $9 + 16$, or 25 so that $c = \sqrt{25} = 5$ and so the hypotenuse and sides of this triangle are commensurable, standing in the ratio of 5:4 and 5:3 and all three are rational.

But what if the sides of the triangle are equal to one another, say $a = 1$ and $b = 1$? Then, $c^2 = 1^2 + 1^2$, or $1 + 1$, or 2 so that $c =$ what? In both cases c is a perfectly definite length, but in the first case all three sides are commensurable in that the unit (1) exactly measures all three as equal to 5, 4, and 3. But in the second case the hypotenuse is incommensurable with its sides, for there is no measure that will exactly measure both, and hence in this case c is irrational.

Of course, in the second case we may say that $c = \sqrt{2}$ and claim

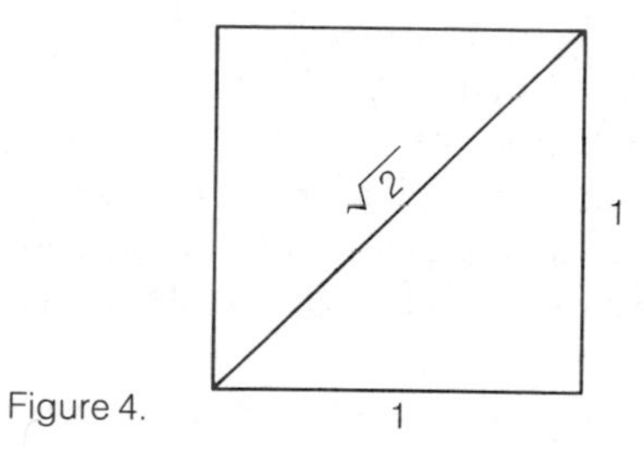

Figure 4.

that it is a perfectly definite number. Yet it certainly is *not* definite in the way that the hypotenuse of the triangle is, where it definitely ends at its two extremities in meeting the sides. In fact, evaluated, $\sqrt{2}$ is an unending decimal, 1.4142 . . . , and although we may extend it as much as we like, we will never reach a quantity which when multiplied by itself will exactly equal the whole number 2.

The hypotenuse of an isosceles right triangle is the diagonal of a square. Hence one can obtain as many examples of incommensurables and irrationals as one can make squares. But how can it be proven in general that the diagonal of a square is always an irrational? It is not a question of actual physical measurement, for that is always inaccurate, not perfectly exact mathematically. How can it be proven that exact arithmetical measure of the diagonal is impossible?

The general proof, which is noticed by Aristotle in *Prior Analytics* (I.23; *GBWW,* Vol. 8, p. 58a) and is found in some editions of Euclid as X.117 goes as follows (*see* fig. 4):

To prove: That the diagonal of a square is incommensurable with its side, or that $\sqrt{2}$ is an irrational number.

To show: $\sqrt{2}$ cannot be expressed as a ratio of two whole numbers.

(1) Suppose that $\sqrt{2}$ *is* rational, then it can be expressed as a ratio of two whole numbers, say m/n, where the ratio or fraction is in its lowest terms, so that m and n are not both even numbers, but one is odd.
$\sqrt{2} = m/n$.
(2) $\sqrt{2} \cdot \sqrt{2} = m/n \cdot m/n$, multiplying each side by itself.
(3) $2 = m^2/n^2$, expressing the result of the multiplication.
(4) $2n^2 = m^2$, multiplying both sides by n^2, and canceling n^2/n^2.
(5) $\therefore m^2$ is even, since it is divisible by 2 (Book VII, Definition 6).
(6) $\therefore m$ is even, since the square of an even number is even (IX.21).
(7) Let $m = 2p$, since m is an even number by step (6) and therefore divisible by 2.
(8) $m^2 = 2n^2$ by step (4).
(9) $2n^2 = (2p)^2 = 4p^2$ from step (7) and step (8).

(10) $n^2 = 2p^2$, by dividing (9) by 2.

(11) n then is even, again by IX.21. But this is contrary to the hypothesis that not both m and n are even as in step (1).

(12) Therefore the contradictory of (1) must be true, since if one contradictory is false, the other must be true. So $\sqrt{2}$ is not rational but irrational and cannot be expressed as a ratio of two whole numbers.

(13) The side of a square then is incommensurable with its diagonal and both cannot be exactly measured by the same measure.

Since there is no lack of whole numbers, it may seem strange that there should be something for which no number can be found that will measure it. Yet with infinitely many numbers and infinitely many lines, we still cannot find one that will exactly measure both the side and the diagonal of a square. The ancients considered it a marvel, a mystery, and according to an ancient story the discovery of the incommensurable caused a scandal among the Pythagoreans, since it exposed a defect in their mathematics; legend has it that the man who made it public knowledge was killed. It seemed to expose in the very nature of things something resistant to reason and its ambitions: an irrational not only in the mathematical sense that there was no ratio among whole numbers to express the relation, but something irrational in the sense of being opposed to reason itself. Yet it was also something eminently worth thinking about, and Plato thought it a disgrace that old men should play checkers rather than ponder the mystery of the irrational and incommensurable (*Laws* VII.820; *GBWW,* Vol. 7, p. 729c).

Modern mathematics claims to have no difficulty in overcoming the incommensurable. It has done so merely by inventing a new kind of number, the surd or irrational number, of which the square root of two is an instance, with "$\sqrt{2}$" being treated as a whole number. Euclid might not have been so easily satisfied, even if he had possessed a more developed arithmetic. The Greek number notation was as cumbersome as the Roman, if not more so. It used the letters of the alphabet with a horizontal stroke above the letter, beginning with $\bar{\alpha}$ (alpha) for 1, $\bar{\beta}$ (beta) for 2, $\bar{\iota}$ (iota) for 10, $\bar{\kappa}$ (kappa) for 20, and so on, and since there was no indication of place-value, the relation between numbers was not immediately evident, as it is, for example, in 5, 50, and 500, but not at all in the Greek equivalents of $\bar{\varepsilon}$ (epsilon), $\bar{\nu}$ (nu), and $\bar{\varphi}$ (phi).

The value in whole numbers of $\sqrt{2}$ is at best an approximation, not as definite and exact as 2. Greek mathematicians did not like to work with approximate values but preferred to be absolutely exact and certain. So too, Greek philosophers had an ideal of knowledge as *epistéme* that is necessary and absolutely certain. It tells something of the difference between the ancients and moderns in that modern philosophers as well as mathematicians have given up the ideal of a necessary and certain truth and now satisfy themselves—believe they *have* to satisfy themselves—with probabilities and approximations.

Yet in one way mathematics still retains its preference for the definite and exact. Modern mathematics has as its arithmetical basis the system of natural numbers, integers, or whole numbers, and it is with reference to them that the other kinds of numbers have been invented. Thus one of the best modern surveys, *What is Mathematics?*, by Courant and Robbins, begins with an account of the natural numbers, claiming that "number is the basis of modern mathematics," and has as its guiding principle that "all mathematical statements should be reducible ultimately to statements about the natural numbers, 1, 2, 3, . . ." and they cite with approval the words of the great nineteenth-century mathematician Leopold Kronecker that "God created the natural numbers; everything else is man's handiwork."

Geometrical algebra

Euclid in Book II continues the investigation of a subject he had already begun, namely that of the transformation of areas. In I.44, which has been described by Sir Thomas Heath, his translator and commentator, as "one of the most impressive in all geometry," he shows how to transform a parallelogram of any shape into a triangle with the same angle and of equal area, where one side is of any given length, i.e., as a unit. The second book continues the investigation, but with the transformation limited to squares and rectangles. Almost half of the propositions of Book II are dependent upon I.47, and in the course of the book, Euclid achieves a complete generalization of that theorem as holding for any triangle, not just for right-angled triangles. II.12 establishes the relation for obtuse-angled and II.13 for acute-angled triangles, in effect establishing the law of cosines that $c^2 = a^2 + b^2 - 2ab \cos C$, in which C is the angle opposite side c.

The contents of the second book have been called geometrical algebra, since in it Euclid shows how to solve geometrically problems that now are solved by algebra. The geometrical equivalents are fairly obvious:

Addition $a + b$ is effected by extending a line A by line B,
Multiplication ab by constructing a rectangle with lines A and B as sides,
Division a/b by the ratio of line A to line B,
Extraction of $\sqrt{a}$ by constructing a square equal to a given rectangle.

To see the equivalence, consider the very simple first proposition stating that given two straight lines, one of which is cut into any number

Figure 5. Book II, Proposition 4.

(1) Given: a straight line cut randomly into segments *a* and *b*.
(2) Construct a square on $a + b$.
(3) Construct a square on *b*.
(4) Construct rectangles *ab* as shown.

$$(a + b)^2 = a^2 + b^2 + 2ab$$

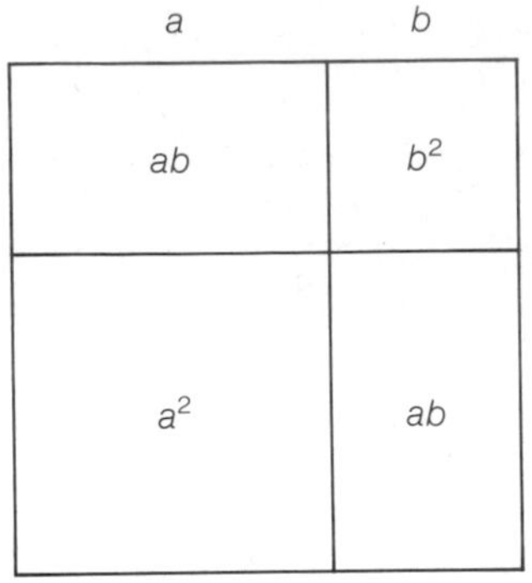

of segments, the rectangle contained by the two straight lines is equal to the rectangles contained by the uncut straight lines and each of the segments. Euclid represents the uncut line by *A* and the other by *BC* cut at points *D* and *E*. To simplify, let us represent the uncut line by *a* and the cut line by $b + c + d$. We have then to prove that $a(b + c + d) = ab + ac + ad$. To prove it we construct a rectangle on the cut line $b + c + d$ with side equal to *a*, which we know that we can do from our ability to construct a line at right angles and so perpendicular to another (I.11), to make one line equal to another (I.3), and to make a line parallel to another (I.31). By extending to this parallel line of length *a* lines at right angles to it and equal respectively to *b*, *c*, and *d* we obtain rectangles *ab*, *ac*, *ad*, all of which are contained within the rectangle $a(b + c + d)$. Thus geometrically we have proven the equivalent of the algebraic distributive law for multiplication.

Proposition II.4 proves that the square on the whole of a straight line is equal to the square of its two segments and twice the rectangle contained by the segments. This is the geometrical equivalent of $(a + b)^2 = a^2 + b^2 + 2ab$, as construction makes evident (*see* fig. 5).

The final proposition of the book, II.14, shows how to construct a square equal to a given rectilineal figure. First, a rectangular parallelogram is made equal to the figure by I.45. The problem then is to find a square equal to a rectangle, i.e., to solve $x^2 = ab$, thus geometrically extracting the square root, since the side of the square is the length *x*.

Book III of the *Elements* contains the geometry of the circle and properties regarding the center, chords, tangents, and segments of it.

Book IV consists entirely of problems in inscribing and circumscribing figures with circles, beginning with the three-sided triangle and progressing successively through four-sided figures, the regular pentagon and hexagon, and ending with the construction within a circle of a regular polygon with fifteen angles and sides. Because of its importance later in the work, it is worth noting how to construct a regular pentagon as given in IV.11 (fig. 6).

Overcoming the irrational

Books V and X are said, by those who know, to be the greatest and most perfect of the thirteen books of Euclid's *Elements,* for in them he shows how to deal with irrational and incommensurable quantities as readily as with rational and commensurable ones.

Book V develops a theory of proportion and similitude. Of the eighteen definitions with which it begins, a few are basic for understanding what is going on. First, the definition of *part* and *multiple* (Book V, Definitions 1, 2). By a part we must understand a proper or aliquot part, i.e., the less of a greater, which exactly measures the greater without either diminution or augmentation. Thus the numbers 1, 2, and 3 are each a part of 6, whereas 4 is not. A multiple defines the greater in relation to the less as that which is exactly measured by the less. Thus 6 is a multiple of 1, 2, and 3, but not of 4. Euclid speaks of "measuring" rather than "dividing," perhaps because it is more appropriate to a geometry of congruence. Thus a measures (or is a divisor or a factor) of b if there is some whole number c such that $b = ca$.

Ratio (*logos*) is defined in Definition 3 as a sort of relation in respect of size between two magnitudes of the same kind. "Of the same kind" is used so as to exclude such a comparison as that of a line with a number, a line with a plane, or a time with a space. For a ratio must be between number and number, line and line, and so on. As for "in respect of size," a ratio is a relation of quantity, as of equal, greater, or less than. Quantities are said to "have a ratio to one another" when they are capable of exceeding one another when multiplied together (Definition 4). Note that it is the capacity of exceeding, not of equaling, that defines a ratio. There is a ratio between 2 and 4, and it is possible to multiply each by numbers so as to obtain a result that is equal. But this is not the case for all magnitudes. The side and diameter of a square have a ratio to one another which is the same in all squares, yet the relation is irrational, for there are no numbers that will multiply them so as to make them equal to one another, notwithstanding that it

Figure 6. The Regular Pentagon
(a simplified version of IV.11).

(1) Draw a circle on diameter *AC*.
(2) Erect perpendicular *DB*.
(3) Bisect *DC* at *E*.
(4) Join *EB*.
(5) Make *EF* = *EB*.
(6) With distance *BF* mark off on the circle *BG, GH, HK, KL*.
(7) Join to form the regular pentagon *BGHKL*.

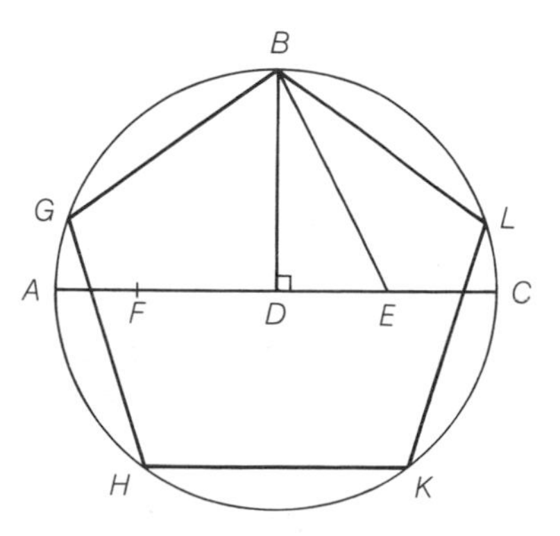

is always possible to make one exceed the other by multiplying by some number. This definition thus makes it possible to bring together under one head both the irrational and the rational. The test is provided in the next two definitions of sameness of ratio or proportionality (*analogon*).

Sameness of ratio, defined in Definition 5, involves four quantities, say a, b, c, d, two relations, a is to b and c is to d $(a : b)$ and $(c : d)$, and two multiples, say m and n. Now take any equimultiples of a and c, i.e., ma and mc, and any equimultiples of b and d, say nb and nd. Then sameness of ratio is defined as holding, for example, that

$$a : b = c : d$$

when, if $ma > nb$ then $mc > nd$
or if $ma = nb$ then $mc = nd$
or if $ma < nb$ then $mc < nd$.

Whereas a ratio holds only between quantities of the same kind, proportionality, as the sameness of ratios, can hold between things of different kinds, thereby making possible the comparison of magnitudes with numbers, and, still more generally, between any kinds of things that can be quantified. It thus provides the basis of measurement. Measurement involves at least three elements: a relation between things, a relation between numbers, and a relation between things and numbers. It is thus a relation between relations, i.e., a proportion. Thus a distance of five miles is to one mile or to a standard unit of length as the number five is to one.

Proportionality so defined also makes possible the comparison of the irrational, thereby overcoming as it were its incommensurability. As a simple example, consider again the relation between the sides and diameters of two squares, one of which has side $e = 1$ and the other $f = 2$, so that the diameters will be respectively $g = \sqrt{2}$ and $h = \sqrt{8}$. The sides and diameters are proportional, i.e., side e is to side f as diameter g is to diameter h, where the rational sides are compared with each other and the irrational diameters. Now according to Definition 5 they are proportional if me stands in the same relation of equal to, greater than, or less than nf that mg does to nh. To test let $m = 1$ and $n = 2$, then we have

$$\begin{aligned} me : nf &= mg : nh \\ 1 \cdot 1 < 2 \cdot 2 &= 1\sqrt{2} < 2\sqrt{8} \\ \text{so} \quad 1 : 2 &= \sqrt{2} : \sqrt{8}. \end{aligned}$$

In the course of Book V Euclid establishes many properties of proportions, among them the following:

if $a : b = c : d$ then $a : c = b : d$ by V.16,

or, in terms of our example,

$$\text{if } 1 : 2 = \sqrt{2} : \sqrt{8}, \text{ then } 1 : \sqrt{2} = 2 : \sqrt{8},$$

thereby establishing a definite relation between the rational side and the irrational diameter.

Geometrical arithmetic

After developing the theory of proportions, Euclid turns to apply it to the geometry of the plane in Book VI and then, in Books VII through IX, to numbers. The definitions for all three arithmetical books are given at the beginning of Book VII. The numbers, as has already been noted, are limited to integers or whole numbers. This is clear from the second definition which says that a number is "a multitude composed of units," which also indicates that zero is not considered a number. The definition of a part of a number (Definition 3) is identical with the first definition in the fifth book, except that the word *number* is substituted for *magnitude.* A number is a prime number when it is measured by no number but one (Definition 11)—or itself, one should add—and numbers are prime to one another when one is their only common measure (Definition 12). A number that is not prime is called composite (Definition 13). Multiplication is defined in terms of addition, one number being added to itself as many times as there are units in the other (Definition 15). The definition for proportional numbers (Definition 20) parallels that for proportion in Book V, Definition 5, and the correlation is proven in VII.20, which shows that if numbers $a : b = c : d$ then $ad = bc$ and conversely.

The thirty-nine propositions of the seventh book are mainly concerned with establishing various properties of numerical proportions and of prime numbers, and ways of finding the greatest common measure and the least common multiple of two numbers. Book VIII deals mostly with numbers that are in continued proportion, or what is now called geometrical progression, i.e., a series of terms such that the consequent of one is also the antecedent of another, as in $a : b = b : c$. The common term is the geometrical mean between the other two numbers; thus 6 is the geometrical mean between 9 and 4 because $9 : 6 = 6 : 4$. Terms in a geometrical progression form a geometric series. The ninth book continues the study of such progressions and concludes its study in IX.35 with a proposition that Sir Thomas Heath, the editor of the *Elements,* described as "perhaps the most interesting in the arithmetical books, since it gives a method, and a very elegant one, of summing any series of terms in geometrical progression."

To see Euclid's method in these books it is worth considering a few examples. For this purpose, among the very best propositions are those for finding the greatest common divisor (or measure) of two numbers and the proof that there is no greatest prime number. These two are not only highly important in mathematics, but Euclid proves them in a way that is practically identical with that still in use today.

The method for finding the greatest common divisor of two numbers is still known as Euclid's algorithm. It is formulated in VII.2 as the problem of finding the greatest common measure of two given numbers not prime to one another. Euclid represents numbers by lines and imagines one line being cut off successively from the other, but for us it is clearer to use numerals.

(1) Given two numbers, a and b, let $a = 187$ and $b = 77$.
(2) Find the largest number that will exactly divide both 187 and 77.
(3) 77 divides 187 by 2, with 33 as a remainder.
(4) 33 divides 77 by 2, with 11 as a remainder.
(5) 11 divides 33 by 3, with 0 as a remainder.
Therefore 11 is the greatest common divisor of 187 and 77.

Proof *per impossibile:*
(6) Suppose 11 is not the greatest common divisor. Let it be $m > 11$.
(7) m must divide $187 - (2 \cdot 77)$ as in (3) above.
(8) m must divide $77 - (2 \cdot 33)$ as in (4) above.
(9) But $77 - (2 \cdot 33) = 11$.
(10) $m = 11$ and $m > 11$ according to supposition (6), which is impossible.
Therefore, 11 is the greatest common divisor of 187 and 77.

Of course, Euclid's proof is general and not limited to any particular numbers, but it is simple enough to replace the numbers used as illusration by letters representing any whole numbers, thus:

(1) Let a and b represent any whole numbers > 0 or 1, and let c, d, p, q, r also represent numbers.
(2) b divides a by some number, with $p + c$ as remainder.
(3) c divides b by some number, with $q + d$ as remainder.
(4) d divides c by some number, with $r + 0$ as remainder.

Or the process is to be continued until there is no remainder, in which case d or the last divisor with no remainder is the greatest common divisor of a or b. If you never reach a divisor that does not divide evenly without a remainder the magnitudes are incommensurable (X.2) or the numbers are prime to one another.

The famous number theorist G. H. Hardy cited the proof for the existence of an infinity of prime numbers, along with that for the irrationality of $\sqrt{2}$, as eminent examples of beauty and high seriousness in mathematics. Euclid's proof occurs as Proposition IX.20, stating that "prime numbers are more than any assigned multitude of prime numbers." The proof depends upon two propositions proved earlier in Book VII, each of which is interesting in itself. The one, VII.31, is that any composite number is measured by some prime number, which is to say that any non-prime is a product of primes. The other, VII.36, is the method for finding the least common multiple of three numbers, which in the case of primes is their product. Here, then, is a modified version of Euclid's proof that there is no greatest prime number:

(1) Given: Prime numbers a, b, and c.
(2) To show: That there are more prime numbers than these.
(3) Let d be the least common multiple of a, b, and c, $d = abc$, the product of the three, by VII.36.
(4) Let $e = d + 1$.
(5) e is either prime or it is not. If e is prime we have shown what we set out to show, namely that there are more primes than a, b, and c.
(6) If e is not prime, it is a composite number and is a product of some prime number, by VII.31, say f, such that e is divisible by f.
(7) f cannot be the same as a, b, or c, for if it were there would be a contradiction.
(8) If f were the same as a, b, or c, it would divide d, since d is the least common multiple of a, b and c by (3) above.
(9) But f also divides e according to (6).
(10) Since $e = d + 1$, f then also divides the indivisible unit, which is absurd.
(11) f then cannot be the same as a, b, or c as supposed in (8). Yet it is prime according to (6).

Therefore we have found another prime beside those given. Since the process could be repeated with any multitude of primes, we have shown that there is no greatest prime number.

The divine proportion

Euclid's geometry, according to Kepler, contains two great treasures. One of them, the Pythagorean theorem, he compared to a measure of gold, while the other, which he called a precious jewel, is the division of a line in extreme and mean ratio. The two are treasures not only because of their beauty, but also because of their value and what one can obtain with them. We have already witnessed some of the power of the Pythagorean theorem. That of extreme and mean ratio is still greater and more wondrous, so much so that Kepler called it the divine proportion; still later it also came to be known as the golden section or ratio.

It is in Book VI, Proposition 30, that Euclid shows how to cut a given straight line in extreme and mean ratio. This ratio is defined in Book VI, Definition 2, as the ratio in which the whole line is to the greater segment as the greater is to the less. Thus the problem is to divide a line into two segments, say a and b, where b is the greater, such that

$$(a + b) : b = b : a.$$

Here the extreme terms are $(a + b)$, the whole line, and a, the smaller segment, while b, the greater, is the mean between the two. The construction is simple, since one need only construct a rectangle contained by the whole and one of the segments equal to the square on the remaining segment (fig. 7).

So stated, it is evident at once that the problem is identical with that of II.11, which is to say that we have again an instance of geometrical algebra. The rectangle is represented by $a(a + b)$ and the square by b^2 such that

$$a(a + b) = b^2$$

or

$$a^2 + ab = b^2$$

or

$$0 = b^2 - ab - a^2.$$

Thus we have a quadratic equation to solve, which is done geometrically by finding where to cut the line so as to obtain the segment b. Since Euclid takes the unit (1) to be indivisible, let us suppose the given line $= 2$. Then we must cut it into two segments such that

$$a + b = 2$$

$$b = 2 - a.$$

The proportion we seek:

$$(a + b) : b = b : a$$

or

$$2 : (2 - a) = (2 - a) : a$$

or

$$(2 - a)^2 = 2a$$

or

$$a^2 - 4a + 4 = 2a$$

or

$$a^2 - 6a + 4 = 0.$$

To solve, we apply the formula for solving a quadratic equation, which, for an equation of the form $ax^2 + bx + c = 0$, is

$$x = \frac{-b \pm \sqrt{b^2 - 4ac}}{2a}.$$

In our equation the coefficients corresponding to a, b, and c are, respectively, 1, 6, and 4. Substituting accordingly in the formula, we obtain

$$a = \frac{6 \pm \sqrt{36 - 16}}{2}$$

$$a = \frac{6 \pm \sqrt{20}}{2} = \frac{6 - 4.472\ldots}{2}$$

$$a = 0.764\ldots$$

$$b = 2 - a = 1.236\ldots$$

Thus, in this case, the divine proportion is

$$2 : 1.236\ldots = 1.236\ldots : 0.764\ldots$$

Again, as in the case of the diameter of a square, we encounter the mystery of the irrational. The given line has a perfectly definite length, terminating at its two extremities, and can be measured exactly (mathematically) as equal to two units. Yet, when it is divided according to the divine proportion, we find that out of the infinite multitude of whole numbers there is not one that will exactly measure (or divide) either segment an exact number of times. To obtain an approximation we have to resort to irrational numbers with the unending decimal.

As Euclid proves in XIII.5, the divine proportion maintains a surprising pattern in that it is additive. Thus if the greater of the two segments

Figure 7. Book VI, Proposition 30. To cut a given finite straight line in extreme and mean ratio.

Book II, Proposition 11. The same result by a simpler construction: to cut a given straight line so that the rectangle contained by the whole and one of the segments is equal to the square on the remaining segment.

(1) Let AB be the given straight line.
(2) Erect perpendicular to AB line $BA' = AB$.
(3) Bisect line BA' at point C.
(4) Join AC.
(5) With center C and radius CB cut AC at D.
(6) With center A and radius AD cut AB at E.
Line AB is then cut at E in extreme and mean ratio.

Proof:

(7) Let $AE = AD = b$, and let $EB = a$.
Since $CD = BC = \frac{1}{2} BA' = \frac{1}{2} BA$,

$\therefore CD = BC = \frac{a+b}{2}$.

(8) Then $a : b = b : (a + b)$.
(9) For in right-angled triangle ABC, by I.47,

$$\left(b + \frac{a+b}{2}\right)^2 = (a+b)^2 + \left(\frac{a+b}{2}\right)^2$$

$$b^2 = ab + a^2$$

$\therefore$ The square on b = the rectangle $a(a + b)$.

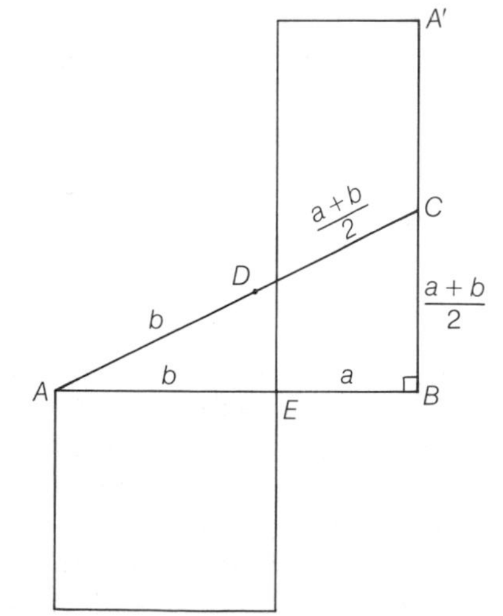

is added to the whole line the resulting line will maintain the same proportion, the previous whole line now becoming the greater segment of the new line. To illustrate, let us first simplify. This proportion has been called φ (phi) after the first letter in the name of the great Greek sculptor, Phidias. Starting then with a line divided into two so that $a + b = 1$, with b as the larger segment, and adding a length equal to the larger segment again, so as to obtain a new line, and continuing the process, we obtain the following results:

$$\begin{array}{ll} \varphi_0 \; a + b & = 1.000 \\ \varphi_1 \; (a + b) + b & = 1.618 \ldots \\ \varphi_2 \; [(a + b) + b] + (a + b) & = 2.618 \ldots \\ \varphi_3 \; \{[(a + b) + b] + (a + b)\} + [(a + b) + b] & = 4.236 \ldots \\ \ldots\ldots & \ldots\ldots \\ \varphi_6 & = 17.944 \ldots \\ \varphi_7 & = 29.034 \ldots \\ \ldots\ldots & \\ \varphi_n = \varphi_{n-2} + \varphi_{n-1} & \end{array}$$

As can be seen, any term in the sequence is the sum of the previous two. Still more surprising, the ratio of any two successive terms maintains the same φ proportion. Thus

$$\varphi_7 : \varphi_6 = 29.034 : 17.944 = \varphi_1 = 1.618.$$

There is a sequence of whole numbers that possesses the same additive property in that, starting with any two numbers, the third is the sum of the preceding two. This is the so-called Fibonacci series, named after its founder, Leonardo of Pisa Fibonacci (b. *c.* 1170). Here is a list of the first ten Fibonacci numbers:

1, 1, 2, 3, 5, 8, 13, 21, 34, 55 . . .

This sequence has the property that the ratio of any two successive numbers approximates the value of φ_1. Thus the 35th and 36th Fibonacci numbers are respectively 9,227,465 and 14,930,352, and their ratio is 1.6180339 . . . . In this way the sequence always provides a whole number approximation to the value of φ, that of 8 to 5 being the commonest.

Such being some of the wonders of the divine proportion, what use does Euclid make of it? Remembering that II.11 is its equivalent, we find its first use in IV.10–14, dealing with the construction of a regular pentagon. However, it is in the final book that it comes into its glory. The first six propositions of Book XIII establish certain properties of the proportion. XIII.8 proves that the diagonals of a regular pentagon cut each other at their intersections according to the same proportion. But the proportion comes to its greatest and most significant use in the analysis of the five regular solids, which is the culminating conclusion of the whole thirteen books, and which has won for the proportion the name of divine. For the reason, we must look to Plato, since these solids came to be known as the Platonic figures because of his interest in them.

It is in the dialogue entitled *Timaeus* that Plato tells the story of how the god made the world (53c–56c; *GBWW,* Vol. 7, pp. 458b–59d). The basic roots of material things, corresponding to fire, air, water, and earth, are the regular solids, the tetrahedron, octahedron, icosahedron, and cube. These solids have as their elements (*stoicheion*) the triangles out of which they are formed as the building blocks of the world. But the word *stoicheion* (which furnishes the Greek title for Euclid's work) also means letter, so that the basic triangles can be said to form the words of the book of nature, which amounts in effect to the claim that this book is written in the language of mathematics. The fifth solid—the dodecahedron—the god reserved for the delineation of the universe as a whole (*to pan*).

Since Euclid was a member of Plato's Academy, it is possible that he was so taken with this story that, when he came to compose his *Elements,* he organized his material so that all would lead up to the investigation of these five regular solids.

These solids, as we learn from the definitions of Book XI, are said to be regular because each has its faces, vertices, and edges all equal. They are named after the number of their faces or sides (*hedron*). Thus the dodecahedron is a regular solid contained by twelve pentagons. The constitution of the five according to their number of faces (F), vertices (V), and edges (E) can be tabulated as follows:

	F	V	E
Tetrahedron or Pyramid (triangles)	4	4	6
Hexahedron or Cube (squares)	6	8	12
Octahedron (triangles)	8	6	12
Icosahedron (triangles)	20	12	30
Dodecahedron (pentagons)	12	20	30

Despite the great interest that the Greeks took in these solids and the extensive study they devoted to them, it was not until the eighteenth century that the great Swiss mathematician Leonhard Euler noted that the relation among the three parts can be expressed in the simple formula: $F + V = E + 2$.

Euclid's method of analyzing and determining the properties of the five regular solids consists in constructing a sphere that circumscribes the solid so as to determine the relation of a side or edge of the solid to the radius of the sphere. If the radius is taken as a rational length, the side of the solid can then be compared with the radius so as to

Figure 8. Constructing a Regular Pentagon: Ptolemy's Method, *Almagest*, Book I, ch. 10 (*GBWW*, Vol. 16, pp. 14–15).

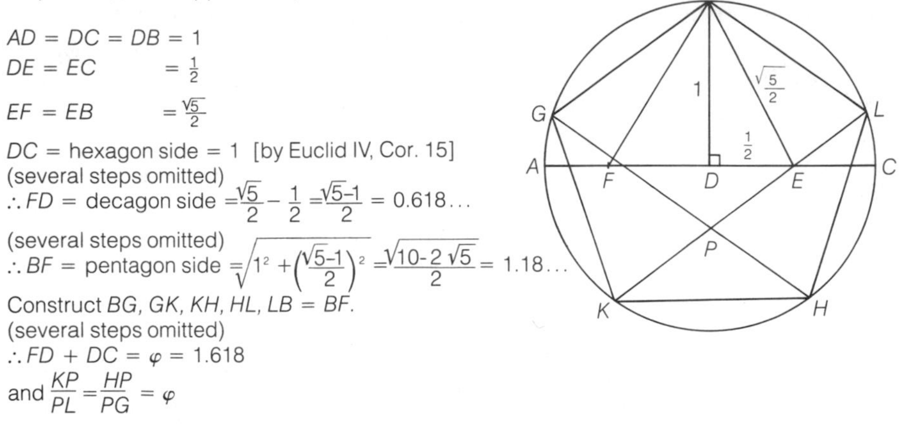

$AD = DC = DB = 1$
$DE = EC = \frac{1}{2}$
$EF = EB = \frac{\sqrt{5}}{2}$
DC = hexagon side = 1 [by Euclid IV, Cor. 15]
(several steps omitted)
$\therefore FD$ = decagon side $= \frac{\sqrt{5}}{2} - \frac{1}{2} = \frac{\sqrt{5}-1}{2} = 0.618\ldots$
(several steps omitted)
$\therefore BF$ = pentagon side $= \sqrt{1^2 + \left(\frac{\sqrt{5}-1}{2}\right)^2} = \frac{\sqrt{10-2\sqrt{5}}}{2} = 1.18\ldots$
Construct $BG, GK, KH, HL, LB = BF$.
(several steps omitted)
$\therefore FD + DC = \varphi = 1.618$
and $\frac{KP}{PL} = \frac{HP}{PG} = \varphi$
B
G
L
A
C
F
D
E
P
K
H
1
$\frac{\sqrt{5}}{2}$
$\frac{1}{2}$

determine whether the two are commensurable or not, and if not what kind of irrational is involved.

In preparation for this task, five propositions of Book IV are essential. IV.10 shows how to construct an isosceles triangle having each of the angles at the base be double the remaining one, i.e., a triangle with base angles equal to 72° and the vertical angle equal to 36°. Since this requires the use of II.11, we know at once that the φ (divine) ratio is involved. The next two propositions show first how to inscribe a regular pentagon within a given circle and then how to circumscribe one about a given circle (IV.11, 12), while the following two show the converse of inscribing and circumscribing a given circle in and about a given pentagon (IV.13, 14).

The first twelve propositions of Book XIII are merely preparatory to the study of the solids. The first six, as already noted, establish certain properties of the φ ratio. Propositions XIII.7–11 demonstrate certain relations in the regular pentagon, hexagon, and decagon, especially determining where the φ ratio appears. Of these the pentagon is the most important, and it is at the intersection of the diagonals drawn from the vertices that φ appears, as shown in Figure 8.

It is not until we reach XIII.13 that actual construction of the solids begins. This gives the construction of a pyramid or tetrahedron, its comprehension in a given sphere (i.e., whose radius can be taken as rational), and the proof that the square on the diameter of the sphere is one and a half times the square on the side of the pyramid. The proof is complicated and becomes more so as we move from consideration of the pyramid (XIII.13) to that of the octahedron (14), on to the cube (in 15), the icosahedron (in 16), and finally to the fifth and most wonderful, the dodecahedron (in 17). However, to see what the various relations are, it is only necessary to consider the comprehensive final proposition, which sets out in a single figure the sides of the five figures and compares them with one another. The construction is simple enough, and it is worth making in order to see where the irrational φ enters in (fig. 9).

Euclid notes with respect to the five solids that three are rational and two irrational when their edges are compared to the radius of the circumscribing sphere. But we must remember, as already noted, that contrary to present usage he calls rational those magnitudes that are commensurable in square only. However, when his results are rendered arithmetically, it becomes clear that all are irrational, but the sides of the icosahedron and dodecahedron are, as it were, more irrational, since they are not commensurable even in square, and it is these two that depend upon the irrational divine proportion.

The relations among the five solids can then be read off from the diagram (fig. 9) and tabulated, along with the arithmetic equivalent, as follows:

$$AF = \text{tetrahedron edge} \quad \tfrac{2}{3}\sqrt{6}\cdot r$$

$$BF = \text{cube edge} \quad \tfrac{2}{3}\sqrt{3}\cdot r$$

$$BE = \text{octahedron edge} \quad \sqrt{2}\cdot r$$

$$BM = \text{icosahedron edge} \quad \tfrac{r}{5}\sqrt{10\,(5-\sqrt{5})}$$

$$BN = \text{dodecahedron edge} \quad \frac{\sqrt{5}-1}{2}\cdot\frac{2}{\sqrt{3}}\cdot r.$$

The presence of the φ ratio is betrayed by the appearance of $\sqrt{5}$ and especially of $\frac{\sqrt{5}-1}{2}$.

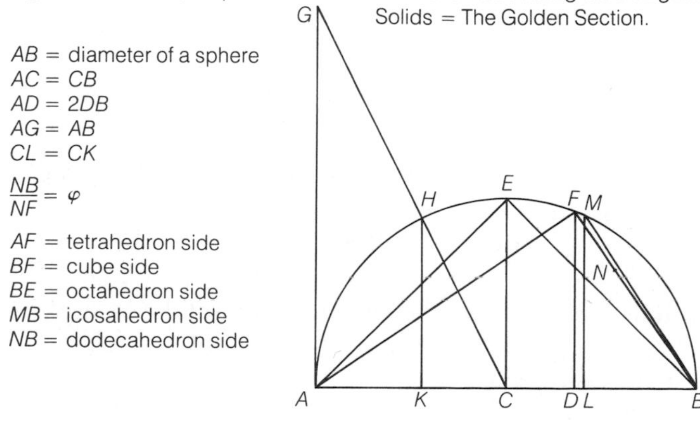

Figure 9. Book XIII, Proposition 18. The Bond of Union Among the 5 Regular Solids = The Golden Section.

The result here presented is in itself a considerable achievement, and worthy to climax the work as a whole. Yet in terms of what might be called mathematical satisfaction a greater is yet to come in the final claim that among the regular convex solids there are and can be five and only these five. The proof depends upon only two things: first the definition that a solid angle cannot be constructed with only two planes or triangles (Book XI, Definition 11), so that it takes three triangles to make the angle of the pyramid, four that of the octahedron, and five that of the icosahedron; second, the theorem that any solid angle is contained by angles less than four right angles, i.e., less than 360° (XI.21). Three squares, i.e., right angles, form the solid angle of the cube, and more than that is impossible. Three regular pentagons form the angle of the dodecahedron, and since the angle of such a pentagon is a right angle plus a fifth (i.e., 108°) more than three cannot form a solid. Thus, given the nature of a regular Euclidean solid, there are and can be only five such—a result that is especially satisfying in that it is definite, certain, and exhausts the possibilities.

As an addendum to this discussion of the five solids, it is worth noting an event that occurred almost 1,900 years later, or, to be exact, on July 19, 1595. On that date Kepler noted down his discovery that "God in creating the universe and regulating the order of the cosmos had in view the five regular bodies [solids] of geometry." (*GBWW,* Vol. 16, p. 841b). In his long hours of observing, measuring, and contemplating the heavens, he claimed to have found the ratios between the five solids in the orbital distances between the planets. Thus, if the orbits are taken as spheres circumscribing one another, the ratios between them are those of the solids arranged thus (*see* fig. 10):

The outermost sphere of Saturn circumscribes
a *cube* inscribed within which is
the sphere of Jupiter circumscribing
a *tetrahedron* inscribed within which is
the sphere of Mars circumscribing
a *dodecahedron* inscribed within which is
the sphere of Earth circumscribing
an *icosahedron* inscribed within which is
the sphere of Venus circumscribing
an *octahedron* inscribed within which is
the sphere of Mercury circumscribing
the central Sun.

The orbital distances and the ratios of the solids do not quite coincide, but Kepler to his delight found that the difference amounted to a harmonic progression making the music of the spheres as the compensating difference.

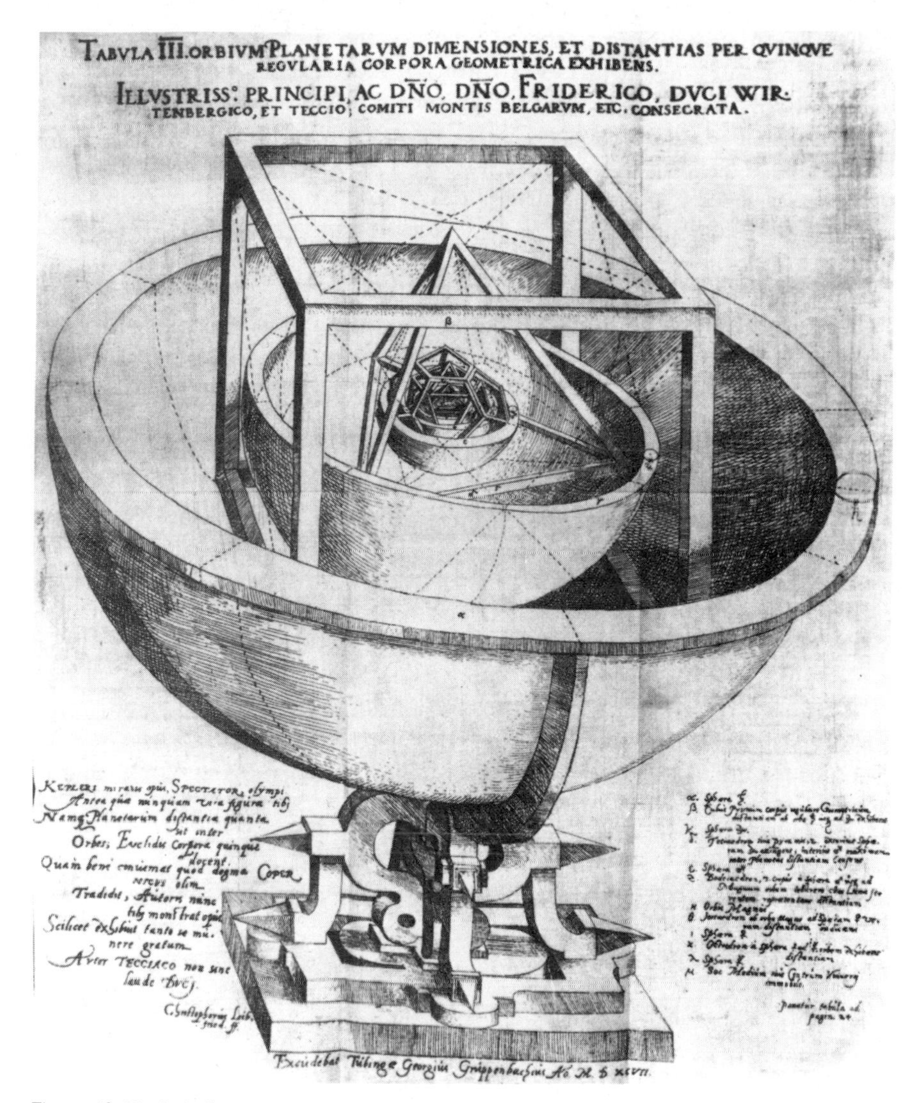

Figure 10. Kepler's figure of the Sun, Earth, and other planets.

Finally, an addendum to the wonders of the divine proportion. From the time of the ancient Greeks (if not from an even earlier time) down to the present it has been a continuing source of fascination and inspiration for artists and architects. There is good evidence that the façade of the Parthenon made use of the φ ratios, that the ground plan as well as the façade of Chartres cathedral is based upon it, while it is known for a fact that Le Corbusier used it as a modular for many of his buildings. Piero della Francesca employed it in many of his paintings and even wrote a treatise on the five solids, and in our own day the Dutch painter Piet Mondrian obviously delighted in it as providing a principle for his geometric paintings. But all this is another and even longer story.

Documentation

Euclid's *Elements* has been cited according to the translation of Thomas L. Heath published in *Great Books of the Western World,* Volume 11.

The Thirteen Books of Euclid's Elements with Introduction and Commentary by T. L. Heath, Cambridge, at the University Press, 1908 (reprint).

H. E. Huntley, *The Divine Proportion: A Study in Mathematical Beauty,* New York, Dover Publications, Inc., 1970.

R. Courant and H. Robbins, *What is Mathematics?,* Oxford University Press, 1941 (reprinted 1978).

J. R. Newman, editor, *The World of Mathematics,* New York, Simon and Schuster, 1956, 4 vols.

PART THREE

Special Features

Maxwell's *Treatise* and the Restoration of the Cosmos

Thomas K. Simpson

Thomas K. Simpson has had a lifelong interest in the relationship between the sciences and the humanities. He is a senior tutor at St. John's College, a school with a program that combines both disciplines, and has carried major responsibility for development of the physics laboratory program there. In addition, he has served as a consultant for the Museum of History and Technology at the Smithsonian Institution, where he researched items in the collection and wrote a guidebook to the exhibits of the Division of Electricity, and also for the Franklin Institute, where he helped evaluate the role of a technological museum in contemporary society.

He studied electrical engineering at the Virginia Polytechnic Institute during 1944–45 and took his B.A. from St. John's in 1950, with military service in between at the Applied Physics Laboratory in Silver Springs, Maryland. Subsequently he earned an M.A. (1955) from Wesleyan University and a Ph.D. in the history of science and technology in 1968 from Johns Hopkins, where his doctoral thesis was a literary-critical study of Maxwell's *Treatise*.

He has written several pieces for scholarly publications, including articles on Maxwell for *Isis* and the *Journal for the History and Philosophy of Science*.

James Clerk Maxwell's *Treatise on Electricity and Magnetism* is clearly a great book—and, at the same time, clearly a great problem. Ever since it was published, in 1873, it has stood as something of an enigma to even the best-intentioned of readers. Although there seems to be no question that the *Treatise* is a classic of physical thought and marks a turning point in our understanding of the natural world, the editors of the *Great Books of the Western World* chose not to include it in their collection; they were no doubt quite right in this judgment in terms of the book's likely usefulness to their readers. Maxwell wrote with constant concern for questions that are no longer regarded as valid, and in this text on electricity and magnetism he sought to achieve philosophical goals which modern readers do not share, and which only seem to render his account obscure. There is even room for doubt whether it is a "book" at all, or some other kind of published entity, a product of the tempo and pressures of the life of science in the modern world.

Thus it is with some misgivings, mixed with a kind of reckless courage, that I invite readers of *The Great Ideas Today* to join me in my journey to a possible-book which I believe is indeed a great work of literature and no less beautiful for the perplexities it incorporates. I have thought that the *Treatise* is a little like a city—not the ordered *polis* which is Plato's Republic, but a teeming modern city, crowded with spirit and life, with activities of all sorts, some converging upon one another, others starting out in directions of their own with remote and unknown destinations, and all guided by a variety of leaders of the present and mythic heroes of the past. If the *Treatise* is such a city, it is an image of what we call "modern science," and if a darkness hangs over Maxwell's work, it may be the shroud that has shadowed our belief in science as a prospect for mankind.

It is popular these days to speak of "scientific revolutions" and their structures, and the renewed recognition of these radical turns of thought has certainly very much illuminated our study of the history of science. Such a "revolution," such a radical turn of thought, is indeed taking place in the pages of Maxwell's *Treatise,* and the fact that the foundations of thought are in flux in the very course of the work itself is part of both the interest and the difficulty of reading it.

But is there not something too pallid in this talk of changes of paradigm? For they are not simply happening, as response to crises in the interpretation of phenomena; the best of them are deeply motivated dialectical thrusts of the human spirit, and the scientist makes his groping way forward under the spell of human concerns much larger than the needs of any special science, or even of science itself. At least, I feel that is the case with the *Treatise.* It is a very human work—unabashedly so, with a major place given, especially, to the warm, genuine figure of Michael Faraday. In its humanity, the *Treatise* seems to me to reach out to some of the largest human questions. The revolution taking place in the pages of this work is turning the world inside out, challenging and perhaps reversing the most fundamental understanding of the nature of science itself, and—I think—undertaking to restore something of the fullness of the cosmos which the Newtonian revolution had, in a sense, emptied with its talk of forces and action-at-a-distance. With the establishment of the concept of the *field,* we might see the end of the Age of Newton and the beginning of the Age of Space, regarded not as void but as configured terrain admitting curvature of mass and density.

But things are not so simple. Entering upon this new world evidently entails totally revising our conceptual structure: we can get the old cosmos back again only in wholly new terms. Here Maxwell's special indirectness and a certain deeply rooted skepticism of the claims of conventional wisdom serve him well in opening the way to a new mode of thought. I see this as a metaphorical transformation of the old, Newtonian physics, so that, remarkably enough, there is included within the pages of Maxwell's *Treatise* a kind of "New *Principia,*" of which the application to electromagnetism in the *Treatise* itself is only one illustration.

Maxwell was a deep admirer of Newton ("that mind without a blemish"), and in certain ways the structure of the *Treatise* becomes assimilated to that of the *Principia.* But Maxwell's "New *Principia*" completely reverses the old, and it does so through such a deliberate and conscious use of analogy and metaphor that it is as if the old *Principia* had come under a spell and were being transformed in a comic Forest of Arden or on Prospero's island. It is out of such a magic transformation that Maxwell draws his revolution, from Newtonian action-at-a-distance and a physics of intangible law, to a restored cosmos once again made whole by contiguity and communication throughout. Ultimately, I think, this implies for Maxwell a new order of intelligibility, not only in the sciences, but for the understanding of history and the human community.

In thus identifying theories of action-at-a-distance as "Newtonian," I do not mean to be making a statement about the dialectical richness of Newton's own thought, as revealed for example in the General Scholium to the *Principia,* or certain of the "Queries" appended to the *Optics* (*GBWW,* Vol. 34, pp. 369–72, 520–44). I am thinking rather of the Newton known to the world through the *Principia* as the book of distance-action determined by strictly formulated mathematical law,

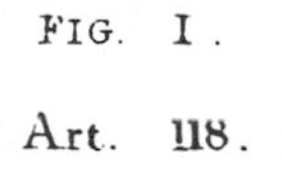

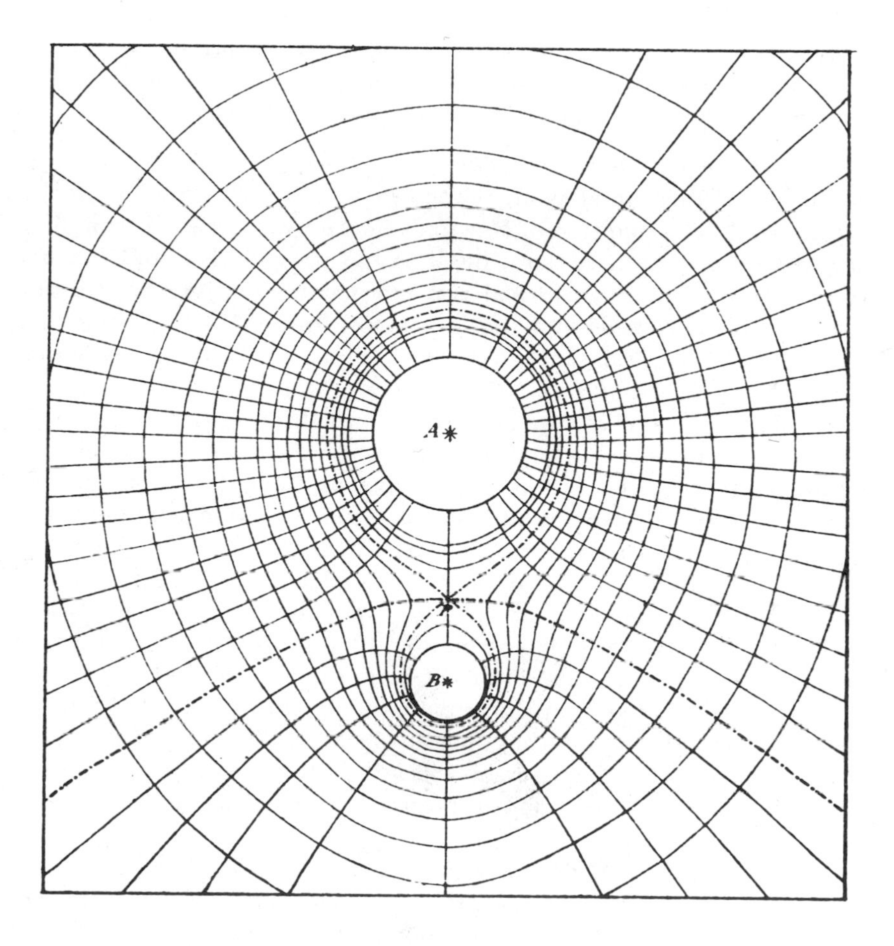

Lines of Force and Equipotential Surfaces.

A = 20. B = 5. P, Point of Equilibrium. AP = $\frac{2}{3}$ AB.

Figure 1. The first figure of James Clerk Maxwell's *Treatise on Electricity and Magnetism*.

and of the long, impressive scientific tradition founded upon this perception. Newton himself certainly speculated relentlessly about possible media, aethereal or otherwise, which might operate between a center of force and a body attracted to it, as between the sun and a planet. But we should remember that Newton had no desire to reduce the operations of nature to mechanics; in particular, the Second Book of the *Principia* is written as a refutation of Descartes and his vortices. When Newton asks,

> What is there in places almost empty of matter, and whence is it that the Sun and planets gravitate towards one another, without dense matter between them? [*Optics,* Query 28; *GBWW,* Vol. 34, p. 529.]

the ultimate answer he is seeking is not anything physical, but "a Being incorporeal, living, intelligent, omnipresent. . . ." Newton is on the track of God. The question of Newton's own understanding is complex, and we cannot pursue it here, but I would suggest that for Newton, physics rightly ends with formal law and action-at-a-distance precisely because this delivers us into the immanent dominion of a being who is "God of Gods, and Lord of Lords" (*Principia,* General Scholium; *GBWW,* Vol. 34, p. 370).

In part, this essay will be an inquiry into the question of whether mathematical physics has a "rhetoric" and will submit to a kind of literary criticism. The "rhetoric" I have in view does not concern ornament, does not exist as an *addition* to the scientific statement, but is intrinsic to it, as the very means by which the statement is made. One point of view would have it that in science the "matter" alone counts, and that questions of "manner" are distractions. This would be a way of understanding the positivist program and would fall in with Hertz's remark, made no doubt from desperation in his attempts to understand Maxwell on the subject of electric charge: "Maxwell's theory is Maxwell's system of equations." Pierre Duhem wrote an entire book, a polemic against Maxwell, in which he attempted to purge electromagnetism of the rhetorical mists in which Maxwell had, in his view, wrapped his subject.[1]

I am encouraged in the alternative view by Maxwell himself, who frequently revealed his preoccupation with questions of form and style. Such questions arise whenever the same thing can be said in more than one way and the choice among these ways makes a difference. Consider this statement from Maxwell's address to the British Association:

> As mathematicians, we perform certain mental operations on the symbols of number or of quantity, and, by proceeding step by step from more simple to more complex operations, we are enabled to express the same thing in many different forms. The equivalence of these different forms, though a necessary consequence of self-evident axioms, is not always, to our minds, self-evident; but the mathematician . . . can

> often transform a perplexing expression into another which explains its meaning in more intelligible language. [*SP* ii/216–17][2]

Maxwell is concerned to master the symbols themselves—to learn to use "analogy," "illustration," and mathematical transformations to wring meaning out of the seemingly abstract and empty forms of mathematical physics, and thus to preserve science for philosophy and the human understanding.

The *Treatise* is, I believe, the work in which he brings to bear all the arts he has developed for this purpose. It is frankly a work dedicated to a rhetorical purpose: Maxwell knows, and explains in his Preface, that there are two general ways, *mathematically equivalent,* in which electromagnetic theory can be presented. They predict the same phenomena; Maxwell acknowledges at the outset that even the most distinctive aspect of his work, the electromagnetic explanation of light, may be predicted equally by the retarded potentials of Ludvig Lorenz. But the difference between two such "equivalent" accounts is precisely the source of the personal energy with which Maxwell writes his *Treatise;* his purpose is to reveal the intellectual consequences of following just one of these alternatives consistently:

> These physical hypotheses, however, are entirely alien from the way of looking at things which I adopt, and one object which I have in view is that some of those who wish to study electricity may, by reading this treatise, come to see that there is another way of treating the subject. . . . [*Tr* i/x][3]

Throughout the *Treatise,* Maxwell throws his equations into that form which will "suggest the ideas" he wishes to present to the reader's mind. These are Faraday's ideas, and the *Treatise,* in my view, can best be understood as a strategic effort to transform the equations of electromagnetic theory into a new structure that captures Faraday's geometrical and physical vision.

Maxwell distinguishes his purpose from that of one who treats all mathematically equivalent forms as equals by saying in the Preface:

> I have therefore taken the part of an advocate rather than that of a judge, and have rather exemplified one method than attempted to give an impartial description of both. [*Tr* i/xi]

It is Maxwell's *advocacy* that I think constitutes this a truly dialectical work. It is governed finally, not by questions of mathematics or laboratory evidence, but by the negation of one path and the affirmation of another according to human criteria not found in the symbols or in the data.

I hasten to remark that this is just one aspect of the *Treatise,* and that in reading it in this rather abstract way as a work of thought we are setting aside the sense in which it very much springs from, and feeds back into, the England of capitalism and the Industrial Revolution. Perhaps in an effort to find a "dialectical" standpoint, we are eliminating from consideration some of the very clues that would lead us to a sense of the larger dialectic in its wholeness, in which the ultimate identity of Maxwell's revolution and the Industrial Revolution would appear. Another reading of the *Treatise,* which I hope to do on another occasion from the point of view of its intersection with measurements, systems of units, economics, and technologies, would give a different picture, complementary to this one. The disarray that readers have found in the book is in part the consequence of these seemingly disparate, but ultimately deeply related, factors. But not everything can be done at once, and we will do well if we can read the *Treatise* at this point from even one consistent point of view.

Faraday and the goal of the *Treatise*

In an extraordinary way, Maxwell's *Treatise on Electricity and Magnetism* presupposes that the reader is already familiar with another book, Faraday's *Experimental Researches in Electricity* (*GBWW,* Vol. 45). Many works refer repeatedly to a single source, but there must be few that *command* their readers as Maxwell does in a footnote: "Read Faraday's *Experimental Researches,* Series i and ii"—advice that might very well apply to any reader of the present essay.[4] For Faraday's work stands as the definition of the goal of the *Treatise:* in some essential way, Maxwell must capture, and as nearly as possible complete, Faraday's project. Thus, the *Treatise* can be seen as a translation into more formal, mathematical terms of Faraday's experimental narrative. But I do not think, as I once did, that this in itself would adequately characterize the relation between the two works, or even that Maxwell would think that translation into formal mathematics or ordered theory would in themselves constitute an improvement on Faraday's original. Rather, it seems to me that Maxwell sets out to capture the spirit of Faraday's work, and to carry it through, as nearly as possible, to the completion Faraday himself sought. In so doing, Maxwell utilizes extensive mathematics and creates something like a formal theoretical system, but these, I think, are merely means to bring greater power to bear on the solution of Faraday's own problem, which, as we shall see, is in no way either analytic or theoretical. Maxwell expresses his dedication to Faraday in strong terms:

> If by anything I have here written I may assist any student in understanding Faraday's modes of thought and expression, I shall regard it as the accomplishment of one of my principal aims—to communicate

> to others the same delight which I have found myself in reading Faraday's *Researches.* [*Tr* i/xi]

It is therefore essential that we begin with some attention to Faraday and his *Researches,* in order to place before ourselves the goal that Maxwell proposes. We have, in effect, to begin with the wrong book: with the *Researches* instead of the *Treatise.*

Faraday developed two concepts which became increasingly significant for him. One was of course his concept of "lines of force." He was impressed by this notion early when he spoke of the lines merely as representations. Toward the end of his work, they bore nearly the whole burden of his thought, and he speculated increasingly about their possible "physical existence." The other fundamental concept was that of the "electrotonic state." This is now unfamiliar to students of science, but for Faraday it was both significant and deeply troubling, and he returned to it, as Maxwell points out, again and again from its introduction in connection with the induction experiments of Series I in 1831, to the end.

In these early experiments, Faraday had been the first to discover that if two circuits are adjacent, the first carrying current and the second including a galvanometer, when the current is interrupted in the first, a brief current is *induced* in the second, as indicated by a deflection of the galvanometer. Essentially, Faraday was convinced that the surge of current in the secondary could not occur unless the primary current had held the secondary circuit in a state of electric *tension,* which was relaxed when the primary current ceased. It was the relaxation of that state of tension which, like the release of a tense spring, caused the galvanometer needle to jump. Faraday had a way of sending off to the university to have a proper scientific term devised to fit his need and, in this case, the result he got was *electrotonic,* from the Greek *tonos,* tension, as in the string of a drawn bow. As we shall see, Maxwell's translation of Faraday's thought turns about these two ideas, the "lines of force" and the "electrotonic state." Maxwell thinks he has found the physical state, the electrotonic state, Faraday was looking for—though not quite in the form Faraday had expected.

For Faraday, these concepts do not function as the elements of a connected *theory* in any formal sense. Faraday was almost totally uneducated in mathematics, a fact that fairly directly reflects the circumstance that he belonged by birth to the working class. It is difficult to grasp the significance of this fact—at once intellectual and social—for science. However brilliantly he succeeded in self-education in other areas, Faraday apparently never felt it necessary to acquire the mathematics he had missed. The result is that he does not have before him with any vividness that universal paradigm of a reasoned deductive system, the geometry of Euclid. He has no working notion of a system of axioms and postulates, or of reasoning leading with logical rigor to universal theorems.

It seems to me that there is in this something of a deliberate rejection, in a spirit which Maxwell may have shared and which may have helped to draw Maxwell to Faraday. We are blessed with the record of a remarkable, revealing exchange of correspondence between Faraday and André-Marie Ampère, the French philosopher and mathematical physicist whose work on electrodynamics Duhem once called "a theory which dispenses with the Frenchman's need to envy the Englishman's pride in the glory of Newton." Here Faraday confronts his opposite, a brilliant mathematical theorist, and in the course of the correspondence Faraday describes his view of his own role:

> . . .I regret that my deficiency in mathematical knowledge makes me dull in comprehending these subjects. I am *naturally skeptical in the matter of theories* and therefore you must not be angry with me for not admitting the one you have advanced immediately.[5]

This skepticism of theory, I believe, turns him away from mathematics almost on principle. Faraday tends to portray mathematicians as operating on a height, while his own work, as experimentalist, lies below, close to nature and to fact. It would be a mistake, I believe, to overlook the element of pride that mixes with humility in his descriptions of his supposedly more modest work. In a moment of triumph following upon the discovery of electromagnetic induction, he wrote to a friend:

> . . .It is quite comfortable to me to find that experiment need not quail before mathematics, but is quite competent to rival it in discovery; and I am amazed to find that what the high mathematicians have announced as the *essential condition* [of one of the phenomena of induction] . . . has so little foundation. . . .[6]

There is more than a suggestion of a moral note in this rejection of theory; in a phrase he used without any hint of apology, Faraday was an "unmathematical philosopher." He speaks an altogether different language from that of the theoretical scientist. He is not stepping hesitantly toward a mathematical physics; he is marching confidently along a different road.

In retrospect, this is a fantastic situation. In the land of Newton, at a time when mathematical physics was again flourishing and the powerful techniques of analytic mathematics had at last made their way from the Continent to England, some of the most creative scientific work of the century was done over a long period of years by a man who had no notion of the *Principia* and did not share either Newton's goals or any appreciation of the power of analytic methods. For Faraday, Newton's classic triumph was essentially meaningless, that triumph which had polarized the intellectual life of Europe for a century. And

Maxwell, who had taken high honors in mathematics at Cambridge, chose this unmathematical philosopher as guide for his own definitive treatise!

How can we understand such a dramatic break in any orderly continuity in the development of science? I think we are witnessing a dialectical questioning of the concept of science itself. In identifying with Faraday's project, Maxwell is not only articulating a new theory of electromagnetism; he is giving science a deliberate new shape.

What, then, is Faraday's concept of science? Despite his proclaimed role as "experimentalist," it is clear that he had one of the most fertile and insistent of speculative minds; in a certain sense, he was constantly producing new hypotheses and his mind was constantly reasoning from them. The result of this, reported in the thousands of paragraphs of the *Experimental Researches* and the equally numerous pages of the *Diary,* is not theory but a vast weaving and unweaving of suspected powers, a process of continual discovery and identification, a great, highly unified formulary for the production and classification of effects.

Faraday, as his biographer John Tyndall proclaimed and all the world agreed, is the great "discoverer"; the paradigm for Faraday is Odysseus rather than Euclid: in a sense he, too, travels from land to land, reporting wonders, guided by legend and myth, rumor or divine love. For Odysseus, the dominant desire is to see men's cities and to know their minds, and to gather all this together in the return to Ithaca. For Faraday, it is to investigate all the powers of nature, and to unveil them as essentially one in the lecture hall at his Royal Institution on Albemarle Street. This is not theoretical physics; as has been suggested, it is essentially chemistry, not in the modern sense of Lavoisier, but as a science of powers in the tradition of van Helmont and Stahl.[7] Faraday recounts his adventures not, I think, as theorist but as *interpreter* of nature, relying on the inherent intelligibility of good narrative. This is science as interpretation, not as theory: what we might call, drawing upon Heidegger, *hermeneutic* science.

The *Experimental Researches* are dense with questions—Faraday's method is that of unremitting inquiry. The very notion of a "series" of researches is, in a sense, that of a chain of linked questions and answers. The underlying question for Faraday is ultimately always the same: what really exists in nature? The practical form that this takes is the *test:* what will happen if I do *this?* Can I produce the phenomenon, the visible or tangible evidence, that will be the sure symptom of the existence of this or that suspected power or state? When the plane of polarized light was rotated on passage through Faraday's "heavy glass" in a strong magnetic field, he announced that he had:

> . . . at last succeeded in *magnetizing and electrifying a ray of light, and in illuminating a magnetic line of force.* [*XR; GBWW,* Vol. 45, p. 595c]

This I believe is symbolic of Faraday's concept of science: to make manifest to the eye what is suspected to exist in nature:

> For if there be such physical lines of magnetic force as correspond (in having a real existence) to the rays of light, it does not seem so very impossible for experiment to touch *them;* and it must be very important to obtain an answer to the inquiry respecting their existence, especially as the answer is likely enough to be in the affirmative.
> [*XR; GBWW,* Vol. 45, p. 832a]

A hypothesis or theory is nothing more than an unresolved suspicion, a part, as Tyndall suggested, of the scaffolding, not of the edifice of science itself, which deals with existences.

Throughout the *Researches,* Faraday sought what he called "contiguity" in nature; understandably, he seeks the same contiguity in the *account* of nature. A work of science should record a completed exploration, a detailed mapping, without gaps, of contiguous substances and powers. It is not merely Faraday's clarity of view and inventiveness that attract Maxwell, but this image of the form physics might take as a physics of contiguity: in a sense, a "field" model of physical explanation itself. In the transformation Maxwell achieved of Faraday's thought, I believe his objective was not only to find mathematical expressions appropriate to Faraday's concepts but to give analytic form to Faraday's vision of an a-theoretic physics through a completed expression of the idea of the electromagnetic field (fig. 1).

Of the two concepts that are so important in Faraday's thought, the "lines of force" and the "electrotonic state," it was curiously the less known "electrotonic state" that seemed to Faraday himself the more fundamental idea, and it is this latter, as we shall see, that Maxwell takes as the key to the translation of Faraday. As we have remarked, it appears early in the *Researches* as the expression of Faraday's perplexity at finding that it is a *change* in the primary current that causes induction. Like other experimenters, he had earlier sought an effect from a *steady* primary current; when, instead, it was the interruption of the primary current that produced the effect, he continued to perceive the pulse in the secondary as evidence of the change in this expected, though never observed, "state." He cannot get this "electrotonic state" out of his head:

> Whilst the wire is subject to either volta-electric or magneto-electric induction, it appears to be in a peculiar state. . . . This electrical condition of matter has not hitherto been recognized, but it probably exerts a very important influence in many if not most of the phenomena produced by currents of electricity. [*XR; GBWW,* Vol. 45, p. 273a]

He has to confess, however, that he found no evidence whatever for the existence of this newly named and announced state:

> This peculiar condition shows no known electrical effects whilst it continues; nor have I yet been able to discover any peculiar powers exerted, or properties possessed, by matter whilst retained in this state.
> [*XR; GBWW,* Vol 45, p. 273b]

He never did. In Series II, he formally withdrew the claim of its existence, though before making his reluctant retraction he had made great efforts to reveal it: he feels strongly that he is in touch with a reality that is present even when the magnetic field is completely at rest. Thirty years after Series I, he reasserts this faith:

> Again and again the idea of an *electro-tonic* state . . . has been forced on my mind; such a state would coincide and become identified with that which would then constitute the physical lines of magnetic force. . . .
> [*XR* ¶3269. Not in *GBWW.*]

Should we say that the "electrotonic state" was, for Faraday, a *theoretical concept* and conclude that Faraday was, after all, a theoretician despite himself? Rather, I think this "state" is theoretical for Faraday only insofar as there is a gap that has not yet been filled in the explanatory series. There is "a link in the chain of effects, a wheel in the physical mechanism of the action, as yet unrecognized." The goal is to fill that gap with something *other* than a speculative concept. As a science reaches completion, theory disappears. Completed science is a-theoretical. With this, I think Maxwell is in deep agreement.

It is useful, finally, to notice what Faraday does *not* ask himself. He does not ask questions about quantitative, functional relationships—about "laws." He does not work with ratios and proportions. Not only does he almost never write an equation, he never asks the kind of question that has an equation as the natural form of its answer.

Faraday's discomfort with the notion of a functional relation in mathematics is revealed poignantly by a remark he made very late in his career, at a time when he had finally been brought into confrontation with the, to him, dreaded and offensive inverse-square law of gravity. He rebels at the formulation: "with a strength VARYING INVERSELY. . . ." The capital letters are his, expressing his outrage at what he considers a blatant violation of the principle of *conservation* of the force: how can it then "vary"? He understands, indeed, the algebraic relation as describing the effect, but the proportion, which for Newton and many generations of scientists after him had fully characterized the force, seems to Faraday utterly unjust to it. "Why, then, talk about the inverse square of the distance?" he says, commenting on a dismissal of his own account by the astronomer-royal, Sir George Airy. "I had to warn my audience against the sound of this law and its supposed opposition on my Friday evening. . . ."

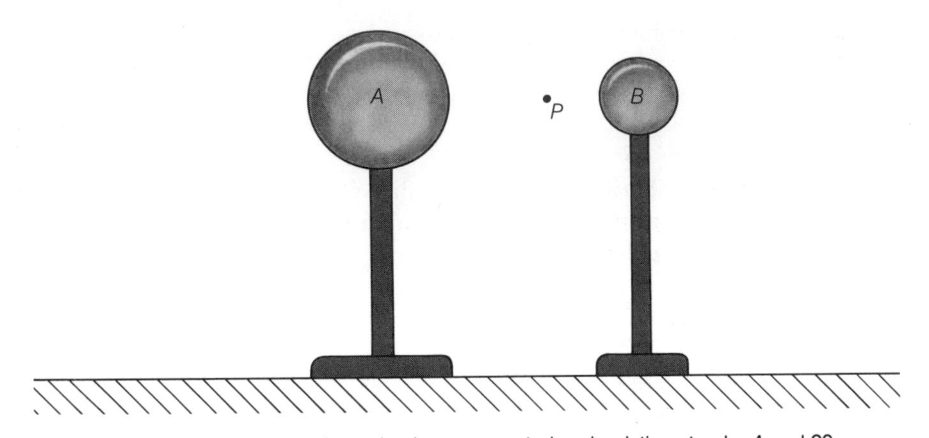

Figure 2. Two positively charged metal spheres, mounted on insulating stands: $A = +20$; $B = +5$. Turn this drawing on its side and you have the arrangement of Figure 1. The figures are printed to scale, so that Figure 2 superimposes on Figure 1.

This is of course a naive view, profoundly naive. Faraday had said:

> Let the imagination go, guiding it by judgment and principle, but holding it in and directing it by *experiment.*[8]

This remark, in its context in the *Diary,* is not a methodological reflection but a Dionysian outcry in the midst of the chase. It is surrounded by a cascade of ideas, as much visionary as experimental, about a wished relation between gravity and electricity. Faraday built the world of the *Experimental Researches* on this assurance of the reality, immediacy, and unity of the world of nature. It is, perhaps, the literary triumph of Maxwell's *Treatise* that he is able to carry this vivid, human insight into mathematical physics itself with such gentleness and conviction, in the process creating a new vision at once of mathematical physics and our relation to nature—even, perhaps, to one another.

A mathematical figure of speech

To "fix our ideas," in a phrase of Maxwell's, we would do well to consider a definite experimental arrangement, as in Figure 2. Here the circles labeled "*A*" and "*B*" represent two positively charged metal spheres, *A* with a charge of 20 units, and *B* with a charge of 5. There is a force of repulsion between them: each is in some way or other able to exert an influence at a distance. For example, *A* could be made to induce a charge on some neutral body at a distance, and Faraday thus tends to refer to this distance-action in terms of "induction." How can we understand the action of a charged body over an intervening distance?

For Faraday, the right interpretation of this situation is crucial. He cannot believe that it is adequately explained by the invocation of a mere mathematical law of action-at-a-distance; something must intervene:

> . . . I was led to suspect that common induction itself was in all cases an *action of contiguous particles* and that electrical action at a distance . . . never occurred except through the influence of the intervening matter. . . . if this be true, the distinction and establishment of such a truth must be of the greatest consequence to our further progress in the investigation of the nature of electric forces.
>
> [*XR; GBWW,* Vol. 45, p. 441c–d]

To carry through the interpretation of electrostatics in Faraday's terms, as the action of an intervening medium, is the challenge Maxwell takes up in Part I of the *Treatise.* Maxwell explains that he will start from the position of traditional theory:

> In the following treatise I propose first to explain the ordinary theory of electrical action, which considers it as depending only on the electrified bodies and on their relative position, without taking account of any phenomena which may take place in the intervening media. In this way we shall establish the law of the inverse square, the theory of the potential, and the equations of Laplace and Poisson. [*Tr* i/62]

This we may refer to as the Old Way, and think of as the way of Newton and the Newtonians, who included most of the mathematicians of electricity in Maxwell's time. It is important to reflect, as mentioned earlier, that Newton's own view of force laws and distance-action was not simple; Maxwell was very much interested in the fact that Newton seems at times to have covered some of the ground that Maxwell himself was about to explore. Here, I am thinking primarily of the tradition of mathematical physics built on the foundation of the *Principia* and formal laws of force acting at a distance.[9]

Newton had concluded in the *Principia:*

> That there is a power of gravity pertaining to all bodies, proportional to the several quantities of matter which they contain.

and that,

> In two spheres gravitating each towards the other, if the matter in places on all sides round about and equidistant from the centres is similar, the weight of either sphere towards the other will be inversely as the square of the distance between their centres.
>
> [*Principia; GBWW,* Vol. 34, p. 282b]

This is Newton's law of gravitation. The corresponding law governing the action of one charged body upon another was given by Coulomb. It had been the great triumph of the early heroes of the mathematical theory of electricity to be able to state such a law for charged bodies and to use it to account for observed electrical phenomena, thereby bringing electrostatics within the fold of the only known mathematical physics, that of an action between two centers of force, along the line which joins them. If we insist on asking *how A* influences *B,* we get only the formal, blank answer, "by virtue of a law. . . ." Indeed, in the *Treatise* Maxwell, true to his promise, develops the theory of such electrical laws very thoroughly. But his intentions lie elsewhere.

To move beyond Newton, Maxwell proposes to use what we might think of as a mathematical figure of speech. He will use a certain mathematical theorem as a bridge between the Old Way and the New, namely that relationship he calls "Thomson's theorem." Without entering here into the details of the mathematical odyssey on which Maxwell embarks, we might simply note that he draws this theorem from a certain storehouse of treasures, a fascinating section, labeled simply "Preliminary," which precedes chapter 1 of the *Treatise* and seems to parallel the Lemmas at the outset of Newton's *Principia.*

The "Preliminary" constitutes an exposition of the mathematical elements that will make possible the development of the science to come. From this Thesaurus of principles (more than a little suggestive, too, of the "topics" of Aristotle and the rhetorical tradition, as libraries of arguments to be brought to bear by the artist, as needed), Maxwell selects "Theorem III," which he proceeds to transform by mathematical artistry into the specific form of Thomson's theorem. This takes the form of an *identity*—not an equation valid only for certain values of the variables, called the "solutions," but an equivalence that holds true for any value of the variables whatever and thus permits the free substitution of one form for the other. Maxwell explains how he will use it:

> In Thomson's theorem, the total energy of the system is expressed in the form of the integral of a certain quantity extended over the whole space between the electrified bodies, and also in the form of an integral extended over the electrified surfaces only. The equality of these two expressions may be thus interpreted physically. We may conceive the physical relation between the electrified bodies, either as the result of the state of the intervening medium, or as the result of a direct action between the electrified bodies at a distance. If we adopt the latter conception, we may determine the law of the action, but we can go no further in speculating on its cause. If, on the other hand, we adopt the conception of action through a medium, we are led to enquire into the nature of that action in each part of the medium. [*TR* i/62–63][10]

The two hypotheses, Maxwell goes on to say, are *mathematically equivalent.* They represent the same quantity, but they express it in such different mathematical forms that they suggest altogether different ideas. Thus this "rhetorical" difference—a difference of "form" without a difference of "content"—can make all the difference between two contrasting views of the world.

Thomson's theorem applies directly to our Figure 2. Here, the two charged bodies repelling one another constitute a system that is tending to fly apart. Like a wound-up spring, it contains stored ("potential") energy. Thomson's theorem will calculate that energy in two ways. The Old Way, taking the presumed charges on the surfaces of the spheres as fundamental, will reckon these by means of a double-integration over the surfaces of the two spheres (the double-integration signifying a double-summation over the two dimensions of the surfaces).

The other side of Thomson's equation suggests the New Way. Here the calculation of the same total energy of the system is carried out over the region surrounding the charged bodies, as a triple-integral representing a summation over the three dimensions of that space. The resulting number, measuring the energy of the compressed system, is the same, reckoned by the Old Way or the New. But if we take the New Way, and sum over space, the question suggests itself immediately, "What is that quantity that we are summing?" It arose out of the mathematical identity, but we might find in it physical significance. Maxwell understands it as an energy density having a value everywhere in the region of the charged bodies, a "region" that has no boundaries. This is not an act of proof, nothing has been logically demonstrated; Maxwell's crucial suggestion, on which he founds field theory in the *Treatise,* is frankly a rhetorical act, one not of demonstration but of interpretation.[11] The field arises, then, as the distribution of this energy density over space; it is the product of Maxwell's vision, and of his skillful mathematical rhetoric, which has shaped the equations so as to bring it to our view. We have entered, with Maxwell, a new conceptual world: what can we make of it?

The view from point "*P*"

Maxwell distinguishes the Old Way and the New as the "direct" and the "inverse" methods:

> In the second chapter we have calculated the potential function and investigated some of its properties on the hypothesis that there is a direct action at a distance between electrified bodies, which is the resultant of the direct actions between the various electrified parts of the bodies.
>
> If we call this the *direct method* of investigation, the *inverse method* will consist in assuming that the potential is a function characterised by properties the same as those which we have already established, and investigating the form of the function.
>
> In the direct method the potential is calculated from the distribution of electricity by a process of integration, and is found to satisfy certain partial differential equations. In the inverse method the partial

> differential equations are supposed given, and we have to find the potential and the distribution of electricity. . . .
>
> The integral, therefore, is the appropriate mathematical expression for a theory of action between particles at a distance, whereas the differential equation is the appropriate expression for a theory of action exerted between contiguous parts of a medium.
>
> [*Tr* i/123–24] [italics added]

The term *differential equation* here envisions a statement, written in terms of derivatives, or rates-of-change of quantities (in electrostatics, rates-of-change in space rather than time), which characterizes the state of affairs everywhere in a region. Such an expression holds true in form at every point, though its specific value changes from point to point. For example, if we wanted to write such a differential equation to characterize the state of affairs in Figure 1, we would need to assert the fact that there are no charges in the space outside of spheres *A* and *B*. Maxwell shows how to write an equation (*Laplace's equation*), in terms of the electric intensity vector, that expresses this.[12] This expression will be known to hold true throughout the field; the problem will be to find the actual values the intensity will have, everywhere, if specific values are set at the boundaries, namely, in this case, at the surfaces of the two spheres (the "boundary conditions").

The resulting distribution of values at all points in the space is what Maxwell calls here "the form of the function" that is to be sought. Change anything—the value at a boundary, or the position of a charge at some point in the midst of the region—and the function will change form, all at once, everywhere. The inverse method sets a problem that can only be solved as a whole. In the direct method, applying Coulomb's law, we can mentally divide each charged surface into a large number of arbitrarily small elements and then total the effect of every element of the surface of sphere *A*, according to the law, upon every element of sphere *B*. Whereas, then, the direct method invites analysis, the inverse method demands a holistic approach; if such a problem is to be solved at all, it must be solved all at once.

Following, then, the inverse method into the new world, we become interested in the space itself, the field. Not only the energy density, which Thomson's theorem gave us, but its other properties must be explored; we need to know what it "looks like." It has a kind of directionality at all points, the directionality of the vector $\boldsymbol{E}$. The inverse method delineates $\boldsymbol{E}$ as a whole pattern, a configuration. Tracing this configuration in connected curves, we get Faraday's lines of electric force, everywhere telling us the shape of the field. The corresponding lines of equal potential (analogous to contour lines on a hillside), running everywhere orthogonal to the lines of $\boldsymbol{E}$, reveal mountains and valleys of complex shapes; Maxwell encourages us to utilize the "eye-knowledge" which diagrams of the field can give us, and he includes a number of these field diagrams as plates accompanying Volume I of the *Treatise.* The first of these plates illustrates the field that arises from the configuration of our spheres *A* and *B;* it is reproduced as Figure 1 of this essay. We would do well to consider what this image portends, for it is in a way a vision of the dialectical principle that motivates the *Treatise.*

Maxwell's figure shows us a *whole,* by contrast with the individual calculations that arise from action-at-a-distance formulas. If such a whole exists, then the question of the world-change becomes that of its significance. In the *direct* method, Maxwell said in the quotation above, "the potential is calculated from the distribution of electricity by a process of integration." "Integration" evidently means in this context a summing up—that is, the gathering of many elements into a totality. The whole is secondary, a consequence; it has the unity merely of marbles in a bag. Can we say that the inverse method carries an opposite significance?

Maxwell's figure, though it too is obtained by a process of integration ("integration" of the differential equation), is an image of continuity, bound everywhere by an equation that speaks of connections. "Integration" seems to have taken on a radically different meaning in the sea change between the direct and the indirect methods. In the first, the parts are primary, and the integration sums them to find their combined effect. In the second, continuity is primary; the process of "integration" in this case finds the single solution that will satisfy the requirements of connectedness throughout. In the first, the integral is a *summation of parts* to constitute a totality; in the second, it is the *symbol of wholeness,* and the invocation of a process in which parts will find their places with respect to a whole that is primary.

Maxwell's close friend, Lewis Campbell, was a student of Jowett's, and it is often noted that, as Maxwell went off to Cambridge to immerse himself in mathematics, Campbell had gone to Oxford to devote himself to Plato.[13] Campbell opened a field of scholarship in his study of the dating of the Platonic dialogues; it is interesting in the present context to note his work as editor of the *Theaetetus* and the *Sophist* (cf. *GBWW,* Vol. 7). Maxwell was very comfortable with Greek and kept in touch with Campbell's work to a certain extent over the years; there are reasons to think that he always had Greek distinctions running in the back of his mind. It might be in order, then, to invoke here the contrast which is so fundamental in those dialogues, the *Theaetetus* and the *Sophist,* between the *all* (*to pan*) and the *whole* (*to holon*). Socrates reminds us of Hesiod's account of a wagon: in one view, the wagon is made up of a hundred planks; in the other, it is that one thing, the *whole,* with respect to which alone any of the parts can have significance (ibid., p. 547d).

Maxwell was certainly not a stranger to this kind of consideration. He believed that the relation between physics and metaphysics was inherently very close. The names hint at it, he thought; it is clear that he felt much more than physical science itself was at stake in this major change of worldviews. The metaphysician, he says, is only the physicist disarmed of all his weapons: while the physicist measures time, space, and mass, the metaphysician struggles to speak of invariant sequence, coexistence, and the nature of matter. Physics has a certain priority; all serious thought must be grounded in consciousness, and hence the metaphysician would do well to enter upon his trade by way of physics.

It is hard not to glance again at the *Theaetetus* and consider the sense in which there is profound truth in Theaetetus's first response to the question, "What is knowledge?"—namely, "Knowledge is *aisthesis*"—which is of course the reason why it is appropriate that Theaetetus, perhaps the best of Socrates' students, comes to him from geometry, the science in which the senses and the mind join in argument. *Aisthesis,* commonly translated "sensation," is perhaps not so far from what Maxwell means by "consciousness"—though worlds separate the choices of the two terms. Maxwell praises, as we have seen, that "eye-knowledge" which his geometrical figure brings to our understanding of the world.

It appears to me that the "inverse method," represented in Figure 1, expresses the inversion not only of mathematical physics and electrostatics but more generally of the liberal arts and the world which they reflect. For example, in a late essay on freedom, Maxwell in effect takes the configuration of this diagram as an image of a new understanding of the operation of the free will.[14] He has wondered aloud whether the development of the physical sciences in the nineteenth century is leading necessarily to an increasing sense of determinism; he concludes that it need not, precisely because of points such as "*P*" in the figure. These are *singular* points, watersheds at which the least force could take us into one valley or the other. No force is required at such a point to change worlds.

The development of the principle of the conservation of energy, Maxwell says, has transformed our idea of the soul: it is no longer the source of motion, as it had been for Aristotle, but, rather, only the guide. He likens this role to that of the "pointsman" (the switch operator) on the railway, who turns the switch points to one side or the other and thereby deflects the course of a train to one or another destination. A simple configuration like that of our figure may have only one such saddle point, but as we go up the scale of being toward greater complexity, such points of indeterminacy multiply. Maxwell sees them as moral turning points, moments of tact, delicacy, and human insight which make crucial differences in our lives. "All great results produced by human endeavor depend on taking advantage of these singular states when they occur," he believes.

Maxwell's notion of singularities could be a rather trivial suggestion in relation to the serious issue of freedom of the will, if it were no more than the observation that points of indeterminacy arise in physical systems. A little reflection on Newton's or Coulomb's law could lead quickly to the same conclusion. I think, however, that the distinction between the merely mechanical concept of instability and Maxwell's insight into free will helps us to see the full significance of the figure and the larger world-change that accompanies the shift from the old to the new view of the integral. For an instability, seen only as an ambivalent outcome of the application of a force law, gives us uncertainty without significance. On the other hand, the point *P* of the figure, seen as a saddle point between two valleys, has significance precisely because the individual decision point is not a point of blind indeterminacy but a point of vision, in which options can be comprehended in their wholeness and relationship. That I think is an interesting insight into free will and is even exemplified in the *Treatise* itself. Rather than teach only his own method, Maxwell seems anxious to probe both the old and the new ways, and insofar as possible to understand them in their significance at this human turning point.

The *Treatise* is a dialectical work, which in its own way is pressing the questions of meaning and being. In insisting on a mode of physics that achieves intelligibility as fully as possible, Maxwell is pioneering in the effort to restore meaning in modern life and to help us understand what is at stake in the threat of its loss. In this sense, the *field* is for Maxwell a paradigm not only for the science of electromagnetism but for the method and structure of science generally, and for human thought, action, and society. The *Treatise* I think tries, as fully as a work of physics can, to achieve the view from point *P*.

Revelation and interpretation

Before he went on to Cambridge, Maxwell was for three years a student at the University of Edinburgh, and many commentators have pointed out the significance that this experience had for his work. In Maxwell's time Edinburgh held firmly to a vision of liberal education entirely different from that at Cambridge. For an honors student at Cambridge the discipline was severe and single-minded. If a student was preparing for honors in mathematics—and this, especially under the influence of William Whewell, was the principal Cambridge track in liberal education—there was little time to spare for other matters.

At Edinburgh, by contrast, the program was broad and balanced, requiring attendance of all students at a wide range of lectures. In no case was the standard of attainment set at the Cambridge level; in place, for example, of total command of Greek, it was rather the goal at Edinburgh to learn through Greek to master language more generally. It was an Edinburgh tradition that lecturers be accessible for general questioning in smaller groups following the lectures. In general, it was an education for men as human beings, not as specialists.[15] The result was that for many students, of whom Maxwell was certainly one, the experience at Edinburgh left a very strong impression and a lifelong commitment to the pursuit of certain fundamental human questions. The concern with determinism and free will discussed above was certainly one of Maxwell's Edinburgh inheritances.

One center of Maxwell's attention at Edinburgh was Sir William Hamilton (not to be confused with the mathematician William Rowan Hamilton of Dublin, who in a very different way was also an important influence on Maxwell.) The Edinburgh Hamilton was famous for his courses of lectures, which all students attended, on logic and metaphysics. Many of the recurrent themes in Maxwell's writings and in his scientific practice are recognizable as Hamiltonian concerns.

Hamilton was, in certain respects at least, a Kantian. At the foundation of his thought lies the principle of "Hamiltonian Relativity":

> . . . the great axiom, that all human knowledge, consequently that all human philosophy, is only of the relative or phaenominal . . . in saying that we know only the relative, I virtually assert that we know nothing absolute.[16]

Our minds, on the other hand, are powerful forces that work upon the phenomena according to laws of the mind's own. There arises the threat of a tyranny of reason, against which Hamilton warns in many ways, for it is a fearsome temptation on the part of the mind, he thinks, to force consciousness into patterns of its own and to proclaim these to be truth. Hamilton particularly suspects philosophical "systems"; he speaks of the "Valhalla of Systems." What then is the right stance toward consciousness? He makes a bold claim:

> . . . philosophy, as the science of truth, requires a renunciation of prejudices. . . . In this, if I may without irreverence compare things human with things divine, Christianity and Philosophy coincide—for truth is equally the end of both. What is the primary condition which our Saviour requires of his disciples? That they throw off their old prejudices, and come with hearts willing to receive knowledge and understandings open to conviction. . . . Philosophy requires an emancipation from the yoke of foreign authority, a renunciation of all blind adhesion to the opinions of our age and country, and a purification of the intellect from all assumptive beliefs.

and then he draws an especially striking proposal:

> Consciousness is to the philosopher what the Bible is to the theologian. Both are revelations of the truth—and both afford the truth to those who are content to receive it, as it ought to be received, with reverence and submission.[17]

This passage points the way to my own thought. It is Hamilton's vision of consciousness as revelatory that I propose as a clue to Maxwell's devotion to Faraday, as well as to his own practice of science. I think Maxwell saw in Faraday the "child," who was ready to purge himself of all prejudices and to approach nature with the conviction that he was in the immediate presence of truth, which he was ready to receive with a full measure of reverence and submission. Hamilton himself goes on to a yet bolder assumption:

> . . . I am . . . bold enough to maintain, that consciousness affords not merely the only revelation, and only criterion of philosophy, but that this revelation is naturally clear. . . .[18]

Consciousness is the equivalent of a sacred text—perhaps it *is* a sacred text—and it will yield truth if we approach it in the appropriate manner. Hamilton may be a "Kantian," but this is not altogether Kant!

Faraday, as we have seen, does not conceive of science in the mode of "theory," which appears to him rather an affront than a model. These quotations from Hamilton, I believe, suggest a point of view from which we might understand Faraday's position and, at the same time, Maxwell's. For if the task of science is to be likened to that of theology in the presence of a sacred text, the mode appropriate to science will not be theory but *interpretation.* Interpretation is a branch of the classic art of rhetoric; it was always important, but it became central with Augustine as the Greek art was brought into the service of Christianity. For Augustine, who most forcefully recast the ancient art in its new role, interpretation (*hermeneuein,* giving us "hermeneutics") was the art that made it possible to read and understand the voice of God in scripture, and indeed, as we see in the *Confessions*—which are an *interpretation* of a life—to "read" the Creation itself as well. All things for Augustine speak of their maker, for one who is able to hear and interpret their message.[19]

Not only Augustine thinks this way. Maxwell's understanding of science—his dedication to interpretation as a way of bringing us closer to nature—is likewise suggestive in spirit, at least in my view, of Heidegger's invocation of hermeneutics in the approach to being, and thus I think it has not been inappropriate to suggest, as I did earlier in this essay, that we meet here a *hermeneutic,* as opposed to a *theoretic,* understanding of science. The field is thus an image of the hermeneutic view of science.

I should say, then, that Maxwell speaks with the Augustinian spirit in *interpreting* the meaning of the inverse method, which he sees as an inversion of our understanding of the cosmos:

> The vast interplanetary and interstellar regions will no longer be regarded as waste places in the universe, which the Creator has not seen

> fit to fill with the symbols of the manifold order of His kingdom. We shall find them to be already full of this wonderful medium; so full, that no human power can remove it from the smallest portion of space, or produce the slightest flaw in its infinite continuity. It extends unbroken from star to star. . . . [*SP* ii/322]

Alexandre Koyré has shown how the Copernican transformation led man out of the "closed world," into the "infinite universe."[20] Newton found the key to interrelation of the elements of the cosmos in the universal law of gravity, but the vast spaces remained void, mediated only by an omnipresent God who is evidently not the God in whom Maxwell places his faith. The question does at this point touch on theology. Newton's God is severe, the "God of power, lordship, dominion"—a God for whom the autocracy of law, and the kind of dark intelligibility law brings, is appropriate. Maxwell has, in his mind, a very different cosmos, a very different God, and a very different concept of intelligibility.

The implications of the "inversion," in Maxwell's interpretation, are pervasive. The integrity, the wholeness we have spoken of in connection with Figure 1, becomes the integrity of the cosmos. The prospect is of a return from the "infinite universe" to the restoration of the ancient cosmos as an ordered, contiguous whole. From the infinite universe, then, to the restored world. Figure 1, so interpreted, becomes the first image of that restoration.

Finally, since we form our human societies on the pattern of the cosmos and vice versa, the restoration of wholeness in the larger world suggests a similar restoration in the society of man. At this point, Maxwell's revolution in the realm of the cosmos has, as its implicit counterpart, that revolution from an "atomic" society to one of contiguity and membership of which Marx writes in the *German Ideology.* Indeed, it is appropriate that the careers of Maxwell and Marx seem to have had one fleeting point of tangency, in a common teacher of mechanics, Robert Willis. Willis's algebra of mechanics has its reflection in Maxwell's chapter "On the Equations of Motion of a Connected System," and in Marx's massive chapter in *Capital* on the analytic principle in capitalism, "Machinery and Modern Industry."[21] The two counterpart chapters reflect the two readings, physical and social, of our Figure 1. But to pursue this thought would require another investigation.

Analogy as an instrument of interpretation

We have seen, in Thomson's theorem, how far a mathematical figure of speech could take us in transforming a world. This transformation came in the early chapters; the *Treatise,* however, works constantly with another rhetorical instrument as well, that of *analogy,* which offers such versatility that it serves in one way or another at every level of investigation. At one extreme, it verges into analytic mathematics itself, as mathematical analogy; at the other, it delivers us to the doorstep of explicit physical theory. Maxwell uses it, not only in this work but in the papers that led up to the *Treatise* and in the books that arose from it, with a special appreciation of the intellectual and strategic alternatives it affords him. He sometimes stops to discuss the role of "analogy" with the reader. Employment of what we might call the right grade of analogy makes it possible to meet the rhetorical criterion Maxwell holds as a standard: to assert all that is justified by the evidence, but no more.

Maxwell returns, in chapter 5 of Part I of the *Treatise,* to ask from a more physical point of view what sort of medium may in fact exist in the space between *A* and *B*? This will not be a specific physical hypothesis, nor a physical *theory* of the field. All that Maxwell explores is the possibility that an analogy can be constructed, by virtue of which the phenomena of electrostatics can be systematically *likened* to those of a physical medium under stress. In this way, our thought is in a way empowered, but in a way it is also suspended. We realize this if we ask just what sort of "medium" we seem to be getting at and look closely at Maxwell's chapter to see what details he gives us. He gives us none; there is a strong suggestion he is playing a kind of game with us, knowing we will be wondering, and saying quite strictly nothing to help us out of our distress. Is this a solid undergoing elastic deformation? He will not say so but only repeats that word, *medium.* It is *like* an elastic solid, and he can use this strict, quantitative analogy to carry out a calculation of the stresses.

The calculated stresses within this metaphoric medium prove to be these: first, a tension along the line of force, which can thus be thought of as stretched like a rope; and second, a stress orthogonal to the line and equal in magnitude to the first. It is evidently a matter of great satisfaction to Maxwell to be able to show us that this is exactly the vision which Faraday had given us. Maxwell cites Faraday's account, and concludes on a note of quiet triumph:

> This is an exact account of the conclusions to which we have been conducted by our mathematical investigation. At every point of the medium there is a state of stress such that there is tension along the lines of force and pressure in all directions at right angles to these lines, the numerical magnitude of the pressure being equal to that of the tension, and both varying as the square of the resultant force at the point.
>
> [*Tr* i/164]

Having won this much ground, Maxwell now undertakes a Circe-like trick which, as a work of rhetoric, may be more disturbing than the inversion of worlds. He returns to the concept with which the whole science of electrostatics began, the concept on which the science is founded, and makes it disappear before our eyes. He shows that "charge" was a work of what Lukács would call "reification," an object of false consciousness bred of living too long in a wrong world.[22] *There is no need for the concept of "charge" in the new world of Maxwell's fields.* There is no "center of force" anywhere. In its place, we will have the very different concept of electric *displacement* throughout the field. Using our new image of an elastic medium, we may consider what happens when a positively charged sphere is placed in the center of a room. The air proves to be *dielectric,* for through the air corresponding apparent negative charges are induced on the walls, floor, and ceiling. With care, we could trace the lines of force from the sphere to those surfaces. With our new insights we could tell ourselves that there is an electric stress everywhere, which Maxwell likes to evaluate in pounds per square inch. This is an instance of induction: the charged sphere, Faraday has said, is *inducing* the wall charges through the dielectric medium of the air.

In this context, Maxwell now introduces his term *displacement:*

> When induction is transmitted through a dielectric, there is in the first place a displacement of electricity in the direction of the induction. For instance, in a Leyden jar, of which the inner coating is charged positively and the outer coating negatively, the direction of the displacement of positive electricity in the substance of the glass is from within outwards. [*Tr* i/166]

Applying this to our case of the charged sphere in the center of a room, we would say: there has been a displacement of positive electricity from the sphere toward the walls. Where, then, is the "charge," that supposed substance on which the science of electricity is founded, and which is the center of all forces? There is, after all, nothing deposited on what have been called "charged" surfaces, but rather a state of affairs, a state of displacement or polarization, throughout the space:

> Thus when the charged conductor is introduced into the closed space [the positively charged sphere into the room, "bringing" electricity with it] there is immediately a displacement of a quantity of electricity equal to the charge through the surface from within outwards, and the whole quantity within the surface remains the same. [*Tr* i/68]

We *thought* we were "bringing" something called "electricity," or "charge," into the room on the "charged" conductor. Actually, by the analogy, we are rearranging the state of affairs in the dielectric medium which fills the room—placing it in a state of stress through a displacement outward from the sphere, to, and *through,* the walls. There is nothing "on" the sphere or "on" the walls. The displacement, and the stress, would be essentially the same if the room were emptied of its air and the experiment were carried out in total vacuum. We have accounted in very different terms for "that apparent charge which is commonly called the Charge of the Conductor." All of this is the consequence of a method not of proof but of interpretation—of entertaining a vivid physical analogy very seriously.

The transformation extended to magnetism

We have followed Maxwell in the transformation of our understanding of electrostatics, but electrostatics is only half of the overall science of electricity and magnetism that Maxwell is addressing in the *Treatise*—and electrostatics is perhaps the easier half. Much more confusing phenomena arise in the domain of magnetism, and especially in relation to "electrodynamics," in which electric currents act magnetically upon one another. In electrostatics we had phenomena which seemed to fit the pattern of the gravitational force between the sun and a planet—Coulomb's law was an easy counterpart to Newton's law of universal gravitation. Maxwell's conversion of thought from Coulomb's law to the field point of view was indeed a delicate maneuver, but it represented a straightforward problem and serves well as a paradigm in which we can study the inverse method and consider its consequences. In electrodynamics, and more generally in the phenomena of magnetism, things are not so clear. Thus, the first electrodynamic phenomenon observed, by Ørsted, was the action of a straight wire carrying current upon a magnetic needle nearby: the poles of the needle were *neither attracted nor repelled* by the wire but were moved in a direction perpendicular of the line joining them to the wire. The effect was rotational, and Faraday in fact showed how to use it to produce a continuous rotational motion. Surely this could not be fitted to the Newtonian model!

It was a moment of special satisfaction for mathematical physics when Ampère succeeded in doing just that—in showing that an inverse-square law could be written which, when applied pair-wise to arbitrarily small current elements, or snippets of current, would account for the observed torque. If mathematical physics were coextensive with laws of force acting at distances along a line of centers, as it seemed, then Ampère had saved the day for mathematical physics, and he was widely celebrated for this victory.

Again, to "fix our ideas" we may think of a particular electrodynamic situation that is in a way a counterpart to the electrostatic arrangement of Figure 2. Here (fig. 3), two wires are carrying current; for simplicity, we may think of them as lying in two parallel planes. Between them will occur a magnetic interaction—an attractive force of one wire upon

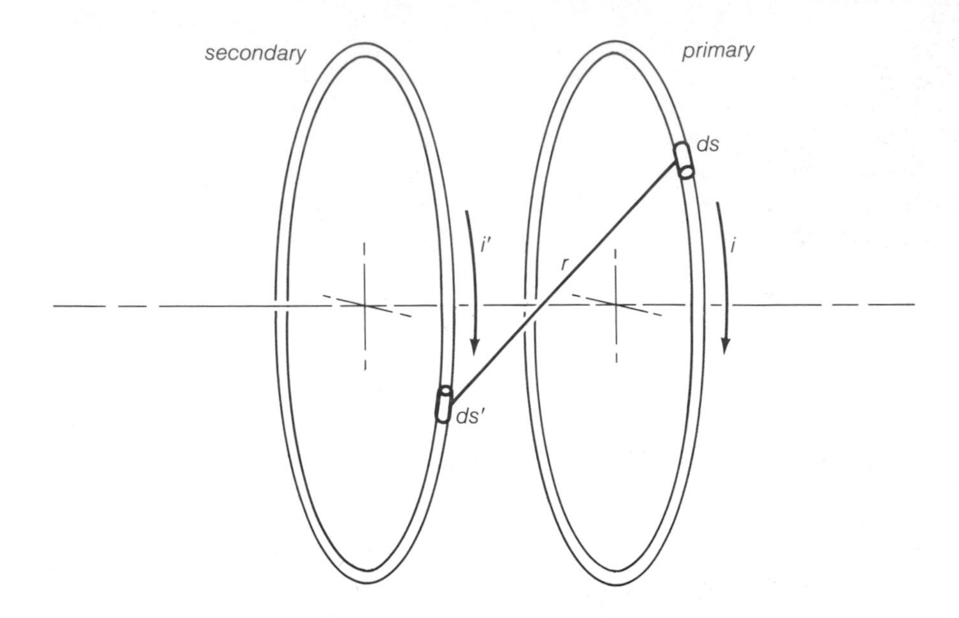

Figure 3. Two circular coils carrying current in parallel planes. If the currents, *i* and *i'*, are flowing as shown, the force between the coils will be attractive; *ds* and *ds'* denote the current elements, and *r* the distance between them, in Ampère's law. If a switch is introduced in the primary, and a galvanometer in the secondary, electromagnetic induction can be demonstrated.

the other if the currents flow as shown in the diagram. Ampère's law applies to two arbitrarily small segments of the two circuits, so-called current elements, *ds* and *ds'*. The law predicts a force along the line *r* joining them, given by a rather complex formula—not at all like the straightforward equation of Coulomb.[23] The very arbitrariness and awkwardness of the formula makes it suspect in Maxwell's eyes: it seems rather imposed on nature than drawn from it. Furthermore, the putative "force" between *ds* and *ds'* can never be demonstrated empirically, for we cannot produce a current in a segment like *ds:* currents by their nature must flow in complete circuits. Ampère's equation must therefore be summed around at least one of the circuits before it can be used, and with that summation, the supposed force along the individual line *r* is completely swallowed up. Thus, the "force" of which Ampère's law speaks can never be observed—and that, in Maxwell's eyes at least, is a very bad sign for any proposed law.

Faraday, of course, takes an utterly different approach to this interaction. We will look at his discussion of the interaction of magnets, rather than the currents of Figure 3, but as the interactions are magnetic in either case, what he says will be applicable to electrodynamics as well. Again, Faraday thinks in terms of events transpiring in the space between the magnets, and again, he delineates this region, the field, in terms of lines of force. If we think for a moment of an isolated magnet, the whole system of its lines of force constitutes for Faraday what he comes to see as an entity, the real locus of the magnetic power, a kind of "atmosphere of power" with a definite, though alterable, form (fig. 4). To designate this spatial object, he again calls on "the advice of a kind friend" to coin an appropriate name. Inasmuch as here the lines suggest to him the form of a winged beetle, the word made to his prescription is *sphondyloid,* or beetlelike (Greek: *sphondylon,* beetle). He defines the newfound *sphondyloid of power* in this way:

> If, in the case of a straight bar-magnet, any one of these lines, *E,* be considered as revolving round the axis of the magnet, it describes a surface; and as the line itself is a closed curve, the surface will form a tube [torus] round the axis and inclose a solid form. Another line of force, *F,* will produce a similar result. The sphondyloid body may be either that contained by the surface of revolution of *E,* or that between the two surfaces of *E* and *F.* . . . [*XR* ¶3271. Not in *GBWW.*]

Faraday has ways of tracing these lines, and even of measuring the power of the total sphondyloid of a given magnet.

He comes to view magnetic actions as taking place primarily between sphondyloids, and only secondarily between the magnets: Thus, as we earlier dispensed with "charge," so now we eliminate the mag-

Figure 4. The sphondyloid of power of a small bar magnet, caught between the sphondyloids of two larger magnets. Iron-filings diagram from Plate V of Faraday's *Diary.* (Compare with Plates III and IV of Volume 3 of Faraday's *Experimental Researches* [redrawn in part as Figure 16 in *GBWW,* Vol. 45, p. 791].)

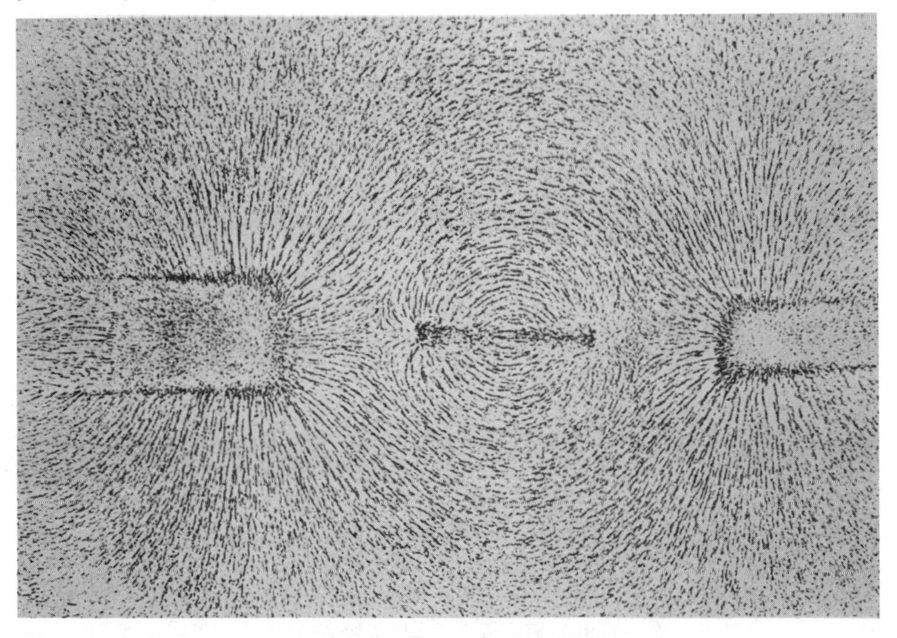

netic "pole." Interactions between magnets take on the proportions of Homeric encounters:

> How easily all these effects present themselves in a consistent form, if read by the principle of representative lines of force! . . . as the [spherical] magnet is approached [by the dominant], its external sphondyloid of power is compressed inwards . . . and at last the magnet is self-contained . . . so that it gives no induced currents. . . . Within that distance the effect of the superior and overpowering force of the great magnet appears . . . which, though it can take partial possession of the little magnet, still, when removed, suffers the force of the latter to develop itself again. . . . [*XR; GBWW,* Vol. 45, p. 847a]

Maxwell, in transforming the mathematics of magnetic interactions from Ampère's form to a field point of view, will take Faraday's depiction of interacting sphondyloids as a guide to the kind of account he will need to produce.

As in the electrostatic case, Maxwell summons a mathematical figure of speech to his aid; we cannot here follow him in this but only report the outcome: the currents of Figure 4 can be shown to be mathematically equivalent to magnetic shells of which they are the boundaries. A *magnetic shell* is an imaginary surface which is magnetized overall in such a way that one face corresponds everywhere to the north pole of a magnet, and the opposite face to the south. In turn, Maxwell borrows from Gauss a powerfully intuitive proposition concerning the potential of a magnetic shell, *M*: the potential at any point *P* is proportional to the solid angle subsumed by the boundary of the shell when seen from that point (fig. 5). The effect of this combination of strategies is to escape completely from the analytic frame of mind of Ampère, and to conceive the magnetic effect as that of the circuit as a *whole.* The mathematical concept of potential catches the spirit of Faraday's imaginative grasp of the magnetic phenomenon as a power in space. By extending the approach of Figure 5 to include the entire region of the magnet, Maxwell is able to grasp the field in the case of magnetism very much as he did in the case of electrostatics, and to conceive again of the whole configured field as incorporating a single potential of the circuit.

The lines of *force* run here, as they did in the electrostatic case, at right angles to the lines connecting points of equal *potential,* or equipotential lines: that is, if we think of the equipotential lines as gravitational "contour" lines, the lines of force run orthogonally to them, or "downhill." All this is depicted in Maxwell's drawing of the combined field of the two circuits of Figure 6. Again, Maxwell has captured in mathematical form the essence of Faraday's insight and has replaced the analytic, formal thinking of Ampère with an integrated, synthetic, and highly intuitive alternative. This is the same conversion of the world

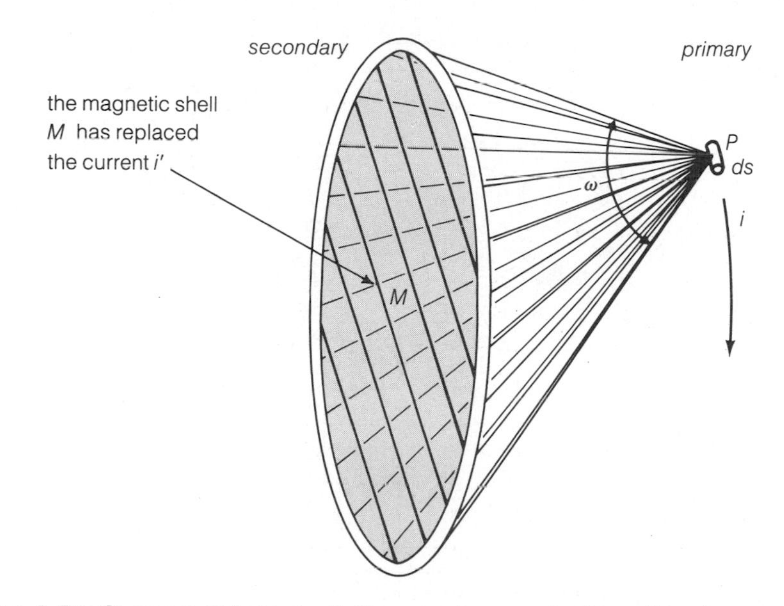

Figure 5. The Gauss potential of a circuit. The secondary current of Figure 3 has been replaced by a magnetic shell, *M* (north face on the right, south on the left), and from the position of *ds* of Figure 3, now denoted *P*, the shell delineates the solid angle *ω*, which measures its potential.

we met in the case of electrostatics, now successfully carried out in the much more complex and elusive realm of magnetic interactions.

At the beginning of chapter 3 of Part IV of the *Treatise,* Maxwell devotes three remarkable pages to a dialectical reflection on these two contrasting understandings of the nature of "science." He draws here again the distinction we have seen earlier between the two contrasting views of the *integral:* as a sum of parts, or as a whole. Ampère, Maxwell says, builds a complex by summation; Faraday begins with the whole and derives the particular from it:

> We are accustomed to consider the universe as made up of parts, and mathematicians usually begin by considering a single particle, and then conceiving its relation to another particle, and so on. This has generally been supposed the most natural method. To conceive of a particle, however, requires a process of abstraction, since all our perceptions are related to extended bodies, so that the idea of the *all* that is in our consciousness at a given instant is perhaps as primitive an idea as that of any individual thing. [*Tr* ii/176–77]

Ampère shut out this wholeness of the act of perception by a deliberate effort to construct a system on the concept of least parts; thus his force law expresses an action between current elements whose relation can never be observed as such in fact. Faraday, proceeding in a way that seems to Maxwell the natural one, accepts what he observes in its immediate unity. He sees magnets as wholes, he sees the patterns of lines

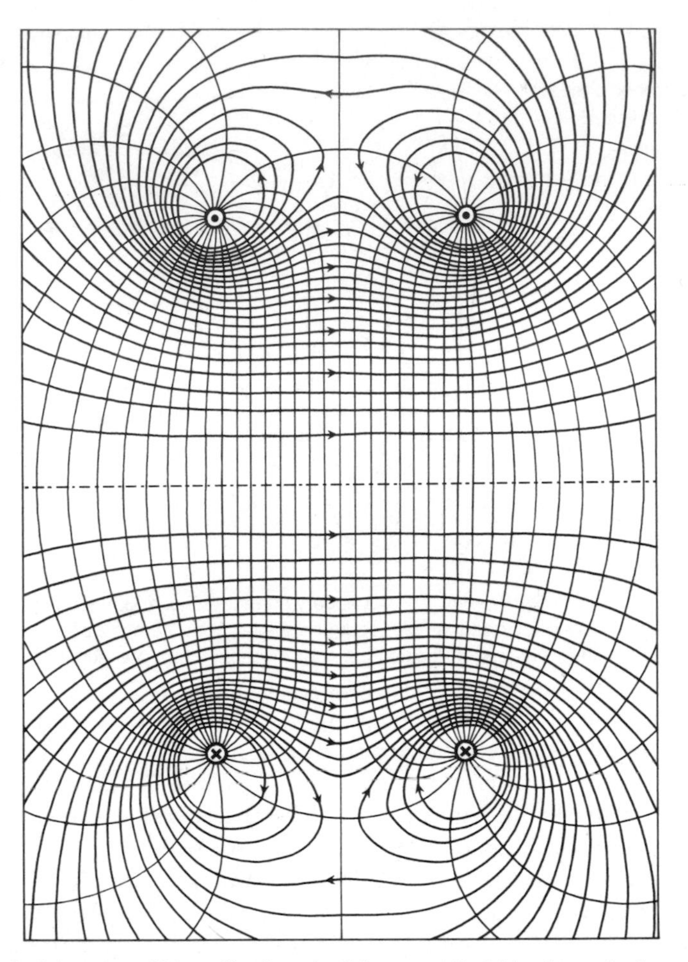

Figure 6. Adaptation of Maxwell's diagram of the magnetic fields of two circular currents (Figure XIX of Volume II of the *Treatise*). This figure represents a vertical section through the circuits of Figure 3. Figure 6 superimposes on Figure 3. The symbol ⊙ represents currents flowing upward; ⊗ represents currents flowing downward into the page. The darker lines represent lines of force. Equipotential lines, running everywhere perpendicular to these, are drawn lighter. (Compare with Figure 9.)

of force in their unity as whole systems, and he names that unity, the "sphondyloid." By the necessities of our mode of perception, a nascent science will be a science of such wholes. Ampère was able to produce a science of another sort only by erasing the record of his actual investigation and by forcing his science to conform to a rigid tradition. Faraday, by his freedom from this discipline, has been able to set his own style and shape his own language. The result is an ability, Maxwell says, "to coordinate his ideas with his facts," and to achieve their expression "in natural, untechnical language." Style is crucial to truth, because only a "natural, untechnical" style will be responsive to nature in the manner of the phenomena themselves. Maxwell says of Faraday:

> This new symbolism consisted of those lines of force extending themselves in every direction from electrified and magnetic bodies, which Faraday in his mind's eye saw as distinctly as the solid bodies from which they emanated. [*SP* ii/318]

In this context, we see how much the metaphor of "the mind's eye" carries with it. As the eye immediately grasps the *whole* in perception, so the mind's eye intuits the concept of field as an extended entity, the system of the lines of force. The field is thought of here essentially as a *whole,* as an entity. Field physics must be close to our immediate intuition of nature, if Maxwell is right about the character of perception.

Electromagnetic induction: from statics to dynamics

Let us turn once again to the phenomenon of electromagnetic induction. When a current flowing in one circuit, the "primary," is started or stopped, a current will be induced in another neighboring "secondary" circuit. In the field view, it is the changing magnetic field of the first circuit that induces the current in the second. But, if a changing field induces currents in other circuits, it should do so in the original circuit as well. This is the phenomenon of "self-induction." Furthermore, by the conservation of energy, the induction must be in a direction to oppose the original change; otherwise, we would have an explosive regeneration of energy. This, too, is in accord with observed phenomena: when a switch in the primary circuit is opened in order to stop current flow, an arc may occur across the points of the switch, the current resisting with a high potential the interruption of its flow.

Maxwell observes, in chapter 4 of Part IV, that this has an inescapable analogy to the flywheel effect in mechanics: the momentum by which a moving mass resists change in its motion. The suggestion becomes very strong that there is, associated with the current, some counterpart to mechanical momentum, which Maxwell comes to call "electrokinetic momentum." It is not literally a momentum of "electricity," for it varies with different geometrical arrangements of the wire (as it would not, for example, if we were speaking of water in a hose). The momentum must in some way be located, not in the wire but in the field. Maxwell's mind moves eagerly in response to this leading thought:

> It is difficult . . . for the mind which has once recognised the analogy between the phenomena of self-induction and those of the motion of material bodies, to abandon altogether the help of this analogy, or to admit that it is entirely superficial and misleading. The fundamental

> dynamical idea of matter, as capable by its motion of becoming the recipient of momentum and of energy, is so interwoven with our forms of thought that, whenever we catch a glimpse of it in any part of nature, we feel that a path is before us leading, sooner or later, to the complete understanding of the subject. . . .
>
> It appears, therefore, that a system containing an electric current is a seat of energy of some kind; and since we can form no conception of an electric current except as a kinetic phenomenon, its energy must be kinetic energy, that is to say, the energy which a moving body has in virtue of its motion. . . .
>
> We are therefore led to enquire whether there may not be some motion going on in the space outside the wire, which is not occupied by the electric current, but in which the electromagnetic effects of the current are manifested. [*Tr* ii/196–98]

Maxwell speaks cautiously, but he is already committed to a perhaps extravagant adventure:

> . . . Has the electric current . . . either momentum or kinetic energy?
>
> We have already shewn that it has something very like momentum, that it resists being suddenly stopped, and that it can exert, for a short time, a great electromotive force.
>
> But a conducting circuit in which a current has been set up has the power of doing work in virtue of this current, and this power cannot be said to be something very like energy, for it is really and truly energy. [*Tr* ii/197]

The energy is "real and true," the momentum is "very like"—fine distinctions of the art of interpretation! We shall see where they lead Maxwell's searching mind.

A new mechanics for a new world

This will be a metaphorical journey. When Maxwell says that we have observed "something *like* momentum," we sense that an analogy is brewing. Maxwell has used analogies extensively before: mathematical analogy in his first paper on electricity, "On Faraday's Lines of Force"; physical analogy in the second paper, "On Physical Lines of Force"; and both kinds in various ways earlier in the *Treatise* itself. Now he is going to travel further with analogy than he has ever done before. Previously, metaphor bridged two systems that were somehow alike. The metaphor spoke of the abstracted likeness, but at each end the cable suspending thought was anchored in *terra firma.* Now Maxwell will propose instead that the suspended thought itself is the reality: from *terra firma* at either end we raise our thoughts to *terra nova* in the intellectual space between. Maxwell has found energy, and something like momentum, in the magnetic field in a pure vacuum: where "nothing" was, there is a thinkable mechanism, running and charged with momentum and kinetic energy.

Here is a kind of being that is real and material, but invisible, intangible, and imponderable. Can we open our thinking to permit the possibility that "matter" is not what we had thought, that very real "matter" could be present in this empty space? Maxwell is indeed asserting the total reality of the field, yet he is not reducing it to a "mechanical system" in the way in which nineteenth-century physicists are accused of having naively tried to do. Rather, he is using metaphorical leverage to raise our thinking to a new level of understanding of what physical reality might entail. I am not sure his critics have fully understood him in this.

Here is Maxwell's announcement of his project:

> What I propose now to do is to examine the consequences of the assumption that the phenomena of the electric current are those of a moving system, the motion being communicated from one part of the system to another by forces, the nature and laws of which we do not yet even attempt to define, because we can eliminate these forces from the equations of motion by the method given by Lagrange for any connected system.
>
> In the next five chapters [chapters 5–9, Part IV, of the *Treatise*] I propose to deduce the main structure of the theory of electricity from a dynamical hypothesis of this kind. . . . [*Tr* ii/198]

To carry out this project will require a highly sophisticated instrument, and Maxwell found what he wanted in what are known as the "Lagrangian equations of motion." This is a set of partial differential equations, which, though published by Lagrange in 1788 in his *Mécanique analytique,* were only becoming widely known in England during the time in which Maxwell was working on electricity and magnetism.[24] They describe in purely analytic terms the motions of a connected mechanical system. The emphasis is on connection, because one special interest of the equations lies in the fact that they eliminate inner connections from explicit consideration. They thereby leave a set of truly independent, "generalized" coordinates with which to describe in observable external terms the state of an inwardly, fully connected system. Any sufficient set of strictly independent coordinates will do. They may be Newtonian displacements, but they need not be—they could be the angular displacement of a knob, the positioning of an odd-shaped cam, or the pull of a string. These are Lagrange's "generalized coordinates," and their time derivatives will be correspondingly "generalized" velocities. We are embarking on a sea of metaphoric displacements, velocities, and their offspring: in Lagrange's equations, they will *act like* their Newtonian counterparts, but they need not *be* the kind of thing Newton was referring to in his laws.

Seen from Maxwell's point of view, Lagrange's equations are sparkling with interest and possibilities, for they begin with the concepts of *connection* and *system;* they look to the *whole,* which they characterize in terms of the scalar energy, and by identifying a set of variables of any sort that is just sufficient to determine a *state* of the system, they make it possible to meet the interpretative ideal of saying exactly what is known and no more.

Maxwell described Lagrange's equations in a parable which is very helpful in understanding their significance to him from what we might call an epistemological point of view. He envisions a group of bell ringers pulling upon ropes connected to a set of bells inaccessible overhead:

> In an ordinary belfry, each bell has one rope which comes down through a hole in the floor to the bellringers' room. But suppose that each rope, instead of acting on one bell, contributes to the motion of many pieces of machinery, and that the motion of each piece is determined not by the motion of one rope alone, but by that of several, and suppose, further, that all this machinery is silent and utterly unknown to the men at the ropes, who can see only as far as the holes in the floor above them.
>
> Supposing all this, what is the scientific duty of the men below? They have full command of the ropes, but of nothing else. They can give each rope any position and any velocity, and they can estimate its momentum by stopping all the ropes at once, and feeling what sort of tug each rope gives. If they take the trouble to ascertain how much work they have to do in order to drag the ropes down to a given set of positions, and to express this in terms of these positions, they have found the potential energy of the system in terms of the known co-ordinates. If they then find the tug on any one rope arising from a velocity equal to unity communicated to itself or to any other rope, they can express the kinetic energy in terms of the co-ordinates and velocities.
>
> These data are sufficient to determine the motion of every one of the ropes when it and all the others are acted on by any given forces. This is all that the men at the ropes can ever know. If the machinery above has more degrees of freedom than there are ropes, the co-ordinates which express these degrees of freedom must be ignored. There is no help for it. [*SP* ii/783–84]

Maxwell, who very much enjoyed a quiet joke, must have taken some satisfaction at the thought of the music that might result.

In what we might call its first level of application, the Lagrangian method is an illustration of the ultimate interpretive instrument in that aspect of the art in which precision of expression is the goal, for it is capable of expressing "all that the men at the ropes can ever know," and no more. By employing just those variables that are accessible and can be measured and controlled, we are able to speak of just what is strictly accessible to us. In this, Lagrange's equations come close to the controlling rhetorical principle of the *Treatise:*

> We must therefore seek for a mode of expression which shall not be capable of expressing too much, and which shall leave room for the introduction of new ideas as these are developed from new facts. [*Tr* ii/7]

At a deeper level of application, the method not only permits a disciplined expression in familiar terms but opens the way to an advance in our understanding through the reformation of the fundamental terms themselves. The electromagnetic field will of course be the machinery of the bells that concerns us. The bell ropes and their velocities become galvanometer deflections and their motions, or the position or motion of a wire near a magnet. We shall be led to introduce a whole new metaphoric language, in which we speak of "electromotive force," "electric current," "electric displacement," or "electrokinetic momentum." In a sense, we have no notion initially what any of these things is. But we may enlarge our notion of force so that it is not a misnomer, or a "mere analogy," to speak, for example, of the electromotive force. Possibly a "force" is something more than we thought.

Perhaps the most difficult concept to deal with on this metaphorical level is "matter" itself, and I would like to take a moment to review some of Maxwell's thoughts about this, and the thoughts, too, of his teacher, William Hamilton of Edinburgh, who I think may help us. Let me start with Hamilton, whom we have already met earlier in this essay. Hamilton insists on the duality of all perception; we invariably, he says, find mixed in our consciousness facts of two kinds—"internal facts" and "external facts." The former testify to an inner reality, the ego, and the latter to an external reality, the non-ego. This duality of perception is ignored, Hamilton complains, by philosophers who are determined to achieve unity and simplicity by the elimination from consideration of one or the other of these components. Embracing both in his "Philosophy of the Conditioned," Hamilton commits himself to what he calls "natural dualism," or "natural realism."

"What is meant," Hamilton asks, "by perceiving the material reality?" He is prepared to answer in terms of "dualism":

> In the first place, it does not mean that we perceive the material reality absolutely and in itself . . . on the contrary, the total and real object of perception is the external object under relation to our sense and faculty of cognition. But though thus relative to us, the object is still . . . the non-ego—the non-ego modified, and relative, it may be, but still the non-ego. . . . Suppose that the total object of consciousness in

> perception is = 12; and suppose that the external reality contributes 6, the material sense 3, and the mind 3—this may enable you to form some rude conjecture of the nature of the object of perception.[25]

Hamilton is willing to assign certain primary qualities to external reality, one of these—*pace* Kant—being "extension." How can "extension" be attributed to external reality, while "space" is asserted (with Kant) to be strictly a condition of our consciousness? Hamilton pauses for a long breath before answering that one:

> To this difficulty, I see only one possible answer. It is this: It cannot be denied that space, as a necessary notion, is native to the mind; but does it follow, that, because there is an *a priori* space, as a form of thought, we may not also have an empirical knowledge of extension, as an element of existence? The former, indeed, may be only the condition through which the latter is possible. . . . But there seems to me no reason to deny, that because we have the one, we may not also have the other. If this be admitted, the whole difficulty is solved. . . .[26]

Hamilton seems to have opened the trapdoor in the ceiling halfway, to glimpse the forbidden things-in-themselves, and to find that there is thus some communication between thought and fact.

In the image of the bell ringers, we can identify the three components of Hamilton's recipe for matter. The six portions of external reality lie sealed from me above the ceiling. Three portions are the laws of operation of my own reason, exercising my "scientific responsibility" to make what I can of the situation. But an interesting three portions of material sense are conveyed by the bell ropes, which communicate between the two realms. Lagrangian theory is a strategy of reason for interpreting the information of the material sense: I think we can say that, in expressing the idea of a connected material system, it mirrors the conditions of reason itself. The principle of relativity tells us that we can know only the configuration of the ropes among themselves, each with respect to the others. There is no absolute reference by which we could measure them more truly. The Philosophy of the Conditioned tells us that we can never assert what is true, simply. But the recipe for matter gives us reason not to despair: we do have a dash of contact with being, and that, I believe, for Maxwell makes it all worthwhile.

There are, Maxwell told his students in experimental physics, two "gateways to knowledge": one by way of the "doctrines of science," the other by way of "those elementary sensations which form the obscure background of all our conscious thoughts." If it is possible to "effect a junction in the citadel of the mind, the position they occupy becomes impregnable." To make this junction is to "wed Thought to Fact"; to effect a mystery. This might be the key to both the content and the style of the *Treatise:* it has dedicated itself to achieving that union inso-

James Clerk Maxwell (1831–79)

far as is possible, by way of the emerging science of electromagnetism and the insights that new science may bring with it. The *Treatise,* I suspect, has more than what is ordinarily regarded as respectable scientific work to do.

Between "Thought" and "Fact," Maxwell sees one link as that of analogy. Analogy builds a bridge, then, between "matter" as sensed and "matter" as known to the mind. All this Maxwell discusses in the speculative essay, "Are There Real Analogies in Nature?," which is reprinted elsewhere in this issue of *The Great Ideas Today.* Thought, he says there, deals in formal relations; whenever the opportunity arises, by a necessity of our natures, we project these relations upon phenomena, thereby *imposing* analogies. Is this only imposition, no more than a "mere projection of our mental machinery on the surface of external things"? I leave it to the reader to turn to Maxwell's essay to see what the answer might seem to be. It was an early essay; the advice to the students of experimental physics was much later. If that latter seems more confident, it may be because the experience in the interval with Lagrangian theory and the *Treatise* has raised Maxwell's spirits in relation to being.

It is significant that Maxwell has his own way of deriving Lagrange's equations in the *Treatise.* Where others, including Lagrange himself, anchor the derivation of the new forms in Newton's laws and Newton's concepts, Maxwell uses the terms of the new science from the beginning. We wake up, so to speak, on the magic island and hear the sounds of Ariel's music. Maxwell above all will not use Newton's fundamental term, *mass.* This is a kind of tacit joke on Newton, to steal his science by refounding it without the use of its primary concept. Other terms, such as *coordinate, velocity, momentum,* or *force,* though familiar in sound, now are used with new meanings—a fact which may only gradually become apparent to the reader. We are indeed under some kind of spell, under a metaphoric charm. Nothing is quite what it seems, nor ever will be, for this is a dialectical turning point, and once a new idea is entertained the world cannot again be the same.

We cannot here trace the unfolding of Lagrange's equations under the guidance of Maxwell's magic, but we may note one or two high points. The beginning is with a statement that sounds like Newton's second law of motion, and Maxwell is no doubt confident we will accept it as such, but in fact it is referring to generalized coordinates and hence bears an altogether new meaning: "The moving force is measured by the rate of increase of the momentum" [*Tr* ii/201]. Except for the relation between them, *force* and *momentum* remain undefined terms—we are, in effect, invited to form ideas of the generalized terms directly. In general, they are not Newtonian force and momentum.

Of the two quantities, "force" and "momentum," it is the former which is treated as intuitively prior, with the result that the edifice of mechanics is built on a new fundamental understanding of force itself. In turn, a generalization of the idea of force means a new approach to the concept of causality, and Maxwell seems indeed to invite this as well. Separating the sensations of effort or resistance from the dynamic idea of force, Maxwell urges us to consider that in dynamics the planets move "like the blessed gods."

Maxwell next introduces the concepts of work and energy, assuming initially that the work done by a force is the product of the force by the space through which it acts. But if force is generalized, then the space which multiplies it must be, as well. The concept of space is opened to generalization in company with the concept of causality. And at last, at the top rather than the base of the edifice, we must encounter mass, as transformed as "space" and "force" have been. It appears merely as the coefficient by which the one-half of the square of the generalized velocity must be multiplied to give the kinetic energy. It bears a new name: not "mass," but the "moment" or "product" of "inertia."

Strictly speaking, perhaps, nothing in the new system has been defined. This might seem to represent resignation, total acceptance of Hamiltonian relativity in its darker aspect. I would rather remember the words about the way in which "Thought weds Fact" and believe that the new mechanics is not a pure formalism but an artfully constructed system of symbols inviting meaning. And it would seem that the encounter with electromagnetism to which we turn now should be the occasion of the epithalamion.

Maxwell, on behalf of the Society for Promoting Christian Knowledge—surely not without the memory of Faraday very much in his mind—prepared a primer of the new mechanics as nearly as possible without recourse to formal mathematics. Always, for Maxwell, the first test of intelligibility of a mathematical structure is restatement in honest prose. *Matter and Motion,* the little book to which I am referring and which also is reprinted in this issue of *The Great Ideas Today,* introduces the new mechanics on an elementary level: "elementary," not in the sense of "easy," for with a little practice analytic mathematics is always the easiest way to go, but in the old and important sense of "elementary." In this book Maxwell states, as accurately and adequately as prose and his skill permit, the real foundations of the new understanding, and in the course of this book he works through to the question which to him is most burning: the argument to Newton's law of universal gravitation. For Maxwell now knows that this law cannot be true. The book is not a diluted account for the nonscientist; rather, it brings the adult reader, scientist or not, to stand with Maxwell and join him in his thoughts as he stares into the heart of the real question, the unresolved prospect that lies ahead: The Twentieth Century, I think it might be called.

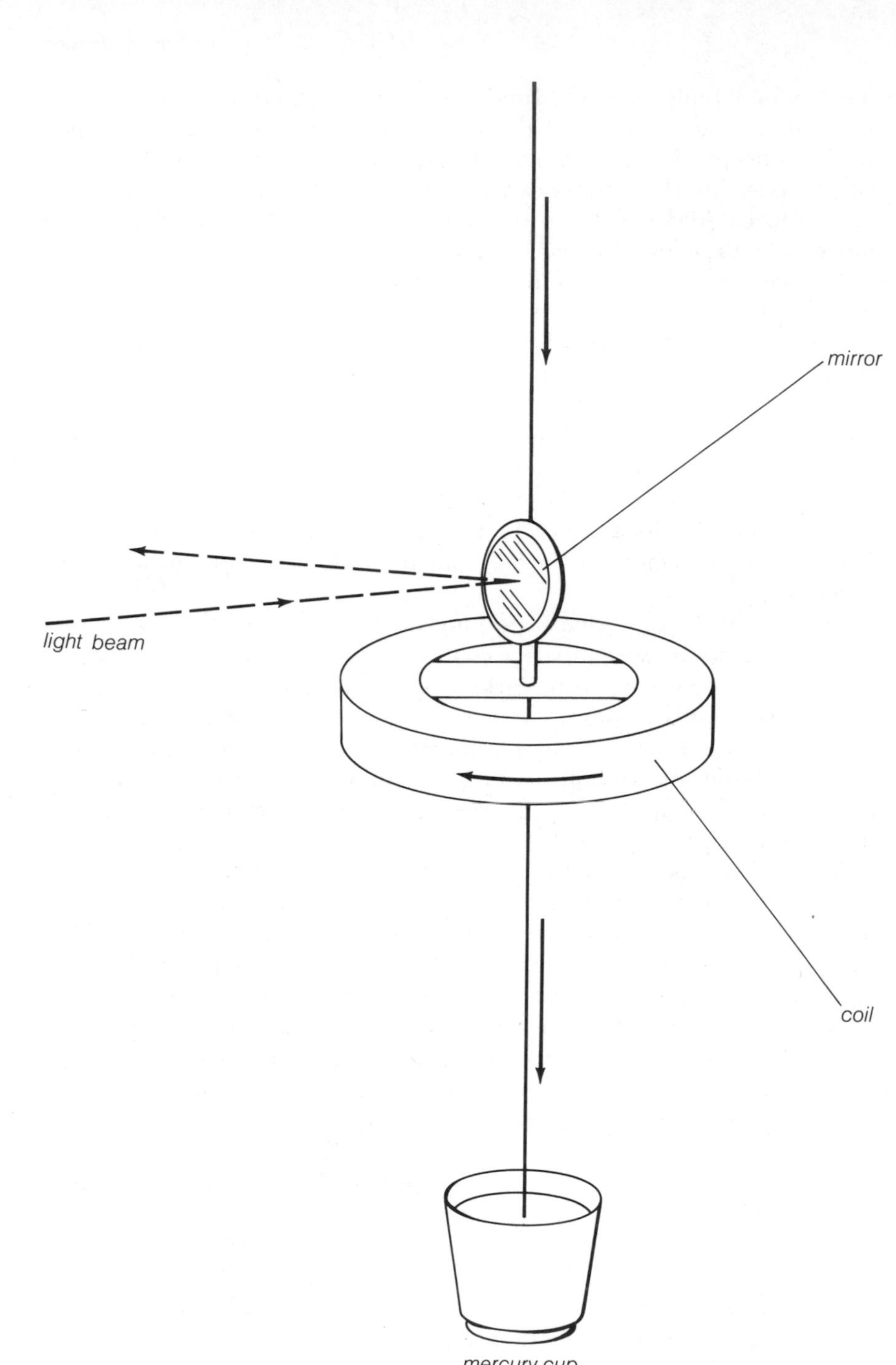

Figure 7. Experiment to detect momentum of a current in a wire. Arrows show direction of current flow: down the suspension wire, around the large coil, and out at the bottom through a mercury cup. [Redrawn from *Tr* ii/217.]

The procession of Maxwell's equations from Lagrange's

Maxwell now breathes life into Lagrange's equations by bringing them to bear on Fact—on the phenomena of electromagnetism. Lagrange's equations presuppose that we are dealing with a single, connected material system, and Maxwell supposes similarly that the electromagnetic field is indeed such a system, yet in Maxwell's application to electromagnetism we find "mechanical" coordinates of very different kinds. One set of coordinates is "mechanical" in the ordinary sense; they are the physical conductors, the wires we can locate in space, and to which we can apply and measure Newtonian forces. Other coordinates, however, are "mechanical" only in a new, extended sense; these are the electrical coordinates: voltages, currents, and charge. Since in neither case do we see the material system to which we suppose they are all connected—the field—we may think of them throughout the following as bell ropes attached to an utterly invisible system. But they are bell ropes of two different categories.

There now follows a marvelous judgment-process, which must have few parallels outside of the realms of theology—for out of this abstract universal schema, we must select the actual terms that describe the electromagnetic world. The parallel I believe Maxwell keeps in mind is Newton's ceremony in "The System of the World," in which our gravitational universe is sorted out of the domain of all possible worlds that was developed in Book I of the *Principia*. In this sense, there might be said to be a *Principia* within the *Treatise:* chapter 5 of the *Treatise* is the new Book I of the *Principia*, while what we might call the Judgment of the Terms in the *Treatise* is the new "System of the World" of Newton's Book III.

Once Maxwell has assigned the generalized coordinates—the electrical measures of the currents, and the mechanical measures of the positions and motions of the wires that conduct them—it is possible to recognize certain of the corresponding coefficients in Lagrange's equations as those that indeed do give rise to known phenomena. Other coefficients, on the other hand, seem to suggest phenomena that have never been seen. Perhaps those terms will have to be omitted as having no application to electromagnetism, but to make certain of this, Maxwell carries out certain novel empirical tests. In effect, the equations demand new, crucial experiments. They are "crucial" in the sense that, if they had succeeded, they would have become classic. Yielding negative results, on the other hand, a classic experiment may go unnoticed—though it is surely no less heroic in its conception, and no less significant in determining which of the possible worlds we live in, than the experiment of the crossroads that yields a positive "discovery."

One of Maxwell's crucial experiments that arises from the equations is diagramed in Figure 7, a drawing reproduced from the *Treatise;* had it succeeded, it would have revealed a momentum of the electric cur-

Figure 8. Maxwell's electrodynamic top, for the detection of a possible cross-coupling between electrokinetic and ordinary mechanical momenta. (Compare with Figure 34 of the *Treatise*, Volume II, page 219.)

rent as flowing in the wire itself. The absence of such an effect confirms for Maxwell his intuition that the real phenomenon to which we give the name "current" is not something that is "in" the wire. Another Lagrangian term suggests a cross-coupling between electrical and mechanical velocities—that is, a force arising from the combined effect of a mechanical velocity and an electric current. Maxwell's "electromagnetic top," depicted in Figure 8, was used to seek this phenomenon, again with a negative result. Maxwell was finding out systematically what world we are in.[27]

Having finished these preliminary judgments—having, in effect, chosen our universe—we now settle to finding the relationship between Lagrangian theory and the electromagnetic phenomena already well known. It will suffice, perhaps, if we watch this process in one representative case. Consider two coupled circuits, a primary and a secondary. Interruption of current in the primary gives rise to a sudden pulse of current in the secondary—stopping the first bell rope gives rise to a significant tug in the second: something is going on "upstairs"! To speak in Lagrangian terminology, the primary current was a generalized "velocity"—that is, the time rate of change of charge (not, we have learned, literally a velocity of flow of anything "in" the wire). Similarly, the "tug" on the secondary rope—the pulse of current revealed by the galvanometer in the secondary circuit—revealed the blocking of a momentum associated with the secondary: again, a generalized "momentum," and not one that corresponds to anything moving "in" the secondary wire. Maxwell speaks of this metaphoric entity of the secondary circuit as an "electrokinetic momentum," and the "tug" arising from its interruption as an "electromotive force." Note that these are strictly correct terms in the context of Lagrangian theory, however much the term "electromotive *force*" may distress modern students who recognize immediately that it is not a Newtonian force.

A metaphoric "mass," represented by an inertial coefficient in Lagrange's equations, relates this velocity in the primary to momentum in the secondary. Where is this Lagrangian mass? Not in the circuits themselves, but in the field: somewhere (or everywhere?) in that "vacuum."

Maxwell now has the task of bringing all this back to Faraday. He has in view a way to draw out of Lagrange the *electrotonic state*, which, as we saw earlier, Faraday himself so long sought but never found. It was that "tug" in the secondary circuit that first led Faraday to believe that some tension was at that moment being released. But what Faraday saw as a *static* tension, Maxwell now perceives dynamically, as the electrokinetic momentum, and the tug not as the impulse from a released spring, but as the reaction of an interrupted flywheel. Faraday's insistent intuition of the importance of that "state" which he could never empirically verify appears now to Maxwell as an important leading clue—a sign that we are dealing, even in the quiescent magnetic field, with a powerful locus of kinetic energy. When we alter the field, we are tampering with the momentum of a very real mechanism—silent, intangible, and indeterminate in form and location as it may be. Its momentum is no less potent for its being known to us only metaphorically. Faraday had sensed its presence. This momentum, then, becomes for Maxwell the central concept of his theory. He finds ways to define an electrokinetic momentum vector at every point in the space surrounding a current; the summation of those vector components around a circuit is the total momentum of the whole current.

Yet we must remember that all of the phenomena we know, and all the values Maxwell is able to assign to the electromagnetic momenta corresponding to points in space, are only tugs on the bell ropes. The value of the field vector at a point is not the momentum *at* that point: it is only the momentum *referred* to that point—the pull on the bell rope, not the thing itself. We may arrive at a complete diagram of the configuration of the field, as in Figure 6, but it remains only a "diagram"—*what* and *where* the field is, we know only to the extent of this complete and quantitative metaphor.

What are known today as "Maxwell's equations" are partial differential equations expressing the relations at every point in the field among the quantities chosen as basic; they are the foundations of Maxwell's account of electromagnetism. Modern texts, taking these as the first principles of a mathematical *theory,* carry four such equations, and it is regarded as the elegance and success of what is called "Maxwell's theory" that more are not needed. Maxwell, on the other hand, wrote a dozen or so; he knew he could get by with fewer, but he thought that, if they suggested further ideas, the more equations he could conceive, the better. I think this suggests that he was not a theorist but an interpreter. Furthermore, watching their procession from Lagrange's equations, he was able to trace in them as they emerged their significance in terms of the dynamical theory—how they told of energy and momentum structures everywhere in the field. Today, I suspect, any physicist who paused to notice this would quickly set it aside as an unfortunate, though not very important, aberration.

The world of light

We have followed one line of Maxwell's thought in his *Treatise* and have seen emerge from it first, the inversion of the world into the image of the electrostatic field, and then the dynamical system of the electromagnetic field. These two now prove to merge very neatly, the electrostatics entering the electromagnetic equations as a potential-energy term. When that has happened, Maxwell finds that the connected system of Lagrange's equations has become a vibrant medium,

Art .496

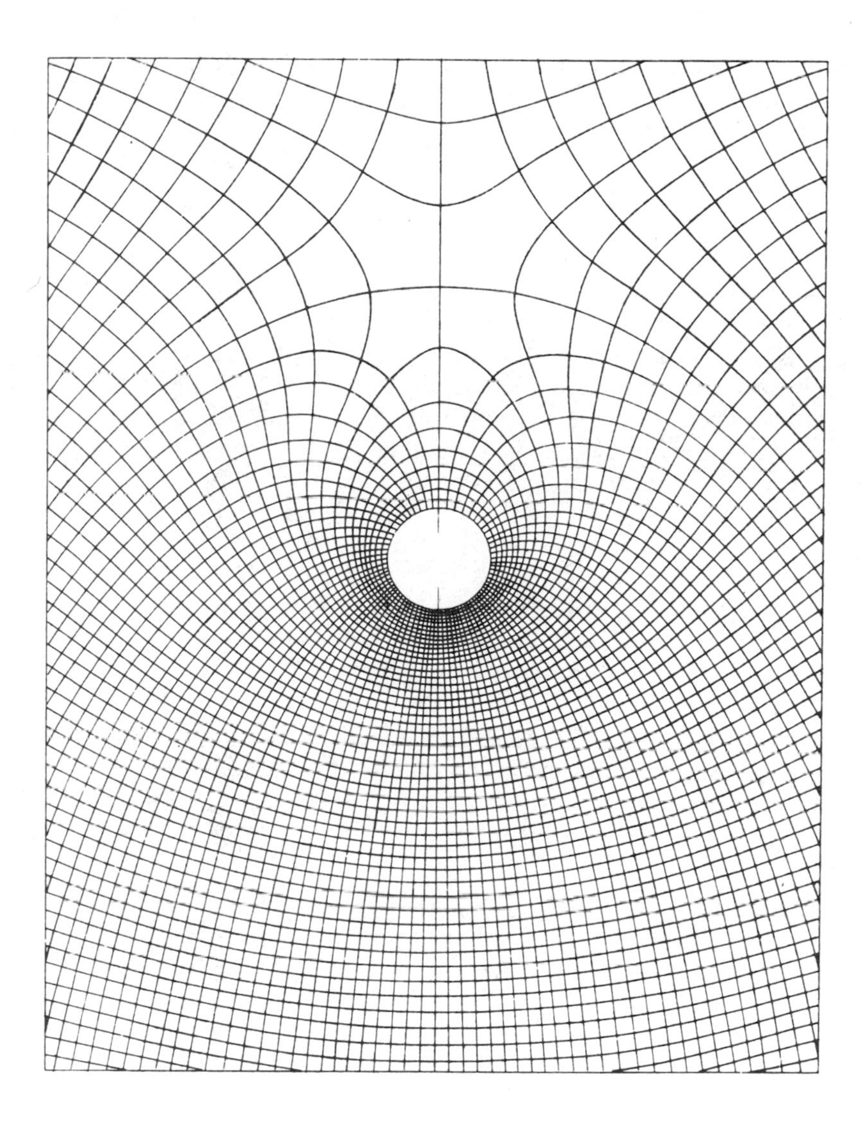

Uniform magnetic field disturbed by an Electric Current in a straight conductor.

A reproduction of Figure XVII from Maxwell's *Treatise on Electricity and Magnetism*.

capable of transmitting an electrical or magnetic disturbance with a very rapid, calculable velocity—calculable, that is, after some exacting measurements have been made.

The story of how those measurements came about is part of another reading of the *Treatise*, the *Treatise* in its context as a kind of Victoria Station in which people from the *Magnetischer Verein* and the Atlantic Cable enterprise are tromping through with their electrodynamometers and coils, while the Duke of Devonshire, as Chancellor of Cambridge University, is overturning the curriculum at Cambridge and fetching Maxwell from his retreat in Scotland to serve as the first professor of experimental physics and to build the Cavendish Laboratory. Out of that mix come the crucial measurements, the *Treatise* in its aspect of practical strategies and skill, which yield the electromagnetic theory of light: the demonstration, to convincing accuracy, that the velocity of propagation in the Lagrangian system is the very velocity of light itself. Light, then, is revealed as one form of electromagnetism. Then that metaphorical electromagnetic "matter" must fill the empty spaces of the cosmos wherever light can carry. This is the light-bearing aether, the discovery of which must have astounded Maxwell: the *electrotonic state* pervades and restores the cosmos, making of it one unified, communicating system.

This is perhaps a rather sad conclusion, for today every schoolchild knows that it turned out there wasn't any aether, and indeed it was rather naive of some old-fashioned gentlemen in the nineteenth century to imagine that there might have been one. We know now that science wasn't meant to deal with questions like that, but rather to write equations, make predictions, do experiments, and revise the results as necessary. In that way, we get on with what matters; the rest is only wasted time and blurred thinking.

I really do wonder whether we have quite understood all this. It would be another study to pursue the question further, but my sense is that between Hamiltonian relativity, which was probably in Maxwell's understanding as inclusive as Einstein's, and the critical and sensitive spirit he grew up with, Maxwell was philosophically ready for anything the twentieth century could bring on—I'm not altogether sure we are all, *post festum,* as ready as he was in anticipation. He was of course keenly aware of relativity questions; he had done a year-cycle spectrometer study looking for aether-drift effects, and one of his last letters was to D. P. Todd at the United States Naval Observatory proposing a study of the moons of Jupiter with this same purpose. In the *Treatise* itself, rather astoundingly, is to be found the theorem concerning moving conductors which can be understood as yielding the "Lorentz-FitzGerald contraction," the apparent "shrinking" of bodies as their speed approaches that of light.[28] Maxwell's convictions about relativity were deeper than any empirical detection of an aether could have shaken—

Art. 487, 702

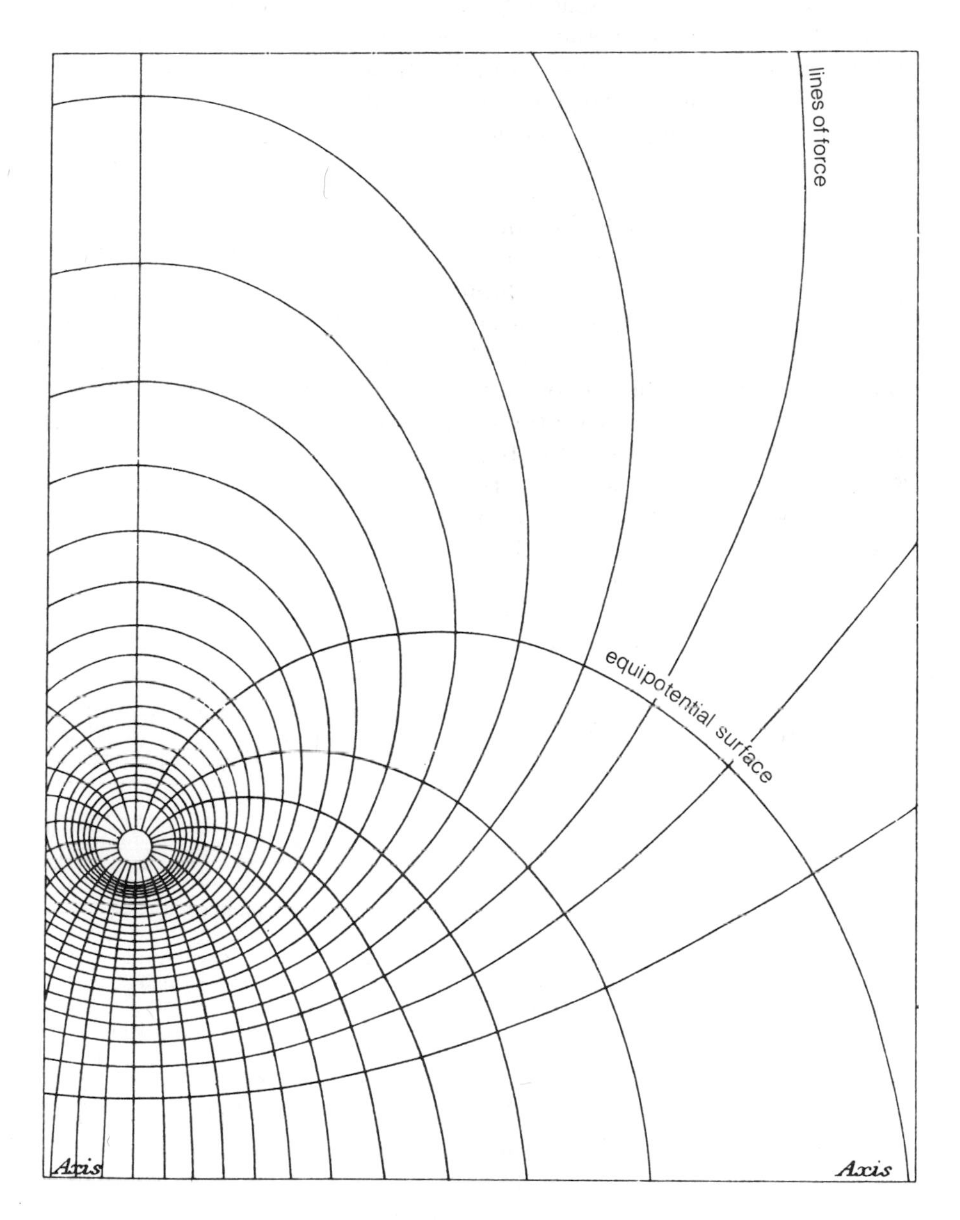

Figure 9. Adaptation of Figure XVIII in Maxwell's *Treatise*.

he would have remained a relativist even if motion relative to an aether had been detected. His derivations of space and time from the phenomena of consciousness were by no means so absolute that he might not have been ready to cut a space-time continuum in various ways.

It is not important whether Maxwell foresaw this or that, or what he might have thought or seen had he lived to a riper age. The question is, I think, what he did see, and what we can find in the *Treatise*, not so much in terms of his having hit on right answers as having found ways to contain the right questions.

What I suppose I would like to ask is this: have we given up on Maxwell's effort to "wed Thought to Fact?" That does not mean going into the laboratory to test a prediction, or taking it out for confirmation on the Nevada flats. It means finding that relation between thought and a real world which gives meaning to what we think, or, put in a more antique style, preserves a relation to being. I think that is the difference between the "theoretical" and the "hermeneutic" approach to science. Maxwell, I have urged, was not a theorist (just count those equations); he was, or sought to be, a messenger. Only that, I think, can explain why Maxwell was not merely interested in Faraday, or primarily concerned with Faraday's results, but was passionately devoted to Faraday as a man. What could that mean? I believe that Maxwell saw in Faraday a fellow interpreter, one who understood the significance and profundity of a text which was sacred because it carried word of being, not in any fancy way, but in a simple, very human sense. Maybe all I am saying is that Maxwell seems to have seen science as a human activity, one that human beings could do, share, care for, and understand. I wonder if the schoolchildren all know, today, that that is a very old-fashioned idea.

---

[1]Pierre Duhem, *Les théories électriques de J. Clerk Maxwell* (Paris: A. Hermann, 1902).

[2]This short-form notation will be used throughout to refer to Maxwell's *Scientific Papers.* W. D. Niven, ed., *The Scientific Papers of James Clerk Maxwell* (2 vols.; Cambridge: Cambridge University Press, 1890). The same edition has been photoprinted by Dover Publications (1952).

[3]Short-form notation for reference to Maxwell's *Treatise.* The first edition was: *A Treatise on Electricity and Magnetism* (2 vols.; Oxford: Clarendon Press, 1873). The edition referred to is not this first edition, however, but the third, edited by J. J. Thomson and published in 1892. It is this which has been photoprinted and reissued by Dover Publications, and which is currently in print.

[4]Short-form notation for reference to Faraday's *Experimental Researches* will be *XR.* Most of the *Researches* are included in *Great Books of the Western World,* and reference will be made to *GBWW* pages where applicable. Any reader with a set of the *Great Books* would do well to read not only Series I and II, as Maxwell recommends, but Series XI as well, and of course to follow the lead of the references made in the course of this article.

[5]Faraday to Ampère, Feb. 2, 1822. L. Pearce Williams, ed., *The Selected Correspondence of Michael Faraday* (2 vols.; Cambridge: Cambridge University Press, 1971), 1, p. 132.

[6]Henry Bence Jones, *The Life and Letters of Faraday* (2 vols.; London: Longmans, Green, and Co., 1870), 2, p. 10.

[7]This point is made by L. Pearce Williams in Lancelot Whyte, ed., *Roger Joseph Boscovich* (London: Allen and Unwin, 1961), p. 1630.

[8]Thomas Martin, ed., *Faraday's Diary* (7 vols. and Index vol.; London: G. Bell & Sons, 1932–36), 7, p. 337.

[9]For a study of the development of Newton's actual thinking in these matters, see the valuable article by Curtis Wilson in last year's edition of *The Great Ideas Today,* "Newton's Path to the *Principia*" (*GIT* 1985, pp. 179–229).

[10]For readers who may be interested in the mathematical forms of theorems discussed in this article, I will make certain of them available in the footnotes. "Thomson's theorem," as presented by Maxwell in the *Treatise* but with the notation somewhat modernized, takes this form:

$$V \iint E_n \, dS = \iiint E^2 d\tau$$

Here, on the left-hand side, E_n is the normal component of the electric intensity vector, $\boldsymbol{E}$, which has the magnitude and direction of the force per unit charge on a very small test charge placed at a point in the region of a charged body. V is the potential, which is uniform over the surface of a charged conducting sphere; and dS is an element of that surface. On the right-hand side, $d\tau$ denotes a volume-element of the space surrounding the sphere, and E is the magnitude of the intensity vector at any point in the space.

[11]Here the act of interpretation consists in arbitrarily separating the integrand on the right-hand side of Thomson's equation, namely, E^2. When expressed in proper units, this quantity, now thought of as an energy density in space, becomes:

$$\omega = \frac{1}{8\pi} E^2 \text{ ergs/cm}^3.$$

[12]Laplace's equation:

$$\frac{\partial^2 V}{\partial x^2} + \frac{\partial^2 V}{\partial y^2} + \frac{\partial^2 V}{\partial z^2} = 0$$

[13]Campbell was Maxwell's original biographer: Lewis Campbell and William Garnett, *The Life of James Clerk Maxwell* (London: Macmillan and Co., 2nd ed., 1884). The significance of his relationship with Maxwell is emphasized by George E. Davie: *The Democratic Intellect: Scotland and Her Universities in the Nineteenth Century* (Edinburgh: Edinburgh University Press, 1962).

[14]"Does the Progress of Physical Science Tend to Give Any Advantage to the Opinion of Necessity . . . ?," Campbell and Garnett, op. cit., pp. 357ff.

[15]Davie, op. cit., especially Part 3.

[16]Sir William Hamilton, *Lectures on Metaphysics and Logic* (2 vols.; Boston: 1859), vol. i (Metaphysics), p. 96.

[17]Ibid., i, p. 58.

[18]Ibid., i. p. 185.

[19]Augustine, *Confessions; GBWW,* Vol. 18.

[20]Alexandre Koyré, *From the Closed World to the Infinite Universe* (New York: Harper, 1958; reprint Peter Smith: 1983), passim.

[21]Karl Marx, *Capital; GBWW,* Vol. 50.

[22]Georg Lukács, "Reification and the Consciousness of the Proletariat," in *History and Class Consciousness* (Cambridge, Mass.: The MIT Press, 1971), pp. 83ff.

[23]Ampère's formula involves the angles θ and θ', which are the angles that the current-elements make with the line which joins them, whose length is r, and the angle ε, which the two current-elements, translated so that they met at a common point, would make with each other. In these terms the equation is:

$$df = \frac{ii'}{r^2} (\cos \varepsilon - 3/2 \cos \theta \cos \theta') \, ds \, ds'.$$

[24]They were popularized especially by Maxwell's friends William Thomson and P. G. Tait, in their *Treatise on Natural Philosophy* (Oxford: 1867).

[25]Hamilton, op. cit., i, p. 357.

[26]Ibid., p. 346.

[27]Maxwell's experiments have been repeated in various forms and have now yielded positive results, representing effects of the coupling of charge and mass in the electron. *See,* for example, S. J. Barnett, "A New Electron-inertia Effect . . . ," *Philosophical Magazine* 12 (1931), pp. 349ff.

[28]This fantasy appears in connection with speculations about the comparison of the electromagnetic and the electrostatic systems of units, at [*Tr* ii/414].

A Revolution in Music: Rousseau, Rameau, and the War of the Opera Houses in Paris in 1752

Maurice Cranston

Maurice Cranston has taught at the London School of Economics since 1959. In 1968 he was elected to the chair of political science formerly held by Harold Laski and Michael Oakeshott. He was born in London in 1920 and was educated at Oxford, where, after his M.A., he received a B.Litt. for a thesis on the freedom of the will. This was later incorporated in his book *Freedom* (1953), which has since run into several editions and established his reputation as a political philosopher. In 1957 he published the definitive biography of John Locke, which won the James Tait Black Memorial Prize, among other literary awards. His other books include *The Mask of Politics* and *What Are Human Rights?* as well as a critical study of Sartre and translations of Rousseau's *Social Contract* and *Discourse on Inequality.* He has written a great deal for radio, notably *Political Dialogues*—imaginary conversations between political philosophers, later published in book form. Professor Cranston taught for four years at the European University Institute in Florence, Italy, and has several times been a visiting professor at Harvard, Dartmouth College, and the University of California in San Diego. He is currently completing a biographical study of Rousseau, of which the first volume, *Jean-Jacques,* was published by W. W. Norton in 1983. His essay on Rousseau's political philosophy appeared in last year's *Great Ideas Today.*

Music in France in the middle of the eighteenth century was not very different from what it had been in the seventeenth century, under Louis XIV. It proclaimed the same Bourbon myth of *gloire* and majesty. It asserted the splendor of kings and the triumph of order. At the opera houses, earthly princes were represented on the stage in the image of gods. Patriotic sentiments were stirred by the sound of trumpets and drums, and love of country was fused into veneration of the Crown. The words, as pompous as the music, were composed in alexandrines and declaimed on the stage with grim solemnity. French opera spoke to the ear much as the architecture of Versailles addressed the eye. It might even claim to have something of that sort of grandeur.

Moreover, the music seemed to be as enduring as the building. The *Alceste* of Jean-Baptiste Lully, for example, was still being performed at the Paris Opéra sixty-five years after the composer's death in 1687. And even when the musicians of the Opéra were not playing Lully, they were usually playing pieces by musicians who composed in the same style, if not always as well. In the work of such musicians as André-Cardinal Destouches, the grand tradition of the Sun King and Versailles had become decidedly worn and dull. But nobody seems to have complained about it until early in the year 1752, when one of the bright young intellectuals connected with the *Encyclopaedia* of Diderot and d'Alembert, a German named Friedrich Melchior Grimm, published a pamphlet of protest, entitled *Lettre sur Omphale,*[1] *Omphale* being an opera by Destouches which had just been put on at the Paris Opéra. Grimm demanded to know why the directors of the opera house had chosen to mount this fifty-year-old work by a dead composer. He protested that the music of *Omphale* had no connection with the words, and that it did nothing to communicate the feelings of the characters in the drama. It was altogether stale, lifeless, and provincial. Music, Grimm argued, was a universal art; but what was heard at the Paris Opéra was a French artifact.

Grimm's attack on *Omphale* had more than one motive. He wanted not only to abolish the established repertory of French opera but to promote Italian opera in its place. Here he was operating hand in glove with a friend and contemporary, the future philosopher Jean-Jacques Rousseau.[2] Rousseau had studied the Italian opera in Italy and had just edited for publication in Paris a work by one of the new Italian operatic composers, Giovanni Battista Pergolesi, entitled *La serva padrona*.[3] Grimm's pamphlet had been timed to coincide with the visit to France of an Italian opera company led by Eustachio Bambini. They brought with them works by Scarlatti, Leo, Jommelli, Vinci, and, first and foremost, Pergolesi. These were practically all comic operas, *opera buffa,* as opposed to the *tragédies lyriques* favored by the French composers. Their music aimed to please rather than to improve the listener. Their productions required no elaborate theatrical machinery, very few singers, and a fairly small orchestra; and they were scored to melodic music, of which the *aria,* or song, was the most conspicuous feature.

It was not the first time Italian opera had been heard in Paris, but in 1752 it suddenly became fashionable. Pergolesi's *La serva padrona* was the great success of the season. Grimm followed up his attack on *Omphale* with another pamphlet, a somewhat Teutonic attempt at wit called *Le Petit prophète de Boehmischbroda*.[4] It is the story of a boy who comes from Bohemia to investigate the present state of music in Paris. He discovers that the French, once the chosen people of music, have lost the art. But hope is not lost. Providence has sent an Italian composer to save French music by the example of his work. If his lesson is ignored there will be no salvation for opera in France. That composer is named as Pergolesi.

If only because Grimm was German, his criticisms of French opera were not allowed to pass unanswered. A stream of pamphlets defending French music appeared under the names of such authors as Mairobert, Cazotte, Castel, La Morlière, Blainville, Fréron, Bonneval, and Morand. The main line of their argument was that the French opera derived from the French dramatic theatre, from the great tradition of Racine, Corneille, and Molière. French composers had the same desire as had French dramatists to impose the discipline of reason on the chaos of human thought. French music, its defenders claimed, was a classical art.

Grimm's rejoinder was that French music was not so much classical as old-fashioned. But whether he was right or wrong, the difference between French and Italian opera was not simply a difference between tragedy and comedy. It was a difference between two sorts of music. French music was academic and authoritarian; it had much in common with the metaphysics of Descartes, which had come to be incorporated into the Bourbon ideology or order, hierarchy, and system—a system in which the monarchy was as central to the kingdom as God was central to the universe. Italian music, by contrast, was natural and spontaneous and seemed to obey no fixed laws at all. This, perhaps, was the secret of its appeal to Grimm and the other Encyclopaedists—for Diderot,[5] d'Alembert,[6] and Holbach[7] all promptly joined Grimm in writing pamphlets in praise of the Italian opera.

So there they were, the smart young philosophers of the Enlighten-

Jean-Jacques Rousseau

ment—not as famous in the early 1750s as they afterward became—but already affording powerful intellectual support for a change in musical taste. Naturally, their qualifications to speak on the subject were challenged.

Somebody did so in verse:

> Are men of science fit arbiters of artistic pleasure,
> Are we to defer to them on what concerns aesthetic taste?[8]

There was undoubtedly a certain vulgarity in the Italian opera which was offensive to many fastidious Parisian ears. Even the subject of *La serva padrona* was unlikely to appeal to a conservative upper-class public, if that public knew enough Italian to follow what was going on. For Pergolesi's opera is all about a maidservant tricking her bachelor master into marrying her, with the happiest of outcomes: all of which conveyed the impertinent message that a maid is as good as a mistress.

One champion of French music protested that Italian music was all very well for peasants, and for the common people to sing in the streets of Naples. French music, he added, was designed for a cultivated public. Discipline and education were needed to master it, even to enjoy it. Italian music, by contrast, was a kind of demotic or plebeian art—crude, simple, and free.[9]

This "freedom" was just what the progressive philosophers of the *Encyclopaedia* liked about it. For they considered themselves, above all things, as being dedicated to the ideal of freedom. D'Alembert entered the controversy with a pamphlet to which he gave the significant title of *De la Liberté de la musique*.

> I am astonished in a century when so many authors busy themselves writing about freedom of trade, freedom of marriage, freedom of the press, and freedom in art, that nobody has so far written about freedom in music . . . for freedom in music entails freedom to feel, and freedom to feel means freedom to think, and freedom to think means freedom to act, and freedom to act means the ruin of states—so let us keep the French opera as it is, if we wish to preserve the kingdom—and let us put a brake on singing, if we do not want to have liberty in speaking to follow soon afterward.[10]

It was war—war between the champions of the traditional French opera and the champions of the Italian opera. They called it the *Querelle des Bouffons,* but it was more than a quarrel in the theatre. It was part of a greater confrontation between conservatives and radicals of France. An English observer, Lady Morgan, points out in a record of the period:

> Paris was divided into two formidable musical factions, which were not without their political color. The privileged class cried out against

> innovation, even in crochets and quavers; and the noble and the rich, the women and the court clung to the monotonous discords of Lully, Rameau, and Mondonville, as belonging to the ancient and established order of things; while the musical connoisseurs and amateurs, the men of talent, genius and letters, were enthusiastic for nature, taste and Italian music.[11]

Rameau—there was a name which Grimm and the other critics of French music hesitated to utter. They considered him an intellectual like themselves. Indeed, Diderot had once tried to persuade him to write on musical subjects for the *Encyclopaedia*. D'Alembert went so far as to prepare a popular version of one of Rameau's books on musical theory; and in his *Preliminary Discourse* to the first volume of the *Encyclopaedia* he wrote:

> Monsieur Rameau has carried the practice of his art to such a high degree of perfection that he has become at once a model and an object of jealousy for a great many musicians. . . . And what distinguishes him most particularly is that he has reflected so fruitfully on the theory of music. . . . [He is] a composer-philosopher. . . . [12]

There was something absurd about this posture of d'Alembert and Grimm and the other Encyclopaedists—in attacking French opera and yet still praising the leading French operatic composer; for Rameau had long since replaced Lully as the most prolific contributor to the French *théâtre lyrique*. He had done a certain amount to reform and lighten the French opera. He had developed the role of the ballet and there were plenty of shepherds and shepherdesses in his operas to offer light relief from gods and kings. But he was nevertheless the outstanding exponent of the French tradition in music.

Rameau had had as many as six operas performed in Paris in twelve months between 1748 and 1749,[13] a triumph only halted because the Comte d'Argenson, who disliked his bad manners, had productions of his works limited to two a year.[14] He was universally acknowledged to be the greatest French musician of his day. He was also France's leading musical theorist, recognized as such throughout Europe. A formidable figure. It is no wonder that the Encyclopaedists were intimidated by him. And yet from the ranks of the Encyclopaedists there emerged a David to challenge this Goliath—Pergolesi's editor, Rousseau.

Rousseau in 1753 was 41 years old, and he had only recently emerged from a long hard struggle to make his way in the world. But he had arrived. His portrait by Maurice-Quentin de la Tour was exhibited at the Paris salon that summer beside those of d'Alembert, Duclos, and other fashionable intellectuals of the time.[15] Rousseau had published only one important essay, his *Discourse on the Sciences and the Arts,* but it had won a prize at Dijon, and its publication in Paris in 1750 had been one of the most talked-about events of the season. Then he established

Scene vi from Rousseau's opera *Le Devin du village (The Village Soothsayer).*

himself almost overnight as an authority on music. He was engaged by Diderot to do the job that Rameau had turned down of writing articles on musical subjects for the *Encyclopaedia,* which became a sort of Bible of the Enlightenment. Rousseau wrote some two hundred articles on music for it. Moreover, at Fontainebleau he had an enormous fashionable success as the composer of an opera—in the "Italian" style—called *Le Devin du village.* Rousseau describes the occasion in his *Confessions*:

> [In the theatre at Fontainebleau] I was wretchedly ill-at-ease, but when the performance began my fears were banished. . . . I was surrounded by murmurs of delight and admiration. The growing excitement soon reached a point when it infected the whole audience. . . . I noticed all around me the whispering of women . . . who said to one another under their breath, "It's delightful; it's delicious: there is not a note that doesn't speak to the heart." . . . I surrendered myself fully to the pleasure and the taste of glory.[16]

Rousseau was henceforth at the head of musical controversy in France. It would be a mistake, however, to suppose that he was in the same ideological camp as those Encyclopaedists who supported Italian music because it was "progressive." He had already proclaimed in the *Discourse on the Sciences and the Arts* that he had no faith in progress. Nor was he especially democratic in his outlook. It is instructive to compare the libretto of Rousseau's opera *Le Devin du village* with that of Pergolesi's *La serva padrona. Le Devin du village* introduces a shepherdess who is distressed because her sweetheart has gone off with an aristocratic lady. In the end, love prevails because the village soothsayer helps to restore the shepherd to the shepherdess, and the two are happily and properly united—a very different tale from that of Pergolesi's opera where a servant is shown to be the right bride for the master. The message of *La serva padrona* is egalitarian; in Rousseau's opera the argument is that people should find love and happiness in their own station in society and not try to trespass across the barriers of class.[17]

It is hardly astonishing that *Le Devin du village* should have given such pleasure to the King at Fontainebleau, for however "radical" the music, the libretto is plainly conservative, and although the King felt duty-bound to protect French music against Italian competition, he could hardly conceal the fact that he personally enjoyed Rousseau's Italian-style music more than that of the French composers. Indeed, after the success of *Le Devin du village* Rousseau could have received a royal pension if only he had had the grace to pay his respects to the King.

He had decided, however, to resist all temptations of worldly glory in order to preserve his integrity as a moralist and critic. And he proved himself the most devastating and eloquent of critics, especially in his treatment of Rameau:

> We have to recognize a distinct talent in Monsieur Rameau, and much ardor, a musical brain, a great knowledge of harmonic movements and all kinds of effects. He has plenty of skill in adapting, distorting, ornamenting and embellishing other people's creations, and making them his own. He has very little facility for invention. He has more cleverness than creativeness; more knowledge than genius; and if he ever had genius it is suffocated by too much knowledge. . . . [Monsieur Rameau's theoretical writings are no less remarkable,] . . . but what is most singular about them is that they have acquired a great reputation without being read.[18]

We can perhaps detect a personal hostility to Rameau in Rousseau's words, and it was undoubtedly in his heart. Rameau and Rousseau had known each other, and disliked each other, for several years. They had first met in 1742 on decidedly unequal terms. Rameau was then already over sixty and at the height of his fame: Rousseau was thirty years younger, an obscure fellow from Geneva who had come to Paris with a project for a new musical notation and the score of an operatic ballet called *Les Muses galantes*. Rousseau's project was turned down by the Academy of Sciences, and when his ballet was given a private performance, Rameau declared the music to be a worthless mixture of plagiarism and bad composition. Rousseau described the experience in a letter to a friend in the country:

> Can you believe that my music put Monsieur Rameau in a very bad temper? He claimed it was too good to be my own work. As a result I had to make revisions, and the success of these only made him more bitterly angry. So that finally I—who have always been Rameau's most fervent admirer—have become the victim of his brutality.[19]

Rousseau did not forget or forgive. The *Querelle des Bouffons,* followed by the success of his *Devin du village,* gave him his opportunity to settle accounts with Rameau.[20] He transformed the Encyclopaedists' attack on an ill-defined musical tradition into an attack on Rameau and Rameau's philosophy of music.

Rameau's first instinct was to ignore the impudent Swiss upstart, but with Rousseau installed as chief musicologist of the *Encyclopaedia,* he realized he could no longer afford to do so. As a result, it was not only Rousseau himself who stopped composing music to write about the theory of music; Rameau was forced to do the same.[21] In the following years Rameau produced a succession of books and pamphlets: among others, *Observations sur notre instinct pour la musique, Erreurs sur la musique dans l'Encyclopédie, Réponse à MM. les éditeurs de l'Encyclopédie, Code de la musique pratique.*[22]

Rousseau, on his side, produced not only more articles on music for the *Encyclopaedia* but an equally long series of writings on musical theory: *Lettre sur la musique française, Dissertation sur la musique moderne, Lettre à Monsieur Raynal, Examen de deux principes avancés par Monsieur Rameau,* and *Sur la musique militaire*[23] besides his *Dictionnaire de musique.*

However much personal bitterness may have animated this controversy, it turned into something very important—important to the history of music, and indeed to the history of culture. For it was here that Rousseau first expounded what we call his romanticism: and he did so in process of refuting Rameau's rationalism.

Rameau took very seriously the role of a philosopher of music. He argued that the purpose of music was not simply to please the ear but to give us knowledge of reality. Scientists had explained that the universe was a systematic whole, intelligible to reason. The purpose of music was to provide, through the testimony of hearing, a double confirmation of the rational order of the universe. "When we think," he wrote, "of the infinite relations that the fine arts have to one another, and to the sciences, it is only logical to conclude that they are governed by one and the same principle. That principle is harmony."[24]

Rameau went even further in his claims for harmony. Harmony was not only the central principle of music, it was the first principle of all the arts. And because harmony was more readily discernible in music than in any other form, music should be recognized as "the first of the arts."[25]

Rousseau agreed that music was the first of the arts, but he asserted that its ruling principle was not harmony but melody.[26] It was only because music could do more than any other art that it was entitled to priority:

> The musician can depict things we cannot hear, while it is impossible for the painter to paint things we cannot see, and it is the great genius of an art which acts only by movement, to use movement even to provide the image of repose. Slumber, the calm of night, solitude, even silence are among the scenes that music can depict. Sometimes sound produces the effect of silence, sometimes silence the effect of sound, just as a man dozes during a steady monotonous reading and then awakes, startled, when the reading ceases. . . . The art of the musician consists in substituting for the invisible image of the object, that of the movements which its presence excites in the mind of the spectator. Not only does the musician move the waves of the sea at will, fan the flames of a fire, make streams flow, rain fall and torrents rush down, he can magnify the horror of a burning desert, darken the walls of a dungeon, or he can calm a storm, soften the air and lighten the sky, and spread, with his orchestra, a fresh breeze through the woods.[27]

Reality for Rousseau is visible palpable nature, and music, he says, can conjure up that nature. It can also, of course, express human feeling which is nature, so to speak, within us; and the expression of feeling is achieved through melody. Thus, when Rousseau and Rameau quarreled over melody and harmony they were concerned with something more than music; their dispute was about reality itself.

Where Rameau, in his Cartesian manner, demanded unity, Rousseau was content with variety; where Rameau looked for fixed rules in music as in mathematics, Rousseau claimed that music was logically different from mathematics, and that musical styles must vary as nature varied. It was the genius of melody that it could express what was natural, whereas harmony was essentially artificial, an invention of the mind.

Rameau insisted that anyone who thought melody prior to harmony did not understand the true character of music. To deny harmony was to repudiate all those sciences which were based on the same mathematical principles of proportion and progression. Melody was an important part of music, but it was generated by the harmonic arrangement of sounds. Hence the man who understood only melody understood only little about music, while the man who had mastered harmony understood almost everything. It was the great marvel of music, Rameau suggested, to be at the same time an art of science. The laws of music and the laws of geometry ruled on the same foundations. Indeed, music could claim to be the first of the sciences for the same reasons that made it the first of the arts.[28]

Rousseau clung equally tenaciously to his belief in the priority of melody. Thus we find him, for example, in the article on *mélodie* in his *Dictionnaire de musique,* arguing that whereas harmony serves a subordinate purpose in holding the different parts of a musical composition together, melody provides the force and energy and the flow of music; while harmony may speak to the ear, melody speaks to the heart.[29]

The controversy between Rousseau and Rameau became more embittered as it became more personal. In his pamphlet called *Erreurs sur la musique dans l'Encyclopédie* Rameau went out of his way to find mistakes that might be attributed to Rousseau. Rousseau, for his part, did nothing to moderate his hostility toward Rameau as a composer. He wrote that Rameau had produced a remarkable comic opera, *Platée,* but that it was not to be compared to "Italian works of *opera buffa:* a fat goose cannot fly like a swallow." He commended Rameau's *recitativi* with faint praise: they were "less natural, but more varied than those of Lully, admirable in a very few scenes, bad in almost all the others"; as for Rameau's "over-elaborate accompaniments, . . . all these beautiful refinements of the art, all these imitations, repetitions, bass harmonies and counterpoints," they were "so many deformed monsters, monuments of bad taste which ought to be relegated to the cloister as their last resting place."[30]

Rameau was disappointed by the reception of his writings on the philosophy of music. Although a certain coolness was beginning to

Jean-Philippe Rameau (1683–1764)

be felt between Rousseau and his fellow Encyclopaedists, the editors, Diderot and d'Alembert, and most of the others rallied to Rousseau's side against Rameau. The fact is that they disapproved Rameau's metaphysics. D'Alembert, a professional geometer, protested in his article "Fondamentale" in the *Encyclopaedia* that it was ridiculous to confuse the rules that govern geometry with the features that give pleasure in music. Diderot, in a preface to the sixth volume of the *Encyclopaedia,* scoffed at the suggestion that geometry is founded on harmony and that all sciences must be compared to music.

At the same time, Rousseau also alienated many of his friends by turning his attack on Rameau's kind of music into an attack on French music in general. At the end of his *Lettre sur la musique française* Rousseau wrote:

> I believe I have shown that there is neither measure nor melody in French music, because the French language does not permit it; that French song is only a continual clamor unendurable to any ear unprepared for it, that its harmony is crude and unexpressive and proclaims only a scholar's padding; that French arias are not arias, that French recitative is not recitative, that the French have no music and cannot have any; and that if they ever do, it will be so much the worse for them.[31]

Harsh words, and naturally they gave offense. Grimm in his newsletter reported that Rousseau's *Lettre sur la musique française* had created a great stir in Paris: "The French will forgive anything if it is amusing, but [Rousseau] reasons earnestly, and with great hatchet blows overthrows all the altars that have been solemnly erected to the genius of French music."[32]

So many complaints about Rousseau's *Lettre* were addressed to the Comte d'Argenson, the minister responsible for the theatres, that an order was drawn up to have Rousseau expelled from France as an undesirable alien. The order was only revoked, it seems, on the intervention of d'Argenson's son, the Marquis de Voyer, who "loved Italian opera."[33] A chronicler reported on 5 December 1753 that Rousseau was deliberately jostled in the crowded pit of the Opera House: "He cried out that he was being suffocated, and on being told that that was no bad thing, he left the theatre."[34] The mayor of Paris withdrew the free pass to which Rousseau was entitled as an operatic composer.

But he refused to give up attending the opera. A friend who was an officer in the Mousquetaires accompanied him as a bodyguard, and as he paid for his ticket under protest he was made to understand that "the public, even at the height of its hostility to [him], was scandalized" at the injustice done to a musician by the municipal authorities.[35]

Over thirty replies[36] to the *Lettre sur la musique française* were published. The conservative journalist Élie Fréron, who had been fairly moderate in his criticisms of Rousseau's earlier writings, having doubtless recognized in the author of the *Discourse on the Sciences and the Arts* sentiments even more reactionary than his own, attacked the *Lettre* unmercifully. In his *L'Année littéraire,* Fréron described Rousseau as a "Swiss missionary" who had no right to speak of "*our* language" or "*our* music"—and even went so far as to describe Rousseau's *Le Devin du village* as a patchwork of tunes that the composer has pillaged from the Italian musicians during his "three years in Venice"[37] (Rousseau had actually spent rather less than one year there).[38] The author of the *Lettre* was also mocked on the stage—at the Comédie Française in a farce called *Les Adieux du goût* by Portelance and Patu—but at least in this case he was put together with the other Encyclopaedists as an object of ridicule.

Some supporters of Italian music feared that the aggressive tone of Rousseau's *Lettre* would only alienate the public and drive them to support the traditional French opera as a matter of patriotic principle. The Président de Brosses, for example, wrote to his brother saying, "Jean-Jacques, with his frenzied essay has done us a great injury, antagonizing the whole nation by the intemperate manner in which he has defended the right ideas."[39]

All the agitation provoked by earlier pamphleteering in the *Querelle des Bouffons* had come to be centered on Rousseau himself. His *Confessions* contains a passage which has puzzled many readers:

> [In 1753] the Parlement [of Paris] had just been exiled [by the King]; unrest was at its height; all the signs pointed to an early uprising. My [*Lettre sur la musique française*] appeared, and all other quarrels were immediately forgotten. No one thought of anything but the danger to French music, and the only uprising that took place was against me. The battle was so fierce that the nation was never to recover from it. . . . If I say that my writings may have averted a political revolution in France, people will think me mad; nevertheless it is a very real truth. . . .[40]

It is ironic that the philosopher most often named as being responsible for the French Revolution should have seen himself as a man who prevented a revolution taking place, but there is no reason to think him mad for making the claim.[41] Ever since the death of Louis XIV in 1715 there had been a constant struggle for power in France between the monarchy, seated at Versailles, and the French *parlements,* and notably that of Paris. It was a continuation of the conflict between the Crown and aristocracy which had erupted into civil war in previous centuries. Louis XIV had secured absolute power in the seventeenth century by refusing to allow the *parlements* to meet, but on his death, leaving an infant child as successor, the *parlement* of Paris was reconvened by the Regent, the Duc d'Orléans, who saw no other means of validating his own claim to rule in the child's name. Once reanimated, the *parlements*—which were not elected legislative bodies like the English parliament, but courts of law composed of noblemen—refused to be silenced. Indeed, they became increasingly demanding in their claims for a share in the sovereignty of the kingdom. In 1753 the King—Louis XV—decided that the *parlements* had overreached themselves and become a threat to his government; and in November of that year he issued an edict to dissolve the Paris *parlement* and replace it with a Royal Chamber. It appeared to many observers that the *parlement* would resist this move by force. Paris seemed to be on the brink of rebellion.

The intellectuals—or *philosophes*—gathered around Diderot's *Encyclopaedia* surveyed these events with a certain indifference. Those who took their political ideas from Montesquieu leaned toward the *parlements,* but there was in the 1750s no equally committed champion of the *parlements'* cause; those intellectuals—and they were more numerous—who shared Voltaire's antipathy to the political ambitions of the nobility were fairly sympathetic to the King's absolutist policy; but feelings on the subject were muted among the Encyclopaedists, as indeed they proved to be among the—predominantly bourgeois—educated classes generally. Paris at that time was not particularly interested in politics.

But is it conceivable that a musical dispute could have diverted aggression that would otherwise have gone into a political revolt? Others besides Rousseau believed it. Mercier, in his *Tableau de Paris,* writes: "Ah, how the government ought to cherish the opera! The theatrical factions made all the other factions disappear."[42] Even Grimm reported in his *Correspondance littéraire* that the public was "much more interested in the quarrel provoked by Rousseau's *Lettre* than in the Royal Chamber and its affairs."[43] Cultural questions were taken seriously in mid-eighteenth-century Paris, and Rousseau's attack on French music put many people into a frenzy of anger. He claims in the *Confessions* that the orchestra at the Paris Opéra actually "plotted to have me assassinated as I left the building,"[44] and although this is probably sheer fantasy, it is a well-attested fact that the musicians at the Opéra burned him in effigy.

Rousseau felt himself to be persecuted, even as Rameau felt himself to be betrayed. But in a very important sense Rousseau had succeeded where Rameau had failed. Rousseau had propelled French music into a new direction: away from the artificial constraints of the seventeenth century toward the creative freedom of the future. Rameau lost heart and produced very little work in the remaining years of his life—one or two ballets, a comic opera, and one last *tragédie lyrique*. He was a lonely and unhappy man.

The Encyclopaedists kept up their attacks on Rameau, even when they quarreled with Rousseau; and Diderot became even more aggressive than d'Alembert. Rameau's operas, he wrote, "will receive the

Giovanni Battista Pergolesi (1710–36)

burial of the Italian virtuosos, a thing which he foresaw and which made him sullen and sad and crabbed; for there is no more cross-grained creature . . . than an author threatened with outliving his reputation."[45]

Some modern critics, such as Edward Dent, have been hardly more charitable: "The Italians won the 'war of the bouffons,' as it was called . . . because their little operas were human and alive, while Rameau was an ageing man, a supreme master, but master of a dying tradition."[46]

All this is only partly true. As a philosopher, Rameau was well and truly defeated by Rousseau. But as a composer he had contributed something by his example to the birth of the new kind of music which Rousseau heralded. Rameau had studied in Italy and was no enemy of Italian music. In several of his works, and especially in what he regarded as his minor works, there is just as much melody as there is in *Le Devin du village*. So that even if Rameau was the supreme champion of the baroque tradition of French music, he was not simply an exponent of baroque music.

Diderot was mistaken in saying that Rameau had outlived his reputation, but Rameau did cease to be fashionable and he underwent a long period of neglect after his death; it was not until the late nineteenth century, and his "rediscovery" by Saint-Saens—who was the inspiration behind the editing of his operas—that Rameau began to achieve the classical status which is now recognized to be his. On the other hand, Rousseau provoked what can fairly be called a revolution in music. Rationalism was overthrown.

Rousseau by the example of his *Devin du village* and his doctrine of the supremacy of melody over harmony had introduced a new "moment" in the history of Western taste. On the musical stage he prepared the way for Mozart, whose *Bastien und Bastienne* is based on the *Devin du village,* and for the operas of Gluck, who brought new life to the French opera after the death of Rameau. Gluck once wrote: "The study I have made of this great man's [Rousseau's] works on music . . . have filled me with admiration. I was left with the profound conviction that if he had chosen to devote himself to the application of this art, he would have been able to achieve the prodigious effects which the ancients attributed to music."[47]

Rousseau is commonly said to have introduced the age of romanticism by his novel *La Nouvelle Héloïse,* which came out in 1761. He seems first to have used the word *romantic* even later, in the fifth of his *Rêveries du promeneur solitaire,*[48] written in 1776. I have tried to show that he had already formulated his romanticism, as a writer on music in the 1750s.

Today Rousseau's writings on music seem to have faded altogether from public consciousness. They are not reproduced in either of the standard present-day editions of his *Oeuvres complètes*—that edited in three volumes by Michel Launay or that edited in four volumes [to date] for the Bibliothèque de la Pléiade by Bernard Gagnebin and others.[49] Nor has any new English translation been undertaken for many years. Yet in the eighteenth century, Rousseau's musical works were published in French in several editions and they were included in full in the earliest collected works.[50] An English translation by William Waring of the *Dictionnaire de musique* was printed in London in 1779 and reprinted several times before the end of the century.[51]

It is strange that our own age, which has taken so much interest in Rousseau's social and ethical ideas, should have failed to recognize the importance of what he had to say about music. For it was as a writer on music that he prepared the world to receive his teaching in other fields. The writings on music hold the key to the meaning of his philosophy and do much to explain the magnitude of its influence.

Abbreviations used in notes

C.C.	*Correspondance complète de J.-J. Rousseau.* Edited by R. A. Leigh. Geneva, Banbury, and Oxford, 1965–.
C.T.W.	*Complete Theoretical Writings of J.-P. Rameau.* Edited by Erwin R. Jacobi. American Institute of Musicology, 1967–72.
J.J.	Maurice Cranston. *Jean-Jacques: The Early Life and Work of Jean-Jacques Rousseau.* New York and London, 1983.
O.C.	*Oeuvres complètes de J.-J. Rousseau.* Edited for the Bibliothèque de la Pléiade by Bernard Gagnebin, Marcel Raymond, *et al.* Paris, 1959–.
Q.B.	*La Querelle des Bouffons.* Edited by Denise Launay. Geneva, 1973.
Tiersot	Julien Tiersot. *J.-J. Rousseau.* Paris, 1920.
Wokler	Robert Wokler. "Rousseau on Rameau and Revolution," edited by R. F. Brissenden and J. C. Eade. *Studies in the Eighteenth Century,* Vol. 6. Canberra, 1979, pp. 251–83.

[1]The text of this pamphlet is reproduced in *Q.B.* I, pp. 1–54.

[2]Grimm and Rousseau met soon after Grimm arrived in France from Germany as governor to the young Prince Frederick of Saxe-Coburg. A shared love of music united them in a friendship which Rousseau described as "at first so very delectable, but afterwards so disastrous." (*O.C.* I, p. 350). Grimm, undoubtedly envious of Rousseau's fame as a writer, achieved his greatest success as author of a newsletter, the *Correspondance littéraire,* which circulated reports of French cultural and artistic life to subscribers throughout Europe.

[3]See *J.J.*, pp. 262–67.

[4]*Q.B.* I, pp. 132–92.

[5]Denis Diderot's greatest achievement was the *Encyclopaedia.* He devoted over twenty-five years to the editing of it, and it stands as the most important single monument of the French Enlightenment. A contemporary of Rousseau, he became a close friend of his in the 1740s when they met as two ambitious young men from the provinces seeking literary fame in Paris. Diderot's most notable contribution to the *Querelle des Bouffons* was a pamphlet entitled *Arrêt rendu à l'amphithéâtre de l'Opéra,* in which he posed as an author seeking to mediate between the two parties but in fact depicted the Italian opera in a favorable, and the French opera in a wholly unfavorable, light. (See *J.J.*, p. 277).

[6]Jean Le Rond d'Alembert was coeditor of the *Encyclopaedia* with Diderot in its earlier years but withdrew from the enterprise when it came to be opposed by the authorities. A physicist by training, he took an intense interest in the theoretical aspects of musical sounds. In the year of the *Querelle des Bouffons,* 1752, he produced a book called *Éléments de musique* based on Rameau's work; but a few months later he became sternly critical of Rameau's philosophy of music.

[7]Baron d'Holbach, the principal contributor to the *Encyclopaedia* on the applied sciences, and the central figure, as a wealthy host, of the social life of the Parisian intelligentsia, wrote several pamphlets in support of Italian music, notably *Lettre à une dame . . . sur l'état présent de l'Opéra* (*Q.B.* I, pp. 119–31).

[8]Cited in Alfred R. Oliver, *The Encyclopedists as Critics of Music* (New York: 1947), p. 92.

[9]Pierre de Morand, *Justification de la musique française* (Paris: 1754).

[10]*Q.B.* III, pp. 2216–17.

[11]Lady Morgan, *France* (London: 1817), vol. II, pp. 127–28.

[12]*Encyclopédie,* vol. I, p. xxxii.

[13]*See* Cuthbert Girdlestone, *Jean-Philippe Rameau* (New York: 1969), p. 481.

[14]Ibid. p. 483. Rameau was said to be "the rudest mortel, the most uncouth and the most unsocial of his time"; Charles Collé, *Journal et mémoires* (Paris: 1868), vol. II, p. 375.

[15]It was of this portrait that Diderot complained: "I looked for the censor of our literature, the Cato, the Brutus of our age . . . instead I saw the composer of *Le Devin du village* well-dressed, well-powdered and ridiculously seated on a cane chair." Jules Assézat and Maurice Tourneux, eds., *Oeuvres complètes de Diderot* (Paris: 1875–77), vol. X, pp. 483–84.

[16]*O.C.* I, pp. 378–79.

[17]Rousseau's famous novel *La Nouvelle Héloïse,* published some years later (in 1761), deals with the impossibility of love between a bourgeois tutor, Saint-Preux, and his aristocratic pupil, Julie. The social laws which proscribed marriage between the classes were treated by Rousseau almost as laws of nature.

[18]Cited by Tiersot, pp. 119–20.

[19]*C.C.* II, p. 87.

[20]Wokler, pp. 251–56.

[21]Rameau thought well of his own achievement: "I owe my discoveries in music entirely to the laws of nature of which the body of sound offers us a model, and the observation of which is at the same time so simple and so illuminating that the musician of today, together with the geometer, listens to me, understands me and imitates me." *C.T.W.* V, pp. 359–60.

[22]All these works are reproduced in *C.T.W.*

[23]These writings are reproduced in *Collection complète des Oeuvres de J.-J. Rousseau* (Paris: Chez Lequien, 1821), vol. XIII, together with other short works on music by Rousseau.

[24]*C.T.W.* V, p. 130. Elsewhere, Rameau wrote: "Music is usually divided into harmony and melody, although the latter is only a part of the former, and it is enough to understand harmony in order to be perfectly instructed in all the properties of music.

. . ." *C.T.W.* I, p. 31. And in another place: "Music is a physico-mathematical science; sound is the physical object, and the relationships between different sounds constitute the mathematical object. Its end is to please and to excite different passions in us. . . . The judgment of the ear is always solid, and however obscure it is without the help of reason, it still adds to the light of reason, once the latter has suggested to us the basis of our judgment. It is a double confirmation for us thus to see reason and hearing agree together." *C.T.W.* III, pp. 29, 53.

[25]*C.T.W.* V, p. 124.

[26]In his *Lettre sur la musique française,* Rousseau writes: "In music it is necessary that the whole thing should communicate at the same time a melody to the ear and an idea to the mind. This unity of melody seems to me to be an indispensable rule, not less important in music than the unity of action in tragedy, since it is based on the same principle and directed to the same end." (*Q.B.* I, p. 708.)

[27]Charles Porset, ed., *Essai sur l'origine des langues* (Bordeaux: 1970), pp. 175–76.

[28]*C.T.W.* III, p. 157.

[29]*Dictionnaire de musique,* in *Oeuvres complètes* (Paris: 1906), vol. VII, p. 157.

[30]Cited in Tiersot, pp. 120–21.

[31]*Q.B.* I, pp. 763–64. Elsewhere in the same work, Rousseau wrote: "The impossibility of inventing pleasing songs compels the [French] composers to turn their energies to the side of harmony, and for lack of real beauties to introduce artificial beauties, which have the sole merit of being difficult to contrive; in place of good music, they construct a scholarly music; to make up for song, they multiply accompaniments . . . to avoid insipidity, they increase the confusion; they think they are making music; but they are only making noise." Ibid., pp. 678–79.

[32]Maurice Tourneux, ed., *Correspondance littéraire philosophique et critique par Grimm, Diderot, Raynal, Meister, etc.* (Paris: 1877–82), vol. II, p. 307.

[33]Cited by Leigh, *C.C.* II, p. 330.

[34]Ibid.

[35]*O.C.* I, p. 385.

[36]*See* Richebourg, *op.cit.*, pp. 38–84.

[37]*C.C.* II, p. 244.

[38]*J.J.*, pp. 169–92.

[39]*C.C.* II, p. 251.

[40]*O.C.* I, p. 384.

[41]Robert Wokler analyzes this situation in his forthcoming book, *The Social Thought of J.-J. Rousseau.*

[42]Cited in *J.J.*, p. 283.

[43]Tourneux, *op.cit.,* vol. II, p. 313.

[44]*O.C.* I, p. 385.

[45]*See* Eve Kisch, "Rameau and Rousseau," *Music and Letters* 23, no. 2 (April 1941), p. 114.

[46]Quoted in ibid., p. 113.

[47]H. and E. H. Mueller von Asow, eds., *Collected Correspondence and Papers of C. W. Gluck* (London: 1962), p. 31.

[48]C. E. Butterworth, trans., *The Reveries of the solitary walker* (New York: 1979), p. 62.

[49]It is proposed to devote the forthcoming fifth volume of the Pléiade edition to Rousseau's musical writings.

[50]The Geneva edition in 33 volumes, 1782–89; the Neûchatel edition in 33 volumes, 1792; and the Brussels edition in 46 volumes, 1804.

[51]Excerpts in English translation from the *Dictionnaire de musique* had already appeared in *A Musical Dictionary,* published by J. Robson in London in 1769.

An Introduction to Mesopotamian Thought: The *Gilgamesh* Epic

George Anastaplo

George Anastaplo has long been a student of our legal system. His career began in 1950 when, after graduating at the top of his law school class at the University of Chicago, he was denied admission to the Illinois Bar because of his opinions about the fundamental right of revolution. These opinions had led to questions being put to him about possible political affiliations, which questions he on principle refused to answer. Ever since an adverse ruling on his case (over strong dissent) by the U.S. Supreme Court in 1961, appeals for his admission to the bar have been made from time to time by prominent lawyers. Mr. Anastaplo himself prefers to let the matter stand as it is, so that, as he says, "observers, including professors as well as students of law, may be obliged to think about these matters—and thereby to reflect upon their profession and the rule of law."

Mr. Anastaplo is professor of law at Loyola University of Chicago and lecturer in the liberal arts at the University of Chicago. Among his books are *The Constitutionalist: Notes on the First Amendment* (1971); *Human Being and Citizen: Essays on Virtue, Freedom and the Common Good* (1975); and *The Artist as Thinker: From Shakespeare to Joyce* (1983). Forthcoming are his books *The Constitution of 1787* and *The American Moralist: Essays on Law, Ethics and Government.* He is also the author of a book-length series of lectures entitled *Constitutions of 1787,* published in the Fall 1986 issue of the *Loyola University Law Journal* (Chicago, Ill.). His essay on *The Bhagavad Gītā* appeared in last year's *Great Ideas Today.*

Mother, mother, what shall we do?
The leaves are turning brown!
Wetness shines on gray porch roofs,
Fog hides all our town.

Daughter, daughter, calm yourself
The whole world's death is a little thing.
Take your toys to another room;
Play a while till spring.
—Sara Prince Anastaplo, *First Fall*[1]

Prologue

Five thousand years ago the story was first told of a king, Gilgamesh, who was in some ways bad, in other ways good.[2] The power of this story is attested to by the great expanse that it covered, both in time and in space—for it appeared in various ancient Mesopotamian countries (and in as many languages) and over more than a thousand years.[3] And yet it was a story that could be lost, perhaps in part because its central issues, or assumptions, became obsolete, at least until modern times.[4]

It is useful to provide, at the outset, a summary of the principal story about Gilgamesh, who seems to have been a historical ruler in what we now know as the Middle East.[5] In fact, two summaries would be useful, if not even three, which is particularly appropriate on this occasion, considering how much use is made in the *Gilgamesh* epic itself of repetitions.[6]

Our first summary is taken from a guide to world literature, which reads,

> *Gilgamesh:* a Babylonian epic poem (*c.* 2000 B.C.). From ancient records it is known that this poem was once more than twice as long as what has survived from it. In its present form it is pieced together from nearly 30,000 tablets or fragments in three languages. The poem tells the adventures of Gilgamesh, who begins as a harsh ruler, has a terrific battle with a primitive figure [Enkidu] and then becomes his staunch friend, loses this friend, tries vainly to regain him, and finally confers with his shade in the land of the dead. The poem, like most primitive epics, is probably pieced together from a good many stories originally

> independent. One of the most interesting sections is the Babylonian tale of the Flood (Tablet XI), which is a remarkable parallel to the story of Noah's Flood in Genesis. The final section, which describes the world after death, is a literal translation from a Sumerian poem.[7]

It is in this final section (Tablet XII) that Gilgamesh confers with the shade of his dead friend, Enkidu.[8]

Our next summary adds a couple of essential points to the first summary we have used. It is taken from the editorial comment introducing the epic in the Speiser translation:

> The theme of this epic is essentially a secular one. The poem deals with such earthy things as man and nature, love and adventure, friendship and combat—all masterfully blended into a background for the stark reality of death. The climactic struggle of the protagonist to change his eventual fate, by learning the secret of immortality from the hero of the Great Flood of long ago [Utnapishtim], ends in failure; but with the failure comes a sense of quiet resignation. For the first time in the history of the world a profound experience on such a heroic scale has found expression in a noble style. The scope and sweep of the epic, and its sheer poetic power, give it a timeless appeal. In antiquity, the influence of the poem spread to various tongues and cultures. Today it captivates student and poet alike.[9]

The considerable interest in this epic in modern times began with a fascination with its account of the Great Flood, something that very much caught the attention of Westerners steeped in the Bible. This happened when the *Gilgamesh* epic was rediscovered by English archaeologists at Nineveh in the second half of the nineteenth century.[10] The account of the Flood, which is particularly intriguing because of its parallels to the account in Genesis, did not originate in any of the stories about Gilgamesh.[11] But this Flood account is used by our poet to illuminate the primary concerns of the *Gilgamesh* epic, namely *eros* (that is, life and desire) and *death* (which, I will suggest, is understood to be critical to life).[12]

We turn now to our third summary, a somewhat more detailed one, which I have put together.[13] Gilgamesh, at the outset of this twelve-tablet Akkadian-language poem, is condemned by his people, especially by the nobles, as arrogant: he seems to be taking advantage of a royal sexual prerogative with the brides of the city of Uruk,[14] and he seems to be assigning wearisome tasks to the young men. Complaints against him are heard by the gods. It seems to be taken for granted by our poet and by his audience that, of course, the gods will do something about this tyrannical king, who is recognized as a mighty man.[15] The response of the gods is a complicated one, beginning with the immediate creation of another powerful man, evidently fully grown, who looks very much like Gilgamesh.[16] This is Enkidu: he is shaggy-haired all over his body; he is endowed with a head of hair like a woman's; he knows neither people nor land. In fact, he lives among the animals, moving about with them as they feed and drink.[17]

But whereas Gilgamesh had caused problems for his fellow men in the city, Enkidu causes problems for them in the countryside (or desert), since he is adept at filling pits and springing traps, thereby protecting from hunters the animals with which he associates. And so a hunter complains to his father, who advises him to go to King Gilgamesh for help. When the hunter does go to Uruk to complain to Gilgamesh, the king responds in the very way that the hunter's father had anticipated:[18] a harlot is sent out from Uruk into the wild to display her charms to Enkidu, who responds as anticipated and is thereby tamed, so much so that his animal companions flee from him thereafter.[19]

The now civilized Enkidu, upon learning of Gilgamesh's notorious practice with the maids of Uruk, is shocked. Enkidu, aided by the harlot with whom he has been consorting, hastens to Uruk and stations himself at the building in which Gilgamesh goes to the women. Gilgamesh and Enkidu grapple ferociously outside the bridal chamber; the king prevails but, instead of killing his antagonist, he befriends him. They become inseparable companions and, so far as we know, Gilgamesh has nothing further to do with the maids of Uruk. (The harlot had anticipated what in fact happens, that Gilgamesh would have dreams that announced both his encounter and his future relations with Enkidu. Other dreams punctuate the story, anticipating again and again what is to happen.[20])

At Gilgamesh's insistence, and despite the protests of Enkidu and the concerns of the elders of Uruk, the two companions go to a distant land (to the Cedar Forest) to destroy the monstrous Humbaba.[21] Humbaba tries to surrender to them, but Enkidu insists upon his death. Earlier Enkidu had had to encourage Gilgamesh to continue the expedition, but thereafter had had to be encouraged himself by Gilgamesh.[22]

The two triumphant companions return home to great acclaim. There then follows in the center of the epic (Tablets VI and VII), the fatal encounter with Ishtar, a goddess who (to draw on Greek counterparts) seems to combine the eroticism of "glorious Aphrodite," the warlikeness of Athena, and the fertility of Ceres. Thus, the narrator tells us,

> Gilgamesh washed his grimy hair, polished his weapons,
> The braid of his hair he shook out against his back.
> He cast off his soiled things, put on his clean ones,
> Wrapped a fringed cloak about and fastened a sash.
> When Gilgamesh had put on his tiara,
> Glorious Ishtar raised an eye at the beauty of Gilgamesh:
> "Come, Gilgamesh, be thou my lover!"[23]

The goddess then describes for him all the good things she will provide him as his wife. The king's response is unequivocal: he makes it clear, all too clear, that he wants nothing to do with her, dismissing her as unreliable. He recites a catalog of a half-dozen others whom she has loved, and who suffered because of her attentions.[24]

Gilgamesh's frank rebuke of Ishtar enrages her.[25] She goes to her father, Anu, who seems to be the first of the gods, demanding revenge. This leads, with certain precautions (lest all mankind be wiped out), to the despatch against Gilgamesh of the voracious Bull of Heaven. We are surprised to see that the two companions, Gilgamesh and Enkidu, are able to deal with this divine instrument, killing it and dedicating its heart, with appropriate ceremonies, to the god Shamash (who has helped them against the Bull, as well as against Humbaba). Enkidu, however, adds insult to injury by throwing the right thigh of the Bull of Heaven at Ishtar, whom he sees hovering nearby and who is most disturbed by the turn of events.[26]

The heroic pair have gone too far. The gods confer, concluding that one of the heroes must die—and Enkidu is settled upon. He wastes away, and Gilgamesh becomes depressed by the decline and then the death of Enkidu.[27] His strong reaction to the death of his companion drives him to wander far (reverting to the primitive condition in which Enkidu had once been?). This long journey ends in a distant land where there is to be found Utnapishtim and his wife, who survived the Great Flood long before and who have never died.[28] During his journey, Gilgamesh is repeatedly told that he cannot avoid death. Utnapishtim tells him the same thing, even as he describes how he and his wife happened to survive the Great Flood and to win deathlessness. Finally, however, Utnapishtim tells Gilgamesh about a plant, which Gilgamesh then secures from the bottom of the sea, and which Utnapishtim says can be used to rejuvenate him. With this in hand, Gilgamesh starts home.[29]

On the way home, he is robbed of his plant by a serpent,[30] and so, bereft, he returns to Uruk with Utnapishtim's boatman.[31] By now Gilgamesh is more or less reconciled to his mortality. The eleventh tablet, and the story proper, concludes with Gilgamesh's showing the boatman the walls of Uruk and the temple of Ishtar. On this occasion he uses words that echo the opening lines of the first tablet of our epic.

The twelfth tablet tells a separate, yet related, story:[32] Gilgamesh drops into the underworld some treasures which have been given him by Ishtar; Enkidu, who is still alive at the beginning of this tablet, volunteers to fetch them, but he does not follow the prudent instructions given him by Gilgamesh and so is permanently trapped in the underworld.[33] But Gilgamesh manages to secure thereafter an interview with the shade of Enkidu, who conveys to him what it means to be dead—the decay and the dissolution. The conclusion of the twelfth tablet is lost; but the fragments we do have indicate that Enkidu also tells

Gilgamesh about the burial rites and services that should be provided the dead by survivors, as well as about the consequences of disposing of corpses without proper ceremony. Thus, it would seem, the twelfth (and final) tablet advocates a systematized response to death.[34]

This, then, is the *Gilgamesh* epic. More details will come to light as I comment on various intriguing features of this five-thousand-year-old story, a story which has been called "the most significant literary creation of the whole of ancient Mesopotamia."[35]

I.

One challenging feature of this epic is the ambiguity in the character of Gilgamesh himself. He exhibits remarkable shifts between heroic strength and an all too human weakness (if not even sensuality and cowardice).[36]

Thus, Gilgamesh can dare much. He volunteers to challenge the terrible Humbaba, believing this to be the means for eliminating evil from the world.[37] Gilgamesh is heroic, but not philosophical; in fact, at times he can seem shallow. Even so, he is introduced as "he who saw everything to the ends of the land."[38]

Yet Gilgamesh is shown early as lustful, creating dissension (at least among the nobility) because of his exercise of certain rights with brides (and because of the attendant rigor evidently used to divert the young men of the city).[39] In a sense, that is, difficulties follow upon his being at the outset too much the disciple of Ishtar, the very goddess against whom he later rebels, with dire consequences for his companion.[40]

Thereafter Gilgamesh becomes remarkably demoralized, not only by the death of Enkidu, but even more by the prospect of his own death. He frantically strives to avoid death: those whom he encounters in his journey to secure immortality are quite struck by his shattered demeanor, especially considering his exploits and reputation.[41]

Thus Gilgamesh runs to extremes, whether in his pursuit of the erotic or in his turning away from it, whether in his contempt for death or in his abhorrence of it. Perhaps Mesopotamian life was always marked by these critical ambiguities.[42] Perhaps, also, deep ambiguity may naturally be found in any way of life that makes as much of sexuality and the female element in its *public* life as the Mesopotamians evidently did.[43]

II.

We have already noticed the importance of Ishtar, the goddess who can be understood to stand for life itself. We have also noticed that Gilgamesh has a dramatic encounter with her (around which the twelve tablets turn), an encounter that proves decisive to the plot, leading to Enkidu's death and to what Gilgamesh does thereafter.[44]

This encounter obscures, however, just how much peaceful collaboration there is between Gilgamesh and Ishtar, both before this fateful encounter and after it. It becomes evident, upon examination, that mankind has to rely upon Ishtar continuously. Thus, Gilgamesh learns from Utnapishtim how troubled Ishtar had been upon seeing mankind threatened by the Great Flood.[45] She had very much resented, on that occasion, the death of the creatures for whose existence she considered herself responsible. At the end of the eleventh tablet we can hear Gilgamesh acknowledging the importance of the Temple of Ishtar as he shows off to a stranger the marvels of his city, Uruk.[46]

That Ishtar is somehow responsible for life itself is evident again and again. Thus, a barmaid encountered by Gilgamesh in the course of his pursuit of immortality seems to be an Ishtar figure: she counsels him to enjoy himself while he can, making much of food and drink and of one's association with spouse and children.[47] Indeed, Ishtar seems to be so much responsible for life that she can even threaten Anu on one occasion with bringing back to "life" on earth all of the dead, who would thus outnumber and overwhelm the living.[48]

There are other questionable features in Ishtar's character as well. These may be seen in the bridal rights that Gilgamesh has exercised, evidently as king. Ambiguities may also be seen in the perhaps related institution of temple-harlotry, which may have been drawn upon in civilizing Enkidu.[49] On the other hand, the catalog of grievances which Gilgamesh hurls at Ishtar, in rejecting her overtures, should be examined more carefully than the king himself seems to have been able to do. That is, it is far from certain that the fates of the six lovers there described (Gilgamesh would have been her seventh) were as undeserved, or as much a reproach to Ishtar, as Gilgamesh seems to believe.[50] In fact, one can see running through these grievances references to developments that contributed to the furtherance of civilization, as happened also in the case of the use of the harlot with Enkidu.[51]

One must wonder, in short, whether Gilgamesh is able to face up to what Ishtar really means. Indeed, one must wonder, did Enkidu become for Gilgamesh a temporary substitute for the erotic? It is indicated, in several ways, that Enkidu is somehow female in his relation with Gilgamesh: for example, the head hair of Enkidu; the dreams of Gilgamesh, in which things are encountered that stand for Enkidu and are responded to as if female; and, of course, the intensity of the relationship between the two.[52] Certainly, the death of Enkidu provokes the quite unexpected reaction we have already noticed, a reaction which suggests that the loss of Enkidu dramatizes problems for Gilgamesh (perhaps with both death and the erotic) that he may have had all along.[53]

III.

One is induced by this epic to wonder about the status of death, and hence of immortality, for mankind. Enkidu, we remember, becomes quite unlike the brutes he has freely associated with after his sexual encounter with the harlot. The brutes, it can be said, really know nothing about the erotic, if only because the truly erotic has a rational component to it.[54] Should it not be said that they do not know anything about death either, if only because they do not understand the difference between life and death?[55] Thus, both eroticism and consciousness of mortality require understanding and are otherwise related as well.

Gilgamesh, early in the story, is quite sensible about death. When Enkidu tries to discourage the dangerous expedition against the fierce Humbaba, Gilgamesh replies,[56]

> Who, my friend, can scale heaven?
> Only the gods live forever under the sun.
> As for mankind, numbered are their days;
> Whatever they achieve is but the wind![57]

And he adds, "A name that endures I will make for me!"[58]

Thereafter, Gilgamesh engages in the slaughter both of Humbaba and of the Bull of Heaven. The killings do not sober him; rather, he exults in these exploits. But the dying and death of Enkidu move him to despair, "moaning bitterly like a wailing woman."[59] Much has been made of Enkidu as someone who looks like Gilgamesh, has his strength, and so forth.[60] So the death of Enkidu means that, evidently for the first time, Gilgamesh has seen someone very much like himself die.[61] That this death is not in battle, or from any obvious affliction, suggests that it is due to the very nature (and hence to the inevitable limitations) of man. Death, or his own vulnerability, is brought close to home when Gilgamesh, after seven days and seven nights of watchful waiting and wailing over Enkidu's corpse, sees a worm come out of his nose.[62]

The despairing Gilgamesh is told several times that death cannot be avoided.[63] Perhaps most eloquent is the counsel of Utnapishtim, the immortal survivor of the Great Flood, which counsel includes these words:

> Do we build a house forever?
>   Do we seal contracts forever?
> Do brothers divide shares forever?
> Does hatred persist forever in the land?
> Does the river forever raise up and bring on floods?
> The dragon-fly leaves its shell
> That its face might but glance at the face of the sun.
> Since the days of yore there has been no permanence;
> The resting and the dead, how alike they are!
> Do they not compose a picture of death,
> The commoner and the noble,
>   Once they are near to their fate?[64]

Death is likened to sleep on more than one occasion in this epic.[65] The implications of this resemblance are suggested by an episode between Gilgamesh, Utnapishtim, and Utnapishtim's wife. The weary Gilgamesh falls asleep, despite a determination not to (as a test of his eligibility for fending off death?). He sleeps for seven days but he insists, upon awakening, that he has slept only one night. He has to be disproved by the precautions Utnapishtim has taken in marking the passage of time (by the daily baking of wafers).[66] There is nothing explicitly said by the poet or grasped by Gilgamesh as to one critical lesson of this episode: if one can sleep a week without knowing it, and without "missing" it, why not years or decades also? And if so, why should death matter?[67]

We recall that the plant recommended by Utnapishtim is not something that grants perpetual deathlessness but merely rejuvenation, and even that plant is lost before Gilgamesh can get home. He does not thereupon try to go back to get more of that plant. Rather, he continues homeward, as if at last recognizing that his effort to fend off mortality had always been a hopeless venture.[68] But then, do we not know that the normal human being accepts death from a surprisingly early age? It takes very few observations or experiences to persuade us of the general mortality of all the living things we encounter.

IV.

Gilgamesh ends up being reconciled to death just as he has been reconciled to eros. In both cases, the reconciliation may reflect a certain hopelessness, if not even desperation, thereby testifying to a limited understanding. That is, he finally accepts that which all somehow sense and adapt themselves to, many somewhat more naturally than does Gilgamesh.

The connection between death and eros is several times indicated. It may be seen most dramatically perhaps in the gods, who live primarily, if not only, through the mortals they get involved with. Consider the implications of words addressed by Gilgamesh to the deathless Utnapishtim shortly after they first meet:

> As I look upon thee, Utnapishtim,
> Thy features are not strange; even as I art thou.
> Thou art not strange at all; even as I art thou.
> My heart had regarded thee as resolved to do battle,
> Yet thou liest indolent upon thy back!
> Tell me, how joinedst thou the Assembly of the gods,
> In thy quest for life?[69]

Utnapishtim then tells the story of the Great Flood.

The fact that the ancient Utnapishtim resembles Gilgamesh as much as he does suggests that we have here still another substitute for Gilgamesh, an anticipation of his contemporary Enkidu. Utnapishtim has transcended mortality somehow, evidently because of his great cunning.[70] But consider the price paid by Utnapishtim—a price of which Gilgamesh does not seem to appreciate the full significance:

> My heart had regarded thee as resolved to do battle,
> Yet thou liest indolent upon thy back!

Is not Gilgamesh, even though he does not seem to realize it, much more vital, much more alive, than the indolent Utnapishtim? We, in turn, can learn from all this something which the battle-oriented Gilgamesh may not learn as he wrestles with his condition.[71]

The erotic element is life-seeking, and life-giving; and it can be fully what it is (with its capacity to evoke the splendid) because of the possibility, nay, the inevitability, of death. The intimate relation between eros and death may be reflected in the status of the female element in this epic (and in the civilization which made this epic possible). Thus we have such graphic females as the harlot, as the mother of Gilgamesh, as "glorious Ishtar" herself, as the barmaid, and as Utnapishtim's wife.

The female is again and again presented in this story as the source of critical instruction and help. This may point up the importance of the erotic as life-serving. Are women particularly life-giving and hence death-averting? Does not the male element in this story tend to be identified more with death and destruction (as is the male god Enlil, who had commissioned Humbaba to guard the Cedar Forest, and who had long before visited the Flood upon mankind)?[72]

Did the civilization in which this story flourished go too far in its subservience to the female element? That may be seen, perhaps, in the institution of temple-harlots dedicated to Ishtar. One can usefully compare to this institution that of the Vestal Virgins in Rome. One is also reminded of how vigorously both the Israelite prophets and the early Christians attacked as abominations the kind of erotic worship associated with Ishtar.[73] Even so, there are some marvelous women in this story.

V.

Perhaps it is because women are so prominent that dreams are as important here as they are. Certainly, the interpretation of dreams is evidently a special (but not the exclusive) province of women. As we have noticed, a harlot anticipates Gilgamesh's dreams about Enkidu. When the dreams do come, Gilgamesh goes to his mother for an authoritative interpretation.[74]

Dreams are tools in the service of men: they provide access to knowledge of what will be, perhaps (at least in part) by providing one with insights into one's own character. Evidently dreams are not understood to have been sent as messengers of the gods, strictly speaking. Utnapishtim was not "told" by any god about the Flood and about the boat he would need—all this evidently came to him in a dream (albeit at the prompting of a god). This, it seems, is not understood to be a *telling* by any god, since it is still up to the human being to figure out the meaning of what he has received. Do dreams reflect what we all somehow sense? Are they a special kind of thinking done by human beings? Does this suggest that everything is somehow interconnected?[75]

The gods rarely dream in Mesopotamian literature. Perhaps they do not have to, because most of them are not vulnerable in the way that human beings are. Perhaps, therefore, women are more prone than men to be adept with dreams because they tend to be more vulnerable than men.

VI.

To say that the gods are not time-bound in the way that human beings are is not to say that they are omnipotent or omniscient. Consider, for example, what happens to the Bull of Heaven sent by the gods to punish Gilgamesh: it is killed by Gilgamesh and Enkidu. Or consider, much earlier, the fact that the god powerful enough to bring on the Great Flood could not destroy all of mankind as he had planned.[76]

I have suggested that the gods may live primarily, if not only, through the human beings with whom they become involved, at least in our epic. The gods are often portrayed as being very much like men in critical respects. They too can be intimidated by, and can cower in the face of, the storm that brings on the Flood. Later, they can respond greedily to the savor of the sacrifice offered by Utnapishtim.[77]

Perhaps it is because the gods are very much like men in certain respects that human beings can keep track of what they are doing. (Enkidu reports to Gilgamesh after their killing of the Bull of Heaven that the gods have just had a conference about them.) Certainly the men in the *Gilgamesh* epic are often very much aware of what the gods are up to, seen most dramatically perhaps in Gilgamesh's awareness of Ishtar's passion for him, which he resists so passionately.[78]

The two most dramatic gods in this story seem to be Ishtar, with her emphasis upon the erotic (or upon life), and Enlil, with his emphasis upon the destructive (or upon death). Far less dramatic, but perhaps even more impressive, may be the gods (and especially Anu?) who set into motion the action of this epic. Cannot the entire story be seen as a complicated divine response to the opening complaints about the arrogant Gilgamesh? All that happens thereafter *may* be seen as part of a great plan to instruct Gilgamesh, and other human beings who watch and learn, about the perils of arrogance (if not about the limitations of kingship itself).[79] This means, among other things, that Gilgamesh must be made to appreciate what that erotic element means which he is so cavalierly exploiting; the king must be made to appreciate how vulnerable even he is to death. Thus he must come to terms, in a complicated way, with both the erotic and the mortal.

VII.

And so, at the end of the eleventh tablet (where the story can be said "properly" to end) Gilgamesh is shown celebrating the walls and the temple of Uruk. The king has thereby returned to his political (and priestly?) duties, having abandoned self-gratification either in the form of mere personal satisfaction (whether through sexuality or through adventures) or in the perhaps related form of a desperate quest for personal immortality on earth.

A proper (Mesopotamian?) recognition of the erotic may be seen, at the end, in Gilgamesh's deference to the Temple of Ishtar; a proper (political?) recognition of death may be seen in his admiration for the city walls. Temples and walls are monuments to life, and to the preservation of life in the face of death, including the indolence (a kind of death) which can accompany such human deathlessness as Utnapishtim displays.

It may well be that the twelfth (and final) tablet, an epilogue of sorts, may present a story that tells, in still another way, how life and death may be reconciled. Perhaps there is something fitting (if not even providential) in the mutilated condition of this particular tablet, which reminds us once again of how vulnerable human things can be. The story in the twelfth tablet does seem to indicate that one's last days are best served by the family and by the city, which make possible the proper rituals and a fitting burial upon death. Although the decay and the irrevocability of death are emphasized in Enkidu's report from the underworld, there may also be an indication of better and worse earthly ways to respond to this inevitable fate. One depends upon one's survivors, at least for one's burial with appropriate rituals, if not also for life-sustaining memory. To speak of survivors, of proper burial, and of memory is to look to the city and to the family—and thus, in still another way, it is to depend upon the city walls without and upon the Temple of Ishtar within.[80]

Epilogue

It seems that the poet responsible for this epic—for the final (and best) version of *Gilgamesh*—simply could not leave it at *eleven* tablets. Certainly, it is evident throughout the story that *twelve* is an important number for the Mesopotamians (as is *seven*). In any event, the adding of the final tablet (whether as the twelfth or not) was deliberate: it was taken, as I have reported, from a poem which is also found standing alone in Mesopotamian literature. This addition can be understood to tell in still another way the entire story of the relations of Gilgamesh and Ishtar and of the effect upon Gilgamesh of Enkidu's death. Perhaps this is a retelling for the benefit of those who need something more, or something other, than the more complicated story told in the first eleven tablets of the epic.[81]

Perhaps, also, if we knew more about the conclusion of this twelfth tablet, we could better explain what it is doing here. This reminds us of how much has depended already upon the generations of dedicated and resourceful scholars who have put this epic back together again, starting with the remarkable excavations at Nineveh a century ago and the meticulous assembly thereafter of thousands upon thousands of pieces. These scholars have retrieved this story from the dustbins of history. The account of their heroic efforts, and of their ingenuity, is itself engaging.[82]

Even more interesting is the question of how much the poet responsible for the final version of this epic was himself aware of with respect to the things I have noticed. There is exhibited here a considerable sophistication, much of which is (I have suggested) related to the status of the female element in Mesopotamian affairs. That is to say, the opinions reflected here are anything but primitive, however colored (if not distorted) they may be by an acceptance of forms of the erotic which require further attention, especially from that perspective which looks to nature for a proper understanding of both eros and death, if not for a proper understanding of understanding itself.[83]

I trust I have said enough to suggest that we have here, in the poet of the *Gilgamesh* epic, a mind to be reckoned with, someone who is remarkably adept in suggesting the complexities in the world.[84] These enduring complexities require the most careful weighing of oppositions if one is to understand, and hence to accept, how things truly are.

---

[1]See also George Anastaplo, *The Artist as Thinker: From Shakespeare to Joyce* (Athens, Ohio: Swallow Press/Ohio University Press, 1983), pp. 422–24; *The Constitutionalist: Notes on the First Amendment* (Dallas: Southern Methodist University Press, 1971), p. 767 n. 184.

The remarkable concern with death in our *Gilgamesh* story (see note 41 below) is reflected in John Gardner's comment on the final tablet of that story:

> The tablet is now half in ruin; much of what it says had fallen into the cracks of time. All we know for sure is that it's good to have sons, probably bad to fall from the mast of a ship into nothingness, good to die quickly and painlessly, good to die in battle, bad to die in the wilderness, unnoticed, and unspeakably bad to die unloved. Mainly what we know is that to die at all is a terrible thing, but to die without having truly lived—without having loved and left loved ones—is to be garbage surviving through eternity on garbage.

"Notes on Gilgamesh, Tablet XII," *MSS,* 2 (1983), pp. 159–64; quoted in John Gardner and John Maier, *Gilgamesh* (New York: Alfred A. Knopf, 1984), pp. 256–57. See Section VII of this article. See also note 29 below.

Compare the essay, "On Death: One by One, Yet All Together," in Anastaplo, *Human Being and Citizen: Essays on Virtue, Freedom, and the Common Good* (Athens, Ohio: Swallow Press/Ohio University Press, 1975), pp. 214f.

[2]King David comes to mind, as does Achilles. See notes 16, 36, and 62, below. See, on Gilgamesh's oppressiveness, Jeffrey H. Tigay, *The Evolution of the Gilgamesh Epic* (Philadelphia: University of Pennsylvania Press, 1982), pp. 180f. (Professor Tigay's book has been widely acclaimed, not least as a most useful distillation of what scholars have

worked out over the past century about the considerably varied fragments on Gilgamesh that we now have.) "The most renowned of ancient Near Eastern heroes is Gilgamesh, who has been dubbed 'the hero par excellence of the ancient world' and 'the hero without peer of the entire ancient Near East.' " John H. Marks, "*Gilgamesh:* An Afterword," in Herbert Mason, *Gilgamesh: A Verse Narrative* (New York: New American Library, Mentor Book, 1972), p. 117 (quoting S. N. Kramer). The name of the hero, as worked out from the cuneiform tablets, has been written various ways in modern times. See, e.g., Gardner and Maier, *Gilgamesh,* pp. 43 ("Bilgamesh"), 282–83; *The Babylonian Legends of the Creation* (London: British Museum, 1921), p. 2 ("Gizdubar" and "Gilgamish"); R. Campbell Thompson, ed., *The Epic of Gilgamesh: Text, Transliteration, and Notes* (Oxford: Clarendon Press, 1930), pp. 8–10. There is no generally accepted account of what the name means.

[3]Professor Tigay speaks of the known written stages of the story extending "over a period of at least 1,500 years down to the manuscripts of its final version." Tigay, *Evolution,* p. 1. "When this epic was first unearthed in the mid-nineteenth century, the tablets discovered were from its latest and best-known version, that of the first millennium B.C.E. . . . [It] is an epic poem covering twelve tablets in its latest version and written in Akkadian, the main Semitic language of ancient Babylonia and Assyria." Ibid., p. 3. (It is this final version that I refer to in this article as "our epic." See note 13 below.)

"The earliest legends we have about Gilgamesh are found in Sumerian lays of the late third millennium B.C. By a process of sifting out, adaptation, and radical transformation, probably in the early second millennium B.C., these legends were reworked into a single epic." William L. Moran, "Ut-napishtim Revisited," *New York Times Book Review,* Nov. 11, 1984, p. 13. "During the seventh century B.C., to which the greater part of the available tablets date back, the Gilgamesh Epic consisted of twelve large tablets, each of which contained about three hundred lines, with the exception of the twelfth, which had only about half as many lines." Alexander Heidel, *The Gilgamesh Epic and Old Testament Parallels,* 2nd ed. (Chicago: University of Chicago Press, 1949), p. 1. See, for an inventory of the ancient texts, Tigay, *Evolution,* pp. 304–7. See, on the many peoples of Western Asia who made use of the cuneiform ("wedge-shaped") script of the Sumerians (the Akkadians, Assyrians, Babylonians, Hittites, Hurrians, Canaanites, and Elamites), Samuel Noah Kramer, "Sumerian Literature, A General Survey," in G. Ernest Wright, ed., *The Bible and the Ancient Near East* (Garden City, N.Y.: Doubleday & Co., Anchor Books, 1965), p. 340. (It should be noticed that I know none of the languages which the *Gilgamesh* tablets use.)

[4]See note 49 below. "Mesopotamia" is usually taken to refer to that region of southwestern Asia between the Tigris and Euphrates rivers, extending from the mountains of Asia Minor to the Persian Gulf. It is possible that the extent of the influence of the Gilgamesh story, and the forms that story took over millennia (including shifts in the rankings of the gods), reflected political and social developments in that region. Thus the colophon for Tablet IX of the epic identifies the tablet as having been made at the "Palace of Ashurbanipal, king of the world, king of Assyria." Heidel, *The Gilgamesh Epic,* p. 68. (The Hebrew Bible has come down to us in its integrity, even though *not* preserved on anything so durable as clay. It did have a people constantly using, and hence preserving, it—and this, perhaps, because it was somehow sounder in its understanding of things? See Anastaplo, "How to Read the Constitution of the United States," *Loyola University of Chicago Law Journal,* vol. 17 (1985), pp. 55–64; also, "The Constitution of 1787: A Commentary," *Loyola University of Chicago Law Journal,* vol. 18 (1986), p. 1f. See as well notes 11 and 57 below. What should the preservation, or mutilation, of a text be taken to say about the role of divine providence? Machiavelli, in his preface to the *Discourses,* says he will "write on all the books of Titus Livy which have not been intercepted by the malignity of the times.")

Perhaps contributing to the considerable interest in the *Gilgamesh* today is the heightened sensitivity in our time to both death and eros (as in the desperate art of Pablo Picasso in his last years). It should be noticed that the Babylonian world, too, was quite sophisticated in commerce, having developed various kinds of contracts and perhaps even insurance. "We could almost say that anything so profoundly human as the image of Gilgamesh was bound to reappear, yet we are still surprised to learn that one of the very oldest stories of man is so inherently contemporary." Mason, *Gilgamesh: A Verse Narrative,* p. 100. Certainly it is more "contemporary" than the Hebrew Bible or Classic Greek stories, where the concern for death tends to be muted. Compare, however, Euripides, *Alcestis* [*GBWW,* Vol. 5, pp. 237–47]. See note 42 below.

[5]"This Sumerian king, who reigned in his city, Uruk, around 2650 B.C., achieved fame and honor unique in Mesopotamian history, and for more than 2,000 years he was celebrated in cult and legend, only to disappear under the sands of Iraq and the ruins of Mesopotamian civilization. But then he reappeared a little more than a century ago—'Out of dark night where lay/The crowns of Nineveh,' in Yeats's phrase. . . ." Moran, "Ut-napishtim Revisited," p. 13. "The Sumerian tales, the earliest known literary embodiment of Gilgamesh's adventures, are separated from his lifetime by several centuries. According to the *Sumerian King List,* Gilgamesh was the fifth king of the first dynasty of Uruk, which historians place in the Second Early Dynastic Period of Sumer (ca. 2700–2500)." Tigay, *Evolution,* p. 13. "For the centuries between Gilgamesh's lifetime (between 2700 and 2500) and the earliest literary texts about him (2100–2000) or their forerunners, the narratives about him are generally presumed to have undergone a process of oral development and transmission." Ibid., p. 15. See also Gardner and Maier, *Gilgamesh,* p. 60.

Gilgamesh is more than once referred to in our story as two-thirds god, one-third human. His mother, Ninsun, is clearly a goddess. Lugalbanda is sometimes said to have been his father; and he is sometimes said to be a god, sometimes not. See, e.g., Heidel, *The Gilgamesh Epic,* pp. 4–5; Tigay, *Evolution,* p. 76 n. 10 and p. 185; Mason, *Gilgamesh,* p. 99. But whatever combination of parents is posited, the puzzle remains of how the two-thirds/one-third ratio was developed. One of the solutions resorted to takes this form: "The problem thus raised casts doubt on the full-human paternity of his father, and therefore it is conceivable that . . . his father was a male vampire and neither fully divine nor mortal, by whatever daemonogenetic Mendelism the result may have been brought about." Thompson, *The Epic of Gilgamesh,* p. 9. A simpler solution may be called for: We are familiar with stories about the matings of gods and humans (as in the case of Achilles' parents). But we are also familiar with stories about matings in which the supposed male parent is human but in which the real male parent is divine (as in the case of Heracles' birth). In the latter sort of situation, can there not be said to be three parents involved? And if the mother is a goddess, the supposed father a human, and the real father a god, then the offspring could be said to have been two-thirds divine, one-third human (especially if the supposed human father helped raise him, thereby imparting to him some of his mortality). (Perhaps even more intriguing is to have the supposed father be divine and the real father human, making the child clearly mortal "biologically.") It is not irrelevant here that there is a tradition that Gilgamesh, like Heracles, eventually came to be regarded as a god. See Tigay, *Evolution,* p. 13. See also note 51 below.

[6]See Tigay, *Evolution,* pp. 101–3, 234. "Is *Gilgamesh* a great epic poem, even in its fragmentary state (for several portions are still missing)? I believe that it is. Is it comparable to Homer's *Iliad* and *Odyssey* or Virgil's *Aeneid*? No. Looked at from a purely literary standpoint, it falls short of Homer on several counts. First there is the irritating habit of Sumerian poets of repeating themselves. . . . [Still,] *Gilgamesh* is a poem of truly epic sweep and power. Its main theme is eternal: Man in his youth, prideful and adventurous, enjoying his brief period of self-fulfillment, even glory, followed by the tragedy of sickness, old age, and death." Leonard Cottrell, "Introduction," in William Ellery Leonard, trans., *Gilgamesh* (Lunenburg, Vt.: Made for the members of the Limited Editions Club, Avon, Conn., at the Stinehour Press, 1974), pp. vii–viii. "If not pushed too far, 'epic' is useful, but it does not translate a Sumerian or Akkadian term." Gardner and Maier, *Gilgamesh,* p. 37.

One advantage of Mesopotamian repetitiveness is that one can get a fairly reliable sense of the plot of a story, even when the text is badly mutilated. Thus, all but one of the principal adventures recapitulated by Gilgamesh toward the end of the story are by then familiar to us. (The one exception is the lion-hunting expedition to which he refers.) I do not directly concern myself with any of the Gilgamesh stories not included in our twelve-tablet "epic." See note 13 below.

[7]Calvin S. Brown, ed., *The Reader's Companion to World Literature* (New York: New American Library, Mentor Book, 1956), p. 186. The first summary ever of the story is found in the opening lines of the first tablet of the epic.

[8]The twelfth tablet is discussed in Section VII of this article.

[9]It is the E. A. Speiser translation which is drawn upon both for the version that appears in this volume of *The Great Ideas Today* (see Part Four) and for my own quotations and

discussion. (Texts in several languages, and from different times, are used in the Speiser array.) My citations are to the translation as found in James B. Pritchard, ed., *Ancient Near Eastern Texts Relating to the Old Testament,* 3rd ed. (Princeton, N.J.: Princeton University Press, 1969), pp. 72f. (which is supplemented there by the S. N. Kramer translation of the Sumerian texts). Hereafter, this volume will be cited as *A.N.E.T.*

I have also found useful the Heidel translation (note 3 above), the Leonard translation (note 6 above), the Mason translation (note 2 above), and the Gardner-Maier translation (note 2 above, which includes a detailed summary of each of the six columns of each of the twelve tablets). Generations of scholars have found useful Thompson, ed., *The Epic of Gilgamesh: Text, Transliteration, and Notes* (note 2 above).

The condition of the text of the *Gilgamesh* is still so incomplete, however, that it is not yet possible to subject it to the kind of detailed analysis which I have been able to attempt with the Confucian *Analects* and the *Bhagavad Gītā*. (See the 1984 and 1985 volumes of *The Great Ideas Today.*)

[10]"Most of the manuscripts of the late version were discovered in the remains of Ashurbanipal's library (destroyed in 612 [B.C.E.] at Nineveh in northeastern Mesopotamia). . . ." Tigay, *Evolution,* p. 130. See note 4 above. See also the text at note 82 below.

[11]There are devoted to the Flood, indirectly if not directly, two of the twelve tablets on which the *Gilgamesh* epic is inscribed. The modern reader can even find "the terrifying description of the Flood [to be] more powerful and evocative than that of the Bible." Cottrell, "Introduction," p. xi. It is reported that "the Flood was accepted in Assyria as a definite event." Thompson, *The Epic of Gilgamesh,* p. 71 n. 6. See, on the Flood, Heidel, *The Gilgamesh Epic,* pp. 224f.; Tigay, *Evolution,* pp. 214f.

I cannot attempt, on this occasion, to deal with the significance of the fact that various biblical stories are generally considered by scholars to have been written long after their counterparts in Mesopotamian literature were written. (I do not know what the accepted scholarly opinion is today as to which tradition was the earlier in *oral* form.) A proper discussion of these matters presupposes an understanding of the Bible in its integrity. Only then can one begin to understand divergences in the Bible from other traditional accounts of similar episodes. See Leo Strauss, "On the Interpretation of Genesis," *L'Homme,* vol. XXI (Jan.–March 1981), p. 5; Robert Sacks, "The Lion and the Ass: A Commentary on the *Book of Genesis,*" *Interpretation,* vol. 8/2, 3 (May 1980), p. 29f. (the uses made of *Gilgamesh* at pp. 75 and 96 may be in need of correction). See also note 4 above, and notes 42, 57, and 70 below.

[12]The story of the Great Flood in our *Gilgamesh* epic was evidently taken from other accounts now available (in parts) to us. The same is true of various other stories in the epic (such as that in Tablet XI). See Section VII of this article.

[13]I work here, as throughout this article, primarily from the final version of the epic. Earlier versions are drawn upon wherever the final version is too fragmented, so long as the earlier versions are not contradicted by the final version. See Tigay, *Evolution,* pp. 3f., 241f. Any summary is likely to reflect considerable commentary, if only in the determination of what is noticed.

[14]Uruk (the Biblical Erech; the modern Warka) was a city-state in what is now southern Iraq. It was on the Euphrates River, just a few miles north of what we know as the Persian Gulf. (The Gulf went considerably further north at that time than it does now, since it has been filled in by deposits from the Euphrates.) Uruk, which is also referred to as Uruk-land and as Uruk-Eanna (reflecting its Temple of Anu and Ishtar), is almost at the same latitude as Jerusalem.

See, on Gilgamesh and the *jus primae noctis,* Tigay, *Evolution,* pp. 182–84. See also notes 20 and 39 below.

[15]"The pattern of oppression, outcry, divine response was a known pattern in accounts of the gods' sending or creating a new character." Ibid., p. 191. "This is a stock pattern, known in several variations in cuneiform literature, in both mythological and historiographic texts." Ibid., p. 180. Does this pattern tend to ignore the place of nature (and hence of chance?) in human affairs? See note 77 below.

[16]Consider the use by Zeus of Hector and the Trojans in response to Achilles' grievance against Agamemnon in the *Iliad.* Hector, when he puts on Achilles' armor, stripped from the body of Patroclus, looks very much like Achilles. See note 40 below.

[17]One can be reminded of Rousseau's *Discourse upon the Origin and Foundation of the*

Inequality Among Mankind (available in excellent English editions prepared by Roger D. and Judith R. Masters for St. Martin's Press, and by Victor Gourevitch for Harper & Row). [Cf. *GBWW*, Vol. 38.] See notes 64 and 83 below.

[18]On other occasions, such prescience is described as the result of interpreting a dream. See, on dreams, the text at note 20 as well as notes 28 and 70 below.

[19]One can be reminded of Delilah, a Philistine woman, who was loved by Samson and who betrayed him to the Philistines. See Judges 16:4f. (She is evidently distinguished from the harlot he earlier consorted with, which consorting had *not* affected his strength. See Judges 16:1–3. Perhaps such appetites made the Delilah episode possible, however.)

The harlot with whom Enkidu consorts seems respectable enough, as well as good-natured and intelligent. Translators usually identify her as a temple-harlot. See, e.g., Leonard, *Gilgamesh,* p. 6 n. 1: "One of the sacred prostitutes at the temple of Ishtar (Astarte)" (after having referred to her in the text as "a priestess"). (Translators do not seem to agree as to whether this harlot is named in the epic. Would not lack of a name suggest that any of the temple-harlots could have done what this one did?) See, on institutional harlots, *Harper's Bible Dictionary,* M. S. Miller and J. L. Miller, eds. (New York: Harper & Brothers, 1959), p. 246:

> Wisdom writers knew and denounced their traits (Prov. 7:5ff., 29:3). Major prophets likened the apostasies of Israel and Judah to the harlotries of whores who frequented green trees and cultic mountain centers (Jer. 3:6, 8; Ezek. 16:15, 17, 20, 22, 30–52; Hos. 4:15). The Canaanite temples and Syrian shrines that Israel knew were often brothels where priests, priestesses, and cultists engaged in impure rites glorifying reproductive processes. The early Christian Church soon made a pronouncement against harlotry (Acts 15:20, 29), and combated it in cosmopolitan centers by teaching that the body is the temple of the Holy Spirit (I Cor. 6:12–20).

See also the text at note 73, and note 49 below. See, on Ishtar, the text at note 23. See also Deut. 23:18; Judges 2:13, 10:6; I Kings 11:5; II Kings 23:13; Jer. 44:17f.

The response of the animals to the post-harlot Enkidu (*Gilgamesh,* I, iv, 22–29), for "he now had wisdom, broader understanding," is followed by this note in the Speiser translation: "The general parallel to Gen. 3:7 is highly suggestive." (*A.N.E.T.,* p. 75 n. 28.) That biblical verse reads, "And the eyes of them both were opened, and they knew that they were naked; and they sewed fig leaves together, and made themselves aprons." See the text at note 54. The harlot tells Enkidu, after their week-long encounter, that he was now wise, having "become like a god." *Gilgamesh,* I, iv, 33 (*A.N.E.T.,* p. 75). See Genesis 3:5: "you shall be as gods, knowing good and evil."

It is traditional to regard love as a civilizing force, as may be seen in the transformation of both Elizabeth and Darcy in Jane Austen's *Pride and Prejudice.*

[20]Nothing seems to be said about what the source is of the many dreams reported and interpreted in our epic, except perhaps in the case of the warning about the Flood which comes to Utnapishtim. See note 70 below. Was there, among the ancient Mesopotamians, an opinion about dream sources, etc., which was too obvious to state? To what extent are we to consider Gilgamesh as having been instructed by his dreams about how he should deal with Enkidu when he overcomes him? Thus, such dreams could be as much guidance as prediction. In any event, Gilgamesh's struggle with Enkidu may have told him something about himself. Later on, Enkidu's various pieces of advice to Gilgamesh (whether or not derived from dreams) may have reflected aspects of Gilgamesh himself. See note 74 below.

Enkidu's dismay upon learning of Gilgamesh's practice with the maids of Uruk suggests that the practice was grounded in custom, not in nature. But may not such a custom have dynastic, if not eugenic, uses, since it makes it likely (if the ruler is as remarkable as Gilgamesh) that the oldest child (the heir of the family?) will be significantly stronger than his siblings as well as on good terms with the royal family?

[21]It used to be said that the expedition against Humbaba (Huwawa in the Hittite language, Hubaba in the Assyrian language) was to "the cedar forests in the Lebanon region." See, e.g., Abraham Malamat, "Campaigns to the Mediterranean by Iahdunlim and Other Mesopotamian Rulers," *Assyriological Studies* (Studies in Honor of Benno Landsberger on His Seventy-Fifth Birthday), No. 16, p. 373. (I happened, while a stu-

dent at the University of Chicago, to see Professor Landsberger in action: particularly engaging was the way he used to order the oddest assortment of things by telephone from Marshall Field's—and get them! This was a personal touch perhaps worthy of ancient Mesopotamian relations between gods and men.)

A shift in scholarly opinion about the location of the Cedar Forest is recorded in Gardner and Maier, *Gilgamesh,* p. 106:

> The cedar forest to which the two men will travel is to be located in what is now Syria, probably the Anti-Lebanon range of mountains. This is the beginning of the adventure that is known also from the Sumerian poem, "Gilgamesh and the Land of the Living," from the Old Babylonian *The Epic of Gilgamesh,* and from a Hittite version of the story. The cedar forest was probably in the east, in what is now Iran, and may represent a precious commodity for the relatively treeless southern Mesopotamia. The story of Gilgamesh's heroism may well have had political, economic, and historical motives behind it. The Akkadian versions have shifted the action to the west.

Gilgamesh's apprehensive mother, in praying to the sun-god Shamash for her son as he embarks upon the expedition against Humbaba, asks Shamash, "Why, having given me Gilgamesh for a son, with a restless heart didst thou endow him?" (*Gilgamesh,* III, ii, 10–11; *A.N.E.T.,* p. 81, Assyrian Version.)

[22]This was after Enkidu's arm had been temporarily paralyzed upon opening the gate of the forest. See *Gilgamesh,* IV, vi, 23f. (*A.N.E.T.,* p. 82).

One can be reminded by Enkidu's urging the perhaps hesitant Gilgamesh to kill Humbaba of Pylades' urging Orestes to kill Clytemnestra (in Aeschylus's *The Libation Bearers* [*GBWW,* Vol. 5, titled *Choephoroe*]).

[23]*Gilgamesh,* VI, 1f. (*A.N.E.T.,* p. 83).

[24]*Gilgamesh,* VI, 24f. (*A.N.E.T.,* p. 84). One can be reminded here of Euripides' Hippolytus. See notes 25, 26, and 76 below.

[25]*Gilgamesh,* VI, 79f. (*A.N.E.T.,* p. 84). And here one can be reminded of the spurned Aphrodite in Euripides' *Hippolytus* [*GBWW,* Vol. 5].

[26]*Gilgamesh,* VI, 157f. (*A.N.E.T.,* p. 85). Does Enkidu regard Ishtar as his rival for Gilgamesh's favor? See note 40 below.

Some suggest that Enkidu throws the Bull's phallus at Ishtar. See, e.g., Leonard, *Gilgamesh,* p. 42 n. 2; Thompson, *The Epic of Gilgamesh,* p. 81 n. 161.

The Bull of Heaven has been identified with famine. See, e.g., ibid., p. 82 l. 23; *Gilgamesh,* VI, 101f. (*A.N.E.T.,* pp. 84–85). The Bull does kill three hundred men before being killed by Gilgamesh and Enkidu. One is reminded here, but only up to a point, of the bull sent against Hippolytus in Euripides' play. See note 76 below.

[27]Is Gilgamesh particularly moved by Enkidu's death because he recognizes that it is Gilgamesh's debts Enkidu is paying?

[28]Utnapishtim is generally understood to mean "he found life." An older name for this man is Atrahasis, which means "exceedingly wise." See Tigay, *Evolution,* p. 229; *A.N.E.T.,* p. 90 n. 164; Gardner and Maier, *Gilgamesh,* p. 65. Atrahasis is used only once in our epic, at XI, 187 (*A.N.E.T.,* p. 95), when the god Ea explains how Utnapishtim had escaped drowning in the Flood. See note 70 below. See, on the Sumerian stories about the relations of Ea and Atrahasis, S. N. Kramer, *Mythologies of the Ancient World* (New York: Doubleday & Co.; Anchor Books, 1961), pp. 126–27.

Noah, we should remember, never escaped death altogether. See the text at note 70.

[29]It was because Utnapishtim's wife urged that something be done for Gilgamesh that he was told about the plant. Gilgamesh always did depend much on women. (The plant is prickly, which suggests that a price must be paid for whatever it offers.)

Opinions differ as to why Gilgamesh did not eat the plant immediately. "The purpose of this plant was to grant rejuvenated life; and it was to be eaten after a person had reached old age. For this reason Gilgamesh does not eat the plant at once but decides to wait until after his return to Uruk, until he has become an 'old man.' . . ." Heidel, *The Gilgamesh Epic,* p. 92 n. 211. Compare Gardner and Maier, *Gilgamesh,* pp. 31–32:

> There is, of course, no possibility of avoiding death in *Gilgamesh.* The agonizing journey does not give Gilgamesh hope of personal immortality; nor does it bring Enkidu back to life. Yet, Gilgamesh is cleansed. He puts on the great garment after he casts

> away the filthy skins he had been wearing. He does return to Uruk, to his kingship, and to Ishtar. (It is important to notice that the magical plant, "The-Old-Man-Will-Be-Made-Young," given him by Utnapishtim, is not devoured by Gilgamesh. He intends to offer it, rather like the eucharist, to the citizens of Uruk. We take this as a symbol of the full renewal of Gilgamesh's public, i.e., priestly and kingly, role; and the altruism marks the transcendence of mere egoistic values.)

See also ibid., p. 251. There may be something sentimental about this interpretation and about the interpretation quoted in note 1 above.

One can be reminded by this "magical plant" of another such plant, that made available to Odysseus in order to be able to withstand the deadly power of Circe. It is in that context alone that "nature" is used by Homer. See *Odyssey* X, 277 et seq.

[30]The plant that brings back youth is not allowed much time in the story. Is not that often the way with rejuvenating things: they are likely to be temporary in their unnatural effects? See note 35 below.

The timing of the serpent here is quite different from that of the serpent in Genesis: there, the serpent acts to deprive man of what he already has; here, the serpent acts to acquire for itself something that man wants for himself (there is nothing "personal" in what the serpent does here, in that the primary end is not to hurt man but to help the serpent?). Does Gilgamesh ever see the serpent? Did Adam?

[31]"In the loss of the plant Gilgamesh sees a sign that he should leave the ship behind and proceed by land. The boatman goes along, for, according to [XI, 235], he apparently has been banished [by Utnapishtim] from the shores of the blessed for bringing Gilgamesh there." Heidel, *The Gilgamesh Epic,* p. 92 n. 215. In any event, Gilgamesh does return home with something of Utnapishtim's.

[32]It translates a much older Sumerian story. See note 81 below.

[33]That is, Enkidu dies. The Leonard translation avoids the obvious problem which is posed by having Enkidu alive at the beginning of the twelfth tablet. It makes the opening conversation between Gilgamesh and Enkidu a conversation between Ninsun (Gilgamesh's mother) and Gilgamesh, with Gilgamesh preparing to commune with the already dead Enkidu. Leonard, *Gilgamesh,* pp. 101f. This is hardly instructive, except as a reminder that what the poet does here truly bears thinking about. See note 81 below.

[34]One can be reminded of Antigone's concerns. Gilgamesh had done well by Enkidu at his death, providing him both elaborate burial rituals and a statue. One can also be reminded of Odysseus's conversations with both Elpenor and Achilles in Hades. Consider, on the other hand, Socrates' expressed lack of concern, in the *Phaedo* [*GBWW,* Vol. 7], as to what is to be done with his lifeless body. Compare the dread exhibited in like circumstances by Cyrus in Xenophon's *Cyropaedia* (the very Cyrus who had once gloated over corpses on the battlefield). See Xenophon, *Cyropaedia,* I, iv, 24; VIII, vii, 25.

[35]Tigay, *Evolution,* p. 10 (quoting S. N. Kramer). "The Gilgamesh epic is a powerful tale in almost any telling. Rilke once called it the greatest thing one could experience, and many consider it the supreme literary achievement of the ancient world before Homer. It has something of the qualities Henry Moore once said he admired in Mesopotamian art—bigness and simplicity without decorative trimming." Moran, "Ut-napishtim Revisited," p. 13.

A classical scholar has provided this useful interpretive summary of the *Gilgamesh* epic:

> The myth exemplifies, through a single legendary figure, the various attitudes to death that humans tend to adopt: theoretical acceptance, utterly destroyed by one's first close acquaintance with it in someone loved; revulsion from the obscenity of physical corruption; the desire to surmount death in one's own private case, either by means of a lasting reputation or by the desperate fantasy that oneself could be immortal. Finally, a kind of resignation—but before that, perhaps, an attempt to delay death by emulating youth.

G. S. Kirk, *Myth: Its Meaning and Functions in Ancient and Other Cultures* (Cambridge: Cambridge University Press, 1970), pp. 144–45. See note 30 above.

[36]One can be reminded of this kind of shift when one compares the Achilles found first in the *Iliad* and then in the Hades scene in the *Odyssey* [*GBWW,* Vol. 4]. See Kirk, *Myth,* pp. 108, 223.

[37]How he got this notion (which is not borne out by the killing of Humbaba) is not clear.

[38]This identification of him may also be seen in colophons. And yet are we not meant by the poet to see, and to understand, things that Gilgamesh does not? See note 81 below.

[39]It should be noticed that Gilgamesh was looked to as a savior by the hunter and his family at the very time he was considered oppressive within Uruk. One could attempt to distinguish city tastes from country tastes, but there is also the fact that Enkidu (or is he no longer really a country man?) is shocked when he learns of Gilgamesh's sexual conduct in Uruk. See the text at note 20. Even so, is there not something properly royal in Gilgamesh's refusal to surrender himself completely to Ishtar? See notes 50 and 51 below.

[40]Thus, the gods destroy the same Enkidu that they had fashioned to use in order to control Gilgamesh. See note 16 above. Does Gilgamesh ever learn the origins (or purpose) of Enkidu? Of course, the death of Enkidu may itself be part of the divine plan to curb Gilgamesh. See the text at note 16 and note 79 below.

Does Ishtar strike at Enkidu because she sees him as a substitute for herself with Gilgamesh? See note 26 above. Is her proposal to Gilgamesh, in effect, an invitation to him to return to his old practices with the maids of Uruk? See notes 51 and 78 below. Were those practices (a kind of Sacred Marriage between Goddess and King?) related to fertility rites? But see note 49 below.

[41]See *Gilgamesh,* X, i, 34f.; iii, 1f. (*A.N.E.T.,* pp. 90–91, Assyrian Version). It seems to have been "the most persistent tradition" in the stories about Gilgamesh that he "was beset by a fear of death." See Paul Garelli, ed., *Gilgameš et sa légende* (Paris: Librairie C. Klincksieck, 1960), p. 51 (by W. G. Lambert).

[42]That there is something about the Mesopotamian region itself which helps account for how things have always been done (and thought?) there is suggested by the presence there today of practices which scholars look to in order to explain obscure passages in the *Gilgamesh.* Consider the following sampling: "the usual method of sitting in the East when there is no stool" (Thompson, *The Epic of Gilgamesh,* p. 79); "the boat must be a light skiff or *bellam,* such as the Arabs of the southern marshes use to this day, either poled or paddled" (ibid., p. 85); "The punting-pole of the Mesopotamian skiff to-day has a knob of bitumen at the upper end and a metal socket or ferule at the lower end" (ibid., p. 85); "There are several methods in vogue in the Near East of making bread; the commonest shape is that of the flat disk of thin bread varying in size, but usually about a foot in diameter. This is probably one of the earliest forms of bread, and it is shown on the Hittite Sculptures. . . . " (ibid., p. 87); "Gilgamish follows the custom of the pearl-divers of Bahrain, long celebrated for its pearl-fisheries [in using large stones to accelerate his descent]. . . . " (ibid., p. 88); "Some good photographs of reed houses [such as Utnapishtim's] have recently been published [in the *National Geographic Magazine,* LXXXII (1942), 410–11]" (Heidel, *The Gilgamesh Epic,* p. 80 n. 166); "To press the carrying strap against [the forehead]; for this method [of lifting and carrying], which is witnessed on the Ur Standard and is still practiced in modern Iraq. . . . " (*A.N.E.T.,* p. 76 n. 40). See also Gardner and Maier, *Gilgamesh,* pp. 229–30, 233 (on a large Sumerian boat made of reed-bundles built by Thor Heyerdahl). See as well note 52 below. Do we not see in these examples indications of how poetry depends on an imitation of nature? Another facet of the poetic imitation of nature may be seen in the samples collected in note 84 below. See also note 83 below.

Thus, various remarkable continuities testify to the extent to which climate and resources (and, indeed, nature) may shape manners and customs over millennia. Consider, for example, what Machiavelli made of such factors:

> In our time, the examples of these two different kinds of government are those of the Turk and of the King of France. . . . Whoever considers, then, the one and the other of these states, will find that it is difficult to acquire the state of the Turk, but [once] conquered, it is easy to hold. And you will find, on the contrary, that it is in some respects easier to take the state of France, but that it is more difficult to hold on to it. . . .
>
> Now, if you will consider the nature of Darius' government, you will find it similar to the kingdom of the Turk. Therefore it was necessary for Alexander first to smash it all and seize the field; after which victory, with Darius dead, the state was left

> secure for Alexander. . . . But it is impossible to possess states ordered like that of France with such quiet. From whence arose each of the many rebellions of Spain, of France, and of Greece against the Romans, because of the many principates which existed in those states.

The Prince (L. P. de Alvarez translation; Dallas: University of Dallas Press, 1984), chap. IV. [Cf. *GBWW,* Vol. 23, p. 7.]

Consider also how Mesopotamia can be distinguished by Thorkild Jacobsen from Egypt:

> How the Egyptian and the Mesopotamian civilizations came to acquire these very different moods—one trusting, the other distrusting, man's power and ultimate significance—is not an easy question. The "mood" of a civilization is the outcome of processes so intricate and so complex as to defy precise analysis. We shall therefore merely point to a single factor which would seem to have played a considerable role—the factor of environment. . . .
>
> Mesopotamian civilization grew up in an environment which was signally different [from Egyptian civilization]. We find there, of course, the same great cosmic rhythms—the change of the seasons, the unwavering sweep of sun, moon, and stars—but we also find an element of force and violence which was lacking in Egypt. The Tigris and Euphrates are not like the Nile; they may rise unpredictably and fitfully, breaking man's dykes and submerging his crops. There are scorching winds which smother man in dust, threaten to suffocate him; there are torrential rains which turn all firm ground into a sea of mud and rob man of his freedom of movement: all travel bogs down. Here, in Mesopotamia, Nature stays not her hand; in her full might she cuts across and overrides man's will, makes him feel to the full how slightly he matters.
>
> The mood of Mesopotamian civilization reflects this. Man is not tempted to overrate himself when he contemplates powers in nature such as the thunderstorm and the yearly flood. Of the thunderstorm the Mesopotamian said that its "dreadful flares of light cover the land like a cloth."

H. and H. A. Frankfort, eds., *Before Philosophy: The Intellectual Adventure of Ancient Man* (London: Penguin Books, 1949), pp. 137–39. See note 57 below.

Consider as well how far the case for the importance of "materialistic" factors may be taken:

> I have chosen this lowly topic [of the consumption of onions in ancient Mesopotamia] as a modest expression of protest against such esoteric and, in the present state of our knowledge, seemingly fruitless pursuits as those devoted to the study of the resurrection of Tammuz and of the Sumerian beliefs in afterlife. This is not a question of the relative importance of studies devoted to grammar, lexicon, or material culture as against those dealing with theological and metaphysical matters. The question is simply that of priorities. As all man's ideas about things divine are human, it is my firm belief that we shall never know what was the nectar of the gods until we learn what was the daily bread of the people.

I. J. Gelb, "The Philadelphia Onion Archive," *Assyriological Studies,* No. 16 (1965), p. 62. Even so, one must wonder what it means to say that "all man's ideas about things divine are human." See note 11 above. And it is only prudent to keep in mind, as we consider these prosaic matters, this observation: "It is safer to try to understand the low in the light of the high than the high in the light of the low. In doing the latter one necessarily distorts the high, whereas in doing the former one does not deprive the low of the freedom to reveal itself fully as what it is." Leo Strauss, *Spinoza's Critique of Religion* (New York: Schocken Books, 1965), p. 2. Not irrelevant here, especially considering Gilgamesh's surprising response to the death of Enkidu, are Mr. Strauss's remarks upon being "struck by the awesome, unfathomable experience of death, of the death of one near and dear to us." See Anastaplo, *The Artist as Thinker,* pp. 270–71. Gilgamesh "was to become the archetype of royal mortality." Kirk, *Myth,* pp. 9–10. See also ibid., pp. 231–32.

[43]Is not the female element naturally more intimate and hence private (as well as

somewhat prosaic)? Consider, in Aeschylus's *Oresteia* [*GBWW,* Vol. 5], the juxtaposition of the female Furies (who guard the home) and Apollo (who looks out for kings). (See Gardner and Maier, *Gilgamesh,* p. 49 n. 42.) Consider also that Socrates does go home at the very end of Plato's *Symposium* [*GBWW,* Vol. 7]. Does not a home usually depend upon the female (and the resulting family life)? (The female element, aside from Socrates' own use of Diotima in his talk, had been muted in the many fine speeches on love the day before.) Consider, as well, the recourse to a prosaic everyday life in the concluding lines of the song at the end of Shakespeare's *Love's Labour's Lost* [*GBWW,* Vol. 26, p. 284d].

[44]See the text at notes 23–26.

[45]*Gilgamesh,* XI, 116–23 (*A.N.E.T.,* p. 94).

[46]The stranger is Utnapishtim's boatman. See note 31 above. Collaboration between Ishtar and Gilgamesh may be seen in Tablet XII of our epic. See also S. N. Kramer, *Gilgamesh and the Ḫuluppu-Tree* (Chicago: University of Chicago Press, 1938).

[47]*Gilgamesh,* X, iii, 1f. (*A.N.E.T.,* p. 90) (the Old Babylonian Version is drawn upon here since the Akkadian-language version is badly mutilated in places). See note 13 above. (Most translators use "ale-wife" instead of "barmaid.")

It is sometimes said that "Gilgamesh [left no] son to [his] father." Thompson, *The Epic of Gilgamesh,* p. 72. Also sometimes said is that Gilgamesh left a son and successor. See ibid., p. 9; Tigay, *Evolution,* p. 168 n. 17. In our *Gilgamesh* there is no reference to any children of Gilgamesh. This poet may have preferred to leave that an open question.

[48]*Gilgamesh,* VI, 99–100 (*A.N.E.T.,* p. 84). This is when Ishtar seeks revenge after having been spurned by Gilgamesh. See note 84 below.

[49]One must wonder, however, whether the poet, or his audience, ever regarded temple-harlotry as questionable—and, if not, what this says about his or their understanding of things. (Should not a similar question be asked about Shakespeare's treatment of Jews in *The Merchant of Venice* and the expected response of his audience? [*GBWW,* Vol. 26].)

See, on Babylonian temple-harlotry, Herodotus, *History,* I, 99 [*GBWW,* Vol. 6, p. 45a]. See also note 19 above. The response by Herodotus assures us that we are not being modern provincials in our own negative response to this institution. (Is the Middle Eastern institution of the harem related? There, too, sexuality is being mismanaged. See note 73 below. Compare the widespread resort of Christianity to institutional celibacy. See the Koran, Sura 57, end.)

Upon confronting temple-harlotry one wonders, "What *could* they have been thinking of?" And one must also wonder whether it is possible truly to understand such people, especially when Sacred Marriage is confused with institutionalized prostitution. See note 40 above. What is for them the meaning of sexuality, of divinity, of nature? We can see in Aristotle an account of what happens when male and female mate, how children (and the family) result, how the family can be extended, and how eventually the village and the city emerge. But should not the Aristotelian be shocked to have simple, healthy sexuality transformed into the kind of institution so much taken for granted (it seems) in ancient Mesopotamia? See the text at note 4. See also the text at note 73.

[50]See note 24 above. Does Gilgamesh resent being chosen, rather than choosing (as he had done, for example, with the maids of Uruk and then with Enkidu)? A transition may be seen here by some from a matriarchal to a patriarchal society. See note 39 above and 75 below.

[51]Central to this array of lovers (with Gilgamesh selected as the seventh) is a stallion: "Then a stallion thou lovedst, famed in battle; the whip, the spur, and the lash thou ordainedst for him." *Gilgamesh,* VI, 53–54 (*A.N.E.T.,* p. 84). Certainly, Ishtar is not ashamed of having tamed the stallion: she can even offer Gilgamesh chariot horses which "shall be famed for racing." *Gilgamesh,* VI, 20 (*A.N.E.T.,* p. 84). Perhaps it can be said that Gilgamesh "identifies" himself with the stallion.

I suspect the poet of our epic appreciated at least as much as we can the salutary consequences of various of the six developments that Gilgamesh regards as grievances. (Had not some of her lovers been properly punished for misconduct or presumptuousness? See Kirk, *Myth,* p. 104.) The purposefulness of this listing *in our epic* is suggested, it seems to me, by the following report (the import of which may not have been noticed by the scholars):

> In *Gilgamesh and the Bull of Heaven,* according to Kramer, the gifts offered Gilgamesh by the goddess Inanna (the Sumerian counterpart of Ishtar) are quite different from

> those that Ishtar offers in [our] epic; scholars have since come to doubt that Inanna proposed to Gilgamesh at all in the Sumerian tale.

Tigay, *Evolution,* p. 24. Thus, "her spurned proposal of marriage to Gilgamesh may have been original with the Akkadian versions." Ibid., p. 70. (The first of the allegedly ill-treated lovers Gilgamesh brings up is Tammuz, "the lover of [her] youth." Would not the poet have expected his thoughtful reader to recognize the considerable regard Ishtar had had for Tammuz? See S. H. Langdon, *Tammuz and Ishtar; A Monograph upon Babylonian Religion and Theology* (Oxford: Clarendon Press, 1914). Compare Kramer, *Mythologies of the Ancient World,* pp. 106–15. Particularly intriguing is this observation: "The worship of this goddess from the earliest period centred at Erech, modern Warka, a city in the extreme south of Mesopotamia, on the eastern bank of the Euphrates. The epic of Gilgamish relates that this city was founded by Gilgamish, who as we have seen was a deified king and identified with Tammuz." Ibid., p. 54. See note 81 below.

Be all this as it may, cannot it be said that Ishtar proposed to Gilgamesh as perhaps Gilgamesh's goddess mother had done to Gilgamesh's human father? Does Gilgamesh's rejection of Ishtar suggest that there will not be another Gilgamesh? "For Ishtar's lovers compare Diodorus, II. 8, about Semiramis. . . ." Thompson, *The Epic of Gilgamesh,* p. 81. See note 5 above. See also note 40 above. For a modern version of this episode, see Robert Silverberg, *Gilgamesh the King* (Toronto: Bantam Books, 1985), pp. 174f., 291f.

[52]See *Gilgamesh,* e.g., I, v, 25f.; V, i, 5 (*A.N.E.T.,* pp. 75–76, 82). Consider also Enkidu's distress upon hearing about Gilgamesh's Humbaba proposal. *Gilgamesh,* III, i, 13f. (*A.N.E.T.,* pp. 78–79, Old Babylonian Version). See as well the text at note 59.

Is sexuality a substitute for the deepest friendship (possible only between males?)? "To this day, one can see young Arab men in the Near East walking with interlocked fingers without any implications of homosexuality." Tigay, *Evolution,* p. 184 n. 22. See note 42 above.

[53]We are not the only ones surprised by Gilgamesh's response to the death of Enkidu: those whom he encounters on his way to Utnapishtim also express surprise. See note 41 above.

[54]See note 19 above and note 83 below. See also Anastaplo, *Human Being and Citizen,* p. 123 (on obscenity). The culmination of the erotic, or at least one remarkable manifestation of it, may be philosophy. See note 71 below.

[55]See Edwin Muir, "The Animals" [*GIT* 1984, p. 383]; Anastaplo, *The Artist as Thinker,* pp. 357–62. See also note 68 below. See as well *GIT* 1984, pp. 384f.

[56]*Gilgamesh,* III, iv, 5–8 (*A.N.E.T.,* p. 79, Old Babylonian Version).

[57]Compare this observation on the durability of the clay tablets used by the ancient Mesopotamians:

> Clay tablets can be baked as hard as brick so that they endure forever. Our paper today decomposes, and does not last a fraction of the time that the Gilgamesh tablets have already survived. Clay is also by its nature fireproof. When a library burns down today, the books perish. When the libraries of Mesopotamia burned down, the ashes of the buildings simply buried the clay tablets for future archaeologists to find. The only effect fire has on tablets is to bake them harder and preserve them better than ever.

Cyrus H. Cordon, "Origins of the Gilgamesh Epic," in Anita Feagles, *He Who Saw Everything: The Epic of Gilgamesh* (New York: Young Scott Books, 1966), pp. 57–58. It has been noticed that the Egyptians expected their greatest buildings to last "forever," while the Mesopotamians expected theirs to crumble away. See Frankfort and Frankfort, eds., *Before Philosophy,* p. 137; note 42 above. But the Mesopotamian clay tablets seem to have outlasted Egyptian papyrus, "all other things being equal." See notes 4 and 11 above.

[58]*Gilgamesh,* III, v, 7 (*A.N.E.T.,* p. 80, Old Babylonian Version).

[59]*Gilgamesh,* VIII, ii, 3 (*A.N.E.T.,* p. 87). Of course, neither Humbaba nor the Bull of Heaven was human. See note 26 above.

[60]*Gilgamesh,* II, v, 13f. (*A.N.E.T.,* p. 78, Old Babylonian Version).

[61]We are not told in our epic whether Gilgamesh ever knew his father. Only in the twelfth tablet is there any serious indication of a life beyond the grave, and *that* is hardly attractive. See Heidel, *The Gilgamesh Epic,* pp. 137f. ("Death and the Afterlife").

[62]See, e.g., *Gilgamesh,* X, ii, 1–9 (*A.N.E.T.*, pp. 89–90, Old Babylonian Version). Compare II Samuel 12:18–23. See also note 35 above.

[63]See, e.g., *Gilgamesh,* X, i, 5f.; iii, lf. (*A.N.E.T.*, pp. 89, 90, Old Babylonian Version).

[64]*Gilgamesh,* X, vi, 26–35 (*A.N.E.T.*, pp. 92–93). Have there not "always" (naturally) been for mankind "days of yore"?

[65]See Tigay, *Evolution,* p. 5 n. 2; Anastaplo, *Human Being and Citizen,* p. 219.

[66]See *Gilgamesh,* XI, 200f. (*A.N.E.T.*, p. 95). Utnapishtim warns his wife here about Gilgamesh, "Since to deceive is human, he will seek to deceive thee." Does not Utnapishtim "project" onto Gilgamesh his own legendary cunning? See the text at note 70.

[67]See the concluding lines of Plato's *Apology* [*GBWW,* Vol. 7, pp. 211–12].

[68]See *Gilgamesh,* XI, 290f. (*A.N.E.T.*, p. 96). The snake does become deathless, but it *is* only a snake. See Aldous Huxley, *After Many a Summer Dies the Swan* (New York: Harper, 1939), pp. 42–44, 345–46, 349–56. See also the text at note 55 above.

[69]*Gilgamesh,* XI, 1–7 (*A.N.E.T.*, p. 93).

[70]Utnapishtim (pursuant to instructions from the god Ea) deceives his fellow citizens as to why he is building a boat, thereby inducing others (who are no less deserving of salvation than he is?) to help him build. *Gilgamesh,* XI, 34f. (*A.N.E.T.*, p. 93). "It was his cunning, however, rather than his heroic deeds (Herakles) or his piety (Noah), that marked him as special." Gardner and Maier, *Gilgamesh,* p. 7.

Is the cunning of old Ea to be contrasted to the wisdom of the god-of-light Shamash? See Gardner and Maier, *Gilgamesh,* pp. 291f., 299–300. "Ea's speech is about language. Only the cunning one, the poet, can lead into the archaic and lead us back to Uruk." Ibid., p. 300. What *is* the poet of the *Gilgamesh* suggesting about what *he* is doing? Our epic "has the god instruct the hero in a ruse to fool the townspeople, whereas the [older] version simply described its perpetration by the hero. . . ." Tigay, *Evolution,* p. 224. Does the poet want us to wonder whether Utnapishtim is to be believed when he says that he got all this, including instructions in deception, from Ea? See note 81 below.

In any event, is not Ea presented as deceiving the other gods (especially Enlil) as to what *he* did in warning Utnapishtim? "It was not I who disclosed the secret of the great gods. I let Atrahasis see a dream, and he perceived the secret of the gods." *Gilgamesh,* XI, 185–86 (*A.N.E.T.*, p. 95). Why is the old name (Atrahasis) used here for Utnapishtim? Is something "premodern" in the relations of gods and men being alluded to?

No reason is given for the Flood except the unexamined enmity of one god, who was opposed by the other gods. Enlil is angry that anyone escaped destruction, and then quixotically he grants two of the survivors deathlessness. *Gilgamesh,* XI, 189f. (*A.N.E.T.*, p. 95). Do not the differences among the gods, evident again and again in the *Gilgamesh,* suggest that such gods do not really know what they are doing? See Plato, *Euthyphro* 8A, 9C–D [*GBWW,* Vol. 7, pp. 194b–c, 195a–b]. Perhaps, indeed, they are not truly gods?

[71]It has been suggested that the lounging Utnapishtim is really imitating "the resting figures of the gods," thus combining in him the human and the divine. See Gardner and Maier, *Gilgamesh,* p. 228. But may not this also suggest that there is something deeply questionable about the lives of the gods themselves? Is there an intimation in *Gilgamesh* anticipating what is developed by Plato about the necessity of eros for the highest development of the life of reason (that is, of philosophy)? See notes 43 and 54 above. Life as fully life must have an erotic element—otherwise one has the indolent Mycroft Holmes instead of an energetic Sherlock Holmes?

[72]Of course, Ishtar had tried to destroy (the anti-erotic?) Gilgamesh with the Bull of Heaven—and on that occasion the male god Anu had been concerned to provide for the general protection of mankind. The male god Shamash had also been protective of Gilgamesh.

[73]Do we not also see in all this some indication of the pervasive Mesopotamian attitude toward the erotic that Muhammad had to deal with (and come to terms with) when he came along in nearby Arabia? (His way was different from both Judaism and Christianity. See note 19 above. Muhammad condemned those who pray to "female beings." Koran, Sura 4, l. 117. See note 50 above.) The pervasive Middle Eastern eroticism is suggested by Montesquieu's *Persian Letters.* Even Solomon, we should remember, had a harem.

The seduction of Enkidu by the harlot did not depend on language or ideas but rather on an elementary (even animalistic) appeal. The story is frank (but not so vivid as the Gardner and Maier translation?) about what was done—and perhaps it is even more significant that both the hunter's father and Gilgamesh "naturally" resorted to the use of the harlot as a remedy. This bears upon what I have suggested about a critical problem being that temple-harlotry is evidently not seen as a problem by the Mesopotamians. See note 49 above.

The harlot, in describing to Enkidu the merits of Uruk, spoke of it as a place where "each day is made a holiday." *Gilgamesh,* I, v, 8 (*A.N.E.T.,* p. 75). What does the poet suggest about the everyday life of Uruk when he can later have Utnapishtim describe the holiday spirit among his fellow citizens who are doomed for destruction? *Gilgamesh,* XI, 70f. (*A.N.E.T.,* p. 93). Is not holidaying often an effort to forget about death?

See, on the perverted place of the erotic among the pagans, and Christianity as a cure for that, G. K. Chesterton, *St. Francis of Assisi* (New York: Doran, 1924), pp. 36f. ("Venus was nothing but venereal vice." Ibid., p. 43).

[74]Later, of course, Gilgamesh and Enkidu interpret their own dreams, perhaps because they have learned something about the art from the women they have associated with. The dreams in our epic are seen as *predictions* rather than as *disguises* (for one's passions, etc.). Should *we* interpret these dreams as they are interpreted in the story? Or can we (should we? are we intended to? are we able to?) go beyond where the people in the story go? That is, are the dreams even more revealing than they are taken in the story to be? See on the difficulty of subjecting ancient dream reports to psychoanalytical inquiry, A. Leo Oppenheim, *The Interpretation of Dreams in the Ancient Near East* (Philadelphia: American Philosophical Society, 1956), pp. 185, 219. See also note 20 above.

[75]See, on what Ea says he did and did not do in alerting Utnapishtim about the Flood, note 70 above. See, on the interconnectedness of all things, Plato, *Meno* 81C–E [*GBWW,* Vol. 7, p. 180a–b].

[76]Compare the overpowering bull sent by Poseidon in Euripides' *Hippolytus: that* divine agent is not going to be killed by any mortals! See note 26 above.

[77]See *Gilgamesh,* XI, 112f., 159–61 (*A.N.E.T.,* pp. 94, 95). (Again and again, one must wonder how Utnapishtim is supposed to *know* what he does about the doings and sayings of the gods. Perhaps the gods have nothing better to do than to tell him stories?) The conduct of the gods in response to the sacrifice calls to mind Aristophanes' *Birds* [*GBWW,* Vol. 5]. Compare Tigay, *Evolution,* pp. 228–29.

In any event, it seems to be assumed throughout that the gods are responsible for famines, floods, etc. Such depredations are not regarded as simply natural occurrences, it seems. See note 15 above and note 82 below.

[78]But then, one might have wondered, why had Gilgamesh "dolled" himself up, if not to win such esteem as Ishtar responded with? And had he done so only in order to be able to repel (somewhat perversely?) the advances by Ishtar which (naturally?) follow upon such esteem? See notes 40 and 51 above.

[79]See the end of note 42 above. We can again be reminded of the doings of Anu, and of the Zeus of the *Iliad.* See notes 16 and 40 above. (Anu, as the first among the gods, if not the god of creation, is made much more of in other Mesopotamian stories. Enlil, it should be noticed, is *not* the god of the underworld.)

[80]See, on Gilgamesh's own descendants, note 47 above. See, on the burial of Socrates, note 34 above.

What is the significance, for us, of the fact that this story was almost permanently lost? Does this not point up the problem with any attempt to guarantee one's memory in the distant future? Yet we recall that Confucius could be described as the man who "knows it's no use, but keeps on doing it." See Anastaplo, "An Introduction to Confucian Thought," *GIT* 1984, p. 169 n. 100. See also note 4 above.

[81]Uses of both *seven* and *twelve* abound in our epic and, evidently, elsewhere in Mesopotamian literature. See, on the importance of *twelve* in ancient Mesopotamia, Eric Voegelin, *Order and History* (Baton Rouge: Louisiana State University Press, 1956), vol. I, pp. 29–35.

Perhaps the most important fact about the twelfth tablet is something so obvious that it can easily be overlooked: the poet of our epic evidently wanted to make it apparent that he has here, as distinct from what he has done elsewhere throughout the epic, incorporated the old material he took from the tradition with very few changes. He thereby puts the perceptive reader on notice that he is perhaps providing an orthodox alternative in the twelfth tablet to the unorthodox probing of fundamental issues in the first eleven tablets. See note 33 above. See, on anticipations of Tablet XII in Tablet VI, Kirk, *Myth,* p. 143 n. 11.

The poet of our epic can be understood to see things differently from his predecessors. He differs as well, it seems, from Gilgamesh himself, whose accounts of his career (as he meets strangers on his way to Utnapishtim) and whose exhibition of walls and temple back in Uruk suggest the sort of thing he said when he recorded "all his toil . . . on a stone stela." *Gilgamesh,* I, i, 8 (*A.N.E.T.,* p. 73). See note 51 above.

An indication of Mesopotamian opinions about the relation of body to soul may be seen in the instructions Gilgamesh gives, in the twelfth tablet, to Enkidu before his Descent. *Gilgamesh,* XII, 10f. (*A.N.E.T.,* p. 97). (Enkidu is quite rash in the twelfth tablet, just as he had been in the earlier account [with the assault on Ishtar], contributing "once again" to his premature death. He generally is even less thoughtful than Gilgamesh.)

One of the changes made by the poet upon appending to our epic (with relatively few changes) the story portion now found in the twelfth tablet, is the addition of an appeal to the moon god Sin. *Gilgamesh,* XII, 62–69 (*A.N.E.T.,* p. 98). Perhaps this is a playful allusion to the name of the poet traditionally associated with our epic, Sin Leqi-Unninni.

[82]See, e.g., Thompson, *The Epic of Gilgamesh,* pp. 5–6; Heidel, *The Gilgamesh Epic,* pp. 2–3. One can see again and again (especially upon consulting Professor Tigay's detailed compilation of the work of so many of his predecessors) how much we rely upon scrupulous, hardworking, and quite learned scholars to establish the texts we (sometimes perhaps too cavalierly) speculate about.

[83]See, for my suggestions about the absence of the notion of *nature* in both the Confucian and the Hindu thought of antiquity, my articles in *The Great Ideas Today,* 1984 and 1985. Similar suggestions can be made about ancient Mesopotamian thought. See note 77 above. Compare note 42 above. (But here, at least, the modern reader is not likely to be misled by translators improperly using *nature* upon rendering the *Gilgamesh* into English. In fact, I do not recall any instance of the use of *nature* in any of the translations I have consulted. It might be instructive to consider why translations of this epic have been more careful than translations of the *Analects* or of the *Bhagavad Gītā* in this respect.) See, for challenging suggestions about "the [primarily intuitive] confrontation between nature and culture" in the *Gilgamesh* epic, Kirk, *Myth,* pp. 148, 152. See also ibid., pp. 145f., 151. See as well note 17 above.

[84]The quality of this poet, or at least of the tradition upon which he so aptly draws, is further suggested by this sampling of a half-dozen passages which retain their appeal even in translation: (1) an apprehensive Enkidu says to Gilgamesh, "A cry, my friend, chokes my throat" (literally, "has bound my neck veins"); (2) Ishtar warns her father Anu, "I will raise up the dead eating and alive, so that the dead shall outnumber the living!"; (3) a startled Enkidu awakens from a dream to ask, "My friend, why are the great gods in council?"; (4) a bereaved Gilgamesh asks, "When I die, shall I not be like Enkidu?"; (5) a god advises Utnapishtim before the Great Flood, "Tear down this house, build a ship! Give up possessions, seek thou life. Forswear worldly goods, and keep the soul alive!"; (6) the storm of the Flood begins, "The wide land was shattered like a pot! For one day the south-storm blew, gathering speed as it blew, submerging the mountains, overtaking the people like a battle. No one can see his fellow, nor can the people be recognized from heaven"; (7) Utnapishtim reports on what happened after the Flood subsided, "When the seventh day arrived, I sent forth and set free a dove. The dove went forth, but came back; since no resting-place for it was visible, she turned round. Then I sent forth and set free a swallow. The swallow went forth, but came back; since no resting-place for it was visible, she turned round. Then I sent forth and set free a raven. The raven went forth and, seeing that the waters had diminished, he eats, circles, caws, and turns not round. Then I let out all to the four winds and offered a sacrifice." *Gilgamesh,* III, ii, 40; VI, 99–100; VI, 194; IX, i, 3; XI, 24–26; XI, 107–112; XI, 145f. (Pritchard, ed., *Ancient Near Eastern Texts,* pp. 79, 84, 85, 88, 93, 94, 94–95). See note 42 above.

NOTE TO THE READER

The articles in this issue of *The Great Ideas Today* suggest many entries to *Great Books of the Western World.* These are listed in the *Syntopicon,* to which any reader who wishes to pursue the issues that have been raised or think about the texts from which they can be seen to come should turn.

For example, Professor Kuspit's essay on modern art takes us at once to Chapter 4, ART, where entries under Topic 2*b* dealing with the role of matter and form in artistic production, Topic 3 on art as imitation, Topic 5 having to do with the human sources of art, and Topic 7, which lists passages in the *Great Books* devoted to the enjoyment of the arts, both in terms of the pleasure they give and the judgment as to their quality we may be inclined to make, are all relevant.

Leo Kadanoff sends us elsewhere—to Chapter 9, CHANCE, the readings listed at Topic 1*b* on the coincidence of causes (one thinks particularly of the Lucretian atoms); also to Chapter 10, CHANGE, Topics 1 through 5, where passages will be found on the nature of change, its principal constituents, the causes and effects of motion, the ideas of motion and rest, and the ways that motion is measured; and then perhaps to Chapter 67, PHYSICS, where discussions of the relation between natural philosophy and mathematics are listed at Topic 1*b,* and where at Topic 3 will be found passages on the actual role of mathematics in the natural sciences.

With respect to Lord Quinton's essay on animals and our largely self-serving conceptions of them, one should begin, of course, with Chapter 2, ANIMAL, where a number of topics suggest themselves. See in particular passages at Topic 1*a*(1), (2), and (3) on animal sensitivity; animal memory, imagination, and intelligence; and animal emotions; also the readings under Topics 1*c*(1) and (2) on the comparison of human and nonhuman animals as well as the comparison of animal with human intelligence; also those under Topic 1*e* on the conception of animals as machines or automata. See, further, the readings at Topic 12 having to do with the taming of animals, the use and abuse of them by men, and the kind of friendship or love that can exist between animals and human beings.

On the same subject, consult as well Chapter 51, MAN, the readings at Topics 1*a*, *b*, and *c* on the comparison between human beings and animals (which will be to some extent repetitive of passages previously listed), and the readings at Topic 4*c* on man's rational powers and the problem of similar powers in other animals; see also the readings at Topic 10*e* on man's conception of his place in the universe as compared with that of other animals. And look as well at Chapter 30, GOOD AND EVIL, Topics 3*a* and 5*a*, for discussions of the relation between man and the good, along with Chapter 60, NATURE, Topic 5*a*, where further passages of the same kind are listed.

So far as Dialectic is concerned, as it too is one of the Great Ideas, passages dealing with it will be found listed in Chapter 18, DIALECTIC. See Topics 1, 4, 5, and 6, especially, where passages defining dialectic, relating it to philosophy and science, and distinguishing it from rhetoric (the difference is, in part, that between proof and persuasion) will be found, as well as readings on the difference between dialectic and sophistry. One should consult also Chapter 77, REASONING, the readings at Topic 5*c*, where passages will be found on the opposition of rational arguments.

And, with respect to Euclid, one should consult the readings listed in Chapter 15, DEFINITION, Topic 5, concerned with definition and demonstration; Chapter 20, EDUCATION, where readings on the methods of learning and the various kinds of learning are listed; Chapter 52, MATHEMATICS, Topics 3*a* and *b*, which deal more specifically with demonstration and construction in mathematical terms, along with Topics 4*b* and *c*, which have to do with geometry and also with proportions and equations; and, once more, Chapter 77, REASONING, where readings are listed at Topics 4*a–d* on the types of reasoning are relevant, as are those at Topics 5*b*(2) and (3) devoted to definitions used as a means of reasoning, and to the theory of demonstrations.

Some of these same chapters should be consulted in connection also with Mr. Simpson's essay on Clerk Maxwell among this year's "Special Features." Particularly important is Chapter 54, MECHANICS, where the Introduction itself ought to be read, and where passages in the *Great Books* on the foundations of mechanics, especially Topics 1*a* and 1*b;* on the subject of motion, void, and medium, Topic 5*d;* on the concept of force, Topics 6*d*(1), (2), and (3); on magnetic force, 7*d*(2); and on electromagnetic fields, 7*e*(3)—all contribute something to our knowledge of the subject. But see also Chapter 10, CHANGE, the readings at Topic 7*c*(3) on absolute and relative motion; also those in Chapter 61, NECESSITY AND CONTINGENCY, at Topic 3*c;* at Topic 6*a* in Chapter 78, RELATION; and in Chapter 89, SPACE, the passages listed under Topics 2*a*, 2*c*, and 3*b*, of which the last, having to do with the relation of physical and mathematical space, is perhaps most nearly fundamental.

To proceed to the subject of music, Maurice Cranston's discussion of the controversy between Rousseau and Jean-Philippe Rameau in the eighteenth century takes us once more to Chapter 4, ART, where Topics 7*a* and *b* on the enjoyment of art are relevant, as is Topic 8 on the relation between art and emotion, and so is Topic 10*b*, concerning regulation of the arts and the problem of censorship.

And in connection with the *Gilgamesh* epic, on which Professor Anastaplo comments this year, see passages listed in Chapter 34, HISTORY, Topic 4*a*(4), on the hero; in Chapter 48, LIFE AND DEATH, Topics 8*a*, *c*, and *d*, where the instinct for self-preservation, the attitude of the hero toward death, and the ceremonials of death are discussed; in Chapter 50, LOVE, where love and hate as passions and acts of will are taken up; and in Chapter 69, POETRY, where Topic 2, the readings on myth and legend, and Topic 4*a*, those on epic poetry, both have some bearing on the matter.

These same passages bear, of course, on the *Gilgamesh* epic itself, which appears in this year's volume among the "Additions to the Great Books Library." As for Clerk Maxwell's *Matter and Motion,* readings in Chapter 53, MATTER, especially passages at 1*a,* 2*a* and *b,* 3*a,* and 4*a,* will be found helpful in relation to Maxwell's *Matter and Motion;* and in the same connection, see, once more, Chapter 54, MECHANICS, this time the passages at Topics 1*a* and *b* on the laws of motion, and also possibly those at Topic 6*c* on velocity, acceleration, and momentum.

Maxwell's papers and lectures, of which three are reprinted in the volume, also send us to the *Great Books.* For example, on "On Action at a Distance," consult Chapter 54, MECHANICS, Topic 6*d*(2); on "Ether," consult the same chapter at Topic 7*a*(4); and with respect to the question whether there are real analogies in nature or not, readings in Chapter 8, CAUSE, Topics 5*b* and *c;* in Chapter 54, MECHANICS, Topics 2*c* and 3*a;* in Chapter 60, NATURE, Topics 1*c,* 3*a, b,* and *c,* along with Topic 4*a* are relevant, while in Chapter 78, RELATION, many of the readings under Topic 1 on the general theory of relation; Topic 4, on relation in the order of thought and knowledge; Topic 5, on order as a system of relationships or related things; and Topic 6*a,* at least, on absolute and relative with respect to space, time, and motion, have something to do with Maxwell's wide-ranging discussion.

And finally, in connection with the story by Henry James with which this volume ends, a reader should not forget that passages listed in Chapter 4, ART, especially those at Topic 5 on the sources of art in experience, imagination, and inspiration, are to the point of the problem faced by the artist in that tale.

PART FOUR

Additions to the Great Books Library

The Epic of Gilgamesh

Editor's Introduction

What is known as the *Gilgamesh* epic is the story of a certain Gilgamesh, king of Uruk (the Biblical Erech, now Warka, in southern Mesopotamia not far from the Persian Gulf—what is now Iraq) in very ancient times. The most nearly complete surviving version of the tale is in Akkadian characters, and indeed was found a century and a half ago, or at least it began to be found, with the first excavations of ancient Nineveh, where the remains of the great library of Assurbanipal, king of the Assyrians, were discovered—clay tablets covered with cuneiform (wedge-shaped) writing. It was clear then, however, that this was a translation from the Sumerian, and parts of the story in that language were subsequently discovered in the ruins of Nippur, Ur, and other cities of the region, all indicating not only literary existence at least as far back as the second millennium B.C. but dealing with events (of which other, fragmentary accounts have since been found) that appear to have occurred in the third.

The story thus dates from the biblical epoch between the time of Abraham and that of Noah, a time mostly taken up with genealogy in the Book of Genesis, though it is also the period of the Tower of Babel. Of this era nothing is known except through archaeological digs, which have uncovered enough of ancient Sumerian civilization to indicate that it was well-developed in cities and irrigation systems, as well as a written language, before it was overcome by Semitic conquests from surrounding Arab lands. The evidence indicates that there were indeed great Floods, of which one, while apparently not the one that Genesis relates (so far as that can be historically identified) is described in the *Gilgamesh* epic, of which it forms the best-preserved portion.

There was also, it now appears, an actual Gilgamesh, who reigned in Uruk sometime—perhaps 2700 B.C.—in the first half of the third millennium. Of him not much is known beyond conjecture save that he was a just judge and great builder, one who erected walls at Uruk that became famous and lasted until the city was conquered some time later by Sargon, a Semite king who caused them to be pulled down. Other exploits may be inferred from the epic itself, as that Gilgamesh ventured as far as northern Syria or southern Turkey where there were great forests from which he brought back cedar wood to build his city.

Sumerian sources for the *Gilgamesh* epic consist of five poems. They deal with Gilgamesh in "the Land of the Living," with his death (in fragmentary form), with the Bull of Heaven, and with the story of the deluge, which was not at first included in the epic. However, this last was sufficiently established so that the Assyrians—the librarians, as we may say, of Assurbanipal, somewhat like the old scribes of Israel—accepted it as part of the canon, although they did not accept stories of one Enmerkar, a forerunner of Gilgamesh on the throne of Uruk, nor poems in which the hero is Lugulbanda, which various compilers before them had assembled.

The components of what became the *Gilgamesh* epic, and these apocryphal writings, suggest an origin older than the earliest Sumerian tablets (which, again, are much older than the Akkadian ones of Assurbanipal's day) and allow us to suppose that the epic was originally conceived in preliterate times, much as certain older tales that were incorporated into the *Iliad* and the *Odyssey*. The difference is that Homer (if there was a Homer) made whole the parts on which he drew, whereas the uncertain fit of parts of the *Gilgamesh* epic is evident. What the entire epic was, at least in its later form, we may never know, notwithstanding the fact that new fragments continue to be recovered from time to time. We only assume that it *was* a whole—that is, an entire, finished work—in the Akkadian translation that was buried with the rest of Assurbanipal's library after the conquest of Nineveh in 612 B.C. If it was not, the parts of it were certainly well known in that Assyrian age and had been for at least a thousand years. The many strains that contribute to it are, moreover, the one surviving body of literature from those ancient times, where outside of Mesopotamia—in Crete, let us say, or Anatolia—only commercial records have been found.

The following modern translation, by E. A. Speiser, is from the Akkadian (Assyrian). The "tablets" correspond to the actual clay tablets from which the version here is taken. Dots indicate missing portions of lines as well as lines that have vanished *in toto* through tablets being broken or having become unreadable. We omit brackets, parentheses, and italics—originally used by the translator to indicate restorations, interpolations (of varying degrees of authenticity), and doubtful translations—for the sake of ease in reading. Some of the translator's notes and textual observations have been retained for this reprinting, and some editorial notes and interpolations of our own have been supplied and are indicated by brackets. We have also added a glossary of names to help in identifying characters and places which are called differently in the different versions of the poem.

The Epic of Gilgamesh

Tablet I

i

He who saw everything to the ends of
the land,
Who all things experienced,
considered all!
. . . together . . . ,
. . . of wisdom, who all things. . . .
The hidden he saw, laid bare the
undisclosed.
He brought report of before the Flood,
Achieved a long journey, weary
and worn.
All his toil he engraved on a stone stela.
Of ramparted Uruk the wall he built,
Of hallowed Eanna, the pure sanctuary.
Behold its outer wall, whose cornice is like
copper,
Peer at the inner wall, which none can
equal! (12)
Seize upon the threshold, which is
from of old!
Draw near to Eanna, the dwelling of
Ishtar,
Which no future king, no man, can equal.
Go up and walk on the walls of Uruk,
Inspect the base terrace, examine the
brickwork:
Is not its brickwork of burnt brick?
Did not the Seven Sages* lay its
foundations?

(Remainder of the column broken away. A Hittite fragment corresponds in part with the damaged initial portion of our column ii and hence appears to contain some of the material from the end of the first column. We gather from this fragment that several gods had a hand in fashioning Gilgamesh, whom they endowed with superhuman size. At length, Gilgamesh arrives in Uruk.)

ii

Two-thirds of him is god, one-third
of him is human.
The form of his body . . .
. . . . (3–7)
. . . like a wild ox lofty . . . ;
The onslaught of his weapons verily has
no equal.
By the drum are aroused his
companions.†
The nobles of Uruk are gloomy in their
chambers:
"Gilgamesh leaves not the son to his
father; (12)
Day and night is unbridled his arrogance.
Is this Gilgamesh, the shepherd of
ramparted Uruk?
Is this our shepherd, bold, stately, wise?
Gilgamesh leaves not the maid to her
mother,
The warrior's daughter, the noble's
spouse!"
The gods hearkened to their plaint,
The gods of heaven Uruk's lord
they . . . :
"Did not Aruru bring forth this strong
wild ox? (20)
The onslaught of his weapons verily has
no equal.

---

*The seven sages who brought civilization to seven of the oldest cities.

†This may indicate that the drum, normally an instrument intended for civic or religious use, is being abused by Gilgamesh for personal purposes.

By the drum are aroused his companions.
Gilgamesh leaves not the son to his father;
Day and night is unbridled his arrogance.
Is this the shepherd of ramparted Uruk?
Is this their . . . shepherd,
Bold, stately, and wise? . . .
Gilgamesh leaves not the maid to her mother,
The warrior's daughter, the noble's spouse!"
When Anu had heard out their plaint,
The great Aruru they called: (30)
"Thou, Aruru, didst create the man;
Create now his double;
His stormy heart let him match.
Let them contend, that Uruk may have peace!"
When Aruru heard this,
A double of Anu she conceived within her.
Aruru washed her hands,
Pinched off clay and cast it on the steppe.
On the steppe she created valiant Enkidu,
Offspring of . . . , essence of Ninurta.
Shaggy with hair is his whole body,
He is endowed with head hair like a woman.
The locks of his hair sprout like Nisaba.
He knows neither people nor land;
Garbed is he like Sumuqan.
With the gazelles he feeds on grass,
With the wild beasts he jostles at the watering-place, (40)
With the teeming creatures his heart delights in water.
Now a hunter, a trapping-man,
Faced him at the watering-place.
One day, a second, and a third
He faced him at the watering-place.
When the hunter saw him, his face became motionless.
He and his beasts went into his house,
Sore afraid, still, without a sound,
While his heart was disturbed, overclouded his face.
For woe had entered his belly;
His face was like that of a wayfarer from afar. (50)

iii

The hunter opened his mouth to speak,
Saying to his father:
"My father, there is a fellow who has come from the hills,
He is the mightiest in the land; strength he has.
Like the essence of Anu, so mighty his strength!
Ever he ranges over the hills,
Ever with the beasts he feeds on grass.
Ever sets he his feet at the watering-place.
I am so frightened that I dare not approach him!
He filled in the pits that I had dug,
He tore up my traps which I had set, (10)
The beasts and creatures of the steppe
He has made slip through my hands.
He does not allow me to engage in fieldcraft!

His father opened his mouth to speak,
Saying to the hunter:
"My son, in Uruk there lives Gilgamesh.
No one is there more mighty than he.
Like the essence of Anu, so mighty is his strength!
Go, then, toward Uruk set thy face,
Speak to him of the power of the man.
Let him give thee a harlot-lass.* Take her with thee;
Let her prevail against him by dint of greater might. (20)
When he waters the beasts at the watering-place,

*[In ancient Babylon this term was not derogatory and may even denote a temple-prostitute, part of the cult of the worship of Ishtar. For a similar Babylonian custom, recorded hundreds of years later, *see* Herodotus, *History; GBWW,* Vol. 6, p. 45a. *See also* George Anastaplo's essay on the *Gilgamesh* elsewhere in this volume (especially sec. IV) for a discussion of the erotic element in the epic.]

She shall pull off her clothing, laying bare
her ripeness.
As soon as he sees her, he will draw near
to her.
Reject him will his beasts that grew up on
his steppe!"
Giving heed to the advice of his father,
The hunter went forth to Gilgamesh.
He took the road, in Uruk he set his foot:
" . . . Gilgamesh . . . ,
There is a fellow who has come from the
hills,
He is the mightiest in the land; strength
he has. (30)
Like the essence of Anu, so mighty his
strength!
Ever he ranges over the hills,
Ever with the beasts he feeds on grass,
Ever sets he his feet at the watering-
place.
I am so frightened that I dare not
approach him!
He filled in the pits that I had dug,
He tore up my traps which I had set,
The beasts and creatures of the steppe
He has made slip through my hands.
He does not allow me to engage in
fieldcraft!"
Gilgamesh says to him, to the hunter:
"Go, my hunter, take with thee a
harlot-lass.
When he waters the beasts at the
watering-place, (42)
She shall pull off her clothing, laying bare
her ripeness.
As soon as he sees her, he will draw near
to her.
Reject him will his beasts that grew up on
his steppe!"
Forth went the hunter, taking with him a
harlot-lass.
They took the road, going straight on
their way.
On the third day at the appointed spot
they arrived.
The hunter and the harlot sat down in
their places.
One day, a second day, they sat by the
watering-place. (50)
The wild beasts came to the watering-
place to drink.

iv

The creeping creatures came, their heart
delighting in water.
But as for him, Enkidu, born in the
hills—
With the gazelles he feeds on grass,
With the wild beasts he drinks at the
watering-place,
With the creeping creatures his heart
delights in water—
The lass beheld him, the savage-man,
The barbarous fellow from the depths of
the steppe:
"There he is, O lass! Free thy breasts,
Bare thy bosom that he may possess thy
ripeness!
Be not bashful! Welcome his ardor! (10)
As soon as he sees thee, he will draw near
to thee.
Lay aside thy cloth that he may rest
upon thee.
Treat him, the savage, to a woman's
task!
Reject him will his wild beasts that grew
up on his steppe,
As his love is drawn unto thee."
The lass freed her breasts, bared her
bosom,
And he possessed her ripeness.
She was not bashful as she welcomed
his ardor.
She laid aside her cloth and he rested
upon her.
She treated him, the savage, to a woman's
task,
As his love was drawn unto her. (20)
For six days and seven nights Enkidu
comes forth,
Mating with the lass.
After he had had his fill of her charms,
He set his face toward his wild beasts.
On seeing him, Enkidu, the gazelles
ran off,
The wild beasts of the steppe drew away
from his body.

Startled was Enkidu, as his body became taut,
His knees were motionless—for his wild beasts had gone.
Enkidu had to slacken his pace—it was not as before;
But he now had wisdom, broader understanding.
Returning, he sits at the feet of the harlot. (30)
He looks up at the face of the harlot,
His ears attentive, as the harlot speaks;
The harlot says to him, to Enkidu:
"Thou art wise, Enkidu, art become like a god!
Why with the wild creatures dost thou roam over the steppe?
Come, let me lead thee to ramparted Uruk,
To the holy temple, abode of Anu and Ishtar,
Where lives Gilgamesh, accomplished in strength,
And like a wild ox lords it over the folk."
As she speaks to him, her words find favor, (40)
His heart enlightened, he yearns for a friend.
Enkidu says to her, to the harlot:
"Up, lass, escort thou me,
To the pure sacred temple, abode of Anu and Ishtar,
Where lives Gilgamesh, accomplished in strength,
And like a wild ox lords it over the folk.
I will challenge him and will boldly address him,

v

I will shout in Uruk: 'I am he who is mighty!
I am the one who can alter destinies,
He who was born on the steppe is mighty; strength he has.' "
"Up then, let us go, that he may see thy face.
I will show thee Gilgamesh; where he is I know well.
Come then, O Enkidu, to ramparted Uruk,
Where people are resplendent in festal attire,
Where each day is made a holiday,
Where . . . lads . . . ,
And lasses . . . of figure. (10)
Their ripeness . . . full of perfume.
They drive the great ones from their couches!
To thee, O Enkidu, who rejoicest in living,
I will show Gilgamesh, the joyful man!
Look thou at him, regard his face;
He is radiant with manhood, vigor he has.
With ripeness gorgeous is the whole of his body,
Mightier strength has he than thou,
Never resting by day or by night.
O Enkidu, renounce thy presumption!
Gilgamesh—of him Shamash is fond;
Anu, Enlil, and Ea have broadened his wisdom. (22)
Before thou comest down from the hills,
Gilgamesh will see thee in his dreams in Uruk: . . .

(Remaining lines of the Assyrian Version of Tablet I are here omitted since the Old Babylonian Version of Tablet II takes up at this point.)

Tablet II

OLD BABYLONIAN VERSION

i

Gilgamesh arose to reveal the dream,
Saying to his mother:*
"My mother, in the time of night
I felt joyful and I walked about
In the midst of the nobles.
The stars appeared in the heavens,
The essence of Anu descended towards me. (8)
I sought to lift it; it was too heavy for me!

*[Ninsunna. *See* glossary.]

I sought to move it; move it I could not!
Uruk-land was gathered about it,
While the nobles kissed its feet.
As I set my forehead,*
They gave me support.
I raised it and brought it to thee."
The mother of Gilgamesh, who knows all,
Says to Gilgamesh:
"Forsooth, Gilgamesh, one like thee
Was born on the steppe,
And the hills have reared him.
When thou seest him, as over a woman
thou wilt rejoice (20)
The nobles will kiss his feet;
Thou wilt embrace him and . . . him;
Thou wilt lead him to me."
He lay down and saw another
Dream: he says to his mother:
"My mother, I saw another
. . . in the confusion. In the street
Of broad-marted Uruk
There lay an axe, and
They were gathered round it. (30)
That axe, strange was its shape.
As soon as I saw it, I rejoiced.
I loved it, and as though to a woman,
I was drawn to it.
I took it and placed it
At my side."
The mother of Gilgamesh, who knows all,
Says to Gilgamesh:
. . . .

ii

"Because I made it vie with thee."
While Gilgamesh reveals his dream,
Enkidu sits before the harlot.
. . . the two of them.
Enkidu forgot where he was born.
For six days and seven nights Enkidu
came forth
Mating with the lass.
Then the harlot opened her mouth,
Saying to Enkidu: (10)
"As I look at thee, Enkidu, thou art
become like a god;
Wherefore with the wild creatures
Dost thou range over the steppe?
Up, I will lead thee
To broad-marted Uruk,
To the holy temple, the abode of Anu,
Enkidu, arise, I will lead thee
To Eanna, the abode of Anu,
Where lives Gilgamesh, accomplished
in deeds,
And thou, like . . . , (20)
Wilt love him like thyself.
Up, arise from the ground,
The shepherd's bed!"
He hearkened to her words, approved her
speech;
The woman's counsel
Fell upon his heart.
She pulled off her clothing;
With one piece she clothed him,
With the other garment
She clothed herself. (30)
Holding on to his hand,
She leads him like a mother
To the board of shepherds,
The place of the sheepfold.
Round him the shepherds gathered.
. . . .

iii

The milk of wild creatures
He was wont to suck.
Food they placed before him;
He gagged, he gaped
And he stared.
Nothing does Enkidu know
Of eating food;
To drink strong drink
He has not been taught.
The harlot opened her mouth, (10)
Saying to Enkidu:
"Eat the food, Enkidu,
As is life's due;
Drink the strong drink, as is the custom
of the land."
Enkidu ate the food,
Until he was sated;
Of strong drink he drank

*To press the carrying strap against it.

Seven goblets.
Carefree became his mood and cheerful,
His heart exulted (20)
And his face glowed.
He rubbed the shaggy growth,
The hair of his body,
Anointed himself with oil,
Became human.
He put on clothing,
He is like a groom!
He took his weapon
To chase the lions,
That shepherds might rest at night. (30)
He caught wolves,
He captured lions,
The chief cattlemen could lie down;
Enkidu is their watchman,
The bold man,
The unique hero!
To . . . he said:
. . . .

iv

. . . .
He made merry.
When he lifted his eyes, (10)
He beheld a man.
He says to the harlot:
"Lass, fetch the man!
Why has he come hither?
His name let me hear."
The harlot called the man,
Going up to him and saying to him:
"Sir, whither hastenest thou?
What is this thy toilsome course?"
The man opened his mouth, (20)
Saying to Enkidu:
"Into the meeting-house he has intruded,
Which is set aside for the people,
. . . for wedlock.
On the city he has heaped defilement,
Imposing strange things on the hapless city.
For the king of broad-marted Uruk
The drum of the people is free for nuptial choice. (30)
For Gilgamesh, king of broad-marted Uruk,
The drum of the people is free
For nuptial choice,
That with lawful wives he might mate!
He is the first,
The husband comes after.
By the counsel of the gods it has so been ordained.
With the cutting of his umbilical cord
It was decreed for him!"
At the words of the man
His* face grew pale.
. . . .

v

. . . .
Enkidu walks in front
And the lass behind him.
When he entered broad-marted Uruk,
The populace gathered about him. (10)
As he stopped in the street
Of broad-marted Uruk,
The people were gathered,
Saying about him:
"He is like Gilgamesh to a hair!
Though shorter in stature,
He is stronger of bone.
. . . . (18)
He is the strongest in the land; strength he has.
The milk of wild creatures
He was wont to suck.
In Uruk there will be a constant clatter of arms."
The nobles rejoiced:
"A hero has appeared
For the man of proper mien!
For Gilgamesh, the godlike,
His equal has come forth."
For Ishhara the bed
Is laid out.
Gilgamesh . . . ,
At night . . . ,
As he approaches,
Enkidu stands in the street
To bar the way

*[Enkidu's.]

To Gilgamesh
. . . in his might.
. . . .

vi

. . . .
Gilgamesh . . .
On the steppe . . .
Sprouts. . . .
He rose up and . . .
Before him. (10)
They met in the Market-of-the-Land.
Enkidu barred the gate
With his foot,
Not allowing Gilgamesh to enter.
They grappled each other,
Holding fast like bulls.
They shattered the doorpost,
As the wall shook.
Gilgamesh and Enkidu
Grappled each other, (20)
Holding fast like bulls;
They shattered the doorpost,
As the wall shook.
As Gilgamesh bent the knee—
His foot on the ground—
His fury abated
And he turned away.
When he had turned away,
Enkidu to him
Speaks up, to Gilgamesh:
"As one alone thy mother
Bore thee,
The wild cow of the steer-folds,
Ninsunna!
Raised up above men is thy head.
Kingship over the people
Enlil has granted thee!"

Tablet III

OLD BABYLONIAN VERSION

(From fragments of text it is clear that Gilgamesh has decided on an expedition against monstrous Huwawa, who lives in the Cedar Forest. Enkidu tries to dissuade him, but Gilgamesh's determination is apparent from the following lines of the Old Babylonian Version:)

Gilgamesh opened his mouth, (3)
Saying to Enkidu:
"Who, my friend can scale heaven?
Only the gods live forever under the sun.
As for mankind, numbered are their
days;
Whatever they achieve is but the wind!
Even here thou art afraid of death.
What of thy heroic might? (10)
Let me go then before thee,
Let my mouth call to me, 'Advance,
fear not!'
Should I fall, I shall have made me
a name:
'Gilgamesh'—they will say—against fierce
Huwawa
Has fallen!' Long after
My offspring has been born in my
house,"

(From the fragmentary text of Tablets IV and V it is clear that the hazardous expedition of the two heroes against Huwawa is successful.)

Tablet VI

He* washed his grimy hair, polished his
weapons,
The braid of his hair he shook out against
his back.
He cast off his soiled things, put on his
clean ones,
Wrapped a fringed cloak about and
fastened a sash.
When Gilgamesh had put on his tiara,
Glorious Ishtar raised an eye at the
beauty of Gilgamesh:
"Come, Gilgamesh, be thou my lover!
Do but grant me of thy fruit.
Thou shalt be my husband and I will be
thy wife.

*Gilgamesh.

I will harness for thee a chariot of lapis
and gold, (10)
Whose wheels are gold and whose horns
are brass.
Thou shalt have storm-demons to hitch
on for mighty mules.
In the fragrance of cedars thou shalt enter
our house.
When our house thou enterest,
Threshold and dais shall kiss thy feet!
Humbled before thee shall be kings,
lords, and princes!
The yield of hills and plain they shall
bring thee as tribute.
Thy goats shall cast triplets, thy sheep
twins,
Thy he-ass in lading shall surpass
thy mule.
Thy chariot horses shall be famed for
racing, (20)
Thine ox under yoke shall not have
a rival!"

Gilgamesh opened his mouth to speak,
Saying to glorious Ishtar:
"What am I to give thee, that I may take
thee in marriage?
Should I give oil for the body, and
clothing?
Should I give bread and victuals?
. . . food fit for divinity,
. . . drink fit for royalty.
. . . . (29–31)
. . . if I take thee in marriage?
Thou art but a brazier which goes out in
the cold;
A back door which does not keep out
blast and wind-storm;
A palace which crushes the valiant . . . ;
A turban whose cover . . . ;
Pitch which soils its bearers;
A waterskin which soaks through its
bearer;
Limestone which springs the stone
rampart;
Jasper which . . . enemy land; (40)
A shoe which pinches the foot of its
owner!
Which lover didst thou love forever?
Which of thy shepherds pleased thee for
all time?
Come, and I will name for thee thy lovers

Of . . . .
For Tammuz, the lover of thy youth,
Thou hast ordained wailing year af-
ter year.
Having loved the dappled shepherd-bird,
Thou smotest him, breaking his wing.
In the groves he sits, crying 'My wing!'*
Then thou lovedst a lion, perfect in
strength;
Seven pits and seven thou didst dig for
him. (5
Then a stallion thou lovedst, famed
in battle;
The whip, the spur, and the lash thou
ordainedst for him.
Thou decreedst for him to gallop seven
leagues,
Thou decreedst for him the muddied
to drink;
For his mother, Silili, thou ordainedst
wailing!
Then thou lovedst the keeper of the her
Who ash-cakes ever did heap up for thee
Daily slaughtered kids for thee; (6
Yet thou smotest him, turning him into
a wolf,
So that his own herd boys drive him off,
And his dogs bite his thighs.
Then thou lovedst Ishullanu, thy father'
gardener,
Who baskets of dates ever did bring
to thee,
And daily did brighten thy table.
Thine eyes raised at him, thou didst go
to him:
'O my Ishullanu, let us taste of thy vigor
Put forth thy "hand" and touch our
"modesty!" '
Ishullanu said to thee: (7
'What dost thou want with me?
Has my mother not baked, have I
not eaten,

*Akkadian *kappi,* plainly a wordplay on t
cry of the bird.

That I should taste the food of stench and foulness?
Does reed-work afford cover against the cold?'
As thou didst hear this his talk,
Thou smotest him and turnedst him into a mole.
Thou placedst him in the midst of . . . ;
He cannot go up . . . nor can he come down . . .
If thou shouldst love me, thou wouldst treat me like them."

When Ishtar heard this,
Ishtar was enraged and mounted to heaven. (80)
Forth went Ishtar before Anu, her father,
To Antum, her mother, she went and said:
"My father, Gilgamesh has heaped insults upon me!
Gilgamesh has recounted my stinking deeds,
My stench and my foulness."
Anu opened his mouth to speak,
Saying to glorious Ishtar:
"But surely, thou didst invite . . . ,
And so Gilgamesh has recounted thy stinking deeds, (90)
Thy stench and thy foulness."

Ishtar opened her mouth to speak,
Saying to Anu, her father:
"My father, make me the Bull of Heaven that he smite Gilgamesh,
And fill Gilgamesh . . . !
If thou dost not make me the Bull of Heaven,
I will smash the doors of the nether world,
I will . . . ,
I will raise up the dead eating and alive,
So that the dead shall outnumber the living!" (100)

Anu opened his mouth to speak,
Saying to glorious Ishtar:
"If I do what thou askest of me,
There will be seven years of barren husks.
Hast thou gathered grain for the people?
Hast thou grown grass for the beasts?"

Ishtar opened her mouth to speak,
Saying to Anu, her father: (108)
"Grain for the people I have stored,
Grass for the beasts I have provided.
If there should be seven years of husks,
I have gathered grain for the people,
I have grown grass for the beasts."

(Lines 114–28 are too fragmentary for translation. It is plain, however, that Anu did Ishtar's bidding, for the Bull comes down and kills hundreds of men with his first two snorts.)

With his third snort he sprang at Enkidu.
Enkidu parried his onslaught. (130)
Up leaped Enkidu, seizing the Bull of Heaven by the horns.
The Bull of Heaven hurled his foam in his face,
Brushed him with the thick of his tail.

Enkidu opened his mouth to speak,
Saying to Gilgamesh:
"My friend, we have gloried. . . ."

(Lines 137–51 mutilated, but the course of the battle is made plain by the following:)

Between neck and horns he thrust his sword. (152)
When they had slain the Bull, they tore out his heart,
Placing it before Shamash.
They drew back and did homage before Shamash.
The two brothers sat down.

Then Ishtar mounted the wall of ramparted Uruk,
Sprang on the battlements, uttering a curse:
"Woe unto Gilgamesh because he insulted me
By slaying the Bull of Heaven!"
When Enkidu heard this speech of Ishtar, (160)

He tore loose the right thigh of the Bull
of Heaven
And tossed it in her face:
"Could I but get thee, like unto him
I would do unto thee.
His entrails I would hang at thy side!"
Thereupon Ishtar assembled the votaries,
The pleasure-lasses and the
temple-harlots.
Over the right thigh of the Bull of Heaven
she set up a wail.
But Gilgamesh called the craftsmen, the
armorers,
All of them.
The artisans admire the thickness of his
horns: (170)
Each is cast from thirty minas of lapis;
The coating on each is two fingers thick;
Six measures of oil, the capacity of
the two,
He offered as ointment to his god,
Lugalbanda.
He brought them and hung them in his
princely bed-chamber.

In the Euphrates they washed their hands,
They embraced each other as they
went on,
Riding through the market-street of
Uruk. (178)
The people of Uruk are gathered to gaze
upon them.
Gilgamesh to the lyre maids of Uruk
Says these words:
"Who is most splendid among the heroes?
Who is most glorious among men?"
"Gilgamesh is most splendid among the
heroes,
Gilgamesh is most glorious among men."
. . . . (186–88)

Gilgamesh in his palace holds a
celebration.
Down lie the heroes on their beds of
night. (190)
Also Enkidu lies down, a dream
beholding.
Up rose Enkidu to relate his dream,
Saying to his friend:
"My friend, why are the great gods in
council?"

Tablet VII

(The first two columns of this tablet, Enkidu's dream, are missing in the Assyrian Version used here. The text picks up, after his dream, with the following lines:)

". . . . . Then daylight came."
And Enkidu answered Gilgamesh:
"Hear the dream which I had last night:
Anu, Enlil, Ea, and heavenly Shamash
Were in council.
And Anu said to Enlil:
'Because the Bull of Heaven they have
slain, and Huwawa
They have slain, therefore'—said Anu—
'the one of them
Who stripped the mountains of the cedar
Must die!'
But Enlil said: 'Enkidu must die;
Gilgamesh, however, shall not die!' (10)

Then heavenly Shamash answered
valiant Enlil:
'Was it not at my command
That they slew the Bull of Heaven and
Huwawa?
Should now innocent
Enkidu die?' But Enlil turned
In anger to heavenly Shamash: 'Because,
much like
One of their comrades, thou didst daily
go down to them.' "
Enkidu lay down ill before Gilgamesh.
And as his* tears were streaming down,
he said:
"O my brother, my dear brother! Me
they would
Clear at the expense of my brother!"
Furthermore: (20)
"Must I by the spirit of the dead
Sit down, at the spirit's door,
Never again to behold my dear brother
with mine eyes?"

*Referring to Gilgamesh.

(The remainder is lost. In a deathbed review of his life, Enkidu seems to bemoan the events that had led up to this sorry state, cursing the successive steps in his fated life. One of his curses, preserved in an Assyrian fragment, is directed against the gate that lamed his hand.)

Enkidu . . . lifted up his eyes, (36)
Speaking with the door as though it were
human:
"Thou door of the woods, uncompre-
hending,
Not endowed with understanding!
At twenty leagues away I found choice
thy wood, (40)
Long before I beheld the lofty cedar.
There is no counterpart of thy wood in
the land.
Six dozen cubits is thy height, two dozen
thy breadth. . . .
Thy pole, thy pole-ferrule, and thy pole-
knob. . . .
A master-craftsman in Nippur built
thee. . . .
Had I known, O door, that this would
come to pass
And that this thy beauty . . . ,
I would have lifted the axe, would
have . . . ,
I would have set a reed frame upon
thee!"

(A long gap follows. When the text sets in again, Enkidu—continuing his bitter survey—invokes the curse of Shamash upon the hunter [who had first discovered him].)

iii

". . . destroy his wealth, diminish
his power!
May his way be repugnant before thee.
May the beasts he would trap escape from
before him.
Let not the hunter attain the fullness of
his heart!"
Then his heart prompted him to curse the
harlot-lass:
"Come, lass, I will decree thy fate,
A fate that shall not end for all eternity!
I will curse thee with a great curse,
An oath, whose curses shall soon over-
take thee.
. . . surfeit of thy charms.
. . . . (11–17)
. . . shall cast into thy house.
. . . the road shall be thy dwelling place,
The shadow of the wall shall be thy
station, (20)
. . . thy feet,
The besotted and the thirsty shall smite
thy cheek!
. . . . (23–30)
Because me thou hast . . .
And because . . . upon me."
When Shamash heard these words of his
mouth,
Forthwith he called down to him from
heaven:
"Why, O Enkidu, cursest thou the
harlot-lass,
Who made thee eat food fit for divinity,
And gave thee to drink wine fit for
royalty,
Who clothed thee with noble garments,
And made thee have fair Gilgamesh for a
comrade?
And has not now Gilgamesh, thy bosom
friend, (40)
Made thee lie on a noble couch?
He has made thee lie on a couch of
honor,
Has placed thee on the seat of ease, the
seat at the left,
That the princes of the earth may kiss
thy feet!
He will make Uruk's people weep over
thee and lament,
Will fill joyful people with woe over thee.
And, when thou art gone,
He will his body with uncut
hair invest,
Will don a lion skin and roam over the
steppe."

When Enkidu heard the words of valiant
Shamash,
. . . his vexed heart grew quiet.

(Short break. Relenting, Enkidu changes his curse into a blessing. He addresses himself once again to the girl:)

iv

"May . . . return to thy place. . . .
Kings, princes, and nobles shall love thee.
None shall on account of thee smite his
thigh.*
Over thee shall the old man shake
his beard.
. . . the young shall unloose his girdle.
. . . carnelian, lapis, and gold.
May he be paid back who defiled thee,
May his home be emptied, his heaped-up
storehouse. (8)
To the presence of the gods the priest
shall let thee enter,
On thy account shall be forsaken the wife,
though a mother of seven."
. . . Enkidu, whose mood is bitter,
. . . lies down all alone.
That night he pours out his feelings to his
friend:
"My friend, I saw a dream last night:
The heavens moaned, the earth
responded;
. . . I stood alone.
. . . his face was darkened.
Like unto . . . was his face.
. . . like the talons of an eagle were
his claws.
. . . he overpowered me. (20)
. . . he leaps.
. . . he submerged me.
. . . . (23–30)
. . . . . . he transformed me,
So that my arms were . . . like those of
a bird.
Looking at me, he leads me to the House
of Darkness,
The abode of Irkalla,
To the house which none leave who have
entered it,
On the road from which there is no
way back,
To the house wherein the dwellers are
bereft of light,
Where dust is their fare and clay
their food.
They are clothed like birds, with wings
for garments, (38)
And see no light, residing in darkness.
In the House of Dust, which I entered,
I looked at rulers, their crowns put away;
I saw princes, those born to the crown,
Who had ruled the land from the
days of yore.
These doubles of Anu and Enlil were
serving meat roasts;
They were serving bake meats and
pouring
Cool water from the waterskins.
In the House of Dust, which I entered,
Reside High Priest and acolyte,
Reside incantatory and ecstatic,
Reside the laver-anointers of the
great gods,
Resides Etana, resides Sumuqan.
Ereshkigal lives there, Queen of the
nether world, (50)
And Belit-Seri, recorder of the nether
world, kneels before her.
She holds a tablet and reads out to her.
Lifting up her head, she beheld me:
Saying: 'Who has brought this one
hither?' "

(The remainder of the tablet in the Assyrian Version is missing. The following fragment may be relevant.)

"Remember all my travels with him! (4)
My friend saw a dream whose portents
were unfavorable:
The day on which he saw the dream was
ended.
Stricken is Enkidu, one day, a second day.
Enkidu's suffering, on his bed, increases.
A third day, a fourth day. . . .
A fifth day, a sixth, and a seventh; (10)
An eighth, a ninth, and a tenth day,
Enkidu's suffering, on his bed, increases.
An eleventh and a twelfth day. . . .

---

*In derision or embarrassment.

Stricken is Enkidu on his bed of pain!
At length he called Gilgamesh and said to him:
'My friend, . . . has cursed me!
Not like one fallen in battle shall I die,
For I feared the battle. . . .
My friend, he who is slain in battle is blessed.
But as for me, ...' "

Tablet VIII

i

With the first glow of dawn Gilgamesh said to his friend:
"Enkidu, thy mother a gazelle, a wild ass thy father, produced thee.
They whose mark is their tails reared thee, and the cattle
Of the steppe and of all the pastures.
May the tracks of Enkidu in the Cedar Forest
Weep for thee, may they not hush night and day.
May the elders of wide, ramparted Uruk weep for thee.
May weep for thee
The finger that is extended behind us in blessing.
May weep for thee
And echo the countryside as though it were thy mother.
May weep for thee . . .
In whose midst we . . . May weep for thee bear, hyena, panther,
Tiger, hart, leopard, lion; oxen, deer, ibex, (10)
And the wild creatures of the steppe.
May weep for thee the river Ula . . .
By whose banks we used to walk.
May weep for thee the pure Euphrates, where we drew
Water for the skin. May weep for thee
The warriors of wide, ramparted Uruk
. . . we slew the Bull . . . May weep for thee . . .
Who in Eridu extolled thy name. May weep for thee . . .
Who . . . extolled thy name. May weep for thee . . .
Who provided . . . grain for thy mouth. May weep for thee . . .
Who put salve on thy back. May weep for thee . . .
Who put ale in thy mouth. May weep for thee the harlot
Who anointed thee with fragrant oil.
May weep for thee . . . (20)
Of the harem who brought to thee
The wife and the ring of thy choice.
May brothers weep for thee like sisters
. . . and may they let grow long
Their head-hair over thee . . . !"

ii

"Hear me, O elders and give ear unto me!
It is for Enkidu, my friend, that I weep,
Moaning bitterly like a wailing woman.
The axe at my side, my hand's trust,
The dirk in my belt, the shield in front of me,
My festal robe, my richest trimming—
An evil demon rose up and robbed me!
O my younger friend, thou chasedst
The wild ass of the hills, the panther of the steppe!
Enkidu, my younger friend, thou who chasedst
The wild ass of the hills, the panther of the steppe!
We who have conquered all things, scaled the mountains, (10)
Who seized the Bull and slew him,
Brought affliction on Hubaba, who dwelled in the Cedar Forest!
What, now, is this sleep that has laid hold on thee?
Thou art benighted and canst not hear me!"
But he lifts not up his eyes;
He touched his heart, but it does not beat.
Then he veiled his friend like a bride . . . ,

Storming over him like a lion,
Like a lioness deprived of her whelps.
He paces back and forth before the couch, (20)
Pulling out his hair and strewing it . . . ,
Tearing off and flinging down his finery,
As though unclean!
With the first glow of dawn, Gilgamesh. . . .
Then Gilgamesh issued a call to the land:
"O smith, . . . ,
Coppersmith, goldsmith, lapidary! Make my friend . . . !"
Then he fashioned a statue for his friend,
The friend whose stature . . . :
" . . . , of lapis is thy breast, of gold thy body, ..."

iii

"On a couch of honor I made thee lie,
I placed thee on the seat of ease, the seat at the left,
That the princes of the earth might kiss thy feet!
Over thee I will make Uruk's people weep and lament,
Joyful people I will fill with woe over thee.
And, when thou art gone,
I shall invest my body with uncut hair,
And, clad in a lion skin, I shall roam over the steppe!"

With the first glow of dawn, Gilgamesh
Loosened his band. . . .

(The remainder of the tablet is missing or too fragmentary for translation, with the exception of the following lines:)

v

With the first glow of dawn, Gilgamesh fashioned . . . , (45)
Brought out a large table of elammaqu wood,
Filled with honey a bowl of carnelian,
Filled with curds a bowl of lapis,
. . . he decorated and exposed to the sun.

Tablet IX

i

For Enkidu, his friend, Gilgamesh
Weeps bitterly, as he ranges over the steppe:
"When I die, shall I not be like Enkidu?
Woe has entered my belly.
Fearing death, I roam over the steppe.
To Utnapishtim, Ubar-Tutu's son,
I have taken the road to proceed in all haste.
When arriving by night at mountain passes,
I saw lions and grew afraid,
I lifted my head to Sin to pray. (10)
To . . . of the gods went out my orisons.
. . . preserve thou me!"
As at night he lay, he awoke from a dream.
There were . . . , rejoicing in life.
He raised his axe in his hand,
He drew the dirk from his belt.
Like an arrow he descended among them.
He smote them and hacked away at them.

(The remainder of Tablet IX gives the adventures of Gilgamesh as he passes successfully the darkness of the mountain range of Mashu guarded by scorpion-men.)

Tablet X

OLD BABYLONIAN VERSION

i

" . . . .
With their skins he clothes himself, as he eats flesh.
. . . , O Gilgamesh, which has not happened
As long as my wind drives the waters."

Shamash was distraught, as he betook
himself to him;
He says to Gilgamesh:
"Gilgamesh, whither rovest thou?
The life thou pursuest thou shalt not find."
Gilgamesh says to him, to valiant
Shamash:
"After marching and roving over the
steppe, (10)
Must I lay my head in the heart of
the earth
That I may sleep through all the years?
Let mine eyes behold the sun
That I may have my fill of the light!
Darkness withdraws when there is
enough light.
May one who indeed is dead behold yet
the radiance of the sun!"

ii

(Beginning lost. Gilgamesh is addressing Siduri, the ale-wife:)

"He who with me underwent all
hardships—
Enkidu, whom I loved dearly,
Who with me underwent all hardships—
Has now gone to the fate of mankind!
Day and night I have wept over him.
I would not give him up for burial—
In case my friend should rise at my
plaint—
Seven days and seven nights, (8)
Until a worm fell out of his nose.
Since his passing I have not found life,
I have roamed like a hunter in the midst
of the steppe.
O ale-wife, now that I have seen thy
face,
Let me not see the death which I ever
dread."
The ale-wife said to him, to Gilgamesh:

iii

"Gilgamesh, whither rovest thou?
The life thou pursuest thou shalt not find.
When the gods created mankind,
Death for mankind they set aside,
Life in their own hands retaining.
Thou, Gilgamesh, let full be thy belly,
Make thou merry by day and by night.
Of each day make thou a feast of
rejoicing,
Day and night dance thou and play!
Let thy garments be sparkling fresh, (10)
Thy head be washed; bathe thou in
water.
Pay heed to the little one that holds on to
thy hand,
Let thy spouse delight in thy bosom!
For this is the task of mankind!"

. . . .

iv

In his wrath he* shatters them.†
When he returned, he goes up to him.‡
Sursunabu his eyes behold.
Sursunabu says to him, to Gilgamesh:
"Tell me, thou, what is thy name?
I am Sursunabu, he of Utanapishtim the
Faraway."
Gilgamesh said to him, to Sursunabu:
"As for me, Gilgamesh is my name,
Who have come from Uruk-Eanna,
Who have traversed the mountains, (10)
A distant journey, as the sun rises.
O Sursunabu, now that I have seen
thy face,
Show me Utanapishtim the Faraway."
Sursunabu says to him, to Gilgamesh.

. . . .

(The Assyrian Version of Tablet X gives the episodes of the meetings with Siduri and with Sursunabu and an account of the crossing of the Waters of Death to the abode of Utnapishtim. The concluding part of Tablet X follows:)

*[Gilgamesh.]

†Apparently the mysterious "Stone Things." [To judge from a Hittite fragment, these were stone figures of unusual properties kept by Sursunabu the boatman.]

‡To the boatman.

v

Gilgamesh also said to him, to
Utnapishtim: (23)
"That now I might come and behold
Utnapishtim,
Whom they call the Faraway,
I ranged and wandered over all the lands,
I traversed difficult mountains,
I crossed all the seas!
My face was not sated with sweet sleep,
I fretted myself with wakefulness;
I filled my joints with misery.
I had not reached the ale-wife's house,
When my clothing was used up. (30)
I slew bear, hyena, lion, panther,
Tiger, stag, and ibex—
The wild beasts and creeping things
of the steppe.
Their flesh I ate and their skins I
wrapped about me."
. . . .

(The beginning of the last column is broken away, except for the conclusion of the sage observations of Utnapishtim:)

vi

"Do we build a house forever? (26)
Do we seal contracts forever?
Do brothers divide shares forever?
Does hatred persist forever in the land?
Does the river forever raise up and bring
on floods?
The dragon-fly leaves its shell (30)
That its face might but glance at the face
of the sun.
Since the days of yore there has been no
permanence;
The resting and the dead, how alike
they are!
Do they not compose a picture of death,
The commoner and the noble,
Once they are near to their fate?
The Anunnaki, the great gods,
foregather;
Mammetum, maker of fate, with them the
fate decrees:
Death and life they determine.
But of death, its days are not revealed."

Tablet XI*

Gilgamesh said to him, to Utnapishtim the
Faraway:
"As I look upon thee, Utnapishtim,
Thy features are not strange; even as I
art thou.
Thou art not strange at all; even as I
art thou.
My heart had regarded thee as resolved
to do battle,
Yet thou liest indolent upon thy back!
Tell me, how joinedst thou the Assembly
of the gods,
In thy quest of life?"

Utnapishtim said to him, to Gilgamesh:
"I will reveal to thee, Gilgamesh, a
hidden matter
And a secret of the gods will I tell
thee: (10)
Shurippak—a city which thou knowest,
And which on Euphrates' banks is
situate—
That city was ancient, as were the gods
within it,
When their heart led the great gods to
produce the flood.
There were Anu, their father,
Valiant Enlil, their counselor,
Ninurta, their assistant,
Ennuge, their irrigator. (18)
Ninigiku-Ea was also present with them;
Their words he repeats to the reed-hut:†
'Reed-hut, reed-hut! Wall, wall!
Reed-hut, hearken! Wall, reflect!

---

*[The discovery of this tablet, with its many parallels to the biblical Flood (cf. *Genesis*, chaps. 6–9), created great interest in the nineteenth-century search for more tablets of the epic. Later excavations indicate the possibility that early biblical authors were familiar with the story.]

†Presumably, the dwelling place of Utnapishtim. Ea addresses him through the barrier of the wall.

Man of Shuruppak, son of Ubar-Tutu,
Tear down this house, build a ship!
Give up possessions, seek thou life.
Forswear worldly goods and keep the soul alive!
Aboard the ship take thou the seed of all living things.
The ship that thou shalt build, (28)
Her dimensions shall be to measure,
Equal shall be her width and her length.
Like the Apsu thou shalt ceil her.'
I understood, and I said to Ea, my lord:
'Behold, my lord, what thou hast thus ordered,
I will be honored to carry out.
But what shall I answer the city, the people and elders?'
Ea opened his mouth to speak,
Saying to me, his servant:
'Thou shalt then thus speak unto them:
"I have learned that Enlil is hostile to me,
So that I cannot reside in your city, (40)
Nor set my foot in Enlil's territory.
To the Deep I will therefore go down,
To dwell with my lord Ea.
But upon you he will shower down abundance,
The choicest birds, the rarest fishes.
The land shall have its fill of harvest riches.
He who at dusk orders the husk-greens,
Will shower down upon you a rain of wheat." '*

With the first glow of dawn,
The land was gathered about me.
. . . . (50–53)
The little ones carried bitumen,
While the grown ones brought all else that was needful.
On the fifth day I laid her framework.
One whole acre was her floor space,
Ten dozen cubits the height of each of her walls,
Ten dozen cubits each edge of the square deck.†
I laid out the contours and joined her together.
I provided her with six decks, (60)
Dividing her thus into seven parts.
Her floor plan I divided into nine parts.
I hammered water-plugs into her.
I saw to the punting-poles and laid in supplies.
Six 'sar' measures‡ of bitumen I poured into the furnace,
Three sar of asphalt I also poured inside.
Three sar of oil the basket-bearers carried,
Aside from the one sar of oil which the calking consumed, (68)
And the two sar of oil which the boatman stowed away.
Bullocks I slaughtered for the people,
And I killed sheep every day.
Must, red wine, oil, and white wine
I gave the workmen to drink, as though river water,
That they might feast as on New Year's Day.
I opened . . . ointment, applying it to my hand.
On the seventh day the ship was completed.
The launching was very difficult,
So that they had to shift the floor planks above and below,
Until two-thirds of the structure had gone into the water.

Whatever I had I laded upon her: (80)
Whatever I had of silver I laded upon her;
Whatever I had of gold I laded upon her;
Whatever I had of all the living beings I laded upon her.
All my family and kin I made go aboard the ship.
The beasts of the field, the wild creatures of the field,

---

*As has long been recognized, these lines feature wordplays in that both *kukku* and *kibāti* may designate either food or misfortune.

†The ship was thus an exact cube.

‡The *sar* was the number 3,600. If the measure understood here was the *sūtu,* then each *sar* designated about 8,000 gallons.

All the craftsmen I made go aboard.
Shamash had set for me a stated time:
'When he who orders unease at night,
Will shower down a rain of blight,
Board thou the ship and batten up the entrance!'
That stated time had arrived:
'He who orders unease at night, showers down a rain of blight.' (90)
I watched the appearance of the weather.
The weather was awesome to behold.
I boarded the ship and battened up the entrance.
To batten down the whole ship, to Puzur-Amurri, the boatman,
I handed over the structure together with its contents.

With the first glow of dawn,
A black cloud rose up from the horizon.
Inside it Adad thunders, (98)
While Shullat and Hanish go in front,
Moving as heralds over hill and plain.
Erragal tears out the posts;*
Forth comes Ninurta and causes the dikes to follow.
The Anunnaki lift up the torches,
Setting the land ablaze with their glare.
Consternation over Adad reaches to the heavens,
Who turned to blackness all that had been light.
The wide land was shattered like a pot!
For one day the south-storm blew,
Gathering speed as it blew, submerging the mountains,
Overtaking the people like a battle. (110)
No one can see his fellow,
Nor can the people be recognized from heaven.
The gods were frightened by the deluge,
And, shrinking back, they ascended to the heaven of Anu.
The gods cowered like dogs
Crouched against the outer wall.
Ishtar cried out like a woman in travail,
The sweet-voiced mistress of the gods moans aloud:
'The olden days are alas turned to clay,
Because I bespoke evil in the Assembly of the gods.
How could I bespeak evil in the Assembly of the gods, (120)
Ordering battle for the destruction of my people,
When it is I myself who give birth to my people!
Like the spawn of the fishes they fill the sea!'
The Anunnaki gods weep with her,
The gods, all humbled, sit and weep,
The lips drawn tight, . . . one and all.
Six days and six nights
Blows the flood wind, as the south-storm sweeps the land.
When the seventh day arrived,
The flood-carrying south-storm subsided in the battle,
Which it had fought like an army. (130)
The sea grew quiet, the tempest was still, the flood ceased.
I looked at the weather: stillness had set in,
And all of mankind had returned to clay.
The landscape was as level as a flat roof.
I opened a hatch, and light fell upon my face.
Bowing low, I sat and wept,
Tears running down on my face.
I looked about for coast lines in the expanse of the sea:
In each of fourteen regions
There emerged a region-mountain.
On Mount Nisir the ship came to a halt. (140)
Mount Nisir held the ship fast,
Allowing no motion.
One day, a second day, Mount Nisir held the ship fast,
Allowing no motion
A third day, a fourth day, Mount Nisir held the ship fast,
Allowing no motion.

---

*Of the world dam.

A fifth, and a sixth day, Mount Nisir held the ship fast,
Allowing no motion.

When the seventh day arrived,
I sent forth and set free a dove.
The dove went forth, but came back;
Since no resting-place for it was visible, she turned round.
Then I sent forth and set free a swallow.
The swallow went forth, but came back; (150)
Since no resting-place for it was visible, she turned round.
Then I sent forth and set free a raven.
The raven went forth and, seeing that the waters had diminished,
He eats, circles, caws, and turns not round.
Then I let out all to the four winds
And offered a sacrifice.
I poured out a libation on the top of the mountain.
Seven and seven cult-vessels I set up,
Upon their pot-stands I heaped cane, cedarwood, and myrtle.
The gods smelled the savor,
The gods smelled the sweet savor, (160)
The gods crowded like flies about the sacrificer.
When at length as the great goddess* arrived,
She lifted up the great jewels which Anu had fashioned to her liking:
'Ye gods here, as surely as this lapis
Upon my neck I shall not forget,
I shall be mindful of these days, forgetting them never.
Let the gods come to the offering;
But let not Enlil come to the offering,
For he, unreasoning, brought on the deluge
And my people consigned to destruction.'
When at length as Enlil arrived, (170)
And saw the ship, Enlil was wroth,
He was filled with wrath over the Igigi gods:
'Has some living soul escaped?
No man was to survive the destruction!'
Ninurta opened his mouth to speak,
Saying to valiant Enlil:
'Who, other than Ea, can devise plans?
It is Ea alone who knows every matter.'
Ea opened his mouth to speak,
Saying to valiant Enlil:
'Thou wisest of gods, thou hero,
How couldst thou, unreasoning, bring on the deluge?
On the sinner impose his sin, (180)
On the transgressor impose his transgression!
Yet be lenient, lest he be cut off,
Be patient, lest he be dislodged!
Instead of thy bringing on the deluge,
Would that a lion had risen up to diminish mankind!
Instead of thy bringing on the deluge,
Would that a wolf had risen up to diminish mankind!
Instead of thy bringing on the deluge,
Would that a famine had risen up to lay low mankind!
Instead of thy bringing on the deluge,
Would that pestilence had risen up to smite down mankind!
It was not I who disclosed the secret of the great gods.
I let Atrahasis see a dream,
And he perceived the secret of the gods.
Now then take counsel in regard to him!'
Thereupon Enlil went aboard the ship.
Holding me by the hand, he took me aboard. (190)
He took my wife aboard and made her kneel by my side.
Standing between us, he touched our foreheads to bless us.
'Hitherto Utnapishtim has been but human.
Henceforth Utnapishtim and his wife shall be like unto us gods.
Utnapishtim shall reside far away, at the mouth of the rivers!'

*Ishtar.

Thus they took me and made me reside far away,
At the mouth of the rivers.
But now, who will for thy sake call the gods to Assembly
That the life which thou seekest thou mayest find?
Up, lie not down to sleep
For six days and seven nights."
As he sits there on his haunches, (200)
Sleep fans him like the whirlwind.
Utnapishtim says to her, to his spouse:
"Behold this hero who seeks life!
Sleep fans him like a mist."
His spouse says to him, to Utnapishtim the Faraway:
"Touch him that the man may awake,
That he may return safe on the way whence he came,
That through the gate by which he left he may return to his land."
Utnapishtim says to her, to his spouse:
"Since to deceive is human, he will seek to deceive thee. (210)
Up, bake for him wafers, put them at his head,
And mark on the wall the days he sleeps."
She baked for him wafers, put them at his head,
And marked on the wall the days he slept.
His first wafer is dried out
The second is gone bad, the third is soggy;
The crust of the fourth has turned white;
The fifth has a moldy cast,
The sixth still is fresh-colored;
The seventh—just as he touched him the man awoke. (218)

Gilgamesh says to him, to Utnapishtim the Faraway:
"Scarcely had sleep surged over me,
When straightway thou dost touch and rouse me!"
Utnapishtim says to him, to Gilgamesh:
"Go, Gilgamesh, count thy wafers,
That the days thou hast slept may become known to thee:
Thy first wafer is dried out,
The second is gone bad, the third is soggy;
The crust of the fourth has turned white;
The fifth has a moldy cast,
The sixth still is fresh-colored.
The seventh—at this instant thou hast awakened." (228)
Gilgamesh says to him, to Utnapishtim the Faraway:
"What then shall I do, Utnapishtim,
Whither shall I go,
Now that the Bereaver has laid hold on my members?
In my bedchamber lurks death,
And wherever I set my foot, there is death!"

Utnapishtim says to him, to Urshanabi, the boatman:
"Urshanabi, may the landing-place not rejoice in thee,
May the place of crossing renounce thee!
To him who wanders on its shore, deny thou its shore!
The man thou hast led hither, whose body is covered with grime,
The grace of whose members skins have distorted,
Take him, Urshanabi, and bring him to the washing-place.
Let him wash off his grime in water clean as snow, (240)
Let him cast off his skins, let the sea carry them away,
That the fairness of his body may be seen.
Let him renew the band round his head,
Let him put on a cloak to clothe his nakedness,
That he may arrive in his city,
That he may achieve his journey.
Let not his cloak have a moldy cast,
Let it be wholly new."
Urshanabi took him and brought him to the washing-place.
He washed off his grime in water clean as snow.

He cast off his skins, the sea carried them away,
That the fairness of his body might be seen. (250)
He renewed the band round his head,
He put on a cloak to clothe his nakedness,
That he might arrive in his city,
That he might achieve his journey.
The cloak had not a moldy cast, but was wholly new.
Gilgamesh and Urshanabi boarded the boat,
They launched the boat on the waves and they sailed away.

His spouse says to him, to Utnapishtim the Faraway:
"Gilgamesh has come hither, toiling and straining.
What wilt thou give him that he may return to his land?" (260)
At that he, Gilgamesh, raised up his pole,
To bring the boat nigh to the shore.
Utnapishtim says to him, to Gilgamesh:
"Gilgamesh, thou hast come hither, toiling and straining.
What shall I give thee that thou mayest return to thy land?
I will disclose, O Gilgamesh, a hidden thing,
And a secret of the gods I will tell thee:
This plant, like the buckthorn is its. . . .
Its thorns will prick thy hands just as does the rose.
If thy hands obtain the plant, thou wilt find new life." (270)
No sooner had Gilgamesh heard this,
Than he opened the water-pipe,*
He tied heavy stones to his feet.
They pulled him down into the deep and he saw the plant.
He took the plant, though it pricked his hands.
He cut the heavy stones from his feet.
The sea cast him up upon its shore.

Gilgamesh says to him, to Urshanabi, the boatman:
"Urshanabi, this plant is a plant apart,
Whereby a man may regain his life's breath.
I will take it to ramparted Uruk, (280)
Will cause . . . to eat the plant . . . !
Its name shall be 'Man Becomes Young in Old Age.'
I myself shall eat it
And thus return to the state of my youth."
After twenty leagues they broke off a morsel,
After thirty further leagues they prepared for the night.
Gilgamesh saw a well whose water was cool.
He went down into it to bathe in the water.
A serpent snuffed the fragrance of the plant;
It came up from the water and carried off the plant.
Going back it shed its slough.

Thereupon Gilgamesh sits down and weeps, (290)
His tears running down over his face.
He took the hand of Urshanabi, the boatman:
"For whom, Urshanabi, have my hands toiled?
For whom is being spent the blood of my heart?
I have not obtained a boon for myself.
For the earth-lion have I effected a boon!
And now the tide will bear it twenty leagues away!
When I opened the water-pipe and . . . the year,

*The opening of the pipe apparently took place in connection with Gilgamesh's dive (cf. also below, line 298). But the details remain obscure. In the *Eridu Creation Story* [another ancient Mesopotamian text], the same term is used, perhaps for a pipe connecting with a source of sweet waters which would nourish the miraculous plant.

I found that which has been placed as a sign for me: I shall withdraw,
And leave the boat on the shore!" (300)
After twenty leagues they broke off a morsel,
After thirty further leagues they prepared for the night.
When they arrived in ramparted Uruk,
Gilgamesh says to him, to Urshanabi, the boatman:
"Go up, Urshanabi, walk on the ramparts of Uruk.
Inspect the base terrace, examine its brickwork,
If its brickwork is not of burnt brick,
And if the Seven Wise Ones laid not its foundation!
One sar is city,* one sar orchards,
One sar margin land; further the precinct of the Temple of Ishtar.
Three sar and the precinct comprise Uruk."

Tablet XII

(Contents and circumstantial evidence mark this tablet as an inorganic appendage to the epic proper. The basic theme is concluded with the hero's failure to attain his quest. Moreover, the last lines of Tablet XI are the same as the final lines of the introduction to the entire work [I, i, 16–19]. . . . The Akkadian Version of the present tablet is a translation of the second part of a Sumerian legend. The first part—disregarded by the Akkadian translator—is fortunately extant. . . . Since the beginning is essential as an introduction to Tablet XII, it may be summarized briefly, as follows:

Shortly after the creation of the universe, a tree growing on the bank of the Euphrates was uprooted by the south wind. Inanna [Ishtar] took the floating trunk and planted it in her garden in Uruk. She intended to use it, in due time, as timber for her bed and chair. When several hostile beings interfered with Inanna's plan, Gilgamesh came to her rescue. In gratitude, Inanna made from the base of the tree a pukku, *probably a magic Drum, and from the crown a* mikkū, *apparently a Drumstick of similar magic potency, and gave them both to Gilgamesh. One day both these precious objects fell into the nether world. Gilgamesh sought to retrieve them but could not. Lamenting his loss, he cried "O my* pukku, *O my* mikkū." *It is at this point that the Akkadian translation, known to us as Tablet XII, sets in, a fact witnessed by the catch-line at the end of Tablet XI. . . .)*

"That time when I verily had the Drum in the carpenter's house,
When the carpenter's wife was verily like my mother who bore me,
When the carpenter's daughter was verily like my younger sister!
Lo, who will bring up the Drum from the nether world?"
Who will bring up the Drumstick from the nether world?
Enkidu says to him, to Gilgamesh, his lord:
"My lord, why criest thou and why is so ill thy heart?
Lo, I will bring up the Drum from the nether world,
I will bring up the Drumstick from the nether world."
Gilgamesh says to him, to Enkidu, his servant: (10)
"If thou wilt go down to the nether world,
I will speak a word to thee, take my word;
My admonitions heed thou well:
Clean raiment thou shalt not put on!
As a sojourner they would mark thee.
With sweet oil from the cruse thou shalt not anoint thee!
At its fragrance they would gather about thee.

*[The *sar,* again, is the number 3,600. Some unit of area must be understood with it here.]

A throw stick into the nether world thou shalt not hurl!
Those struck with the throw stick would surround thee.
A staff into thy hands thou shalt not take! (20)
The spirits would tremble on thy account.
Sandals to thy feet thou shalt not fasten,
A sound against the nether world thou shalt not make,
Thy wife whom thou lovest thou shalt not kiss,
Thy wife whom thou hatest thou shalt not strike,
Thy son whom thou lovest thou shalt not kiss,
Thy son whom thou hatest thou shalt not strike!
The wailing of the nether world would seize thee!"—
"She who rests, she who rests,
The mother of Ninazu, she who rests;
Her holy shoulders are not covered with raiment, (30)
Her cruse-shaped breasts are not wrapped with cloth."
To his lord's admonitions Enkidu gave no heed.
He put on clean raiment:
They marked him as a sojourner.
With sweet oil from the cruse he anointed himself:
At the fragrance of it they gathered about him.
He hurled the throw stick into the nether world:
Those struck with the throw stick surrounded him.
A staff he took into his hand:
The spirits trembled on his account.
Sandals to his feet he fastened, (40)
A sound against the nether world he made,
He kissed his beloved wife,
He struck his hated wife,
He kissed his beloved son,
He struck his hated son:
The wailing of the nether world seized him.
"She who rests, she who rests,
The mother of Ninazu, she who rests;
Her holy shoulders are not covered with raiment,
Her cruse-shaped breasts are not wrapped with cloth."
She allowed not Enkidu to ascend from the nether world. (50)
Namtar did not seize him, Fever did not seize him;
The nether world seized him.
Nergal's unsparing deputy did not seize him;
The nether world seized him.
On the battlefield of men he did not fall;
The nether world seized him!
Then my lord, the son of Ninsun,
Weeping over Enkidu, his servant,
Went all alone to Ekur, the temple of Enlil:
"Father Enlil, lo, my Drum fell into the nether world,
My Drumstick fell into the nether world;
Namtar did not seize him, Fever did not seize him;
The nether world seized him.
Nergal's unsparing deputy did not seize him; (60)
The nether world seized him.
On the battlefield of men he did not fall;
The nether world seized him!"
Father Enlil did not intercede for him in the matter;
To Ur he went:
"Father Sin, lo, my Drum fell into the nether world,
My Drumstick fell into the nether world.
Enkidu, whom I sent to bring them up, the nether world seized.
Namtar did not seize him, Fever did not seize him;
The nether world seized him.
Nergal's unsparing deputy did not seize him;
The nether world seized him.
On the battlefield of men he did not fall;

The nether world seized him!"
Father Sin did not intercede for him in the matter;
To Eridu he went:
"Father Ea, lo, my Drum fell into the nether world, (70)
My Drumstick fell into the nether world.
Enkidu, whom I sent to bring them up, the nether world seized.
Namtar did not seize him, Fever did not seize him;
The nether world seized him.
Nergal's unsparing deputy did not seize him;
The nether world seized him.
On the battlefield of men he did not fall;
The nether world seized him!"
Father Ea did intercede for him in the matter.
He said to Nergal, the valiant hero:
"O valiant hero, Nergal . . . ,
Open forthwith a hole in the earth,
That the spirit of Enkidu may issue forth from the nether world, (80)
That to his brother he might tell the ways of the nether world."
Nergal, the valiant hero, hearkened to Ea,
Scarcely had he opened a hole in the earth,
When the spirit of Enkidu, like a wind-puff,
Issued forth from the nether world.
They embraced and kissed each other.
They exchanged counsel, sighing at each other:
"Tell me, my friend, tell me, my friend,
Tell me the order of the nether world which thou hast seen."
"I shall not tell thee, I shall not tell thee!
But if I tell thee the order of the nether world which I have seen, (90)
Sit thou down and weep!"
". . . I will sit down and weep."
"My body . . . , which thou didst touch as thy heart rejoiced,
Vermin devour as though an old garment.
My body . . . , which thou didst touch as thy heart rejoiced,
. . . is filled with dust."
He cried "Woe!" and threw himself in the dust,
Gilgamesh cried "Woe!" and threw himself in the dust.
" . . . has thou seen?" "I have seen."

(The text here is mutilated or lost, except for the following fragment:)

" . . . ?" "I have seen: (2′)
. . . weeps over it."
" . . . ?" "I have seen:
. . . eats bread."
" . . . ?" "I have seen:
. . . drinks water."
" . . . hast thou seen?" "I have seen:
. . . his heart rejoices."
" . . . hast thou seen?" "I have seen: (10′)
Like that of a good scribe is his arm bared.
. . . he enters the palace."
" . . . hast thou seen?" "I have seen:
Like a beautiful standard. . . ."
. . . . (119–44)
"Him who fell down from the mast hast thou seen?"
"I have seen:
Scarcely . . . the pegs are pulled out."
"Him who died a sudden death hast thou seen?"
"I have seen:
He lies upon the night couch and drinks pure water."
"Him who was killed in battle hast thou seen?"
"I have seen:
His father and his mother raise up his head, (150)
And his wife weeps over him."
"Him whose corpse was cast out upon the steppe hast thou seen?"
"I have seen:
His spirit finds no rest in the nether world."
"Him whose spirit has no one to tend it hast thou seen?"
"I have seen:
Lees of the pot, crumbs of bread, offals of the street he eats."

Ancient Nineveh at night. The surviving version of the *Gilgamesh* epic, translated into Akkadian, was found with the excavations of Nineveh, where the remains of the great library of Assurbanipal, king of the Assyrians, were discovered.

Glossary

Names which appear only once and are sufficiently defined in the text are omitted from this glossary.

Adad. The rain god.

Anu. God of the sky, father of the gods.

Anunnaki. Offspring of Anu who reigned in the nether world as judges of the dead.

Apsu. The fresh underground waters that fathered Ea.

Aruru. Goddess of the stony, rocky ground; goddess of birth.

Atrahasis. "Exceeding Wise," an epithet of Utnapishtim.

Ea. God of the sweet, fresh waters in the earth, known for his cleverness. Probably one of Anu's children.

Eanna. The temple of Anu and Ishtar in Uruk.

Enkidu. A wild man created by the goddess Aruru out of clay. He was made in order to contend with Gilgamesh but instead became his friend and companion.

Enlil. God of winds and agriculture, creator of the hoe.

Ennuge. God of irrigation; inspector of canals.

Ereshkigal. Also called Irkalla. Queen of the nether world and sister of Ishtar.

Eridu. City on the Persian Gulf which had a great temple to Ea.

Erragal. See *Nergal.*

Etana. King of Kish (a city constantly at war with Uruk), who was carried to heaven by an eagle.

Gilgamesh. Hero of the epic; son of the goddess Ninsunna and fifth king of Uruk after the Flood.

Hanish. With Shullat, one of the divine heralds of storm and bad weather.

Hubaba. Assyrian form of Huwawa.

Huwawa. Divinely appointed guardian of the Cedar Forest.

Igigi. The gods of the heavens.

Irkalla. Another name for Ereshkigal.

Ishhara. A form of Ishtar.

Ishtar. Powerful goddess of love and fertility; also goddess of war. Daughter of Sin.

Lugalbanda. Husband to Ninsunna, Gilgamesh's mother. A king of Uruk, a god, and a shepherd; himself the hero of a cycle of Sumerian poems.

Namtar. The god of plague and death.

Nergal. Also called Erragal. Underworld god with the power of life and death. Sometimes appears as the husband of Ereshkigal.

Ninazu. "Water sprinkler," husband of Ereshkigal.

Ninigiku-Ea. Epithet of Ea.

Ninsun. Variant form of Ninsunna.

Ninsunna. A minor goddess noted for wisdom. Mother of Gilgamesh and wife of the legendary hero Lugalbanda.

Ninurta. God of thunderstorms, floods, and the plough. One of Enlil's sons.

Nisaba. Goddess of grain.

Shamash. Also Utu-Shamash. The sun god and judge of the gods. Husband and brother of Ishtar.

Shullat. With Hanish, one of the divine heralds of storm and bad weather.

Shurippak. One of the oldest Mesopotamian cities. Home of Utnapishtim before the Flood. (Var.: Shuruppak)

Siduri. The divine wine-maker and brewer. Possibly a form of Ishtar.

Sin. The moon god. Father of Shamash and Ishtar, son of Enlil.

Sumuqan. God of cattle.

Sursunabu. The boatman who ferries daily across the Waters of Death. Sumerian Urshanabi.

Ubar-Tutu. A king of Shurippak, one of the oldest cities in Mesopotamia. Utnapishtim's father.

Ur. One of the most important ancient Mesopotamian cities.

Urshanabi. See *Sursunabu.*

Uruk. Ancient Mesopotamian city ruled by a succession of kings, of which Gilgamesh was the fifth.

Utanapishtim. Assyrian form of Utnapishtim.

Utnapishtim. The Mesopotamian hero of the Flood. After the Flood the gods granted immortality to him and his wife.

Utu-Shamash. See *Shamash.*

Matter and Motion

James Clerk Maxwell

MANUALS OF ELEMENTARY SCIENCE.

MATTER AND MOTION.

BY

J. CLERK MAXWELL,

M.A., LL.D. Edin., F.R.SS. L. & E.,

Honorary Fellow of Trinity College, and Professor of Experimental Physics in the University of Cambridge.

PUBLISHED UNDER THE DIRECTION OF THE COMMITTEE OF GENERAL LITERATURE AND EDUCATION, APPOINTED BY THE SOCIETY FOR PROMOTING CHRISTIAN KNOWLEDGE.

LONDON:
SOCIETY FOR PROMOTING CHRISTIAN KNOWLEDGE;
SOLD AT THE DEPOSITORIES:
77, GREAT QUEEN STREET, LINCOLN'S INN FIELDS;
4, ROYAL EXCHANGE; 48, PICCADILLY;
AND BY ALL BOOKSELLERS.

NEW YORK: POTT, YOUNG & CO.

1876.

Editor's Introduction

Most of what is required to be said about James Clerk Maxwell is said by Mr. Simpson elsewhere in these pages, writing on both Maxwell's *Treatise on Electricity and Magnetism* and, immediately following this introduction, on his *Matter and Motion,* which is thereafter reprinted.

Some biographical details are nevertheless appropriate to add. Maxwell, who became by general consent the greatest mathematical physicist of his time (1831–79), and who probably ranks, with those who keep score in such matters, second only to Newton in the magnitude of his theoretical insights into science, was born in Scotland, the son of a well-off countryman who sent him to school in Edinburgh, as well as to the university there. At the age of nineteen—when he was already the author of two papers published by the Royal Society of Edinburgh, one of them a fully worked theory of photoelastic stress having to do with color vision (Newton also, it will be recalled, began as a student of optics)—he went on to Cambridge. There at Trinity College in 1854 he narrowly missed being senior wrangler in the mathematical tripos, arguably the most difficult examination of its kind in the world at that time (its kind including a great deal of physics, by the way, along with mathematics), and graduated overall with high honors.

Maxwell could probably have had a fellowship with such a record, but he preferred returning home to his father, a widower, of whom he was particularly fond, and took an appointment at a college in Aberdeen. However, in 1860, when he failed to receive the professorship he wanted at the University of Edinburgh, he accepted an offer from King's College, London, where over the next five years he accomplished some of his best work. Among his productions were papers on the kinetic theory of gases (leading eventually to the book called *Theory of Heat,* published in 1877) and on physical lines of force, which of course was prefatory to his eventual magnum opus, *A Treatise on Electricity and Magnetism* (1873).

His debt to Michael Faraday, who is in some sense the spirit of this great work, in which he has somewhat the position that Socrates has in the dialogues of Plato, is indicated in these pages by Mr. Simpson, as indeed it was acknowledged with entire generosity by Maxwell himself. He had become familiar with Faraday's *Experimental Researches in Electricity* (*GBWW,* Vol. 45) while at Cambridge, and he had delivered a paper, "On Faraday's Lines of Force," to the Cambridge Philosophical Society within two years of his graduation.

Aware as he was that Faraday knew no mathematics, yet convinced that his scientific insights were fundamentally correct, Maxwell had resolved, as he said, that before he began the study of electricity, he would "read no mathematics on the subject" until he had read Faraday's account of his experiments. "As I proceeded with the study of Faraday," he went on, "I perceived that his method of conceiving the phenomena was also a mathematical one, though not exhibited in the conventional form of mathematical symbols." To which he added that he had "also found that these methods were capable of being expressed in the ordinary mathematical forms, and thus compared with those of the professed mathematicians."

His own work then became, as he indicated, and as Mr. Simpson explains in detail, a kind of translation of Faraday's work into mathematical terms, retaining, however, Faraday's conception of physics as against that of the conventional mathematicians of the day.

Of course Maxwell, because he did know mathematics, went further than Faraday in establishing the connection between electricity and magnetism, so far, indeed, that he exceeded the state of experimental research in that day. Hence the *Treatise* came to be regarded, ironically, as having chiefly a kind of speculative, merely mathematical, importance.

Not until Hertz verified experimentally Maxwell's predictions as to field theory was the magnitude of his work fully appreciated. Indeed it is Hertz (who—also ironically—was interested only in Maxwell's equations, not in Faraday's ways of looking at things), who created Maxwell's reputation as perhaps the foremost theoretician of the age. His stature was subsequently recognized also by Einstein, who called his equations "the most important event in physics since Newton's time."

Matter and Motion, to which Mr. Simpson has kindly provided an introduction that appears immediately following these remarks, was published in 1877 as an effort to explain, in as nontechnical manner as possible, the conception of physics, and indeed of all science, at which Maxwell by then had arrived—a conception in which the field, as distinct from particular bodies, had become the organizing element. It was written while Maxwell was working as director of the Cavendish Laboratory at Cambridge, which at its inception (1871) he had been asked to design, and which he created as one of the great institutions of its kind in the world. It was shortly after *Matter and Motion* appeared that Maxwell, while still director of this laboratory, became ill and died at the early age of forty-seven.

Following *Matter and Motion* in this volume will be found reprints of three short papers by Maxwell, each of which has some bearing on the positions taken by him in the works under discussion here. The papers are, in order, "Are There Real Analogies in Nature?" from Lewis Campbell and William Garnett, *The Life of James Clerk Maxwell,* 2nd ed. (London: Macmillan and Co., 1884), pp. 348–55; "On Action at a Distance," reprinted in W. D. Niven, editor, *The Scientific Papers of James Clerk Maxwell,* 2 vols. (New York: Dover Publications, 1952), Vol. II, pp. 311–23; and "Ether," from the *Encyclopædia Britannica,* 9th ed., Vol. VIII, pp. 568–72.

In these papers some footnotes have been eliminated, and the names only of the most important figures cited by Maxwell have been editorially identified. "Are There Real Analogies in Nature?" was one of a number of essays written by Maxwell for the "Apostles" Club at Cambridge University between 1853 and 1856 and is regarded as a serious exposition of his views on certain philosophical questions. "On Action at a Distance" appeared originally in the Proceedings of the Royal Institution of Great Britain, to whose members it was addressed.

On *Matter and Motion,* by Thomas K. Simpson

Maxwell's little book *Matter and Motion* is of the sort that is easily overlooked. It is brief, modest, and admittedly "elementary"; at first scanning, it seems not to get very far with the subject of mechanics. There are few equations, it is not replete with illustrations or examples, and there are no worked problems. It is also well over a century out of date. In sum, then, it seems at best the kind of introductory text one might recommend to a beginner whose ultimate ambitions lay in other directions.

The error entailed in such a judgment has to do, I suspect, with our understanding of the term *elementary.* In ordinary parlance the word suggests the superficial, the simplified—something watered down for beginners. Though Maxwell certainly is aiming his book at beginners, I think he has the opposite notion of what is elementary, or what it might mean to place ourselves at the threshold of a science. The elements of a science lie not on its surface but in its depths. They are few, and in a sense uncomplicated, and in that respect they are appropriate for beginners: indeed, beginners may be in a better position to appreciate them than experts, whose long experience with complexities often makes the simplest things invisible.

Maxwell is evidently concerned, himself, with the foundations of this science of mechanics, and he seems to enjoy taking his case for their reformulation, not to his fellow scientists, but to the workingman. Maxwell taught over the years in classes of adult education, and this little treatise, as the title page tells us, was published by the Committee of General Literature and Education of the Society for Promoting Christian Knowledge. As I discuss elsewhere in this issue of *The Great Ideas Today,* Maxwell was greatly drawn to the figure of Michael Faraday, a brilliantly productive scientist who was innocent of any knowledge of mathematics beyond the operations of arithmetic. It seems important to Maxwell to be able to express the outcome of sophisticated mathematical investigations in plain prose, "forms of words," as he says, which can be understood by the unmathematical reader.

At the time *Matter and Motion* was published, Maxwell was heavily engaged in a new enterprise at Cambridge University. He had recently been appointed the university's first professor of experimental physics; he was launching the new Cavendish Laboratory, and in connection with this assignment he was giving lectures on mechanics, electricity and magnetism, and heat to students who were not skilled in mathematics. This was a sharp turn for him from his own background, for as a student at Cambridge he had taken honors in the "mathematical" examinations, which in fact covered much of the mathematical physics of the day, and he had only recently published his *Treatise on Electricity and Magnetism* and a text for Cambridge students who were studying that subject within the context of a severe discipline in analytic mathematics. In his lectures at the Cavendish, then, Maxwell was regularly translating his mathematical ideas into new nonmathematical formulations, using models, illustrative experiments, and careful prose. Out of this was coming his *Elementary Treatise in Electricity and Magnetism,* which very unfortunately he did not complete before his death. I presume the present *Matter and Motion* represents the kind of foundation he was laying in mechanics for his nonmathematical Cambridge students. Maxwell makes it clear that he himself prefers this *elementary* mode of presentation; he does not think of it as intellectually inferior or inappropriate to the subject.

It is evident that Maxwell approaches the foundations of mechanics with the spirit of a reformer. Not only does he set out to purge certain important errors, but even in a science as old and established as mechanics, he sees a new kind of possibility which will come with a reformation of the elements. The beginning students, then, immediately find themselves caught up in a workshop in which the most fundamental of the physical sciences is undergoing reconstruction. The reader of *Matter and Motion* is in a specially privileged position, joining with Maxwell in reshaping the first of the sciences.

Certainly *Matter and Motion* is unlike other elementary texts, of

Maxwell's time or ours. The reader is in a sense given no quarter but taken straight to the heart of the difficulty. There is no preliminary *terra firma* in Maxwell's book: we don't begin with "simple" cases, in which a stone stands firmly on the ground and a lever is applied to it, or a ball is dropped from a given height at a given time, to fall a specified distance. Instead, from the outset we find ourselves dealing with systems of bodies, whose positions are defined, not with respect to a fixed earth, but in relation to one another. Such a system, we are told, may be small or it may be the whole universe. The term *configuration* is introduced immediately thereafter, very abstractly, as "the assemblage of relative positions."

Two themes are thus introduced in full earnestness from the beginning: that of the wholeness of a *system* of bodies, the whole to be treated as an entity prior to the separate consideration of its parts; and that of the relativity of all of our accounts of physical systems. Without arguing that *Matter and Motion* itself had any particular influence, we can see that it stands at a historical turning point in physics, and that it very consciously is transforming the foundations of mechanics. The new concept which has made it possible to take the system as the object of scientific reasoning is that of *energy*, with the principle of its conservation. The principle of relativity, which in *Matter and Motion* goes hand in hand with that of the wholeness of the system, Maxwell probably takes more directly from metaphysical convictions.

It is important to Maxwell to make clear that this is a treatise not about physics but about abstract dynamics, that is, a science of axiomatic principles and their consequences, to be contrasted with physics, which takes observed phenomena into consideration. Throughout *Matter and Motion*, Maxwell dwells on consideration of our most fundamental ideas: ideas of time, of space, of matter, force, and energy. They are the subject matter of this treatise, and one of its major concerns is to reshape, clarify, and purify these ideas and the science based on them. Thus, it is not at all inappropriate that in Article 15 he explicitly turns to "a few points relating to the metaphysics" of the subject of space. In so doing, he joins issue with Descartes in a way which might suggest not only his disagreement but a deeper affinity of purpose. Descartes, Maxwell goes on to say in Article 16, was very wrong about the definition of matter, not having understood its identification with the principle of inertia, and hence was in turn wrong about the idea of space. Matter, Maxwell insists, is one thing, space, another—Descartes had in effect identified them.

With this fundamental correction, however, I think Maxwell comes close to pursuing the Cartesian goal of a study of mechanics from the point of view of thought alone: in abstract dynamics we are dealing with pure concepts. Thus the Cartesian title, alluding to the two principles of the Cartesian account of the physical world, is telling us where Maxwell stands. Whereas Newtonian *forces* must be expressed between specific bodies, it is possible to work with the *energy* of an entire system as a whole. Each configuration of a conservative system will correspond to a definite energy, and from state to state of such a system we will pass through definite energy changes. In these terms, dynamics can mount to the higher ground of the "configuration" and characterize systems of wholes and their relationships as its primary concern. Thus Maxwell points out that where Newton spoke of a "force" of one body on another, the larger view is that of "stress," which sees the relativity of the two bodies in their mutuality.

All this takes us, however, directly to what is probably the central thesis of *Matter and Motion,* surely a powerful insight into the central problem of dynamics as well as the future course of physics: the principle of relativity. Maxwell is unyielding on this concept, which he sees as belonging to our ideas themselves, not as contingent upon the phenomena of the world. Our common words seem to speak of absolutes, and to make a distinction between, for example, "relative" and "absolute" space. But for Maxwell it is a fundamental, metaphysical truth that "All our knowledge, both of time and place, is essentially relative" (art. 18).

Maxwell must feel, then, that Newton was on the wrong track in "conceiving" absolute time and space as the foundations of the mathematical theory of mechanics, and then recognizing by contrast that phenomenal time and space are relative. Rather, the foundations of dynamics must speak of these concepts as *inherently* relativistic. Einstein, not Maxwell, carries this through to completion for both space and time; but Maxwell here certainly defines the task.

One way to present such a relativistic view of a system to the mind of the reader is by way of a diagram, and for Maxwell the notion of a diagram as a representation of a physical system is very important. As scientific editor of the Ninth Edition of the *Encyclopædia Britannica,* he introduced an article, which he wrote himself, on "Diagrams"—a topic that would not have occurred to most editors. There are many instances of diagrams in *Matter and Motion,* because they express both our knowledge and its limitations in a single image. Maxwell gives us diagrams, not only of the positions of systems of bodies, but of displacements, velocities, and accelerations. The important thing about his diagrams is that they have no origins—that is, they do not locate their points with respect to a supposed coordinate system: there is no frame of reference. Points are located and move and accelerate only with respect of one another:

> This diagram of displacements (without an origin) will then represent neither more nor less than all we can ever know about the displacement of the system (art. 22).

If Maxwell is to remain true to the principle of relativity as he states it, the difficulty is not that we are doomed to ignorance, but that position and displacement are *inherently* relative: there is, in truth, no origin.

In Article 29 of *Matter and Motion,* Maxwell presents the diagrams of position and velocity in a way that dramatizes, I believe, his insight concerning relativity. The diagram of position is rightly labeled "Diagram of Configuration," since in a sense *position* would suggest absolute location, whereas the term *con-figuration* expresses immediately the fact that the only "figure" that emerges is a pattern of points relative to one another. Maxwell has presented this diagram of configuration, not only without an origin, but printed as bright dots on a black field, so that not even the paper appears to us as *terra firma;* the bodies which make up a system appear naked, like points of light in the night sky. Between them there are no absolute measures of distance any more than there are in the cosmos.

The transformed dynamics that emerges from the pages of *Matter and Motion* is not a mere structure of thought but a working instrument at the cutting edge of science—these dynamic ideas are, Maxwell says, "scientific," i.e., science-*making*. The reader in effect is invited to stand with Maxwell at the borders of the unknown, and to survey with him the terrain which lies beyond. Ultimately, Maxwell perceives that a completed dynamics would be coextensive with the whole of physical science, projected into "dynamical form."

Maxwell refers the reader to the efforts he is currently making to accomplish this dynamical theory in the realm of electromagnetism, in his *Treatise on Electricity and Magnetism* (1873). The dynamical approach brings to each physical problem only the conviction that it can be described in the abstract terms of dynamics; it is thus the minimal, and hence safest, hypothesis. Maxwell sees, as well, in Article 148, its promise for molecular physics.

One problem, however, constitutes the burden of the latter part of the book: the problem of the aether. Maxwell says, "Energy cannot exist except in connection with matter." But energy, in the form of light and heat, traverses the space between the sun and the earth. Hence, there must be matter "existing in the interplanetary spaces" and, in fact, "disseminated through the whole of the visible universe (art. 108). This "matter," the "aether," cannot be gravitational in proportion to its mass. Yet Newton, by means of experiments reported in the *Principia,* demonstrated that *all* matter exerts a gravitational force corresponding to its mass. Beginning with Chapter VII, Maxwell therefore very carefully reviews the theory of the pendulum and its application to the measurement of the gravitational constant. In Chapter VIII he concludes, notwithstanding the experimental evidence, that "it is still extremely doubtful whether the medium of light and electricity is a gravitating substance, though it is certainly material and has mass" (art.

145). The implicit question, standing as it does simply as an enigma, in effect sets the stage for much of the physics of the twentieth century.

In reflecting on the relation between *Matter and Motion* and the physics of the twentieth century, it is important to recall the breadth of Maxwell's claim for the inherent relativity of the concepts of time and space. It is sometimes supposed that Maxwell, in searching for that matter which conveyed the energies of light and electricity, hoped to find an absolute reference frame and thereby escape the implications of relativity. Maxwell makes clear in this text, I believe, that his sense of relativity cuts much deeper than that:

> To discover the existence of a medium, and to determine our velocity with respect to it by observation on the motion of bodies, is a legitimate scientific inquiry, but supposing all this done we should have discovered, not an error in the laws of motion, but a new fact in science (art. 48).

Motion relative to an aether would then be an important *physical* fact, but it would not alter the foundations of dynamics. Those are relativistic in their very conception. As I conclude in an article elsewhere in this volume, Maxwell would, then, remain a relativist even in the face of the discovery of a universal aether. The insights of this little "elementary" treatise cut very deep.

Matter and Motion

Contents

Chapter I. Introduction

Article 1. Nature of physical science

Physical science is that department of knowledge which relates to the order of nature, or, in other words, to the regular succession of events.

The name of physical science, however, is often applied in a more or less restricted manner to those branches of science in which the phenomena considered are of the simplest and most abstract kind, excluding the consideration of the more complex phenomena, such as those observed in living beings.

The simplest case of all is that in which an event or phenomenon can be described as a change in the arrangement of certain bodies. Thus the motion of the moon may be described by stating the changes in her position relative to the earth in the order in which they follow one another.

In other cases we may know that some change of arrangement has taken place, but we may not be able to ascertain what that change is.

Thus when water freezes we know that the molecules or smallest parts of the substance must be arranged differently in ice and in water. We also know that this arrangement in ice must have a certain kind of symmetry, because the ice is in the form of symmetrical crystals, but we have as yet no precise knowledge of the actual arrangement of the molecules in ice. But whenever we can completely describe the change of arrangement we have a knowledge, perfect so far as it extends, of what has taken place, though we may still have to learn the necessary conditions under which a similar event will always take place.

Hence the first part of physical science

relates to the relative position and motion of bodies.

Article 2. Definition of a material system

In all scientific procedure we begin by marking out a certain region or subject as the field of our investigations. To this we must confine our attention, leaving the rest of the universe out of account till we have completed the investigation in which we are engaged. In physical science, therefore, the first step is to define clearly the material system which we make the subject of our statements. This system may be of any degree of complexity. It may be a single material particle, a body of finite size, or any number of such bodies, and it may even be extended so as to include the whole material universe.

Article 3. Definition of internal and external

All relations or actions between one part of this system and another are called *internal* relations or actions.

Those between the whole or any part of the system and bodies not included in the system are called *external* relations or actions. These we study only so far as they affect the system itself, leaving their effect on external bodies out of consideration. Relations and actions between bodies not included in the system are to be left out of consideration. We cannot investigate them except by making our system include these other bodies.

Article 4. Definition of configuration

When a material system is considered with respect to the relative position of its parts, the assemblage of relative positions is called the *configuration* of the system.

A knowledge of the configuration of the system at a given instant implies a knowledge of the position of every point of the system with respect to every other point at that instant.

Article 5. Diagrams

The configuration of material systems may be represented in models, plans, or diagrams. The model or diagram is supposed to resemble the material system only in form, not necessarily in any other respect.

A plan or a map represents on paper in two dimensions what may really be in three dimensions and can only be completely represented by a model. We shall use the term *diagram* to signify any geometrical figure, whether plane or not, by means of which we study the properties of a material system. Thus, when we speak of the configuration of a system, the image which we form in our minds is that of a diagram, which completely represents the configuration, but which has none of the other properties of the material system. Besides diagrams of configuration we may have diagrams of velocity, of stress, etc., which do not represent the form of the system, but by means of which its relative velocities or its internal forces may be studied.

Article 6. A material particle

A body so small that, *for the purposes of our investigation,* the distances between its different parts may be neglected, is called a *material particle.*

Thus in certain astronomical investigations the planets, and even the sun, may be regarded each as a material particle, because the difference of the actions of different parts of these bodies does not come under our notice. But we cannot treat them as material particles when we investigate their rotation. Even an atom, when we consider it as capable of rotation, must be regarded as consisting of many material particles.

The diagram of a material particle is of course a mathematical point, which has no configuration.

Article 7. Relative position of two material particles

The diagram of two material particles consists of two points, as, for instance, A and B.

The position of B relative to A is indicated by the direction and length of the straight line $\overline{AB}$ drawn *from A to B*. If you start from A and travel in the direction indicated by the line $\overline{AB}$ and for a distance equal to the length of that line, you will get to B. This direction and distance may be indicated equally well by any other line, such as $\overline{ab}$, which is parallel and equal to $\overline{AB}$. The position of A with respect to B is indicated by the direction and length of the line $\overline{BA}$, drawn *from B to A*, or the line $\overline{ba}$, equal and parallel to $\overline{BA}$.

It is evident that $\overline{BA} = -\overline{AB}$.

In naming a line by the letters at its extremities, the order of the letters is always that in which the line is to be drawn.

Article 8. Vectors*

The expression $\overline{AB}$, in geometry, is merely the name of a line. Here it indicates the operation by which the line is drawn, that of carrying a tracing point in a certain direction for a certain distance. As indicating an operation, $\overline{AB}$ is called a *vector*, and the operation is completely defined by the direction and distance of the transference. The starting point, which is called the *origin* of the vector, may be anywhere.

To define a finite straight line we must state its origin as well as its direction and length. All vectors, however, are regarded as equal which are parallel (and drawn toward the same parts) and of the same magnitude.

Any quantity, such, for instance, as a velocity or a force, which has a definite direction and a definite magnitude may be treated as a vector and may be indicated in a diagram by a straight line whose direction is parallel to the vector, and whose length represents, according to a determinate scale, the magnitude of the vector.

Article 9. System of three particles

Let us next consider a system of three particles.

Its configuration is represented by a diagram of three points, A, B, C.

Figure 1

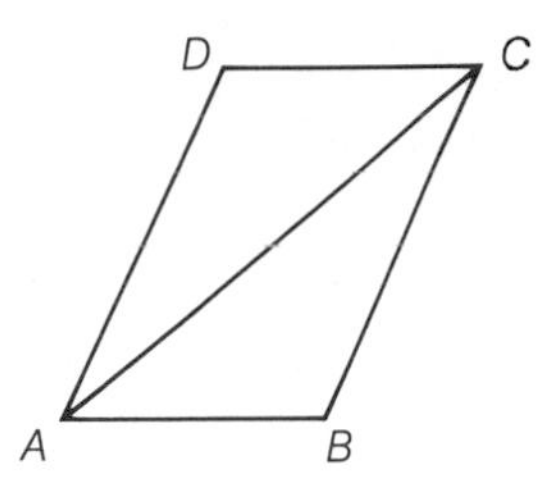

The position of B with respect to A is indicated by the vector $\overline{AB}$, and that of C with respect to B by the vector $\overline{BC}$.

It is manifest that from these data, when A is known we can find B and then C, so that the configuration of the three points is completely determined.

The position of C with respect to A is indicated by the vector $\overline{AC}$, and by the last remark the value of $\overline{AC}$ must be deducible from those of $\overline{AB}$ and $\overline{BC}$.

*[In reading *Matter and Motion,* we are sharing Maxwell's thinking at a time when the concepts of the vector and vector notation were still in the process of taking form. The editors have therefore chosen to follow Maxwell's own notation as reflected in the first edition of *Matter and Motion* as closely as possible, denoting a line segment representing a vector, for example, as in this section, by a bar printed over the letter pair: $\overline{AB}$, rather than by any more modern notation. In this, Maxwell's text has been followed rigorously except in cases which seem to be unambiguous instances of oversight in the first edition.]

The result of the operation $\overline{AC}$ is to carry the tracing point from A to C. But the result is the same if the tracing point is carried first from A to B and then from B to C, and this is the sum of the operations $\overline{AB} + \overline{BC}$.

Article 10. Addition of vectors

Hence the rule for the addition of vectors may be stated thus: From any point as origin draw the successive vectors in series, so that each vector begins at the end of the preceding one. The straight line from the origin to the extremity of the series represents the vector which is the sum of the vectors.

The order of addition is indifferent; for if we write $\overline{BC} + \overline{AB}$ the operation indicated may be performed by drawing $\overline{AD}$ parallel and equal to $\overline{BC}$, and then joining $\overline{DC}$, which, by Euclid, I. 33, is parallel and equal to $\overline{AB}$, so that by these two operations we arrive at the point C in whichever order we perform them.

The same is true for any number of vectors, take them in what order we please.

Article 11. Subtraction of one vector from another

To express the position of C with respect to B in terms of the positions of B and C with respect to A, we observe that we can get from B to C either by passing along the straight line BC or by passing from B to A and then from A to C. Hence

$\overline{BC} = \overline{BA} + \overline{AC}$.

$= \overline{AC} + \overline{BA}$ since the order of addition is is different.

$= \overline{AC} - \overline{AB}$ since $\overline{AB}$ is equal and opposite to $\overline{BA}$.

Or the vector $\overline{BC}$, which expresses the position of C with respect to B, is found by subtracting the vector of B from the vector of C, these vectors being drawn to B and C respectively from any common origin A.

Article 12. Origin of vectors

The positions of any number of particles belonging to a material system may be defined by means of the vectors drawn to each of these particles from some one point. This point is called the origin of the vectors, or, more briefly, the origin.

This system of vectors determines the configuration of the whole system; for if we wish to know the position of any point B with respect to any other point A, it may be found from the vectors $\overline{OA}$ and $\overline{OB}$ by the equation

$$\overline{AB} = \overline{OB} - \overline{OA}.$$

We may choose any point whatever for the origin, and there is for the present no reason why we should choose one point rather than another. The configuration of the system—that is to say, the position of its parts with respect to each other—remains the same, whatever point be chosen as origin. Many inquiries, however, are simplified by a proper selection of the origin.

Article 13. Relative position of two systems

If the configurations of two different systems are known, each system having its own origin, and if we then wish to include both systems in a larger system, having, say, the same origin as the first of the two systems, we must ascertain the position of the origin of the second system with re-

Figure 2

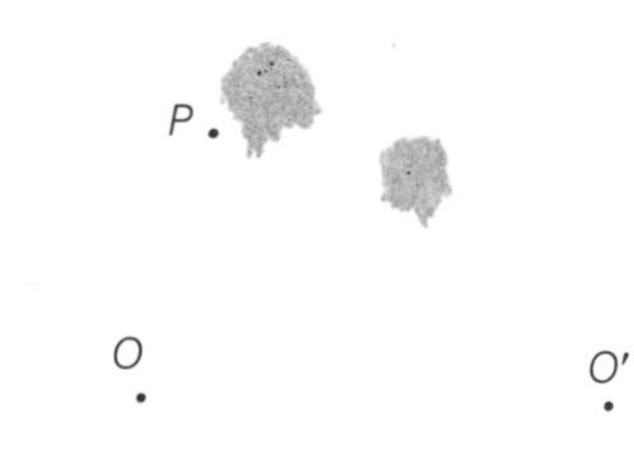

spect to that of the first, and we must be able to draw lines in the second system parallel to those in the first.

Then, by Article 9, the position of a point P of the second system, with respect to the first origin, O, is represented by the sum of the vector $\overline{OP}$ of that point with respect to the second origin, O' and the vector $\overline{OO'}$ of the second origin, O' with respect to the first, O.

Article 14. Three data for the comparison of two systems

We have an instance of this formation of a large system out of two or more smaller systems, when two neighbouring nations, having each surveyed and mapped its own territory, agree to connect their surveys so as to include both countries in one system. For this purpose three things are necessary.

1st. A comparison of the origin selected by the one country with that selected by the other.

2nd. A comparison of the directions of reference used in the two countries.

3rd. A comparison of the standards of length used in the two countries.

1. In civilized countries latitude is always reckoned from the equator, but longitude is reckoned from an arbitrary point, as Greenwich or Paris. Therefore, to make the map of Britain fit that of France, we must ascertain the difference of longitude between the Observatory of Greenwich and that of Paris.

2. When a survey has been made without astronomical instruments, the directions of reference have sometimes been those given by the magnetic compass. This was, I believe, the case in the original surveys of some of the West India islands. The results of this survey, though giving correctly the local configuration of the island, could not be made to fit properly into a general map of the world till the deviation of the magnet from the true north at the time of the survey was ascertained.

3. To compare the survey of France with that of Britain, the metre, which is the French standard of length, must be compared with the yard, which is the British standard of length.

The yard is defined by Act of Parliament 18 and 19 Vict. c. 72, July 30, 1855, which enacts "that the straight line or distance between the centres of the transverse lines in the two gold plugs in the bronze bar deposited in the office of the Exchequer shall be the genuine standard yard at 62° Fahrenheit, and if lost, it shall be replaced by means of its copies."

The metre derives its authority from a law of the French Republic in 1795. It is defined to be the distance between the ends of a certain rod of platinum made by Borda, the rod being at the temperature of melting ice. It has been found by the measurements of Captain Clarke that the metre is equal to 39.37043 British inches.

Article 15. On the idea of space

We have now gone through most of the things to be attended to with respect to the configuration of a material system. There remain, however, a few points relating to the metaphysics of the subject, which have a very important bearing on physics.

We have described the method of combining several configurations into one system which includes them all. In this way we add to the small region which we can explore by stretching our limbs the more distant regions which we can reach by walking or by being carried. To these we add those of which we learn by the reports of others, and those inaccessible regions whose position we ascertain only by a process of calculation, till at last we recognize that every place has a definite position with respect to every other place, whether the one place is accessible from the other or not.

Thus from measurements made on the earth's surface we deduce the position of the centre of the earth relative to known objects, and we calculate the number of cubic miles in the earth's volume quite independently of any hypothesis as to what may exist at the centre of the earth, or in any other place beneath that thin layer of the crust of the earth which alone we can directly explore.

Article 16. Error of Descartes

It appears, then, that the distance between one thing and another does not depend on any material thing between them, as Descartes seems to assert when he says (*Princip. Phil.,* II. 18) that if that which is in a hollow vessel were taken out of it without anything entering to fill its place, the sides of the vessel, having nothing between them, would be in contact.

This assertion is grounded on the dogma of Descartes, that the extension in length, breadth, and depth which constitute space is the sole essential property of matter. "The nature of matter," he tells us, "or of body considered generally, does not consist in a thing being hard, or heavy, or coloured, but only in its being extended in length, breadth, and depth" (*Princip.,* II. 4). By thus confounding the properties of matter with those of space, he arrives at the logical conclusion that if the matter within a vessel could be entirely removed, the space within the vessel would no longer exist. In fact he assumes that all space must be always full of matter.

I have referred to this opinion of Descartes in order to show the importance of sound views in elementary dynamics. The primary property of matter was indeed distinctly announced by Descartes in what he calls the "First Law of Nature" (*Princip.,* II. 37): "That every individual thing, so far as in it lies, perseveres in the same state, whether of motion or of rest."

We shall see when we come to Newton's laws of motion that in the words "so far as in it lies," properly understood, is to be found the true primary definition of matter, and the true measure of its quantity. Descartes, however, never attained to a full understanding of his own words (*quantum in se est*), and so fell back on his original confusion of matter with space—space being, according to him, the only form of substance, and all existing things but affections of space. This error runs through every part of Descartes' great work, and it forms one of the ultimate foundations of the system of Spinoza. I shall not attempt to trace it down to more modern times, but I would advise those who study any system of metaphysics to examine carefully that part of it which deals with physical ideas.

We shall find it more conducive to scientific progress to recognize, with Newton, the ideas of time and space as distinct, at least in thought, from that of the material system whose relations these ideas serve to coordinate.

Article 17. On the idea of time

The idea of time in its most primitive form is probably the recognition of an order of sequence in our states of consciousness. If my memory were perfect, I might be able to refer every event within my own experience to its proper place in a chronological series. But it would be difficult, if not impossible, for me to compare the interval between one pair of events and that between another pair—to ascertain, for instance, whether the time during which I can work without feeling tired is greater or less now than when I first began to study. By our intercourse with other persons, and by our experience of natural processes which go on in a uniform or a rhythmical manner, we come to recognize the possibility of arranging a system of chronology in which all events whatever, whether relating to ourselves or to others, must find their place. Of any two events, say the actual disturbance at the star in Corona Borealis, which caused the luminous effects examined spectroscopically by Mr. Huggins on the 16th May, 1866, and the mental suggestion which first led Professor Adams or M. Leverrier to begin the researches which led to the discovery, by Dr. Galle, on the 23rd September, 1846, of the planet Neptune, the first named must have occurred either before or after the other, or else at the same time.

Absolute, true, and mathematical time is conceived by Newton as flowing at a constant rate, unaffected by the speed or slowness of the motions of material things. It is also called *duration.* Relative, apparent, and common time is duration as estimated by the motion of bodies, as by days, months, and years. These measures of time may be regarded as provisional, for the progress of astronomy has taught us to measure the inequality in the lengths of days, months, and years, and thereby to reduce the apparent time to a more uniform scale, called *mean solar time.*

Article 18. Absolute space

Absolute space is conceived as remaining always similar to itself and immovable. The arrangement of the parts of space can no more be altered than the order of the portions of time. To conceive them to move from their places is to conceive a place to move away from itself.

But as there is nothing to distinguish one portion of time from another except the different events which occur in them, so there is nothing to distinguish one part of space from another except its relation to the place of material bodies. We cannot describe the time of an event except by reference to some other event, or the place of a body except by reference to some other body. All our knowledge, both of time and place, is essentially relative. When a man has acquired the habit of putting words together, without troubling himself to form the thoughts which ought to correspond to them, it is easy for him to frame an antithesis between this relative knowledge and a so-called absolute knowledge, and to point out our ignorance of the absolute position of a point as an instance of the limitation of our faculties. Anyone, however, who will try to imagine the state of a mind conscious of knowing the absolute position of a point will ever after be content with our relative knowledge.

Article 19. Statement of the general maxim of physical science

There is a maxim which is often quoted, that "The same causes will always produce the same effects."

To make this maxim intelligible we must define what we mean by the same causes and the same effects, since it is manifest that no event ever happens more than once, so that the causes and effects cannot be the same in *all* respects. What is really meant is that if the causes differ only as regards the absolute time or the absolute place at which the event occurs, so likewise will the effects.

The following statement, which is equivalent to the above maxim, appears to be more definite, more explicitly connected with the ideas of space and time, and more capable of application to particular cases:

"The difference between one event and another does not depend on the mere difference of the times or the places at which they occur, but only on differences in the nature, configuration, or motion of the bodies concerned."

It follows from this, that if an event has occurred at a given time and place, it is possible for an event exactly similar to occur at any other time and place.

There is another maxim which must not be confounded with that quoted at the beginning of this article, which asserts that "Like causes produce like effects."

This is only true when small variations in the initial circumstances produce only small variations in the final state of the system. In a great many physical phenomena this condition is satisfied; but there are other cases in which a small initial variation may produce a very great change in the final state of the system, as when the displacement of the points causes a railway train to run into another instead of keeping its proper course.

Chapter II. On Motion

Article 20. Definition of displacement

We have already compared the position of different points of a system at the same instant of time. We have next to compare the position of a point at a given instant with its position at a former instant, called the *epoch.*

The vector which indicates the final position of a point with respect to its position at the epoch is called the *displacement* of that point. Thus if A_1 is the initial and A_2 the final position of the point A, the line $\overline{A_1A_2}$ is the displacement of A, and any vector $\overline{oa}$ drawn from the origin o parallel and equal to $\overline{A_1A_2}$ indicates this displacement.

Article 21. Diagram of displacement

If another point of the system is displaced from B_1 to B_2 the vector $\overline{ob}$ parallel and equal to $\overline{B_1B_2}$ indicates the displacement of B.

Figure 3

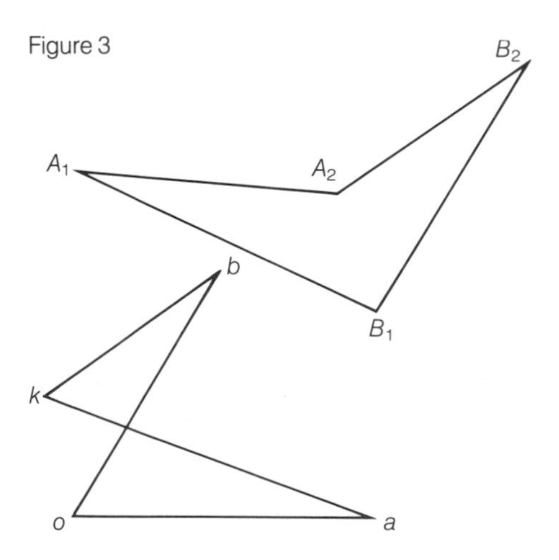

In like manner the displacement of any number of points may be represented by vectors drawn from the same origin o. This system of vectors is called the *diagram of displacement.* It is not necessary to draw actual lines to represent these vectors; it is sufficient to indicate the points a, b, etc., at the extremities of the vectors. The diagram of displacement may therefore be regarded as consisting of a number of points, a, b, etc., corresponding with the material particles, A, B, etc., belonging to the system, together with a point o, the position of which is arbitrary, and which is the assumed origin of all the vectors.

Article 22. Relative displacement

The line $\overline{ab}$ in the diagram of displacement represents the displacement of the point B with respect to A.

For if in the diagram of displacement (fig. 3) we draw $\overline{ak}$ parallel and equal to $\overline{B_1A_1}$, and in the same direction, and join $\overline{kb}$, it is easy to show that $\overline{kb}$ is equal and parallel to $\overline{A_2B_2}$.

For the vector $\overline{kb}$ is the sum of the vectors $\overline{ka}$, $\overline{ao}$, and $\overline{ob}$, and $\overline{A_2B_2}$ is the sum of $\overline{A_2A_1}$, $\overline{A_1B_1}$, and $\overline{B_1B_2}$. But of these, $\overline{ka}$ is the same as $\overline{A_1B_1}$, $\overline{ao}$ is the same as $\overline{A_2A_1}$, and $\overline{ob}$ is the same as $\overline{B_1B_2}$, and by Article 10 the order of summation is indifferent, so that the vector $\overline{kb}$ is the same, in direction and magnitude, as $\overline{A_2B_2}$. Now $\overline{ka}$, or $\overline{A_1B_1}$, represents the original position of B with respect to A, and $\overline{kb}$, or $\overline{A_2B_2}$, represents the final position of B with respect to A. Hence $\overline{ab}$ represents the displacement of B with respect to A, which was to be proved.

In Article 20 we purposely omitted to say whether the origin to which the original configuration was referred, and that to which the final configuration is referred, are absolutely the same point, or whether, during the displacement of the system, the origin also is displaced.

We may now, for the sake of argument, suppose that the origin is absolutely fixed, and that the displacements represented by $\overline{oa}$, $\overline{ab}$, etc., are the absolute displacements. To pass from this case to that in which the origin is displaced we have only to take A, one of the movable points, as origin. The absolute displacement of A being represented by $\overline{oa}$, the displacement of B with respect to A is represented, as we have seen, by $\overline{ab}$, and so on for any other points of the system.

The arrangement of the points a, b, etc., in the diagram of displacement is therefore the same, whether we reckon the displacements with respect to a fixed point or a displaced point; the only difference is that we adopt a different origin of vectors in the diagram of displacements, the rule being that whatever point we take, whether fixed or moving, for the origin of the diagram of configuration, we take the corresponding point as origin in the diagram of displacement. If we wish to indicate the fact that we are entirely ignorant of the absolute displacement in space of any point of the system, we may do so by constructing the diagram of displacements as a mere system of points, without indicating in any way which of them we take as the origin.

This diagram of displacements (without an origin) will then represent neither more nor less than all we can ever know about the displacement of the system. It consists simply of a number of points, a, b, c, etc., corresponding to the points A, B, C, of the material system, and a vector, as $\overline{ab}$ represents the displacement of B with respect to A.

Article 23. Uniform* displacement

When the displacements of all points of a material system with respect to an external point are the same in direction and magnitude, the diagram of displacement is reduced to two points—one corresponding to the external point, and the other to each and every point of the displaced system. In this case the points of the system are not displaced with respect to one another, but only with respect to the external point.

This is the kind of displacement which occurs when a body of invariable form moves parallel to itself. It may be called uniform displacement.

Article 24. On motion

When the change of configuration of a system is considered with respect only to its state at the beginning and the end of the process of change, and without reference to the time during which it takes place, it is called the displacement of the system.

When we turn our attention to the process of change itself, as taking place during a certain time and in a continuous manner, the change of configuration is ascribed to the motion of the system.

Article 25. On the continuity of motion

When a material particle is displaced so as to pass from one position to another, it can only do so by traveling along some course or path from the one position to the other.

At any instant during the motion the particle will be found at some one point of the path, and if we select any point of the path, the particle will pass that point once

*When the simultaneous values of a quantity for different bodies or places are equal, the quantity is said to be *uniformly* distributed in space.

Figure 4

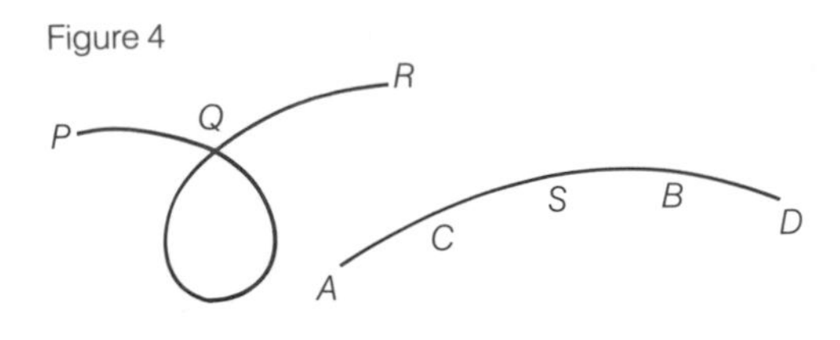

at least* during its motion.

This is what is meant by saying that the particle describes a continuous path. The motion of a material particle which has continuous existence in time and space is the type and exemplar of every form of continuity.

Article 26. On constant† velocity

If the motion of a particle is such that in equal intervals of time, however short, the displacements of the particle are equal and in the same direction, the particle is said to move with constant velocity.

It is manifest that in this case the path of the body will be a straight line, and the length of any part of the path will be proportional to the time of describing it.

The rate or speed of the motion is called the velocity of the particle, and its magnitude is expressed by saying that it is such a distance in such a time, as, for instance, ten miles an hour, or one metre per second. In general we select a unit of time, such as a second, and measure velocity by the distance described in unit of time.

If one metre be described in a second and if the velocity be constant, a thousandth or a millionth of a metre will be described in a thousandth or a millionth of a second. Hence, if we can observe or calculate the displacement during any interval of time, however short, we may deduce the distance which would be described in a longer time with the same velocity. This result, which enables us to state the velocity during the short interval of time, does not depend on the body's actually continuing to move at the same rate during the longer time. Thus we may know that a body is moving at the rate of ten miles an hour, though its motion at this rate may last for only the hundredth of a second.

Article 27. On the measurement of velocity when variable

When the velocity of a particle is not constant, its value at any given instant is measured by the distance which would be described in a unit of time by a body having the same velocity as that which the particle has at that instant.

Thus when we say that at a given instant, say one second after a body has begun to fall, its velocity is 980 centimetres per second, we mean that if the velocity of a particle were constant and equal to that of the falling body at the given instant, it would describe 980 centimetres in a second.

It is specially important to understand what is meant by the velocity or rate of motion of a body, because the ideas which are suggested to our minds by considering the motion of a particle are those which Newton made use of in his method of Fluxions,‡ and they lie at the foundation of the great extension of exact science which has taken place in modern times.

---

*If the path cuts itself so as to form a loop, as *P, Q, R* (fig. 4), the particle will pass the point of intersection, *Q*, twice, and if the particle returns on its own path, as in the path *A, B, C, D*, it may pass the same point, *S*, three or more times.

†When the successive values of a quantity for successive instants of time are equal, the quantity is said to be *constant.*

‡According to the method of Fluxions, when the value of one quantity depends on that of another, the rate of variation of the first quantity with respect to the second may be expressed as a velocity, by imagining the first quantity to represent the displacement of a particle, while the second flows uniformly with the time.

Article 28. Diagram of velocities

If the velocity of each of the bodies in the system is constant, and if we compare the configurations of the system at an interval of a unit of time, then the displacements, being those produced in unit of time in bodies moving with constant velocities, will represent those velocities according to the method of measurement described in Article 26.

If the velocities do not actually continue constant for a unit of time, then we must imagine another system consisting of the same number of bodies, and in which the velocities are the same as those of the corresponding bodies of the system at the given instant but remain constant for a unit of time. The displacements of this system represent the velocities of the actual system at the given instant.

Another mode of obtaining the diagram of velocities of a system at a given instant is to take a small interval of time, say the nth part of the unit of time, so that the middle of this interval corresponds to the given instant. Take the diagram of displacements corresponding to this interval and magnify all its dimensions n times. The result will be a diagram of the *mean* velocities of the system during the interval. If we now suppose the number n to increase without limit the interval will diminish without limit, and the mean velocities will approximate without limit to the actual velocities at the given instant. Finally, when n becomes infinite the diagram will represent accurately the velocities at the given instant.

Article 29. Properties of the diagram of velocities (fig. 5)

Figure 5

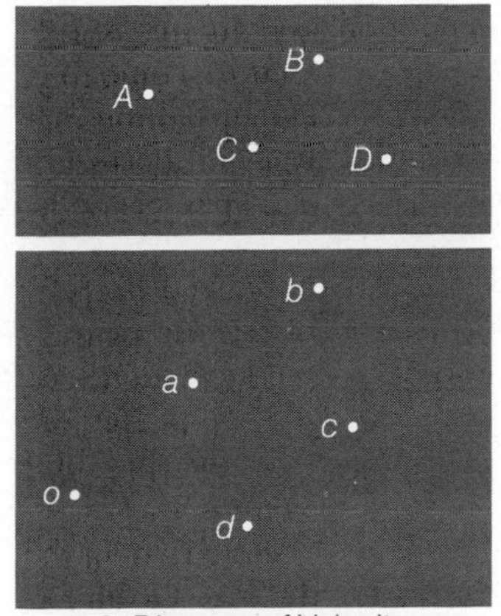

2 Diagram of Velocity.

The diagram of velocities for a system consisting of a number of material particles consists of a number of points, each corresponding to one of the particles.

The velocity of any particle B with respect to any other, A, is represented in direction and magnitude by the line $\overline{ab}$ in the diagram of velocities, drawn from the point a, corresponding to A, to the point b, corresponding to B.

We may in this way find, by means of the diagram, the relative velocity of any two particles. The diagram tells us nothing about the absolute velocity of any point; it expresses exactly what we can know about the motion and no more. If we choose to imagine that $\overline{oa}$ represents the absolute velocity of A, then the absolute velocity of any other particle, B, will be represented by the vector $\overline{ob}$, drawn from o as origin to the point b, which corresponds to B.

But as it is impossible to define the position of a body except with respect to the position of some point of reference, so it is impossible to define the velocity of a body, except with respect to the velocity of the point of reference. The phrase "absolute velocity" has as little meaning as "absolute position." It is better, therefore, not to distinguish any point in the diagram of velocity as the origin, but to regard the diagram as expressing the relations of all the velocities without defining the absolute value of any one of them.

Article 30. Meaning of the phrase "at rest"

It is true that when we say that a body is at rest we use a form of words which appears to assert something about that body considered in itself, and we might imagine that the velocity of another body, if reckoned with respect to a body at rest, would be its true and only absolute velocity. But the phrase "at rest" means in ordinary language "having no velocity with respect to that on which the body stands," as, for instance, the surface of the earth or the deck of a ship. It cannot be made to mean more than this.

It is therefore unscientific to distinguish between rest and motion, as between two different states of a body in itself, since it is impossible to speak of a body being at rest or in motion except with reference, expressed or implied, to some other body.

Article 31. On change of velocity

As we have compared the velocities of different bodies at the same time, so we may compare the relative velocity of one body with respect to another at different times.

Figure 6

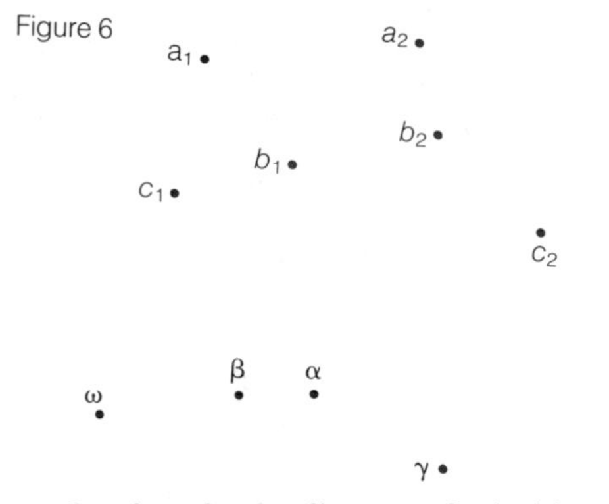

If a_1, b_1, c_1 be the diagram of velocities of the system of bodies *A, B, C,* in its original state, and if a_2, b_2, c_2 be the diagram of velocities in the final state of the system, then if we take any point ω as origin and draw $\overline{\omega a}$ equal and parallel to $\overline{a_1a_2}$, $\overline{\omega\beta}$ equal and parallel to $\overline{b_1b_2}$, $\overline{\omega\gamma}$ equal and parallel to $\overline{c_1c_2}$, and so on, we shall form a diagram of points a, β, γ, etc., such that any line $\overline{a\beta}$ in this diagram represents in direction and magnitude the change of the velocity of *B* with respect to *A*. This diagram may be called the diagram of *total accelerations.*

Article 32. On acceleration

The word *acceleration* is here used to denote any change in the velocity, whether that change be an increase, a diminution, or a change of direction. Hence, instead of distinguishing, as in ordinary language, between the acceleration, the retardation, and the deflection of the motion of a body, we say that the acceleration may be in the direction of motion, in the contrary direction, or transverse to that direction.

As the displacement of a system is defined to be the change of the configuration of the system, so the *total acceleration* of the system is defined to be the change of the velocities of the system. The process of constructing the diagram of total accelerations by a comparison of the initial and final diagrams of velocities is the same as that by which the diagram of displacements was constructed by a comparison of the initial and final diagrams of configuration.

Article 33. On the rate of acceleration

We have hitherto been considering the total acceleration which takes place during a certain interval of time. If the rate of acceleration is constant, it is measured by the total acceleration in a unit of time. If the rate of acceleration is variable, its value at a given instant is measured by the total acceleration in unit of time of a point whose acceleration is constant and equal to that of the particle at the given instant.

It appears from this definition that the method of deducing the rate of acceleration from a knowledge of the total acceleration in any given time is precisely analogous to that by which the velocity at any instant is deduced from a knowledge of the displacement in any given time.

The diagram of total accelerations constructed for an interval of the *n*th part of the unit of time, and then magnified *n* times, is a diagram of the mean rates of acceleration during that interval, and by taking the interval smaller and smaller, we ultimately arrive at the true rate of acceleration at the middle of that interval.

As rates of acceleration have to be considered in physical science much more frequently than total accelerations, the word *acceleration* has come to be employed in the sense in which we have hitherto used the phrase "rate of acceleration."

In future, therefore, when we use the word *acceleration* without qualification, we mean what we have here described as the rate of acceleration.

Article 34. Diagram of accelerations

The diagram of accelerations is a system of points, each of which corresponds to one of the bodies of the material system, and is such that any line $\alpha\beta$ in the diagram represents the rate of acceleration of the body B with respect to the body A.

It may be well to observe here that in the diagram of configuration we use the capital letters, A, B, C, etc., to indicate the relative position of the bodies of the system; in the diagram of velocities we use the small letters, a, b, c, to indicate the relative velocities of these bodies; and in the diagram of accelerations we use the Greek letters, α, β, γ, to indicate their relative accelerations.

Article 35. Acceleration a relative term

Acceleration, like position and velocity, is a relative term and cannot be interpreted absolutely.

If every particle of the material universe within the reach of our means of observation were at a given instant to have its velocity altered by compounding therewith a new velocity, the same in magnitude and direction for every such particle, all the relative motions of bodies within the system would go on in a perfectly continuous manner, and neither astronomers nor physicists, though using their instruments all the while, would be able to find out that anything had happened.

It is only if the change of motion occurs in a different manner in the different bodies of the system that any event capable of being observed takes place.

Chapter III. On Force

Article 36. Kinematics and kinetics

We have hitherto been considering the motion of a system in its purely geometrical aspect. We have shown how to study and describe the motion of such a system, however arbitrary, without taking into account any of the conditions of motion which arise from the mutual action between the bodies.

The theory of motion treated in this way is called *kinematics*. When the mutual action between bodies is taken into account, the science of motion is called *kinetics*, and when special attention is paid to force as the cause of motion, it is called *dynamics.*

Article 37. Mutual action between two bodies—stress

The mutual action between two portions of matter receives different names according to the aspect under which it is studied, and this aspect depends on the extent of the material system which forms the subject of our attention.

If we take into account the whole phenomenon of the action between the two portions of matter, we call it *stress.* This stress, according to the mode in which it acts, may be described as attraction, repulsion, tension, pressure, shearing stress, torsion, etc.

Article 38. External force

But if, as in Article 2, we confine our attention to one of the portions of matter, we see, as it were, only one side of the transaction—namely, that which affects the portion of matter under our consideration—and we call this aspect of the phenomenon, with reference to its effect, an *external force* acting on that portion of matter, and with reference to its cause we call it the *action* of the other portion of matter. The opposite aspect of the stress is called the *reaction* on the other portion of matter.

Article 39. Different aspects of the same phenomenon

In commercial affairs the same transaction between two parties is called buying when we consider one party, selling when we consider the other, and trade when we take both parties into consideration.

The accountant who examines the records of the transaction finds that the two parties have entered it on opposite sides of their respective ledgers, and in comparing the books he must in every case bear in mind in whose interest each book is made up.

For similar reasons in dynamical investigations we must always remember which of the two bodies we are dealing with, so that we may state the forces in the interest of that body and not set down any of the forces on the wrong side of the account.

Article 40. Newton's laws of motion

External or "impressed" force considered with reference to its effect—namely, the alteration of the motions of bodies—is completely defined and described in Newton's three laws of motion. [Cf. *GBWW,* Vol. 34, p. 14.]

The first law tells us under what conditions there is no external force.

The second shows us how to measure the force when it exists.

The third compares the two aspects of the action between two bodies, as it affects the one body or the other.

Article 41. The first law or motion

Law I. *Every body perseveres in its state of rest or of moving uniformly in a straight line, except insofar as it is made to change that state by external forces.*

The experimental argument for the truth of this law is that in every case in which we find an alteration of the state of motion of a body, we can trace this alteration to some action between that body and another, that is to say, to an external force. The existence of this action is indicated by its effect on the other body when the motion of that body can be observed. Thus the motion of a cannonball is retarded, but this arises from an action between the projectile and the air which surrounds it, whereby the ball experiences a force in the direction opposite to its relative motion, while the air, pushed forward by an equal force, is itself set in motion and constitutes what is called the *wind* of the cannonball.

But our conviction of the truth of this law may be greatly strengthened by considering what is involved in a denial of it. Given a body in motion. At a given instant let it be left to itself and not acted on by any force. What will happen? According to Newton's law it will persevere in moving uniformly in a straight line, that is, its velocity will remain constant both in direction and magnitude.

If the velocity does not remain constant let us suppose it to vary. The change of velocity, as we saw in Article 31, must have a definite direction and magnitude. By the maxim of Article 19, this variation must be the same whatever be the time or place of the experiment. The direction of the change of motion must therefore be determined either by the direction of the motion itself or by some direction fixed in the body.

Let us, in the first place, suppose the law to be that the velocity diminishes at a certain rate, which for the sake of the argument we may suppose so slow that by no experiments on moving bodies could we have detected the diminution of velocity in hundreds of years.

The velocity referred to in this hypothetical law can only be the velocity referred to a point absolutely at rest. For if it is a relative velocity its direction as well as its magnitude depends on the velocity of the point of reference.

If, when referred to a certain point, the body appears to be moving northward with diminishing velocity, we have only to refer it to another point moving northward with a uniform velocity greater than that of the body, and it will appear to be moving southward with increasing velocity.

Hence the hypothetical law is without meaning, unless we admit the possibility of defining absolute rest and absolute velocity.

Even if we admit this as a possibility, the hypothetical law, if found to be true, might be interpreted, not as a contradiction of Newton's law, but as evidence of the resisting action of some medium in space.

To take another case. Suppose the law to be that a body, not acted on by any force, ceases at once to move. This is not only contradicted by experience, but it leads to a definition of absolute rest as the state which a body assumes as soon as it is freed from the action of external forces.

It may thus be shown that the denial of Newton's law is in contradiction to the only system of consistent doctrine about space and time which the human mind has been able to form.

Article 42. On the equilibrium of forces

If a body moves with constant velocity in a straight line, the external forces, if any, which act on it, balance each other or are in equilibrium.

Thus if a carriage in a railway train moves with constant velocity in a straight line, the external forces which act on it—such as the traction of the carriage in front of it pulling it forward, the drag of that behind it, the friction of the rails, the resistance of the air acting backward, the weight of the carriage acting downward, and the pressure of the rails acting upward—must exactly balance each other.

Bodies at rest with respect to the surface of the earth are really in motion, and their motion is not constant nor in a straight line. Hence the forces which act on them are not exactly balanced. The apparent weight of bodies is estimated by the upward force required to keep them at rest relatively to the earth. The apparent weight is therefore rather less than the attraction of the earth, and makes a smaller angle with the axis of the earth, so that the combined effect of the supporting force and the earth's attraction is a force perpendicular to the earth's axis just sufficient to cause the body to keep to the circular path which it must describe if resting on the earth.

Article 43. Definition of equal times

The first law of motion, by stating under what circumstances the velocity of a moving body remains constant, supplies us with a method of defining equal intervals of time. Let the material system consist of two bodies which do not act on one another, and which are not acted on by any body external to the system. If one of these bodies is in motion with respect to the other, the relative velocity will, by the first law of motion, be constant and in a straight line.

Hence intervals of time are equal when the relative displacements during those intervals are equal.

This might at first sight appear to be nothing more than a definition of what we mean by equal intervals of time, an expression which we have not hitherto defined at all.

But if we suppose another moving system of two bodies to exist, each of which is not acted upon by any body whatever, this second system will give us an independent method of comparing intervals of time.

The statement that equal intervals of time are those during which equal displacements occur in any such system is therefore equivalent to the assertion that the comparison of intervals of time leads to the same result whether we use the first system of two bodies or the second system as our timepiece.

We thus see the theoretical possibility of comparing intervals of time however distant, though it is hardly necessary to remark that the method cannot be put in practice in the neighbourhood of the earth, or any other large mass of gravitating matter.

Article 44. The second law of motion

Law II. *Change of motion is proportional to the impressed force and takes place in the direction in which the force is impressed.*

By *motion* Newton means what in modern scientific language is called *momentum,* in which the quantity of matter moved is taken into account as well as the rate at which it travels.

By impressed force he means what is now called *impulse,* in which the time during which the force acts is taken into account as well as the intensity of the force.

Article 45. Definition of equal masses and of equal forces

An exposition of the law therefore involves a definition of equal quantities of matter and of equal forces.

We shall assume that it is possible to cause the force with which one body acts on another to be of the same intensity on different occasions.

If we admit the permanency of the properties of bodies this can be done. We know that a thread of caoutchouc when stretched beyond a certain length exerts a tension which increases the more the thread is elongated. On account of this property the thread is said to be elastic. When the same thread is drawn out to the same length it will, if its properties remain constant, exert the same tension. Now let one end of the thread be fastened to a body, *M,* not acted on by any other force than the tension of the thread, and let the other end be held in the hand and pulled in a constant direction with a force just sufficient to elongate the thread to a given length. The force acting on the body will then be of a given intensity, F. The body will acquire velocity, and at the end of a unit of time this velocity will have a certain value, V.

If the same string be fastened to another body, N, and pulled as in the former case, so that the elongation is the same as before, the force acting on the body will be the same, and if the velocity communicated to N in a unit of time is also the same, namely V, then we say of the two bodies M and N that they consist of equal quantities of matter, or, in modern language, they are equal in mass. In this way, by the use of an elastic string, we might adjust the masses of a number of bodies so as to be each equal to a standard unit of mass, such as a pound avoirdupois, which is the standard of mass in Britain.

Article 46. Measurement of mass

The scientific value of the dynamical method of comparing quantities of matter is best seen by comparing it with other methods in actual use.

As long as we have to do with bodies of exactly the same kind, there is no difficulty in understanding how the quantity of matter is to be measured. If equal quantities of the substance produce equal effects of any kind, we may employ these effects as measures of the quantity of the substance.

For instance, if we are dealing with sulfuric acid of uniform strength, we may estimate the quantity of a given portion of it in several different ways. We may weigh it, we may pour it into a graduated vessel and so measure its volume, or we may ascertain how much of a standard solution of potash it will neutralize.

We might use the same methods to estimate a quantity of nitric acid if we were dealing only with nitric acid; but if we wished to compare a quantity of nitric acid with a quantity of sulfuric acid we should obtain different results by weighing, by measuring, and by testing with an alkaline solution.

Of these three methods, that of weighing depends on the attraction between the acid and the earth, that of measuring depends on the volume which the acid occupies, and that of titration depends on its power of combining with potash.

In abstract dynamics, however, matter is considered under no other aspect than as that which can have its motion changed by the application of force. Hence any two bodies are of equal mass if equal forces applied to these bodies produce, in equal times, equal changes of velocity. This is the only definition of equal masses which can be admitted in dynamics, and it is applicable to all material bodies, whatever they may be made of.

It is an observed fact that bodies of equal mass, placed in the same position relative to the earth, are attracted equally toward the earth, whatever they are made of; but this is not a doctrine of abstract dynamics, founded on axiomatic principles, but a fact discovered by observation and verified by the careful experiments of Newton,* on the times of oscillation of hollow wooden balls suspended by strings of the same length and containing gold, silver, lead, glass, sand, common salt, wood, water, and wheat.

The fact, however, that in the same geographical position the weights of equal masses are equal is so well established that no other mode of comparing masses than that of comparing their weights is ever made use of, either in commerce or in science, except in researches undertaken for the special purpose of determining in absolute measure the weight of unit of mass at different parts of the earth's surface. The method employed in these researches is essentially the same as that of Newton,

---

*_Principia_, Book III, Prop. 6 [_GBWW_, Vol. 34, p. 279].

namely, by measuring the length of a pendulum which swings seconds.

The unit of mass in this country is defined by the Act of Parliament (18 and 19 Vict. c. 72, July 30, 1855) to be a piece of platinum marked "P. S., 1844, 1 lb." deposited in the office of the Exchequer, which "shall be and be denominated the Imperial Standard Pound Avoirdupois." One seven-thousandth part of this pound is a grain. The French standard of mass is the "Kilogramme des Archives," made of platinum by Borda. Professor Miller finds the kilogram equal to 15432.34874 grains.

Article 47. Numerical measurement of force

The unit of force is that force which, acting on the unit of mass for the unit of time, generates a unit of velocity.

Thus the weight of a gram—that is to say, the force which causes it to fall—may be ascertained by letting it fall freely. At the end of one second its velocity will be about 981 centimetres per second if the experiment be in Britain. Hence the weight of a gram is represented by the number 981 if the centimetre, the gram, and the second are taken as the fundamental units.

It is sometimes convenient to compare forces with the weight of a body and to speak of a force of so many pounds weight or gram weight. This is called *gravitation measure.* We must remember, however, that though a pound or a gram is the same all over the world, the weight of a pound or a gram is greater in high latitudes than near the equator, and therefore a measurement of force in gravitation measure is of no scientific value unless it is stated in what part of the world the measurement was made.

If, as in Britain, the units of length, mass, and time are one foot, one pound, and one second, the unit of force is that which, in one second, would communicate to one pound a velocity of one foot per second. This unit of force is called a *poundal.*

In the French metric system the units are one centimetre, one gram, and one second. The force which in one second would communicate to one gram a velocity of one centimetre per second is called a *dyne.*

Since the foot is 30.4797 centimetres and the pound is 453.59 grams, the poundal is 13825.38 dynes.

Article 48. Simultaneous action of forces on a body

Now let a unit of force act for a unit of time upon a unit of mass. The velocity of the mass will be changed, and the total acceleration will be unity in the direction of the force.

The magnitude and direction of this total acceleration will be the same whether the body is originally at rest or in motion. For the expression "at rest" has no scientific meaning, and the expression "in motion," if it refers to relative motion, may mean anything, and if it refers to absolute motion can only refer to some medium fixed in space. To discover the existence of a medium, and to determine our velocity with respect to it by observation on the motion of bodies, is a legitimate scientific inquiry, but supposing all this done we should have discovered, not an error in the laws of motion, but a new fact in science.

Hence the effect of a given force on a body does not depend on the motion of that body.

Neither is it affected by the simultaneous action of other forces on the body. For the effect of these forces on the body is only to produce motion in the body, and this does not affect the acceleration produced by the first force.

Hence we arrive at the following form of the law. *When any number of forces act on a body, the acceleration due to each force is the same in direction and magnitude as if the others had not been in action.*

When a force, constant in direction and magnitude, acts on a body, the total acceleration is proportional to the interval of time during which the force acts.

For if the force produces a certain total acceleration in a given interval of time, it will produce an equal total acceleration in the next because the effect of the force does not depend upon the velocity which the body has when the force acts on it. Hence in every equal interval of time there will be an equal change of the velocity, and the total change of velocity from the beginning of the motion will be proportional to the time of action of the force.

The total acceleration in a given time is proportional to the force.

For if several equal forces act in the same direction on the same body in the same direction, each produces its effect independently of the others. Hence the total acceleration is proportional to the number of the equal forces.

Article 49. On impulse

The total effect of a force in communicating velocity to a body is therefore proportional to the force and to the time during which it acts conjointly.

The product of the time of action of a force into its intensity if it is constant, or its mean intensity if it is variable, is called the *impulse* of the force.

There are certain cases in which a force acts for so short a time that it is difficult to estimate either its intensity or the time during which it acts. But it is comparatively easy to measure the effect of the force in altering the motion of the body on which it acts, which, as we have seen, depends on the impulse.

The word *impulse* was originally used to denote the effect of a force of short duration, such as that of a hammer striking a nail. There is no essential difference, however, between this case and any other case of the action of force. We shall therefore use the word *impulse* as above defined, without restricting it to cases in which the action is of an exceptionally transient character.

Article 50. Relation between force and mass

If a force acts on a unit of mass for a certain interval of time, the impulse, as we have seen, is measured by the velocity generated.

If a number of equal forces act in the same direction, each on a unit of mass, the different masses will all move in the same manner and may be joined together into one body without altering the phenomenon. The velocity of the whole body is equal to that produced by one of the forces acting on a unit of mass.

Hence the force required to produce a given change of velocity in a given time is proportional to the number of units of mass of which the body consists.

Article 51. On momentum

The numerical value of the *momentum* of a body is the product of the number of units of mass in the body into the number of units of velocity with which it is moving.

The momentum of any body is thus measured in terms of the momentum of a unit of mass moving with a unit of velocity, which is taken as the unit of momentum.

The direction of the momentum is the same as that of the velocity, and as the velocity can only be estimated with respect to some point of reference, so the particular value of the momentum depends on the point of reference which we assume. The momentum of the moon, for example, will be very different according as we take the earth or the sun for the point of reference.

Article 52. Statement of the second law of motion in terms of impulse and momentum

The change of momentum of a body is numerically equal to the impulse which produces it and is in the same direction.

Article 53. Addition of forces

If any number of forces act simultaneously on a body, each force produces an acceleration proportional to its own magnitude (Art. 48). Hence if in the diagram of accelerations (Art. 34) we draw from any origin a line representing in direction and magnitude the acceleration due to one of the forces, and from the end of this line another representing the acceleration due to another force, and so on, drawing lines for each of the forces taken in any order, then the line drawn from the origin to the extremity of the last of the lines will represent the acceleration due to the combined action of all the forces.

Since in this diagram lines which represent the accelerations are in the same proportion as the forces to which these accelerations are due, we may consider the lines as representing these forces themselves. The diagram, thus understood, may be called a *diagram of forces,* and the line from the origin to the extremity of the series represents the *resultant force.*

An important case is that in which the set of lines representing the forces terminate at the origin so as to form a closed figure. In this case there is no resultant force, and no acceleration. The effects of the forces are exactly balanced, and the case is one of equilibrium. The discussion of cases of equilibrium forms the subject of the science of *statics.*

It is manifest that since the system of forces is exactly balanced, and is equivalent to no force at all, the forces will also be balanced if they act in the same way on any other material system, whatever be the mass of that system. This is the reason why the consideration of mass does not enter into statical investigations.

Article 54. The third law of motion

Law III. *Reaction is always equal and opposite to action, that is to say, the actions of two bodies upon each other are always equal and in opposite directions.*

When the bodies between which the action takes place are not acted on by any other force, the changes in their respective momenta produced by the action are equal and in opposite directions.

The changes in the velocities of the two bodies are also in opposite directions but not equal, except in the case of equal masses. In other cases the changes of velocity are in the inverse ratio of the masses.

Article 55. Action and reaction are the partial aspects of a stress.

We have already (Art. 37) used the word *stress* to denote the mutual action between two portions of matter. This word was borrowed from common language and invested with a precise scientific meaning by the late Professor Rankine, to whom we are indebted for several other valuable scientific terms.

As soon as we have formed for ourselves the idea of a stress, such as the *tension* of a rope or the *pressure* between two bodies, and have recognized its double aspect as it affects the two portions of matter between which it acts, the third law of motion is seen to be equivalent to the statement that all force is of the nature of stress, that stress exists only between two portions of matter, and that its effects on these portions of matter (measured by the momentum generated in a given time) are equal and opposite.

The stress is measured numerically by

the force exerted on either of the two portions of matter. It is distinguished as a tension when the force acting on either portion is toward the other, and as a pressure when the force acting on either portion is away from the other.

When the force is inclined to the surface which separates the two portions of matter the stress cannot be distinguished by any term in ordinary language but must be defined by technical mathematical terms.

When a tension is exerted between two bodies by the medium of a string, the stress, properly speaking, is between any two parts into which the string may be supposed to be divided by an imaginary section or transverse interface. If, however, we neglect the weight of the string, each portion of the string is in equilibrium under the action of the tensions at its extremities, so that the tensions at any two transverse interfaces of the string must be the same. For this reason we often speak of the tension of the string as a whole, without specifying any particular section of it, and also the tension between the two bodies, without considering the nature of the string through which the tension is exerted.

Article 56. Attraction and repulsion

There are other cases in which two bodies at a distance appear mutually to act on each other, though we are not able to detect any intermediate body, like the string in the former example, through which the action takes place. For instance, two magnets or two electrified bodies appear to act on each other when placed at considerable distances apart, and the motions of the heavenly bodies are observed to be affected in a manner which depends on their relative position.

This mutual action between distant bodies is called *attraction* when it tends to bring them nearer, and *repulsion* when it tends to separate them.

In all cases, however, the action and reaction between the bodies are equal and opposite.

Article 57. The third law true of action at a distance

The fact that a magnet draws iron toward it was noticed by the ancients, but no attention was paid to the force with which the iron attracts the magnet. Newton, however, by placing the magnet in one vessel and the iron in another, and floating both vessels in water so as to touch each other, showed experimentally that as neither vessel was able to propel the other along with itself through the water, the attraction of the iron on the magnet must be equal and opposite to that of the magnet on the iron, both being equal to the pressure between the two vessels. [*GBWW,* Vol. 34, p. 22.]

Having given this experimental illustration, Newton goes on to point out the consequence of denying the truth of this law. For instance, if the attraction of any part of the earth, say a mountain, upon the remainder of the earth were greater or less than that of the remainder of the earth upon the mountain, there would be a residual force, acting upon the system of the earth and the mountain as a whole, which would cause it to move off, with an ever-increasing velocity, through infinite space.

Article 58. Newton's proof not experimental

This is contrary to the first law of motion, which asserts that a body does not change its state of motion unless acted on by *external* force. It cannot be affirmed to be contrary to experience, for the effect of an inequality between the attraction of the earth on the mountain and the mountain on the earth would be the same as that of a force equal to the difference of these attractions acting in the direction of the line joining the centre of the earth with the mountain.

If the mountain were at the equator, the earth would be made to rotate about an axis parallel to the axis about which it would otherwise rotate, but not passing exactly through the centre of the earth's mass.

If the mountain were at one of the poles, the constant force parallel to the earth's axis would cause the orbit of the earth about the sun to be slightly shifted to the north or south of a plane passing through the centre of the sun's mass.

If the mountain were at any other part of the earth's surface, its effect would be partly of the one kind and partly of the other.

Neither of these effects, unless they were very large, could be detected by direct astronomical observations, and the indirect method of detecting small forces, by their effect in slowly altering the elements of a planet's orbit, presupposes that the law of gravitation is known to be true. To prove the laws of motion by the law of gravitation would be an inversion of scientific order. We might as well prove the law of addition of numbers by the differential calculus.

We cannot, therefore, regard Newton's statement as an appeal to experience and observation, but rather as a deduction of the third law of motion from the first.

Chapter IV. On the Properties of the Centre of Mass of a Material System

Article 59. Definition of a mass-vector

We have seen that a vector represents the operation of carrying a tracing point from a given origin to a given point.

Let us define a mass-vector as the operation of carrying a given mass from the origin to the given point. The direction of the mass-vector is the same as that of the vector of the mass, but its magnitude is the product of the mass into the vector of the mass.

Thus if $\overline{OA}$ is the vector of the mass A, the mass-vector is $\overline{OA} \cdot A$.

Article 60. Centre of mass of two particles

If A and B are two masses, and if a point C be taken in the straight line $\overline{AB}$, so that $\overline{BC}$ is to $\overline{CA}$ as A to B, then the mass-vector of a mass $A + B$ placed at C is equal to the sum of the mass-vectors of A and B.

Figure 7

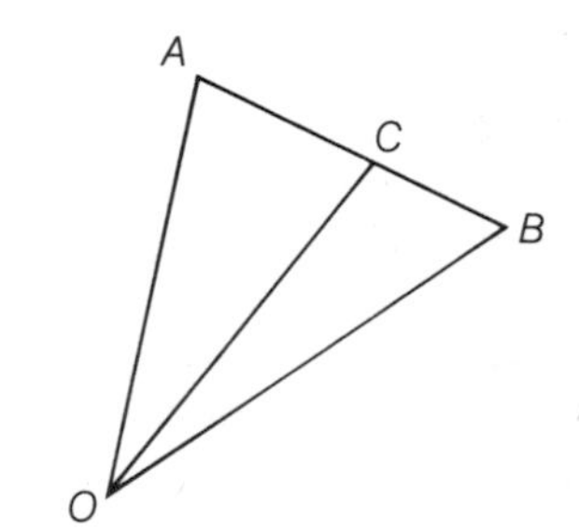

$$\text{For } \overline{OA} \cdot A + \overline{OB} \cdot B$$
$$= (\overline{OC} + \overline{CA})\, A + (\overline{OC} + \overline{CB})\, B.$$
$$= \overline{OC}\, (A + B) + \overline{CA} \cdot A + \overline{CB} \cdot B.$$

Now the mass-vectors $\overline{CA} \cdot A$ and $\overline{CB} \cdot B$ are equal and opposite, and so destroy each other, so that $\overline{OA} \cdot A + \overline{OB} \cdot B = \overline{OC}\, (A + B)$ or, C is a point such that if the masses of A and B were concentrated at C, their mass-vector from any origin O would be the same as when A and B are in their actual positions. The point C is called the *centre of mass* of A and B.

Article 61. Centre of mass of a system

If the system consists of any number of particles, we may begin by finding the centre of mass of any two particles, and substituting for the two particles a particle equal to their sum placed at their centre of mass. We may then find the centre of mass of this particle, together with the third particle of the system, and place the sum of the three particles at this point, and so on till we have found the centre of mass of the whole system.

The mass-vector drawn from any origin to a mass equal to that of the whole system placed at the centre of mass of the system is equal to the sum of the mass-vectors drawn from the same origin to all the particles of the system.

It follows, from the proof in Article 60, that the point found by the construction here given satisfies this condition. It is plain from the condition itself that only one point can satisfy it. Hence the construction must lead to the same result, as to the position of the centre of mass, in whatever order we take the particles of the system.

The centre of mass is therefore a definite point in the diagram of the configuration of the system. By assigning to the different points in the diagrams of displacement, velocity, total acceleration, and rate of acceleration, the masses of the bodies to which they correspond, we may find in each of these diagrams a point which corresponds to the centre of mass and indicates the displacement, velocity, total acceleration, or rate of acceleration of the centre of mass.

Article 62. Momentum represented as the rate of change of a mass-vector

In the diagram of velocities, if the points o, a, b, c correspond to the velocities of the origin O and the bodies A, B, C, and if p be the centre of mass of A and B placed at a

Figure 8

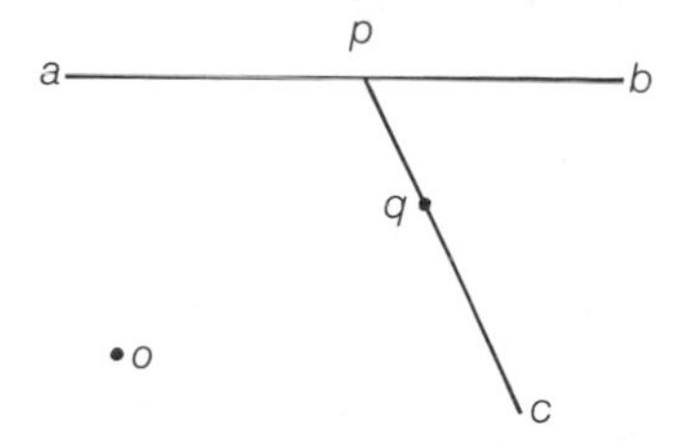

and b respectively, and if q is the centre of mass of $A + B$ placed at p and C at c, then q will be the centre of mass of the system of bodies A, B, C at a, b, c, respectively.

The velocity of A with respect to O is indicated by the vector $\overline{oa}$, and that of B and C by $\overline{ob}$ and $\overline{oc}$. $\overline{op}$ is the velocity of the centre of mass of A and B, and oq that of the centre of mass of A, B, and C, with respect to O.

The momentum of A with respect to O is the product of the velocity into the mass, or $\overline{oa} \cdot A$, or what we have already called the mass-vector, drawn from o to the mass A at a. Similarly the momentum of any other body is the mass-vector drawn from o to the point on the diagram of velocities corresponding to that body, and the momentum of the mass of the system concentrated at the centre of mass is the mass-vector drawn from o to the whole mass at q.

Since, therefore, a mass-vector in the diagram of velocities is what we have already defined as a momentum, we may state the property proved in Article 61, in terms of momenta, thus: The momentum of a mass equal to that of the whole system, moving with the velocity of the centre of mass of the system, is equal in magnitude and parallel in direction to the sum of the momenta of all the particles of the system.

Article 63. Effect of external forces on the motion of the centre of mass

In the same way in the diagram of total acceleration the vectors $\overline{\omega\alpha}$, $\overline{\omega\beta}$, drawn from

Figure 9

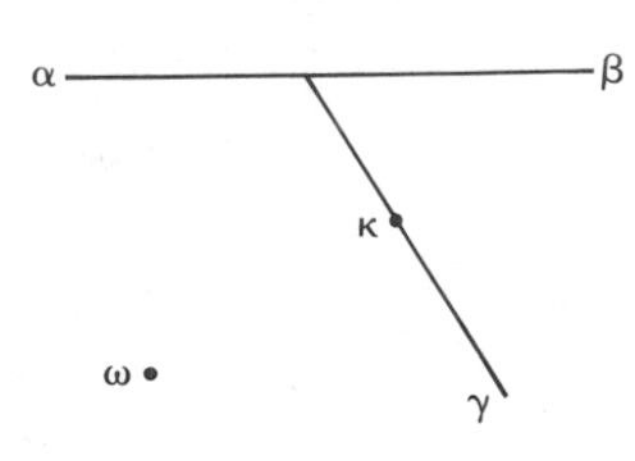

the origin, represent the change of velocity of the bodies *A, B,* etc., during a certain interval of time. The corresponding mass-vectors, $\overline{\omega\alpha}\cdot A$, $\overline{\omega\beta}\cdot B$, etc., represent the corresponding changes of momentum, or, by the second law of motion, the impulses of the forces acting on these bodies during that interval of time. If κ is the centre of mass of the system, $\overline{\omega\kappa}$ is the change of velocity during the interval, and $\overline{\omega\kappa}\,(A + B + C)$ is the momentum generated in the mass concentrated at the centre of gravity. Hence, by Article 61, the change of momentum of the imaginary mass equal to that of the whole system concentrated at the centre of mass is equal to the sum of the changes of momentum of all the different bodics of the system.

In virtue of the second law of motion we may put this result in the following form:

The effect of the forces acting on the different bodies of the system in altering the motion of the centre of mass of the system is the same as if all these forces had been applied to a mass equal to the whole mass of system, and coinciding with its centre of mass.

Article 64. The motion of the centre of mass of a system is not affected by the mutual action of the parts of the system.

For if there is an action between two parts of the system, say *A* and *B,* the action of *A* on *B* is always, by the third law of motion, equal and opposite to the reaction of *B* on *A*. The momentum generated in *B* by the action of *A* during any interval is therefore equal and opposite to that generated in *A* by the reaction of *B* during the same interval, and the motion of the centre of mass of *A* and *B* is therefore not affected by their mutual action.

We may apply the result of the last article to this case and say that, since the forces on *A* and on *B* arising from their mutual action are equal and opposite, and since the effect of these forces on the motion of the centre of mass of the system is the same as if they had been applied to a particle whose mass is equal to the whole mass of the system, and since the effect of two forces equal and opposite to each other is zero, the motion of the centre of mass will not be affected.

Article 65. First and second laws of motion

This is a very important result. It enables us to render more precise the enunciation of the first and second laws of motion, by defining that by the velocity of a body is meant the velocity of its centre of mass. The body may be rotating, or it may consist of parts, and be capable of changes of configuration, so that the motions of different parts may be different, but we can still assert the laws of motion in the following form:

Law I. The centre of mass of the system perseveres in its state of rest, or of uniform motion in a straight line, except insofar as it is made to change that state by forces acting on the system from without.

Law II. The change of momentum of the system during any interval of time is measured by the sum of the impulses of the external forces during that interval.

Article 66. Method of treating systems of molecules

When the system is made up of parts which are so small that we cannot observe them, and whose motions are so rapid and so variable that even if we could observe them we could not describe them, we are still able to deal with the motion of the centre of mass of the system, because the internal forces which cause the variation of the motion of the parts do not affect the motion of the centre of mass.

Article 67. By the introduction of the idea of mass we pass from point-vectors, point displacements, velocities, total accelerations, and rates of acceleration, to mass-vectors, mass displacements, momenta, impulses, and moving forces.

In the diagram of rates of acceleration (fig. 9, Art. 63) the vectors $\overline{\omega\alpha}$, $\overline{\omega\beta}$, etc., drawn from the origin, represent the rates of acceleration of the bodies *A, B,* etc., at a given instant, with respect to that of the origin *O.*

The corresponding mass-vectors, $\overline{\omega\alpha} \cdot A$, $\overline{\omega\beta} \cdot B$, etc., represent the forces acting on the bodies *A, B,* etc.

We sometimes speak of several forces acting on a body, when the force acting on the body arises from several different causes, so that we naturally consider the parts of the force arising from these different causes separately.

But when we consider force, not with respect to its causes, but with respect to its effect—that of altering the motion of a body—we speak not of the forces but of the force acting on the body, and this force is measured by the rate of change of the momentum of the body and is indicated by the mass-vector in the diagram of rates of acceleration.

We have thus a series of different kinds of mass-vectors corresponding to the series of vectors which we have already discussed.

We have, in the first place, a system of mass-vectors with a common origin, which we may regard as a method of indicating the distribution of mass in a material system, just as the corresponding system of vectors indicates the geometrical configuration of the system.

In the next place, by comparing the distribution of mass at two different epochs, we obtain a system of mass-vectors of displacement.

The rate of mass displacement is momentum, just as the rate of displacement is velocity.

The change of momentum is impulse, as the change of velocity is total acceleration.

The rate of change of momentum is moving force, as the rate of change of velocity is rate of acceleration.

Article 68. Definition of a mass-area

When a material particle moves from one point to another, twice the area swept out by the vector of the particle multiplied by the mass of the particle is called the mass-area of the displacement of the particle with respect to the origin from which the vector is drawn.

If the area is in one plane, the direction of the mass-area is normal to the plane, drawn so that, looking in the positive direction along the normal, the motion of the particle round its area appears to be the direction of the motion of the hands of a watch.

If the area is not in one plane, the path of the particle must be divided into portions so small that each coincides sensibly with a straight line, and the mass-areas corresponding to these portions must be added together by the rule for the addition of vectors.

Article 69. Angular momentum

The rate of change of a mass-area is twice the mass of the particle into the triangle, whose vertex is the origin and whose base is the velocity of the particle measured along the line through the particle in the direction of its motion. The direction of this mass-area is indicated by the normal drawn according to the rule given above.

The rate of change of the mass-area of a particle is called the *angular momentum* of the particle about the origin, and the sum of the angular momenta of all the particles is called the angular momentum of the system about the origin.

The angular momentum of a material system with respect to a point is, therefore, a quantity having a definite direction as well as a definite magnitude.

The definition of the angular momentum of a particle about a point may be expressed somewhat differently as the product of the momentum of the particle with respect to that point into the perpendicular from that point on the line of motion of the particle at that instant.

Article 70. Moment of a force about a point

The rate of increase of the angular momentum of a particle is the continued product of the rate of acceleration of the velocity of the particle into the mass of the particle into the perpendicular from the origin on the line through the particle along which the acceleration takes place. In other words, it is the product of the moving force acting on the particle into the perpendicular from the origin on the line of action of this force.

Now the product of a force into the perpendicular from the origin on its line of action is called the *moment* of the force about the origin. The axis of the moment, which indicates its direction, is a vector drawn perpendicular to the plane passing through the force and the origin, and in such a direction that, looking along this line in the direction in which it is drawn, the force tends to move the particle round the origin in the direction of the hands of a watch.

Hence the rate of change of the angular momentum of a particle about the origin is measured by the moment of the force which acts on the particle about that point.

The rate of change of the angular momentum of a material system about the origin is in like manner measured by the geometric sum of the moments of the forces which act on the particles of the system.

Article 71. Conservation of angular momentum

Now consider any two particles of the system. The forces acting on these two particles, arising from their mutual action, are equal, opposite, and in the same straight line. Hence the moments of these forces about any point as origin are equal, opposite, and about the same axis. The sum of these moments is therefore zero. In like manner the mutual action between every other pair of particles in the system consists of two forces, the sum of whose moments is zero.

Hence the mutual action between the bodies of a material system does not affect the geometric sum of the moments of the forces. The only forces, therefore, which need be considered in finding the geometric sum of the moments are those which are external to the system—that is to say, between the whole or any part of the system and bodies not included in the system.

The rate of change of the angular momentum of the system is therefore measured by the geometric sum of the moments of the external forces acting on the system.

If the directions of all the external forces pass through the origin, their moments are zero, and the angular momentum of the system will remain constant.

When a planet describes an orbit about the sun, the direction of the mutual action between the two bodies always passes through their common centre of mass.

Hence the angular momentum of either body about their common centre of mass remains constant, so far as these two bodies only are concerned, though it may be affected by the action of other planets. If, however, we include all the planets in the system, the geometric sum of their angular momenta about their common centre of mass will remain absolutely constant, whatever may be their mutual actions, provided no force arising from bodies external to the whole solar system acts in an unequal manner upon the different members of the system.

Chapter V. On Work and Energy

Article 72. Definitions

Work *is the act of producing a change of configuration in a system in opposition to a force which resists that change.*

Energy *is the capacity of doing work.*

When the nature of a material system is such that if, after the system has undergone any series of changes, it is brought back in any manner to its original state, the whole work done by external agents on the system is equal to the whole work done by the system in overcoming external force, the system is called a conservative system.

Article 73. Principle of conservation of energy

The progress of physical science has led to the discovery and investigation of different forms of energy, and to the establishment of the doctrine that all material systems may be regarded as conservative systems, provided that all the different forms of energy which exist in these systems are taken into account.

This doctrine, considered as a deduction from observation and experiment, can, of course, assert no more than that no instance of a nonconservative system has hitherto been discovered.

As a scientific or science-producing doctrine, however, it is always acquiring additional credibility from the constantly increasing number of deductions which have been drawn from it, and which are found in all cases to be verified by experiment.

In fact the doctrine of the conservation of energy is the one generalized statement which is found to be consistent with fact, not in one physical science only, but in all.

When once apprehended it furnishes to the physical inquirer a principle on which he may hang every known law relating to physical actions, and by which he may be put in the way to discover the relations of such actions in new branches of science.

For such reasons the doctrine is commonly called the *principle of the conservation of energy.*

Article 74. General statement of the principle of the conservation of energy

The total energy of any material system is a quantity which can neither be increased nor diminished by any action between the parts of the system, though it may be transformed into any of the forms of which energy is susceptible.

If, by the action of some agent external to the system, the configuration of the system is changed, while the forces of the system resist this change of configuration, the external agent is said to do work on the system. In this case the energy of the system is increased by the amount of work done on it by the external agent.

If, on the contrary, the forces of the system produce a change of configuration which is resisted by the external agent, the system is said to do work on the external agent, and the energy of the system is diminished by the amount of work which it does.

Work, therefore, is a transference of energy from one system to another; the system which gives out energy is said to do work on the system which receives it, and the amount of energy given out by the first system is always exactly equal to that received by the second.

If, therefore, we include both systems in one larger system, the energy of the total system is neither increased nor diminished by the action of the one partial system on the other.

Article 75. Measurement of work

Work done by an external agent on a material system may be described as a change in the configuration of the system taking place under the action of an external force tending to produce that change.

Thus, if one pound is lifted one foot from the ground by a man in opposition to the force of gravity, a certain amount of work is done by the man, and this quantity is known among engineers as one foot-pound.

Here the man is the external agent, the material system consists of the earth and the pound, the change of configuration is the increase of the distance between the matter of the earth and the matter of the pound, and the force is the upward force exerted by the man in lifting the pound, which is equal and opposite to the weight of the pound. To raise the pound a foot higher would, if gravity were a uniform force, require exactly the same amount of work. It is true that gravity is not really uniform but diminishes as we ascend from the earth's surface, so that a foot-pound is not an accurately known quantity, unless we specify the intensity of gravity at the place. But for the purpose of illustration we may assume that gravity is uniform for a few feet of ascent, and in that case the work done in lifting a pound would be one foot-pound for every foot the pound is lifted.

To raise twenty pounds of water ten feet high requires two hundred foot-pounds of work. To raise one pound ten feet high requires ten foot-pounds, and as there are twenty pounds the whole work is twenty times as much, or two hundred foot-pounds.

The quantity of work done is, therefore, proportional to the product of the numbers representing the force exerted and the displacement in the direction of the force.

In the case of a foot-pound the force is the weight of a pound—a quantity which, as we know, is different in different places. The weight of a pound expressed in absolute measure is numerically equal to the intensity of gravity, the quantity denoted by g, the value of which in poundals to the pound varies from 32.227 at the pole to 32.117 at the equator and diminishes without limit as we recede from the earth. In dynes to the gram it varies from 978.1 to 983.1. Hence, in order to express work in a uniform and consistent manner, we must multiply the number of foot-pounds by the number representing the intensity of gravity at the place. The work is thus reduced to foot-poundals. We shall always understand work to be measured in this manner and reckoned in foot-poundals when no other system of measurement is mentioned. When work is expressed in foot-pounds the system is that of *gravitation-measures,* which is not a complete system unless we also know the intensity of gravity at the place.

In the metrical system the unit of work is the *erg,* which is the work done by a dyne acting through a centimetre. There are 421393.8 ergs in a foot-poundal.

Article 76. Potential energy

The work one by a man in raising a heavy body is done in overcoming the attraction between the earth and that body. The energy of the material system, consisting of the earth and the heavy body, is thereby increased. If the heavy body is the leaden weight of a clock, the energy of the clock is increased by winding it up, so that the clock is able to go for a week in spite of the friction of the wheels and the resistance of the air to the motion of the pendulum and also to give out energy in other forms, such as the communication of the vibrations to the air, by which we hear the ticking of the clock.

When a man winds up a watch he does work in changing the form of the mainspring by coiling it up. The energy of the mainspring is thereby increased, so that as it uncoils itself it is able to keep the watch going.

In both these cases the energy communicated to the system depends upon a change of configuration.

Article 77. Kinetic energy

But in a very important class of phenomena the work is done in changing the velocity of the body on which it acts. Let us take as a simple case that of a body moving without rotation under the action of a force. Let the mass of the body be M pounds, and let a force of F poundals act on it in the line of motion during an interval of time, T seconds. Let the velocity at the beginning of the interval be V and that at the end V' feet per second, and let the distance traveled by the body during the time be S feet. The original momentum is MV, and the final momentum is MV', so that the increase of momentum is $M(V' - V)$, and this, by the second law of motion, is equal to FT, the *impulse* of the force F acting for the time T. Hence—

$$FT = M(V' - V). \qquad (1)$$

Since the velocity increases uniformly with the time, the mean velocity is the arithmetical mean of the original and final velocities, or $\frac{1}{2}(V' + V)$.

We can also determine the mean velocity by dividing the space S by the time T, during which it is described.

$$\text{Hence } \frac{S}{T} = \tfrac{1}{2}(V' + V). \qquad (2)$$

Multiplying the corresponding members of equations (1) and (2) each by each we obtain—

$$FS = \tfrac{1}{2}MV'^2 - \tfrac{1}{2}MV^2. \qquad (3)$$

Here FS is the work done by the force F acting on the body while it moves through the space S in the direction of the force, and this is equal to the excess of $\frac{1}{2}MV'^2$ above $\frac{1}{2}MV^2$. If we call $\frac{1}{2}MV^2$, or half the product of the mass, into the square of the velocity, the *kinetic energy* of the body at first, then $\frac{1}{2}MV'^2$ will be the kinetic energy after the action of the force F through the space S. The energy is here expressed in foot-poundals.

We may now express the equation in words by saying that the work done by the force F in changing the motion of the body is measured by the increase of the kinetic energy of the body during the time that the force acts.

We have proved that this is true when the interval of time is so small that we may consider the force as constant during that time, and the mean velocity during the interval as the arithmetical mean of the velocities at the beginning and end of the interval. This assumption, which is exactly true when the force is constant, however long the interval may be, becomes in every case more and more nearly true as the interval of time taken becomes smaller and smaller. By dividing the whole time of action into small parts, and proving that in each of these the work done is equal to the increase of the kinetic energy of the body, we may, by adding the successive portions of the work and the successive increments of energy, arrive at the result that the total work done by the force is equal to the total increase of kinetic energy.

If the force acts on the body in the direction opposite to its motion, the kinetic energy of the body will be diminished instead of being increased, and the force, instead of doing work on the body, will act as a resistance, which the body, in its motion, overcomes. Hence a moving body, as long as it is in motion, can do work in overcoming resistance, and the work done by the moving body is equal to the diminution of its kinetic energy, till at last, when the body is brought to rest, its kinetic energy is exhausted, and the whole work it has done is then equal to the whole kinetic energy which it had at first.

We now see the appropriateness of the name *kinetic energy,* which we have hitherto used merely as a name to denote the product $\frac{1}{2}MV^2$. For the energy of a body has been defined as the capacity which it has of doing work, and it is measured by the work which it can do. The *kinetic* energy of a body is the energy it has in virtue of being in *motion,* and we have now shown that its value is expressed by $\frac{1}{2}MV^2$ or $\frac{1}{2}MV \times V$, that is, half the product of its momentum into its velocity.

Article 78. Oblique forces

If the force acts on the body at right angles to the direction of its motion it does no work on the body, and it alters the direction but not the magnitude of the velocity. The kinetic energy, therefore, which depends on the square of the velocity, remains unchanged.

If the direction of the force is neither coincident with, nor at right angles to, that of the motion of the body we may resolve the force into two components, one of which is at right angles to the direction of motion, while the other is in the direction of motion (or in the opposite direction).

The first of these components may be left out of consideration in all calculations about energy, since it neither does work on the body nor alters its kinetic energy.

The second component is that which we have already considered. When it is in the direction of motion it increases the kinetic energy of the body by the amount of work which it does on the body. When it is in the opposite direction the kinetic energy of the body is diminished by the amount of work which the body does against the force.

Hence in all cases the increase of kinetic energy is equal to the work done on the body by external agency, and the diminution of kinetic energy is equal to the work done by the body against external resistance.

Article 79. Kinetic energy of two particles referred to their centre of mass

The kinetic energy of a material system is equal to the kinetic energy of a mass equal to that of the system moving with the velocity of the centre of mass of the system, together with the kinetic energy due to the motion of the parts of the system relative to its centre of mass.

Let us begin with the case of two particles whose masses are A and B, and whose velocities are represented in the diagram of velocities by the lines $\overline{oa}$ and $\overline{ob}$. If c is the centre of mass of a particle equal to A placed at a, and a particle equal to B placed

Figure 10

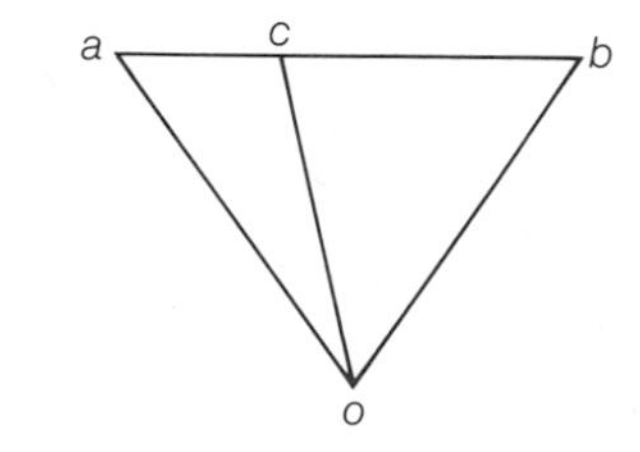

at b, then $\overline{oc}$ will represent the velocity of the centre of mass of the two particles.

The kinetic energy of the system is the sum of the kinetic energies of the particles, or

$$T = \tfrac{1}{2}A\,\overline{oa}^2 + \tfrac{1}{2}B\,\overline{ob}^2 .$$

Expressing $\overline{oa}^2$ and $\overline{ob}^2$ in terms of $\overline{oc}$, $\overline{ca}$ and $\overline{cb}$ and the angle $oca = \theta$.

$$\begin{aligned} T = &\tfrac{1}{2}A\,\overline{oc}^2 + \tfrac{1}{2}A\,\overline{ca}^2 - A\,\overline{oc}\cdot\overline{ca}\cos\theta. \\ &+ \tfrac{1}{2}B\,\overline{oc}^2 + \tfrac{1}{2}B\,\overline{cb}^2 - B\,\overline{oc}\cdot\overline{cb}\cos\theta. \end{aligned}$$

But since c is the centre of mass of A at a, and B at b,

$$A\cdot\overline{ca} + B\cdot\overline{cb} = 0.$$

Hence adding

$$T = \tfrac{1}{2}(A+B)\,\overline{oc}^2 + \tfrac{1}{2}A\,\overline{ca}^2 + \tfrac{1}{2}B\,\overline{cb}^2,$$

or, the kinetic energy of the system of two particles A and B is equal to that of a mass equal to $(A + B)$ moving with the velocity of the centre of mass, together with that of the motion of the particles relative to the centre of mass.

Article 80. Kinetic energy of a material system referred to its centre of mass

We have begun with the case of two particles, because the motion of a particle is assumed to be that of its centre of mass, and we have proved our proposition true for a system of two particles. But if the proposition is true for each of two material systems taken separately, it must be true of the system which they form together. For if we now suppose $\overline{oa}$ and $\overline{ob}$ to represent the velocities of the centres of mass of two material systems A and B, then $\overline{oc}$ will represent the velocity of the centre of mass of the combined system $A + B$, and if T_A represents the kinetic energy of the motion of the system A relative to its own centre of mass, and T_B the same for the system B, then if the proposition is true for the systems A and B taken separately, the kinetic energy of A is

$$\tfrac{1}{2}A\,\overline{oa}^2 + T_A,$$

and that of B $\quad \tfrac{1}{2}B\,\overline{ob}^2 + T_B.$

The kinetic energy of the whole is therefore

$$\tfrac{1}{2}A\,\overline{oa}^2 + \tfrac{1}{2}B\,\overline{ob}^2 + T_A + T_B,$$

or,

$$\tfrac{1}{2}(A+B)\,\overline{oc}^2 + \tfrac{1}{2}A\,\overline{ca}^2 + T_A + \tfrac{1}{2}B\,\overline{cb}^2 + T_B.$$

The first term represents the kinetic energy of a mass equal to that of the whole system moving with the velocity of the centre of mass of the whole system.

The second and third terms, taken together, represent the kinetic energy of the system A relative to the centre of gravity of the whole system, and the fourth and fifth terms represent the same for the system B.

Hence if the proposition is true for the two systems A and B taken separately, it is true for the system compounded of A and B. But we have proved it true for the case of two particles; it is therefore true for three, four, or any other number of particles, and therefore for any material system.

The kinetic energy of a system referred to its centre of mass is less than its kinetic energy when referred to any other point.

For the latter quantity exceeds the former by a quantity equal to the kinetic energy of a mass equal to that of the whole system moving with the velocity of the centre of mass relative to the other point, and since all kinetic energy is essentially positive, this excess must be positive.

Article 81. Available kinetic energy

We have already seen in Article 64 that the mutual action between the parts of a material system cannot change the velocity of the centre of mass of the system. Hence that part of the kinetic energy of the system which depends on the motion of the centre of mass cannot be affected by any action internal to the system. It is therefore impossible, by means of the mutual action of the parts of the system, to convert this part of the energy into work. As far as the system itself is concerned, this energy is unavailable. It can be converted into work only by means of the action between this system and some other material system external to it.

Hence if we consider a material system unconnected with any other system, its available kinetic energy is that which is due to the motions of the parts of the system relative to its centre of mass.

Let us suppose that the action between the parts of the system is such that after a certain time the configuration of the system becomes invariable, and let us call this process the solidification of the system. We have shown that the angular momentum of the whole system is not changed by any mutual action of its parts. Hence if the original angular momentum is zero, the system, when its form becomes invariable, will not rotate about its centre of mass, but if it moves at all will move parallel to itself, and the parts will be at rest relative to the centre of mass. In this case therefore the whole available energy will be converted into work by the mutual action of the parts during the solidification of the system.

If the system has angular momentum, it will have the same angular momentum when solidified. It will therefore rotate about its centre of mass, and will therefore still have energy of motion relative to its centre of mass, and this remaining kinetic energy has not been converted into work.

But if the parts of the system are allowed to separate from one another in directions perpendicular to the axis of the angular momentum of the system, and if the system when thus expanded is solidified, the remaining kinetic energy of rotation round the centre of mass will be less and less the greater the expansion of the system, so that by sufficiently expanding the system we may make the remaining kinetic energy as small as we please, so that the whole kinetic energy relative to the centre of mass of the system may be converted into work within the system.

Article 82. Potential energy

The potential energy of a material system is the capacity which it has of doing work depending on other circumstances than the motion of the system. In other words, potential energy is that energy which is not kinetic.

In the theoretical material system which we build up in our imagination from the fundamental ideas of matter and motion, there are no other conditions present except the configuration and motion of the different masses of which the system is composed. Hence in such a system the circumstances upon which the energy must depend are motion and configuration only, so that, as the kinetic energy depends on the motion, the potential energy must depend on the configuration.

In many real material systems we know that part of the energy does depend on the configuration. Thus the mainspring of a watch has more energy when coiled up than when partially uncoiled, and two bar magnets have more energy when placed side by side with their similar poles turned the same way than when their dissimilar poles are placed next each other.

Article 83. Elasticity

In the case of the spring we may trace the connection between the coiling of the spring and the force which it exerts somewhat further by conceiving the spring divided (in imagination) into very small parts or elements. When the spring is coiled up, the form of each of these small parts is altered, and such an alteration of the form of a solid body is called a *strain*.

In solid bodies strain is accompanied with internal force or stress; those bodies in which the stress depends simply on the strain are called *elastic*, and the property of exerting stress when strained is called *elasticity*.

We thus find that the coiling of the spring involves the strain of its elements, and that the external force which the spring exerts is the resultant of the stresses in its elements.

We thus substitute for the immediate relation between the coiling of the spring and the force which it exerts, a relation between the strains and stresses of the elements of the spring; that is to say, for a single displacement and a single force, the relation between which may in some cases be of an exceedingly complicated nature, we substitute a multitude of strains and an equal number of stresses, each strain being connected with its corresponding stress by a much more simple relation.

But when all is done, the nature of the connection between configuration and force remains as mysterious as ever. We can only admit the fact, and if we call all such phenomena phenomena of elasticity, we may find it very convenient to classify them in this way, provided we remember that by the use of the word *elasticity* we do not profess to explain the cause of the connection between configuration and energy.

Article 84. Action at a distance

In the case of the two magnets there is no visible substance connecting the bodies between which the stress exists. The space between the magnets may be filled with air or with water, or we may place the magnets in a vessel and remove the air by an air-pump, till the magnets are left in what is commonly called a vacuum, and yet the mutual action of the magnets will not be altered. We may even place a solid plate of glass or metal or wood between the magnets, and still we find that their mutual action depends simply on their relative position and is not perceptibly modified by placing any substance between them, unless that substance is one of the magnetic metals. Hence the action between the magnets is commonly spoken of as *action at a distance*.

Attempts have been made, with a certain amount of success,* to analyze this action at a distance into a continuous distribution of stress in an invisible medium, and thus to establish an analogy between the magnetic action and the action of a spring or a rope in transmitting force; but still the general fact that strains or changes of configuration are accompanied by stresses or internal forces, and that thereby energy is stored up in the system so strained, remains an ultimate fact which has not yet been explained as the result of any more fundamental principle.

Article 85. Theory of potential energy more complicated than that of kinetic energy

Admitting that the energy of a material system may depend on its configuration, the mode in which it so depends may be much more complicated than the mode in which the kinetic energy depends on the motion of the system. For the kinetic energy may be calculated from the motion of the parts of the system by an invariable method. We multiply the mass of each part by half the square of its velocity and take the sum of all such products. But the potential energy arising from the mutual action of two parts of the system may depend on the relative position of the parts in a manner which may be different in different instances. Thus when two billiard

**See* Clerk Maxwell's *Treatise on Electricity and Magnetism*, Vol. II, Art. 641.

balls approach each other from a distance, there is no sensible action between them till they come so near one another that certain parts appear to be in contact. To bring the centres of the two balls nearer, the parts in contact must be made to yield, and this requires the expenditure of work.

Hence in this case the potential energy is constant for all distances greater than the distance of first contact and then rapidly increases when the distance is diminished.

The force between magnets varies with the distance in a very different manner, and in fact we find that it is only by experiment that we can ascertain the form of the relation between the configuration of a system and its potential energy.

Article 86. Application of the method of energy to the calculation of forces

A complete knowledge of the mode in which the energy of a material system varies when the configuration and motion of the system are made to vary is mathematically equivalent to a knowledge of all the dynamical properties of the system. The mathematical methods by which all the forces and stresses in a moving system are deduced from the single mathematical formula which expresses the energy as a function of the variables have been developed by Lagrange, Hamilton, and other eminent mathematicians, but it would be difficult even to describe them in terms of the elementary ideas to which we restrict ourselves in this book. An outline of these methods is given in my *Treatise on Electricity,* Part IV, Chapter V, Article 553, and the application of these dynamical methods to electromagnetic phenomena is given in the chapters immediately following.

But if we consider only the case of a system at rest, it is easy to see how we can ascertain the forces of the system when we know how its energy depends on its configuration.

For let us suppose that an agent external to the system produces a displacement from one configuration to another, then if in the new configuration the system possesses more energy than it did at first, it can have received this increase of energy only from the external agent. This agent must therefore have done an amount of work equal to the increase of energy. It must therefore have exerted force in the direction of the displacement, and the mean value of this force, multiplied into the displacement, must be equal to the work done. Hence the mean value of the force may be found by dividing the increase of energy by the displacement.

If the displacement is large this force may vary considerably during the displacement, so that it may be difficult to calculate its mean value; but since the force depends on the configuration, if we make the displacement smaller and smaller the variation of the force will become smaller and smaller, so that at last the force may be regarded as sensibly constant during the displacement.

If, therefore, we calculate for a given configuration the *rate* at which the energy increases with the displacement, by a method similar to that described in Articles 27, 28, and 33, this rate will be numerically equal to the force exerted by the external agent in the direction of the displacement.

If the energy diminishes instead of increasing as the displacement increases, the system must do work on the external agent, and the force exerted by the external agent must be in the direction opposite to that of displacement.

Article 87. Specification of the direction of forces

In treatises on dynamics the forces spoken of are usually those exerted by the external agent on the material system. In treatises on electricity, on the other hand, the forces spoken of are usually those exerted by the electrified system against an external agent which prevents the system from moving. It is necessary, therefore, in reading any statement about forces, to ascertain whether the force spoken of is to be regarded from the one point of view or the other.

We may in general avoid any ambiguity by viewing the phenomenon as a whole, and speaking of it as a stress exerted between two points or bodies, and distinguishing it as a tension or a pressure, an attraction or a repulsion, according to its direction. See Article 55.

Article 88. Application to a system in motion

It thus appears that from a knowledge of the potential energy of a system in every possible configuration we may deduce all the external forces which are required to keep the system in that configuration. If the system is at rest, and if these external forces are the actual forces, the system will remain in equilibrium. If the system is in motion the force acting on each particle is that arising from the connections of the system (equal and opposite to the external force just calculated), together with any external force which may be applied to it. Hence a complete knowledge of the mode in which the potential energy varies with the configuration would enable us to predict every possible motion of the system under the action of given external forces, provided we were able to overcome the purely mathematical difficulties of the calculation.

Article 89. Application of the method of energy to the investigation of real bodies

When we pass from abstract dynamics to physics—from material systems, whose only properties are those expressed by their definitions, to real bodies, whose properties we have to investigate—we find that there are many phenomena which we are not able to explain as changes in the configuration and motion of a material system.

Of course if we begin by assuming that the real bodies are systems composed of matter, which agrees in all respects with the definitions we have laid down, we may go on to assert that all phenomena are changes of configuration and motion, though we are not prepared to define the kind of configuration and motion by which the particular phenomena are to be explained. But in accurate science such asserted explanations must be estimated, not by their promises, but by their performances. The configuration and motion of a system are facts capable of being described in an accurate manner, and therefore, in order that the explanation of a phenomenon by the configuration and motion of a material system may be admitted as an addition to our scientific knowledge, the configurations, motions, and forces must be specified and shown to be consistent with known facts, as well as capable of accounting for the phenomenon.

Article 90. Variables on which the energy depends

But even when the phenomena we are studying have not yet been explained dynamically, we are still able to make great use of the principle of the conservation of energy as a guide to our researches.

To apply this principle, we in the first place assume that the quantity of energy in a material system depends on the state of that system, so that for a given state there is a definite amount of energy.

Hence the first step is to define the different states of the system, and when we have to deal with real bodies we must define their state with respect not only to the configuration and motion of their visible parts, but if we have reason to suspect that the configuration and motion of their invisible particles influence the visible phenomenon, we must devise some method of estimating the energy thence arising.

Thus pressure, temperature, electric potential, and chemical composition are variable quantities, the values of which serve to specify the state of a body, and in general the energy of the body depends on the values of these and other variables.

Article 91. Energy in terms of the variables

The next step in our investigation is to determine how much work must be done by external agency on the body in order to make it pass from one specified state to another.

For this purpose it is sufficient to know the work required to make the body pass from a particular state, which we may call the *standard state,* into any other specified state. The energy in the latter state is equal to that in the standard state, together with the work required to bring it from the standard state into the specified state. The fact that this work is the same through whatever series of states the system has passed from the standard state to the specified state is the foundation of the whole theory of energy.

Since all the phenomena depend on the variations of the energy of the body, and not on its total value, it is unnecessary, even if it were possible, to form any estimate of the energy of the body in its standard state.

Article 92. Theory of heat

One of the most important applications of the principle of the conservation of energy is to the investigation of the nature of heat.

At one time it was supposed that the difference between the states of a body when hot and when cold was due to the presence of a substance called caloric, which existed in greater abundance in the body when hot than when cold. But the experiments of Rumford on the heat produced by the friction of metal, and of Davy on the melting of ice by friction, have shown that when work is spent in overcoming friction, the amount of heat produced is proportional to the work spent.

The experiments of Hirn have also shown that when heat is made to do work in a steam-engine, part of the heat disappears, and that the heat which disappears is proportional to the work done.

A very careful measurement of the work spent in friction, and of the heat produced, has been made by Joule, who finds that the heat required to raise one pound of water from 39° F to 40° F is equivalent to 772 foot-pounds of work at Manchester, or 24,858 foot-poundals.

From this we may find that the heat required to raise one gram of water from 3° C to 4° C is 42,000,000 ergs.

Article 93. Heat a form of energy

Now, since heat can be produced it cannot be a substance; and since whenever mechanical energy is lost by friction there is a production of heat, and whenever there is a gain of mechanical energy in an engine there is a loss of heat; and since the quantity of energy lost or gained is proportional to the quantity of heat gained or lost, we conclude that heat is a form of energy.

We have also reasons for believing that the minute particles of a hot body are in a state of rapid agitation, that is to say, that each particle is always moving very swiftly, but that the direction of its motion alters so often that it makes little or no progress from one region to another.

If this be the case, a part, and it may be a very large part, of the energy of a hot body must be in the form of kinetic energy.

But for our present purpose it is unnecessary to ascertain in what form energy exists in a hot body; the most important fact is that energy may be measured in the form of heat, and since every kind of energy may be converted into heat, this gives us one of the most convenient methods of measuring it.

Article 94. Energy measured as heat

Thus when certain substances are placed in contact chemical actions take place, the substances combine in a new way, and the new group of substances has different chemical properties from the original group of substances. During this process mechanical work may be done by the expansion of the mixture, as when gunpowder is fired; an electric current may be produced, as in the voltaic battery; and heat may be generated, as in most chemical actions.

The energy given out in the form of mechanical work may be measured directly, or it may be transformed into heat by friction. The energy spent in producing the electric current may be estimated as heat by causing the current to flow through a conductor of such a form that the heat generated in it can easily be measured. Care must be taken that no energy is transmitted to a distance in the form of sound or radiant heat without being duly accounted for.

The energy remaining in the mixture, together with the energy which has escaped, must be equal to the original energy.

Andrews, Favre and Silbermann, and others have measured the quantity of heat produced when a certain quantity of oxygen or of chlorine combines with its equivalent of other substances. These measurements enable us to calculate the excess of the energy which the substances concerned had in their original state, when uncombined, above that which they have after combination.

Article 95. Scientific work to be done

Though a great deal of excellent work of this kind has already been done, the extent of the field hitherto investigated appears quite insignificant when we consider the boundless variety and complexity of the natural bodies with which we have to deal.

In fact the special work which lies before the physical inquirer in the present state of science is the determination of the quantity of energy which enters or leaves a material system during the passage of the system from its standard state to any other definite state.

Article 96. History of the doctrine of energy

The scientific importance of giving a name to the quantity which we call kinetic energy seems to have been first recognized by Leibnitz, who gave to the product of the mass by the square of the velocity the name of *Vis Viva*. This is twice the kinetic energy.

Newton, in the "Scholium to the Laws of Motion," expresses the relation between the rate at which work is done by the external agent, and the rate at which it is given out, stored up, or transformed by any machine or other material system, in the following statement, which he makes in order to show the wide extent of the application of the third law of motion. [Cf. *GBWW,* Vol. 34, p. 24.]

"If the action of the external agent is estimated by the product of its force into its velocity, and the reaction of the resistance in the same way by the product of the velocity of each part of the system into the resisting force arising from friction, cohesion, weight, and acceleration, the action and reaction will be equal to each other, whatever be the nature and motion of the system." That this statement of Newton's implicitly contains nearly the whole doctrine of energy was first pointed out by Thomson and Tait.

The words *action* and *reaction* as they occur in the enunciation of the third law of motion are explained to mean *forces,* that is to say, they are the opposite aspects of one and the same stress.

In the passage quoted above a new and different sense is given to these words by estimating action and reaction by the product of a force into the velocity of its point of application. According to this definition the action of the external agent is the rate at which it does work. This is what is meant by the *power* of a steam-engine or other prime mover. It is generally expressed by the estimated number of ideal horses which would be required to do the work at the same rate as the engine, and this is called the *horsepower* of the engine.

When we wish to express by a single word the rate at which work is done by an agent we shall call it the *power* of the agent, defining the power as the work done in the unit of time.

The use of the term *energy,* in a precise and scientific sense, to express the quantity of work which a material system can do, was introduced by Dr. Young.*

Article 97. On the different forms of energy

The energy which a body has in virtue of its motion is called kinetic energy.

A system may also have energy in virtue of its configuration, if the forces of the system are such that the system will do work against external resistance while it passes into another configuration. This energy is called *potential energy.* Thus when a stone has been lifted to a certain height above the earth's surface, the system of two bodies, the stone and the earth, has potential energy and is able to do a certain amount of work during the descent of the stone. This potential energy is due to the fact that the stone and the earth attract each other, so that work has to be spent by the man who lifts the stone and draws it away from the earth, and after the stone is lifted the attraction between the earth and the stone is capable of doing work as the stone descends. This kind of energy, therefore, depends upon the work which the forces of the system would do if the parts of the system were to yield to the action of these forces. This is called the "sum of the tensions" by Helmholtz in his celebrated memoir on the "Conservation of Energy."† Thomson called it *statical energy;* it has also been called *energy of position;* but Rankine introduced the term *potential energy*—a very felicitous expression, since it not only signifies the energy which the system has not in actual possession, but only has the power to acquire, but it also indicates its connection with what has been called (on other grounds) the *potential function.*

The different forms in which energy has been found to exist in material systems have been placed in one or other of these two classes—*kinetic energy,* due to motion, and *potential energy,* due to configuration.

Thus a hot body, by giving out heat to a colder body, may be made to do work by causing the cold body to expand in opposition to pressure. A material system, therefore, in which there is a nonuniform distribution of temperature has the capacity of doing work, or energy. This energy is now believed to be kinetic energy, due to a motion of agitation in the smallest parts of the hot body.

Gunpowder has energy, for when fired it is capable of setting a cannonball in motion. The energy of gunpowder is *chemical energy,* arising from the power which the constituents of gunpowder possess of arranging themselves in a new manner when exploded, so as to occupy a much larger

**Lectures on Natural Philosophy,* Lecture VIII.

†Berlin, 1847. Translated in Taylor's *Scientific Memoirs,* February 1853.

volume than the gunpowder does. In the present state of science chemists figure to themselves chemical action as a rearrangement of particles under the action of forces tending to produce this change of arrangement. From this point of view, therefore, chemical energy is potential energy.

Air, compressed in the chamber of an air-gun, is capable of propelling a bullet. The energy of compressed air was at one time supposed to arise from the mutual repulsion of its particles. If this explanation were the true one its energy would be potential energy. In more recent times it has been thought that the particles of the air are in a state of motion, and that its pressure is caused by the impact of these particles on the sides of the vessel. According to this theory the energy of compressed air is kinetic energy.

There are thus many different modes in which a material system may possess energy, and it may be doubtful in some cases whether the energy is of the kinetic or the potential form. The nature of energy, however, is the same in whatever form it may be found. The quantity of energy can always be expressed as that of a body of a definite mass moving with a definite velocity.

Chapter VI. Recapitulation

Article 98. Retrospect of abstract dynamics

We have now gone through that part of the fundamental science of the motion of matter which we have been able to treat in a manner sufficiently elementary to be consistent with the plan of this book.

It remains for us to take a general view of the relations between the parts of this science, and of the whole to other physical sciences, and this we can now do in a more satisfactory way than we could before we had entered into the subject.

Article 99. Kinematics

We began with kinematics, or the science of pure motion. In this division of the subject the ideas brought before us are those of space and time. The only attribute of matter which comes before us is its continuity of existence in space and time—the fact, namely, that every particle of matter, at any instant of time, is in one place and in one only, and that its change of place during any interval of time is accomplished by moving along a continuous path.

Neither the force which affects the motion of the body, nor the mass of the body, on which the amount of force required to produce the motion depends, come under our notice in the pure science of motion.

Article 100. Force

In the next division of the subject force is considered in the aspect of that which alters the motion of a mass.

If we confine our attention to a single body, our investigation enables us, from observation of its motion, to determine the direction and magnitude of the resultant force which acts on it, and this investigation is the exemplar and type of all researches undertaken for the purpose of the discovery and measurement of physical forces.

But this may be regarded as a mere application of the definition of a force and not as a new physical truth.

It is when we come to define equal forces as those which produce equal rates of acceleration in the same mass, and equal masses as those which are equally accelerated by equal forces, that we find that these definitions of equality amount to the assertion of the physical truth that the comparison of quantities of matter by the forces required to produce in them a given acceleration is a method which always leads to consistent results, whatever be the absolute values of the forces and the accelerations.

Article 101. Stress

The next step in the science of force is that in which we pass from the consideration of a force as acting on a body to that of its being one aspect of that mutual action between two bodies, which is called by Newton *action* and *reaction,* and which is now more briefly expressed by the single word *stress.*

Article 102. Relativity of dynamical knowledge

Our whole progress up to this point may be described as a gradual development of the doctrine of relativity of all physical phenomena. Position we must evidently acknowledge to be relative, for we cannot describe the position of a body in any terms which do not express relation. The ordinary language about motion and rest does not so completely exclude the notion of their being measured absolutely, but the reason of this is that in our ordinary language we tacitly assume that the earth is at rest.

As our ideas of space and motion become clearer, we come to see how the whole body of dynamical doctrine hangs together in one consistent system.

Our primitive notion may have been that to know absolutely where we are, and in what direction we are going, are essential elements of our knowledge as conscious beings.

But this notion, though undoubtedly held by many wise men in ancient times, has been gradually dispelled from the minds of students of physics.

There are no landmarks in space; one portion of space is exactly like every other portion, so that we cannot tell where we are. We are, as it were, on an unruffled sea, without stars, compass, soundings, wind, or tide, and we cannot tell in what direction we are going. We have no log which we can cast out to take a dead reckoning by; we may compute our rate of motion with respect to the neighbouring bodies, but we do not know how these bodies may be moving in space.

Article 103. Relativity of force

We cannot even tell what force may be acting on us; we can only tell the difference between the force acting on one thing and that acting on another.

We have an actual example of this in our everyday experience. The earth moves round the sun in a year at a distance of 91,520,000 miles, or 1.473×10^{13} centimetres. It follows from this that a force is exerted on the earth in the direction of the sun, which produces an acceleration of the earth in the direction of the sun of about 0.019 in feet and seconds, or about $\frac{1}{1680}$ of the intensity of gravity at the earth's surface.

A force equal to the sixteen-hundredth part of the weight of a body might be easily measured by known experimental methods, especially if the direction of this force were differently inclined to the vertical at different hours of the day.

Now, if the attraction of the sun were exerted upon the solid part of the earth, as distinguished from the movable bodies on which we experiment, a body suspended by a string, and moving with the earth, would indicate the difference between the solar action on the body and that on the earth as a whole.

If, for example, the sun attracted the earth and not the suspended body, then at sunrise the point of suspension, which is rigidly connected with the earth, would be drawn toward the sun, while the suspended body would be acted on only by the earth's attraction, and the string would appear to be deflected away from the sun by a sixteen-hundredth part of the length of the string. At sunset the string would be deflected away from the setting sun by an equal amount; and as the sun sets at a different point of the compass from that at which he rises the deflections of the string would be in different directions, and the difference in the position of the plumb line at sunrise and sunset would be easily observed.

But instead of this, the attraction of gravitation is exerted upon all kinds of matter equally at the same distance from the attracting body. At sunrise and sunset the centre of the earth and the suspended body are nearly at the same distance from the sun, and no deflection of the plumb line due to the sun's attraction can be observed at these times. The attraction of the sun, therefore, insofar as it is exerted equally upon all bodies on the earth, produces no effect on their relative motions. It is only the differences of the intensity and direction of the attraction acting on different parts of the earth which can produce any effect, and these differences are so small for bodies at moderate distances that it is only when the body acted on is very large, as in the case of the ocean, that their effect becomes perceptible in the form of tides.

Article 104. Rotation

In what we have hitherto said about the motion of bodies, we have tacitly assumed that in comparing one configuration of the system with another, we are able to draw a line in the final configuration parallel to a line in the original configuration. In other words, we assume that there are certain directions in space which may be regarded as constant, and to which other directions may be referred during the motion of the system.

In astronomy, a line drawn from the earth to a star may be considered as fixed in direction, because the relative motion of the earth and the star is in general so small compared with the distance between them that the change of direction, even in a century, is very small. But it is manifest that all such directions of reference must be indicated by the configuration of a material system existing in space, and that if this system were altogether removed, the original directions of reference could never be recovered.

But though it is impossible to determine the absolute velocity of a body in space, it is possible to determine whether the direction of a line in a material system is constant or variable.

For instance, it is possible by observations made on the earth alone, without reference to the heavenly bodies, to determine whether the earth is rotating or not.

So far as regards the geometrical configuration of the earth and the heavenly bodies, it is evidently all the same

Whether the sun, predominant in heaven,
Rise on the earth, or earth rise on the sun;
He from the east his flaming road begin,
Or she from west her silent course advance
With inoffensive pace that spinning sleeps
On her soft axle, while she paces even,
*And bears thee soft with the smooth air along.**

The distances between the bodies composing the universe, whether celestial or terrestrial, and the angles between the lines joining them are all that can be ascertained without an appeal to dynamical principles, and these will not be affected if any motion of rotation of the whole system, similar to that of a rigid body about an axis, is combined with the actual motion; so that from a geometrical point of view the Copernican system, according to which the earth rotates, has no advantage, except that of simplicity, over that in which the earth is supposed to be at rest, and the apparent

*[Milton, *Paradise Lost; GBWW,* Vol. 32, p. 235b.]

motions of the heavenly bodies to be their absolute motions.

Even if we go a step further and consider the dynamical theory of the earth rotating round its axis, we may account for its oblate figure, and for the equilibrium of the ocean and of all other bodies on its surface, on either of two hypotheses—that of the motion of the earth round its axis, or that of the earth not rotating but caused to assume its oblate figure by a force acting outward in all directions from its axis, the intensity of this force increasing as the distance from the axis increases. Such a force, if it acted on all kinds of matter alike, would account not only for the oblateness of the earth's figure but for the conditions of equilibrium of all bodies at rest with respect to the earth.

It is only when we go further still, and consider the phenomena of bodies which are in motion with respect to the earth, that we are really constrained to admit that the earth rotates.

Article 105. Newton's determination of the absolute velocity of rotation

Newton was the first to point out that the absolute motion of rotation of the earth might be demonstrated by experiments on the rotation of a material system. For instance, if a bucket of water is suspended from a beam by a string, and the string twisted so as to keep the bucket spinning round a vertical axis, the water will soon spin round at the same rate as the bucket, so that the system of the water and the bucket turns round its axis like a solid body. [*GBWW,* Vol. 34, p. 11.]

The water in the spinning bucket rises up at the sides and is depressed in the middle, showing that in order to make it move in a circle a pressure must be exerted toward the axis. This concavity of the surface depends on the absolute motion of rotation of the water and not on its relative rotation.

For instance, it does not depend on the rotation relative to the bucket. For at the beginning of the experiment, when we set the bucket spinning, and before the water has taken up the motion, the water and the bucket are in relative motion, but the surface of the water is flat, because the water is not rotating but only the bucket.

When the water and the bucket rotate together, there is no motion of the one relative to the other, but the surface of the water is hollow, because it is rotating.

When the bucket is stopped, as long as the water continues to rotate its surface remains hollow, showing that it is still rotating though the bucket is not.

It is manifestly the same, as regards this experiment, whether the rotation be in the direction of the hands of a watch or the opposite direction, provided the rate of rotation is the same.

Now let us suppose this experiment tried at the North Pole. Let the bucket be made, by a proper arrangement of clockwork, to rotate either in the direction of the hands of a watch, or in the opposite direction, at a perfectly regular rate.

If it is made to turn round by clockwork once in twenty-four hours (sidereal time) the way of the hands of a watch laid face upward, it will be rotating as regards the earth, but not rotating as regards the stars.

If the clockwork is stopped, it will rotate with respect to the stars, but not with respect to the earth.

Finally, if it is made to turn round once in twenty-four hours (sidereal time) in the opposite direction, it will be rotating with respect to the earth at the same rate as at first, but instead of being free from rotation as respects the stars, it will be rotating at the rate of one turn in twelve hours.

Hence if the earth is at rest, and the stars moving round it, the form of the surface will be the same in the first and last case; but if the earth is rotating, the water will be rotating in the last case but not in the first, and this will be made manifest by the water rising higher at the sides in the last case than in the first.

The surface of the water will not be really concave in any of the cases supposed, for the effect of gravity acting toward the centre of the earth is to make the surface convex, as the surface of the sea is, and the rate of rotation in our experiment is not sufficiently rapid to make the surface concave. It will only make it slightly less convex than the surface of the sea in the last case, and slightly more convex in the first.

But the difference in the form of the surface of the water would be so exceedingly small that with our methods of measurement it would be hopeless to attempt to determine the rotation of the earth in this way.

Article 106. Foucault's pendulum

The most satisfactory method of making an experiment for this purpose is that devised by M. Foucault.

A heavy ball is hung from a fixed point by a wire, so that it is capable of swinging like a pendulum in any vertical plane passing through the fixed point.

In starting the pendulum care must be taken that the wire, when at the lowest point of the swing, passes exactly through the position it assumes when hanging vertically. If it passes on one side of this position, it will return on the other side, and this motion of the pendulum round the vertical instead of through the vertical must be carefully avoided, because we wish to get rid of all motions of rotation either in one direction or the other.

Let us consider the angular momentum of the pendulum about the vertical line through the fixed point.

At the instant at which the wire of the pendulum passes through the vertical line, the angular momentum about the vertical line is zero.

The force of gravity always acts parallel to this vertical line, so that it cannot produce angular momentum round it. The tension of the wire always acts through the fixed point, so that it cannot produce angular momentum about the vertical line.

Hence the pendulum can never acquire angular momentum about the vertical line through the point of suspension.

Hence when the wire is out of the vertical, the vertical plane through the centre of the ball and the point of suspension cannot be rotating; for if it were, the pendulum would have an angular momentum about the vertical line.

Now let us suppose this experiment performed at the North Pole. The plane of vibration of the pendulum will remain absolutely constant in direction, so that if the earth rotates, the rotation of the earth will be made manifest.

We have only to draw a line on the earth parallel to the plane of vibration, and to compare the position of this line with that of the plane of vibration at a subsequent time.

As a pendulum of this kind properly suspended will swing for several hours, it is easy to ascertain whether the position of the plane of vibration is constant as regards the earth, as it would be if the earth is at rest, or constant as regards the stars, if the stars do not move round the earth.

We have supposed, for the sake of simplicity in the description, that the experiment is made at the North Pole. It is not necessary to go there in order to demonstrate the rotation of the earth. The only region where the experiment will not show it is at the equator.

At every other place the pendulum will indicate the rate of rotation of the earth with respect to the vertical line at that place. If at any instant the plane of the pendulum passes through a star near the horizon either rising or setting, it will continue to pass through that star as long as it is near the horizon. That is to say, the horizontal part of the apparent motion of a star on the horizon is equal to the rate of rotation of the plane of vibration of the pendulum.

It has been observed that the plane of vibration appears to rotate in the opposite direction in the Southern Hemisphere, and by a comparison of the rates at various places the actual time of rotation of the earth has been deduced without reference to astronomical observations. The mean value, as deduced from these experiments by Messrs. Galbraith and Houghton in their *Manual of Astronomy,* is 23 hours 53 minutes 37 seconds. The true time of rotation of the earth is 23 hours 56 minutes 4 seconds mean solar time.

Article 107. Matter and energy

All that we know about matter relates to the series of phenomena in which energy is transferred from one portion of matter to another, till in some part of the series our bodies are affected, and we become conscious of a sensation.

By the mental process which is founded on such sensations we come to learn the conditions of these sensations, and to trace them to objects which are not part of ourselves, but in every case the fact that we learn is the mutual action between bodies. This mutual action we have endeavoured to describe in this treatise. Under various aspects it is called *force, action and reaction,* and *stress,* and the evidence of it is the change of the motion of the bodies between which it acts.

The process by which stress produces change of motion is called *work,* and, as we have already shown, work may be considered as the transference of energy from one body or system to another.

Hence, as we have said, we are acquainted with matter only as that which may have energy communicated to it from other matter, and which may, in its turn, communicate energy to other matter.

Energy, on the other hand, we know only as that which in all natural phenomena is continually passing from one portion of matter to another.

Article 108. Test of a material substance

Energy cannot exist except in connection with matter. Hence since, in the space between the sun and the earth, the luminous and thermal radiations, which have left the sun and which have not reached the earth, possess energy, the amount of which per cubic mile can be measured, this energy must belong to matter existing in the interplanetary spaces; and since it is only by the light which reaches us that we become aware of the existence of the most remote stars, we conclude that the matter which transmits light is disseminated through the whole of the visible universe.

Article 109. Energy not capable of identification

We cannot identify a particular portion of energy or trace it through its transformations. It has no individual existence, such as that which we attribute to particular portions of matter.

The transactions of the material universe appear to be conducted, as it were, on a system of credit. Each transaction consists of the transfer of so much credit or energy from one body to another. This act of transfer or payment is called *work.* The energy so transferred does not retain any character by which it can be identified when it passes from one form to another.

Article 110. Absolute value of the energy of a body unknown

The energy of a material system can only be estimated in a relative manner.

In the first place, though the energy of the motion of the parts relative to the centre of mass of the system may be accurately defined, the whole energy consists of this together with the energy of a mass equal to that of the whole system moving with the velocity of the centre of mass. Now this latter velocity—that of the centre of mass—can be estimated only with reference to some body external to the system, and the value which we assign to this velocity will be different according to the body which we select as our origin.

Hence the estimated kinetic energy of a material system contains a part, the value of which cannot be determined except by the arbitrary selection of an origin. The only origin which would not be arbitrary is the centre of mass of the material universe, but this is a point the position and motion of which are quite unknown to us.

Article 111. Latent energy

But the energy of a material system is indeterminate for another reason. We cannot reduce the system to a state in which it has no energy, and any energy which is never removed from the system must remain unperceived by us, for it is only as it enters or leaves the system that we can take any account of it.

We must, therefore, regard the energy of a material system as a quantity of which we may ascertain the increase or diminution as the system passes from one definite condition to another. The absolute value of the energy in the standard condition is unknown to us, and it would be of no value to us if we did know it, as all phenomena depend on the variations of the energy, and not on its absolute value.

Article 112. A complete discussion of energy would include the whole of physical science.

The discussion of the various forms of energy—gravitational, electromagnetic, molecular, thermal, etc.—with the conditions of the transference of energy from one form to another, and the constant dissipation of the energy available for producing work, constitutes the whole of physical science, insofar as it has been developed in the dynamical form under the various designations of Astronomy, Electricity, Magnetism, Optics, Theory of the Physical States of Bodies, Thermodynamics, and Chemistry.

Chapter VII. The Pendulum and Gravity

Article 113. On uniform motion in a circle

Let M (fig. 11) be a body moving in a circle with velocity V.

Let $\overline{OM} = r$ be the radius of the circle.

The direction of the velocity of M is that of the tangent to the circle. Draw $\overline{OV}$ parallel to this direction through the centre of the circle and equal to the distance described in unit of time with velocity V, then $\overline{OV} = V$.

If we take O as the origin of the diagram of velocity, V will represent the velocity of the body at M.

As the body moves round the circle, the point V will also describe a circle, and the velocity of the point V will be to that of M as $\overline{OV}$ to $\overline{OM}$.

Figure 11

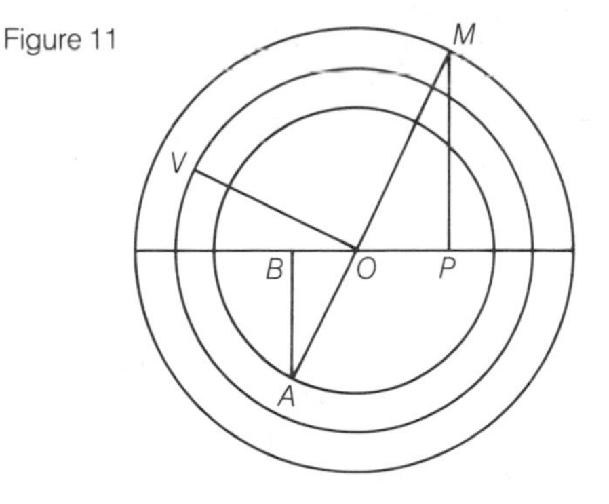

If, therefore, we draw $\overline{OA}$ in $\overline{MO}$ produced, and therefore parallel to the direction of motion of V, and make $\overline{OA}$ a third proportional to $\overline{OM}$ and $\overline{OV}$, and if we assume O as the origin of the diagram of rate of acceleration, then the point A will represent the velocity of the point V, or, what is the same thing, the rate of acceleration of the point M.

Hence, when a body moves with uniform velocity in a circle, its acceleration is directed toward the centre of the circle and is a third proportional to the radius of the circle and the velocity of the body.

The force acting on the body M is equal to the product of this acceleration into the mass of the body, or if F be this force

$$F = \frac{MV^2}{r}.$$

Article 114. Centrifugal force

This is the force which must act on the body M in order to keep it in the circle of radius v, in which it is moving with velocity V.

The direction of this force is toward the centre of the circle.

If this force is applied by means of a string fastened to the body, the string will be in a state of tension. To a person holding the other end of the string this tension will appear to be directed toward the body M, as if the body M had a tendency to move away from the centre of the circle which it is describing.

Hence this latter force is often called *centrifugal force*.

The force which really acts on the body, being directed toward the centre of the circle, is called *centripetal force*, and in some popular treatises the centripetal and centrifugal forces are described as opposing and balancing each other. But they are merely the different aspects of the same stress.

Article 115. Periodic time

The time of describing the circumference of the circle is called the *periodic time*. If π represents the ratio of the circumference of a circle to its diameter, which is 3.14159 . . . , the circumference of a circle of radius r is $2\pi r$, and since this is described in the periodic time T with velocity V, we have

$$2\pi r = VT.$$

Hence $$F = 4\pi^2 M \frac{r}{T^2}.$$

The rate of circular motion is often expressed by the number of revolutions in unit of time. Let this number be denoted by n, then

$$nT = 1$$

and $F = 4\pi^2 Mrn^2$.

Article 116. On simple harmonic vibrations

If while the body M (fig. 11) moves in a circle with uniform velocity another point P moves in a fixed diameter of the circle, so as to be always at the foot of the perpendicular from M on that diameter, the body P is said to execute *simple harmonic vibrations*.

The radius, r, of the circle is called the *amplitude* of the vibration.

The periodic time of M is called the *periodic time* of vibration.

The angle which $\overline{OM}$ makes with the positive direction of the fixed diameter is called the *phase* of the vibration.

Article 117. On the force acting on the vibrating body

The only difference between the motions of M and P is that M has a vertical motion compounded with a horizontal motion which is the same as that of P. Hence the velocity and the acceleration of the two bodies differ only with respect to the vertical part of the velocity and acceleration of M.

The acceleration of P is therefore the horizontal component of that of M, and since the acceleration of M is represented by $\overline{OA}$, which is in the direction of $\overline{MO}$ produced, the acceleration of P will be represented by $\overline{OB}$, where B is the foot of the perpendicular from A on the horizontal diameter. Now by similar triangles OMP, OAB

$$\overline{OM} : \overline{OA} :: \overline{OP} : \overline{OB}.$$

But $\overline{OM} = r$ and $\overline{OA} = -4\pi^2 \frac{r}{T^2}$. Hence

$$\overline{OB} = -\frac{4\pi^2}{T^2}\overline{OP} = -4\pi^2 n^2\,\overline{OP}.$$

In simple harmonic vibration, therefore, the acceleration is always directed toward the centre of vibration and is equal to the distance from that centre multiplied by $4\pi^2 n^2$, and if the mass of the vibrating body is P, the force acting on it at a distance x from O is $4\pi^2 n^2 Px$.

It appears, therefore, that a body which executes simple harmonic vibrations in a straight line is acted on by a force which varies as the distance from the centre of vibration, and the value of this force at a given distance depends only on that distance, on the mass of the body, and on the square of the number of vibrations in unit of time, and is independent of the amplitude of the vibrations.

Article 118. Isochronous vibrations

It follows from this that if a body moves in a straight line and is acted on by a force directed toward a fixed point on the line and varying as the distance from that point, it will execute simple harmonic vibrations, the periodic time of which will be the same whatever the amplitude of vibration.

If for a particular kind of displacement of a body, as turning round an axis, the force tending to bring it back to a given position varies as the displacement, the body will execute simple harmonic vibrations about that position, the periodic time of which will be independent of their amplitude.

Vibrations of this kind, which are executed in the same time whatever be their amplitude, are called *isochronous vibrations.*

Article 119. Potential energy of the vibrating body

The velocity of the body when it passes through the point of equilibrium is equal to that of the body moving in the circle, or $V = 2\pi rn$, where r is the amplitude of vibration and n is the number of double vibrations per second.

Hence the kinetic energy of the vibrating body at the point of equilibrium is

$$\tfrac{1}{2}MV^2 = 2\pi^2 Mr^2 n^2$$

where M is the mass of the body.

At the extreme elongation, where $x = r$, the velocity, and therefore the kinetic energy, of the body is zero. The diminution of kinetic energy must correspond to an equal increase of potential energy. Hence if we reckon the potential energy from the configuration in which the body is at its point of equilibrium, its potential energy when at a distance r from this point is $2\pi^2 Mn^2 r^2$.

This is the potential energy of a body which vibrates isochronously and executes n double vibrations per second when it is at rest at the distance, r, from the point of equilibrium. As the potential energy does not depend on the motion of the body, but only on its position, we may write it

$$2\pi^2 Mn^2 x^2,$$

where x is the distance from the point of equilibrium.

Article 120. The simple pendulum

The simple pendulum consists of a small heavy body called the bob, suspended from a fixed point by a fine string of invariable length. The bob is supposed to be so small that its motion may be treated as that of a material particle, and the string is supposed to be so fine that we may neglect its mass and weight. The bob is set in motion so as to swing through a small angle in a vertical plane. Its path, therefore, is an arc of a circle, whose centre is the point of suspension, O, and whose radius is the length of the string, which we shall denote by l.

Figure 12

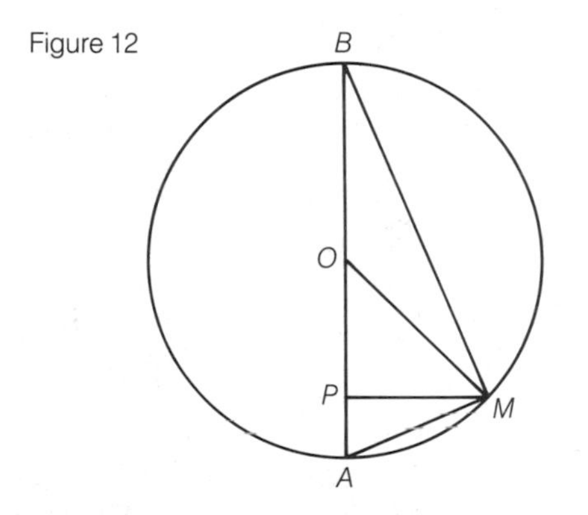

Let O (fig. 12) be the point of suspension and $\overline{OA}$ the position of the pendulum when hanging vertically. When the bob is at M it is higher than when it is at A by the height $\overline{AP} = \dfrac{\overline{AM}^2}{\overline{AB}}$ where $\overline{AM}$ is the chord of the arc ALM and $\overline{AB} = 2l$.

If M be the mass of the bob and g the intensity of gravity, the weight of the bob will be Mg and the work done against gravity during the motion of the bob from A to M will be $Mg\overline{AP}$. This, therefore, is the potential energy of the pendulum when the bob is at M, reckoning the energy zero when the bob is at A.

We may write this energy

$$\frac{Mg}{2l}\overline{AM}^2.$$

The potential energy of the bob when displaced through any arc varies as the square of the chord of that arc.

If it had varied as the square of the arc itself in which the bob moves, the vibrations would have been strictly isochronous. As the potential energy varies more slowly than the square of the arc, the period of each vibration will be greater when the amplitude is greater.

For very small vibrations, however, we may neglect the difference between the chord and the arc, and denoting the arc by x we may write the potential energy

$$\frac{Mg}{2l}x^2.$$

But we have already shown that in harmonic vibrations the potential energy is $2\pi^2Mn^2x^2$.

Equating these two expressions and clearing fractions we find

$$g = 4\pi^2n^2l,$$

where g is the intensity of gravity, π is the ratio of the circumference of a circle to its diameter, n is the number of vibrations of the pendulum in unit of time, and l is the length of the pendulum.

Article 121. A rigid pendulum

If we could construct a pendulum with a bob so small and a string so fine that it might be regarded for practical purposes as a simple pendulum, it would be easy to determine g by this method. But all real pendulums have bobs of considerable size, and in order to preserve the length invariable the bob must be connected with the point of suspension by a stout rod, the mass of which cannot be neglected. It is always possible, however, to determine the length of a simple pendulum whose vibrations would be executed in the same manner as those of a pendulum of any shape.

The complete discussion of this subject would lead us into calculations beyond the limits of this treatise. We may, however, arrive at the most important result without calculation as follows.

The motion of a rigid body in one plane may be completely defined by stating the motion of its centre of mass, and the motion of the body round its centre of mass.

The force required to produce a given change in the motion of the centre of mass depends only on the mass of the body (Art. 63).

The moment required to produce a given change of angular velocity about the centre of mass depends on the distribution of the mass, being greater the further the different parts of the body are from the centre of mass.

If, therefore, we form a system of two particles rigidly connected, the sum of the masses being equal to the mass of a pendulum, their centre of mass coinciding with that of the pendulum, and their distances from the centre of mass being such that a couple of the same moment is required to produce a given rotatory motion about the centre of mass of the new system as about that of the pendulum, then the new system will for motions in a certain plane be dynamically equivalent to the given pendulum, that is, if the two systems are moved in the same way the forces required to guide the motion will be equal. Since the two particles may have any ratio, provided the sum of their masses is equal to the mass of the pendulum, and since the line joining them may have any direction provided it passes through the centre of mass, we may arrange them so that one of the particles corresponds to any given point of the pendulum, say, the point of suspension P (fig. 13). The mass of this

Figure 13

particle, and the position and mass of the other at Q, will be determinate. The position of the second particle, Q, is called the *centre of oscillation*. Now in the system of two particles, if one of them, P, is fixed and the other, Q, allowed to swing under the action of gravity, we have a simple pendulum. For one of the particles, P, acts as the point of suspension, and the other, Q, is at an invariable distance from it, so that the connection between them is the same as if they were united by a string of length $l = \overline{PQ}$.

Hence a pendulum of any form swings in exactly the same manner as a simple pendulum whose length is the distance from the centre of suspension to the centre of oscillation.

Article 122. Inversion of the pendulum

Now let us suppose the system of two particles inverted, Q being made the point of suspension and P being made to swing. We have now a simple pendulum of the same length as before. Its vibrations will therefore be executed in the same time. But it is dynamically equivalent to the pendulum suspended by its centre of oscillation.

Hence if a pendulum be inverted and suspended by its centre of oscillation its vibrations will have the same period as before, and the distance between the centre of suspension and that of oscillation will be equal to that of a simple pendulum having the same time of vibration.

It was in this way that Captain Kater determined the length of the simple pendulum which vibrates seconds.

He constructed a pendulum which could be made to vibrate about two knife edges, on opposite sides of the centre of mass and at *unequal* distances from it.

By certain adjustments, he made the time of vibration the same whether the one knife edge or the other were the centre of suspension. The length of the corresponding simple pendulum was then found by measuring the distance between the knife edges.

Article 123. Illustration of Kater's pendulum

Figure 14

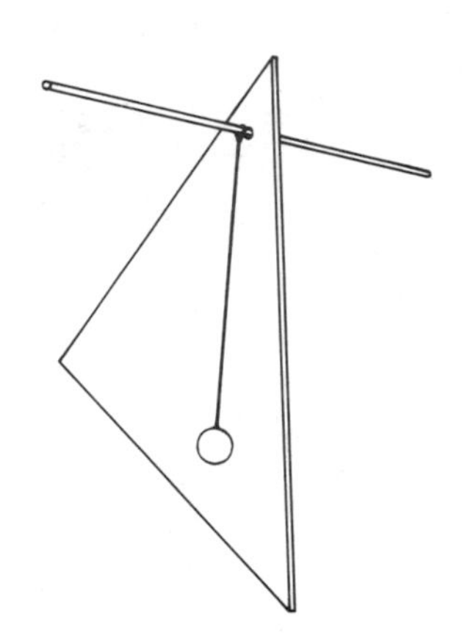

The principle of Kater's pendulum may be illustrated by a very simple and striking experiment. Take a flat board of any form (fig. 14), and drive a piece of wire through it near its edge, and allow it to hang in a vertical plane, holding the ends of the wire by the finger and thumb. Take a small bullet, fasten it to the end of a thread and allow the thread to pass over the wire, so that the bullet hangs close to the board. Move the hand by which you hold the wire horizontally in the plane of the board, and observe whether the board moves forward or backward with respect to the bullet. If it moves forward lengthen the string, if backward shorten it till the bullet and the board move together. Now mark the point of the board opposite the centre of the bullet and fasten the string to the wire. You will find that if you hold the wire by the ends and move it in any manner, however sudden and irregular, in the plane of the board, the bullet will never quit the marked spot on the board.

Hence this spot is called the centre of oscillation, because when the board is oscillating about the wire when fixed it oscillates as if it consisted of a single particle placed at the spot.*

It is also called the centre of percussion, because if the board is at rest and the wire is suddenly moved horizontally the board will at first begin to rotate about the spot as a centre.

Article 124. Determination of the intensity of gravity

The most direct method of determining g is, no doubt, to let a body fall and find what velocity it has gained in a second, but it is very difficult to make accurate observations of the motion of bodies when their velocities are so great as 981 centimetres per second, and besides, the experiment would have to be conducted in a vessel from which the air has been exhausted, as the resistance of the air to such rapid motion is very considerable, compared with the weight of the falling body.

The experiment with the pendulum is much more satisfactory. By making the arc of vibration very small, the motion of the bob becomes so slow that the resistance of the air can have very little influence on the time of vibration. In the best experiments the pendulum is swung in an airtight vessel from which the air is exhausted.

Besides this, the motion repeats itself, and the pendulum swings to and fro hundreds, or even thousands, of times before the various resistances to which it is exposed reduce the amplitude of the vibrations till they can no longer be observed.

---

*[Maxwell's meaning seems to be this: When the board is oscillating as a pendulum about the wire as a fixed support, the board oscillates as if it were a simple pendulum with its mass concentrated as a single particle placed at the spot. Accordingly, the editors have seen fit to extend the wire in this diagram to the other side of the board (the left-hand side of the diagram). This is the only alteration we have made to any of Maxwell's original diagrams.]

Thus the actual observation consists not in watching the beginning and end of one vibration, but in determining the duration of a series of many hundred vibrations, and thence deducing the time of a single vibration.

The observer is relieved from the labour of counting the whole number of vibrations, and the measurement is made one of the most accurate in the whole range of practical science by the following method.

Article 125. Method of observation

A pendulum clock is placed behind the experimental pendulum, so that when both pendulums are hanging vertically the bob, or some other part of the experimental pendulum, just hides a white spot on the clock pendulum, as seen by a telescope fixed at some distance in front of the clock.

Observations of the transit of "clock stars" across the meridian are made from time to time, and from these the rate of the clock is deduced in terms of "mean solar time."

The experimental pendulum is then set swinging, and the two pendulums are observed through the telescope. Let us suppose that the time of a single vibration is not exactly that of the clock pendulum but a little more.

The observer at the telescope sees the clock pendulum always gaining on the experimental pendulum, till at last the experimental pendulum just hides the white spot on the clock pendulum as it crosses the vertical line. The time at which this takes place is observed and recorded as the *first positive coincidence.*

The clock pendulum continues to gain on the other, and after a certain time the two pendulums cross the vertical line at the same instant in opposite directions. The time of this is recorded as the *first negative coincidence.* After an equal interval of time there will be a second positive coincidence, and so on.

By this method the clock itself counts the number, N, of vibrations of its own pendulum between the coincidences. During this time the experimental pendulum has executed one vibration less than the clock. Hence the time of vibration of the experimental pendulum is $\frac{N}{N-1}$ seconds of clock time.

When there is no exact coincidence, but when the clock pendulum is ahead of the experimental pendulum at one passage of the vertical and behind at the next, a little practice on the part of the observer will enable him to estimate at what time between the passages the two pendulums must have been in the same phase. The epoch of coincidence can thus be estimated to a fraction of a second.

Article 126. Estimation of error

The experimental pendulum will go on swinging for some hours, so that the whole time to be measured may be ten thousand or more vibrations.

But the error introduced into the calculated time of vibration, by a mistake even of a whole second in noting the time of vibration, may be made exceedingly small by prolonging the experiment.

For if we observe the first and the nth coincidence, and find that they are separated by an interval of N seconds of the clock, the experimental pendulum will have lost n vibrations, as compared with the clock, and will have made $N - n$ vibrations in N seconds. Hence the time of a single vibration is $T = \frac{N}{N-n}$ seconds of clock time.

Let us suppose, however, that by a mistake of a second we note down the last coincidence as taking place $N + 1$ seconds after the first. The value of T as deduced from this result would be

$$T' = \frac{N+1}{N+1-n}$$

and the error introduced by the mistake of a second will be

$$T' - T = \frac{N+1}{N+1-n} - \frac{N}{N-n}$$

$$= \frac{n}{(N+1-n)(N-n)}$$

If N is 10,000 and n is 100, a mistake of one second in noting the time of coincidence will alter the value of T only about one-millionth part of its value.

Chapter VIII. Universal Gravitation

Article 127. Newton's method

The most instructive example of the method of dynamical reasoning is that by which Newton determined the law of the force with which the heavenly bodies act on each other.

The process of dynamical reasoning consists in deducing from the successive configurations of the heavenly bodies, as observed by astronomers, their velocities and their accelerations, and in this way determining the direction and the relative magnitude of the force which acts on them.

Kepler had already prepared the way for Newton's investigation by deducing from a careful study of the observations of Tycho Brahe the three laws of planetary motion which bear his name. [See *GBWW,* Vol. 16, pp. 845–1004.]

Article 128. Kepler's laws

Kepler's laws are purely kinematical. They completely describe the motion of the planets, but they say nothing about the forces by which these motions are determined.

Their dynamical interpretation was discovered by Newton.

The first and second law relate to the motion of a single planet.

Law I. The areas swept out by the vector drawn from the sun to a planet are proportional to the times of describing them. If h denotes twice the area swept out in unit of time, twice the area swept out in time t will be ht, and if P is the mass of the planet, Pht will be the mass-area, as defined in Article 68. Hence the angular momentum of the planet about the sun, which is the rate of change of the mass-area, will be Ph, a constant quantity.

Hence, by Article 70, the force, if any, which acts on the planet must have no moment with respect to the sun, for if it had it would increase or diminish the angular momentum at a rate measured by the value of this moment.

Hence, whatever be the force which acts on the planet, the direction of this force must always pass through the sun.

Article 129. Angular velocity

Definition. The angular velocity of a vector is the rate at which the angle increases which it makes with a fixed vector in the plane of its motion.

If ω is the angular velocity of a vector, and r its length, the rate at which it sweeps out an area is $\frac{1}{2}\omega r^2$. Hence, $h = \omega r^2$, and since h is constant, ω, the angular velocity of a planet's motion round the sun, varies inversely as the square of the distance from the sun.

This is true whatever the law of force

may be, provided the force acting on the planet always passes through the sun.

Article 130. Motion about the centre of mass

Since the stress between the planet and the sun acts on both bodies, neither of them can remain at rest. The only point whose motion is not affected by the stress is the centre of mass of the two bodies.

Figure 15

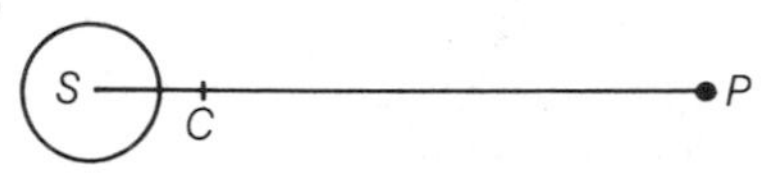

If r is the distance $\overline{SP}$ (fig. 15), and if C is the centre of mass, $\overline{SC} = \dfrac{Pr}{S + P}$ and $\overline{CP} = \dfrac{Sr}{S+P}$. The angular momentum of P about C is $P\omega \dfrac{S^2r^2}{(S + P)^2} = \dfrac{PS^2h}{(S + P)^2}$.

Article 131. The orbit

We have already made use of diagrams of configuration and of velocity in studying the motion of a material system. These diagrams, however, represent only the state of the system at a given instant; and this state is indicated by the relative position of points corresponding to the bodies forming the system.

It is often, however, convenient to represent in a single diagram the whole series of configurations or velocities which the system assumes. If we suppose the points of the diagram to move so as continually to represent the state of the moving system, each point of the diagram will trace out a line, straight or curved.

On the diagram of configuration, this line is called, in general, the *path* of the body. In the case of the heavenly bodies it is often called the *orbit.*

Article 132. The hodograph

On the diagram of velocity the line traced out by each moving point is called the *hodograph* of the body to which it corresponds.

The study of the hodograph, as a method of investigating the motion of a body, was introduced by Sir W. R. Hamilton. The hodograph may be defined as the path traced out by the extremity of a vector which continually represents, in direction and magnitude, the velocity of a moving body.

In applying the method of the hodograph to a planet, the orbit of which is in one plane, we shall find it convenient to suppose the hodograph turned round its origin through a right angle, so that the vector of the hodograph is perpendicular instead of parallel to the velocity it represents.

Article 133. Kepler's second law

Law II. The orbit of a planet with respect to the sun is an ellipse, the sun being in one of the foci.

Let *APQB* (fig. 16) be the elliptic orbit.

Figure 16

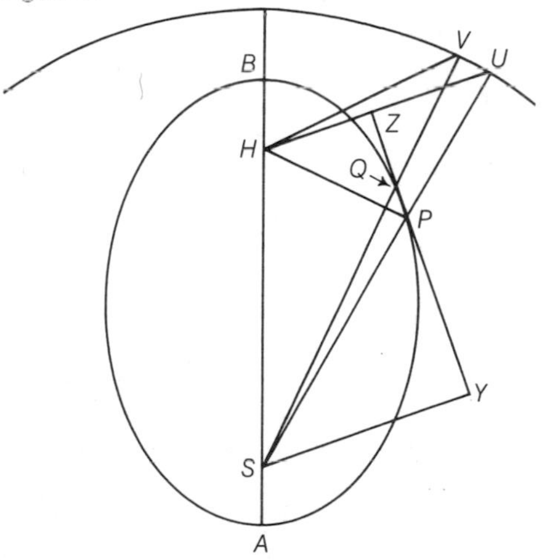

Let S be the sun in one focus, and let H be the other focus. Produce $\overline{SP}$ to U, so that $\overline{SU}$ is equal to the transverse axis $\overline{AB}$, and join $\overline{HU}$, then $\overline{HU}$ will be proportional and perpendicular to the velocity at P.

For bisect $\overline{HU}$ in Z and join $\overline{ZP}$, $\overline{ZP}$ will be a tangent to the ellipse at P; let $\overline{SY}$ be a perpendicular from S on this tangent.

If v is the velocity at P, and h twice the area swept out in unit of time, $h = v\overline{SY}$.

Also if b is half the conjugate axis of the ellipse $\overline{SY} \cdot \overline{HZ} = b^2$.

Now $\overline{HU} = 2\overline{HZ}$; hence

$$v = \tfrac{1}{2}\frac{h}{b^2}\,\overline{HU}.$$

Hence $\overline{HU}$ is always proportional to the velocity, and it is perpendicular to its direction. Now $\overline{SU}$ is always equal to $\overline{AB}$. Hence the circle whose centre is S and radius $\overline{AB}$ is the hodograph of the planet, H being the origin of the hodograph.

The corresponding points of the orbit and the hodograph are those which lie in the same straight line through S.

Thus P corresponds to U and Q to V.

The velocity communicated to the body during its passage from P to Q is represented by the geometrical difference between the vectors $\overline{HU}$ and $\overline{HV}$, that is, by the line $\overline{UV}$, and it is perpendicular to this arc of the circle and is therefore, as we have already proved, directed toward S.

If PQ is the arc described in unit of time, then $\overline{UV}$ represents the acceleration, and since $\overline{UV}$ is on a circle whose centre is S, $\overline{UV}$ will be a measure of the angular velocity of the planet about S. Hence the acceleration is proportional to the angular velocity, and this by Article 129 is inversely as the square of the distance $\overline{SP}$. Hence the acceleration of the planet is in the direction of the sun and is inversely as the square of the distance from the sun.

This, therefore, is the law according to which the attraction of the sun on a planet varies as the planet moves in its orbit and alters its distance from the sun.

Article 134. Force on a planet

Since, as we have already shown, the orbit of the planet with respect to the centre of mass of the sun and planet has its dimensions in the ratio of S to $S + P$ to those of the orbit of the planet with respect to the sun, if $2a$ and $2b$ are the axes of the orbit of the planet with respect to the sun, the area is πab, and if T is the time of going completely round the orbit, the value of h is

$$2\pi\,\frac{ab}{T}.$$

The velocity with respect to the sun is therefore

$$\pi\,\frac{a}{Tb}\,\overline{HU}.$$

With respect to the centre of mass it is

$$\frac{S}{S+P}\,\frac{\pi a}{Tb}\,\overline{HU}.$$

The acceleration of the planet toward the centre of mass is

$$\frac{S}{S+P}\,\frac{\pi a}{Tb}\,\overline{UV}$$

and the impulse on the planet whose mass is P is therefore

$$\frac{S \cdot P}{S+P}\,\frac{\pi a}{Tb}\,\overline{UV}.$$

Let t be the time of describing PQ, then twice the area SPQ is

$$ht = \omega r^2 t$$

$$\text{and } \overline{UV} = 2a\omega t = 2a\,\frac{h}{r^2}\,t = 4\pi\,\frac{a^2 b}{Tr^2}\,t.$$

Hence the force on the planet is

$$F = 4\pi^2\,\frac{S \cdot P}{S+P}\,\frac{a^3}{T^2 r^2}.$$

This then is the value of the stress or attraction between a planet and the sun in terms of their masses P and S, their mean distance a, their actual distance r, and the periodical time T.

Article 135. Interpretation of Kepler's third law

To compare the attraction between the sun and different planets, Newton made use of Kepler's third law.

Law III. The squares of the time of different planets are proportional to the cubes of their mean distances.

In other words $\frac{a^3}{T^2}$ is a constant, say $\frac{C}{4\pi^2}$

Hence
$$F = C\frac{S \cdot P}{S+P}\frac{1}{r^2}.$$

In the case of the smaller planets their masses are so small, compared with that of the sun, that $\frac{S}{S+P}$ may be put equal to 1, so that $F = CP\frac{1}{r^2}$ or the attraction on a planet is proportional to its mass and inversely as the square of its distance.

Article 136. Law of gravitation

This is the most remarkable fact about the attraction of gravitation, that at the same distance it acts equally on equal masses of substances of all kinds. This is proved by pendulum experiments for the different kinds of matter at the surface of the earth. Newton extended the law to the matter of which the different planets are composed. [See *GBWW,* Vol. 34, pp. 276–82.]

It had been suggested, before Newton proved it, that the sun as a whole attracts a planet as a whole, and the law of the inverse square had also been previously stated, but in the hands of Newton the doctrine of gravitation assumed its final form.

Every portion of matter attracts every other portion of matter, and the stress between them is proportional to the product of their masses divided by the square of their distance.

For if the attraction between a gram of matter in the sun and a gram of matter in a planet at distance r is $\frac{C}{r^2}$ where C is a constant, then if there are S grams in the sun and P in the planet the whole attraction between the sun and one gram in the planet will be $\frac{CS}{r^2}$, and the whole attraction between the sun and the planet will be $C\frac{SP}{r^2}$.

Comparing this statement of Newton's "Law of Universal Gravitation" with the value of F formerly obtained we find

$$C\frac{S \cdot P}{r^2} = 4\pi^2\frac{S \cdot P}{S+P}\frac{a^3}{T^2r^2}.$$

$$\text{or}\quad 4\pi^2a^3 = C\,(S+P)\,T^2.$$

Article 137. Amended form of Kepler's third law

Hence Kepler's third law must be amended thus:

The cubes of the mean distances are as the squares of the times multiplied into the sum of the masses of the sun and the planet.

In the case of the larger planets, Jupiter, Saturn, etc., the value of $S + P$ is considerably greater than in the case of the earth and the smaller planets. Hence the periodic times of the larger planets should be somewhat less than they would be according to Kepler's law, and this is found to be the case.

In the following table the mean distances (a) of the planets are given in terms of the mean distance of the earth, and the periodic time T in terms of the sidereal year:

Planet	a	T	a^3	T^2	$a^3 - T^2$
Mercury	0.387098	0.24084	0.0580046	0.0580049	−0.0000003
Venus	0.72333	0.61518	0.378451	0.378453	−0.0000002
Earth	1.0000	1.00000	1.00000	1.00000	
Mars	1.52369	1.88082	3.53746	3.53747	−0.00001
Jupiter	5.20278	11.8618	140.832	140.701	+0.131
Saturn	9.53879	29.4560	867.914	867.658	+0.256
Uranus	19.1824	84.0123	7058.44	7058.07	+0.37
Neptune	30.037	164.616	27100.0	27098.4	+1.6

It appears from the table that Kepler's third law is very nearly accurate, for a^3 is very nearly equal to T^2, but that for those planets whose mass is less than that of the earth—namely, Mercury, Venus, and Mars—a^3 is less than T^2, whereas for Jupiter, Saturn, Uranus, and Neptune, whose mass is greater than that of the earth, a^3 is greater than T^2.

Article 138. Potential energy due to gravitation

The potential energy of the gravitation between the bodies S and P may be calculated when we know the attraction between them in terms of their distance. The process of calculation by which we sum up the effects of a continually varying quantity belongs to the integral calculus, and though in this case the calculation may be explained by elementary methods, we shall rather deduce the potential energy directly from Kepler's first and second laws.

These laws completely define the motion of the sun and planet, and therefore we may find the kinetic energy of the system corresponding to any part of the elliptic orbit. Now, since the sun and planet form a conservative system, the sum of the kinetic and potential energy is constant, and therefore when we know the kinetic energy we may deduce that part of the potential energy which depends on the distance between the bodies.

Article 139. Kinetic energy of the system

To determine the kinetic energy we observe that the velocity of the planet with respect to the sun is, by Article 133,

$$v = \tfrac{1}{2}\frac{h}{b^2}\,\overline{HU}.$$

The velocities of the planet and the sun with respect to the centre of mass of the system are respectively

$$\frac{S}{S+P}\,v \quad \text{and} \quad \frac{P}{S+P}\,v.$$

The kinetic energies of the planet and the sun are therefore

$$\tfrac{1}{2}P\frac{S^2v^2}{(S+P)^2} \quad \text{and} \quad \tfrac{1}{2}S\,\frac{P^2}{(S+P)^2}\,v^2$$

and the whole kinetic energy is

$$\tfrac{1}{2}\,\frac{S\cdot P}{S+P}\,v^2 = \tfrac{1}{4}\,\frac{S\cdot P}{S+P}\,\frac{h^2}{b^4}\,\overline{HU}^2.$$

To determine v^2 in terms of $\overline{SP}$ or r, we observe that by the law of areas

$$v\cdot\overline{SY} = h = \frac{2\pi ab}{T} \qquad (1)$$

also by a property of the ellipse

$$\overline{HZ} \cdot \overline{SY} = b^2 \qquad (2)$$

and by the similar triangles HZP and SYP

$$\frac{\overline{SY}}{\overline{HZ}} = \frac{\overline{HP}}{\overline{SP}} = \frac{r}{2a - r} \qquad (3)$$

multiplying (2) and (3) we find

$$\overline{SY}^2 = \frac{b^2 r}{2a - r}.$$

Hence by (1)

$$v^2 = \frac{4\pi^2 a^2 b^2}{T^2} \frac{1}{\overline{SY}^2} = \frac{4\pi^2 a^2}{T^2} \left(\frac{2a}{r} - 1\right)$$

and the kinetic energy of the system is

$$\frac{4\pi^2 a^3}{T^2} \frac{S \cdot P}{S + P} \left(\frac{1}{r} - \frac{1}{2a}\right)$$

and this by the equation at the end of Article 136 becomes

$$C \cdot S \cdot P \left(\frac{1}{r} - \frac{1}{2a}\right)$$

where C is the constant of gravitation.

This is the value of the kinetic energy of the two bodies S and P when moving in an ellipse of which the transverse axis is $2a$.

Article 140. Potential energy of the system

The sum of the kinetic and potential energies is constant, but its absolute value is by Article 110 unknown, and not necessary to be known.

Hence if we assume that the potential energy is of the form

$$K - C \cdot S \cdot P \frac{1}{r}$$

the second term, which is the only one depending on the distance, r, is also the only one which we have anything to do with. The other term K represents the work done by gravitation while the two bodies originally at an infinite distance from each other are allowed to approach as near as their dimensions will allow them.

Article 141. The moon is a heavy body

Having thus determined the law of the force between each planet and the sun, Newton proceeded to show that the observed weight of bodies at the earth's surface and the force which retains the moon in her orbit round the earth are related to each other according to the same law of the inverse square of the distance.

This force of gravity acts in every region accessible to us, at the top of the highest mountains and at the highest point reached by balloons. Its intensity, as measured by pendulum experiments, decreases as we ascend; and although the height to which we can ascend is so small compared with the earth's radius that we cannot from observations of this kind infer that gravity varies inversely as the square of the distance from the centre of the earth, the observed decrease of the intensity of gravity is consistent with this law, the form of which had been suggested to Newton by the motion of the planets.

Assuming, then, that the intensity of gravity varies inversely as the square of the distance from the centre of the earth, and knowing its value at the surface of the earth, Newton calculated its value at the mean distance of the moon.

His first calculations were vitiated by his adopting an erroneous estimate of the dimensions of the earth. When, however, he had obtained a more correct value of this quantity he found that the intensity of gravity calculated for a distance equal to that of the moon was equal to the force required to keep the moon in her orbit.

He thus identified the force which acts between the earth and the moon with that which causes bodies near the earth's surface to fall toward the earth.

Article 142. Cavendish's experiment

Having thus shown that the force with which the heavenly bodies attract each other is of the same kind as that with which bodies that we can handle are attracted to the earth, it remained to be shown that bodies such as we can handle attract one another.

The difficulty of doing this arises from the fact that the mass of bodies which we can handle is so small compared with that of the earth, that even when we bring the two bodies as near as we can the attraction between them is an exceedingly small fraction of the weight of either.

We cannot get rid of the attraction of the earth, but we must arrange the experiment in such a way that it interferes as little as is possible with the effects of the attraction of the other body.

The apparatus devised by the Rev. John Michell for this purpose was that which has since received the name of the *torsion balance.* Michell died before he was able to make the experiment, but his apparatus afterward came into the hands of Henry Cavendish, who improved it in many respects and measured the attraction between large leaden balls and small balls suspended from the arms of the balance. A similar instrument was afterward independently invented by Coulomb for measuring small electric and magnetic forces, and it continues to be the best instrument known to science for the measurement of small forces of all kinds.

Article 143. The torsion balance

The torsion balance consists of a horizontal rod suspended by a wire from a fixed support. When the rod is turned round by an external force in a horizontal plane it twists the wire, and the wire, being elastic, tends to resist this strain and to untwist itself. This force of torsion is proportional to the angle through which the wire is twisted, so that if we cause a force to act in a horizontal direction at right angles to the rod at its extremity, we may, by observing the angle through which the force is able to turn the rod, determine the magnitude of the force.

The force is proportional to the angle of torsion and to the fourth power of the diameter of the wire and inversely to the length of the rod and the length of the wire.

Hence, by using a long fine wire and a long rod, we may measure very small forces.

Figure 17

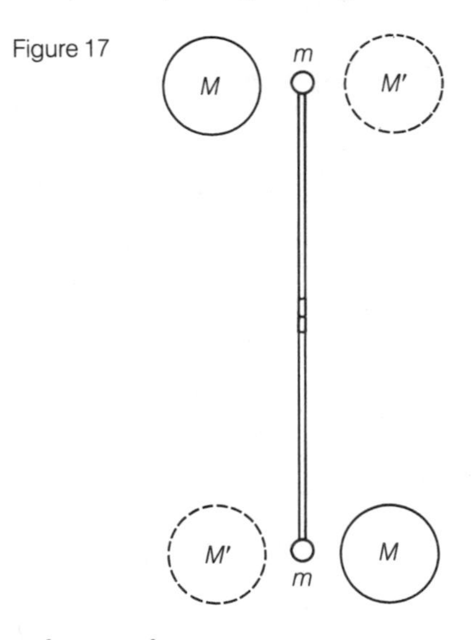

In the experiment of Cavendish two spheres of equal mass, *m,* are suspended from the extremities of the rod of the torsion balance. We shall for the present neglect the mass of the rod in comparison with that of the spheres. Two larger spheres of equal mass, *M,* are so arranged that they can be placed either at *M* and *M* or at *M′* and *M′*. In the former position they tend by their attraction on the smaller

Henry Cavendish. (After the portrait by Alexander.)

spheres, m and m, to turn the rod of the balance in the direction of the arrows. In the latter position they tend to turn it in the opposite direction. The torsion balance and its suspended spheres are enclosed in a case, to prevent their being disturbed by currents of air. The position of the rod of the balance is ascertained by observing a graduated scale as seen by reflection in a vertical mirror fastened to the middle of the rod. The balance is placed in a room by itself, and the observer does not enter the room but observes the image of the graduated scale with a telescope.

Article 144. Method of the experiment

The time, T, of a double vibration of the torsion balance is first ascertained, and also the position of equilibrium of the centres of the suspended spheres.

The large spheres are then brought up to the positions MM, so that the centre of each is at a distance from the position of equilibrium of the centre of the suspended sphere.

No attempt is made to wait till the vibrations of the beam have subsided, but the scale-divisions corresponding to the extremities of a single vibration are observed, and are found to be distant x and y respectively from the position of equilibrium. At these points the rod is, for an instant, at rest, so that its energy is entirely potential, and since the total energy is constant, the potential energy corresponding to the position x must be equal to that corresponding to the position y.

Figure 18

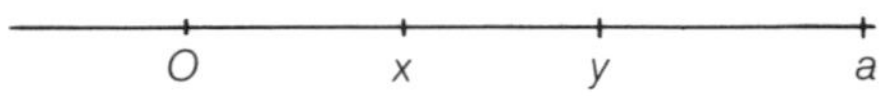

O x y a

Now if T be the time of a double vibration about the point of equilibrium O, the potential energy due to torsion when the scale reading is x is, by Article 119,

$$\frac{2\pi^2 m}{T^2}x^2$$

and that due to the gravitation between m and M is, by Article 140,

$$K - C\frac{mM}{a-x}.$$

The potential energy of the whole system in the position x is therefore

$$K - C\frac{mM}{a-x} + \frac{2\pi^2 m}{T^2}x^2.$$

In the position y it is

$$K - C\frac{mM}{a-y} + \frac{2\pi^2 m}{T^2}y^2$$

and since the potential energy in these two positions is equal,

$$CmM\left(\frac{1}{a-y} - \frac{1}{a-x}\right) = \frac{2\pi^2 m}{T^2}(y^2 - x^2).$$

Hence $C = \frac{2\pi^2}{MT^2}(x+y)(a-x)(a-y)$.

By this equation C, the constant of gravitation, is determined in terms of the observed quantities, M the mass of the large spheres in grams, T the time of a double vibration in seconds, and the distances x, y, and a in centimetres.

According to Baily's experiments, $C = 6.5 \times 10^{-8}$. If we assume the unit of mass, so that at a distance unity it would produce an acceleration unity, the centimetre and the second being units, the unit of mass would be about 1.537×10^7 grams, or 15.37 tons. This unit of mass reduces C, the constant of gravitation, to unity. It is therefore used in the calculations of physical astronomy.

Article 145. Universal gravitation

We have thus traced the attraction of gravitation through a great variety of natural phenomena and have found that the law established for the variation of the force at different distances between a planet and the sun also holds when we compare the attraction between different planets and the sun, and also when we compare the attraction between the moon and the earth with that between the earth and heavy bodies at its surface. We have also found that the gravitation of equal masses at equal distances is the same whatever be the nature of the material of which the masses consist. This we ascertain by experiments on pendulums of different substances, and also by a comparison of the attraction of the sun on different planets, which are probably not alike in composition. The experiments of Baily on spheres of different substances placed in the torsion balance confirm this law.

Since, therefore, we find in so great a number of cases occurring in regions remote from each other that the force of gravitation depends on the mass of bodies only, and not on their chemical nature or physical state, we are led to conclude that this is true for all substances.

For instance, no man of science doubts that two portions of atmospheric air attract one another, although we have very little hope that experimental methods will ever be invented so delicate as to measure or even to make manifest this attraction. But we know that there is attraction between any portion of air and the earth, and we find by Cavendish's experiment that gravitating bodies, if of sufficient mass, gravitate sensibly toward each other, and we conclude that two portions of air gravitate toward each other. But it is still extremely doubtful whether the medium of light and electricity is a gravitating substance, though it is certainly material and has mass.

Article 146. Cause of gravitation

Newton, in his *Principia,* deduces from the observed motions of the heavenly bodies the fact that they attract one another according to a definite law.

This he gives as a result of strict dynamical reasoning, and by it he shows how not only the more conspicuous phenomena but all the apparent irregularities of the motions of these bodies are the calculable results of this single principle. In his *Principia* he confines himself to the demonstration and development of this great step in the science of the mutual action of bodies. He says nothing about the means by which bodies are made to gravitate toward each other. We know that his mind did not rest at this point—that he felt that gravitation itself must be capable of being explained, and that he even suggested an explanation depending on the action of an ethereal medium pervading space. But with that wise moderation which is characteristic of all his investigations, he distinguished such speculations from what he had established by observation and demonstration and excluded from his *Principia* all mention of the cause of gravitation, reserving his thoughts on this subject for the "Queries" printed at the end of his *Opticks.* [See *GBWW,* Vol. 34, pp. 516–44.]

The attempts which have been made since the time of Newton to solve this difficult question are few in number and have not led to any well-established result.

Article 147. Application of Newton's method of investigation

The method of investigating the forces which act between bodies, which was thus pointed out and exemplified by Newton in the case of the heavenly bodies, was followed out successfully in the case of electrified and magnetized bodies by Cavendish, Coulomb, and Poisson.

The investigation of the mode in which the minute particles of bodies act on each other is rendered more difficult from the fact that both the bodies we consider and their distances are so small that we cannot perceive or measure them, and we are therefore unable to observe their motions as we do those of planets, or of electrified and magnetized bodies.

Article 148. Methods of molecular investigations

Hence the investigations of molecular science have proceeded for the most part by the method of hypothesis, and comparison of the results of the hypothesis with the observed facts.

The success of this method depends on the generality of the hypothesis we begin with. If our hypothesis is the extremely general one that the phenomena to be investigated depend on the configuration and motion of a material system, then if we are able to deduce any available results from such an hypothesis, we may safely apply them to the phenomena before us.

If, on the other hand, we frame the hypothesis that the configuration, motion, or action of the material system is of a certain definite kind, and if the results of this hypothesis agree with the phenomena, then, unless we can prove that no other hypothesis would account for the phenomena, we must still admit the possibility of our hypothesis being a wrong one.

Article 149. Importance of general and elementary properties

It is therefore of the greatest importance in all physical inquiries that we should be thoroughly acquainted with the most general properties of material systems, and it is for this reason that in this book I have rather dwelt on these general properties than entered on the more varied and interesting field of the special properties of particular forms of matter.

Three Papers

James Clerk Maxwell

1. Are There Real Analogies in Nature?

In the ancient and religious foundation of Peterhouse there is observed this rule, that whoso makes a pun shall be counted the author of it, but that whoso pretends to find it out shall be counted the publisher of it, and that both shall be fined. Now, as in a pun two truths lie hid under one expression, so in an analogy one truth is discovered under two expressions. Every question concerning analogies is therefore the reciprocal of a question concerning puns, and the solutions can be transposed by reciprocation. But since we are still in doubt as to the legitimacy of reasoning by analogy, and as reasoning even by paradox has been pronounced less heinous than reasoning by puns, we must adopt the direct method with respect to analogy, and then, if necessary, deduce by reciprocation the theory of puns.

That analogies appear to exist is plain in the face of things, for all parables, fables, similes, metaphors, tropes, and figures of speech are analogies, natural or revealed, artificial or concealed. The question is entirely of their reality. Now, no question exists as to the possibility of an analogy without a mind to recognize it—that is rank nonsense. You might as well talk of a demonstration or refutation existing unconditionally. Neither is there any question as to the occurrence of analogies to our minds. They are as plenty as reasons, not to say blackberries. For, not to mention all the things in external nature which men have seen as the projections of things in their own minds, the whole framework of science, up to the very pinnacle of philosophy, seems sometimes a dissected model of nature, and sometimes a natural growth on the inner surface of the mind. Now, if in examining the admitted truths in science and philosophy, we find certain general principles appearing throughout a vast range of subjects, and sometimes reappearing in some quite distinct part of human knowledge; and if, on turning to the constitution of the intellect itself, we think we can discern there the reason for this uniformity in the form of a fundamental law of the right action of the intellect, are we to conclude that these various departments of nature in which analogous laws exist have a real interdependence; or that their relation is only apparent and owing to the necessary conditions of human thought?

There is nothing more essential to the right understanding of things than a perception of the relations of *number*. Now the very first notion of number implies a previous act of intelligence. Before we can count any number of things we must pick them out of the universe and give each of them a fictitious unity by definition. Until we have done this, the universe of sense is neither one nor many, but indefinite. But yet, do what we will, nature seems to have a certain horror of partition. Perhaps the most natural thing to count "one" for is a man or human being, but yet it is very difficult to do so. Some count by heads, others by souls, others by noses; still there is a tendency either to run together into masses or to split up into limbs. The dimmed outlines of phenomenal things all merge into one another unless we put on the focusing glass of theory, and screw it up sometimes to one pitch of definition and sometimes to another, so as to see down into different depths through the great millstone of the world.

As for space and time, any man will tell you that "it is now known and ascertained that they are merely modifications of our own minds." And yet if we conceive of the mind as absolutely indivisible and capable of only one state at a time, we must admit that these states may be arranged in chronological order, and that this is the only real order of these states. For we have no reason to believe, on the ground of a given succession of simple sensations, that differences in position, as well as in order of occurrence, exist among the causes of these sensations. But yet we are convinced of the coexistence of different objects at the same time, and of the identity of the same object at different times. Now if we admit that we can think of difference independent of sequence, and of sequence without difference, we have admitted enough on which to found the possibility of the ideas of space and time.

But if we come to look more closely into these ideas, as developed in human beings, we find that *their* space has triple extension but is the same in all directions, without behind or before, whereas time extends only back and forward and always goes forward.

To inquire why these peculiarities of these fundamental ideas are so would require a most painful if not impossible act of self-exenteration; but to determine whether there is anything in nature corresponding to them, or whether they are mere projections of our own mental machinery on the surface of external things, is absolutely necessary to appease the cravings of intelligence. Now it appears to me that when we say that space has three dimensions, we not only express the impossibility of conceiving a fourth dimension, coordinate with the three known ones, but assert the objective truth that points may differ in position by the independent variation of three variables. Here, therefore, we have a *real* analogy between the constitution of the intellect and that of the external world.

With respect to time, it is sometimes assumed that the consecution of ideas is a fact precisely the same kind as the sequence of events in time. But it does not appear that there is any closer connection between these than between mental difference and difference of position. No doubt it is possible to assign the accurate date of every act of thought, but I doubt whether a chronological table drawn up in this way would coincide with the sequence of ideas of which we are conscious. There is an analogy, but I think not an identity, between these two orders of thoughts and things. Again, if we know what is at any assigned point of space at any assigned instant of time, we may be said to know all the events of nature. We cannot conceive any other thing which it would be necessary to know; and, in fact, if any other necessary element does exist, it never enters into any phenomenon so as to make it differ from what it would be on the supposition of space and time being the only necessary elements.

We cannot, however, think any set of thoughts without conceiving of them as depending on reasons. These reasons, when spoken of with relation to objects, get the name of causes, which are reasons, analogically referred to objects instead of thoughts. When the objects are mechanical, or are considered in a mechanical point of view, the causes are still more strictly defined and are called *forces.*

Now if we are acquainted not only with the events but also with the forces, in nature, we acquire the power of predicting events not previously known.

This conception of cause, we are informed, has been ascertained to be a notion of invariable sequence. No doubt invariable sequence, if observed, would suggest the notion of cause, just as the end of a poker painted red suggests the notion of heat, but although a cause without its invariable effect is absurd, a cause by its apparent frustration only suggests the notion of an equal and opposite cause.

Now the analogy between reasons, causes, forces, principles, and moral rules is glaring, but dazzling.

A reason or argument is a conductor by which the mind is led from a proposition to a necessary consequence of that proposition. In pure logic reasons must all tend in the same direction. There can be no conflict of reasons. We may lose sight of them or abandon them but cannot pit them against one another. If our faculties were indefinitely intensified, so that we could see all the consequences of any admission, then all reasons would resolve themselves into one reason, and all demonstrative truth would be one proposition. There would be no room for plurality of reasons, still less for conflict. But when we come to causes of phenomena and not reasons of truths, the conflict of causes, or rather the mutual annihilation of effects, is manifest. Not but what there is a tendency in the human mind to lump up all causes and give them an aggregate name, or to trace chains of causes up to their knots and asymptotes. Still we see, or seem to see, a plurality of causes at work, and there are some who are content with plurality.

Those who are thus content with plurality delight in the use of the word *force* as applied to cause. *Cause* is a metaphysical word implying something unchangeable and always producing its effect. *Force,* on the other hand, is a scientific word, signifying something which always meets with opposition, and often with successful opposition, but yet never fails to do what it can in its own favour. Such are the physical forces with which science deals, and their maxim is that might is right, and they call themselves laws of nature. But there are other laws of nature which determine the form and action of organic structure. These are founded on the forces of nature, but they seem to do no work except that of direction. Ought they to be called forces? A force does work in proportion to its strength. These *direct* forces to work after a model. They are *molds,* not forces. Now since we have here a standard from which deviation may take place, we have, besides the notion of *strength,* which belongs to force, that of *health,* which belongs to organic law. Organic beings are not conscious of organic laws, and it is not the conscious being that takes part in them, but another set of laws now appear in very close connection with the conscious being. I mean the laws of thought. These may be interfered with by organic laws, or by physical disturbances, and no doubt every such interference is regulated by the laws of the brain and of the connection between the medulla and the process of thought. But the thing to be observed is, that the laws which regulate the *right* process of the intellect are identical with the most abstract of all laws, those which are found among the relations of necessary truths, and that though these are mixed up with, and modified by, the most complex systems of phenomena in physiology and physics, they must be recognized as supreme among the other laws of thought. And this supremacy does not consist in superior strength, as in physical laws, nor yet, I think, in reproducing a type as in organic laws, but in being right and true; even when other causes have been for a season masters of the brain.

When we consider voluntary actions in general, we think we see causes acting like forces on the willing being. Some of our motions arise from physical necessity, some from irritability or organic excitement, some are performed by our machinery without our knowledge, and some evidently are due to us and our volitions. Of these, again, some are merely a repetition of a customary act, some are due to the attractions of pleasure or the pressure of constrained activity, and a few show some indications of being results of distinct acts of the will. Here again we have a continuation of the analogy of cause. Some had supposed that in will they had found the only true cause, and that all physical causes are only apparent. I need not say that this doctrine is exploded.

What we have to observe is that new elements enter into the nature of these higher causes, for mere abstract reasons are simply absolute; forces are related by their strength; organic laws act toward resemblances to types; animal emotions tend to that which promotes the enjoyment of life; and will is in great measure actually subject to all these, although certain other laws of *right,* which are abstract and demonstrable, like those of reason, are *supreme* among the laws of will.

Now the question of the reality of analogies in nature derives most of its interest from its application to the opinion that the phenomena of nature, being varieties of motion, can only differ in complexity, and therefore the only way of studying nature is to master the fundamental laws of motion first and then examine what kinds of complication of these laws must be studied in order to obtain true views of the universe. If this theory be true, we must look for indications of these fundamental laws throughout the whole range of science, and not least among those remarkable products of organic life, the results of cerebration (commonly called "thinking"). In this case, of course, the resemblances between the laws of different classes of phenomena should hardly be called analogies, as they are only transformed identities.

If, on the other hand, we start from the study of the laws of thought (the abstract, logical laws, not the *physio*-logical), then these apparent analogies become merely repetitions by reflection of certain necessary modes of action to which our minds are subject. I do not see how, upon either hypothesis, we can account for the existence of one set of laws of which the supremacy is necessary, but to the operation contingent. But we find another set of laws, the operation of which is inflexible when once in action but depends in its beginnings on some act of volition. The theory of the consequences of actions is greatly perplexed by the fact that each act sets in motion many trains of machinery, which react on other agents and come into regions of physical and metaphysical chaos from which it is difficult to disentangle them. But if we could place the telescope of theory in proper adjustment, to see not the physical events which form the subordinate foci of the disturbance propagated through the universe but the moral foci where the true image of the original act is reproduced, then we shall recognize the fact that when we clearly see any moral act, then there appears a moral necessity for the trains of consequences of that act, which are spreading through the world to be concentrated on some focus, so as to give a true and complete image of the act in its moral point of view. All that bystanders see is the physical act, and some of its immediate physical consequences, but as a partial pencil of light, even when not adapted for distinct vision, may enable us to see an *object,* and not merely light, so the partial view we have of any act, though far from perfect, may enable us to see it morally as an act, and not merely physically as an event.

If we think we see in the diverging trains of physical consequences not only a capability of forming a true image of the act but also of reacting upon the agent, either directly or after a long circuit, then perhaps we have caught the idea of *necessary* retribution as the legitimate consequence of all moral action.

But as this idea of *necessary* reaction of the consequences of action is derived only from a few instances, in which we have guessed at such a law among the necessary laws of the universe, and we have a much more distinct idea of *justice,* derived from those laws which we necessarily recognize as supreme, we connect the idea of retribution much more with that of *justice* than with that of *cause and effect.* We therefore regard retribution as the result of *interference* with the mechanical order of things, and intended to vindicate the supremacy of the right order of things, but still we suspect that the two orders of things will eventually dissolve into one.

I have been somewhat diffuse and confused on the subject of moral law, in order to show to what length analogy will carry the speculations of men. Whenever they see a relation between two things they know well, and think they see there must be a similar relation between things less known, they reason from the one to the other. This supposes that although pairs of things may differ widely from each other, the *relation* in the one pair may be the same as in the other. Now, as in a scientific point of view the *relation* is the most important thing to know, a knowledge of the one thing leads us a long way toward a knowledge of the other. If all that we know is relation, and if all the relations of one pair of things correspond to those of another pair, it will be difficult to distinguish the one pair from the other, although not presenting a single point of resemblance, unless we have some difference of relation to something else whereby to distinguish them. Such mistakes can hardly occur except in mathematical and physical analogies, but if we are going to study the constitution of the individual mental man, and draw all our arguments from the laws of society on the one hand, or those of the nervous tissue on the other, we may chance to convert useful helps into wills-of-the-wisp. Perhaps the "book," as it has been called, of nature is regularly paged; if so, no doubt the introductory parts will explain those that follow, and the methods taught in the first chapters will be taken for granted and used as illustrations in the more advanced parts of the course; but if it is not a "book" at all, but a *magazine,* nothing is more foolish to suppose that one part can throw light on another.

Perhaps the next most remarkable analogy is between the principle, law, or plan according to which all things are made suitably to what they have to do, and the intention which a man has of making things which will work. The doctrine of final causes, although productive of barrenness in its exclusive form, has certainly been a great help to inquirers into nature; and if we only maintain the existence of the analogy, and allow observation to determine its form, we cannot be led far from the truth.

There is another analogy which seems to be supplanting the other on its own ground, which lies between the principle, law, or plan, according to which the forms of things are made to have a certain community of type, and that which induces human artists to make a set of different things according to varieties of the same model. Here apparently the final cause is analogy or homogeneity, to the exclusion of usefulness.

And last of all we have the secondary forms of crystals bursting in upon us, and sparkling in the rigidity of mathematical necessity, and telling us neither of harmony of design, usefulness, or moral significance—nothing but spherical trigonometry and Napier's analogies. It is because we have blindly excluded the lessons of these angular bodies from the domain of human knowledge that we are still in doubt about the great doctrine that the only laws of matter are those which our minds must fabricate, and the only laws of mind are fabricated for it by matter.

2. On Action at a Distance*

I have no new discovery to bring before you this evening. I must ask you to go over very old ground and to turn your attention to a question which has been raised again and again ever since men began to think.

The question is that of the transmission of force. We see that two bodies at a distance from each other exert a mutual influence on each other's motion. Does this mutual action depend on the existence of some third thing, some medium of communication, occupying the space between the bodies, or do the bodies act on each other immediately, without the intervention of anything else?

The mode in which Faraday was accustomed to look at phenomena of this kind differs from that adopted by many other modern inquirers, and my special aim will be to enable you to place yourselves at Faraday's point of view, and to point out the scientific value of that conception of *lines of force* which, in his hands, became the key to the science of electricity.

When we observe one body acting on another at a distance, before we assume that this action is direct and immediate, we generally inquire whether there is any material connection between the two bodies; and if we find strings, or rods, or mechanism of any kind, capable of accounting for the observed action between the bodies, we prefer to explain the action by means of these intermediate connections, rather than to admit the notion of direct action at a distance.

Thus, when we ring a bell by means of a wire, the successive parts of the wire are first tightened and then moved, till at last the bell is rung at a distance by a process in which all the intermediate particles of the wire have taken part one after the other. We may ring a bell at a distance in other ways, as by forcing air into a long tube, at the other end of which is a cylinder with a piston which is made to fly out and strike the bell. We may also use a wire; but instead of pulling it, we may connect it at one end with a voltaic battery, and at the other with an electromagnet, and thus ring the bell by electricity.

Here are three different ways of ringing a bell. They all agree, however, in the circumstance that between the ringer and the bell there is an unbroken line of communication, and that at every point of this line some physical process goes on by which the action is transmitted from one end to the other. The process of transmission is not instantaneous but gradual; so that there is an interval of time after the impulse has been given to one extremity of the line of communication, during which the impulse is on its way but has not reached the other end.

It is clear, therefore, that in many cases the action between bodies at a distance may be accounted for by a series of actions between each successive pair of a series of bodies which occupy the intermediate space; and it is asked, by the advocates of mediate action, whether, in those cases in which we cannot perceive the intermedi-

*[From the *Proceedings of the Royal Institution of Great Britain,* vol. 7.]

ate agency, it is not more philosophical to admit the existence of a medium which we cannot at present perceive than to assert that a body can act at a place where it is not.

To a person ignorant of the properties of air, the transmission of force by means of that invisible medium would appear as unaccountable as any other example of action at a distance, and yet in this case we can explain the whole process and determine the rate at which the action is passed on from one portion to another of the medium.

Why then should we not admit that the familiar mode of communicating motion by pushing and pulling with our hands is the type and exemplification of all action between bodies, even in cases in which we can observe nothing between the bodies which appears to take part in the action?

Here for instance is a kind of attraction with which Professor Guthrie* has made us familiar. A disk is set in vibration and is then brought near a light suspended body, which immediately begins to move toward the disk, as if drawn toward it by an invisible cord. What is this cord? Sir W. Thomson† has pointed out that in a moving fluid the pressure is least where the velocity is greatest. The velocity of the vibratory motion of the air is greatest nearest the disk. Hence the pressure of the air on the suspended body is less on the side nearest the disk than on the opposite side, the body yields to the greater pressure and moves toward the disk.

The disk, therefore, does not act where it is not. It sets the air next it in motion by pushing it, this motion is communicated to more and more distant portions of the air in turn, and thus the pressures on opposite sides of the suspended body are rendered unequal, and it moves toward the disk in consequence of the excess of pressure. The force is therefore a force of the old school—a case of *vis a tergo*—a shove from behind.

The advocates of the doctrine of action at a distance, however, have not been put to silence by such arguments. What right, say they, have we to assert that a body cannot act where it is not? Do we not see an instance of action at a distance in the case of a magnet, which acts on another magnet not only at a distance but with the most complete indifference to the nature of the matter which occupies the intervening space? If the action depends on something occupying the space between the two magnets, it cannot surely be a matter of indifference whether this space is filled with air or not, or whether wood, glass, or copper be placed between the magnets.

Besides this, Newton's law of gravitation, which every astronomical observation only tends to establish more firmly, asserts not only that the heavenly bodies act on one another across immense intervals of space but that two portions of matter, the one buried a thousand miles deep in the interior of the earth, and the other a hundred thousand miles deep in the body of the sun, act on one another with precisely the same force as if the strata beneath which each is buried had been nonexistent. If any medium takes part in transmitting this action, it must surely make some difference whether the space between the bodies contains nothing but this medium, or whether it is occupied by the dense matter of the earth or of the sun.

But the advocates of direct action at a distance are not content with instances of this kind, in which the phenomena, even at first sight, appear to favour their doctrine. They push their operations into the enemy's camp and maintain that even when the action is apparently the pressure of contiguous portions of matter, the contiguity is only apparent—that a space *always* intervenes between the bodies which act on each other. They assert, in short, that so far from action at a distance being im-

*[Frederick Guthrie (1833–86).]

†[Sir William Thomson, Lord Kelvin (1824–1907).]

possible, it is the only kind of action which ever occurs, and that the favourite old *vis a tergo* of the schools has no existence in nature and exists only in the imagination of schoolmen.

The best way to prove that when one body pushes another it does not touch it is to measure the distance between them. Here are two glass lenses, one of which is pressed against the other by means of a weight. By means of the electric light we may obtain on the screen an image of the place where the one lens presses against the other. A series of coloured rings is formed on the screen. These rings were first observed and first explained by Newton. The particular colour of any ring depends on the distance between the surfaces of the pieces of glass. Newton formed a table of the colours corresponding to different distances, so that by comparing the colour of any ring with Newton's table, we may ascertain the distance between the surfaces at that ring.* The colours are arranged in rings because the surfaces are spherical, and therefore the interval between the surfaces depends on the distance from the line joining the centres of the spheres. The central spot of the rings indicates the place where the lenses are nearest together, and each successive ring corresponds to an increase of about the 4,000th part of a millimetre in the distance of the surfaces.

The lenses are now pressed together with a force equal to the weight of an ounce; but there is still a measurable interval between them, even at the place where they are nearest together. They are not in optical contact. To prove this, I apply a greater weight. A new colour appears at the central spot, and the diameters of all the rings increase. This shows that the surfaces are now nearer than at first, but they are not yet in optical contact, for if they were, the central spot would be black. I therefore increase the weights, so as to press the lenses into optical contact.

But what we call optical contact is not real contact. Optical contact indicates only that the distance between the surfaces is much less than a wavelength of light. To show that the surfaces are not in real contact, I remove the weights. The rings contract, and several of them vanish at the centre. Now it is possible to bring two pieces of glass so close together that they will not tend to separate at all but adhere together so firmly that when torn asunder the glass will break, not at the surface of contact, but at some other place. The glasses must then be many degrees nearer than when in mere optical contact.

Thus we have shown that bodies begin to press against each other while still at a measurable distance, and that even when pressed together with great force they are not in absolute contact but may be brought nearer still, and that by many degrees.

Why, then, say the advocates of direct action, should we continue to maintain the doctrine, founded only on the rough experience of a prescientific age, that matter cannot act where it is not, instead of admitting that all the facts from which our ancestors concluded that contact is essential to action were in reality cases of action at a distance, the distance being too small to be measured by their imperfect means of observation?

If we are ever to discover the laws of nature, we must do so by obtaining the most accurate acquaintance with the facts of nature, and not by dressing up in philosophical language the loose opinions of men who had no knowledge of the facts which throw most light on these laws. And as for those who introduce æthereal, or other media, to account for these actions, without any direct evidence of the existence of such media, or any clear understanding of

*[*Optics,* bk. 2, pts. 1, 2; *GBWW,* Vol. 34, pp. 457–78.]

how the media do their work, and who fill all space three and four times over with æthers of different sorts, why the less these men talk about their philosophical scruples about admitting action at a distance the better.

If the progress of science were regulated by Newton's first law of motion, it would be easy to cultivate opinions in advance of the age. We should only have to compare the science of today with that of fifty years ago; and by producing, in the geometrical sense, the line of progress, we should obtain the science of fifty years hence.

The progress of science in Newton's time consisted in getting rid of the celestial machinery with which generations of astronomers had encumbered the heavens, and thus "sweeping cobwebs off the sky."

Though the planets had already got rid of their crystal spheres, they were still swimming in the vortices of Descartes. Magnets were surrounded by effluvia, and electrified bodies by atmospheres, the properties of which resembled in no respect those of ordinary effluvia and atmospheres.

When Newton demonstrated that the force which acts on each of the heavenly bodies depends on its relative position with respect to the other bodies, the new theory met with violent opposition from the advanced philosophers of the day, who described the doctrine of gravitation as a return to the exploded method of explaining everything by occult causes, attractive virtues, and the like.

Newton himself, with that wise moderation which is characteristic of all his speculations, answered that he made no pretense of explaining the mechanism by which the heavenly bodies act on each other. To determine the mode in which their mutual action depends on their relative position was a great step in science, and this step Newton asserted that he had made. To explain the process by which this action is effected was a quite distinct step, and this step Newton, in his *Principia,* does not attempt to make.

But so far was Newton from asserting that bodies really do act on one another at a distance, independently of anything between them, that in a letter to Bentley, which has been quoted by Faraday, he says:

It is inconceivable that inanimate brute matter should, without the mediation of something else, which is not material, operate upon and affect other matter without mutual contact, as it must do if gravitation, in the sense of Epicurus, be essential and inherent in it. . . . That gravity should be innate, inherent, and essential to matter, so that one body can act upon another at a distance, through a vacuum, without the mediation of anything else, by and through which their action and force may be conveyed from one to another, is to me so great an absurdity, that I believe no man who has in philosophical matters a competent faculty of thinking can ever fall into it.

Accordingly, we find in his *Optical Queries,* and in his letters to Boyle, that Newton had very early made the attempt to account for gravitation by means of the pressure of a medium, and that the reason he did not publish these investigations "proceeded from hence only, that he found he was not able, from experiment and observation, to give a satisfactory account of this medium, and the manner of its operation in producing the chief phenomena of nature."

The doctrine of direct action at a distance cannot claim for its author the discoverer of universal gravitation. It was first asserted by Roger Cotes, in his preface to the *Principia,* which he edited during Newton's life. According to Cotes, it is by experience that we learn that all bodies gravitate. We do not learn in any other way that they are extended, movable, or solid. Gravitation, therefore, has as much right to be considered an essential property of matter as extension, mobility, or impenetrability.

And when the Newtonian philosophy gained ground in Europe, it was the opinion of Cotes rather than that of Newton that became most prevalent, till at last Boscovich* propounded his theory, that matter is a congeries of mathematical points, each endowed with the power of attracting or repelling the others according to fixed laws. In his world, matter is unextended, and contact is impossible. He did not forget, however, to endow his mathematical points with inertia. In this some of the modern representatives of his school have thought that he "had not quite got so far as the strict modern view of 'matter' as being but an expression for modes or manifestations of 'force'."

But if we leave out of account for the present the development of the ideas of science and confine our attention to the extension of its boundaries, we shall see that it was most essential that Newton's method should be extended to every branch of science to which it was applicable—that we should investigate the forces with which bodies act on each other in the first place, before attempting to explain *how* that force is transmitted. No men could be better fitted to apply themselves exclusively to the first part of the problem than those who considered the second part quite unnecessary.

Accordingly Cavendish, Coulomb, and Poisson, the founders of the exact sciences of electricity and magnetism, paid no regard to those old notions of "magnetic effluvia" and "electric atmospheres," which had been put forth in the previous century, but turned their undivided attention to the determination of the law of force, according to which electrified and magnetized bodies attract or repel each other. In this way the true laws of these actions were discovered, and this was done by men who never doubted that the action took place at a distance, without the intervention of any medium, and who would have regarded the discovery of such a medium as complicating rather than as explaining the undoubted phenomena of attraction.

We have now arrived at the great discovery by Ørsted of the connection between electricity and magnetism. Ørsted found that an electric current acts on a magnetic pole, but that it neither attracts it nor repels it but causes it to move round the current. He expressed this by saying that "the electric conflict acts in a revolving manner."

The most obvious deduction from this new fact was that the action of the current on the magnet is not a push-and-pull force but a rotatory force, and accordingly many minds were set a-speculating on vortices and streams of æther whirling round the current.

But Ampère, by a combination of mathematical skill with experimental ingenuity, first proved that two electric currents act on one another, and then analyzed this action into the resultant of a system of push-and-pull forces between the elementary parts of these currents.

The formula of Ampère, however, is of extreme complexity, as compared with Newton's law of gravitation, and many attempts have been made to resolve it into something of greater apparent simplicity.

I have no wish to lead you into a discussion of any of these attempts to improve a mathematical formula. Let us turn to the independent method of investigation employed by Faraday in those researches in electricity and magnetism which have made this Institution one of the most venerable shrines of science.

No man ever more conscientiously and systematically laboured to improve all his powers of mind than did Faraday from the very beginning of his scientific career. But whereas the general course of scientific method then consisted in the application of the ideas of mathematics and astronomy

---

*[Ruggero Boscovich (1711–87).]

to each new investigation in turn, Faraday seems to have had no opportunity of acquiring a technical knowledge of mathematics, and his knowledge of astronomy was mainly derived from books.

Hence, though he had a profound respect for the great discovery of Newton, he regarded the attraction of gravitation as a sort of sacred mystery, which, as he was not an astronomer, he had no right to gainsay or to doubt, his duty being to believe it in the exact form in which it was delivered to him. Such a dead faith was not likely to lead him to explain new phenomena by means of direct attractions.

Besides this, the treatises of Poisson and Ampère are of so technical a form that to derive any assistance from them the student must have been thoroughly trained in mathematics, and it is very doubtful if such a training can be begun with advantage in mature years.

Thus Faraday, with his penetrating intellect, his devotion to science, and his opportunities for experiments, was debarred from following the course of thought which had led to the achievements of the French philosophers and was obliged to explain the phenomena to himself by means of a symbolism which he could understand, instead of adopting what had hitherto been the only tongue of the learned.

This new symbolism consisted of those lines of force extending themselves in every direction from electrified and magnetic bodies, which Faraday in his mind's eye saw as distinctly as the solid bodies from which they emanated.

The idea of lines of force and their exhibition by means of iron filings was nothing new. They had been observed repeatedly, and investigated mathematically, as an interesting curiosity of science. But let us hear Faraday himself, as he introduces to his reader the method which in his hands became so powerful.

*It would be a voluntary and unnecessary abandonment of most valuable aid if an experimentalist, who chooses to consider magnetic power as represented by lines of magnetic force, were to deny himself the use of iron filings. By their employment he may make many conditions of the power, even in complicated cases, visible to the eye at once; may trace the varying direction of the lines of force and determine the relative polarity; may observe in which direction the power is increasing or diminishing; and in complex systems may determine the neutral points or places where there is neither polarity nor power, even when they occur in the midst of powerful magnets. By their use probable results may be seen at once, and many a valuable suggestion gained for future leading experiments.**

Experiment on lines of force

In this experiment each filing becomes a little magnet. The poles of opposite names belonging to different filings attract each other and stick together, and more filings attach themselves to the exposed poles, that is, to the ends of the row of filings. In this way the filings, instead of forming a confused system of dots over the paper, draw together, filing to filing, till long fibres of filings are formed, which indicate by their direction the lines of force in every part of the field.

The mathematicians saw in this experiment nothing but a method of exhibiting at one view the direction in different places of the resultant of two forces, one directed to each pole of the magnet; a somewhat complicated result of the simple law of force.

But Faraday, by a series of steps as remarkable for their geometrical definiteness as for their speculative ingenuity, imparted to his conception of these lines of force a clearness and precision far in advance of

*[*Experimental Researches in Electricity*, ¶3234; *GBWW*, Vol. 45, p. 793c.]

that with which the mathematicians could then invest their own formulae.

In the first place, Faraday's lines of force are not to be considered merely as individuals but as forming a system, drawn in space in a definite manner so that the number of the lines which pass through any area, say of one square inch, indicates the intensity of the force acting through the area. Thus the lines of force become definite in number. The strength of a magnetic pole is measured by the number of lines which proceed from it; the electrotonic state of a circuit is measured by the number of lines which pass through it.

In the second place, each individual line has a continuous existence in space and time. When a piece of steel becomes a magnet, or when an electric current begins to flow, the lines of force do not start into existence each in its own place, but as the strength increases new lines are developed within the magnet or current and gradually grow outward, so that the whole system expands from within, like Newton's rings in our former experiment. Thus every line of force preserves its identity during the whole course of its existence, though its shape and size may be altered to any extent.

I have no time to describe the methods by which every question relating to the forces acting on magnets or on currents, or to the induction of currents in conducting circuits, may be solved by the consideration of Faraday's lines of force. In this place they can never be forgotten. By means of this new symbolism, Faraday defined with mathematical precision the whole theory of electromagnetism, in language free from mathematical technicalities, and applicable to the most complicated as well as the simplest cases. But Faraday did not stop here. He went on from the conception of geometrical lines of force to that of physical lines of force. He observed that the motion which the magnetic or electric force tends to produce is invariably such as to shorten the lines of force and to allow them to spread out laterally from each other. He thus perceived in the medium a state of stress, consisting of a tension, like that of a rope, in the direction of the lines of force, combined with a pressure in all directions at right angles to them.

This is quite a new conception of action at a distance, reducing it to a phenomenon of the same kind as that action at a distance which is exerted by means of the tension of ropes and the pressure of rods. When the muscles of our bodies are excited by that stimulus which we are able in some unknown way to apply to them, the fibres tend to shorten themselves and at the same time to expand laterally. A state of stress is produced in the muscle, and the limb moves. This explanation of muscular action is by no means complete. It gives no account of the cause of the excitement of the state of stress, nor does it even investigate those forces of cohesion which enable the muscles to support this stress. Nevertheless, the simple fact that it substitutes a kind of action, which extends continuously along a material substance, for one of which we know only a cause and an effect at a distance from each other induces us to accept it as a real addition to our knowledge of animal mechanics.

For similar reasons we may regard Faraday's conception of a state of stress in the electromagnetic field as a method of explaining action at a distance by means of the continuous transmission of force, even though we do not know how the state of stress is produced.

But one of Faraday's most pregnant discoveries, that of the magnetic rotation of polarized light, enables us to proceed a step farther. The phenomenon, when analyzed into its simplest elements, may be described thus: Of two circularly polarized rays of light, precisely similar in configuration, but rotating in opposite directions, that ray is propagated with the greater velocity which rotates in the same direction as the electricity of the magnetizing current.

It follows from this, as Sir W. Thomson has shown by strict dynamical reasoning, that the medium when under the action of magnetic force must be in a state of rotation—that is to say, that small portions of the medium, which we may call molecular vortices, are rotating, each on its own axis, the direction of this axis being that of the magnetic force.

Here, then, we have an explanation of the tendency of the lines of magnetic force to spread out laterally and to shorten themselves. It arises from the centrifugal force of the molecular vortices.

The mode in which electromotive force acts in starting and stopping the vortices is more abstruse, though it is of course consistent with dynamical principles.

We have thus found that there are several different kinds of work to be done by the electromagnetic medium if it exists. We have also seen that magnetism has an intimate relation to light, and we know that there is a theory of light which supposes it to consist of the vibrations of a medium. How is this luminiferous medium related to our electromagnetic medium?

It fortunately happens that electromagnetic measurements have been made from which we can calculate by dynamical principles the velocity of propagation of small magnetic disturbances in the supposed electromagnetic medium.

This velocity is very great, from 288 to 314 millions of metres per second, according to different experiments. Now the velocity of light, according to Foucault's experiments, is 298 millions of metres per second. In fact, the different determinations of either velocity differ from each other more than the estimated velocity of light does from the estimated velocity of propagation of small electromagnetic disturbance. But if the luminiferous and the electromagnetic media occupy the same place, and transmit disturbances with the same velocity, what reason have we to distinguish the one from the other? By considering them as the same, we avoid at least the reproach of filling space twice over with different kinds of æther.

Besides this, the only kind of electromagnetic disturbances which can be propagated through a nonconducting medium is a disturbance transverse to the direction of propagation, agreeing in this respect with what we know of that disturbance which we call light. Hence, for all we know, light also may be an electromagnetic disturbance in a nonconducting medium. If we admit this, the electromagnetic theory of light will agree in every respect with the undulatory theory, and the work of Thomas Young and Fresnel will be established on a firmer basis than ever, when joined with that of Cavendish and Coulomb by the keystone of the combined sciences of light and electricity—Faraday's great discovery of the electromagnetic rotation of light.

The vast interplanetary and interstellar regions will no longer be regarded as waste places in the universe, which the Creator has not seen fit to fill with the symbols of the manifold order of His kingdom. We shall find them to be already full of this wonderful medium; so full, that no human power can remove it from the smallest portion of space, or produce the slightest flaw in its infinite continuity. It extends unbroken from star to star; and when a molecule of hydrogen vibrates in the Dog Star, the medium receives the impulses of these vibrations and, after carrying them in its immense bosom for three years, delivers them in due course, regular order, and full tale into the spectroscope of Mr. Huggins,* at Tulse Hill.

But the medium has other functions and operations besides bearing light from man to man, and from world to world, and giving evidence of the absolute unity of the metric system in the universe. Its minute parts may have rotatory as well as vibratory motions, and the axes of rotation form

---

*[Sir William Huggins (1824–1910).]

those lines of magnetic force which extend in unbroken continuity into regions which no eye has seen, and which, by their action on our magnets, are telling us in language not yet interpreted what is going on in the hidden underworld from minute to minute and from century to century.

And these lines must not be regarded as mere mathematical abstractions. They are the directions in which the medium is exerting a tension like that of a rope, or rather, like that of our own muscles. The tension of the medium in the direction of the earth's magnetic force is in this country one grain weight on eight square feet. In some of Dr. Joule's experiments, the medium has exerted a tension of 200 pounds weight per square inch.

But the medium, in virtue of the very same elasticity by which it is able to transmit the undulations of light, is also able to act as a spring. When properly wound up, it exerts a tension, different from the magnetic tension, by which it draws oppositely electrified bodies together, produces effects through the length of telegraph wires, and, when of sufficient intensity, leads to the rupture and explosion called lightning.

These are some of the already discovered properties of that which has often been called vacuum, or nothing at all. They enable us to resolve several kinds of action at a distance into actions between contiguous parts of a continuous substance. Whether this resolution is of the nature of explication or complication, I must leave to the metaphysicians.

3. Ether

Ether, or Æther (*αἰθήρ*, probably from *αἴθω*, I burn, though Plato in his *Cratylus** derives the name from its perpetual motion—*ὅτι ἀεὶ θεῖ περὶ τὸν ἀέρα ῥέων, ἀειθεὴρ δικαίως ἂν καλοῖτο*), a material substance of a more subtle kind than visible bodies, supposed to exist in those parts of space which are apparently empty.

The hypothesis of an æther has been maintained by different speculators for very different reasons. To those who maintained the existence of a plenum as a philosophical principle, nature's abhorrence of a vacuum was a sufficient reason for imagining an all-surrounding æther, even though every other argument should be against it. To Descartes, who made extension the sole essential property of matter, and matter a necessary condition of extension, the bare existence of bodies apparently at a distance was a proof of the existence of a continuous medium between them.

But besides these high metaphysical necessities for a medium, there were more mundane uses to be fulfilled by æthers. Æthers were invented for the planets to swim in, to constitute electric atmospheres and magnetic effluvia, to convey sensations from one part of our bodies to another, and so on, till all space had been filled three or four times over with æthers. It is only when we remember the extensive and mischievous influence on science which hypotheses about æthers used formerly to exercise that we can appreciate the horror of æthers which sober-minded men had during the eighteenth century, and which, probably as a sort of hereditary prejudice, descended even to the late Mr. John Stuart Mill.

The disciples of Newton maintained that in the fact of the mutual gravitation of the heavenly bodies, according to Newton's law, they had a complete quantitative account of their motions; and they endeavoured to follow out the path which Newton had opened up by investigating and measuring the attractions and repulsions of electrified and magnetic bodies, and the cohesive forces in the interior of bodies, without attempting to account for these forces.

Newton himself, however, endeavoured to account for gravitation by differences of pressure in an æther; but he did not publish his theory, "because he was not able from experiment and observation to give a satisfactory account of this medium, and the manner of its operation in producing the chief phenomena of nature."

On the other hand, those who imagined æthers in order to explain phenomena could not specify the nature of the motion of these media and could not prove that the media, as imagined by them, would produce the effects they were meant to explain. The only æther which has survived is that which was invented by Huygens to explain the propagation of light.† The evidence for the existence of the luminiferous æther has accumulated as additional phenomena of light and other radiations have been discovered; and the properties of this medium, as deduced from the phenomena of light, have been found to be precisely

---

*[410b; *GBWW*, Vol. 7, p. 98d.]

†[Christiaan Huygens, *Treatise on Light; GBWW*, Vol. 34.]

those required to explain electromagnetic phenomena.

Function of the æther in the propagation of radiation

The evidence for the undulatory theory of light will be given in full, under the article on LIGHT, but we may here give a brief summary of it so far as it bears on the existence of the æther.

That light is not itself a substance may be proved from the phenomenon of interference. A beam of light from a single source is divided by certain optical methods into two parts, and these, after traveling by different paths, are made to reunite and fall upon a screen. If either half of the beam is stopped, the other falls on the screen and illuminates it, but if both are allowed to pass, the screen in certain places becomes dark and thus shows that the two portions of light have destroyed each other.

Now, we cannot suppose that two bodies when put together can annihilate each other; therefore light cannot be a substance. What we have proved is that one portion of light can be the exact opposite of another portion, just as $+a$ is the exact opposite of $-a$, whatever a may be. Among physical quantities we find some which are capable of having their signs reversed, and others which are not. Thus a displacement in one direction is the exact opposite of an equal displacement in the opposite direction. Such quantities are the measures, not of substances, but always of processes taking place in a substance. We therefore conclude that light is not a substance but a process going on in a substance, the process going on in the first portion of light being always the exact opposite of the process going on in the other at the same instant, so that when the two portions are combined no process goes on at all. To determine the nature of the process in which the radiation of light consists, we alter the length of the path of one or both of the two portions of the beam, and we find that the light is extinguished when the difference of the length of the paths is an odd multiple of a certain small distance called a half wavelength. In all other cases there is more or less light; and when the paths are equal, or when their difference is a multiple of a whole wavelength, the screen appears four times as bright as when one portion of the beam falls on it. In the ordinary form of the experiment these different cases are exhibited simultaneously at different points of the screen, so that we see on the screen a set of fringes consisting of dark lines at equal intervals, with bright bands of graduated intensity between them.

If we consider what is going on at different points in the axis of a beam of light at the same instant, we shall find that if the distance between the points is a multiple of a wavelength the same process is going on at the two points at the same instant, but if the distance is an odd multiple of half a wavelength the process going on at one point is the exact opposite of the process going on at the other.

Now, light is known to be propagated with a certain velocity (3.004×10^{10} centimetres per second in vacuum, according to Cornu). If, therefore, we suppose a movable point to travel along the ray with this velocity, we shall find the same process going on at every point of the ray as the moving point reaches it. If, lastly, we consider a fixed point in the axis of the beam, we shall observe a rapid alternation of these opposite processes, the interval of time between similar processes being the time light takes to travel a wavelength.

These phenomena may be summed up in the mathematical expression

$$u = A \cos (nt - px + a)$$

which gives u, the phase of the process, at a point whose distance measured from a fixed point in the beam is x, and at a time t.

We have determined nothing as to the nature of the process. It may be a displacement, or a rotation, or an electrical disturbance, or indeed any physical quantity which is capable of assuming negative as well as positive values. Whatever be the nature of the process, if it is capable of being expressed by an equation of this form, the process going on at a fixed point is called a *vibration;* the constant A is called the *amplitude;* the time $2\pi/n$ is called the *period;* and $nt - px + a$ is the *phase.*

The configuration at a given instant is called a *wave,* and the distance $2\pi/p$ is called the *wavelength.* The velocity of propagation is n/p. When we contemplate the different parts of the medium as going through the same process in succession, we use the word *undulatory* to denote this character of the process without in any way restricting its physical nature.

A further insight into the physical nature of the process is obtained from the fact that if the two rays are polarized, and if the plane of polarization of one of them be made to turn round the axis of the ray, then when the two planes of polarization are parallel the phenomena of interference appear as above described. As the plane turns round, the dark and light bands become less distinct, and when the planes of polarization are at right angles, the illumination of the screen becomes uniform, and no trace of interference can be discovered.

Hence the physical process involved in the propagation of light must not only be a directed quantity or vector capable of having its direction reversed, but this vector must be at right angles to the ray, and either in the plane of polarization or perpendicular to it. Fresnel supposed it to be a displacement of the medium perpendicular to the plane of polarization. Maccullagh and Neumann supposed it to be a displacement in the plane of polarization. The comparison of these two theories must be deferred till we come to the phenomena of dense media.

The process may, however, be an electromagnetic one, and as in this case the electric displacement and the magnetic disturbance are perpendicular to each other, either of these may be supposed to be in the plane of polarization.

All that has been said with respect to the radiations which affect our eyes, and which we call light, applies also to those radiations which do not produce a luminous impression on our eyes, for the phenomena of interference have been observed, and the wavelengths measured, in the case of radiations which can be detected only by their heating or by their chemical effects.

Elasticity, tenacity, and density of the æther

Having so far determined the geometrical character of the process, we must now turn our attention to the medium in which it takes place. We may use the term *æther* to denote this medium, whatever it may be.

In the first place, it is capable of transmitting energy. The radiations which it transmits are able not only to act on our senses, which of itself is evidence of work done, but to heat bodies which absorb them; and by measuring the heat communicated to such bodies, the energy of the radiation may be calculated.

In the next place this energy is not transmitted instantaneously from the radiating body to the absorbing body but exists for a certain time in the medium.

If we adopt either Fresnel's or Maccullagh's form of the undulatory theory, half of this energy is in the form of potential energy, due to the distortion of elementary portions of the medium, and half in the form of kinetic energy, due to the motion of the medium. We must therefore regard the æther as possessing elasticity similar to that of a solid body, and also as having a finite density. If we take Pouillet's estimate of 1.7633 as the number of gram-centigrade units of heat produced by direct sunlight falling on a square centimetre in a minute, this is equivalent to 1.234×10^6 ergs per second. Dividing this by 3.004×10^{10}, the velocity of light in centimetres per second, we get for the energy in a cubic centimetre 4.1×10^{-5} ergs. Near the sun the energy in a cubic centimetre would be about 46,000 times this, or 1.886 ergs. If we further assume, with Sir W. Thomson, that the amplitude is not more than one hundredth of the wavelength, we have $Ap = 2\pi/100$, or about 1/16; so that we have—

Energy per cubic centimetre	$= \frac{1}{2}\rho V^2 A^2 p^2 =$		1.886 ergs.
Greatest tangential stress per square centimetre	$=$	$\rho V^2 Ap$	$=$ 30.176 dynes.
Coefficient of rigidity of æther	$=$	ρV^2	$=$ 842.8.
Density of æther	$=$	ρ	$=$ 9.36×10^{-19}.

The coefficient of rigidity of steel is about 8×10^{11}, and that of glass 2.4×10^{11}.

If the temperature of the atmosphere were everywhere 0° C, and if it were in equilibrium about the earth supposed at rest, its density at an infinite distance from the earth would be 3×10^{-346} which is about 3×10^{327} times less than the estimated density of the æther. In the regions of interplanetary space the density of the æther is therefore very great compared with that of the attenuated atmosphere of interplanetary space, but the whole mass of æther within a sphere whose radius is that of the most distant planet is very small compared with that of the planets themselves.

The æther distinct from gross matter

When light travels through the atmosphere it is manifest that the medium through which the light is propagated is not the air itself, for in the first place the air cannot transmit transverse vibrations, and the normal vibrations which the air does transmit travel about a million times slower than light. Solid transparent bodies, such as glass and crystals, are no doubt capable of transmitting transverse vibrations, but the velocity of transmission is still hundreds of thousands times less than that with which light is transmitted through these bodies. We are therefore obliged to suppose that the medium through which light is propagated is something distinct from the transparent medium known to us, though it interpenetrates all transparent bodies and probably opaque bodies too.

The velocity of light, however, is different in different transparent media, and we must therefore suppose that these media take some part in the process, and that their particles are vibrating as well as those of the æther, but the energy of the vibrations of the gross particles must be very much smaller than that of the æther, for otherwise a much larger proportion of the incident light would be reflected when a ray passes from vacuum to glass or from glass to vacuum than we find to be the case.

Relative motion of the æther

We must therefore consider the æther within dense bodies as somewhat loosely connected with the dense bodies, and we have next to inquire whether, when these dense bodies are in motion through the great ocean of æther, they carry along with them the æther they contain, or whether the æther passes through them as the water of the sea passes through the meshes of a net when it is towed along by a boat. If it were possible to determine the velocity of light by observing the time it takes to travel between one station and another on the earth's surface, we might, by comparing the observed velocities in opposite directions, determine the velocity of the æther with respect to these terrestrial stations. All methods, however, by which it is practicable to determine the velocity of light from terrestrial experiments depend on the measurement of the time required for the double journey from one station to the other and back again, and the increase of this time on account of a relative velocity of the æther equal to that of the earth in its orbit would be only about one hundred millionth part of the whole time of transmission and would therefore be quite insensible.

The theory of the motion of the æther is hardly sufficiently developed to enable us to form a strict mathematical theory of the aberration of light, taking into account the motion of the æther. Professor Stokes,* however, has shown that, on a very probable hypothesis with respect to the motion of the æther, the amount of aberration would not be sensibly affected by that motion.

The only practicable method of determining directly the relative velocity of the æther with respect to the solar system is to compare the values of the velocity of light deduced from the observation of the eclipses of Jupiter's satellites when Jupiter is seen from the earth at nearly opposite points of the ecliptic.

Arago† proposed to compare the deviation produced in the light of a star after passing through an achromatic prism when the direction of the ray within the prism formed different angles with the direction of motion of the earth in its orbit. If the æther were moving swiftly through the prism, the deviation might be expected to be different when the direction of the light was the same as that of the æther, and when these directions were opposite.

The present writer arranged the experiment in a more practicable manner by using an ordinary spectroscope, in which a plane mirror was substituted for the slit of the collimator. The cross wires of the observing telescope were illuminated. The light from any point of the wire passed through the object glass and then through the prisms as a parallel pencil till it fell on the object glass of the collimator, and came to a focus at the mirror, where it was reflected, and after passing again through the object glass it formed a pencil passing through each of the prisms parallel to its original direction, so that the object glass of the observing telescope brought it to a focus coinciding with the point of the cross wires from which it originally proceeded. Since the image coincided with the object, it could not be observed directly, but by diverting the pencil by partial reflection at a plane surface of glass, it was found that the image of the finest spider line could be distinctly seen, though the light which formed the image had passed twice through three prisms of 60°. The apparatus was first turned so that the direction of the light in first passing through the second prism was that of the earth's motion in its orbit. The apparatus was afterward placed so that the direction of the light was opposite to that of the earth's motion. If the deviation of the ray by the prisms was increased or diminished for this reason in the first journey, it would be diminished or increased in the return journey, and the image would appear on one side of the object. When the apparatus was turned round it would appear on the other side. The experiment was tried at different times of the year, but only negative results were obtained.

*[Sir George Stokes (1819–1903).]
†[François Arago (1786–1853).]

We cannot, however, conclude absolutely from this experiment that the æther near the surface of the earth is carried along with the earth in its orbit, for it has been shown by Professor Stokes that according to Fresnel's hypothesis the relative velocity of the æther within the prism would be to that of the æther outside inversely as the square of the index of refraction, and that in this case the deviation would not be sensibly altered on account of the motion of the prism through the æther.

Fizeau,* however, by observing the change of the plane of polarization of light transmitted obliquely through a series of glass plates, obtained what he supposed to be evidence of a difference in the result when the direction of the ray in space was different, and Angström obtained analogous results by diffraction. The writer is not aware that either of these very difficult experiments has been verified by repetition.

In another experiment of M. Fizeau, which seems entitled to greater confidence, he has observed that the propagation of light in a stream of water takes place with greater velocity in the direction in which the water moves than in the opposite direction, but that the change of velocity is less than that which would be due to the actual velocity of the water, and that the phenomenon does not occur when air is substituted for water. This experiment seems rather to verify Fresnel's theory of the æther; but the whole question of the state of the luminiferous medium near the earth, and of its connection with gross matter, is very far as yet from being settled by experiment.

Function of the æther in electromagnetic phenomena

Faraday conjectured that the same medium which is concerned in the propagation of light might also be the agent in electromagnetic phenomena. "For my own part," he says,

> *considering the relation of a vacuum to the magnetic force and the general character of magnetic phenomena external to the magnet, I am more inclined to the notion that in the transmission of the force there is such an action, external to the magnet, than that the effects are merely attraction and repulsion at a distance. Such an action may be a function of the æther; for it is not at all unlikely that, if there be an æther, it should have other uses than simply the conveyance of radiations.*†

This conjecture has only been strengthened by subsequent investigations.

Electrical energy is of two kinds, electrostatic and electrokinetic. We have reason to believe that the former depends on a property of the medium in virtue of which an electric displacement elicits an electromotive force in the opposite direction, the electromotive force for unit displacement being inversely as the specific inductive capacity of the medium.

The electrokinetic energy, on the other hand, is simply the energy of the motion set up in the medium by electric currents and magnets, this motion not being confined to the wires which carry the currents, or to the magnet, but existing in every place where magnetic force can be found.

Electromagnetic Theory of Light

The properties of the electromagnetic medium are therefore as far as we have gone similar to those of the luminiferous medium, but the best way to compare them is to determine the velocity with which an electromagnetic disturbance would be propagated through the medium. If this

*[Armand Fizeau (1819–96).]

†[*Experimental Researches in Electricity,* ¶3075; *GBWW,* Vol. 45, p. 759b–c.]

should be equal to the velocity of light, we would have strong reason to believe that the two media, occupying as they do the same space, are really identical. The data for making the calculation are furnished by the experiments made in order to compare the electromagnetic with the electrostatic system of units. The velocity of propagation of an electromagnetic disturbance in air, as calculated from different sets of data, does not differ more from the velocity of light in air, as determined by different observers, than the several calculated values of these quantities differ among each other.

If the velocity of propagation of an electromagnetic disturbance is equal to that of light in other transparent media, then in nonmagnetic media the specific inductive capacity should be equal to the square of the index of refraction.

Boltzmann has found that this is very accurately true for the gases which he has examined. Liquids and solids exhibit a greater divergence from this relation, but we can hardly expect even an approximate verification when we have to compare the results of our sluggish electrical experiments with the alternations of light, which take place billions of times in a second.

The undulatory theory, in the form which treats the phenomena of light as the motion of an elastic solid, is still encumbered with several difficulties.

The first and most important of these is that the theory indicates the possibility of undulations consisting of vibrations normal to the surface of the wave. The only way of accounting for the fact that the optical phenomena which would arise from these waves do not take place is to assume that the æther is incompressible.

The next is that, whereas the phenomena of reflection are best explained on the hypothesis that the vibrations are perpendicular to the plane of polarization, those of double refraction require us to assume that the vibrations are in that plane.

The third is that, in order to account for the fact that in a doubly refracting crystal the velocity of rays in any principal plane and polarized in that plane is the same, we must assume certain highly artificial relations among the coefficients of elasticity.

The electromagnetic theory of light satisfies all these requirements by the single hypothesis that the electric displacement is perpendicular to the plane of polarization. No normal displacement can exist, and in doubly refracting crystals the specific dielectric capacity for each principal axis is assumed to be equal to the square of the index of refraction of a ray perpendicular to that axis, and polarized in a plane perpendicular to that axis. Boltzmann has found that these relations are approximately true in the case of crystallized sulfur, a body having three unequal axes. The specific dielectric capacity for these axes are respectively

4.773 3.970 3.811

and the squares of the indices of refraction

4.576 3.886 3.591.

Physical constitution of the æther

What is the ultimate constitution of the æther? Is it molecular or continuous?

We know that the æther transmits transverse vibrations to very great distances without sensible loss of energy by dissipation. A molecular medium, moving under such conditions that a group of molecules once near together remain near each other during the whole motion, may be capable of transmitting vibrations without much dissipation of energy, but if the motion is such that the groups of molecules are not merely slightly altered in configuration but entirely broken up, so that their component molecules pass into new types of grouping, then in the passage from one type of grouping to another the energy of regular vibrations will be frittered away into that of the irregular agitation which we call heat.

We cannot therefore suppose the constitution of the æther to be like that of a gas, in which the molecules are always in a state of irregular agitation, for in such a medium a transverse undulation is reduced to less than one five-hundredth of its amplitude in a single wavelength. If the æther is molecular, the grouping of the molecules must remain of the same type, the configuration of the groups being only slightly altered during the motion.

Mr. S. Tolver Preston has supposed that the æther is like a gas whose molecules very rarely interfere with each other, so that their mean path is far greater than any planetary distances. He has not investigated the properties of such a medium with any degree of completeness, but it is easy to see that we might form a theory in which the molecules *never* interfere with each other's motion of translation but travel in all directions with the velocity of light; and if we further suppose that vibrating bodies have the power of impressing on these molecules some vector property (such as rotation about an axis) which does not interfere with their motion of translation, and which is then carried along by the molecules, and if the alternation of the average value of this vector for all the molecules within an element of volume be the process which we call light, then the equations which express this average will be of the same form as that which expresses the displacement in the ordinary theory.

It is often asserted that the mere fact that a medium is elastic or compressible is a proof that the medium is not continuous but is composed of separate parts having void spaces between them. But there is nothing inconsistent with experience in supposing elasticity or compressibility to be properties of every portion, however small, into which the medium can be conceived to be divided, in which case the medium would be strictly continuous. A medium, however, though homogeneous and continuous as regards its density, may be rendered heterogeneous by its motion, as in Sir W. Thomson's hypothesis of vortex-molecules in a perfect liquid.

The æther, if it is the medium of electromagnetic phenomena, is probably molecular, at least in this sense.

Sir W. Thomson has shown that the magnetic influence on light discovered by Faraday depends on the direction of motion of moving particles, and that it indicates a rotational motion in the medium when magnetized. See also Maxwell's *Electricity and Magnetism,* art. 806, etc.

Now, it is manifest that this rotation cannot be that of the medium as a whole about an axis, for the magnetic field may be of any breadth, and there is no evidence of any motion the velocity of which increases with the distance from a single fixed line in the field. If there is any motion of rotation, it must be a rotation of very small portions of the medium each about its own axis, so that the medium must be broken up into a number of molecular vortices.

We have as yet no data from which to determine the size or the number of these molecular vortices. We know, however, that the magnetic force in the region in the neighbourhood of a magnet is maintained as long as the steel retains its magnetization, and as we have no reason to believe that a steel magnet would lose all its magnetization by the mere lapse of time, we conclude that the molecular vortices do not require a continual expenditure of work in order to maintain their motion, and that therefore this motion does not necessarily involve dissipation of energy.

No theory of the constitution of the æther has yet been invented which will account for such a system of molecular vortices being maintained for an indefinite time without their energy being gradually dissipated into that irregular agitation of the medium which, in ordinary media, is called heat.

Whatever difficulties we may have in forming a consistent idea of the constitution of the æther, there can be no doubt that the interplanetary and interstellar spaces are not empty but are occupied by a material substance or body, which is certainly the largest and probably the most uniform body of which we have any knowledge.

Whether this vast homogeneous expanse of isotropic matter is fitted not only to be a medium of physical interaction between distant bodies, and to fulfil other physical functions of which, perhaps, we have as yet no conception, but also, as the authors of the *Unseen Universe** seem to suggest, to constitute the material organism of beings exercising functions of life and mind as high or higher than ours are at present, is a question far transcending the limits of physical speculation.

---

*[*The Unseen Universe; or, Physical Speculations on a Future State,* published anonymously, but later, in a "sequel" to it, ascribed to the well-known scientists Balfour Stewart and P. G. Tait, entitled *Paradoxical Philosophy* (London: Macmillan & Co., 1878).]

The Madonna of the Future

Henry James

Editor's Introduction

Henry James, who has appeared in two previous issues of *The Great Ideas Today* (most recently the 1982 edition) and, such is his distinction as a storyteller, may well appear again, was much concerned as a writer with what nowadays we call the creative process, and so with the artist as a human being. His views upon this subject may seem in some ways dated, at least as expressed in his tales. For example, "The Lesson of the Master" and "The Author of Beltraffio," published in the 1880s, deal with what he regarded as the conflict between life and art, as does *The Tragic Muse,* a novel of 1890. In the first, the "lesson" which a distinguished author drills into his would-be disciple is not to be like him, because at the height of his success he has lost the passion and the hunger that would make him a fit model to follow—an admonition that seems quaint enough in this age of the professional. Similarly, the notion of the artist as a pagan, in the sense of "The Author of Beltraffio" (a figure patterned not on Robert Louis Stevenson, as gossip once had it, but on his contemporary John Addington Symonds), who could be regarded as dangerously immoral for lack of orthodox religious faith, is of another time, indeed was hardly vital, as an idea, to the extent imagined, in James's own day.

Even "The Madonna of the Future," a still earlier story (1873), here reprinted, seems extravagant in its supposition of an artist *manqué* who spends his entire life preparing for a masterpiece he never begins—though some such situation is found, after all, in so contemporary a work as *The Plague,* by Albert Camus, one of whose characters cannot get beyond the first sentence of the novel he intends to write, since he is never satisfied with the words he has put down.

The predicament of the artist in James's story, who feels that as an American he is among "the disinherited of Art," who must make up from resources within himself for "the poor little barren artificial deposit" of American perception, living the while in exile, seems likewise far removed from the artists discussed by Professor Kuspit elsewhere in these pages—artists who have been at the very center, the suggestion is, of the painting and sculpture of their time, which may therefore be fairly called an American time in art. This is so even if we recognize that James's own view is that of the narrator in the tale, who insists that such American disadvantages are beside the point, which is to get on with the task and "do something fine"—a counsel sufficiently modern, perhaps.

What really sets James off from our own time is, however, as we may think, his conviction that art and the artist, properly considered, are moral in their aim. Such a word would be likely, we feel, to make the artists of our day embarrassed if they assumed it, unless it were meant that art and the artist should have integrity, should be true to themselves, which certainly is part of what James meant. But he meant something more. He meant that the artist has some responsibility to life, that he *makes* life in the sense that he gives it interest and importance—brings it, so to say, to its fullest realization through his depiction of it, which has therefore necessarily a moral dimension. He renders actual the potential of life, we might say in Aristotelian terms, understanding—so James thought—what at its best it could reveal.

In this conviction James meant to steer between aesthetes such as Walter Pater, whose belief in craft he shared, and self-styled journalists such as H. G. Wells, whose vitality he admired, the difference being, in each case, that he thought them lacking in any sufficient sense of purpose. Intensity—living, as Pater urged, "with a hard, gemlike flame"—was not enough, any more than was what Wells called "technique," by which he meant the ability to write a successful novel, for the Jamesian ideal. And while the moral sort of purpose James himself had in mind is likely to appear irrelevant—since extrinsic—to art as at present we understand and practice it, we might remember that for James himself, the "life" he celebrated, far from being independent of art, was something only art was able to achieve, and of which the measure was, for him, "the amount of felt life concerned in producing it." In this he was a quite determined rebel, despite his good manners, utterly at odds with the notion of maintaining a code of behavior for its own sake, and ruthless in his exposure of the folly and blindness of those who tried to do that. And so, in all, he is perhaps not so distant a figure as he may appear to us, for he would have respected the seriousness of the artists discussed here by Professor Kuspit, even if he could have made little of their materials and nothing whatever, probably, of their modes.

Of course, much of this general attitude formed itself in James's mind relatively late in his career. At the time he published "The Madonna of the Future" he was only thirty years old, but lately (1869) set out from America on the European tour—the famous "passionate pilgrimage"—which had such a formative influence upon him. No part of that experience was of more consequence to him than Italy, to which he returned over and over again during his life, and on which he drew for so many of his novels and tales, among them this early example.

The Madonna of the Future

We had been talking about the masters who had achieved but a single masterpiece—the artists and poets who but once in their lives had known the divine afflatus and touched the high level of perfection. Our host had shown us a charming little cabinet picture by a painter whose name we had never heard, and who, after this single spasmodic bid for fame, had appeared to relapse into obscurity and mediocrity. There was some discussion as to the frequency of this inconsequence; during which I noted H—— sit silent, finishing his cigar with a meditative air and looking at the picture, which was being handed round the table. "I don't know how common a case it is," he said at last, "but I've seen it. I've known a poor fellow who painted his one masterpiece, and who"—he added with a smile—"didn't even paint that. He made his bid for fame and missed it." We all knew H—— for a clever man who had seen much of men and manners and had a great stock of reminiscences. Someone immediately questioned him further, and while I was engrossed with the raptures of my neighbour over the precious object in circulation he was induced to tell his tale. If I were to doubt whether it would bear repeating, I should only have to remember how that charming woman our hostess, who had left the table, ventured back in rustling rose-colour, to pronounce our lingering a want of gallantry, and, then finding us under the spell, sank into her chair in spite of our cigars and heard the story out so graciously that when the catastrophe was reached she glanced across and showed me a tear in each of her beautiful eyes.

It relates to my youth and to Italy: two very fine things! (H—— began.) I had arrived late in the evening at Florence and, while I finished my bottle of wine at supper, had fancied that, tired traveler though I was, I might pay such a place a finer compliment than by going vulgarly to bed. A narrow passage wandered darkly away out of the little square before my hotel and looked as if it bored into the heart of Florence. I followed it and at the end of ten minutes emerged upon a great piazza filled only with the mild autumn moonlight. Opposite rose the Palazzo Vecchio, like some huge civic fortress, with the great bell tower springing from its embattled verge even as a mountain-pine from the edge of a cliff. At the base, in the great projected shadow, gleamed certain dim sculptures which I wonderingly approached. One of the images, on the left of the palace door, was a magnificent colossus who shone through the dusky air like a sentinel roused by some alarm and in whom I at once recognized Michael Angelo's famous David. I turned with a certain relief from his heroic sinister strength to a slender figure in bronze poised beneath the high light loggia which opposes the free and elegant span of its arches to the dead masonry of the palace; a figure supremely shapely and graceful, markedly gentle almost, in spite of his holding out with his light nervous arm the snaky head of the slaughtered Gorgon. His name—as, unlike the great David, he still stands there—is Perseus, and you may read his story not in the Greek mythology but in the memoirs of Benvenuto Cellini. Glancing from one of these fine fellows to the other, I probably uttered some irrepressible commonplace of praise, for, as if provoked by my voice, a man rose from the steps of the loggia, where he had been sitting in the shadow, and addressed me in proper English—a small slim personage clad in some fashion of black velvet tunic (as it seemed) and with a mass of auburn hair, which shimmered in the moonlight, escaping from a little beretto of the *cinquecento.* In a tone of the most insinuating deference he proceeded to appeal to me for my "impressions." He was romantic, fantastic, slightly unreal. Hovering in that consecrated neighbourhood he might have passed for the genius of esthetic hospitality—if the genius of esthetic hospitality wasn't commonly some shabby little custode who flourishes a calico pocket-handkerchief and openly resents the divided franc. This analogy was made nonetheless complete by his breaking into discourse as I threw myself diffidently back upon silence.

"I've known Florence long, sir, but I've never known her so lovely as tonight. It's as if the ghosts of her past were abroad in the empty streets. The present is sleeping; the past hovers about us like a dream made visible. Fancy the old Florentines strolling up in couples to pass judgment on the last performance of Michael, of Benvenuto! We should come in for a precious lesson if we might overhear what they say. The plainest burgher of them, in his cap and gown, had a taste in the matter. That was the prime of art, sir. The sun stood high in heaven, and his broad and equal blaze made the darkest places bright and the dullest eyes clear. We live in the evening of time. We grope in the grey dusk, carrying each our poor little taper of selfish and painful wisdom, holding it up to the great models and to the dim idea, and seeing nothing but overwhelming greatness and dimness. The days of illumination are gone. But do you take my refreshing idea"—and he grew suddenly almost familiar in this visionary fervour—"my idea that the light of that time rests upon us here for an hour? I've never seen the David so grand, the Perseus so fair! Even the inferior productions of John of Bologna and of Baccio Bandinelli seem to realize the artist's dream. I feel as if the moonlit air were charged with the secrets of the masters, and as if, standing here in religious attention, we might—well, witness a revelation!" Perceiving at this moment, I suppose, my halting comprehension reflected in my puzzled face, this interesting rhapsodist paused and blushed. Then with a melancholy smile: "You think me a moonstruck charlatan, I suppose. It's not my habit to hang about the piazza and pounce upon innocent tourists. But tonight, I confess, I'm under the charm. And then, somehow, I seemed to take you too for an artist!"

"I'm not an artist, I'm sorry to say, as you must understand the term. But pray make no apologies. I *am* also under the charm, and your eloquent remarks," I declared, "have only deepened it."

"If you're not an artist, you're worthy to be one!" he returned with flattering frankness. "A young man who arrives at Florence late in the evening and, instead of going prosaically to bed or hanging over the travelers' book at his hotel, walks forth without loss of time to render homage to these blest objects is a young man after my own heart!"

The mystery was suddenly solved; my friend was the most characteristic of compatriots. He would *have* to be one of "us," of the famished race—for we were at least a pair—to take the situation so to heart. "Nonetheless so, I trust," I answered, "if the young man is a sordid New Yorker."

"New Yorkers have often been munificent patrons of art!" he answered urbanely.

For a moment I was alarmed. Was his irrepressible passion mere Yankee enterprise?—was he simply a desperate brother of the brush who had posted himself here to extort an "order" from a sauntering tourist? But I wasn't called to defend myself. A great brazen note broke suddenly from the far-off summit of the bell tower above us and sounded the first stroke of midnight. My companion started, apologized for detaining me and prepared to retire. But he seemed to offer so lively a promise of further entertainment that I was loath to part with him and suggested we should proceed homeward together. He cordially assented; so we turned out of the Piazza, passed down before the statued arcade of the Uffizi and came out upon the Arno. What course we took I hardly remember, but we roamed far and wide for an hour, my companion delivering by snatches a positively moon-touched esthetic lecture. I listened in puzzled fascination, wondering who the deuce he might be. He confessed with a melancholy but all-respectful headshake to an origin identical with my own. "We're the disinherited of Art! We're condemned to be superficial! We're excluded from the magic circle! The soil of American perception is a poor little barren artificial deposit! Yes, we're wedded to imperfection! An American, to excel, has just ten times as much to learn as a European! We lack the deeper sense! We have neither taste nor tact nor force! How *should* we have them? Our crude and garish climate, our silent past, our deafening present, the constant pressure about us of unlovely conditions, are as void of all that nourishes and prompts and inspires the artist as my sad heart is void of bitterness in saying so! We poor aspirants must live in perpetual exile."

"You seem fairly at home in exile," I made answer, "and Florence seems to me a very easy Siberia. But do you know my own thought? Nothing is so idle as to talk about our want of a nursing air, of a kindly soil, of opportunity, of inspiration, of the things that help. The only thing that helps is to do something fine. There's no law in our glorious Constitution against that. Invent, create, achieve. No matter if you've to study fifty times as much as one of these. What else are you an artist for? Be you our Moses," I added, laughing and laying my hand on his shoulder, "and lead us out of the house of bondage!"

"Golden words, golden words, young man!"—my friend rose to it beautifully. " 'Invent, create, achieve'! Yes, that's our business; I know it well. Don't take me, in heaven's name, for one of your barren complainers, of the falsely fastidious, who have neither talent nor faith! I'm at work!"—and he glanced about him and lowered his voice as if this were quite a peculiar secret—"I'm at work night and day. I've undertaken, believe me, a creation. I'm no Moses; I'm only a poor patient artist; but it would be a fine thing if I were to cause some slender stream of beauty to flow in our thirsty land! Don't think me a monster of conceit," he went on as he saw me smile at the avidity with which he adopted my illustration; "I confess that I *am* in one of those moods when great things seem possible! This is one of my—shall I say inspired?—nights: I dream waking! When the south wind blows over Florence at midnight it seems to coax the soul from all the fair things locked away in her churches and galleries; it comes into my own little studio with the moonlight; it sets my heart beating too deeply for rest. You see I'm always adding a thought to my conception. This evening I felt I couldn't sleep unless I had communed with the genius of Buonarotti!"

He seemed really to know his Florence through and through and had no need to tell me he loved her. I saw he was an old devotee and had taken her even from the first to his heart. "I owe her everything," he put it—"it's only since I came here that I've really lived, intellectually and esthetically speaking. One by one all profane desires, all mere worldly aims, have dropped away from me and left me nothing but my pencil, my little notebook"—he tapped his breast pocket—"and the worship of the pure masters, those who were pure because they were innocent and those who were pure because they were strong!"

"And have you been very productive all this time?" I found myself too interested to keep from asking.

He was silent awhile before replying. "Not in the vulgar sense! I've chosen never to manifest myself by imperfection. The good in every performance I've reabsorbed into the generative force of new creations; the bad—there's always plenty of that—I've religiously destroyed. I may say with some satisfaction that I've not added a grain to the rubbish of the world. As a proof of my conscientiousness"—and he stopped short, eyeing me with extraordinary candour, as if the proof were to be overwhelming—"I've never sold a picture! 'At least no merchant traffics in my heart!' Do you remember that divine line in Browning? My little studio has never been profaned by superficial feverish mercenary work. It's a temple of labour but of leisure! Art is long. If we work for ourselves of course we must hurry. If we work for *her* we must often pause. She can wait!"

This had brought us to my hotel door, somewhat to my relief, I confess, for I had begun to feel unequal to the society of a genius of this heroic strain. I left him, however, not without expressing a friendly hope that we should meet again. The next morning my curiosity had not abated; I was anxious to see him by common daylight. I counted on meeting him in one of the many art-haunts of the so rich little city, and I was gratified without delay. I found him in the course of the morning in the Tribune of the Uffizi—that little treasure-chamber of world-famous things. He had turned his back on the Venus de' Medici and, with his arms resting on the rail that protects the pictures and his head buried in his hands, was lost in the contemplation of that superb neighbouring triptych of Andrea Mantegna—a work which has neither the material splendour nor the commanding force of some of its neighbours, but which, glowing there with the loveliness of patient labour, suits possibly a more constant need of the soul. I looked at the picture for some time over his shoulder; at last, with a heavy sigh, he turned away and our eyes met. As he recognized me he coloured for the consciousness of what I brought back: he recalled perhaps that he had made a fool of himself overnight. But I offered him my hand with a frankness that assured him I was no scoffer. I knew him by his great nimbus of red hair; otherwise he was much altered. His midnight mood was over, and he looked as haggard as an actor by daylight. He was much older than I had supposed, and had less bravery of costume and attitude. He seemed quite the poor patient artist he had proclaimed himself, and the fact that he had never sold a picture was more conceivable doubtless than commendable. His velvet coat was threadbare and his short slouched hat, of an antique pattern, revealed a rustiness that marked it an "original" and not one of the picturesque reproductions that members of his craft sometimes affect. His eye was mild and heavy, and his expression singularly gentle and acquiescent; the more so for a certain pale facial spareness which I hardly knew whether to refer to the consuming fire of genius or to a meagre diet. A very little talk, however, cleared his brow and brought back his flow.

"And this is your first visit to these enchanted halls?" he cried. "Happy, thrice happy youth!"—with which, taking me by the arm, he prepared to lead me to each of the preeminent works in turn and show me the flower of the array. Before we left the Mantegna, however, I felt him squeeze me and give it a loving look. "*He* was not in a hurry," he murmured. "*He* knew nothing of 'raw Haste, half-sister to Delay'!" How sound a critic he might have been didn't seem to me even then to concern me—it so served that he was an amusing one; overflowing with opinions and theories, sympathies and aversions, with disquisition and gossip and anecdote. He inclined more than I approved to the sentimental proposition, was too fond, I thought, of superfine shades and of discovering subtle intentions and extracting quintessences. At moments too he plunged into the sea of metaphysics and floundered awhile in waters that were not for my breasting. But his abounding knowledge and frequent felicities told a touching story of long attentive hours in all such worshipful companies; there was a reproach to my wasteful saunterings in his systematic and exhaustive attack. "There are two moods," I remember his saying, "in which we may walk through galleries—the critical and the ideal. They seize us at their pleasure, and we can never tell which is to take its turn. The critical, oddly, is the genial one, the friendly, the condescending. It relishes the pretty trivialities of art, its vulgar cleverness, its conscious graces. It has a kindly greeting for anything which looks as if, according to his light, the painter had enjoyed doing it—for the little Dutch cabbages and kettles, for the taper fingers and breezy mantles of late-coming Madonnas, for the little blue-hilled, broken-bridged, pastoral, classical landscapes. Then there are the days of fierce, fastidious longing—solemn church-feasts of the taste or the faith—when all vulgar effort and all petty success is a weariness and everything but the best, the best of the best, disgusts. In these hours we're relentless aristocrats of attitude. We'll not take Michael for granted, we'll not swallow Raphael whole!"

The gallery of the Uffizi is not only rich in its possessions, but peculiarly fortunate in that fine architectural accident or privilege which unites it—with the breadth of river and city between them—to the princely extent of the Pitti. The Louvre and the Vatican hardly give you such a sense of sustained enclosure as those long passages projected over street and stream to establish an inviolate transition between the two palaces of art. We paced the clear tunnel in which those precious drawings by eminent hands hang chaste and grey above the swirl and murmur of the yellow Arno, and reached the grand-ducal, the palatial saloons. Grand-ducal as they are, they must be pronounced imperfect showrooms, since, thanks to their deep-set windows and their massive mouldings, it is rather a broken light that reaches the pictured walls. But here the masterpieces hang thick, so that you see them in a deep diffused lustre of their own. And the great chambers, with their superb dim ceilings, their outer wall in splendid shadow and the sombre opposite glow of toned canvas and gleaming gold, make themselves almost as fine a picture as the Titians and Raphaels they imperfectly reveal. We lingered briefly before many a Raphael and Titian; but I saw my friend was impatient and I suffered him at last to lead me directly to the goal of our journey—the most tenderly fair of Raphael's virgins, the Madonna of the Chair. Of all the fine pictures of the world, it was to strike me at once as the work with which criticism has least to do. None betrays less effort, less of the mechanism of success and of the irrepressible discord between conception and result that sometimes faintly invalidates noble efforts. Graceful, human, near to our sympathies as it is, it has nothing of manner, of method, nothing almost of style; it blooms there in a softness as rounded and as instinct with harmony as if it were an immediate exhalation of genius. The figure imposes on the spectator a spell of submission which he scarce knows whether he has given to heavenly purity or to earthly charm. He is intoxicated with the fragrance of the tenderest blossom of maternity that ever bloomed among men.

"That's what I call a fine picture," said my companion after we had gazed awhile in silence. "I've a right to say so, for I've copied it so often and so carefully that I could repeat it now with my eyes shut. Other works are of Raphael: this is Raphael himself. Others you can praise, you can qualify, you can measure, explain, account for: this you can only love and admire. I don't know in what seeming he walked here below while this divine mood was upon him; but after it surely he could do nothing but die—this world had nothing more to teach him. Think of it awhile, my friend, and you'll admit that I'm not raving. Think of his seeing that spotless image not for a moment, for a day, in a happy dream or a restless fever-fit, not as a poet in a five minutes' frenzy—time to snatch his phrase and scribble his immortal stanza; but for days together, while the slow labour of the brush went on, while the foul vapours of life interposed and the fancy ached with tension, fixed, radiant, distinct, as we see it now! What a master, certainly! But ah what a seer!"

"Don't you imagine," I fear I profanely asked, "that he had a model, and that some pretty young woman—"

"As pretty a young woman as you please! It doesn't diminish the miracle. He took his hint of course, and the young woman possibly sat smiling before his canvas. But meanwhile the painter's idea had taken wings. No lovely human outline could charm it to vulgar fact. He saw the fair form made perfect; he rose to the vision without tremor, without effort of wing; he communed with it face to face and resolved into finer and lovelier truth the purity which completes it as the fragrance completes the rose. That's what they call idealism; the word's vastly abused, but the thing's good. It's my own creed at any rate. Lovely Madonna, model at once and muse, I call you to witness that I too am an idealist!"

"An idealist then"—and I really but wanted to draw him further out—"an idealist is a gentleman who says to Nature in the person of a beautiful girl: 'Go to, you're all wrong! Your fine's coarse, your bright's dim, your grace is *gaucherie.* This is the way you should have done it!' Isn't the chance against him?"

He turned on me at first almost angrily—then saw that I was but sowing the false to reap the true. "Look at that picture," he said, "and cease your irreverent mockery! Idealism is *that!* There's no explaining it; one must feel the flame. It says nothing to Nature, or to any beautiful girl, that they won't both forgive. It says to the fair woman: 'Accept me as your artist-friend, lend me your beautiful face, trust me, help me, and your eyes shall be half my masterpiece.' No one so loves and respects the rich realities of nature as the artist whose imagination intensifies them. He knows what a fact may hold—whether Raphael knew, you may judge by his inimitable portrait, behind us there, of Tommaso Inghirami—but his fancy hovers above it as Ariel in the play hovers above the sleeping prince. There's only one Raphael, but an artist may still be an artist. As I said last night, the days of illumination are gone; visions are rare; we've to look long to have them. But in meditation we may still cultivate the ideal; round it, smooth it, perfect it. The result, the result"—here his voice faltered suddenly and he fixed his eyes for a moment on the picture; when they met my own again they were full of tears—"the result may be less than this, but still it may be good, it may be *great!*" he cried with vehemence. "It may hang somewhere, through all the years, in goodly company, and keep the artist's memory warm. Think of being known to mankind after some such fashion as this; of keeping pace with the restless centuries and the changing world; of living on and on in the cunning of an eye and a hand that belong to the dust of ages, a delight and a law to remote generations; of making beauty more and more a force and purity more and more an example!"

"Heaven forbid," I smiled, "that I should take the wind out of your sails! But doesn't it occur to you that besides being strong in his genius Raphael was happy in a certain good faith of which we've lost the trick? There are people, I know, who deny that his spotless Madonnas are anything more than pretty blondes of that period, enhanced by the Raphaelesque touch, which they declare to be then as calculating and commercial as any other. Be that as it may, people's religious and esthetic needs went arm in arm, and there was, as I may say, a demand for the Blessed Virgin, visible and adorable, which must have given firmness to the artist's hand. I'm afraid there's no demand now."

My friend momentarily stared—he shivered and shook his ears under this bucketful of cold water. But he bravely kept up his high tone. "There's always a demand—that ineffable type is one of the eternal needs of man's heart; only pious souls long for it in silence, almost in shame. Let it appear and their faith grows brave. How *should* it appear in this corrupt generation? It can't be made to order. It could indeed when the order came trumpet-toned from the lips of the Church herself and was addressed to genius panting with inspiration. But it can spring now only from the soil of passionate labour and culture. Do you really fancy that while from time to time a man of complete artistic vision is born into the world such an image can perish? The man who paints it has painted everything. The subject admits of every perfection—form, colour, expression, composition. It can be as simple as you please and yet as rich; as broad and free and yet as full of delicate detail. Think of the chance for flesh in the little naked nestling child, irradiating divinity; of the chance for drapery in the chaste and ample garment of the mother. Think of the great story you compress into that simple theme. Think above all of the mother's face and its ineffable suggestiveness, of the mingled burden of joy and trouble, the tenderness turned to worship and the worship turned to far-seeing pity. Then look at it all in perfect line and lovely colour, breathing truth and beauty and mastery."

"*Anch' io son pittore!*" I laughed. "Unless I'm mistaken *you* have a masterpiece on the stocks. If you put all that in, you'll do more than Raphael himself did. Let me know when your picture's finished, and wherever in the wide world I may be I'll post back to Florence and pay my respects to—the *Madonna of the future!*"

His face, at this, had a flush of consciousness, and he seemed to sigh half in protest, half in resignation. "I don't often mention my picture by name. I detest this modern custom of premature publicity. A great work needs silence, privacy, mystery. And then, do you know, people are so cruel, so frivolous, so unable to imagine a man's wishing to paint a Madonna at this time of day, that I've been laughed at, positively laughed at, sir!"—and his poor, guilty blush deepened. "I don't know what has prompted me to be so frank and trustful with you. You look as if you wouldn't laugh at me. My dear young man"—and he laid his hand on my arm—"I'm worthy of respect. Whatever my limitations may be, I'm honest. There's nothing grotesque in a pure ambition or in a life devoted to it."

II

There was something so admirably candid in his look and tone that further questions seemed to savour just then of indiscretion. I had repeated opportunity to put as many as I would, however, for after this we spent much time together. Daily, for a fortnight, we met under agreement that he should help me to intimacy with the little treasure-city. He knew it so well and had studied it with so pious a patience, he was so deeply versed both in its greater and its minor memories, he had become in short so fond and familiar a Florentine, that he was an ideal *valet de place* and I was glad enough to leave dryer documents at home and learn what I wanted from his lips and his example. He talked of Florence as a devoted old lover might still speak of an old incomparable mistress who remained proof against time; he liked to describe how he had lost his heart to her at first sight. "It's the fashion to make all cities of the feminine gender, but as a rule it's a monstrous mistake. Is Florence of the same sex as New York, as Chicago, as London, as Liverpool? She's the sole perfect lady of them all; one feels toward her as some sensitive aspiring youth feels to some beautiful older woman with a 'history.' She fills you with a presumptuous gallantry." This disinterested passion seemed to stand my friend instead of the common social ties; he led a lonely life and cared for nothing but his work. I was duly flattered by his having taken my uninstructed years into his favour and by his generous sacrifice of precious hours to my society. We spent them in historic streets and consecrated nooks, in churches and convents and galleries, spent them above all in study of those early paintings in which Florence is so rich, returning ever and anon, with restless sympathies, to find in these tender blossoms of art a fragrance and savour more precious than the full-fruited knowledge of the later works. We lingered often in the mortuary chapel of San Lorenzo, where we watched Michael Angelo's dim-visaged warrior sit like some awful Genius of Doubt and brood behind his eternal mask upon the mysteries of life. We stood more than once in the little convent chambers where Fra Angelico wrought as if an angel indeed had held his hand, and gathered that sense of scattered dews and early bird-notes which makes an hour among his relics resemble a morning stroll in some monkish garden. We did all this and much more—wandered into obscure shrines, damp courts, and dusty palace-rooms, in quest of lingering hints of fresco and lurking treasures of sculpture.

I was more and more impressed with my companion's remarkable singleness of purpose. Everything became a pretext for one of his high-flown excursions. Nothing could be seen or said that didn't lead him sooner or later to a glowing discourse on the true, the beautiful and the good. If my friend was not a genius, he was certainly a natural rhapsodist, or even a harmless madman; and I found the play of his temper, his humour, and his candid and unworldly character as quaint as if he had been a creature from another planet. He seemed indeed to know very little of this one, and lived and moved altogether in his boundless province of art. A creature more unsullied by the accidents of life it's impossible to conceive, and I sometimes questioned the reality of an artistic virtue, an esthetic purity, on which some profane experience hadn't rubbed off a little more. It was hard to have to accept him as of our own hardheaded stock; but after all there could be no better sign of his American star than the completeness of his reaction in favour of vague profits. The very heat of his worship was a mark of conversion; those born within sight of the temple take their opportunities more for granted. He had, moreover, all our native mistrust for intellectual discretion and our native relish for sonorous superlatives. As a critic he rather ignored proportion and degree; his recognitions had a generous publicity, his discriminations were all discoveries. The small change of appreciation seemed to him in fine no coin for a gentleman to handle; and yet with all this overflow of opinion and gesture he remained in himself a mystery. His professions were practically, somehow, all masks and screens, and his personal allusions, as to his ambiguous background, mere wavings of the dim lantern. He was modest and proud, in other words, and never spoke of his domestic matters. He was evidently poor, and yet must have had some slender independence, since he could afford to make so merry over the fact that his culture of ideal beauty had never brought him a penny. His poverty, I supposed, was his motive for neither inviting me to his lodging nor mentioning its whereabouts. We met either in some public place or at my hotel, where I entertained him as freely as I might without appearing to be prompted by charity. He appeared for the most part hungry, and this was his nearest approach to human grossness. I made a point of never seeming to cross a certain line with him, but, each time we met, I ventured to make some respectful allusion to the *magnum opus,* to inquire, if I might, as to its health and progress. "We're getting on, with the Lord's help," he would say with a bravery that never languished; "I think we can't be said not to be doing well. You see I've the grand advantage that I lose no time. These hours I spend with you are pure profit. They bring me in a harvest of incentives. Just as the truly religious soul is always at worship, the genuine artist is always in labour. He takes his property wherever he finds it—he learns some precious secret from every object that stands up in the light. If you but knew—in connection with something to be done—of the rapture of observing and remembering, of applying one's notes. I take in at every glance some hint for light, for colour, for style. When I get home I pour out my treasures into the lap of my Madonna. Oh, I'm not idle! *Nulla dies sine linea.*"

III

I had been introduced meanwhile to an American lady whose drawing room had long formed an attractive place of reunion for strangers of supposed distinction. She lived on a fourth floor and was not rich; but she offered her visitors very good tea, little cakes at option, and conversation not quite to match. Her conversation had mainly a high esthetic pitch, for Mrs. Coventry was famously "artistic." Her apartment was a sort of miniature Pitti Palace. She possessed "early masters" by the dozen—a cluster of Peruginos in her dining room, a Giotto in her boudoir, an Andrea del Sarto over her drawing-room chimneypiece. Surrounded by these treasures and by innumerable bronzes, mosaics, majolica dishes, and little worm-eaten diptychs covered with angular saints on gilded backgrounds, she enjoyed the dignity of a social high-priestess of the arts. She always wore on her bosom a huge, if reduced, copy of the Madonna della Seggiola. Gaining her ear quietly one evening I asked her whether she knew among our compatriots in the place of a certain eccentric but charming Mr. Theobald.

"Know him, know poor Theobald?"—her answer was as public as if I had owed it to the bell-crier. "All Florence knows him, his flamed-coloured locks, his black velvet coat, his interminable harangues on the Beautiful and his wondrous Madonna that mortal eye has never seen and that mortal patience has quite given up expecting."

"Really," I asked, "you don't believe in his wondrous Madonna?"

"My dear ingenuous youth," rejoined my shrewd friend, "has he made a convert of you? Well, we all believed in him once; he came down upon Florence—that is on our little colony here—and took the town by storm. Another Raphael, at the very least, had been born among men, and our poor dear barbarous country was to have the credit of him. Hadn't he the very hair of Raphael flowing down on his shoulders? The hair, alas—it's his difficulty—appears to have to do duty for the head! We swallowed him whole, however; we hung on his lips and proclaimed his genius from the housetops. The women were dying to sit to him for their portraits and be made immortal like Leonardo's Gioconda. We decided that his manner was a good deal like Leonardo's—'esoteric' and indescribable and fascinating. Well, it has all remained esoteric, and nobody can describe what nobody has ever seen. The months, the years have passed and the miracle has hung fire; our master has never produced his masterpiece. He has passed hours in the galleries and churches, posturing, musing, and gazing; he has talked more about his subject—about every subject—than any human being before has ever talked about anything, but has never put brush to canvas. We had all subscribed, as it were, to the great performance; but as it never came off people began to ask for their money again. I was one of the last of the faithful; I carried devotion so far as to sit to him for my head. If you could have seen the horrible creature he made of me, you'd recognize that even a woman with no more vanity than will tie her bonnet straight must have cooled off then. The man didn't know the very alphabet of drawing. His strong point, he intimated, was his sentiment; but is it a consolation, when one has been painted a fright, to know that the man has particularly enjoyed doing it? One by one, I confess, we fell away from the faith, and Mr. Theobald didn't lift his little finger to preserve us. At the first hint that we were tired of waiting and that we should like the show to begin he was off in a huff. 'Great work requires time, contemplation, privacy, mystery! O ye of little faith!' We answered that we didn't insist on a great work; that the five-act tragedy might come at his convenience; that we merely asked for something to keep us from yawning, some light little *lever de rideau.* On that the poor dear man took his stand as a genius misconceived and persecuted, a martyr to his opinions, and washed his hands of us from that hour! No, I believe he does me the honour to consider me the head and front of the conspiracy formed to nip his glory in the bud—a bud that has taken twenty years to blossom. Ask him if he knows me, and he'll tell you I'm a horribly ugly old woman who has vowed his destruction because he doesn't see his way to paint her in the style of Titian's Flora. I'm afraid that since then he has had none but chance followers, innocent strangers like yourself, who have taken him at his word. The mountain's still in labour; I haven't heard that the mouse has been born. I pass him once in a while in the galleries, and he fixes his great dark eyes on me with a sublimity of indifference, as if I were a bad copy of a Sassoferrato! It's ever so long now since I heard that he was making studies for a Madonna who was to be a *résumé* of all the other Madonnas of the Italian school—like that antique Venus who borrowed a nose from one great image and an ankle from another. It's certainly a grand idea. The parts may be fine, but when I think of my unhappy portrait I tremble for the whole. He has communicated this *trouvaille,* under pledge of solemn secrecy, to fifty chosen spirits, to everyone he has ever been able to buttonhole for five minutes. I suppose he wants to get an order for it, and he's not to blame; for goodness knows how he lives. I see by your blush"—my friend freely proceeded—"that you've been honoured with his confidence. You needn't be ashamed, my dear young man; a man of your age is none the worse for a certain generous credulity. Only allow me this word of advice: keep your credulity out of your pockets! Don't pay for the picture till it's delivered. You haven't been treated to a peep at it, I imagine? No more have your fifty predecessors in the faith. There are people who doubt there's any picture to be seen. I shouldn't myself be surprised if, when one runs him to earth, one finds scarce more than in that terrible little tale of Balzac's—a mere mass of incoherent scratches and daubs, a jumble of dead paint!"

I listened to this bold sketch in silent wonder. It had a painfully plausible sound, it set the seal on shy suspicions of my own. My hostess was satirical, but was neither unveracious nor vindictive. I determined to let my judgment wait upon events. Possibly she was right, but if she was wrong she was cruelly wrong. Her version of my friend's eccentricities made me impatient to see him again and examine him in the light of public opinion. On our next meeting I at once asked him if he knew Mrs. Coventry. He laid his hand on my arm with a sadder, though perhaps sharper, look than had ever yet come into his face. "Has she got *you* into training? She's a most vain woman. She's empty and scheming, and she pretends to be serious and kind. She prattles about Giotto's second manner and Vittoria Colonna's liaison with 'Michael'—

one would suppose Michael lived across the way and was expected in to take a hand at whist—but she knows as little about art, and about the conditions of production, as I know about the stock market. She profanes sacred things," he more vehemently went on. "She cares for you only as someone to hand teacups in that horrible humbugging little parlour with its trumpery Peruginos! If you can't dash off a new picture every three days and let her hand it round among her guests, she tells them you're a low fraud and that they must have nothing to do with you."

This attempt of mine to test Mrs. Coventry's understanding of our poor friend was made in the course of a late afternoon walk to the quiet old church of San Miniato, on one of the hilltops which directly overlook the city, from whose gates you are guided to it by a stony and cypress-bordered walk, the most fitting of avenues to a shrine. No spot is more propitious to rest and thought than the broad terrace in front of the church, where, lounging against the parapet, you may glance in slow alternation from the black and yellow marbles of the church façade, seamed and cracked with time and wind-sown with a tender flora of their own, down to the full domes and slender towers of Florence and over to the blue sweep of the wide-mouthed cup of mountains in whose hollow this choicest handful of the spoils of time has been stored away for keeping. I had proposed, as a diversion from the painful memories evoked by Mrs. Coventry's name, that Theobald should go with me the next evening to the opera, where some work rarely played was to be given. He declined, as I half-expected, for I had noted that he regularly kept his evenings in reserve and never alluded to his manner of passing them. "You've reminded me before," I put to him, "of that charming speech of the Florentine painter in Alfred de Musset's *Lorenzaccio: 'I do no harm to anyone. I pass my days in my studio. On Sunday I go to the Annunziata or to Santa Maria; the monks think I have a voice; they dress me in a white gown and a red cap, and I take a share in the choruses; sometimes I do a little solo: these are the only times I go into public. In the evening, I visit my sweetheart; when the night is fine, we pass it on her balcony.'* I don't know whether you've a sweetheart or whether she has a balcony. But if you *are* so happy it's certainly better than trying to hold out against a third-rate prima donna."

He made no immediate answer, but at last he turned to me solemnly. "Can you look upon a beautiful woman with reverent eyes?"

"Really," I said, "I don't pretend to be sheepish, but I should be sorry to think myself impudent." And I asked him what in the world he meant. When at last I had assured him that if the question was of his giving me such an exhibition I would accept it on the terms he should impose, he made known to me—with an air of religious mystery—that it was in his power to introduce me to the most beautiful woman in Italy: "A beauty with a beautiful soul."

"Upon my word," I said, "you're extremely fortunate. I'm not less so, but you do keep cards up your sleeve."

"This woman's beauty," he returned, "is a revelation, a lesson, a morality, a poem! It's my daily study." Of course after this I lost no time in reminding him of what, before we parted, had taken the shape of a promise. "I feel somehow," he had said, "as if it were a violation of that privacy in which I've always studied and admired her. Therefore what I'm doing for you—well, my friend, is friendship. No hint of her existence has ever fallen from my lips. But with too great a familiarity we're apt to lose a sense of the real value of things, and you'll perhaps throw some new light on what I show you and offer a fresher appreciation."

We went accordingly by appointment to a certain ancient house in the heart of Florence—the precinct of the Mercato

Vecchio—and climbed a dark, steep staircase to its highest flight. Theobald's worshipped human type seemed hung as far above the line of common vision as his artistic ideal was lifted over the usual practice of men. He passed without knocking into the dark vestibule of a small apartment where, opening an inner door, he ushered me into a small saloon. The room affected me as mean and sombre, though I caught a glimpse of white curtains swaying gently at an open window. At a table, near a lamp, sat a woman dressed in black, working at a piece of embroidery. As my guide entered she looked up with a serene smile; then, seeing me, she made a movement of surprise and rose with stately grace. He stepped nearer, taking her hand and kissing it with an indescribable air of immemorial usage. As he bent his head she looked at me askance and had, I thought, a perfectly human change of colour.

"This is the sublime Serafina!"—Theobald frankly waved me forward. "And this is a friend and a lover of the arts," he added, introducing me. I received a smile, a curtsey, and a request to be seated.

The most beautiful woman in Italy was a person of a generous Italian type and of a great simplicity of demeanour. Seated again at her lamp with her embroidery, she seemed to have nothing whatever to say. Theobald, bending to her in a sort of Platonic ecstasy, asked her a dozen paternally tender questions about her health, her state of mind, her occupations and the progess of her needlework, which he examined minutely and summoned me to admire. It was one of the pieces of some ecclesiastical vestment—ivory satin wrought with an elaborate design of silver and gold. She made answer in a full rich voice, but with a brevity I couldn't know whether to attribute to native reserve or to the profane constraint of my presence. She had been that morning to confession; she had also been to market and had bought a chicken for dinner. She felt very happy; she had nothing to complain of except that the people for whom she was making her vestment and who furnished her materials should be willing to put such rotten silver thread into the garment, as one might say, of the Lord. From time to time, as she took her slow stitches, she raised her eyes and covered me with a glance which seemed at first to express but a placid curiosity, but in which, as I saw it repeated, I thought I perceived the dim glimmer of an attempt to establish an understanding with me at the expense of our companion. Meanwhile, as mindful as possible of Theobald's injunction of reverence, I considered the lady's personal claims to the fine compliment he had paid her.

That she was indeed a beautiful woman I recognized as soon as I had recovered from the surprise of finding her without the freshness of youth. Her appearance was of the sort which, in losing youth, loses little of its greater merit, expressed for the most part as it was in form and structure and, as Theobald would have said, in "composition." She was broad and ample, low-browed and large-eyed, dark and pale. Her thick brown hair hung low beside her cheek and ear and seemed to drape her head with a covering as chaste and formal as the veil of a nun. The poise and carriage of this head were admirably free and noble, and all the more effective that their freedom was at moments discreetly corrected by a little sanctimonious droop which harmonized admirably with the level gaze of her dark and quiet eye. A strong serene physical nature, with the placid temper which comes of no nerves and no troubles, seemed this lady's comfortable portion. She was dressed in plain dull black, save for a dark blue kerchief which was folded across her bosom and exposed a glimpse of her massive throat. Over this kerchief was suspended a little silver cross. I admired her greatly, yet with a considerable reserve. A certain mild intellectual apathy was the very mark of her complexion and form, and always seemed to round and enrich them; but this bourgeoise Egeria, if I viewed her right, betrayed rather a vulgar stagnation of mind. There might have once been a dim spiritual light in her face, but it had long since begun to wane. And furthermore, in plain prose, she was growing stout. My disappointment amounted very nearly to complete disenchantment when Theobald, as if to facilitate my covert inspection, declaring that the lamp was very dim and that she would ruin her eyes without more light, rose and addressed himself to a couple of candles on the mantelpiece, which he lighted and transferred to the table. In this improved clearness I made our hostess out a very mature person. She was neither haggard nor worn nor grey, but she was thick and coarse. The beautiful soul my friend had promised me seemed scarce worth making such a point of; it dwelt in no deeper principle than some accident of quietude, some matronly mildness of lip and brow. I should have been ready even to pronounce her sanctified bend of the head nothing more inward than the trick of a person always working at embroidery. It might have been even a slightly more sinister symptom, for in spite of her apparently admirable dullness this object of our all-candid homage practically dropped a hint that she took the situation rather less seriously than her friend. When he rose to light the candles she looked across at me with a quick intelligent smile and tapped her forehead with her forefinger; then, as from a sudden feeling of compassionate loyalty to poor Theobald I preserved a blank face, she gave a little shrug and resumed her work.

What was the relation of this singular couple? Was he the most ardent of friends or the most discreet of lovers? Did she regard him as an eccentric swain whose benevolent admiration of her beauty she was not ill-pleased to humour at the small cost of having him climb into her little parlour and gossip of summer nights? With her decent and sombre dress, her simple gravity and that fine piece of priestly stitching, she looked like some pious lay-member of a sisterhood living by special permission outside her convent walls. Or was she maintained here aloft by her admirer in comfortable leisure, so that he might have before him the perfect eternal type, uncorrupted and untarnished by the struggle for existence? Her shapely hands, I observed, were very fair and white; they lacked the traces of what is called honest toil.

"And the pictures, how do they come on?" she asked of Theobald after a long pause.

"Oh, in their own fine, quiet way! I've here a friend whose sympathy and encouragement give me new faith and ardour."

Our hostess turned to me, gazed at me a moment rather inscrutably, and then, repeating the vivid reference to the contents of our poor friend's head she had used a minute before, "He has a magnificent genius!" she said with perfect gravity.

"I'm inclined to think so"—I was amused in spite of myself.

"Eh, why do you smile?" she cried. "If you doubt what I say, you must see the *santo bambino!*" And she took the lamp and conducted me to the other side of the room, where, on the wall, in a plain black frame, hung a large drawing in red chalk. Beneath it was attached a little bowl for holy water. The drawing represented a very young child, entirely naked, half-nestling back against his mother's gown, but with his two little arms outstretched as in the act of benediction. It had been thrown off with singular freedom and directness, but was nonetheless vivid with the sacred bloom of infancy. A dimpled elegance and grace, which yet didn't weaken its expression, recalled the touch of Correggio. "That's what he can do!" said my hostess. "It's the blessed little boy I lost. It's his very image, and the Signor Teobaldo, a generous person if there ever was one, gave it me as a gift. He has given me many things besides!"

I looked at the picture for some time—

certainly it had a charm. Turning back to our friend I assured him that if it were hung amid the drawings in the Uffizi and labeled with a glorious name it would bravely hold its own. My praise seemed to give him joy; he pressed my hands—his eyes filled with tears. I had apparently quickened his desire to expatiate on the history of the drawing, for he rose and took leave of our companion, kissing her hand with the same mild ardour as before. It occurred to me that the offer of a similar piece of gallantry on my own part might help me to know what manner of woman she was. When she felt my intention she withdrew her hand, dropped her eyes solemnly, and made me a severe curtsey. Theobald took my arm and led me rapidly into the street.

"And what do you think of the sublime Serafina?" he cried with anxiety.

"She's certainly a fine figure of a woman," I answered without ceremony.

He eyed me an instant askance and then seemed hurried along by the current of remembrance. "You should have seen the mother and the child together, seen them as I first saw them—the mother with her head draped in a shawl, a divine trouble in her face and the bambino pressed to her bosom. You'd have said, I'm sure, that Raphael had found his match in common chance. I was coming back one summer night from a long walk in the country when I met this apparition at the city gate. The woman held out her hand and I hardly knew whether to say 'What do you want?' or to fall down and worship. She asked for a little money and received what I gave her with the holy sweetness with which the Santissima Vergine receives the offerings of the faithful. I saw she was beautiful and pale—she might have stepped out of the stable of Bethlehem! I gave her money and helped her on her way into the town. I had guessed her story. She too was a maiden mother, but she had been turned out into the world in her shame. I felt in all my pulses that here was my subject marvelously realized. It was as if I had had like one of the monkish artists of old a miraculous vision. I rescued the poor creatures, cherished them, watched them as I would have done some precious work of art, some lovely fragment of fresco discovered in a mouldering cloister. In a month—as if to deepen and sanctify the sadness and sweetness of it all—the poor little child died. When she felt he was going she lifted him up to me for ten minutes—so as not to lose him *all*—and I made that sketch. You saw a feverish haste in it, I suppose; I wanted to spare the poor little mortal the pain of his position. After that I doubly valued the mother. She's the simplest, sweetest, most natural creature that ever bloomed in this brave old land of Italy. She lives in the memory of her child, in her gratitude for the scanty kindness I've been able to show her, and in her simple instinctive imperturbable piety. She's not even conscious of her beauty; my admiration has never made her vain. Heaven yet knows that I've made no secret what I think of it. You must have taken in the extraordinary clearness and modesty of her look. Was there ever such a truly virginal brow, such a natural classic elegance in the wave of the hair and the arch of the forehead? I've studied her; I may say I know her. I've absorbed her little by little, I've made her my own, my mind's stamped and imbued, and I've determined now to clinch the impression. I shall at last invite her to sit for me!"

" 'At last—at last'?" I repeated in amazement. "Do you mean she has never done so yet?"

"I've not really—since that first time—made her *pose,*" he said with a shade of awkwardness. "I've taken notes, you know; I've got my grand fundamental impression. That's the great thing! But I've not actually put her to the inconvenience—so to call it—to which I'd have put a common model."

What had become for the moment of my perception and my tact I'm at a loss to say; in their absence I was unable to repress a headlong exclamation. I was destined to regret it. We had stopped at a turning and beneath a lamp. "My poor friend," I exclaimed, laying my hand on his shoulder, "you've *dawdled!* She's an old, old woman—for a maiden mother."

It was as if I had brutally struck him; I shall never forget the long slow almost ghastly look of pain with which he answered me. "Dawdled?—old, old?" he stammered. "Are you joking?"

"Why, my dear fellow, I suppose you don't take her for anything *but* mature?"

He drew a long breath and leaned against a house, looked at me with questioning, protesting, reproachful eyes. At last starting forward and grasping my arm: "Answer me solemnly: does she seem to you really and truly old? Is she wrinkled, is she faded—am I blind?" he demanded.

Then at last I understood the immensity of his illusion; how, one by one, the noiseless years had ebbed away and left him brooding in charmed inaction, forever preparing for a work forever deferred. It struck me almost as a kindness now to tell him the plain truth. "I should be sorry to say you're blind," I returned, "but I think you're rather unfortunately deceived. You've lost time in effortless contemplation. Your friend was once young and fresh and virginal; but you see that must have been some years ago. Still, she has fine things left. By all means make her sit for you." But I broke down; his face was too horribly reproachful.

He took off his hat and stood passing his handkerchief mechanically over his forehead. " 'Fine things left'?" he stared. "Do you speak as if other people had helped themselves—?"

"Why, my dear man," I smiled, "the years have helped themselves! But she has what the French call—don't they?—*de beaux restes?*"

Oh, how he gaped and how something seemed to roll over him! "I must make my Madonna out of *de beaux restes!* What a masterpiece she'll be! Old—old! Old—old!" he reechoed.

"Never mind her age," I cried, revolted by what I had done; "never mind my impression of her! You have your memory, your notes, your genius. Finish your picture in a month. I pronounce it beforehand a masterpiece and hereby offer you for it any sum you may choose to ask."

He kept staring, but seemed scarce to understand me. "Old—old!" he kept stupidly repeating. "If she's old what am I? If her beauty has faded where, where is my strength? Has life been a dream? Have I worshipped too long? Have I loved too well?" The charm in truth was broken. That the chord of illusion should have snapped at my light accidental touch showed how it had been weakened by excessive tension. The poor fellow's sense of wasted time, of vanished opportunity, surged in upon his soul in waves of darkness. He suddenly dropped his head and burst into tears.

I led him homeward with all possible tenderness, but I attempted neither to check his grief, to restore his equanimity nor to unsay the hard truth. When we reached my hotel I tried to induce him to come in. "We'll drink a glass of wine," I smiled, "to the completion of the Madonna."

With a violent effort he held up his head, mused for a moment with a formidably sombre frown and then, giving me his hand, "I'll finish it," he vowed, "in a month! No, no, in a fortnight! After all I have it *here!*" And he smote his forehead. "Of course she's old! She can afford to have it said of her—a woman who has made twenty years pass like a twelvemonth! Old—old! Why, sir, she shall be eternal!"

I wished to see him safely to his own door, but he waved me back and walked away with an air of resolution, whistling and swinging his cane. I waited a moment—then followed him at a distance and saw him proceed to cross the Santa Trinità

Bridge. When he reached the middle he suddenly paused, as if his strength had deserted him, and leaned upon the parapet gazing over into the Arno. I was careful to keep him in sight; I confess I passed ten very nervous minutes. He recovered himself at last and went his way slowly and with hanging head.

That I had really startled him into a bolder use of his long-garnered stores of knowledge and taste, into the vulgar effort and hazard of production, seemed at first reason enough for his continued silence and absence; but as day followed day without his either calling or sending me a line and without my meeting him in his customary haunts, in the galleries, in the chapel at San Lorenzo, or even strolling between the Arno-side and the great hedge-screen of verdure which, along the drive of the Cascine, throws the fair occupants of the open carriages into such becoming relief—as for more than a week I got neither tidings nor sight of him, I began to fear I might have fatally offended him and that instead of giving a wholesome push to his talent, or at least to his faith, I had done it a real harm. I had a wretched suspicion I might have made him ill. My stay at Florence was drawing to a close, and it was important that before resuming my journey I should assure myself of the truth. Theobald had to the last kept his lodging a secret, and I was at a loss how to follow him up. The simplest course was to make inquiry of the object of his homage who neighboured with the Mercato Vecchio, and I confess that unsatisfied curiosity as to the lady herself counseled it as well. Perhaps I had done her injustice, perhaps she was as immortally fresh and fair as he conceived her. I was at any rate anxious to set eyes once more on the ripe enchantress who had made twenty years, as he had said, pass like a twelvemonth. I repaired accordingly one morning to her abode, climbed the interminable staircase, and reached her door. It stood ajar, and, while I hesitated to enter, a little serving-maid came clattering out with an empty cooking-pot, as if she had just performed some savoury errand. The inner door too was open; so I crossed the little vestibule and reached the room in which I had formerly been received. It hadn't its evening aspect. The table, or one end of it, was spread for a late breakfast, before which sat a gentleman—an individual at least of the male sex—doing execution upon a beef-steak and onions and a bottle of wine. At his elbow, in intimate nearness, was placed the lady of the house. Her attitude, as I arrived, was not that of an enchantress. With one hand she held in her lap a plate of smoking macaroni; with the other she had lifted high in air one of the pendulous filaments of this succulent compound and was in the act of slipping it gently down her throat. On the uncovered end of the table, facing her companion, were ranged half-a-dozen small statuettes, of some snuff-coloured substance resembling terra-cotta. He, brandishing his knife with ardour, was apparently descanting on their merits.

Evidently I darkened the door. My hostess dropped her macaroni—into her mouth, and rose hastily with a harsh exclamation and a flushed face. I forthwith felt sure that the sublime Serafina's secret was still better worth knowing than I had supposed, and that the way to learn it was to take it for granted. I summoned my best Italian, I smiled and bowed and apologized for my intrusion; and in a moment, whether or no I had dispelled the lady's irritation, I had at least made her prudent. I must put myself at my ease; I must take a seat. This was another friend of hers—also an artist, she declared with a smile that had turned to the gracious. Her companion wiped his moustache and bowed with great civility. I saw at a glance that he was equal to the situation. He was presumably the author of the statuettes on the table and knew a money-spending *forestiere* when he saw one. He was a small active man, with a clever, impudent tossed-up nose, a sharp little black eye, conscious of many things at once, and the cocked-up moustache of a trooper. On the side of his head he wore jauntily one of the loose velvet caps affected by sculptors in damp studios, and I observed that his feet were encased in bright "worked" slippers. On Serafina's remarking with dignity that I was the friend of Mr. Theobald he broke out into the fantastic French of which Italians are sometimes so insistently lavish, declaring without reserve that Mr. Theobald was a magnificent genius.

"I am sure I don't know," I answered with a shrug. "If you're in a position to affirm it you've the advantage of me. I've seen nothing from his hand but the bambino yonder, which certainly is fine."

He had it that the bambino was a masterpiece—in the maniera Correggiesca. It was only a pity, he added with a knowing laugh, that the sketch hadn't been made on some good bit of honeycombed old panel. The sublime Serafina hereupon protested that Mr. Theobald was the soul of honour and didn't lend himself to that style of manufacture. "I'm not a judge of genius," she said, "and I know nothing of pictures. I'm a poor, simple widow; but I'm sure *nostro signore* has the heart of an angel and the virtue of a saint. He's my great benefactor," she made no secret of it. The afterglow of the somewhat sinister flush with which she had greeted me still lingered in her cheek and perhaps didn't favour her beauty; I couldn't but judge it a wise custom of Theobald's to visit her only by candlelight. She was coarse and her poor adorer a poet.

"I've the greatest esteem for him," I stated; "it's for that reason I've been so uneasy at not seeing him for ten days. Have you seen him? Is he perhaps ill?"

"Ill? Heaven forbid!" cried Serafina with genuine vehemence.

Her companion uttered a rapid expletive and reproached her with not having been to see him. She hesitated a moment, then simpered the least bit and bridled. "He comes to see me—without reproach! But it wouldn't be the same for me to go to him, though indeed you may almost call him a man of holy life."

"He has the greatest admiration for you," I said. "He'd have been honoured by your visit."

She looked at me a moment sharply. "More admiration than you. Admit that!" Of course I protested with all the eloquence at my command, and my ambiguous hostess then confessed that she had taken no fancy to me on my former visit and that, our friend not having returned, she believed I had poisoned his mind against her. "It would be no kindness to the poor gentleman, I can tell you that," she said. "He has come to see me every evening for years. It's a long friendship! No one knows him as I do."

"I don't pretend to know him or to understand him. I can only esteem and—I think I may say—love him. Nevertheless he seems to me a little—!" And I touched my forehead and waved my hand in the air.

Serafina glanced at her companion as for inspiration. He contented himself with shrugging his shoulders while he filled his glass again. The padrona hereupon treated me to a look of more meaning than quite consorted with her noble blankness. "Ah, but it's for that that *I* love him! The world has so little kindness for such persons. It laughs at them and despises them and cheats them. He's too good for this wicked life. It's his blest imagination that he finds a little Paradise up here in my poor apartment. If he thinks so, how can I help it? He has a strange belief—really I ought to be ashamed to tell you—that I resemble the Madonna Santissima, heaven forgive me! I let him think what he pleases so long as it makes him happy. He was very kind to me once and I'm not one who forgets a favour. So I receive him every evening civilly, and ask after his health, and let him look at me on this side and that. For that matter, I may say it without vanity, I was worth looking at once. And he's not always amusing, *poveretto!* He sits sometimes for an hour without speaking a word, or else he talks away, without stopping, about art and nature and beauty and duty, about fifty fine things that are all so much Latin to me. I beg you to understand that he has never said a word to me I mightn't honourably listen to. He may be a little cracked, but he's one of the blessed saints."

"Eh, eh," cried the man, "the blessed saints were all a little cracked!"

Serafina, I surmised, left part of her story untold; what she said sufficed to make poor Theobald's own statement still more affecting than I had already found its strained simplicity. "It's a strange fortune, certainly," she went on, "to have such a friend as this dear man—a friend who's less than a lover, yet more than a brother." I glanced at her comrade, who continued to smirk in a mystifying manner while he twisted the ends of his moustache between his copious mouthfuls. Was *he* less than a lover? "But what will you have?" Serafina pursued. "In this hard world one mustn't ask too many questions; one must take what comes and keep what one gets. I've kept my *amoroso* for twenty years, and I do hope that, at this time of day, signore, you've not come to turn him against me!"

I assured her I had no such intention, and that I should vastly regret disturbing Mr. Theobald's habits or convictions. On the contrary I was alarmed about him and would at once go in search of him. She gave me his address and a florid account of her sufferings at his non-appearance. She had not been to him for various reasons; chiefly because she was afraid of displeasing him, as he had always made such a mystery of his home. "You might have sent this gentleman!" I however ventured to suggest.

"Ah," cried the gentleman, "he admires Madonna Serafina, but he wouldn't admire me whom he doesn't take for Saint Joseph!" And then confidentially, his finger on his nose: "His taste's terribly severe!"

I was about to withdraw after having promised that I would inform our hostess of my friend's condition, when her companion, who had risen from table and girded his loins apparently for the onset, grasped me gently by the arm and led me before the row of statuettes. "I perceive by your conversation, signore, that you're a patron of the arts. Allow me to request your honourable attention for these modest products of my own ingenuity. They are brand-new, fresh from my atelier, and have never been exhibited in public. I have brought them here to receive the verdict of this dear lady, who's a good critic, for all she may pretend to the contrary. I'm the inventor of this peculiar style of statuette—of subject, manner, material, everything. Touch them, I pray you; handle them freely—you needn't fear. Delicate as they look, it's impossible they should break! My various creations have met with great success. They're especially admired by the American *conoscenti.* I've sent them all over Europe—to London, Paris, Vienna! You may have noticed some little specimens in Paris, on the *grand boulevard*"—he aimed at the French sound of the words—"in a shop of which they constitute the specialty. There's always a crowd about the window. They form a very pleasing ornament for the mantel-shelf of a gay young bachelor, for the boudoir of a pretty woman. You couldn't make a prettier present to a person with whom you should wish to exchange a harmless joke. It's not classic art, signore, of course; but, between ourselves, isn't classic art sometimes rather a bore? Caricature, burlesque, *la charge,* has hitherto been confined to paper, to the pen and pencil. Now it has been my inspiration to introduce it into statuary. For this purpose I've invented a peculiar plastic compound which you will permit me not to divulge. That's my secret, signore! It's as light, you perceive, as cork, and yet firm as alabaster! I frankly confess that I really pride myself as much on this little stroke of chemical ingenuity as upon the other element of novelty in my creations—my types. What do you say to my types, signore? The idea's bold; does it strike you as happy? Cats and monkeys—monkeys and cats—all human life is there! Human life, of course I mean, viewed with the eye of the satirist! To combine sculpture and satire, signore, has been my unprecedented ambition. I flatter myself I've not egregiously failed."

As this jaunty Juvenal of the chimney-piece thus persuasively proceeded he took up his little groups successively from the table, held them aloft, turned them about, rapped them with his knuckles and gazed at them lovingly, his head on one side. They consisted each, with a vengeance, of a cat and a monkey, occasionally draped, in some preposterously sentimental conjunction. They exhibited a certain sameness of motive and illustrated chiefly the different phases of what, in fine terms, might have been called the amorous advance and the amorous alarm; but they were strikingly clever and expressive, and were at once very dreadful little beasts and very natural men and women. I confess, however, that they failed to amuse me. I was doubtless not in a mood to enjoy them, for they seemed to me peculiarly cynical and vulgar. Their imitative felicity was revolting. As I looked askance at the complacent little artist, brandishing them between finger and thumb and caressing them with the fondest eye, he struck me as himself little more than an exceptionally intelligent ape. I mustered an admiring grin, however, and he blew another blast. "My figures are studied from life! I've a little menagerie of monkeys whose frolics I follow by the hour. As for the cats, one has only to look out of one's back window! Since I've begun to examine these expressive little brutes I've made many profound observations. Speaking, signore, to a man of imagination, I may say that my little designs are not without a philosophy of their own. Truly, I don't know whether the cats and monkeys imitate us, or whether it's we who imitate them." I congratulated him on his philosophy, and he resumed: "You'll do me the honour to admit that I've handled my subjects with delicacy. Eh, it was needed, *signore mio.* I've been just a bit free, but not too free—eh, *dica?* Just a scrap of a hint, you know! You may see as much or as little as you please. These little groups, however, are no measure of my invention. If you'll favour me with a call at my studio I think you'll admit that my combinations are really infinite. I likewise execute figures to command. You've perhaps some little motive—the fruit of your philosophy of life, signore—which you'd like to have interpreted. I can promise to work it up to your satisfaction; it shall have as many highlights and sharp accents as you please! Allow me to present you with my card and to remind you that my prices are moderate. Only sixty francs for a little group like that. My statuettes are as durable as bronze—*aere perennius,* signore—and, between ourselves, I think they're more amusing!

As I pocketed his card I turned an eye on Madonna Serafina, wondering whether she had a sense for contrasts. She had picked up one of the little couples and was tenderly dusting it with a feather broom.

What I had just seen and heard had so deepened my compassionate interest in my deluded friend that I took a summary leave, making my way directly to the house designated by this remarkable woman. It was in an obscure corner of the opposite side of the town and presented a sombre and squalid appearance. A withered crone, in the doorway, on my inquiring for Theobald, welcomed me with a mumbled blessing and an expression of relief at the poor gentleman's having at last a caller. His lodging appeared to consist of a single room at the top of the house. On getting no answer to my knock I opened the door, supposing him absent; so that it gave me a certain shock to find him but seated helpless and dumb. His chair was near the single window, facing an easel which supported a large canvas. On my entering he looked up at me blankly, without changing his position, which was that of absolute lassitude and dejection, his arms loosely folded, his legs stretched before him, his head hanging on his breast. Advancing into the room I saw how vividly his face answered to his attitude. He was pale, haggard, and unshaven, and his dull and sunken eye gazed at me without a spark of recognition. My fear had been that he would greet me with fierce reproaches, as the cruelly officious patron who had turned his contentment to bitterness, and I was relieved to find my appearance excite no visible resentment. "Don't you know me?"—I put out my hand. "Have you already forgotten me?"

He made no response, but kept his position stupidly and left me staring about the room. It spoke, the poor place, all plaintively for itself. Shabby, sordid, naked, it contained, beyond the wretched bed, but the scantiest provision for personal comfort. It was bedroom at once and studio—a grim ghost of a studio. A few dusty casts and prints on the walls, three or four old canvases turned face inward and a rusty-looking colour-box formed, with the easel at the window, the sum of its appurtenances. The whole scene savoured horribly of indigence. Its only wealth was the picture on the easel, presumably the famous Madonna. Averted as this was from the door I was unable to see its face; but at last, sickened by my impression of vacant misery, I passed behind Theobald eagerly and tenderly. I can scarcely say I was surprised at what I found—a canvas that was a mere dead blank cracked and discoloured by time. This was his immortal work! Though not surprised, I confess I was powerfully moved, and I think that for five minutes I couldn't have trusted myself to speak. At last my silent nearness affected him; he stirred and turned and then rose, looking at me with a slow return of intelligence. I murmured some kind ineffective nothings about his being ill and needing advice and care, but he seemed absorbed in the effort to recall distinctly what had last passed between us. "You were right," he said with a pitiful smile, "I'm a dawdler! I'm a failure! I shall do nothing more in this world. You opened my eyes, and though the truth is bitter I bear you no grudge. Amen! I've been sitting here for a week face to face with it, the terrible truth, face to face with the past, with my weakness and poverty and nullity. I shall never touch a brush! I believe I've neither eaten nor slept. Look at that canvas!" he went on as I relieved my emotion by an urgent request that he would come home with me and dine. "That was to have contained my masterpiece! Isn't it a promising foundation? The elements of it are all *here.*" And he tapped his forehead with that mystic confidence which had so often marked the gesture for me before. "If I could only transpose them into some brain that has the hand, the will! Since I've been sitting here taking stock of my intellects, I've come to believe that I've the material for a hundred masterpieces. But my hand's paralyzed now and they'll never be painted. I never began! I waited and waited to be worthier to begin—I wasted my life in preparation. While I fancied my creation was growing it was only dying. I've taken the whole business too hard. Michael Angelo didn't when he went at the Lorenzo. He did his best at a venture, and his venture's immortal. *That's* mine!" And he pointed with a gesture I shall never forget at the empty canvas. "I suppose we're a genus by ourselves in the providential scheme—we talents that can't act, that can't do nor dare! We take it out in talk, in study, in plans and promises, in visions! But our visions, let me tell you," he cried with a toss of his head, "have a way of being brilliant, and a man has not lived in vain who has seen the things *I've* seen! Of course you won't believe in them when that bit of worm-eaten cloth is all I have to show for them; but to convince you, to enchant and astound the world, I need only the hand of Raphael. His brain I already have. A pity, you'll say, that I haven't his modesty! Ah, let me boast and babble now—it's all I have left! I'm the half of a genius! Where in the wide world is my other half? Lodged perhaps in the vulgar soul, the cunning ready fingers of some dull copyist or some trivial artisan who turns out by the dozen his easy prodigies of touch! But it's not for me to sneer at him; he at least does something. He's not a dawdler. Well for me if I had been vulgar and clever and reckless, if I could have shut my eyes and taken my leap."

What to say to the poor fellow, what to do for him, seemed hard to determine; I chiefly felt I must break the spell of his present inaction and draw him out of the haunted air of the little room it was such cruel irony to call a studio. I can't say I persuaded him to come forth with me; he simply suffered himself to be led, and when we began to walk in the warm light of day I was able to appreciate his great weakness. Nevertheless he seemed in a manner to revive; he even murmured to me at last that he should like to go to the Pitti Gallery. I shall never forget our melancholy stroll through those gorgeous halls, every picture on whose walls glowed, to my stricken sight, with an insolent renewal of strength and lustre. The eyes and lips of the great portraits reflected for me a pitying scorn of the dejected pretender who had dreamed of competing with their triumphant authors. The celestial candour even of the Madonna of the Chair, as we paused in perfect silence before her, broke into the strange smile of the women of Leonardo. Perfect silence indeed marked our whole progess—the silence of a deep farewell; for I felt in all my pulses, as Theobald, leaning on my arm, dragged one heavy foot after the other, that he was looking his last. When we came out he was so exhausted that instead of taking him to my hotel to dine I called a cab and drove him straight to his own poor lodging. He had sunk into the deepest lethargy; he lay back in the vehicle with his eyes closed, as pale as death, his faint breathing interrupted at intervals by a gasp like a smothered sob or a vain attempt to speak. With the help of the old woman who had admitted me before and who emerged from a dark back court I contrived to lead him up the long, steep staircase and lay him on his wretched bed. To her I gave him in charge while I prepared in all haste to call a doctor. But she followed me out of the room with a pitiful clasping of her hands.

"Poor dear blessed gentleman," she wailed—"is he dying?"

"Possibly. How long has he been so bad?"

"Since a certain night he passed ten days ago. I came up in the morning to make his poor bed, and found him sitting up in his clothes before that great dirty canvas he keeps there. Poor dear strange man, he says his prayers to it! He hadn't been to bed—nor even since then, as you may say. What has happened to him? Has he found out about *quella cattiva donna?*" she panted with a glittering eye and a toothless grin.

"Prove at least that one old woman can be faithful," I said, "and watch him well till I come back." My return was delayed through the absence of the English physician, who was away on a round of visits and whom I vainly pursued from house to house before I overtook him. I brought him to Theobald's bedside none too soon. A violent fever had seized our patient, whose case was evidently grave. A couple of hours later on I knew he had brain-fever. From this moment I was with him constantly, but I am far from wishing fully to report his illness. Excessively painful to witness, it was happily brief. Life burned out in delirium. One night in particular that I passed at his pillow, listening to his wild snatches of regret, of aspiration, of rapture and awe at the phantasmal pictures with which his brain seemed to swarm, comes back to my memory now like some stray page from a lost masterpiece of tragedy. Before a week was over we had buried him in the little

Protestant cemetery on the way to Fiesole. Madonna Serafina, whom I had caused to be informed of his state, had come in person, I was told, to inquire about its progress; but she was absent from his funeral, which was attended but by a scanty concourse of mourners. Half-a-dozen old Florentine sojourners, in spite of the prolonged estrangement that had preceded his death, had felt the kindly impulse to honour his grave. Among them was my friend Mrs. Coventry, whom I found, on my departure, waiting in her carriage at the gate of the cemetery.

"Well," she said, relieving at last with a significant smile the solemnity of our immediate greeting, "and the greatest of all Madonnas? Have you seen her after all?"

"I've seen her," I said; "she's mine—by bequest. But I shall never show her to you."

"And why not, pray?"

"Because you wouldn't understand her!"

She rather glared at me. "Upon my word you're polite!"

"Pardon me—I'm sad and vexed and bitter." And with reprehensible rudeness I marched away. I was impatient to leave Florence; my friend's blighted spirit met my eyes in all aspects. I had packed my trunk to start for Rome that night, and meanwhile, to beguile my unrest, I aimlessly paced the streets. Chance led me at last to the church of San Lorenzo. Remembering poor Theobald's phrase about Michael Angelo—"He did his best at a venture"—I went in and turned my steps to the chapel of the tombs. Viewing in sadness the sadness of its immortal treasures, I could say to myself while I stood there that they needed no ampler commentary than those simple words. As I passed through the church again to leave it, a woman, turning away from one of the side-altars, met me face to face. The black shawl depending from her head draped becomingly the handsome face of Madonna Serafina. She stopped as she recognized me, and I saw she wished to speak. Her brow was lighted and her ample bosom heaved in a way that seemed to portend a certain sharpness of reproach. But some expression of my own then drew the sting from her resentment, and she addressed me in a tone in which bitterness was tempered by an acceptance of anticlimax that had been after all so long and so wondrously postponed. "I know it was you, now, who separated us," she said. "It was a pity he ever brought you to see me! Of course, you couldn't think of me as he did. Well, the Lord gave him, the Lord has taken him. I've just paid for a nine days' mass for his soul. And I can tell you this, signore—I never deceived him. Who put it into his head that I was made to live on holy thoughts and fine phrases? It was his own imagination, and it pleased him to think so. Did he suffer much?" she added more softly and after a pause.

"His sufferings were great, but they were short."

"And did he speak of me?" She had hesitated and dropped her eyes; she raised them with her question, and revealed in their sombre stillness a gleam of feminine confidence which for the moment revived and enhanced her beauty. Poor Theobald! Whatever name he had given his passion it was still her fine eyes that had charmed him.

"Be contented, madam," I answered gravely.

She lowered her lids again and was silent. Then exhaling a full rich sigh as she gathered her shawl together: "He was a magnificent genius!"

I bowed assent and we separated.

Passing through a narrow side street on my way back to my hotel, I noted above a doorway a sign that it seemed to me I had read before. I suddenly remembered it for identical with the superscription of a card that I had carried for an hour in my waistcoat pocket. On the threshold stood the ingenious artist whose claims to public favour were thus distinctly signalized, smoking a pipe in the evening air and giving the finishing polish with a bit of rag to one of his inimitable "combinations." I caught the expressive curl of a couple of tails. He recognized me, removed his little red cap with an obsequious bow, and motioned me to enter his studio. I returned his salute and passed on, vexed with the apparition. For a week afterwards, whenever I was seized among the ruins of triumphant Rome with some peculiarly poignant memory of Theobald's transcendent illusions and deplorable failure, I seemed to catch the other so impertinent and so cynical echo: "Cats and monkeys, monkeys and cats—all human life is there!"

PICTURE CREDITS

*Key to abbreviations used to indicate location of pictures on page: r.—right; l.—left; t.—top; b.—bottom; c.—center; *—courtesy. Abbreviations are combined to indicate unusual placement.*

—FRONTISPIECE * Leo Castelli Gallery, New York **—2** © 1986 Timothy Greenfield-Sanders **—5** Oil on canvas, 68″ × 8′8″; collection, The Museum of Modern Art, New York. Purchase. **—11** Hans Namuth **—15** Oil on canvas, $37\frac{7}{8}''$ × $29\frac{7}{8}''$; collection, The Museum of Modern Art, New York. Gift of Mr. and Mrs. Roy R. Neuberger **—16** Collection of Mr. and Mrs. Graham Gund; agent, Art Resource **—18, 20, 21, 23, 27, 29, 34** * Leo Castelli Gallery, New York **—35** Photograph, Gianfranco Gorgoni * Leo Castelli Gallery, New York **—38** Wooden folding chair, photograph of chair, and photographic enlargement of dictionary definition of chair; $32\frac{3}{8}''$ × $14\frac{7}{8}''$ × $20\frac{7}{8}''$; photo panel, 36″ × $24\frac{1}{8}''$; text panel, $24\frac{1}{8}''$ × $24\frac{1}{2}''$; collection, The Museum of Modern Art, New York. Larry Aldrich Foundation Fund **—46** Michael Alexander/Time Magazine **—52** * The Pace Gallery, New York **—55** Oil on canvas, 98″ × $187\frac{1}{2}''$; collection, Douglas Cramer, Los Angeles, * Mary Boone Gallery, New York **—57** Oil on canvas, 84″ × 108″; collection, Achille Maramotti, Rome, * Mary Boone Gallery, New York **—64** Jet Propulsion Laboratory **—65** (t.) © Georg Gerster—Photo Researchers **—65** (b.) From *Snow Crystals,* by W. A. Bentley and W. J. Humphreys, 1962, Dover Publications, New York **—82** Royal Library, Windsor Castle **—86** From *The Fractal Geometry of Nature,* by Benoit B. Mandelbrot, 1983, W. H. Freeman & Co., New York **—88** Adapted from "Metamagical Themas," Douglas R. Hofstadter, © 1981 by Scientific American Inc. All rights reserved. **—91** (t., r.) From *The Lorenz Equations: Bifurcations, Chaos, and Strange Attractors,* Colin Sparrow, 1982, Springer-Verlag, New York **—94** * B. J. Harris Photographers, London **—99** Alinari/Art Resource **—101** The Cleveland Museum of Natural History **—103, 107** The Bettmann Archive **—112** SEF/Art Resource **—114** Robert L. Dunne—Bruce Coleman, Inc. **—116, 118, 120** Culver Pictures **—130** Linda Koebner—Bruce Coleman, Inc. **—132** AP/Wide World Photos **—135, 140** The Bettmann Archive **—146** Lois/George Cox—Bruce Coleman, Inc. **—150** Philip Jones Griffiths—Magnum **—178** Alinari/Art Resource **—215** Photograph/Charles Eames **—218** * Eric Simpson **—221, 245** Photographs, University of Chicago Department of Special Collections **—248** Adapted from photograph from University of Chicago Department of Special Collections **—255** The Bettmann Archive **—260** * Smithsonian Institution, Museum of History and Technology **—271, 274, 279, 283** The Bettmann Archive **—318, 345, 415** The Bettmann Archive **—420** Culver Pictures **—444** The Bettmann Archive

Now there's a way to identify all your fine books with flair and style. As part of our continuing service to you, Britannica Home Library Service, Inc. is proud to be able to offer you the fine quality item shown on the next page.

Booklovers will love the heavy-duty personalized embosser. Now you can personalize all your fine books with the mark of distinction, just the way all the fine libraries of the world do.

To order this item, please type or print your name, address and zip code on a plain sheet of paper. (Note special instructions for ordering the embosser). Please send a check or money order only (your money will be refunded in full if you are not delighted) for the full amount of purchase, including postage and handling, to:

Britannica Home Library Service, Inc.
Attn: Yearbook Department
Post Office Box 6137
Chicago, Illinois 60680

(Please make remittance payable to: Britannica Home Library Service, Inc.)

Authors

in Great Books of the Western World

Homer
Aeschylus
Sophocles
Herodotus
Euripides
Thucydides
Hippocrates
Aristophanes
Plato
Aristotle
Euclid
Archimedes
Apollonius
Lucretius
Virgil
Plutarch
Tacitus
Epictetus
Nicomachus
Ptolemy
Marcus Aurelius
Galen
Plotinus
Augustine
Thomas Aquinas
Dante
Chaucer
Machiavelli
Copernicus
Rabelais
Montaigne
Gilbert
Cervantes
Francis Bacon
Galileo
Shakespeare
Kepler